COMMUNICATION IN SOCIETY

COMMUNICATION IN SOCIETY

JESS K. ALBERTS
Arizona State University

JUDITH N. MARTIN
Arizona State University

THOMAS K. NAKAYAMA
Northeastern University

Boston Columbus Indianapolis New York San Francisco Upper Saddle River
Amsterdam Cape Town Dubai London Madrid Milan Munich Paris Montréal Toronto Delhi
Mexico City São Paulo Sydney Hong Kong Seoul Singapore Taipei Tokyo

Editor-in-Chief, Communication: Karon Bowers
Editorial Assistant: Megan Sweeney
Director of Development: Meg Botteon
Development Editor: Kristen Desmond LeFevre
Marketing Manager: Blair Tuckman
Associate Development Editor: Angela Pickard
Media Producer: Megan Higginbotham
Production Manager: Raegan Keida Heerema
Associate Managing Editor: Bayani Mendoza de Leon
Managing Editor: Linda Mihatov Behrens
Project Coordination, Interior Design, and Electronic Page Makeup: Integra Software Services, Inc.
Cover Art Director: Anne Bonanno Nieglos
Cover Designer: Joe DePinho
Front Cover Photos: Apomares/iStockphoto; Blend Images/Superstock; Blend images/Superstock
Back Cover Photo: Photoshot
Photo Researcher: Sheila Norman
Image Permission Coordinator: Lee Scher
Manufacturing Manager: Mary Ann Gloriande
Printer and Binder: Courier/Kendallville
Cover Printer: Lehigh-Phoenix Color/Hagerstown

Library of Congress Cataloging-in-Publication Data

Alberts, Jess K.
    Communication in society / Jess K. Alberts, Judith N. Martin, Thomas K. Nakayama.
        p. cm.
    ISBN-13: 978-0-205-62787-5
    ISBN-10: 0-205-62787-0
    1. Communication—Social aspects.   2. Interpersonal communication.   3. Public speaking   I. Martin, Judith N.
II. Nakayama, Thomas K.   III. Title.
    HM1206.A42 2011
    302.5—dc22

                                                                                                    2010023216

2 3 4 5 6 7 8 9 10—CRK—13 12 11

Allyn & Bacon
is an imprint of

PEARSON

www.pearsonhighered.com

ISBN-13: 978-0-205-62787-5
ISBN-10:   0-205-62787-0

BRIEF CONTENTS

PART ONE   COMMUNICATION ESSENTIALS

1 Introduction to Human Communication 2

2 Communication, Perception, and Identity Development 26

3 Verbal Communication 50

4 Nonverbal Communication 76

5 Listening 100

6 Communication Across Cultures 120

7 Communication and New Technologies 144

PART TWO   COMMUNICATING IN DYADS

8 Interpersonal Communication and Relationship Development 174

9 Managing Challenges in Interpersonal Relationships 200

10 Managing Conflict in Interpersonal Relationships 226

PART THREE   COMMUNICATING IN GROUPS

11 Small Group Communication Processes 254

12 Leadership in Groups and Organizations 282

PART FOUR   SPEAKING IN PUBLIC

13 Speaking in Public: Topic Selection and Speech Development 304

14 Speaking in Public: Speech Delivery 334

15 Speaking in Public: Informative Speaking 354

16 Speaking in Public: Persuasive Speaking 370

CONTENTS

To the Instructor xii
Acknowledgments xxi
About the Authors xxi

PART ONE COMMUNICATION ESSENTIALS

1 Introduction to Human Communication 2

The Importance of Studying Human Communication 4
What Is Human Communication? 7
  Components of Human Communication 8
  VISUAL SUMMARY 1.1 Key Components of Human Communication 9
  A Model of Human Communication: Human Communication in Society 12
Communication Ethics 17
  Defining Communication Ethics 18
  Developing Communication Ethics 19
  Communication Ethics in Practice 22
Summary • Key Terms • Chapter Review Questions • Activities • Web
Activities 23
  DID YOU KNOW?
  Too Much Talk Can Lead to Problems 4
  Careers in Communication 6
  COMMUNICATION IN SOCIETY
  Sexual Harassment Usually Starts with Inappropriate Comments 21
  BUILDING YOUR COMMUNICATION SKILLS
  Building a Framework for Thinking Ethically and Making Ethical
    Decisions 22

2 Communication, Perception, and Identity Development 26

What Is Perception? 28
  Selection 28
  Organization 28
  Interpretation 30
What Is Identity? 32
  Identity Exists at Both the Individual and Societal Levels 32
  Identities Are Both Fixed and Dynamic 32
  Identities Are Created Through Interaction 33
  Identities Must Be Seen in Context 33
The Importance of Perception and Identity 34
The Individual, Perception, and Identity 36
  Reflected Appraisals 36
  Social Comparison 37
  Self-Fulfilling Prophecy 38
  Self-Concept 39
  VISUAL SUMMARY 2.1 Identity Development
    Through Communication 41
The Individual, Perception, Identity, and Society 42
  Social Identity 42
  Power, Perception, and Identity 42
  Culture, Perception, and Identity 43
The Ethics of Perceiving and Communicating About Identities 43
  Stereotyping 43
  Prejudice 45
  Stereotyping, Prejudice, and Communication 45
Skills for Improving Perception and Communication About Identities 46
Summary • Key Terms • Chapter Review Questions • Activities • Web
Activities 48
  DID YOU KNOW?
  The Ringtone Adults Cannot Hear 34
  COMMUNICATION IN SOCIETY
  The Smell Report 35
  BUILDING YOUR COMMUNICATION SKILLS
  Communicating About Identities 40
  Refining Your Perceptual Processes 44

3 Verbal Communication 50

What Is Verbal Communication? 52
The Importance of Verbal Communication 52
Verbal Communication and the Individual 53
  Functions of Language 53
  Components of Language 55
  Influences on Verbal Communication 58
  Gender 58
  VISUAL SUMMARY 3.1 Components of Language 59
  Age 60
  Regionality 61
  Ethnicity and Race 62
  Education and Occupation 63
The Individual, Verbal Communication, and Society 63
  Language and Perception 64
  Language and Power 64
  Power and Words 65
  Power and Accent 66
  Power and Identity Labels 68
Ethics and Verbal Communication 69
  Become Aware of the Power of Language 69
  Become Conscious of Your Language Use 70
Improving Your Verbal Communication Skills 70
  Supportive Versus Defensive Communication 70
  Confirming and Disconfirming Communication 71
  "I" Statements 72
Summary • Key Terms • Chapter Review Questions • Activities • Web Activities 73

DID YOU KNOW?
Words of the Year 52
A Little Poem Regarding Computer Spell Checkers 54
No Slang 61
Language Discrimination 67
COMMUNICATION IN SOCIETY
Mind Your (Terror) Language 69
BUILDING YOUR COMMUNICATION SKILLS
Avoiding Bias in Language 66

4 Nonverbal Communication 76

What Is Nonverbal Communication? 78
The Importance of Nonverbal Communication 79
Nonverbal Communication and the Individual 80
    Influences on Nonverbal Communication 80
    Nonverbal Codes 82
    VISUAL SUMMARY 4.1 *Proxemics* 87
The Functions of Nonverbal Messages 92
    Communicating Information 92
    Regulating Interaction 92
    Expressing and Managing Intimacy 93
    Establishing Social Control 93
    Signaling Service-Task Functions 93
The Individual, Nonverbal Communication, and Society 94
    Nonverbal Communication and Power 94
    Nonverbal Communication, Prejudice, and Discrimination 95
Ethics and Nonverbal Communication 96
Improving Your Nonverbal Communication Skills 96
Summary • Key Terms • Chapter Review Questions • Activities • Web Activities 97
    DID YOU KNOW?
    How Much Does Nonverbal Communication Contribute to Meaning? 78
    Territoriality: Maintaining Private and Public Spaces 88
    COMMUNICATION IN SOCIETY
    Etiquette for the World Traveler 83
    BUILDING YOUR COMMUNICATION SKILLS
    Developing Sensitivity to Cross-Cultural Nonverbal Communication 81
    Five Tips for Enhancing Nonverbal Communication Skills 91

5 Listening 100

What Is Listening? 102
The Importance of Listening 102
    VISUAL SUMMARY 5.1 *Stages of Listening* 103
Listening and the Individual 105
    Influences on Listening 106
    Barriers to Listening 110
The Individual, Listening, and Society 114
    Social Hierarchy 114
    Listening in Context 115
    Listening and Community 115
Ethics and Listening 116

Improving Your Listening Skills 117
    Become Aware 117
    Identify Poor Habits 117
    Strive for Mindful Listening 118
Summary • Key Terms • Chapter Review Questions • Activities • Web Activities 118
    DID YOU KNOW?
    Statistically Speaking, How Many People Are Deaf or Hard of Hearing? 111
    COMMUNICATION IN SOCIETY
    Effective Listening Skills of Managers 105
    BUILDING YOUR COMMUNICATION SKILLS
    Do's and Don'ts for Improving Listening Between Men and Women 109
    Are You an Ineffective Listener? 113

6 Communication Across Cultures 120

What Is Intercultural Communication? 122
The Importance of Intercultural Communication 122
    Increased Opportunities for Intercultural Contact 122
    Enhanced Business Effectiveness 124
    Improved Intergroup Relations 124
    Enhanced Self-Awareness 125
Intercultural Communication and the Individual 125
    Intercultural Communication on the Borders 126
    VISUAL SUMMARY 6.1 *Border Dwellers Through Travel* 127
    The Influence of Cultural Values on Communication 132
    A Dialectic Approach 136
The Individual, Intercultural Communication, and Society 138
    Political, Historical, and Social Forces 138
    Intercultural Communication and Power 139
Ethics and Intercultural Communication 140
Improving Your Intercultural Communication Skills 141
    Increase Motivation 141
    Increase Your Knowledge of Self and Others 141
    Avoid Stereotypes 141
Summary • Key Terms • Chapter Review Questions • Activities • Web Activities 142
    DID YOU KNOW?
    Meeting Other Travelers Adds Depth to Argentina Visit 123
    Soaring with Eagles 134
    COMMUNICATION IN SOCIETY
    TV Reality Not Often Spoken of: Race 140
    BUILDING YOUR COMMUNICATION SKILLS
    Sobering Advice for Anyone Contemplating a Cross-Cultural Marriage 130

7 Communication and New Technologies 144

What Is Computer-Mediated Communication? 146
The Importance of Computer-Mediated Communication 147

How Does Computer-Mediated Communication Impact Our Communication Choices? 148
  Media Deficit Approach 148
  VISUAL SUMMARY 7.1 *Media Richness Theory* 150
  Media Augmentation Approach 152
  Social Network Theory 152
Computer-Mediated Communication and the Individual 153
  Managing Identity 153
  Relationship Development 156
The Individual, Communication Technology, and Society 161
  Gender, Age, Ethnicity, and Technology Use 161
  Power, Access, and the Digital Divide 162
  Globalization and the Digital Divide 166
  Closing the Digital Divide 166
Ethics and Computer-Mediated Communication 167
  Ethics and Online Identity 167
  Building Relationships Online 169
Improving Your Computer-Mediated Communication Skills 169
  E-mail Etiquette 169
  Cell Phone Etiquette 169
  Evaluating Internet Information 171
Summary • Key Terms • Chapter Review Questions • Activities • Web Activities 171

  DID YOU KNOW?
  Employers Admit to Disqualifying Candidates Due to Facebook Content 156
  The Ten Commandments of Computer Ethics 168
  COMMUNICATION IN SOCIETY
  Love in the Age of Social Networking 151
  BUILDING YOUR COMMUNICATION SKILLS
  Guidelines for Using Social Networking Sites 158
  Safety Tips for Online Dating 160
  Guidelines for Voice and Text Messaging 170

PART TWO COMMUNICATING IN DYADS

8 Interpersonal Communication and Relationship Development 174

What Is Interpersonal Communication? 176
  Interpersonal Communication Involves Interdependent Parties 176
  Interpersonal Communication Exists on a Continuum 176
  Interpersonal Communication Is Relational 176
The Importance of Interpersonal Communication and Relationships 177
Interpersonal Communication, Relationships, and the Individual 177
  Influences on Relationship Development 177
  Models of Relationship Development 180
  Communicating in Friendships and Romantic Relationships 185
  VISUAL SUMMARY 8.1 *The Dialectical Model of Relationship Development* 186
...iety, Power, Courtship, and Marriage 193
  ...ociety, Power, and Romantic Relationships 193
  ...ciety, Power, and Friendship 195

Ethics and Interpersonal Communication 195
Improving Your Maintenance Skills in Long-Distance Friendships 196
  Maintain Frequent Contact 196
  Encourage Openness 196
  Engage in Positivity 197
  Offer Social Support 197
Summary • Key Terms • Chapter Review Questions • Activities • Web Activities 197

  DID YOU KNOW?
  DNA Dating Site Predicts Chemical Romance 179
  Women's and Men's Flirtation Behaviors Differ 187
  COMMUNICATION IN SOCIETY
  Race and Romantic Relationships in the United States 193
  BUILDING YOUR COMMUNICATION SKILLS
  Strategies for Maintaining Long-Distance Romantic Relationships 178
  Initiating a Conversation 188

9 Managing Challenges in Interpersonal Relationships 200

What Are Relationship Challenges? 202
The Importance of Managing Relationship Challenges 202
The Individual and Relationship Challenges 202
  Developing Social Influence Skills 202
  Managing Aversive Communication Interactions 208
  Relationship Threats 212
  VISUAL SUMMARY 9.1 *Influences on the Perceived Hurtfulness of a Message* 213
The Individual, Relationship Challenges, and Society 219
  Society, Sex Roles, and Relationship Challenges 219
  Society, Emotion, and Relationship Challenges 220
Ethics and Relationship Challenges 222
Improving Your Interpersonal Communication Skills 223
Summary • Key Terms • Chapter Review Questions • Activities • Web Activities 224

  DID YOU KNOW?
  Recognizing a Potential Batterer 216
  COMMUNICATION IN SOCIETY
  Abused Men: The Silent Victims of Domestic Violence 220
  BUILDING YOUR COMMUNICATION SKILLS
  Responding to a Partner's Infidelity 216
  Preventing Sexual Coercion 218

10 Managing Conflict in Interpersonal Relationships 226

What Is Conflict? 228
  Interdependence 228
  Interests 228
  Incompatibilities 229
  Limited Resources 229

The Importance of Managing Conflict Effectively 229
The Individual and Conflict Management 230
    What Purposes Does Conflict Serve? 230
    What Causes Conflict? 231
    Responding to Conflict: Styles and Strategies 232
    Choosing a Conflict Response 237
    Emotion 239
    Problematic Conflict Interactions 240
    VISUAL SUMMARY 10.1 *The Four Horsemen of the Apocalypse* 242
The Individual, Conflict Management, and Society 244
    Power 244
    Culture 245
    Gender 246
Ethics and Conflict Management 247
    Be Truthful 247
    Avoid Name-Calling 247
    Own Your Messages 247
    Avoid Coercion 247
Improving Your Conflict-Management Skills 248
    A Strategic Approach to Conflict Management 248
    The Competence Model of Conflict 249
Summary • Key Terms • Chapter Review Questions • Activities • Web Activities 251
    DID YOU KNOW?
    He Who Cast the First Stone Probably Didn't 241
    COMMUNICATION IN SOCIETY
    Actor Makes the Wrong Call 235
    BUILDING YOUR COMMUNICATION SKILLS
    Tips for Managing and Resolving Conflict 243
    Principles of Interpersonal Conflict 250

PART THREE COMMUNICATING IN GROUPS

11 Small Group Communication Processes 254

What Is Small Group Communication? 256
    A Small Number of People 256
    A Common Purpose 256
    A Connection with Each Other 256
    An Influence on Each Other 256
The Importance of Small Group Communication 257
    Reasons to Study Small Group Communication 257
    Advantages and Disadvantages of Group Work 258
Small Group Communication and the Individual 259
    Types of Communication Roles 259
    Effective Small Group Communication 264
    VISUAL SUMMARY 11.1 *Roles in Groups* 265

The Individual, Small Group Communication, and Society 274
    Power and Group Communication 274
    Cultural Diversity and Small Group Communication 275
Ethics and Small Group Communication 278
Improving Your Small Group Communication Skills 278
Summary • Key Terms • Chapter Review Questions • Activities • Web Activities 279
    DID YOU KNOW?
    Procedures That Help Groups Agree 270
    COMMUNICATION IN SOCIETY
    COINs: The Future of Innovation? 273
    BUILDING YOUR COMMUNICATION SKILLS
    Identifying Roles in Group Situations 262
    How to Handle Conflicts in Meetings 269

12 Leadership in Groups and Organizations 282

What Is Leadership? 284
The Importance of Leadership 285
Leadership and the Individual 285
    The Role of Communication in Leadership 286
    Influences on Leadership 287
Theories of Leadership 290
    Functional Theory 290
    Style Theory 291
    Transformational Leadership Theory 292
    VISUAL SUMMARY 12.1 *Leadership Styles* 293
    Servant Leadership Theory 294
    Toxic Leadership 295
The Individual, Leadership, and Society 296
Ethics and Leadership 298
    Honesty 298
    Respect and Service to Others 299
    Fairness and Justice 299
    Building Community 300
    Moral Leadership 300
Becoming an Effective Leader 300
    Conduct a Leadership Self-Assessment 300
    Search for Leadership Opportunities 301
    Improve Your Strategic Communication Skills 301
Summary • Key Terms • Chapter Review Questions • Activities • Web Activities 302
    DID YOU KNOW?
    Leadership Is an Influence Relationship 284
    COMMUNICATION IN SOCIETY
    Mandela: His Lessons of Leadership 299
    BUILDING YOUR COMMUNICATION SKILLS
    Leading Diverse People 297

PART FOUR SPEAKING IN PUBLIC

13 Speaking in Public: Topic Selection and Speech Development 304

What Is Public Speaking? 306

The Importance of Speaking in Public 306

Establishing Your Reasons for Speaking in Public 307
Identifying Your General Purpose 308
Generating and Selecting Your Topic 308
Identifying Your Specific Purpose 310

Analyzing and Relating to Your Audience 311
What Does Your Audience Know About Your Topic? 312
Who Is Your Audience? 313
What Does Your Audience Know About You? 313
What Does Your Audience Expect from You? 313

Developing Your Speech 314
Narrowing Your Topic 314
Determining Your Main Points 315
Identifying Your Thesis Statement 316
Finding Supporting Materials 317

Organizing Your Speech 321
Developing the Body of Your Speech 321
Selecting Your Organizational Pattern 321
Creating Your Outline 323

Developing Your Transitions, Introduction, and Conclusion 326
Developing Effective Transitions 326
Developing an Effective Introduction 326
Gaining Audience Attention 327
Focusing the Audience's Attention on Your Topic
   by Relating It to Them 328
Giving the Audience an Overview of Your Organizational Pattern 328
Helping the Audience Understand Your Thesis 328
Developing an Effective Conclusion 329
VISUAL SUMMARY 13.1 *Developing Your Speech* 330

Becoming an Ethical Public Speaker 331
*Summary • Key Terms • Chapter Review Questions • Activities • Web
Activities* 331

DID YOU KNOW?
Selected Search Engines and Databases 318
COMMUNICATION IN SOCIETY
Bill Gates, the Great Communicator? 306
BUILDING YOUR COMMUNICATION SKILLS
Communication Event Checklist 307

14 Speaking in Public: Speech Delivery 334

What Is Speech Delivery? 336

The Importance of Speech Delivery 336

Key Issues in Effective Speech Delivery 336
Overcoming Anxiety 336
Preparing Carefully 337
Setting the Tone 339
Considering Language and Style 339
Incorporating Visual Aids 343
Being Aware of Time Limits 345
Choosing a Delivery Method 345
Projecting a Persona 346
Practicing Your Speech 349
VISUAL SUMMARY 14.1 *Key Issues in Effective Speech Delivery* 350

The Individual, Speech Delivery, and Society 351
Ethos, Pathos, and Logos 351

Speech Delivery and Ethics 352
Use Language Sensitively 352
Use Visual Aids Carefully 352
Respect Time Limits 352
*Summary • Key Terms • Chapter Review Questions • Activities • Web
Activities* 352

DID YOU KNOW?
PowerPoint Tips 343
COMMUNICATION IN SOCIETY
Be Cautious with Humor 347
BUILDING YOUR COMMUNICATION SKILLS
Try Relaxing Breathing Exercises 338
The Importance of Dress 341
Stylistic Devices 342
Visual Aids Checklist 344

15 Speaking in Public: Informative Speaking 354

What Is Informative Speaking? 356

The Importance of Informative Speaking 357

Informative Versus Persuasive Speaking 357

Types of Informative Speeches 360
VISUAL SUMMARY 15.1 *Informative Versus Persuasive Speaking* 361
Speeches About "Objects" 362
Speeches About Processes 362
Speeches About Events 362
Speeches About Concepts 363

Organizing Informative Speeches 363
Using a Chronological Pattern 364
Using a Geographical/Spatial Pattern 364
Using a Topical Pattern 365

Tips for Effective Informative Speaking 365
Include Information That Is Accurate and Objective 365
Include Facts That Are Truthful and Can Be Corroborated 366
Include Ideas That Are Accessible to Your Audience 366
Include Visual Aids That Clearly and Accurately Describe Facts 366
Respect the Ideas of the Audience 367

Sample Informative Speech in Outline Form 367

Ethics and Informative Speaking 368

Summary • *Key Terms* • *Chapter Review Questions* • *Activities* • *Web Activities* 369

> **DID YOU KNOW?**
> *Four Types of Informative Speeches* 360
> **COMMUNICATION IN SOCIETY**
> *Informing the Public About the H1N1 Outbreak* 356
> **BUILDING YOUR COMMUNICATION SKILLS**
> *Checklist for Fact Finding* 366

16 Speaking in Public: Persuasive Speaking 370

What Is Persuasive Speaking? 372

The Importance of Persuasive Speaking 373

The Power to Persuade 376
  The Power of Ethos 376
  The Power of Logos 376
  VISUAL SUMMARY 16.1 *The Power to Persuade* 377
  The Power of Pathos 378

Types of Persuasive Speeches 379
  Speeches to Impact the Audience's Attitudes 379
  Speeches to Impact the Audience's Beliefs 380
  Speeches to Impact the Audience's Values 381
  Speeches to Impact the Audience's Behavior 381

Organizing Persuasive Speeches 382
  Using a Problem-Solution or Problem-Solution-Action Pattern 384
  Using a Claim Pattern 385
  Using Monroe's Motivated Sequence 386

Tips for Speaking Persuasively 387
  Select a Topic Appropriate to Persuasion 387
  Organize Your Thesis As a Statement of Fact, Value, or Policy 388
  Establish Credibility Through the Quality of Your Sources 389
  Avoid Misusing Persuasive Language 391

Persuasive Speaking and Ethics 391

Summary • *Key Terms* • *Chapter Review Questions* • *Activities* • *Web Activities* 392

> **DID YOU KNOW?**
> *The Boomerang Effect* 378
> *Fallacies of Reasoning* 382
> **COMMUNICATION IN SOCIETY**
> *The Return of Public Deliberation?* 375
> **BUILDING YOUR COMMUNICATION SKILLS**
> *Research Checklist* 390

GLOSSARY 395
REFERENCES 409
CREDITS 439
INDEX 443

TO THE INSTRUCTOR

Each of us is both an individual and a member of society when we communicate. We know we are individuals whenever we communicate and others communicate with us as individuals. On the other hand, we also know that our communication is interpreted and evaluated against the backdrop of social expectations and social roles. It is this tension between individual identities and social identities that motivated us to write this book. Our goal is to help students learn to think clearly about the complexities of their individual choices when communicating in society.

EFFECTIVE
COMMUNICATION IN SOCIETY
MEANS THINKING CRITICALLY
AND ACTING ETHICALLY

We stress the importance of thinking critically about communication choices and their ethical impact in larger social contexts—because the way people receive and interpret communication is as much a part of the communication process as the sending of messages is. We stress these issues in each chapter through:

Posing *Reflection Questions* that prod students to stop and think critically about important issues in communication.

How do you choose which channel to use when you communicate with others? Do you consider who they are, the topic, the importance of the message, or something else? Overall, do you think you pick the best channel most of the time? If not, what do you need to do to select more appropriately?

Concluding with a dedicated section discussing the ethical implications of the topic addressed in the chapter.

BECOMING AN ETHICAL PUBLIC SPEAKER

We have stressed the importance of ethical communication in all contexts in this book, and public speaking is no exception. According to the authors of *The Speaker's Handbook* (Sprague & Stuart, 2005), effective public speaking involves a commitment to ethical communication principles, including at least two specific guidelines: respect for the integrity of your audience and respect for the integrity of ideas.

Respecting your audience's integrity means recognizing that you have a special kind of power in the public speaking situation. "When audience members entrust you with their time and attention, you take on an obligation to treat them with fairness and concern" (Sprague & Stuart, 2005, p. 33). This means that you do not try to manipulate them into making decisions that might endanger their health or safety and that you do not say anything that might deceive them. Your listeners don't have to agree with what you say, but

EFFECTIVE COMMUNICATION IN SOCIETY MEANS BUILDING STUDENTS' SKILLS AND ENHANCING THEIR UNDERSTANDING

Students benefit from an enhanced understanding of their place in society and how their communication is likely to be interpreted, as this knowledge helps them more effectively use and build their communication skills. To accomplish this, each chapter:

Includes *Building Your Communication Skills* boxes that expose students to a skills-based focus on specific aspects of communication. These boxes give students useful tips to help them enact effective communication practices and immediately increase their communication effectiveness.

Building Your Communication SKILLS

Developing Sensitivity to Cross-Cultural Nonverbal Communication

Most people expect that verbal communication will vary across cultures and anticipate that they will have difficulty communicating in a non-native language. However, fewer people recognize that nonverbal communication can differ considerably across cultures and that they need to be careful when interpreting nonverbal communication cross-culturally. Below we offer you five strategies to help you communicate nonverbally and interpret others' nonverbal communication in unfamiliar cultures.

1. **Observe Closely**. When entering a new culture, set aside your normal understanding of nonverbal signals and anticipate the unexpected. Assume that you do not know the rules, and observe people in the culture carefully to determine patterns of behavior. For example, you may assume that individuals from Japan are happy or amused if they giggle or laugh quietly; however, if you observe their behavior over time and across contexts, you will likely become aware that this behavior often reflects feelings

Concludes with a dedicated section of practical, easy-to-enact instructions in the specific skills students need to improve their communication effectiveness related to the topic addressed in the chapter.

ACTIVITIES

1. Brainstorm a list of informative speech topics. Using the criteria identified in the chapter, narrow your list based on the premise that you will be speaking in each of the following settings:
   a. Your public speaking class
   b. Your dorm
   c. To your 10-year-old brother's friends at an informal gathering
   d. To your coworkers at your office
2. The following is a list of informative speech topics.
   - Facebook
   - Sonia Sotomayor
   - Rachel Maddow
   - Woodstock
   - *Harry Potter*
   - Sushi

For each of the above topics, consider how your informative speech would change, depending on your audience. Below are your different audiences:
   a. Your public speaking class
   b. A fourth-grade class
   c. Your coworkers at your place of employment
   d. A senior citizens' center

For each of the above scenarios, consider how your word choice, content, and framing would differ.

Incorporates *Did You Know?* boxes that highlight interesting aspects of communication and engage student interest in particular topics.

DID YOU KNOW?

Statistically Speaking, How Many People are Deaf or Hard of Hearing?

While listening is generally viewed as a skill, an alternative view is that listening is also impacted strongly by a person's physical ability to hear. This author addresses the question What is the biggest statistical mystery in the deaf and hard-of-hearing community of the United States (and the world)? and tells us that there is little agreement on the answer. How often do you assume that the person listening to you has no hearing impairment? How might this assumption influence the outcomes of your communication encounters?

Previews chapter objectives that students should strive to know by the end of the chapter.

Once you have read this chapter, you will be able to:
- Define verbal communication.
- Identify three reasons for learning about verbal communication.
- Describe the functions and components of language.
- Identify and give an example of each influence on verbal communication.
- Explain the relationship between language and perception.
- Explain the relationship between language and power.
- Discuss ways to communicate more ethically.
- Identify and give an exam

SOCIETY
Language and Perception
Language and Power
Power and Words
Power and Accent
Power and Identity Labels

ETHICS AND VERBAL COMMUNICATION
Become Aware of the Power of

Displays *Visual Summaries* that engage visual learners by using images to graphically illustrate and reinforce important concepts and show the relationships among interconnected elements.

Identity Development Through Communication

VISUAL SUMMARY 2.1

REFLECTED APPRAISAL (THE LOOKING-GLASS SELF)	SOCIAL COMPARISONS	SELF-FULFILLING PROPHECIES
How I see myself is developed through communication with others . . .	**and how I compare myself to others . . .**	**affects how I communicate with them and them with me . . .**
• Interactions with parents and others shape our early identity and sense of ones self.	• Through our interactions with others, we learn what characteristics are valued (or disdained) by others.	• When we expect something to occur, that expectation increases the likelihood that it will.
• The process is repeated with family, friends, teachers, acquaintances, and strangers.	• Then, we assess whether we have more or fewer of those characteristics to determine how we measure up to others in our **identity group**.	• A belief in a particular outcome influences people to act and communicate in ways that make the outcome more likely.
• **Particular others** are important people in our lives who influence aspects of our identity.		• Others can also cause their prophecies about us to come true by communicating with us as though they will come true.
• **Generalized others** are the collection of roles, rules, norms, beliefs, and attitudes endorsed by our community.	**each of which affects my evaluation of myself.**	

Gives students quick, practical information and advice and builds skills through the *Communication Skills for Interview Success* feature, located inside the front and back covers, that they can use to be effective communicators in employment interviews.

COMMUNICATION SKILLS FOR INTERVIEW SUCCESS

Types of Job Interviews: Behavioral Interviews vs. Traditional Interviews

The two most common styles of interviewing used by companies are the traditional job interview and the behavioral interview.

	Behavioral Interviews	Traditional Interviews
Purpose	to identify past work behaviors and/or assess how job candidates are likely to respond to specific situations in the future	to identify whether the interviewee: • has the skills and abilities to perform the job • possesses the enthusiasm and work ethic that the employer expects • will be a team player and fit into the organization

EFFECTIVE COMMUNICATION IN SOCIETY MEANS TAKING RESPONSIBILITY AS AN INDIVIDUAL

This book helps students learn to clearly understand and take responsibility for the complexities of their individual communication choices. We recognize that messages are interpreted differently because of senders' age, gender, race, ethnicity, religion, sexuality, and other social differences that guide society. Differences, however, are not simply markers of how we as individuals are dissimilar; rather, they also point to connections that we have with others who share our gender, age, sexuality, race, ethnicity, religion, and other characteristics. To highlight this message:

THE INDIVIDUAL AND RELATIONSHIP CHALLENGES

Each interaction between people in a relationship is affected by the communication choices of both partners. While you can only control your own behavior, the choices you make impact how others respond to you and, therefore, how the conversation unfolds. This truth was articulated centuries ago in Proverbs 15:1, which states "A soft answer turns away wrath: but grievous words stir up anger" (Holy Bible, KJV, n.d.). Researchers have scientifically established the truth of this saying; they have found that 96 percent of the time, the likelihood that a relational partner will care how you feel is determined by the attitude with which you begin the conversation. More specifically, people who show vulnerability evoke tenderness and caring from others, while those who are critical are met with defensiveness and hostility (Atkinson, 2005). So even if someone approaches you in anger, you can control the course of the conversation by the tone of your response.

Because we cannot discuss every potential problem you might encounter in your close relationships, in this chapter we will explore three categories of relationship challenges we perceive to be the most pervasive and/or potentially destructive to relationships: social influence, aversive communication behaviors, and relationship threats. Let's take each in turn.

Each chapter includes a section that directly applies the topic addressed in the chapter to a discussion of its role in individual communication choices and how those choices interact with societal expectations and norms.

We include an *It Happened to Me* feature, which is composed of vignettes that come from student experiences and are presented in their own voices. These narratives serve to illustrate and clarify communication concepts and highlight the complexity and real-world application of chapter material.

These are just a few questions that might help you develop a list of potential topics. Talk to your friends. Brainstorm with them. Great ideas come out of group discussion!

You may now be considering several topics for your speech, but how do you decide among them? While an almost-infinite number of great speech topics exist, not all topics are equally suited for the circumstances you are going to confront. Public speaking expert Cheryl Hamilton (2009) suggests that for each possible topic, you consider whether it meets the following criteria (pp. 96–98):

The Topic Should Be of Interest to the Speaker

A speech can be especially dry if the speaker is unenthusiastic about

IT HAPPENED TO ME: *Scott*

I am a political science major in my last semester, and instant run-off voting has been my subject of interest since my first year in college. In instant-run-off voting, voters rank-order candidates if no candidate gets a clear majority. The candidate with the least votes is eliminated, and the process is repeated until one candidate obtains a majority of votes. This system is used in some countries and even some states within the United States. It has many advantages, but few people know about it, so I thought it made an excellent choice for my speech topic.

EFFECTIVE COMMUNICATION IN SOCIETY MEANS UNDERSTANDING THE INFLUENCE OF SOCIETY

We help students understand the important influence of the many social roles they occupy—beyond age, gender, race, and sexuality. In addition to being male or female, for example, a person might also be a parent, consumer, voter, manager, and police officer, among other roles. All of these individual characteristics and social roles are important, because an individual's communication is interpreted and evaluated (or "read") based on the social expectations that accompany them. To reinforce this lesson,

Each chapter is includes a section that directly applies the topic addressed in the chapter to a discussion of its role in societal expectations and norms and, in turn, their intersection with individual communication choices.

SOCIETY, POWER, COURTSHIP, AND MARRIAGE

Many people think that relationships depend solely on the individuals involved, that our decision to befriend or become intimate with another person is a matter of choice, and that how we communicate and behave within relationships is strictly a matter of preference. However, society wields strong influences on our choices and behavior. Sometimes these influences are explicit and a matter of law, as in restrictions against marriage between underage teenagers. Other societal influences are more subtle. For example, why is it that 95 percent of all marriages are racially homogenous (United States Bureau of the Census, 1998)? Similarly, why do most couples who marry have a wedding ceremony, and why are

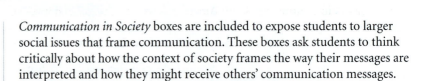

Communication in Society boxes are included to expose students to larger social issues that frame communication. These boxes ask students to think critically about how the context of society frames the way their messages are interpreted and how they might receive others' communication messages.

Communication in SOCIETY

Effective Listening Skills of Managers

In the article summarized below, journalist Martin Kornacki describes the results of recent research emphasizing the importance of line (factory) managers' communication skills. Do you think these findings can be generalized to other work contexts? For example, supervisors in fast food restaurants? Supervisors of departments in white-collar professions?

According to new research findings, line managers' communication skills—especially listening skills—are particularly important during periods of economic downturns.

In a recent news article, journalist Martin Kornacki describes a research study that found that employees who believe that their managers listen to them and answer questions honestly have greater confidence in their organization's future, which then translates into commitment to the organization, and greater productivity—even if the economic outlook is uncertain.

The key seems to be good relationships between managers and workers—fostered by listening skills. Kornacki also

interviewed clinical psychologist Dr Amy Silver, who has worked with organizations in turbulent situations. She emphasizes the role of active listening in establishing solid trusting relationships between line managers and line workers. According to Dr. Silver, the best relationships—characterized by genuineness, empathy and rapport—are built from "active listening by both parties, with slightly more emphasis on the more powerful party to do so." She goes on to say that it's called active listening "because it is easy to listen, but not so easy to truly listen." She also points to many research studies that demonstrate that the quality of the relationship is crucial in determining productivity in business contexts.

Kornacki concludes that companies who do not invest in improving managers' communication skills are generally less productive and these differences between good and poor business practices are highlighted during economic recessions.

SOURCE: Kornacki, M. (2009, April 20). Managers' communication skills put under scrutiny by new research. *TJ online*. Retrieved January 21, 2010 from http://www.trainingjournal.com/news/2069.html#

A WORD ABOUT LANGUAGE

The text's commitment to presenting comprehensive coverage of the complex issues in the field of communication carries with it a responsibility to use language thoughtfully. We recognize the fact that, for complex historical and political reasons, identity labels carry strong denotative meanings that may vary from person to person. Hence, we have used the most inclusive terms possible, given the heterogeneity of opinions within various ethnic and racial groups.

For example, the term *Hispanic* was created and used in 1980 by the U.S. government when collecting census statistics but is rejected by many individuals of Spanish descent. They (and we) prefer *Latina/o* (referring to a U.S. American of Spanish descent from a specific ancestral nation such as Argentina, Mexico, or any other country in Latin America or from Spain). We also use *Mexican American* when referring to individuals coming more directly from Mexico and *Chicana/o* to designate people of Mexican descent with more political consciousness.

Similarly, we use the inclusive term *Asian American,* unless referring to individuals from a specific national origin (e.g., Japan or the Philippines). We use *African American* or *Black* interchangeably, recognizing that some individuals (originating from the Caribbean) prefer the more-inclusive term *Black,* while others prefer *African American.* We also use *Native American* and *American Indian* interchangeably, recognizing that individuals are divided in their preferences for each of these terms.

We should also note that we use *White,* because this is the term preferred by U.S. Americans of European ancestry, rather than *European American.* We believe that this term appropriately emphasizes the racial distinction that is more important than ethnic distinctions in contemporary U.S. society. At the same time, we recognize that some individuals prefer to emphasize their more specific origins (*Japanese American* rather than *Asian American, Yaqui* rather than *Native American,* or *German American* rather than *White*).

Finally, we are learning to think more internationally in our use of language. Many of our neighbors in Central and South America as well as Canada find it offensive when we use the term "American" to refer to ourselves. After all, they are Americans also. Therefore, we prefer the term *U.S. American* in recognition of the fact that we are only one society out of many that make up the continents of North and South America.

RESOURCES IN PRINT AND ONLINE

Name of Supplement	Available in Print	Available Online	Instructor or Student Supplement	Description
Instructor's Manual (ISBN: 0205030882)	√	√	Instructor Supplement	Prepared by Sarah Riforgiate, Arizona State University, the Instructor's Manual includes a wealth of resources for each chapter. There is an annotated Instructional Outline that matches the PowerPoint® presentation package and can be used for planning, developing, and delivering lectures. Discussion Questions, designed to increase student engagement, can also be used for assignments, essay questions, or as review questions for an exam (sample answers are provided). In addition, there are In-Class/Out-of-Class Activities and suggestions for Additional Resources. Available for download at www.pearsonhighered.com/irc (access code required).
Test Bank (ISBN: 0205030033)	√	√	Instructor Supplement	The Test Bank, prepared by Sarah Riforgiate, Arizona State University, consists of more than 1200 thoroughly reviewed assessments, a blend of multiple choice, completion, short answer, and essay questions. Each question is referenced by a correct answer/grading criteria (for essay questions only), page reference, and skill designation. Available for download at www.pearsonhighered.com/irc (access code required)
MyTest (ISBN: 0205030904)		√	Instructor Supplement	This flexible, online test generating software includes all questions found in the printed Test Bank, allowing instructors to create their own personalized exams. Instructors can also edit any of the existing test questions and even add new questions. Other special features of this program include random generation of test questions, creation of alternate versions of the same test, scrambling of question sequence, and test preview before printing. Available at www.pearsonmytest.com (access code required).
PowerPoint® Presentation Package (ISBN: 0205030890)		√	Instructor Supplement	This text-specific package, prepared by Sarah Riforgiate, Arizona State University, is the electronic version of the lecture outlines provided in the Instructor's Manual and provides a basis for your lecture with PowerPoint® slides for each chapter of the book. Available for download at www.pearsonhighered.com/irc (access code required).
Pearson Allyn & Bacon Introduction to Communication Video Library	√		Instructor Supplement	Pearson Allyn & Bacon's Introduction to Communication Video Library contains a range of videos from which adopters can choose. The videos feature a variety of topics and scenarios for communication foundations, interpersonal communication, small group communication, and public speaking. Please contact your Pearson representative for details and a complete list of videos and their contents to choose which would be most useful to your course. Some restrictions apply.
Lecture Questions for Clickers for Introduction to Communication (ISBN: 0205547230)		√	Instructor Supplement	Prepared by Keri Moe, El Paso Community College, an assortment of questions and activities covering culture, listening, interviewing, public speaking, interpersonal conflict and more are presented in a user-friendly PowerPoint® presentation package. These slides will help liven up your lectures and can be used along with the Personal Response System to get students more involved in class discussion. Available at www.pearsonhighered.com/irc (access code required).
A Guide for New Teachers of Introduction to Communication, Fourth Edition (ISBN: 0205750001)	√	√	Instructor Supplement	Prepared by Susanna G. Porter, Kennesaw State University with a new chapter on using MyCommunicationLab by Heather Dillon, Urbana, Illinois, this guide is designed to help new teachers effectively teach the introductory communication course. It is full of first day of class tips, great teaching ideas, a guide to Pearson resources, and sample activities and assignments. Available at www.pearsonhighered.com/irc (access code required).

Name of Supplement	Available in Print	Available Online	Instructor or Student Supplement	Description
Preparing Visual Aids for Presentations, Fifth Edition (ISBN: 020561115X)	√		Student Supplement	Prepared by Dan Cavanaugh, this 32-page visual booklet provides a host of ideas for using today's multimedia tools to improve presentations, including suggestions for planning a presentation, guidelines for designing visual aids and storyboarding, and a walkthrough that shows how to prepare a visual display using PowerPoint® (available for purchase).
Pearson Allyn & Bacon Introduction to Communication Study Site (Open access)		√	Student Supplement	This open access student study resource features practice tests, learning objectives, and Web links organized around the major topics typically covered in the Introduction to Communication course. Available at www.abintrocommunication.com.
Public Speaking in the Multicultural Environment, Second Edition (ISBN: 0205265111)	√		Student Supplement	Prepared by Devorah A. Lieberman, Portland State University, this booklet helps students learn to analyze cultural diversity within their audiences and adapt their presentations accordingly (available for purchase).
The Speech Outline (ISBN: 032108702X)	√		Student Supplement	Prepared by Reeze L. Hanson and Sharon Condon of Haskell Indian Nations University, this workbook includes activities, exercises, and answers to help students develop and master the critical skill of outlining (available for purchase).
Multicultural Activities Workbook (ISBN: 0205546528)	√		Student Supplement	By Marlene C. Cohen and Susan L. Richardson of Prince George's Community College, Maryland, this workbook is filled with hands-on activities that help broaden the content of speech classes to reflect diverse cultural backgrounds. The checklists, surveys, and writing assignments all help students succeed in speech communication by offering experiences that address a variety of learning styles (available for purchase).
Speech Preparation Workbook (ISBN: 013559569X)	√		Student Supplement	Prepared by Jennifer Dreyer and Gregory H. Patton of San Diego State University, this workbook takes students through the stages of speech creation–from audience analysis to writing the speech–and includes guidelines, tips, and easy to fill-in pages (available for purchase).
Study Card for Introduction to Speech Communication (ISBN: 0205474381)	√		Student Supplement	Colorful, affordable, and packed with useful information, the Pearson Allyn & Bacon Study Cards make studying easier, more efficient, and more enjoyable. Course information is distilled down to the basics, helping students quickly master the fundamentals, review a subject for understanding, or prepare for an exam. Because they're laminated for durability, they can be kept for years to come and pulled out whenever students need a quick review (available for purchase).
MyCommunicationLab		√	Instructor & Student Supplement	MyCommunicationLab is a state-of-the-art, interactive and instructive solution for communication courses. Designed to be used as a supplement to a traditional lecture course or to completely administer an online course, MyCommunicationLab combines a Pearson eText, MySearchLab™, MediaShare, multimedia, video clips, activities, research support, tests and quizzes to completely engage students. See next page for more details.

SAVE TIME AND IMPROVE RESULTS WITH **PEARSON** mycommunicationlab

Designed to amplify a traditional course in numerous ways or to administer a course online, **MyCommunicationLab** for Introductory Communication courses combines pedagogy and assessment with an array of multimedia activities –videos, speech preparation tools, assessments, research support, multiple newsfeeds—to make learning more effective for all types of students. Now featuring more resources, including a video upload tool, this new release of **MyCommunicationLab** is visually richer and even more interactive than the previous version—a leap forward in design with more tools and features to enrich learning and aid students in classroom success.

Teaching and Learning Tools

Pearson eText: Identical in content and design to the printed text, a Pearson eText provides students access to their text whenever and wherever they need it. In addition to contextually placed multimedia features in every chapter, the Pearson eText allows students to take notes and highlight, just like a traditional book.

Videos and Video Quizzes: Interactive videos provide students with the opportunity to watch video clips that portray different communication scenarios, interviews with well-known communication scholars, and sample speeches including both professional and student speeches. Many student speeches are annotated with constructive feedback. MyCommunicationLab also offers a number of video-based quizzes that can be assigned and that report to the instructor's gradebook.

Assessment: Online self-assessments in MyPersonalityProfile, including SCAM, PRCA-24, and assessments that test introversion, shyness, and communication competence, help students learn about the different communication styles and assess their own. Instructors can use these tools to show learning over the duration of the course. In addition to MyPersonalityProfile, Pre- and Post-Tests are included in every chapter. The results from these tests create a customized study plan for further review and focus students on areas in which they need to improve.

MyOutline: MyOutline offers step-by-step guidance for writing an effective outline, along with tips and explanations to help students better understand the elements of an outline and how all the pieces fit together. Outlines that students create can be downloaded to their computer, emailed as an attachment, or

saved in the tool for future editing. Instructors can either select from several templates based on our texts, or they can create their own outline template for students to use.

Topic Selector: This interactive tool helps students get started generating ideas and then narrowing down topics. Our Topic Selector is question based, rather than drill-down or simply a list of ideas, in order to help students really learn the process of selecting their topic. Once they have determined their topic, students are directed to credible online sources for guidance with the research process.

ABC News RSS feed: MyCommunicationLab provides an online news feed from ABC News, updated hourly, to help students choose and research group assignments and speeches.

MySearchLab: Pearson's MySearchLab™ is the easiest way for students to start a research assignment or paper. Complete with extensive help on the research process and four databases of credible and reliable source material, MySearchLab ™ helps students quickly and efficiently make the most of their research time. In addition to an extensive research database, MySearchLab™ also includes AutoCite, which assists in the creation of a "Works Cited" document.

Cutting Edge Technology

MediaShare: With our exciting, cutting edge video upload tool, students are able to upload group assignments, interpersonal role plays, and speeches for their instructor and classmates to watch (whether face-to-face or online) and provide online feedback and comments at time-stamped intervals. MediaShare also includes a completely customizable grading rubric for instructors, which allows grades to be imported into most learning management systems. Structured much like a social networking site, MediaShare can help promote a sense of community among students.

Audio Chapter Summaries: Every chapter includes a streaming audio chapter summary, perfect for students reviewing material before a test or instructors reviewing material before class.

Quick and Dirty Tips Podcast: Through an agreement with Quick and Dirty Tips, MyCommunicationLab now features a RSS feed of T*he Public Speaker's Quick and Dirty Tips for Improving Your Communication Skills*, which covers topics such as conflict, negotiation, networking, pronunciation, eye contact, overcoming nervousness, interviewing skills, accent modification, and more!

Online Administration

No matter what course management system you use—or if you do not use one at all, but still wish to easily capture your students' grade and track their performance—Pearson has a **MyCommunicationLab** option to suit your needs. Contact one of Pearson's Technology Specialists for more information and assistance.

A **MyCommunicationLab** access code is no additional cost when packaged with selected Pearson Communication texts. To get started, contact your local Pearson Publisher's Representative at **www.pearsonhighered.com/replocator**.

ACKNOWLEDGMENTS

We are grateful to all the students and instructors who have provided invaluable feedback to us as we wrote this book. Unfortunately, we are not able to list all of the students who provided feedback, but we would like to acknowledge the instructors who have helped to shape and define this book.

REVIEWERS

Dr. Todd A. Allen, *Geneva College*
Phil Backlund, *Central Washington University*
Joshua Borgmann, *Southwestern Community College*
Bob Brown, *Chippewa Valley Technical College*
Peter Croisant, *Geneva College*
Dennis C. Dufer, *St. Louis Community College – Meramec*
Angela Gibson, *Shelton State Community College*
Jacqueline Irwin, *California State University Sacramento*
Pam Joraanstad, *Glendale Community College*
Amie D. Kincaid, *University of Illinois, Springfield*
Jennifer Lehtinen, *SUNY Orange*
Gregg Nelson, *Chippewa Valley Technical College*
Sandra L. Pensoneau-Conway, *Wayne State University*
Kelly Petkus, *Austin Community College*
Elizabeth Ribarsky, *University of Illinois, Springfield*
Kate Simcox, *Messiah College*
Janice K. Vincent, *Jackson State University*
Dan Warren, *Bellevue University*
Diana M. Withers, *Austin Community College*

ADDITIONAL ACKNOWLEDGMENTS

We would also like to thank our colleagues and students for their invaluable assistance and moral support: A special thanks to Professor Nicole Maurantonio (formerly of Northeastern University, now at the University of Richmond) for her invaluable assistance with the public speaking chapters. Our thanks also to Professor Kelly McDonald, Arizona State University, for generously sharing his expertise and relevant material on communication issues in leadership, to Professor Pauline Hope Cheong, Arizona State University, for providing invaluable assistance in framing cutting-edge issues in the CMC chapter, and to Professor Laura A. Janusik (Rockhurst University) for sharing her expertise and materials in recent scholarship on listening.

In addition, we want to express our deepest gratitude to Charee Mooney, our editorial assistant, who worked tirelessly and competently (often at a moment's notice) to gather materials, research various topics, and share her personal experiences and stories. She went far beyond the call of duty to help us complete this project successfully and on time.

Thanks to the Pearson Allyn & Bacon team who made it all happen. Thanks to editor-in-chief Karon Bowers. Thanks also to Susan Messer, development editor, for her enthusiasm and hard work, and to Kristen Desmond LeFevre, development editor, for her important guidance and help in shaping the chapters. We also thank photo researcher Sheila Norman; visual research manager Beth Brenzel, and development manager David Kear. And thanks to project editor Kristin Jobe and editorial assistant Megan Sweeney.

Finally, we thank our partners—James LeRoy, Ronald Chaldu, and David Karbonski—who continue to tolerate our frequent absences with good grace. We give them our deepest thanks for their support throughout this and many other projects.

ABOUT THE AUTHORS

Jess Alberts is President's Professor in the Hugh Downs School of Human Communication at Arizona State University. She is a social scientist who focuses on interpersonal communication and specializes in the study of conflict.

Judith Martin is a professor in the Hugh Downs School of Human Communication at Arizona State University. She is an interpretive scholar whose expertise is in intercultural communication.

Thomas Nakayama is chair and professor in the Department of Communication Studies at Northeastern University. He is a critical scholar who focuses on rhetoric and intercultural communication.

With their different areas of expertise, the authors have created a comprehensive text with a truly balanced approach to the study of human communication.

COMMUNICATION IN SOCIETY

1

INTRODUCTION TO HUMAN COMMUNICATION

On her way to class, Charee called her dad to let him know what time she would arrive home; she then texted a friend to arrange to meet for lunch. While she waited for class to begin, she checked her e-mail and chatted with classmates. When the professor arrived, she turned off her iPhone and listened attentively as the class began.

Most people, like Charee, exist in a sea of communication. They watch television (perhaps too much); attend class lectures; phone, e-mail, and text their friends and family; and are inundated by messages over loudspeakers as they shop for groceries or use public transportation. Given all of this, it is hard to imagine that only 75 years ago, most communication occurred either face to face or via "snail mail." But in fact, throughout much of human history, individuals lived very close to the people they knew. They conducted commerce and maintained relationships primarily with the same small group of people throughout their lives. Today, people maintain relationships with individuals thousands of miles away, and they buy and sell products halfway around the globe on eBay. This instant and widespread access to the world has its benefits, but it also has its costs.

With so many communication options, people need a wider range of communication skills than ever before. Successful communicators must converse effectively face to face; correspond clearly via e-mail; learn when it is appropriate to use text messaging; and absorb the norms and etiquette surrounding cell phones, chat rooms, and video and telephone conferences.

Becoming an effective communicator involves both understanding the components and processes of communication and putting them into practice. As you work in this course to improve your communication skills, you may see positive changes in your relationships, your career, your engagement in civic life, and even in your identity. How many other courses can claim all that?

Once you have read this chapter, you will be able to:

- Discuss the importance of studying human communication.
- Define communication.
- Describe a variety of careers in communication.
- Name and explicate the seven primary components of communication.
- Explain the Human Communication in Society model.
- Understand the ethical responsibilities of speakers and listeners.
- Formulate your own communication ethic.

CHAPTER OUTLINE

THE IMPORTANCE OF STUDYING HUMAN COMMUNICATION

WHAT IS HUMAN COMMUNICATION?
  Components of Human Communication
  A Model of Human Communication: Human Communication in Society

COMMUNICATION ETHICS
  Defining Communication Ethics
  Developing Communication Ethics
  Communication Ethics in Practice

Summary

Key Terms

Chapter Review Questions

Activities

Web Activities

THE IMPORTANCE OF STUDYING HUMAN COMMUNICATION

As you begin this book, two questions may arise. First, you may wonder exactly how the study of human communication differs from other studies of humans, such as psychology. Communication differs from other social science disciplines because it focuses exclusively on the exchange of messages to create meaning. Scholars in communication explore what, when, where, and why humans interact (Emanuel, 2007). They do so to increase our understanding of how people communicate and to help individuals improve their abilities to communicate in a wide variety of contexts. In addition, unlike most social sciences, the study of communication has a long history—reaching back to the classical era of Western civilization when Isocrates, Plato, and Aristotle wrote about the important role of communication in politics, the courts, and learning (National Communication Association Poole & Walther, 2001). However, the ability to speak effectively and persuasively has been valued since the beginning of recorded history. As early as 3200 to 2800 BCE, the Precepts of Kagemni and Ptah-Hopte commented on communication (NCA Pathways, 2003), and the Old Testament acknowledges the importance of communication skills, as when God appoints Aaron Moses' spokesperson (Holy Bible, KJV, n.d.).

Second, you may wonder why you need to study communication; after all, you have probably been doing a reasonably good job of it thus far. And isn't most communication knowledge just common sense? Unfortunately, it is not. If good communication skills were just common sense, then communication would not so often go awry. We would live in a world where misunderstandings rarely occurred; conflicts were easily resolved; and public speakers were organized, clear, and engaging. Instead, communication is a complex activity influenced by a variety of factors, including cultural differences, cognitive abilities, and social norms.

Good communication is not a cure-all for every relationship and career ill, but it can help you attain your goals, establish relationships, and develop your identity. Every day, you use communication to accomplish practical goals such as inviting a friend to see a movie with you, resolving a conflict with a colleague, or persuading the city council to install speed bumps in your neighborhood. Essentially, communication is functional, as it allows you to accomplish the daily tasks of living. However, is it possible to have too much communication? To learn one researcher's answer to this question, see *Did You Know? Too Much Talk Can Lead to Problems.*

DID YOU KNOW?

Too Much Talk Can Lead to Problems

A researcher at the University of Missouri-Columbia has found that girls who talk very extensively about their problems with friends are likely to become more anxious and depressed.

The research on girls' communication was conducted by Amanda Rose, Associate Professor of Psychological Sciences in the College of Arts and Science. The six-month study, which included boys and girls, examined the effects of *co-rumination*—excessively talking with friends about problems and concerns. Rose discovered that girls co-ruminate more than boys, especially in adolescence, and that girls who co-ruminated the most in the fall of the school year were most likely to be more depressed and anxious by the spring.

"When girls co-ruminate, they're spending such a high percentage of their time dwelling on problems and concerns that it probably makes them feel sad and more hopeless about the problems because those problems are in the forefront of their minds. Those are symptoms of depression," Rose said. "In terms of anxiety, co-ruminating likely makes them feel more worried about the problems, including about their consequences. Co-rumination also may lead to depression and anxiety because it takes so

much time, time that could be used to engage in other, more positive activities that could help distract youth from their problems. This is especially true for problems that girls can't control, such as whether a particular boy likes them, or whether they get invited to a party that all of the popular kids are attending."

Ironically, although co-rumination was related to increased depression and anxiety, Rose also found that co-rumination was associated with positive friendship quality, including feelings of closeness between friends. Boys who co-ruminated also developed closer friendships across the school year but did not develop greater depressive and anxiety symptoms over time.

Rose said adolescents should be encouraged to talk about their problems, but only in moderation and without co-ruminating. "They also should engage in other activities, like sports, which can help them take their minds off their problems, especially problems that they can't control," she said.

SOURCE: Adapted from: "Prospective associations of co-rumination with friendship and emotional adjustment." (2007, July 16). http://www.news-medical.net/news/2007/07/16/27624.aspx

Do you ever co-ruminate with friends? If so, what topics do you discuss? How does engaging in this behavior make you feel? Can you think of other communication behaviors or activities that might help you more than co-ruminating does? If so, next time you find yourself excessively talking about your problems with a friend, try one of those activities.

You also use communication to meet people, to develop professional and personal relationships, and to terminate dissatisfying relationships. Communication scholar Steve Duck argues that relationships are primarily communicative (1994). Moreover, the relationships you have with others—including how you think and feel about one another—develop as you communicate. Through your communication interactions, you and your relationship partners develop shared meanings for events, explanations for your past, and a vision of your future together (Alberts, Yoshimura, Rabby, & Loschiavo, 2005; Dixon & Duck, 1993). So, when you tell your romantic partner, "I have never loved anyone as much as I love you, and I never will," you simultaneously redefine your past romantic relationships, create shared meaning for your present relationship, and project a vision of your future together. Similarly, through your communication with friends, coworkers, and acquaintances, you define and redefine your relationships.

Perhaps most fundamentally, your communication interactions with others allow you to establish who you are to them (Gergen, 1982; Mead, 1934). As you communicate, you attempt to reveal yourself in a particular light. For example, when you are at work, you may try to establish yourself as someone who is pleasant, hardworking, honest, and/or powerful. With a new roommate, you may want your communication behavior to suggest that you are responsible, fun, and easygoing. However, at the same time as your communication creates an image of who you are for others, *their* communication shapes your vision of yourself. For example, if your friends laugh at your jokes, compliment you on your sense of humor, and introduce you to others as a funny person, you will probably see yourself as amusing. In these ways, communication helps create both your self-identity and your identity as others perceive it.

Communication has the potential to transform your life—both for the better and for the worse. (To read how one student's communication created a transformation, see *It Happened to Me: Chelsea*.) As many people have discovered, poor or unethical communication can negatively affect lives. How? Communicating poorly during conflict can end relationships, inadequate interviewing skills can result in unemployment, and negative feedback from conversational partners can lessen one's self-esteem. Sometimes communication can have even more significant effects. For example, people who lie under oath may be charged with a crime, as Martha Stewart and others have learned (McCord, Greenhalgh, & Magasin, 2004).

Talking extensively about problems can cause girls to become anxious and depressed.

As you can see from Chelsea's story, developing excellent communication skills can also transform your life for the better. The three authors of this book have all had

students visit months or years after taking our communication classes to tell us what a difference the classes have made in their lives. A student in a public-speaking class reported that, because of her improved presentation skills, she received the raise and promotion she had been pursuing for years. Another student in a conflict and negotiation class revealed that her once-troubled marriage became more stable once she learned to express disagreements better. A third student felt more confident after he took a persuasion class that taught him how to influence people.

Studying human communication may also benefit you by leading you to a new career path. A wide variety of communication careers are available, and a degree in communication can prepare you for many of these. For more information, see *Did You Know? Careers in Communication.*

IT HAPPENED TO ME: *Chelsea*

When the professor asked us to identify a time when communication was transformative, many examples came to mind. Finally, I settled on one involving a negative relationship. In high school, there's usually one person you just don't get along with: boyfriend drama, bad mouthing, you name it. I remember dreading seeing this one girl, and I'm sure she felt the same about me. Graduation came and went, and I completely forgot about her. A year later, I came across her Web page as I was searching for old classmates online. As I thought about how petty our arguments were and how cruel we were to each other, I felt smaller and smaller. So I decided to end it. I used e-mail to apologize for my bad behavior, because with e-mail I felt safer—I could compose my thoughts, avoid a direct confrontation, and give her time to respond. A couple days later, I received an e-mail from her saying she felt the same way and was also sorry for the way she acted. Next week, we're going to have a cup of coffee together to really put the past behind us. Maybe to some people that doesn't seem all that life changing, but after hating this girl for two years, it's an amazing transformation for me.

DID YOU KNOW?

Careers in Communication

Careers in advertising, including: advertising or marketing specialist, copy writer, account executive, sales manager, media planner, media buyer, creative director, media sales representative, public opinion researcher

Careers in communication education, including: language arts coordinator, high school speech teacher, forensics/debate coach, drama director, college or university professor, speech communication department chairperson

Careers in electronic media/radio-television/broadcasting, including: broadcasting station manager, director of broadcasting, film/tape librarian, community relations director, unit manager, film editor, news director, news writer, transmitter engineer, technical director, advertising sales coordinator, traffic/ continuity specialist, media buyer, market researcher, actor, announcer, disc jockey, news anchor, public relations manager, comedy writer, casting director, producer, business manager, researcher, account executive, floor manager, talk show host

Careers in journalism, including: reporter, editor, newscaster, author, copy writer, script writer, publisher, news service researcher, technical writer, acquisitions editor, media interviewer

Careers in public relations, including: publicity manager, advertising manager, marketing specialist, press agent, lobbyist, corporate public affairs specialist, account executive, development officer, fund-raiser, membership recruiter, sales manager, media analyst, media planner, creative director, audience analyst, news writer, public opinion researcher

Careers in theater/performing arts/dramatic arts, including: performing artist, script writer, producer, director, arts administrator, performing arts educator, costume designer, scenic designer, lighting designer, theater critic, makeup artist, stage manager, model, theater professor, casting director

Careers in Fields Related to Communication
Careers in business and communication, including: sales representative, executive manager, personnel manager, public information officer, industrial and labor relations

representative, negotiator, director of corporate communication, customer service representative, newsletter editor, communication trainer, human resources manager, mediator, buyer

Careers in education, including: teacher (elementary and secondary), school counselor, educational researcher, audiovisual specialist, educational administrator, school/university information specialist, director of college news, director of a collegiate information center, educational tester, development officer, educational fund-raiser, alumni officer, college placement officer, college admissions director, college recruiter

Communication and government/political-related careers, including: public information officer, speechwriter, legislative assistant, campaign director, research specialist, program coordinator, negotiator, lobbyist, press secretary, elected official

Careers in health and communication, including: health educator, school health care administrator, medical grants writer, hospital director of communication, clinic public relations director, health communication analyst, research analyst, medical training supervisor, communications manager for federal health agencies, health personnel educator, medical center publications editor, hospice manager, drug rehabilitationist, health care counselor, activities director, marketing director, and health facility fund-raiser

Careers in international relations and negotiations, including: on-air international broadcasting talent, corporate representative, translator, student tour coordinator, diplomat, foreign relations officer, host/hostess for foreign dignitaries, foreign correspondent

Careers in law and communication, including: public defender, corporate lawyer, district attorney, public interest lawyer, private practice lawyer, legal researcher, mediation and negotiation specialist, paralegal researcher, legal secretary, legal reporter, legal educator

Careers in social and human services, including: public administrator, social worker, recreational supervisor, human rights officer, community affairs liaison, park service public relations specialist, philanthropic representative, religious leader, mental counselor

NOTE: These career titles were derived from a survey of communication graduates from 16 colleges and universities that has been supplemented with other jobs clearly in the speech communication field.

SOURCE: Wolvin, A. D. (1998). "Careers in Communication: An update." *Journal of the Association for Communication Administration, 27*, 71–73.

WHAT IS HUMAN COMMUNICATION?

Even though you have been communicating for your entire life, you probably have not given much thought to the process. You may question why we even need to provide a definition for something so commonplace. Although communication is an everyday occurrence, the term covers a wide variety of behaviors that include talking to friends, broadcasting media messages, and e-mailing coworkers. Because the term *communication* is complex and can have a variety of definitions, we need to acquaint you with the definition we will use throughout this text.

Broadly speaking, *human communication* can be defined as *a process in which people generate meaning through the exchange of verbal and nonverbal messages*. In this book, however, we emphasize the influence of individual and societal forces and the roles of culture and context more than other definitions do. Because we believe that these concepts are essential to understanding the communication process completely, we have developed a definition of human communication that includes them. Accordingly, we define **human communication** as a *transactional process in which people generate meaning through the exchange of verbal and nonverbal messages in specific contexts, influenced by individual and societal forces and embedded in culture*. In the following sections, we

human communication
a transactional process in which people generate meaning through the exchange of verbal and nonverbal messages in specific contexts, influenced by individual and societal forces and embedded in culture

will illustrate our definition of human communication and explore the meaning of each of these concepts and their relationships to one another. To do so, we first look at the basic components of communication as highlighted in current definitions. Then, we examine the way in which these components serve as the building blocks of our own model of human communication in society. Finally, we explain how individual and societal influences as well as culture and context contribute to an understanding of the communication process.

Components of Human Communication

Consider the following scenario:

> Charee grew up in the United States and needed to talk to her father, Pham, who was reared in Vietnam, about her desire to attend graduate school out of state. She was worried; she was the first member of her family to attend graduate school and would be the first single family member to move so far away. She hoped to convince her father that it was a good idea for her to go away, while also displaying respect for him as her father and the head of the household. To ensure that things went well, she decided that they should meet at his favorite neighborhood café in the early afternoon so they could talk privately. She rehearsed how she would convey information that he might not be happy to hear and practiced responses to the objections she expected him to raise.

As this example reveals, communication is a complex process that can require considerable thought and planning. The complexity inherent in communication is due in part to the variety of factors that compose and influence it. The seven basic components of communication that Charee—and you—must consider when planning an interaction are *message creation, meaning creation, setting, participants, channels, noise, and feedback*. Each of these features is central to how a communication interaction unfolds. (See *Visual Summary 1.1: Key Components of Human Communication*.) To help you understand this process, we analyze Charee's experiences with her father.

Message Creation

Messages are the building blocks of communication, and the process of taking ideas and converting them into messages is called **encoding;** receiving a message and interpreting its meaning is referred to as **decoding**. Depending on the importance of a message, people are more or less careful in encoding their messages. In our example above, Charee was very concerned with how she encoded her messages to her father. She particularly wanted to communicate to her dad that they would remain close, both to persuade him that she should go to graduate school out of state and to assure him that her leaving would not change their relationship. To accomplish this, she decided to encode her idea into this message: "I promise that I will call at least twice a week, I'll e-mail you every day, and I'll come home for all holidays."

When you communicate, you encode and exchange two types of messages—verbal and nonverbal—and most are symbolic. A **symbol** is something that represents something else and conveys meaning (Buck & Vanlear, 2002). For example, a Valentine's Day heart symbolizes the physical heart, it represents romantic love, and it conveys feelings of love and romance when given to a relational partner. Similarly, the verbal system is composed of linguistic symbols (that is, words), while the nonverbal message system is composed of nonlinguistic symbols such as smiles, laughter, winks, vocal tone, and hand gestures.

When we say *communication is symbolic*, we are describing the fact that the symbols people use—the words they speak and the gestures they use—are arbitrary, or without any inherent meaning (Dickens, 2003). Rather, their meaning is derived as communicators employ agreed-upon definitions. For instance, putting up one's hand palm forward would not mean "stop" unless people in the United States agreed to this meaning, and the word *mother* would not mean a female parent unless speakers of English agreed that it would. Because communicators use symbols to create meaning, different groups often develop distinct words for the same concept. For instance, the common word for a feline house pet is *cat* in

messages
the building blocks of communication events

encoding
taking ideas and converting them into messages

decoding
receiving a message and interpreting its meaning

symbol
something that represents something else and conveys meaning

Key Components of Human Communication

The goal of exchanging symbols—that is, of communicating—is to **create meaning**.

Participants—two or more people who interact.

A **channel** is the means through which a message is conveyed.

Noise refers to any stimulus that can interfere with, or degrade, the quality of a message.

The response to a message is called **feedback**.

Individual forces include your demographic characteristics such as age, race, ethnicity, nationality, gender/sex, sexual orientation, regional identity, and socioeconomic class, as well as such factors as personality and cognitive and physical ability.

Societal Forces include the political, historical, economic, and social structures of a society that influence the value hierarchy and affect how we view specific individual characteristics.

Culture refers to the learned patterns of perceptions, values, and behaviors that a group of people shares.

Context includes the setting, or aspects of the physical environment, in which an interaction occurs, but it also includes which and how many participants are present as well as the specific occasion (for example, a Sunday dinner or a birthday party) during which the interaction unfolds.

English but *neko* in Japanese. Thus, there is no intrinsic connection between most words and their meanings—or gestures and their meanings, as Alyssa discovered during a trip to Europe (see *It Happened to Me: Alyssa*).

As Alyssa's experience reveals, although most people recognize that cultures vary in the words they use for specific ideas and items, they don't always realize that nonverbal gestures can have varied meanings across cultures as well.

Creating messages is the most fundamental requirement for communication to occur, but it is certainly not enough by itself. Messages also need to create similar meanings for everyone involved in the interaction.

IT HAPPENED TO ME: Alyssa

Recently, I traveled in Europe; I had no idea how difficult it would be to communicate, even in England. I spent the first few days navigating London on my own. It was so hard! People tried to help, but because of the differences in word choice and accents, I couldn't fully understand their directions. After London, I went to Italy, where I had an even harder time communicating due to the language barrier. So I resorted to using nonverbal gestures such as pointing, smiling, and thumbs up and down. However, I ran into problems doing this. One night, I ordered wine for a friend and myself. The bartender looked uncertain when he brought the two glasses of wine I'd ordered, so I gave him a "thumbs up" to mean okay, that he had it right. However, to him the gesture meant "one," so he thought I only wanted one glass, and he took the other away. It took us awhile to get the order straight.

Meaning Creation

The goal of exchanging symbols —that is, of communicating—is to create meaning. The messages we send and receive shape meaning beyond the symbols themselves. We also bring to each message a set of experiences, beliefs, and values that help shape specific meanings. This is why people can hear the same message but understand it differently. Charee was aware of this as she planned the conversation with her father. She knew they didn't always have precisely the same meanings for every word. For example, the word *independent* carried positive meanings for her, but she knew it carried more negative and potentially upsetting meanings for her father. Therefore, when talking to her father, she would never argue that going away was good for her because it would make her more independent.

Meaning is made even more complex because, as the example above suggests, each message carries with it two types of meaning—content meaning and relationship meaning. **Content meaning** includes *denotative* and *connotative* meaning. Denotative meaning is the concrete meaning of the message, such as the definition you would find in a dictionary. Connotative meaning describes the meanings suggested by or associated with the message and the emotions triggered by it. For example, denotatively, the word *mother* refers to one's female parent, while connotatively it may include meanings such as warmth, nurturance, and intimacy. **Relationship meaning** describes what the message conveys about the relationship between the parties (Robinson-Smith, 2004; Watzlawick, Beavin, & Jackson, 1967). For example, if a colleague at work tells you to "run some copies of this report," you may become irritated, while you likely wouldn't mind if your boss told you to do the same thing. In both cases, the relationship message may be understood as "I have the right to tell you what to do"—which is probably okay if it comes from your supervisor, but not if it comes from a peer.

Setting

The physical surroundings of a communication event make up its setting. **Setting** includes the location where the communication occurs (in a library versus a bar), environmental conditions (including the temperature, noise, lighting), time of day or day of the week, and the proximity of the communicators. Together, these factors create the physical setting, which affects communication interaction.

Why do you think Charee chose her father's favorite restaurant in the middle of the afternoon as the setting for their conversation? She did so for several reasons. First, her father would be more likely to feel relaxed and in a good mood in a location with which he was familiar. Second, she selected the middle of the afternoon so they would have more privacy and fewer interruptions. Finally, she chose a public setting because she believed that her father would remain calmer in a public than in a private setting, such

content meaning
the concrete meaning of the message and the meanings suggested by or associated with the message and the emotions triggered by it

relationship meaning
what a message conveys about the relationship between the parties

setting
the physical surroundings of a communication event

as at home. As you can see, Charee carefully selected a setting that would be comfortable for both participants and that she believed would enhance her chances for being successful.

Participants

During communication, **participants**—two or more people—interact. The number of participants, as well as their characteristics, influences how the interaction unfolds. Typically, the more characteristics participants share (cultural values, history), the easier they will find it to communicate, because they can rely on their common assumptions about the world.

As Charee planned her conversation, she recognized that she and her father shared a number of important characteristics—respect for elders in the family, a communal approach to relationships, and a desire for harmony. However, she also realized that they differed in important ways. Although she was close to her family, she desired more independence than her father would want for himself or for her; in addition, she believed that it was permissible for young, single women to live away from their families, while she was pretty sure her father didn't agree.

The type of relationship communicators have and the history they share also affect their communication. Whether communicators are family members, romantic partners, colleagues, friends, or acquaintances affects how they frame, deliver, and interpret a message. Because Charee was talking with her father rather than her boyfriend, she focused on displaying respect for his authority and asking (rather than telling) him about wanting to move away for college.

As we have suggested already, the moods and emotions that communicators bring to and experience during their interaction influence it as well. Because Charee wanted to increase the likelihood that the conversation with her father would go well, she tried to create a situation in which he would be in a calmer and happier frame of mind.

Channels

For a message to be transmitted from one participant to another, it must travel through a channel. A **channel** is the means through which a message is conveyed. Historically, the channels people used to communicate with one another were first face-to-face, then letters and newsprint, and yet later through telephone calls, radio, and television. Now we have numerous communication channels due to technology, including instant messaging, mobile instant messaging, e-mail, and videophones.

The channel one selects to communicate a message can affect how the message is perceived and its impact on the relationship. For example, if your romantic partner broke up with you by changing his/her relationship status on Facebook rather than talking to you face-to-face, how would you respond? Because Charee was sensitive to the importance of the communication channel she used with her father, she elected to communicate with him face-to-face; it was a channel her father was familiar with and would find appealing.

Noise

Noise refers to any stimulus that can interfere with, or degrade, the quality of a message. Noise describes external signals such as loud music or voices, a humming air conditioner, or bizarre dress or hairstyles. Noise can come from internal stimuli, such as hunger or sleepiness, and semantic interference, such as when speakers use words you do not know or use a familiar word in an unfamiliar way. If you have ever tried to have a conversation with someone who used highly technical language in a noisy room while you were sleepy, you have experienced a "perfect storm" of noise.

How did the noise factor affect Charee's choices? She chose to meet at a café in the middle of the afternoon to minimize the sources of noise that could interfere with her conversation with her father. Fewer people were likely to be present between lunch and

participants
the people interacting during communication

channel
the means through which a message is transmitted

noise
any stimulus that can interfere with, or degrade, the quality of a message

Text messaging is one channel of communication.

How do you choose which channel to use when you communicate with others? Do you consider who they are, the topic, the importance of the message, or something else? Overall, do you think you pick the best channel most of the time? If not, what do you need to do to select more appropriately?

feedback
the response to a message

human communication in society model
a transactional model of communication that depicts communication as occurring when two or more people create meaning as they respond to each other and their environment.

dinner, so there would be fewer competing voices and sounds, and the wait staff would be less likely to interrupt with meal service, so there would be fewer distractions. By choosing a setting that minimized interference, she improved the chances that her message would be clear.

Feedback

Finally, the response to a message is called **feedback**. Feedback lets a sender know if the message was received and how the message was interpreted. For example, if a friend tells you a joke and you laugh heartily, your laughter serves as feedback that you heard the joke and found it amusing. Similarly, if you fall asleep during a lecture, you provide feedback to your professor that either you are very tired or you find the lecture boring. Thus, your feedback serves as a message to the sender, who then uses the information conveyed to help shape his or her next message.

Although Charee wasn't sure what type of feedback her father would provide or what type she would need to give him, she did spend time anticipating what they each would say. She also knew that she would need to be sensitive to his messages and was prepared to offer feedback that was both supportive and persuasive.

A Model of Human Communication: Human Communication in Society

To help people understand complex processes, scientists and engineers, among others, create visual models to show how all components of a process work together. Scholars of human communication have done the same. They have developed models to reveal how the seven components described above work together to create a communication interaction.

The first such model of human communication depicted communication as a linear process that primarily involved the transfer of information from one person to another (Eisenberg & Goodall, 1997; Laswell, 1948; Shannon & Weaver, 1949). In this model, communication occurred when a sender encoded a message (put ideas into words and symbols) that was sent to a receiver who decoded (interpreted) it. Then, the process was believed to reverse: The receiver became the sender, and the sender became the receiver (Laswell, 1948). (See Figure 1.1.) This model also included the components of noise and channel. Since that time, other, more complex models, such as the Human Communication in Society model, have been created to show a greater variety of factors that interact with one another to influence the communication process.

The **Human Communication in Society model** is a transactional model that, like most previous models, depicts communication as occurring when two or more people create meaning as they respond to each other and their environment. In addition, it is

FIGURE 1.1 A Linear Model of Communication

An early model of communication.

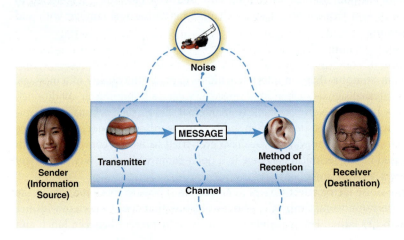

based on a belief in the important roles of individual and societal forces, contexts, and culture in the communication process. We discuss each of these topics in detail below, and to help clarify the concepts, we illustrate how they function during the communication process by once again looking in on Charee's interaction with her father.

After carefully planning for the interaction with her father about her desire to leave home to go to graduate school, Charee engaged in the following conversation with him:

Charee: *Purdue, Illinois, ASU, and Texas all let me in*. (While talking, Charee notices a quizzical look on her father's face.)

Charee: *I mean, all of them accepted me for graduate school.*

Dad: *Oh. How many did you apply to?*

Charee: *Just four. They all accepted me.*

Dad: (frowning, speaking uncertainly) *So where are you gonna go?*

Charee: (looking away, speaking hesitantly) *Uh, Texas, I think.*

Dad: (startled) *Texas?! Why not stay at ASU?*

Charee: (speaking patiently) *Because it's better for my career to go and work with other people. I'll be able to get a better job when I graduate if I can say that I worked with 12 people instead of 6, Dad. Plus, Texas is real high up there in the rankings. It's a good school.*

Dad: (shaking his head, speaking firmly) *Oh. Well, I think you can get a better job if you can show that you're loyal. If you stay at ASU, people will think, "Oh, she can stay at one place and do a good job. She has loyalty."*

Charee: (nodding her head, speaking carefully) *But I have been loyal to ASU for six years. People here know me and how I work. They also know that I can learn and grow somewhere else.*

Dad: *I guess I can see that. I just wish you didn't have to go.*

Communication Is Transactional

To say that *communication is a transaction* captures the fact that (1) each communicator is a sender and receiver *at the same time*, (2) meaning is created as people communicate together, (3) communication is an ongoing process, and (4) previous communication events and relationships influence the meaning of communication (Warren & Yoder, 1998; Watzlawick et al., 1967). What does this mean?

First, all participants to a communication event both receive and send messages simultaneously, even if those messages are sent only nonverbally. As you may have noted, as Charee explained that she was "let in" to four universities, she realized from her father's nonverbal behavior that he was confused. That is, she received his message even as she talked, and he sent a message even as he listened.

Second, as the example above suggests, meaning is not something one person creates and then sends to another person via a message. If that were true, Charee's father would not have been confused by the expression "let in"; Charee's initial message would have been sufficient. Rather, meaning was created as Charee and her dad communicated together; she made a statement, he showed his lack of understanding, and Charee offered more information until they shared similar understandings or meaning (See Figure 1.2).

Third, describing communication as ongoing highlights the fact that it is a process whose specific beginnings and endings can be difficult to discern. All the interactions one has had with individuals in the past influence one's communication in the present, just as a person's current communication affects his or her expectations for and experiences of future interactions. For instance, Charee planned her interaction and communicated with her father based on her previous experiences with him. Specifically, she knew he would rather she stay close to home, so she was prepared to offer arguments for why leaving home for graduate school was best. Her experiences with her father, then, affected the messages she crafted for their conversation. In addition, she recognized that their conversation would impact how they communicated with each other in the future. If he became angry, he would likely communicate with her less or more negatively, which in turn would influence their future interactions, and so on.

FIGURE 1.2 Communication Is Transactional

Meaning is created as people communicate together.

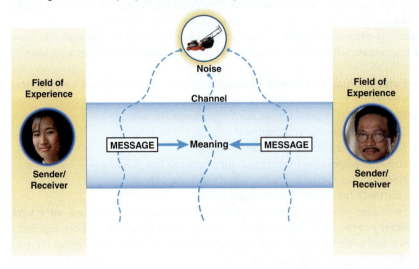

Finally, because communication is ongoing and interactive, when people communicate, they and their conversational partners reaffirm or alter their identities and relationships. Thus, Charee's conversation with her father will likely change how they see each other. He might see her as more adult and independent because of her desire to move away, or he may now perceive her as a less loving child. Similarly, she may view him as less of an authority figure and more of a peer, or she might believe that he is authoritarian and rigid.

Communication Is Influenced by Individual Forces

The individual is a primary focus in communication. Many separate individual forces or characteristics contribute to your identity, and these in turn affect your communication. Individual forces include your demographic characteristics such as age, race, ethnicity, nationality, gender/sex, sexual orientation, regional identity, and socioeconomic class, as well as such factors as personality and cognitive and physical ability. In addition, individual forces include your **field of experience**, such as your education and experiences.

For example, Charee is female, twenty-four, and a college graduate, while her father is a male in his late forties who operates an automotive repair shop. Each of these individual factors influences the way they communicate as well as the ways in which others communicate to and about them. Because of her experiences as a college student, Charee knows what "let in" means and understands that universities often evaluate students who obtain all three degrees at one college negatively when they hire new professors. On the other hand, her father is not aware of this information, and based on his culture and his experiences in the workforce, he understands that loyalty is an important quality in an employee.

The combination of these individual characteristics is unique for every person, so people communicate in distinctive ways. However, every society places limits on the variations that are deemed acceptable. For example, not all men speak assertively, enjoy talking about sports, or "high five" one another. In mainstream U.S. culture, though, many people consider these behaviors as normal for males. Talking in a more "female" style, such as speaking very quietly or politely, talking about fashion, or using "effeminate" nonverbal gestures is typically considered inappropriate for men and boys. If you veer somewhat from the norm, you may be seen as odd, or you might be shunned; if you veer too far from the norm, you may be labeled as mentally ill. So while we are each individuals, society places constraints on the range of our individualism—a topic we discuss later.

Communication Is Influenced by Societal Forces

As we have suggested immediately above, individual differences are not value free. They are arranged in a hierarchy in which some individual characteristics are more highly valued

field of experience
the education, life events, and cultural background that a communicator possesses

than others. For example, being White is often advantageous in U.S. society, being young has advantages over being old, and being physically able is more advantageous than having a disability. How society evaluates these characteristics affects how we talk to, and about, people who display them.

The political, historical, economic, and social structures of a society influence this value hierarchy and affect how we view specific individual characteristics. The historical conditions under which many U.S. racial and ethnic groups arrived in the United States, for instance, continue to affect their identities. For example, many of the earliest Vietnamese immigrants who moved to the United States during and shortly after the Vietnam War had very strong work ethics but were not fluent in English, so they created businesses of their own—as restaurant owners, nail technicians, and other service professionals. Consequently, many people still fail to realize that Vietnamese Americans also work as lawyers, professors, and physicians. Similarly, even though Barack Obama was elected president of the United States, the fact that many African Americans came to the United States as slaves continues to impact the ways in which people think and talk about him.

The values attributed to individual characteristics such as age, sexual orientation, and sex also come from these larger societal forces—whether communicated to us through the media, by our friends and family, or by organizations such as schools, religious institutions, or clubs. For example, the teachings of religious groups shape many people's views on sexual orientation, and because most societies have historically been patriarchal, many continue to value women in the public realm less than they do men.

In Charee's case, two societal forces at work in her interaction with her father are how society views women and how it views parent–child interactions. Pham was reared at a time when males had considerably more power than females and parents were assumed to know what was best for their children. Consequently, he tends to hold the belief that fathers should have considerable power over the decision making of their children—especially their unmarried female children. On the other hand, Charee grew up at a time when men and women were seen as more equal and parents exerted less control over their children's lives.

Social hierarchies wherein men are more valued than women or older people's opinions are considered more worthwhile than younger people's arise from the meanings that societal structures impose on individual characteristics, and communication maintains these hierarchies. For example, cultures that value maleness over femaleness have many more stereotypes and negative terms for women than they do for men. Moreover, these cultures value certain types of communication over others. Thus, women in leadership positions may be criticized for not communicating decisively and directly—a style of communication more commonly associated with men and viewed as the superior form for leaders. We will see how these hierarchies work in more detail in Chapter 3 (verbal communication) and Chapter 4 (nonverbal communication).

Communication Is Influenced by Culture

Communication also is embedded in culture. **Culture** refers to the learned patterns of perceptions, values, and behaviors that a group of people shares. Culture is dynamic and heterogeneous (Martin & Nakayama, 2005), meaning that it changes over time and that despite commonalities, members of cultural groups do not all think and behave alike. You probably belong to many cultures, including those of your gender, ethnicity, occupation, and religion, and each of these cultures will have its own communication patterns.

When you identify yourself as a member of a culture defined by age, ethnicity, or gender, this culture-group identity also becomes one of your individual characteristics. For example, as people move from their teen years into young adulthood, middle age, and old age, they generally transition from one age-related culture to another. Because each cultural group has a unique set of perceptions, values, and behaviors, each also has its own set of communication principles. As you become an adult, then, you probably stop using language you used as a teenager. However, while changing your language is an individual decision, it is influenced by cultural and societal expectations as well.

Culture affects all, or almost all, communication interactions (Schirato & Yell, 1996). More specifically, participants bring their beliefs, values, norms, and attitudes to each

culture
learned patterns of perceptions, values, and behaviors shared by a group of people

interaction, and the cultures to which they belong shape each of these factors. Cultural beliefs also affect how we expect others to communicate. As we discussed above, because he is Vietnamese, Charee's father values family closeness, loyalty, and the role of the father as head of the family. Because she is Vietnamese American, Charee holds many of these same beliefs, but she also values independence and individuality in ways that her father does not.

In addition to participants' cultural backgrounds, the culture in which a communication event takes place impacts how participants communicate. For example, in the United States, politicians routinely mention religion in their public addresses and specifically refer to God; however, in France, because of a stricter separation between church and state, politicians typically avoid mentioning religion or deities in their public communication and would be criticized if they did. Regional culture can also affect participants' expectations of appropriate communication behavior. For instance, southerners in the United States tend to be more nonverbally demonstrative and thus might hug others more than do northeasterners (Andersen, Lustig, & Andersen, 1990). Of course, other cultural differences (ethnic background, religious background) might influence these nonverbal behaviors as well.

Being gay is both an individual and a cultural factor.

Communication Is Influenced by Context

Each communication interaction occurs in a specific context. Context includes the setting—or aspects of the physical environment—in which an interaction occurs, but it also includes which and how many participants are present as well as the specific occasion (for example, a Sunday dinner or a birthday party) during which the interaction unfolds. Context can exert a strong influence on how people communicate with one another. For example, you could argue with your close friend in private when just the two of you are present, during a social event when you are part of a group, during a staff meeting at work, on a television talk show about feuding friends, or in the mall. Can you imagine how each of these contexts would influence your communication? You might be more open if the two of you are alone and in private; you may try to get others involved if you are with friends; you could be more subdued at the mall; you might refrain from mentioning anything too negative on television; or you might be more hostile in an e-mail. It was for this reason that Charee arranged to talk with her father at his favorite restaurant in the afternoon.

The tensions that exist among individual forces, societal forces, cultures, and contexts shape communication and meaning. To help you understand these tensions, let's return yet again to Charee's conversation with her father. Their conversation was influenced by the context (a restaurant), multiple individual forces (each person's age, sex, cultural background, and education), multiple societal forces (the value placed on education, family, sex, and age), as well as their cultures (the meanings of independence, loyalty, and family). Thus, in the conversation between Charee and her father, the context in which the conversation occurred, their individual experiences with higher education, and the cultural meaning of the parent–child relationship all came together to influence the communication interaction. These components and their relationships to one another are depicted in Figure 1.3: The Human Communication in Society Model.

As we stated at the beginning of the chapter and as is revealed in our model, for us, communication is a transactional process in which people generate meaning through the exchange of verbal and nonverbal messages in specific contexts, influenced by individual and societal forces and embedded in culture. This is the definition and model of communication that will guide you as you explore the remainder of this book. After you complete this course, we recommend that you return to this section to assess how your own understanding of the communication process has changed and deepened.

Our goal in presenting this model is to provide you with a framework for organizing your reading and understanding of this complex process we call communication. However, before moving on, we need to discuss one more essential concept that frames and guides all of your communication efforts—ethics.

FIGURE 1.3 The Human Communication in Society Model

The Human Communication in Society model emphasizes both individual and societal forces.

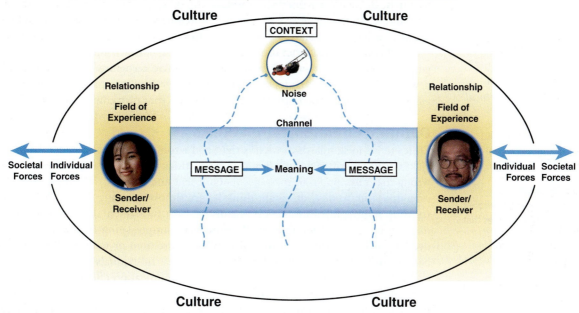

COMMUNICATION ETHICS

In the United States, we appear to be in the midst of a crisis with regard to ethical communication. In the business world, executives at American Insurance Group (AIG) were charged with lying to investors and the public (Verschoor, 2005), and corporate leaders at Global Crossing, WorldCom, Tyco, and Arthur Andersen were investigated or indicted on ethics charges. Unfortunately, ethical communication in the political arena does not appear to be faring much better; recently, Illinois Governor Rod Blagojevich was impeached on ethics charges (Lorg & Pearson, 2009).

Individuals' personal lives are apparently in a state of ethical disarray as well: Approximately 85 percent of surveyed daters admitted having lied to their partners in the previous two weeks (Tolhuizen, 1990), while 74 percent of students admitted to cheating on exams and 84 percent to cheating on written assignments (McCabe & Trevino, 1996). Also, some citizens lie on their tax returns, and some salespeople misrepresent the quality or availability of their products. Given examples such as these, one may wonder if a communication ethic still exists.

We strongly believe that it does. Even if unethical communication is widespread and some people get away with their misbehavior, most people are still held responsible for the messages they create (Barnlund, 1962; Christians & Traber, 1997; Johannesen, 1990). If you spread gossip about your friends, lie to your employer, or withhold information from your family, justifying your behavior by pointing to the ethical failures of others will not excuse you. Those who know you and are close to you still expect you to meet basic standards for ethical communication.

Why are communication ethics so important? First, they sustain professional success. Yes, unethical people may prosper in the short run, but over time, unethical practices catch up with the people who engage in them. To a great extent, your reputation as a person of integrity impacts whether others want to hire you, work for you, or conduct business with you. Once that reputation is damaged, it can be difficult if not impossible to regain; consequently, communicating and behaving ethically is just good business.

Communication ethics are vital to personal relationships as well. Maintaining intimate and caring relationships can be difficult, but it becomes virtually impossible if one communicates unethically by lying, manipulating, or verbally abusing friends and lovers. Intimate

What communication behaviors do you believe are ethical? Unethical? What principles guide your decisions regarding whether a communication behavior is ethical or unethical?

ethics
standards of what is right and wrong, good and bad, moral and immoral

communication ethics
the standards of right and wrong that one applies to messages that are sent and received

relationships are grounded in trust. Without trust, people can't be open and vulnerable with one another—behaviors which are essential to intimacy. When one person abuses that trust by his or her unethical conduct, the other party is often deeply wounded and finds it difficult to ever again be intimate within the relationship. Far too many people have learned the hard way that a lack of ethics destroys relationships.

In this section, we lay out some basic principles of ethical communication. Clearly, these guidelines reflect our own communication ethics. We recognize that all individuals must develop their own ethical codes and that they can alter them over time. We offer the following guidelines simply for you to consider as you develop your own communication ethic.

Defining Communication Ethics

Ethics refers to standards of what is right and wrong, good and bad, moral and immoral (Jaksa & Pritchard, 1994). **Communication ethics** describes the standards of right and wrong that one applies to messages that are sent and received. When you hear the term *communication ethics*, you might think we are simply referring to whether messages are truthful. Although truthfulness is one of the most fundamental ethical standards, communicating ethically requires much more than simply being truthful. It also involves deciding what information can and should be disclosed or withheld and assessing the benefit or harm associated with specific messages. Individuals have a responsibility to evaluate the ethics of their own and others' communication efforts. Similarly, organizations ought to weigh the ethics of sharing or withholding information that might affect the value of their stock shares, and broadcasting companies should decide whether it is ethical to report private information about individuals. Let's look at each of these topics more closely.

Truthfulness

Truthfulness plays a fundamental role in ethical communication for two reasons: First, others expect messages to be truthful; second, messages have consequences. Because people inherently expect speakers to be truthful, we may actually make it easier for them to deceive us (Buller & Burgoon, 1996). If an audience is not suspicious, they probably won't look for cues that the speaker is lying (McCornack & Parks, 1986). However, because of the implicit contract to be honest, discovery of deception can severely damage relationships. The more intimate the relationship, the greater the expectation people have that others will be truthful and the more damaging any deception will be.

As we've implied, messages should be truthful because they have consequences. Your communication can influence the beliefs, attitudes, and behaviors of others. Your communication could persuade a customer to purchase an item, a friend to loan you money, or an acquaintance to become romantically involved with you. The more consequential the outcome of your message, the more you will be held accountable to the truth. For example, you might not be criticized too harshly for exaggerating your salary during a flirtation with a stranger, but an employer will probably consider it unethical if you lie about your salary on a job application.

Sharing or Withholding Information

A related fundamental principle of ethical communication concerns what information should be divulged and what can be withheld. When is withholding information a matter of legitimate privacy, and when is it a matter of inappropriate secrecy? Thus, you have to determine whether to tell your romantic partner the number of sexual partners you have had; news organizations have to decide whether to reveal the names and sexual histories of rape victims; and pharmaceutical companies have to choose how much information to reveal about the side effects of their products.

In our view, a message can be considered legitimately private when other parties have no right to expect access to it. Inappropriate secrecy, on the other hand, occurs when other parties might legitimately expect access to a message that is withheld. This distinction is important, because typically, it is ethical to maintain privacy, but it may be unethical to engage in secrecy.

How does one decide what is private and what is secret? We believe that communicators have an ethical responsibility to share information that other people require to make informed decisions. For example, if you have only dated someone once or twice, you may choose to keep private that you have a sexually transmitted disease. However, if the two of you consider becoming sexually intimate, you have an ethical obligation to reveal the information. Without this information, your partner cannot make an informed decision about whether to engage in sexual contact. What will happen to your relationship if you withhold the information and your partner catches your disease and finds out later that you withheld the information? Similarly, your friends may not need to know that you were fired from your last job for thievery, but your new boss has a legitimate need for access to this information.

On the other hand, revealing information can sometimes be unethical. For example, if you have agreed to maintain confidentiality about a topic, it could be considered unethical to reveal what you know. However, if you violate a confidence because of a higher ethical principle, most people would likely consider your behavior ethical. For example, if you have a duty of confidentiality to your employer but your company engages in illegal toxic dumping, it would likely be more ethical to break this confidence. Here, the ethic of protecting the public health supersedes the ethic of keeping a confidence. However, these are not easy decisions.

Benefit and Harm of Messages

To determine the most ethical choice, you should consider the benefit or harm associated with your messages. A classic example concerns whether it is right to lie to a potential murderer about the whereabouts of the intended victim. A principle of honesty suggests that you should tell the truth. But in this case, once you evaluate the potential harm of sharing versus withholding the information, you might well decide to withhold the information.

More typically, issues of harm and benefit are less clear. For example, if you discover that your best friend's romantic partner is being unfaithful, should you share that information? Will it result in more harm or more benefit? If you know that a relative cheated on her taxes, should you tell the IRS?

Think back for a moment to Charee's conversation with her dad. How might communication ethics be relevant to their conversation? If you think about it for a moment, you might see that a person in Charee's situation could be tempted to lie. If she had told her father that she wasn't accepted at ASU, then she wouldn't have had to worry as much that he would try to persuade her to stay home or that her decision to leave would upset him. However, both because she is an ethical person and because she understands the consequences that unethical behavior can have on relationships, she chose to be open and honest with her father regarding her options and the reasons for her decision.

Because many communication events are complex and the underlying ethical principles are not definitive, you will need to gradually develop your own philosophy of ethical communication and apply it on a case-by-case basis. This is one requirement of being an effective communicator. However, just as you develop your own ethical standards and decisions, others will do so as well, which means that you and others in your life may not always agree.

Developing Communication Ethics

As a communicator, you will face many ambiguous and difficult choices of both a professional and a personal nature. If you develop your own set of communication ethics, you will be better prepared to face these difficult choices. In this section, we provide some guidelines to draw on.

Absolutism Versus Relativism

A fundamental decision in communication ethics concerns how **absolute** or **relative** your ethical standards will be. Will you use the same absolute standards for every communication interaction, or will your ethical choices be relative and depend on each situation? The Greek philosopher Plato and the German philosopher Immanuel Kant conceptualized

absolutism
pertaining to the belief that there is a single correct moral standard that holds for everyone, everywhere, every time

relativism
pertaining to the belief that moral behavior varies among individuals, groups, and cultures, as well as across situations

FIGURE 1.4   Absolutism Versus Relativism

Where would you place yourself on this ethics continuum?

Absolutism   ◄——————————————————————————►   Relativism

the absolutist perspective (Kant, 1949) and both believed that there is a rationally correct, moral standard that holds for everyone, everywhere, every time. Relativists such as French philosopher Jean-Paul Sartre, on the other hand, hold the view that moral behavior varies among individuals, groups, and cultures. They argue that because there is no universal standard of morality, there is no rational way to decide who is correct (Sartre, 1973).

If you hold to the absolutist perspective that lying is always wrong, then in the earlier example regarding the murderer, you would be obligated to reveal the whereabouts of the intended victim. But if you adhere to a relativistic position regarding truth and deception, you would decide in the moment what the most ethical choice was, based on the specific circumstances.

In reality, few people develop an ethical standard that is completely absolute or relative. Instead, absolutism and relativism are the opposite ends of a continuum, and most people's standards lie somewhere along that continuum (see Figure 1.4).

The issue for you is to decide how absolute or relative your ethical standards will be. If you strongly believe that deception is wrong, you may choose the path of deception only when you believe the truth will cause great harm—a standard that falls toward the absolutist end of the continuum. However, if you favor a more relative view, you will consider a variety of factors, in addition to harm, as you make your decisions.

Ethics of Language Use

Another important ethical issue related to message creation centers on the types of language you use—particularly language that refers to others. Most of the time, people do not think about the names they use to describe a group of people or an individual as ethical issues. Although we three authors have our own ideas that we'll present about the ethical use of language, you will need to decide how language choices fit within the ethical perspective you are developing.

Some more obvious examples of unethical language include racial and ethnic slurs and sexist and homophobic references, which we will discuss in more detail in Chapter 3. But less obvious examples exist as well. For example, when you refer to a colleague as an "idiot," to your enemies as "monsters," or to your political opponents as "fascists," you not only denigrate their humanity and their identities, but you shut down open communication and discussion about the salient issues. Similarly, language which sexualizes or objectifies others, especially in the workplace, is unethical; it can also be illegal. To learn more about sexual comments in the workplace, see *Communication in Society: Sexual Harassment Usually Starts with Inappropriate Comments*. Unethical language prevents you from engaging in interactions that allow a more complex view of both the issues and the other person or group.

You may have noticed that some individuals use what might be perceived as negative terms to describe themselves or other members of their group. For example, some gays and lesbians refer to themselves or others as "queer" and "dyke," and some members of ethnic minority groups adopt the ethnic slurs that outsiders have used to demean them. Does this mean that outsiders can use these same terms? Typically, it does not. When members of a group use a negative term, other members of the group usually recognize its intent and know that it is not meant to demean them; however, when an outsider uses the term, group members cannot interpret the intention and therefore may take offense (Brewer & Miller, 1996).

Ethical Responsibilities of Receivers

You may not have thought much about your responsibilities as a receiver of communication, in part because receivers typically are thought of as passive members of a communication interaction (Johannesen, 1990). Recall, however, that we view communication as a transactional process in which communicators both send and receive messages. What do your responsibilities as a receiver entail?

Communication in SOCIETY

Sexual Harassment Usually Starts with Inappropriate Comments

Have you been sexually harassed? If so, was it communicated verbally or nonverbally? At what point should an organization intervene when talk becomes sexual?

According to the Novations Group's annual workplace ridicule survey, sexually offensive remarks were heard more often in 2007 than in 2006. Specifically, 42% of the 546 male and female employees surveyed reported hearing sexually offensive comments in the workplace—up from 34% in 2006.

While a sexually inappropriate remark here or there won't generally rise to the level of a hostile environment, such comments are often a precursor to a viable sex harassment claim. Here are two examples.

1. A male employee tells a female coworker he finds attractive what he'd like to do to her if they were alone. He never touches her, but his comments become more frequent and more graphic.
2. A female employee corners a male colleague and propositions him. Whenever possible thereafter, she brushes against him, gives him a hug, or massages his shoulders.

Too many supervisors dismiss isolated comments until it's too late—until those comments become anything but isolated or the aggressor acts on his/her words. That's why it's imperative that your supervisors immediately discipline employees for:

- making verbal advances or propositions of a sexual nature;
- making graphic verbal commentaries about an individual's body;
- making sexually derogatory comments, epithets, slurs, and jokes; and
- using sexually derogatory words to describe an individual.

Stress to them that they must take disciplinary action even if the complaining employee does not feel physically threatened by the remarks; humiliation is an equal consideration, ruled the 11th Circuit. In the case before it, an executive allegedly "mortified" and "embarrassed" a female employee by failing to dispel rumors that they were a couple; telling people at a company event that she was not his date, but that he wished she were; and publicly offering her and her boyfriend $1 million if she would spend the night with him.

SOURCE: Retrieved March 13, 2010, from http://www.legalworkplace.com/sexual-harassment-inappropriate-comments-elt.aspx

---

Overall, message receivers have a responsibility to listen mindfully (Kruger, 1999), paying close attention to what is being communicated and listening both for what is said and what is left unsaid. This responsibility is particularly great when you must form opinions or make decisions based on information you receive.

Other ethical responsibilities for receivers include *reasoned skepticism* and *healthy feedback* (Johannesen, 1990). **Reasoned skepticism** describes the balance of open-mindedness and critical attitude needed when evaluating others' messages. In order to engage in reasoned skepticism, listeners should ask questions and interrogate speakers to ensure that they have sufficient understanding and information to form an opinion or make a decision. As a corollary, speakers are responsible for listening to their audience and responding accurately to the questions they pose.

Healthy feedback refers to the honest and ethical responses receivers provide to the messages of others. For example, if you hear a racist joke, what do you think would count as healthy feedback? If you believe that racist language is unethical, then your responsibility as an ethical listener would be to refuse to laugh at the joke. You may even let the joke teller know that you find the joke and its language offensive.

One caveat: Interactions sometimes happen in larger contexts in which communicators are not equally empowered to speak freely. So, if your boss tells a sexist joke during a meeting, you may feel constrained from providing healthy feedback. In this case, acting as an ethical receiver may not be healthy for your career! On a larger scale, many people have looked back and questioned why observers of certain historical or political events did not speak up. For example, why didn't more people in Germany speak up or do something to prevent the Holocaust during World War II?

reasoned skepticism
the balance of open-mindedness and critical attitude needed when evaluating others' messages

healthy feedback
the honest and ethical responses receivers provide to the messages of others

In situations of unequal power relations, less-powerful individuals who speak out are vulnerable. Individuals in these situations must choose between speaking up and suffering the consequences, or remaining quiet and wrestling with their consciences. When ethical people remain quiet, they typically do so because they fear for themselves or others. However, this fear can further empower the powerful, creating a "chilling effect" (Roloff & Cloven, 1990) on the oppressed and vulnerable and on their willingness to ask questions. The more powerful the individual or group is in relation to you, the more difficult it may be for you to protest. Deciding how to communicate in these situations is a serious issue, and individuals have reflected on this topic for centuries. You must decide for yourself how much risk you are willing to bear when speaking out against those in power.

Communication Ethics in Practice

In this discussion of ethics, we have offered guidelines for creating your own communication ethics. However, in practice, making ethical choices is not always easy or clear-cut. Many situations arise that are ambiguous, complex, and multilayered. At times, you may not see how you can be ethical and accomplish important goals at the same time. For example, if you know that a friend and classmate has plagiarized a paper, what should you do? Should you keep quiet and maintain your friendship, or should you maintain your personal ethics and tell the instructor? Similarly, if you are a salesperson, how do you respond if a potential client asks whether a competitor's product is as good as yours and you believe it is? Do you tell the truth and thus jeopardize a potential sale? People who tend toward an absolutist view say that you must always tell the truth, so you should only sell a product you truly believe is superior. Others may tell you that no one expects salespeople to be completely truthful in this context; therefore, you are not bound to share your opinion (Diener, 2002; Wokutch & Carson, 1981).

We believe that all communicators need to create an ethical stance based on their own beliefs, values, and moral training. Once *you've* established your ethical stance, you will be prepared to make thoughtful and deliberate communication choices.

To assist you further in creating your own communication ethic, please see *Building Your Communication Skills: Building a Framework for Thinking Ethically and Making Ethical Decisions.*

Building Your Communication SKILLS

Building a Framework for Thinking Ethically and Making Ethical Decisions

This framework for thinking ethically is the product of dialogue and debate at the Markkula Center for Applied Ethics at Santa Clara University. Primary contributors include Manuel Velásquez, Dennis Moberg, Michael J. Meyer, Thomas Shanks, Margaret R. McLean, David DeCosse, Claire André, and Kirk O. Hanson.

Making good ethical decisions requires a trained sensitivity to ethical issues and a practiced method for exploring the ethical aspects of a decision and weighing the considerations that should impact our choice of a course of action. Having a method for ethical decision making is absolutely essential. When practiced regularly, the method becomes so familiar that we work through it automatically without consulting the specific steps.

The more novel and difficult the ethical choice we face, the more we need to rely on discussion and dialogue with others about the dilemma. Only by careful exploration of the problem, aided by the insights and different perspectives of others, can we make good ethical choices in such situations.

We have found the following framework for ethical decision making a useful method for exploring ethical dilemmas and identifying ethical courses of action.

A Framework for Ethical Decision Making

Recognize an Ethical Issue

1. Could this decision or situation be damaging to someone or to some group? Does this decision involve a choice between a good and bad alternative, or perhaps between two "goods" or between two "bads"?

2. Is this issue about more than what is legal or what is most efficient? If so, how?

Get the Facts

3. What are the relevant facts of the case? What facts are not known? Can I learn more about the situation? Do I know enough to make a decision?

4. What individuals and groups have an important stake in the outcome? Are some concerns more important? Why?

5. What are the options for acting? Have all the relevant persons and groups been consulted? Have I identified creative options?

Evaluate Alternative Actions

6. Evaluate the options by asking the following questions:
   - Which option will produce the most good and do the least harm? (The Utilitarian Approach)
   - Which option best respects the rights of all who have a stake? (The Rights Approach)
   - Which option treats people equally or proportionately? (The Justice Approach)
   - Which option best serves the community as a whole, not just some members? (The Common Good Approach)
   - Which option leads me to act as the sort of person I want to be? (The Virtue Approach)

Make a Decision and Test It

7. Considering all these approaches, which option best addresses the situation?

8. If I told someone I respect—or told a television audience—which option I have chosen, what would they say?

Act and Reflect on the Outcome

9. How can my decision be implemented with the greatest care and attention to the concerns of all participants?

10. How did my decision turn out and what have I learned from this specific situation?

SOURCE: Markula Center for Thinking Ethically. (2010). "A framework for thinking ethically." Retrieved March 9, 2010, from http://scu.edu/ethics/practicing/decision/framework.html

SUMMARY

Studying human communication can enrich and transform your life professionally and personally. In order to understand how communication occurs, you need to study it.

The *process* of communication between participants involves sending and receiving verbal and nonverbal messages through specific channels in particular settings. Messages are affected by noise and influenced by feedback. As scholars have studied communication

in depth, they have moved away from seeing the communication process as a *linear* event that involves transmitting a message from a sender to a receiver. Instead, they began to view it as an *interactive* process in which both senders and receivers communicate—senders through message transmission, and receivers through feedback. More recently, researchers have come to view communication as a transactional process in which each participant is both a receiver and a sender, and each interaction is affected by noise, the participants' relationship, and their fields of experience. The approach taken in this book extends the transactional model by emphasizing that all communication interactions are influenced by the intersection of individual and societal forces, that they are embedded in culture, and that they occur in specific contexts.

The ethics of individual communication choices are another essential feature of communication. This is a topic we will return to throughout the book. Key aspects of communication ethics include truthfulness, decisions regarding sharing or withholding information, and the benefit and harm associated with one's choices. Communicators' ethical choices are affected by their position on the continuum of absolutism versus relativism, which in turn influences their language use, how they receive and how they respond to others' communication efforts.

KEY TERMS

absolutism 19
channel 11
communication ethics 18
content meaning 10
culture 15
decoding 8
encoding 8
ethics 18

feedback 12
field of experience 14
healthy feedback 21
human communication 7
human communication in society
   model 12
messages 8
noise 11

participants 11
reasoned skepticism 21
relationship meaning 10
relativism 19
setting 10
symbol 8

CHAPTER REVIEW QUESTIONS

1. What does it mean that communication is a *transactional process*?

2. How does culture impact the communication process?

3. What are the key differences between the human communication in society model and the linear model?

4. What is the difference between privacy and secrecy?

5. What are the ethical responsibilities of receivers?

ACTIVITIES

1. **Guidelines for Responding to Electronic Communication**
Much debate has raged over whether it is appropriate to talk on one's cell phone in restaurants, in front of friends, or in the car. The Federal Aviation Administration is considering whether to allow airline passengers to use their cell phones during flights—and many people are already complaining about the possibility. The widespread use of instant text messaging and the ability to access our e-mail almost anywhere have made the issues surrounding the

appropriate use of electronic communication even more complex. To focus the discussion and guide your own decisions regarding your responses to these types of electronic communication, develop a list of rules for how, when, and with whom it is appropriate to respond.

2. **Creating a Communication Ethic**
Interview three people and ask them to describe the underlying ethic(s) that guide(s) their communication choices. Then write a brief statement that describes your own communication ethic.

3. **Communication Ethics in the Media**
   Watch television for one evening and observe the number of ethical dilemmas related to communication that people and characters confront. Note their response to each dilemma. How many people/characters make choices that you consider ethical? How many do not? What justifications or reasons do people/characters give for their choices? What consequences, if any, are portrayed? What conclusions can you draw about the portrayal of communication ethics on television?

WEB ACTIVITIES

1. Make a list of all of the careers you believe require good communication skills. Then go to the University of North Carolina Wilmington's Career Services page at http://www.uncw.edu/stuaff/career/Majors/communication.htm to examine the list of careers for which a communication degree prepares students. What careers did you list that are not listed on the University of North Carolina Wilmington site? Why do you think the differences exist? Finally, create a list of careers you would post if you were responsible for creating such a site.

2. Go to the National Communication Association's "Famous People with Degrees in Communication" page at http://www.natcom.org/index.asp?bid=342 After reading the page, develop a list of at least ten careers that famous people have pursued after obtaining degrees in communication.

3. Go to http://www.hodu.com/authentic.shtml and read the article on "Strategies for More Authentic Communication." After reading the article, answer the following questions: When are you most likely to lie? What benefits do you think will accrue if you lie? What can you do to increase how ethical you are when you communicate with others?

2

COMMUNICATION, PERCEPTION, AND IDENTITY DEVELOPMENT

A fter the first hall meeting in their dorm, Tavit and Samantha went for coffee to discuss their experiences.

Tavit: What did you think of Bo, our dorm resident?

Samantha: I suppose he's okay. He seemed a little, I don't know, bossy. He was funny, but I don't know if I would feel comfortable going to him with a problem or anything.

Tavit: Really? I liked him a lot. I thought Bo was funny and would be easy to talk to. He's someone I think I could hang out with.

Samantha: He seemed kind of distant to me. I guess we'll have plenty of chances to find out what he is really like during the semester.

As Tavit and Samantha's conversation illustrates, our perceptions of others strongly influence how we respond to and communicate about them. If we perceive people as friendly, fun, and similar to ourselves, we tend to be drawn toward and want to communicate with them. However, if we view individuals as distant, controlling, and quite unlike ourselves, we may try to minimize contact. As the example suggests, however, not everyone perceives and responds to people and events the same way.

Just as our perceptions of others impact how we communicate with them, our perceptions and communication impact how they see themselves. Let's take our scenario above as a case in point. How might Tavit's or Samantha's perceptions affect Bo's perception of himself? If most people perceive him as Tavit does—as amusing and open—and therefore respond to him by laughing and including him in activities, then Bo probably sees himself positively. On the other hand, if most people respond as Samantha did and consequently choose to have little contact with him, Bo may perceive himself more negatively.

As you might expect, then, perception and identity are powerfully intertwined. On the one hand, Samantha's perceptions of Bo affect his identity. At the same time, how Bo views himself and others impacts how he perceives and responds to the world around him. If he has a positive self-image, Bo may perceive that others like him, he might be more optimistic and see the positive aspects of a situation more readily, and he could be less aware of others' negative reactions to him.

For the reasons discussed above, understanding identity development requires that you also understand how the perception process works, and vice versa. In this chapter, we discuss both of these topics and explore how they interact with communication to shape who you are and how you respond to the world. In our discussion of these topics, we first explore how each process works, and then we briefly examine why understanding the processes of perception and identity development is important. Next, we consider both individual and societal influences on these processes. We also address the ethics of perceiving and communicating about identities and end the chapter with suggestions for sharpening your perception and communication about identities.

Once you have read this chapter, you will be able to:

- Explain the perception process.
- Explain how identities are developed.
- Describe the influence of perception on identity development.
- Discuss the importance of perception and identity development.

CHAPTER OUTLINE

WHAT IS PERCEPTION?
  Selection
  Organization
  Interpretation

WHAT IS IDENTITY?
  Identity Exists at Both the Individual and Societal Levels
  Identities Are Both Fixed and Dynamic
  Identities Are Created Through Interaction
  Identities Must Be Seen in Context

THE IMPORTANCE OF PERCEPTION AND IDENTITY

THE INDIVIDUAL, PERCEPTION, AND IDENTITY
  Reflected Appraisals
  Social Comparison
  Self-Fulfilling Prophecy
  Self-Concept

THE INDIVIDUAL, PERCEPTION, IDENTITY, AND SOCIETY
  Social Identity
  Power, Perception, and Identity
  Culture, Perception, and Identity

THE ETHICS OF PERCEIVING AND COMMUNICATING ABOUT IDENTITIES
  Stereotyping
  Prejudice
  Stereotyping, Prejudice, and Communication

SKILLS FOR IMPROVING PERCEPTION AND COMMUNICATION ABOUT IDENTITIES

Summary

Key Terms

Chapter Review Questions

Activities

Web Activities

● Identify factors that influence an individual's perceptions and identity development.
● Understand the ethical consequences of one's perceptions and how one communicates about them.
● Improve your perception and communication about others' identities.

WHAT IS PERCEPTION?

Every day you are confronted with considerable sensory input, both internally and externally. Internally, you may be distracted by hunger, tiredness, or excitement, while externally you are exposed to sounds, smells, and sights that compete for your attention. How do you manage all the information your senses bring to you without being overwhelmed? The answer is that you continuously engage in a variety of processes that limit and structure everything you perceive (Kanizsa, 1979; Morgan, 1977).

Perception refers to the processes of **selection**, **organization**, and **interpretation** of the information you collect through your senses: what you see, hear, taste, smell, and touch. The specific sensory data you select, the ways in which you organize it, and the interpretations you assign to it affect how you communicate. Although these processes tend to happen concurrently and unconsciously, we separate them here to better explain how they function.

Selection

Because people experience more sensory information than they can process, they selectively focus on and remember only part of it. Consciously or unconsciously, you attend to just a narrow range of the array of sensory information available and ignore the remainder, a process called **selective attention**.

The sensory input you select is not random, however (Greenough, Black, & Wallace, 1987). When a range of sensory experiences accost you, various factors affect your selection, including your identity, features of the person or object you have encountered, and your experiences and values. For example, at large social events, you are liable to attend to only one or a few people because you cannot focus on everyone at once. Who captures your focus depends on:

- aspects of your identity—if you are Native American, you may find your attention drawn more to participants who also are Native American;
- features of the person—someone dressed differently from everyone else will likely attract your attention; and
- your goals—if you would like to meet a potential romantic partner, you may pay attention to attractive men or women in your age range.

Organization

After you select the sensory input you will attend to, you must make sense of it. To do this, you organize the information into a recognizable picture that informs your perception of the event or person. How do you do that? You can make sense of the sensory information because of two cognitive principles—*cognitive representation* and *categorization*—that help people organize and respond to their perceptions.

Cognitive Representation

The term **cognitive representation** describes the human ability to form mental models of the world they live in (Gavetti & Levinthal, 2000; Weick, 1995). Think of these models as maps, or sets of instructions, that humans create and then refer to later. For example, you know how to respond to a fire alarm—whether it occurs at school or home or even at a mall—because you have a developed cognitive map for doing so. That is, you have learned that a fire alarm communicates danger and that you should evacuate a building when you hear one. We have fire drills specifically to help people develop maps for fire alarms so

perception
the processes of selection, organization, and interpretation of the information you collect through your senses: what you see, hear, taste, smell, and touch

selection
the process of choosing which sensory information to focus on

organization
the process by which one recognizes what sensory input represents

interpretation
the act of assigning meaning to sensory information

selective attention
consciously or unconsciously attending to just a narrow range of the full array of sensory information available

cognitive representation
the ability to form mental models of the world

that they are familiar with how to respond and can act more instinctively when faced with a real alarm.

You also develop cognitive maps that shape your perceptions of people and communication events. From an early age, children are provided with maps of people who are "safe" (such as family members and police officers) and maps to help them decide who may be dangerous (such as strangers and people who act too familiar with them.) Thus, through their communication efforts, parents help children organize their perceptions of others in particular ways.

Remember: Maps are *representations* of things, not the things themselves. Cognitive maps consist of general outlines to guide you; they are not fixed sets of utterances or events that you memorize. Two specific types of cognitive representations, or maps, that individuals use to organize their perceptions about people and communication are called prototypes and interpersonal scripts.

Prototypes Communication behavior is strongly influenced by prototypes. A **prototype** is the most typical or representative example of a person or concept. For example, many people's prototypical idea

Just as people develop mental models for how to respond in an emergency, they develop mental models for communication behavior.

of a professor is a person who is male, has white hair (and perhaps a beard), and wears a tweed jacket with leather patches. Although a few professors fulfill this prototype, many more do not (just look around your campus). Nonetheless, this prototype persists, in part because of how media depict college instructors.

Prototypes are important because people compare specific individuals to the prototype they have and then communicate with others based on the degree to which they perceive that the individual conforms to that prototype. You likely see this most often when it comes to the issue of gender. People have prototypical ideas of what a "man" or a "woman" is. These prototypes represent idealized versions of masculine and feminine identities. The more an individual resembles your prototype, the more likely you are to communicate with that person in a stereotypical (or prototypical) manner. For example, men who are muscular and tall and have facial hair are often perceived to be very masculine. Consequently, people tend to communicate with them as if they embody typical masculine characteristics, such as having an interest in sports, a heterosexual orientation, and a lack of interest in topics such as fashion, interior design, or personal relationships. Similarly, a man who possesses none of those characteristics may be viewed as not masculine and be communicated with accordingly.

Interpersonal Scripts An **interpersonal script** is a relatively fixed sequence of events you expect to occur during interactions with others; it functions as a guide or template for how to act in particular situations (Burgoon, Berger, & Waldron, 2000; Pearce, 1994). You develop scripts for activities you engage in frequently. Most people have a script for how to meet a new person. For example, when you first meet someone of interest on campus, you probably approach the person, introduce yourself, and ask a question such as "What is your major?" or "Where is your hometown?" Thus, you follow a routine of sorts (Douglas, 1990). Your choice of script or the way in which you alter a script depends on your perceptions of others. If you perceive someone as friendly, attractive, and fun, you may use a different script to initiate a conversation than if you perceive the person as shy, quiet, and withdrawn.

As this discussion suggests, cognitive representations help people navigate the physical and social world. These maps provide guidelines that shape how we communicate with others through the prototypes and interpersonal scripts we develop as we grow up and mature.

prototype
an idealized schema

interpersonal script
a relatively fixed sequence of events that functions as a guide or template for communication or behavior

categorization

a cognitive process used to organize information by placing it into larger groupings of information

label

a name assigned to a category based on one's perception of the category

stereotyping

creating schemas that overgeneralize attributes of a specific group

Categorization

Another type of cognitive process people use to organize information is **categorization**. Categorization is inherent to all languages. The linguistic symbols (or words) individuals use represent the groupings they see around them. Because it is difficult to remember everything, people use groupings that represent larger categories of information or objects (Lakoff, 1987).

For example, you probably lump a lot of information under the category of teacher. What characteristics did you think of when you read the word *teacher*? You probably envisioned a subcategory, such as a professor, coach, or elementary school teacher. However, the concept of teacher has certain features that apply to all subcategories; you understand that *teacher* refers to a person who helps educate you, not someone who takes care of your physical health. Forming and using categories allows you to understand and store information and also makes you a more efficient communicator.

Although grouping is a natural cognitive and perceptual process, it also can lead to misperceptions. Categorizing can cause one to reduce complex individuals to a single category or to expect them to behave in ways consistent with the category, regardless of the circumstance. You might categorize an individual as "stuck up" based on your perception that the person doesn't talk to you or stands apart from others. Once you reduce people to a category, you may communicate with them as if they possess no other characteristics. If you categorize someone as stuck up, you may never talk with them and discover that they are just shy.

When people categorize others, they typically also assign them a **label**. The two activities tend to go hand in hand. Thus, once you place people into groups or categories, you probably assign a label to the category. You may have heard groups of people and the individuals within those groups labeled or described as sorority girls, geeks, or gang members, for instance. Although labeling others can function as a useful shortcut, it also can lead to negative outcomes (Link & Phelan, 2001). When you label people, you tend to view them only through the lens of the label; your expectations, evaluations, and responses to them are influenced by the label(s). Thus, labeling can cause problems even when you use positive labels.

Labels can limit your view of others and even yourself. For example, did your family have a label they used to describe you? Were you the smart one or the well-behaved one or even the goof-off? If you were labeled the goof-off, you may not have been given many opportunities to disprove the label, and your ideas may have been discounted even when they were valid. Gradually, you may have come to discount the value of your own ideas. Of course, sometimes entire groups of people can be labeled in ways that create problems, such as perceiving all Muslims as terrorists, even though surveys show that Muslims reject terrorism as much if not more than non-Muslim Americans (Ballen, 2007).

As you may have guessed, labeling is related to stereotyping. **Stereotyping** occurs when you create schemas that overgeneralize attributes of a group to which others belong (Fiske & Taylor, 1991). You stereotype when you assume that every member of the group possesses certain characteristics. For example, you may assume that most males enjoy talking about sports, as in the example of scripts that we used earlier. So you initiate a conversation with an unfamiliar man by discussing last night's game. Few characteristics, if any, are true of every single member of a group, and if you use the sports opener with every man you meet, you may eventually get a blank stare.

As noted, grouping individuals makes it easy to remember information about them, yet it often leads to inaccurate beliefs and assumptions. When you overgeneralize a group's attributes, you are less able to see the individuality of the people you encounter. Therefore, categorizing others is an activity that requires caution. We will explore the ethics of stereotyping later in this chapter.

Interpretation

After you perceive and organize sensory information, you assign meaning to it (Bruner, 1958, 1991). If your friend passes you on campus and doesn't say hello, you attempt to interpret what the snub means. Did your friend not see you? Is your friend angry at you? Everyone assigns meaning to the information they perceive, but all individuals do not

necessarily assign the same meaning to similar information. Why not? Because people use different frames and make varied attributions about people and events they experience—topics we take up next.

Frames

Structures that shape how people interpret their perceptions are called **frames**. An individual's understanding of an event depends on the frame used to interpret it (Dijk, 1977). If you frame the world as a place full of people who are rude, you are likely to interpret your friend's snub as deliberate, while if your view of the world is that people are nice, you may interpret your friend's failure to say hello as simply not seeing you. In essence, individuals view the world through interpretive frames that guide how they make sense of events (Fisher, 1997).

Individuals' frames develop over time, based on experience, interaction with others, and innate personality (Neale & Bazerman, 1991; Putnam & Holmer, 1992). Because we cannot perceive every aspect of an experience, frames also direct our attention toward some features of an episode and away from others. A bad mood, for example, directs attention to the negative aspects of an event. Usually, people don't become aware of frames until something happens to force them to replace one frame with another. If a friend points out that you are focusing only on the negative, you may become more aware of how your mood is framing, or focusing, your perceptions and interpretations. Your frame can change, then, as new information is introduced.

How should you use this information about framing? Now that you are aware that interpretations of people, events, and objects are influenced by an individual's frames, you should be more critical of your own interpretations. Recognize that your interpretations (as well as those of others) do not necessarily represent the "truth," but simply represent a particular way of viewing the world.

Attribution

How often do you wonder "why did she (or he) do that?" As you observe and interact with others, you probably spend considerable energy attempting to determine the causes of their behavior. At heart, most of us are amateur psychologists who search for the reasons people behave as they do. **Attribution theory** explains the processes we use to judge our own and others' behavior (Fehr, 1993; Spitzberg, 2001). Fritz Heider (1958), a psychologist and professor, said that attribution is the process of drawing inferences about others' behavior. More specifically, *inferences* are the conclusions we draw or interpretations we make based on the information available to us. For example, imagine that your boss's romantic partner receives a promotion at your organization. What conclusion would you draw? What attribution would you make if you called your romantic partner at 3 AM and he or she wasn't home? Although we're constantly being told we shouldn't judge others, attribution theory says we can't help it (Griffin, 1994).

One fundamental attribution we make is whether the cause of an individual's behavior is internal or external. An *internal* cause would be a personality characteristic, while an *external* cause would be situational. Suppose you came home from class one evening and found your roommate in a bad mood. You could attribute the mood to some trait internal to your roommate (she is moody and unpleasant) or to something external (her boss yelled at her). You are particularly likely to make internal attributions when the behavior is unexpected—that is, when it is something that most other people would not do (Kelley, 1973). For instance, if you laugh during a sad movie, people are more likely to attribute your reaction to something about your personality. But when the behavior fits our expectations, we are likely to attribute it to external causes. Therefore, if you cry during a sad movie, people are likely to attribute your behavior to the movie.

Your attributions may also depend on whether you are the actor or the observer of the behavior. You are more likely to attribute your own negative behavior to external causes and your positive actions to internal states (Jong, Koomen, & Mellenbergh, 1988). This is referred to as an **attributional bias**. If you are polite, it is because you have good manners; if you are rude, it is because others mistreated you. These attributions are examples of a

Are you an optimist or a pessimist? Do you think people are inherently generous or self-serving? The answers to these questions, and others like them, reveal how your beliefs shape the frames that in turn influence how you perceive the world. What other frames do you use that influence your interpretations of people and experiences?

frame
a structure that shapes how people interpret their perceptions

attribution theory
explanation of the processes we use to judge our own and others' behavior

attributional bias
the tendency to attribute one's own negative behavior to external causes and one's positive actions to internal states

self-serving bias
the tendency to give one's self more credit than is due when good things happen and to accept too little responsibility for those things that go wrong

fundamental attribution error
the tendency to attribute others' negative behavior to internal causes and their positive behaviors to external causes

identity
who a person is, composed of individual and social categories a person identifies with, as well as the categories that others identify with that person

self-serving bias. Operating under this bias, we tend to give ourselves more credit than is due when good things happen, and we accept too little responsibility for those things that go wrong. Most individuals are harsher judges of other people's behavior than they are of their own. We tend to attribute others' negative behavior to internal causes (such as their personality) and their positive behavior to external causes (such as the situation). This tendency is referred to as the **fundamental attribution error** (Ross, 1977).

Interestingly, when people make attributions about others, they tend to trust negative information they hear more than positive information (Lupfer, Weeks, & Dupuis, 2000). If you hear both positive and negative information about others, you tend to remember and rely on the negative rather than the positive information to formulate your attributions. However, you are not confined to these faulty attributional processes; you can work to overcome them. First, do not assume that you are a mind reader and that the attributions you make are always accurate. Remain aware that your attributions are really just guesses (even if they are educated guesses). You also need to be aware of self-serving biases and work to minimize them. Recognize that we all tend to attribute our own positive actions to ourselves and others' negative actions to themselves. Look for alternative explanations for your own and others' behavior. Lastly, avoid overemphasizing the negative. People have an inclination to remember and to highlight the negative, so try to avoid the negative in your own comments, and balance the positive against the negative in your evaluations of others.

As our discussion thus far reveals, who you are influences how you perceive the world and the people in it. Those perceptions, in turn, influence your own and others' identities. We examine this process next.

WHAT IS IDENTITY?

We have been using the term *identity* throughout this chapter, but what is it really? Identity is tied closely to identification. **Identity** refers to the social categories you identify with as well as the categories that others identify with you. Society creates social categories such as *adolescent* or *adult*, but they only become part of one's identity when one identifies with them. For example, some people perceive themselves as adults once they turn 18, while others don't identify themselves this way until they are out of college or even older. Many social categories exist, and individuals identify with a variety of them during their lifetimes. To help you understand how perception and communication affect identity development, we next examine four essential characteristics of identity.

Identity Exists at Both the Individual and Societal Levels

Jake Harwood, a communication professor, explains this first characteristic of identity: "At the individual (personal identity) level, we are concerned with our difference from other individuals, and the things that make us unique as people. At the collective (social identity) level, we are concerned with our group's differences from other groups and the things that make our group unique" (2006, pp. 84–85). Thus, your individual identities may include athlete, honor student, and poet, while your social identities include your ethnicity, nationality, or socioeconomic class.

We should note that identities are not necessarily only individual *or* social; they can be both, depending on the situation. For example, many readers of this text are U.S. Americans, and their national identity is part of their social identity. Because they are surrounded by other people from the United States, they may not be conscious of this as part of their individual identity. On the other hand, when they travel abroad, their national identity becomes part of their individual identity, because this characteristic often differentiates them from others.

Identities Are Both Fixed and Dynamic

How can identities be both fixed and dynamic? If you think about it, you will realize that certain aspects of our identities, although stable to some extent, actually do change over time. A person may be born male, but as he grows from an infant to a boy to a teenager to a

young man to a middle-aged man and then to an old man, the meanings of his male identity change. He is still a male and still identifies as a male, but what it means to be male alters as he ages, and social expectations change regarding what a man should be (Kimmel, 2005).

Identities Are Created Through Interaction

A third important characteristic of identity is that it is shaped by the relationships, experiences, and communication interactions you share with others. For example, people who travel abroad and then return home may experience stress, but they also experience growth and change—and communication with those they meet as they travel plays a key role in both (Martin & Harrell, 1996). Social identities also can change as people interact with others. In the 1970s, women attended "consciousness-raising" groups to alter how they perceived and performed their identities as females. Women in these groups were encouraged to think of themselves not primarily as wives and mothers but as the professional and social equivalents of men. Women's heightened awareness and dissatisfaction with their social identity prompted them to become involved in a larger social movement. This same shift happened for those who protested against racial discrimination in the 1960s. In these instances, a common social identity brought people together into communities, and these communities in turn improved the position of the particular social identity in society.

Identities Must Be Seen in Context

Fourth, the meaning of identities can be understood only in their historical, cultural, and social contexts (Hecht, Jackson, & Ribeau, 2003; Johnson, 2001). For instance, throughout history, we have had varied notions of what it means to be female (Roth, 2005). Although Cleopatra was the last Egyptian pharaoh and Joan of Arc led the French Army into battle in the fifteenth century, even in their own times they were significant exceptions to the rule.

For much of history, women have been perceived as intellectually inferior, physically delicate, and/or morally weak when compared to men. Because of these beliefs, in many cultures women were denied voting and property rights and even custody of their children in the event of divorce. For example, until 1881, when English women married, all of their property and wealth transferred to their spouses, as did their right to enter into any contracts (Erickson, 1993). In the United States, women didn't win the right to vote until 1920, and it wasn't until 1974 that they were constitutionally guaranteed the right to equal pay for equal work (Imbornoni, 2008).

Contemporary U.S. American women have all the legal rights of men, yet historical conceptions of women still affect how they are positioned in society. For example, on average, women earn 77 percent of men's pay; only 16 of 100 U.S. senators and just 74 of 435 representatives are women (U.S. Census Bureau, 2006); and people in many religions remain opposed to women serving as ministers and priests.

The situation for women in other cultures can be even more challenging. Although women in Saudi Arabia make up 70 percent of those enrolled in universities, they compose just 5 percent of the workforce; their testimony in court is treated as presumption rather than fact; and they live mostly segregated lives (Azuri, 2006). Thus, a hierarchy exists across cultures in which one identity (male) is preferentially treated over another (female). You can probably think of other examples in which preferential treatment was given—or denied—based on race, sexuality, religion, social class, or age (Allen, 2004).

Finally, identities are influenced by social contexts. The meaning a specific identity has and how people respond to it depends on the situation in which people find themselves. For example, Otto's mother is Apache and his father is German. Although he identifies primarily as Apache, while he was growing up, children on the reservation did not perceive him as Native American. Consequently, he was teased and often felt excluded from his community. When he began attending community college, however, he found that looking "Anglo" meant that White students included him in social activities more than they did other Native American students. Thus, his perceived identity varied

depending on the context in which he displayed it. To read how one student feels about her religious identity and the way context affects her willingness to share it, see *It Happened to Me: Elizabeth*.

As Elizabeth reveals, her willingness to display her religious identity is influenced by the social contexts she encounters. If she is unsure of others' religious identities, she conceals her own. But if she encounters someone with a similar identity, she feels comfortable sharing this aspect of herself. Can you think of contexts in which you prefer to conceal aspects of your own identity? If so, what characteristic of the context makes you hesitant to disclose this identity?

Identity and communication are deeply intertwined. Moreover, "identity and communication are mutually reinforcing" (Abrams, O'Connor, & Giles, 2002, p. 237). And as we have noted, perception is central to both identity development and how we communicate. In the next section, we examine why understanding these concepts and their relationships to each other helps you become a better communicator.

IT HAPPENED TO ME: Elizabeth

If I meet someone in a college class, I don't tell them that I'm involved in a church or that I'm a Christian unless they bring it up or it's obvious they are too. I do not want to appear to be a religious nut waiting to shove my belief system down their throat. My belief in Christ is really at the core of who I am, though. When I meet people through work who are in churches, I am open with them about my work, my life, and even my challenges. This is because they are my brothers/sisters in Christ, and that's the culture of what we do—care for, and about, one another.

THE IMPORTANCE OF PERCEPTION AND IDENTITY

As we have discussed thus far, how individuals respond to people, objects, and environments depends largely on the perceptions they have about them. That is, when you communicate, you don't just respond to others' words: You respond to your *perceptions* of the way they look, sound, smell, and, on occasion, feel. For example, considerable research has established that people treat others they perceive as attractive better than those they view as less attractive (Chaiken, 1986; Wilson & Nias, 1999)—which may explain why so many people flock to makeover shows like *What Not to Wear* and *The Biggest Loser*.

However, two people can perceive the same event or person in radically different ways. Why? Our perceptions are affected by individual factors, such as our age or gender, genetic makeup, and experience, as well as by societal forces including culture, historical events, and established social roles and identities. To see how the individual factor of age can affect perceptual abilities, see *Did You Know? The Ringtone Adults Cannot Hear*.

DID YOU KNOW?

The Ringtone Adults Cannot Hear

Are you familiar with mosquito ringtones? If so, do you know how they work to impact individuals' perception of sound?

The mosquito ringtone is based on technology created by Britain's Howard Stapleton, who developed a device described as the "mosquito teen repellent." The device emitted a high-pitched-frequency tone that adults could not hear but that teenagers found annoying. It was used by shopkeepers to disperse teenagers from public spaces where they congregated. Later, inventive students converted the same technology into a ringtone that adults could not hear. This allowed them to receive phone calls and text messages while in class without their teachers being aware of it—that is, provided their teachers were old enough. To test your ability to hear mosquito ringtones at different frequency levels, go to http://www.freemosquitoringtone.org/

Sex, like age, can impact perceptual abilities as well. For instance, women on average have a keener sense of smell than do men, so smell may play a more important role in perception for them (Estroff, 2004; Herz & Inzlicht, 2002). Overall, women may be more positively influenced by smells they find attractive and more negatively by smells they dislike. For more information on this topic, see *Communication in Society: The Smell Report.*

It probably makes sense to you that individual characteristics affect people's perceptions, but you may be questioning how societal forces can do so. To explore the answer to this, let's take the example above about the sense of smell. Just as an individual characteristic (such as sex) determines how sensitive you are to odors, your culture determines how you interpret and value specific smells. In the United States, for example, people typically are encouraged to wear deodorant and colognes to mask their natural body odors (Classen, Howes, & Synott, 1994). However, in some cultures natural body odors are considered desirable, and U.S. Americans may be viewed as smelling antiseptic (Danghel, 1996). How you perceive people who do or don't wear deodorant, then, depends on the culture in which you live. In turn, how you perceive and react to others based on their bodily odors impacts how they see themselves, or their identities.

Identities influence perception as well. They cause people to perceive aspects of their environment and other people in specific ways. For example, because of the frequency of sexual assault in the United States, females may be particularly aware of their environment if it is late at night and they are alone. They may be aware of the level of lighting, who else is around, even small noises. In this case, they perceive the environment quite differently than most men do because they are women (and feel more vulnerable). At the same time, their focus on the environment reinforces their cultural identities as victims.

Identity is important because it features in the communication process in several ways. First, because individuals bring their self-images or identities to each encounter, every communication interaction is affected by their identities. For example, when elderly

Communication in **SOCIETY**

The Smell Report

Have you noticed a difference in sense of smell between the sexes? Why do you think women typically have a keener sense of smell?

Sex-Differences

On standard tests of smelling ability—including odour detection, discrimination and identification—women consistently score significantly higher than men. One researcher has claimed that the superior olfactory ability of females is evident even in newborn babies. One study suggests that sex-difference findings may not be entirely reliable, and that sex differences in olfactory prowess may apply to some odours but not others. It is also possible, however, that many studies have not taken account of the changes in female sensitivity to smell during the menstrual cycle. It is known that female sensitivity to male pheromones (scented sex hormones), for example, is 10,000 times stronger during ovulation than during menstruation. It may be that female smell sensitivity is also generally more acute during this phase. (It has been shown that other senses such as hearing are more acute around ovulation, when women can also hear slightly higher frequencies than at other times.) These fluctuations may account for some inconsistencies in the findings, although hormone cycles cannot explain why female children score higher than male children. In an experiment at the Hebrew University, Jerusalem, women without children held an unrelated infant in their arms for one hour and then were tested for infant smell-recognition. Most were successful. The researchers conclude, "This indicates that the ability to identify infants by their odor is a more general human skill than previously realized." But they didn't test men, so it may only be a general female skill. Other tests have shown, however, that both men and women are able to recognise their own children or spouses by scent. In one well-known experiment, women and men were able to distinguish T-shirts worn by their marriage partners, from among dozens of others, by scent alone. Women are also significantly more likely than men to suffer from "cacosmia"—feeling ill from the smell of common environmental chemicals such as paint and perfume.

ADAPTED FROM: Social Issues Research Centre. www.sirc.org/publik/smell_diffs.html

people talk to teenagers, both groups may have to accommodate for differences in their experiences and language use.

Second, identity plays an important role in intercultural communication, which has become increasingly common in our global, technology-based world. Workers in international companies often have contact with people from other cultures. The more familiar they are with the values related to identity in other cultures, the better prepared they will be. In Japan, for instance, age is seen as a virtue, and older people are treated with great respect (Condon, 1984). In fact, the Japanese have a "respect for the aged" holiday. In the United States, on the other hand, people tend to be valued more for their accomplishments than for their age, and youth is often valued over age. If a young person from the U.S. fails to bestow respect on an older Japanese colleague, the older person may feel insulted and be unwilling to cooperate fully.

Third, understanding identity is useful because so much of U.S. life is organized around and geared toward specific identities (Allen, 2004). In the United States, we have television stations such as *Black Entertainment Television* and *Telemundo*, and magazines like *Ebony* and *More*, which are targeted to groups based on their race, age, and/or sex. We also have entertainment venues such as Disneyland, Sandals, and Club Med, which are developed specifically for families, romantic couples, and singles, respectively. In this identity-based climate, individuals often interact primarily with others who share their identities. Consequently, learning how to communicate effectively with individuals whose identities vary from yours may require considerable thought and effort; being prepared by educating yourself about identities will surely benefit you.

Finally, in identity, individual and societal forces come together to shape communication experiences. That is, although we each possess individual identity characteristics such as social class or nationality, society defines the meanings of those characteristics. Also, we cannot separate our identities—as individuals or as members of society—from our communication experiences. Identity is vital to how meaning is created in communication (Hecht, 1993). We explain this interaction throughout this chapter. We begin first, however, by examining in more detail how individual factors influence one's perception and identity.

In Japan, age is seen as a virtue; consequently they observe a "respect for the aged" holiday.

THE INDIVIDUAL, PERCEPTION, AND IDENTITY

In the field of communication, our understanding of identity development arises out of a theory called symbolic interactionism (Blumer, 1969; Mead, 1934). According to this theory, individuals attribute meaning to objects, actions, and people based on their social, or symbolic, interactions with others. In other words, what you perceive as beautiful, ethical, and even edible is based on what you have heard and experienced during your interactions with others. You likely learned through observing and communicating with others that eating lobster is a luxury but that eating bugs is disgusting. We develop and reveal identities through communication interactions in much the same way. In this section, we explore how one's own and others' perceptions and communication influence identity development.

Reflected Appraisals

reflected appraisals
the idea that people's self-images arise primarily from the ways in which others view them and from the many messages they have received from others about who they are

looking-glass self
the idea that self-image results from the images others reflect back to an individual

A primary influence on identity development is a process called **reflected appraisals** (Sullivan, 1953). The term describes the idea that people's self-images arise primarily from the ways in which others perceive them and from the many messages they receive from others about who they are. This concept also often is referred to as the **looking-glass self** (Cooley, 1902; Edwards, 1990), a term that highlights the idea that your self-image results from the images others reflect back to you.

The process of identity development begins at birth. Although newborns do not at first have a sense of self (Rosenblith, 1992), as they interact with others, their identities develop. How others act toward and respond to them influences how infants build their identities. For example, as infants assert their personalities or temperaments, others respond to those characteristics. Parents of a calm and cheerful baby are strongly drawn to hold and

play with the infant, and they describe the child to others as a "wonderful" baby. On the other hand, parents who perceive their infant as tense and irritable may feel frustrated when they cannot calm their child and might respond more negatively to the infant. They may engage in fewer positive interactions with their baby and describe the child as "difficult." Thus, the parents' perceptions influence their interactions with the baby, which in turn shapes his identity for himself and for the parents, as well as for others who have contact with the family (Papalia, Olds, & Feldman, 2002).

The reflected appraisal process is repeated with family, friends, teachers, acquaintances, and strangers as the individual grows. If as a child you heard your parents say that you were gifted, your teachers praised your classroom performance, and acquaintances commented on how verbal you were, you probably came to see yourself in those ways. Through numerous interactions with other people about your appearance, your abilities, your personality, and your character, you developed your identities as a student, friend, male, or female, among others.

The perceptions of two types of "others" influence this process of identity development. George Herbert Mead (1934) described them as *particular others* and the *generalized other*. **Particular others** are the important people in your life whose perceptions, opinions, and behavior influence the various aspects of your identity. Parents, caregivers, siblings, and close friends are obvious particular others who influence your identity. Some particular others may strongly influence just one of your identities or one aspect of an identity. If you believe your soccer coach perceives you as untalented, you may see yourself as a poor soccer player even if friends and family tell you otherwise.

Your sense of your self also is influenced by your perceptions of the **generalized other**, or the collection of roles, rules, norms, beliefs, and attitudes endorsed by the community in which you live. You come to understand what is valued and important in your community via your interactions with particular others, strangers, and acquaintances; various media such as movies, books, and television; and the social institutions that surround you. For example, if you notice that your family, friends, and even strangers comment on people's appearances, that the media focus on people's attractiveness, and that people who look a certain way seem to get more attention at school and are hired for the best jobs, you develop an internalized view of what the generalized other values with regard to appearance. You compare your perceptions of yourself to the norms for attractiveness in your community, which then affects how this aspect of your identity develops.

Gradually, you begin to see yourself in specific ways, which in turn influences your communication behavior, which further shapes others' views of you, and so on. In this way, individual identities are created and recreated by communication interactions throughout one's life.

However, reflected appraisals aren't the only type of communication interaction that shapes identity. Each of us also engages in a process called *social comparison*, which influences how we perceive and value our identities.

Social Comparison

Not only do we see ourselves as possessing specific characteristics, we also evaluate how desirable those characteristics are. As we discussed, particular and generalized others become the basis for our understanding of which characteristics are valued. For example, Amish children learn through their interactions with family, friends, the church, and their

particular others
the important people in an individual's life whose opinions and behavior influence the various aspects of identity

generalized other
the collection of roles, rules, norms, beliefs, and attitudes endorsed by the community in which a person lives

Social norms reflect the characteristics valued in a culture.

?

To understand how social comparisons affect your identity, answer the following questions: To what groups do you compare yourself most often? How do these comparisons affect the way you see yourself? Are these groups the most appropriate reference groups for you to use? How would you feel if you chose different reference groups?

community that aggression is a negative trait that one should minimize or eliminate (Kraybill, 1989). In contrast, in gangs, aggression is valued and encouraged, and community members learn this as well (Sanders, 1994).

Once we understand what characteristics are valued (or disdained) in our communities, we assess whether we individually possess more or less of them than do others in our communities. We compare our perceptions of ourselves to our perceptions of others to determine how we measure up, and through this social comparison, we evaluate ourselves. In this way, the groups we compare ourselves to—our reference groups—play an important role in shaping how we view ourselves. For example, how would you feel if you earned a 78 on an exam and your grade was the highest in the class? What if 78 were the lowest grade in the class? Your perception of yourself and your abilities is shaped not only by a specific trait but also by how it compares to the traits of others in your reference group. However, your self-evaluation can vary depending on what you use as a reference group. If you compare your appearance to that of your friends, colleagues, and classmates, you may feel pretty good. However, if you use the idealized images of actors and models in magazines and movies, you may not feel as positively about your attractiveness.

Self-Fulfilling Prophecy

Communication interactions also can influence one's identity through a process known as the **self-fulfilling prophecy**, meaning that when an individual expects something to occur, the expectation increases the likelihood that it will. If you believe you can perform well on an exam, you are likely to study and prepare for the exam, which typically results in your doing well. Others also have expectations for you that can influence your behavior as well. For example, if your sales manager believes you are a poor salesperson, she may assign you to a territory where you won't have access to big accounts, and she may refuse to send you to sales conferences where your skills could be honed. If you still succeed, she may believe that you just got lucky. However, because you have a poor territory, don't have the opportunity to enhance your sales skills, and receive no rewards for your successes, you probably will not be a very good salesperson. Thus, the belief in a particular outcome influences people to act and communicate in ways that will make the outcome more likely; in turn, the outcome influences how we perceive ourselves. For example, parents often unwittingly influence how their children perform in math and how their children perceive themselves as mathematicians. If a child hears her mother complain about her own poor math skills and how unlikely it is that her child will do better, the child is unlikely to succeed in math classes. When the child encounters difficulty with math, the messages she heard from her mother may increase the likelihood that she will give up and say, "Well, I'm just not good at math." On the other hand, if a child hears messages that she is good at math, she is more likely to keep trying and work harder when faced with a difficult math problem. This, in turn, will influence her to perceive herself as a competent mathematician.

Self-fulfilling prophecies can have a powerful effect on an individual's performance, especially when they are grounded in stereotypes of one's identity. For example, stereotypes exist that Asian students excel at math, that African American students are less verbally competent than White students, and that females are worse at math and spatial reasoning than are males. Studies have shown that even subtly or implicitly reminding individuals of these stereotypical expectations can impact their performance—a concept called **stereotype threat**.

In one study, African Americans who were simply reminded of race performed significantly worse on a verbal exam than when the issue of race was not mentioned (Steele & Aronson, 1995); and in another study, Asian American students performed better on a math test when reminded of their race (Shih, Pittinsky, & Ambady, 1999). In a similar study, females who were cued to think about gender performed worse on math and spatial-ability tests than when the issue of gender was not raised (McGlone & Aronson, 2006). Yet another study found that White male engineering students solved significantly fewer problems when told that they were part of a study to examine why Asian Americans perform better in math than when told it was simply a timed test (Smith & White, 2002).

These studies reveal that individuals' performances can be enhanced or hampered when they are reminded, even implicitly, of perceptions and expectations related to important identities. This is true not only of sex and gender but also of socioeconomic status

self-fulfilling prophecy
when an individual expects something to occur, the expectation increases the likelihood that it will

stereotype threat
process in which reminding individuals of stereotypical expectations regarding important identities can impact their performance

(Croizet & Claire, 1998) and age. These findings remind us that we need to be careful about creating self-fulfilling prophecies for others and allowing others' perceptions and expectations to become self-fulfilling prophecies for us.

Through repeated communication interactions such as reflected appraisals, social comparisons, and self-fulfilling prophecies, we come to have a sense of who we are. This sense of who we are is referred to as one's *self-concept*.

self-concept
the understanding of one's unique characteristics as well as the similarities to, and differences from, others

Self-Concept

As we have suggested, identity generally continues to evolve; at the same time, individuals have some fairly stable perceptions about themselves. These stable perceptions are referred to as self-concept. **Self-concept** includes your perceptions of your unique characteristics as well as your similarities to, and differences from, others. It is an internal image you hold of yourself. Your self-concept is based on your reflected appraisals and social comparisons. However, reflected appraisals only go so far. When someone describes you in a way that you reject, they have violated your self-concept. For example, if you think of yourself as open and outgoing, and a friend calls you "private," you are likely to think the friend does-n't know you very well. To see how one student responds to others' reflected appraisals that violate her self-concept, read *It Happened to Me: Shannon*.

Shannon's narrative is a good example of how reflected appraisals are rejected when they are inconsistent with one's self-concept. Shannon knows that she is driven, moral, and hard-working, so when people appraise her based on a stereo-

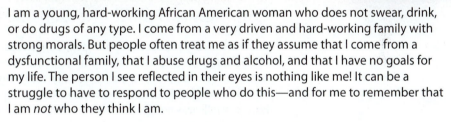

IT HAPPENED TO ME: Shannon

I am a young, hard-working African American woman who does not swear, drink, or do drugs of any type. I come from a very driven and hard-working family with strong morals. But people often treat me as if they assume that I come from a dysfunctional family, that I abuse drugs and alcohol, and that I have no goals for my life. The person I see reflected in their eyes is nothing like me! It can be a struggle to have to respond to people who do this—and for me to remember that I am *not* who they think I am.

type that is at odds with her self-appraisal, she ignores them. However, as she also points out, it can take a concerted effort to disregard such negative evaluations when they occur frequently. When faced with many such negative evaluations, sometimes one's self-concept and self-esteem are affected.

Self-esteem is part of an individual's self-concept: a description of how you evaluate yourself overall. It functions as a lens through which you interpret reflected appraisals and social comparisons, which may make it hard to change. For example, if you have relatively high self-esteem, you may discount negative reflected appraisals and overgeneralize positive ones. So, if a student with high self-esteem fails an exam, he may attribute the failure to external factors (the test was unfair), rather than to himself. On the other hand, a person with low self-esteem is more likely to attribute a failure to the self (I'm not smart enough) than to external factors.

Because self-esteem is such a powerful lens through which you see the world, your self-concept may not be entirely consistent with how others perceive you. If you have ever watched *American Idol*, you probably know what we mean. Many contestants who audition have very high regard for their singing ability, even though the judges do not. Several factors can create such a mismatch. First, individuals' self-image and the feedback they receive may be out of synch because others don't want to hurt their feelings or because they respond negatively when faced with information that contradicts their self-image. Their friends, for example, might not think they have musical talent but compliment them anyway so they won't be upset. Second, if one holds on to an image of the self that is no longer accurate, she/he may have a distorted self-image—or one that doesn't match with how others see them. If you were chubby in grade school, for instance, you may still think of yourself as overweight, even if you are now very slim. Finally, people may not recognize or accept their positive qualities because of modesty or because they value self-effacement. If your social or cultural group discourages people from viewing themselves as better than others, you may only compare yourself to exceptionally attractive or talented people or may refuse to acknowledge your strengths in public settings. In Japanese culture, the appearance of

modesty (*kenkyo*) is highly valued (Davies & Ikeno, 2002). A similar trait of "yieldedness to others" (*glassenheit*) leads the Amish to downplay their accomplishments (Kraybill, 1989).

Because your communication with and about others so strongly affects their self-concepts, you will be a more effective communicator if you work to improve your communication about others' identities. To help you accomplish this, see *Building Your Communication Skills: Communicating About Identities.*

Throughout this discussion of the individual and identity development, we have focused on four concepts: reflected appraisals, social comparison, self-fulfilling prophecies, and self-concept. However, identity development is a circular process in which these concepts are interrelated. For example, reflected appraisals influence your self-concept, which affects your communication behavior, which in turn shapes how others perceive you and, ultimately, what they reflect back to you. Then the process starts all over again. To view an illustration of this process, see *Visual Summary 2.1: Identity Development Through Communication.* To expand the frame of this circular process even further, we next examine how societal factors influence your perceptions, identity, and communication.

Building Your Communication SKILLS

Communicating About Identities

In almost every interaction you have, you discuss others' identities, even if you don't realize it. Whether you're talking about your romantic partner, your professors, your boss, or your roommates, you're usually touching on some aspect of their identities. With this in mind, your relationships will likely improve if you become more mindful of how you talk about them.

Here are four suggestions:

1. ***Avoid overgeneralizing.*** It is tempting to describe someone by relying on the stereotypes of one of their identities. However, doing so is both unfair to the group of individuals who share that identity as well as to the person you are discussing. Instead of negatively categorizing someone's identity, you could simply describe their behavior. For example, instead of describing an unpleasant customer as a "typical New Yorker," you could say that the person spoke abruptly and didn't engage in social pleasantries.

2. ***Examine your attributions.*** Although it is perfectly natural to make attributions about others' behavior, too often people (wrongly) assume that their attributions are correct. So, if you find yourself making negative attributions about others' behavior, stop and ask yourself what other, more positive reasons might exist for their behavior. For example, instead of assuming your colleague leaves work as soon as possible because he is lazy, ask yourself if he might need to pick up children from daycare or have other important responsibilities that affect his behavior.

3. ***Become aware of which identities you focus on most.*** If you focus on one specific identity most —whether it is gender, race, ethnicity, or age—you are probably overlooking other important identities that influence individuals' values, beliefs, and behaviors. Once you become aware of this tendency, stop yourself and focus on other identities the individual possesses. For example, if you find yourself focusing on why old (or young) people engage in certain behaviors, focus instead on their professional, gender, and socioeconomic identities to see if this alternative analysis offers any insight into their choices.

4. ***Ask others for feedback.*** At first, you may resist analyzing your own communication about identities. To help you, you can ask close friends or family members to provide feedback to you on what they have observed about your communication—or to do so while you are talking with them about others. If you identify any of these patterns, you can work to modify them.

Identity Development Through Communication

REFLECTED APPRAISAL (THE LOOKING-GLASS SELF)

How I see myself is developed through communication with others . . .

- Interactions with parents and others shape our early identity and sense of ones self.

- The process is repeated with family, friends, teachers, acquaintances, and strangers.

- **Particular others** are important people in our lives who influence aspects of our identity.

- **Generalized others** are the collection of roles, rules, norms, beliefs, and attitudes endorsed by our community.

SOCIAL COMPARISONS

and how I compare myself to others . . .

- Through our interactions with others, we learn what characteristics are valued (or disdained) by others.

- Then, we assess whether we have more or fewer of those characteristics to determine how we measure up to others in our **identity group**.

each of which affects my evaluation of myself.

SELF-FULFILLING PROPHECIES

affects how I communicate with them and them with me . . .

- When we expect something to occur, that expectation increases the likelihood that it will.

- A belief in a particular outcome influences people to act and communicate in ways that make the outcome more likely.

- Others can also cause their prophecies about us to come true by communicating with us as though they will come true.

SELF CONCEPT

Self-concept

- Self concept is composed of the fairly stable perceptions we have ourselves.

- It includes our understanding of similarities and differences between ourselves and others.

- It is an internal image we have of ourselves and affects the external image we project to others.

- It influences our communication behavior.

- **Self-esteem** the part of self-concept composed of the internal valuation of what we see in the looking glass.

- **Self-respect** the extent to which one feels entitled to regard and respect from self and others.

social identity
the specific identities an individual holds in a society

primary identities
identities such as race, ethnicity, and age that have a consistent and enduring impact on your life

secondary identities
identities such as occupation and marital status that are changeable over the life span and from situation to situation

THE INDIVIDUAL, PERCEPTION, IDENTITY, AND SOCIETY

Although our interactions with others strongly influence our perceptions and identities, societal influences do as well. In this section, we explore three societal influences on individuals' perceptions and identities: social identity, power, and culture.

Social Identity

Social Identity refers to the specific identities an individual holds in a society. These include job positions, familial roles (such as mother or father), and memberships in various organizations. For example, Teri is a mother, a religious leader, a soccer coach, and a community activist. Her identities affect how people perceive and communicate with her in several ways. First, society defines specific expectations for her based on her identities (Kirouac & Hess, 1999). Many people, for example, expect that religious leaders will be especially moral, selfless, and well intentioned. In turn, these perceptions affect the ways in which religious leaders interact with others. If you expect Teri, as a religious leader, to be highly moral, she may work to communicate with you in ways that fulfill your expectations.

Second, the education, training, and/or socialization a person undergoes as she develops her identities influence her perceptions. For example, a police officer may perceive the world as populated with more criminals than the average person does because of the way she has been trained, and other people may perceive her as more masculine than other women because of her identity as a police officer. Each individual's perceptions are unique, based on his or her own identities and characteristics. However, individuals also share certain perceptual realities with others in their power positions in society's hierarchy as well as with others in their cultures—topics we take up next.

Power, Perception, and Identity

Every society has a hierarchy, and in a hierarchy, some people have more power than others. Your relative position of power or lack of power is connected to a great extent to your primary and secondary identities. **Primary identities** (race, ethnicity, age) have the most consistent and enduring impact on your life, while **secondary identities**, such as occupation and marital status, are more changeable over the life span and from situation to situation.

In each culture, some identities are valued over others. In the United States, we value youth and whiteness over age and being a person of color (primary identities), and we value being married and a white-collar professional over being single and blue collared (secondary identities). How you are perceived, and how you interpret the world, is shaped by these identities. For example, in the United States, the dominant perception is that everyone can move up in society through hard work and education ("Middle of the Class," 2005). However, individuals who are born poor and who live in deprived areas with few resources can find it very difficult, no matter how hard they try, to follow the path to "success" as defined by mainstream U.S. culture. Thus, the perceptual reality of people with this identity (e.g., a social class of working poor) will likely differ from the perceptual reality of those higher in the power hierarchy (Douthat, 2005).

Similarly, your racial identity and its position in the racial hierarchy influences your perceptions about the reality of racial bias. It is well documented that White Americans and African Americans historically have had very different perceptions regarding the role of race in the United States (Hacker, 2003). A study conducted after Hurricane Katrina devastated the Gulf Coast revealed a broad divergence in perceptions: When asked whether racial inequality remains a major problem, 71 percent of African Americans replied yes, compared to only 32 percent of Whites (Pew Research Center for the People and the Press, 2005). Interestingly, after President Obama had been in office 100 days, a poll found that 59 percent of African-Americans (and 65 percent of Whites) characterized the relationship between Blacks and Whites in America as "good" (CBS News/New York Times survey, April 27, 2009). Thus, people's perceptions may change as circumstances change.

Culture, Perception, and Identity

Culture strongly influences perception and identity. One way it does so is through its **sensory model**. Every culture has its own sensory model, which means that each culture emphasizes a few of the five senses (Classen, 1990). Moreover, the emphasis placed on one sense over another affects what a culture's members pay attention to and value. People in the United States, for example, tend to give primacy to the visual. Therefore, we tend to value and reward physical attractiveness. On the other hand, people living in the Andes Mountains of South America tend to place more emphasis on what they hear than on what they see (Classen, 1990). Therefore, they prize individuals who are well spoken and who can tell engaging stories.

A culture is composed of a set of shared practices, norms, values, and beliefs (Brislin, 2000; Shore, 1996). Due to learning and socialization, these elements shape individuals' thoughts, feelings, perceptions, and identities. For example, individuals in East Asian cultures often are highly interdependent and place more emphasis on the group than the individual. For this reason, they discourage self-promotion and encourage greater self-criticism than do European North American cultures. By encouraging self-criticism (and then working on self-improvement), the thinking goes, they are contributing to the overall strength of the group (Heine & Lehman, 2004; Markus, Mullally, & Kitayama, 1997). In the United States, however, the emphasis is more often on the individual, and most people are encouraged to distinguish themselves from others. For example, current books on dating and work success teach U.S. Americans how to "brand" themselves like a product. Thus, the dominant culture in the United States encourages people to talk about their success and to refrain from self-disparaging rhetoric. As a result, in East Asia, a modest person would be perceived positively, while the same person may be disparaged in the United States as being overly self-effacing (Kim, 2002).

Because cultural background influences perception and identity, it also influences how people expect communication to occur (Scollon & Wong-Scollon, 1990). In some Native American cultures, individuals perceive strangers as potentially unpredictable, so they may talk little—if at all—until they have established familiarity and trust with the newcomer (Braithwaite, 1990). This approach differs considerably from the customs of some European American cultures in which people view strangers as potential friends and use talk to become acquainted (Krivonos & Knapp, 1975). Now imagine a Native American and a European American from these different communication cultures meeting for the first time. How is each likely to behave? The Native American may remain relatively quiet while observing the new person. The European American most likely will try to engage in a lively conversation and ask a number of questions to draw the other person out. Therefore, the Native American may perceive the European American as pushy and suspicious, while the European American may perceive the Native American as unfriendly or shy (Braithwaite, 1990). Each perceives or evaluates the other's identity based on expectations that were shaped by his or her own cultural perceptions, values, and meanings (Scollon & Wong-Scollon, 1990). To discover how you can refine your perceptual processes and your interpretation of your own and others' identities, see *Building Your Communication Skills: Refining Your Perceptual Processes.*

THE ETHICS OF PERCEIVING AND COMMUNICATING ABOUT IDENTITIES

You might think that ethics play a very small role in perceptual and cognitive processes related to identities. However, as we've discussed throughout this chapter, the ways in which you communicate to and about people are connected to your perceptions and cognitions about their identities. Two ethical issues that arise when people communicate with others based on their perceptions of those individuals' identities are stereotyping and prejudice.

Stereotyping

As noted earlier in the chapter, stereotypes are broad generalizations about an entire class of objects or people based on some knowledge of some aspects of some members

sensory model
model that explains how an individual culture emphasizes a few of the five senses

Building Your Communication SKILLS

Refining Your Perceptual Processes

Before you assume that your perceptions about others are accurate, ask yourself these questions:

- Have you **failed to notice** any relevant information due to selective attention? For example, did you focus on the person's ethnicity rather than on what he or she said?

- Have you used **faulty organizational patterns**? For example, did you attribute someone's poor job performance to their age, ethnicity, race, or sex, or did you attribute it to the individual, to environmental factors, or to your own behavior?

- Have you considered **all possible interpretations** for the information you perceived? For example, if you weren't hired for a job, was it due to the interviewer's sex, ethnicity, or age? Or did you fail to prepare sufficiently for the interview? Could there have been more qualified candidates, or were you not well suited to the position?

- Has your **physical condition** influenced your perceptions? For example, were you tired, angry, or frightened during an exchange with another person? Such physical states can increase the tendency to engage in stereotypical thinking.

- Has your **cultural background** influenced your perceptions? For example, did you perceive politeness as deception?

- Has one of your **social identities** influenced your perception? For example, have you considered how others with different identities might perceive the same issue?

of the class (Brislin, 2000; Stephan & Stephan, 1992). Although stereotyping can cause problems, humans are hard-wired to do it. Historically, the ability to make snap judgments about others—that is, to determine whether someone was part of one's group and therefore safe, or not part of one's group and consequently potentially dangerous—increased one's survivability. Stereotyping, or recognizing characteristics that group members have in common, is not negative in and of itself. It only becomes a problem (1) when we over-rely on it and fail to recognize the diversity that also occurs within groups and/or (2) when we make negative attributions about others based on little personal information, as described in *It Happened to Me: Damien.*

The people who stereotype Damien and other computer programmers likely are engaging in both of the above cognitive errors. They aren't recognizing that many computer programmers, like Damien, are social and socially skilled, and they are basing their beliefs on interactions with a few programmers—

IT HAPPENED TO ME: Damien

Shortly after school started, I decided to join a fraternity and began going to parties on the weekends. Often, when people heard me mention that I was a part-time computer programmer, they would first look shocked and then crack some kind of joke about it, like "Bill Gates, Jr., eh?" I guess it surprises people that I don't have glasses, that I venture out into the sunlight once in a while, and that I engage in some social activities! I realize that their preconceived notions about "techies" have come from somewhere, but, because at least half of my fellow "computer geeks" are far from the nerdy stereotype, it would be nice if people would recognize that we aren't all pale, glasses-wearing, socially awkward nerds!

or perhaps on no interactions at all. Instead, their stereotype may be based on what they have read, images in the media, or information they have obtained from others. Although stereotyping is an understandable and natural cognitive activity, it often leads to polarized understandings of the world as "between me and you, us and them, females and males,

Blacks and Whites" (Ting-Toomey, 1999, p. 149). In turn, polarized thinking frequently leads to a rigid, intolerant view of certain behavior as correct or incorrect (Ting-Toomey, 1999). For example, do you believe it is more appropriate for adult children to live on their own or with their parents before they marry? People with polarized thinking assume that their own cultural beliefs regarding this issue are right or correct instead of recognizing that cultures differ in what is considered appropriate. Stereotyping also can cause problems when it leads to prejudice.

Prejudice

Prejudice occurs when people experience adverse or negative feelings toward a group as a whole or toward an individual because she or he belongs to a group (Rothenberg, 1992). People can experience prejudice against a person or group because of their physical characteristics, perceived ethnicity, age, national origin, religious practices, and a number of other identity categories.

Some television viewers complained that the cast of *Jersey Shore* perpetuated negative stereotypes of Italian Americans.

Given the negative associations most people have with the concept of prejudice, you may wonder why it persists. Researchers believe that prejudice is common and pervasive because it serves specific functions, the two most important of which are *elevating one's self-esteem* and *supporting group values* (Brislin, 2000). Let's explore these concepts.

The **self-esteem** building function of prejudice describes the role it plays in protecting individuals' sense of self-worth. For example, an individual who is not financially successful and whose group members tend not to be financially successful may attribute blame to other groups for hoarding resources and preventing him or her from becoming successful. The less financially successful individual may also look down on groups that are even less financially successful as a way to protect his or her own ego. These attitudes may make people feel better, but they also prevent them from analyzing reasons for their own failure and negatively affect the ways they talk to and about targeted groups. People who look down on groups that are less financially successful may also describe them and talk to them as if they were lazy, incompetent, or not very bright.

Prejudice also serves *to support group values* by allowing people to view their own values, norms, and cultural practices as appropriate and correct. By devaluing other groups' behavior and beliefs, people maintain a solid sense that they are right. Unfortunately, this same function causes group members to denigrate the cultural practices of others. You likely have seen many examples of prejudice supporting group values, as when individuals engage in uncivil arguments and personal attacks over issues such as men's and women's roles, abortion, and politics.

Stereotyping, Prejudice, and Communication

When people stereotype others and/or experience prejudice, they may also communicate to and about these people in a way that denigrates or puts them down based on their identities. Doing so debases others' humanity and shuts down open communication. Examples of unethical communication and behavior related to stereotyping and identity occur when straight people harass individuals they believe are gay, or when people are disrespectful to others based on their perception of the others' race or ethnicity. Although you probably don't engage in such obvious insults to people's identities, do you disparage them in

What kind of stereotypes have others used to categorize you? How did you feel when that occurred? How did you respond? What do you think people should do to minimize their stereotyping of others?

prejudice
experiencing aversive or negative feelings toward a group as a whole or toward an individual because she or he belongs to a group

self-esteem
part of one's self-concept; arises out of how one perceives and interprets reflected appraisals and social comparisons

other, more subtle ways? For example, have you ever referred to someone as "just a home-maker" or "only a dental assistant"?

In addition, if what you attend to and perceive about people first is their skin color, their sex, or their relative affluence, you may find yourself reducing them to this single identity category. Each of us is composed of multiple identities, and even within a specific identity group, individuals may differ widely from one another. Thus, individuals may be offended when others respond to them based only on one of their identities, especially one that is not relevant to the situation at hand. For example, managers in some organizations will not promote mothers of small children to highly demanding positions. They justify this by claiming that the women won't be able to fulfill both their family and their professional roles competently. Although these women may be mothers, their identities as mothers likely are not relevant to their workplace identities and performance—just as men's identities as fathers are rarely seen as relevant to their jobs. Each person is a complex of identities, and each person desires others to recognize his or her multiple and unique identities. You are more likely to communicate ethically if you keep this fact in mind.

SKILLS FOR IMPROVING PERCEPTION AND COMMUNICATION ABOUT IDENTITIES

You now know that your perceptions about others' identities and the ways in which you communicate to people based on those perceptions significantly impact their identity development and self-concepts. However, you may be less aware of the degree to which your perceptions are subject to variance and error due to the variety of steps one goes through in forming them. Because perception plays such a strong role in identity development and communication, you can benefit from improving your perceptual processes and your communication to others based on their identities. What can you do?

First, you can engage in mindfulness. **Mindfulness**, as we discuss in more detail in Chapters 5 and 10, refers to having a clear focus on the activity you are engaged in, with attention to as many specifics of the event as you can (Langer, 1978). People tend to be most mindful when they are engaged in a new or unusual activity. Once an activity becomes habitual, individuals are likely to overlook its details. Mindfulness requires that you bring the same level of attention and involvement to routine perceptual and communication activities as you do to novel ones.

Mindfulness is not natural for most people. Instead of focusing on what is immediately happening in front of them, individuals tend to think about past experiences or future plans. Therefore, if you want to become more mindful of your behavior and interactions, you must practice (and practice and practice). Here are some behaviors you can perform that will help you become more mindful, or present, during your conversations with others if you practice them:

- *Focus on relevant aspects of the interaction*. Instead of letting your mind wander to what you might say next, concentrate on what you and your conversational partner are saying right now. As part of this focus, also pay attention to how you refer to other people and other groups. Are you stereotyping them? Does your language suggest that you are prejudiced against others? In focusing on this, you become more aware both of the other interactant's and your own communication patterns.
- *Focus on different perspectives*. Ask yourself how members of the group you are discussing would view your language choices and communication behavior. Also ask yourself whether you would want a member of the group, or the person him/herself, to hear what you are saying.
- *Draw distinctions between a person/experience and its stereotype*. That is, instead of offering a generalization about an individual or her/his group, recognize that one individual—or one experience—does not constitute the entirety of a group's or individual's characteristics.

mindfulness
having a clear focus on the activity you are engaged in, with attention to as many specifics of the event as you can

- ***Recognize that an individual is different from others in his/her group.*** Realize (and remind yourself) that no matter what experiences you have had with other members of an individual's group, the person you are interacting with/talking about is a unique individual who may share only some or even none of the characteristics you are familiar with from previous interactions.
- ***Note your physical responses and the comments you make to yourself.*** Be attentive to your own prejudices and negative reactions to individuals and groups. Also, remember that your reactions may be more of a statement about *you* than about the other person(s).

Another way to improve your perception and understanding is to clearly separate *facts* from *inferences*. Facts are truths that are verifiable based on observation. Inferences, as mentioned earlier in the chapter, are conclusions we draw or interpretations we make based on the facts. Thus, it may be a fact that Southerners speak more slowly than do people from other regions of the United States, but it is an inference if you conclude that their slow speech indicates slow thought processes.

A third way you can improve your perception of and communication with others is to be empathic toward them. *Empathy* refers to the ability to understand another person's experience from within that person's frame of reference and to do so without judgment. Empathy, then, means that when someone acts differently than you would in a given situation, you try to understand why—based on who that person is and what they have experienced—without evaluating him/her. If, for example, your parents say they don't want you to indulge in your long-time dream of skydiving, how could you respond empathically? You might do so by imagining how fearful a person might feel if a loved one was at risk or even died. Or you could think about how you would feel if your younger sibling or romantic partner wanted to engage in a dangerous behavior.

Empathy is important to communication because, as we discuss above, individuals' responses to others are based on the attributions they make. Because actions typically are ambiguous (that is, you don't know why a person chooses to engage in them), you try to evaluate others' thoughts and intentions to explain their behavior. When you don't know another person or group very well, or at all, you tend to make even more errors in your attributions and reasoning than you do with friends and family. Specifically, you are more likely to make negative attributions about their behavior and personality.

How can you improve your empathy skills? First, you can become more curious about others, their experiences, and how those experiences shape their behavior. To do so, you need to question why others might act as they do, rather than assuming that you know. You also should attempt to explain others' behavior in a variety of ways. If someone cuts you off in traffic, for example, rather than assuming that she/he is being rude and aggressive, think of a variety of reasons why the person might have done so. Perhaps she/he didn't see you, was distracted by a serious personal problem, was responding an emergency, or had children in the car who distracted them. As you can see from this example, when you look for alternative explanations, you should focus on positive intentions and to try to understand others without passing judgment on them or their behavior.

Finally, one communication act in particular will greatly improve your perception and understanding of others—perception checking. That is, check with others to determine if their perceptions match yours. If they do not, you may need to alter your perceptions. For example, Rosario once had an extremely negative reaction to a job candidate who interviewed at her company. She perceived him as arrogant and sexist. However, when she talked with her colleagues, she discovered that no one else had a similarly strong negative response to the candidate. She decided that her perceptions must have been influenced by something in her own background and that she was interpreting his behavior more negatively than she should. In revising her opinion of the candidate, Rosario demonstrated a well-developed sensitivity to the perception side of communication and its impact on how we understand others' identities. All of us can benefit from greater awareness of the assumptions and attributions we make about others.

SUMMARY

Perceptions are based on three interrelated processes—selection, organization, and interpretation of sensory information. Understanding the perception process is important, because individuals' own as well as others' perceptions influence how identities develop. Learning about the influence that perception and communication have on identity development is important for four reasons: (1) How individuals respond to people, objects, and environments depends largely on the perceptions they have about them; (2) individuals' identities influence the perceptions they have about events, people, and their environment; (3) much of U.S. life is organized around and geared toward specific identities; and (4) identity is a key site where individual and societal forces come together to shape communication experiences.

In this chapter, *identity* refers to the social categories people identify with as well as the categories that others identify with them. These identities are developed through four communication processes, including reflected appraisals, social comparisons, self-fulfilling prophecies, and self-concept. In addition to these communication interactions, perception and identity are affected by societal features, such as social identity or role, position in the power hierarchy, and the cultures in which one is raised and lives. Because perception and identity are such important contributors to communication interactions, to ensure that one's perception and communication about others' identities are ethical, one should minimize stereotypical thinking, avoid using denigrating language, and steer clear of reducing people to a single identity category. In addition, one can engage in effective communication about identities by being mindful, separating facts from inferences, being empathic, and engaging in perception checking.

KEY TERMS

attribution theory 31
attributional bias 31
categorization 30
cognitive representation 28
frame 31
fundamental attribution error 32
generalized other 37
identity 32
interpretation 28
label 30
looking-glass self 36

mindfulness 46
organization 28
particular others 37
perception 28
predjudice 45
primary identities 42
prototype 29
reflected appraisals 36
interpersonal script 29
secondary identities 42
selection 28

selective attention 28
self-concept 39
self-esteem 45
self-fulfilling prophecy 38
self-serving bias 32
sensory model 43
social identity 42
stereotype threat 38
stereotyping 30

CHAPTER REVIEW QUESTIONS

1. How do perception and identity influence one another?

2. How important is the role of interpretation in the perception process? What factors most influence how individuals interpret events?

3. How do cognitive maps, plans, and scripts differ from one another? How are they alike?

4. How are identities created through interaction?

5. How do reflected appraisals and social comparisons affect identity development?

6. How can mindfulness improve one's perceptions of and communication about others' identities?

ACTIVITIES

1. In your next conversation, attempt to be mindful for the entire conversation. Be present in the moment and focus on the other person—including what they are wearing, what they are saying, and their nonverbal behavior. Also focus on your own perception and communication processes related to identities. Write a two-page reflection

paper describing what you observed, how easy or difficult it was for you to stay mindful, and what you learned from the experience.

2. List the identities that are most important to you. Some of these identities may not have been discussed in this chapter. Note some situations in which the identities not discussed in the chapter become most relevant and some situations where other identities dominate.

3. For each of the words below, write down your beliefs about the group represented. In other words, provide a list of specific characteristics you believe are typically displayed by members of these groups.

a. fraternity members
b. politicians
c. models
d. hip-hop stars
e. body builders
f. religious leaders

After you have done so, compare your list to the lists created by other members of your class. What characteristics for each group did you have in common? What characteristics differed? Can you think of at least one person from each group who does not display the characteristics you listed? How valid do you think your stereotypes are?

WEB ACTIVITIES

1. Read this essay on personal homepages and identity: **www.aber.ac.uk/media/Documents/short/ webident.html** Then scan some homepages and think about the identity each homepage author is constructing and why you perceive the author's identity as you do. How is someone's identity in everyday life different from his or her identity on a homepage?

2. Go to the homepage of Harvard's Interpersonal Perception and Communication Laboratory at **www.wjh.harvard.edu/~na/** Click on one of the links under "Projects" and read a summary of the project that is being conducted. Write a brief paragraph summarizing what this project will explain about perception and communication.

3

VERBAL COMMUNICATION

My boyfriend is from Boston, and I'm from California. He has a strong East Coast accent, making it hard for me to understand him sometimes. He also uses slang words that I've never heard before. I continually ask him to repeat himself. It's frustrating for both of us, so our deal is that he will try harder to enunciate and I will listen more carefully. The most difficult time was when I visited his hometown of Boston and met all his friends and family. It was a big culture shock at first, but eventually I caught on to the slang and pronunciation.

When you think of *communication,* you probably most often think about the verbal elements of communication—the words people choose, the accents they speak with, and the meanings they convey through language. You may less frequently consider the ways in which verbal communication assists or hinders relationship development, as illustrated in the opening example from our student Yolanda, or its effect on the creation of identities.

In this chapter, we explore the verbal elements of communication and how people use verbal communication to accomplish various goals. First, we define verbal communication and discuss its value as a topic of study. We then describe how language functions for individuals and how societal forces influence verbal communication. Finally, we provide suggestions for communicating more ethically and effectively.

Once you have read this chapter, you will be able to:

- Define verbal communication.
- Identify three reasons for learning about verbal communication.
- Describe the functions and components of language.
- Identify and give an example of each influence on verbal communication.
- Explain the relationship between language and perception.
- Explain the relationship between language and power.
- Discuss ways to communicate more ethically.
- Identify and give an example of confirming and disconfirming communication.
- Identify and give an example of an "I" statement.

CHAPTER OUTLINE

WHAT IS VERBAL COMMUNICATION?

THE IMPORTANCE OF VERBAL COMMUNICATION

VERBAL COMMUNICATION AND THE INDIVIDUAL
 Functions of Language
 Components of Language
 Influences on Verbal Communication
 Gender
 Age
 Regionality
 Ethnicity and Race
 Education and Occupation

THE INDIVIDUAL, VERBAL COMMUNICATION, AND SOCIETY
 Language and Perception
 Language and Power
 Power and Words
 Power and Accent
 Power and Identity Labels

ETHICS AND VERBAL COMMUNICATION
 Become Aware of the Power of Language
 Become Conscious of Your Language Use

IMPROVING YOUR VERBAL COMMUNICATION SKILLS
 Supportive Versus Defensive Communication
 Confirming and Disconfirming Communication
 "I" Statements

Summary

Key Terms

Chapter Review Questions

Activities

Web Activities

WHAT IS VERBAL COMMUNICATION?

Verbal communication generally refers to the written or oral words we exchange, and these words are usually also referred to as language. However, as our opening example shows, verbal communication has to do with more than just the words people speak. It includes pronunciation or accent, the meanings of the words used, and a range of variations in the way people speak a language—depending on their regional backgrounds and other factors.

Language, of course, plays a central role in communication. Some argue that it is our use of language that makes us human. Unlike other mammals, humans use symbols that they can string together to create new words and with which they can form infinite sets of never-before-heard, thought, or read sentences. This ability allows people to be creative and expressive, such as when they coin terms like "googleganger"—nominated by the American Dialect Society as the most creative word for 2007—meaning a person with your name who shows up when you google yourself. You can see other words of the year in *Did You Know? Words of the Year*. Even small children, unschooled in grammar, create their own rules of language by using innate linguistic ability together with linguistic information they glean from the people around them. For example, young children often say "mouses" instead of "mice" because they first learn, and broadly apply, the most common rule for pluralizing—adding an *s*.

DID YOU KNOW?

Words of the Year

Each year, the American Dialect Society identifies words that most dominated the national discourse:

2003: metrosexual (fashion-conscious heterosexual male)

2004: red state, blue state, purple states (together, a representation of the American political map)

2005: truthiness (the quality of preferring concepts or facts one wishes to be true, rather than concepts or facts known to be true—popularized by Steven Colbert)

2006: plutoed (to demote or devalue someone or something, as happened to the former planet Pluto when the General Assembly of the International Astronomical Union decided that Pluto no longer met its definition of a planet)

2007: subprime (a risky or less-than-ideal loan, mortgage, or investment)

2008: bailout (rescue by the government of companies on the brink of failure, including large players in the banking industry)

2009: *tweet* (short message sent via the Twitter.com service)

SOURCE: http://www.americandialect.org/woty.html

To help you better understand the role of language in the communication process, the next section explores seven communicative functions of language as well as four components of language use.

THE IMPORTANCE OF VERBAL COMMUNICATION

Although the nonverbal aspects of communication are important, the verbal elements are the foundation on which meaning is created. If you wonder about the relative importance of the verbal versus nonverbal elements of communication, try to convey nonverbally "I failed my exam because I locked my keys in my car and couldn't get my textbook until well after midnight." You probably don't need to conduct this exercise if you have ever traveled in countries where you didn't speak the language; no doubt you already know that nonverbal communication can only get you so far. We will touch on the importance of

nonverbal communication here and discuss it in depth in Chapter 4. However, in this section, we focus on the central role of the verbal elements in getting a message across.

Verbal communication is also important because of the role it plays in identity and relationship development. As you might remember from our discussion in Chapter 2, individuals develop a sense of self through communication with others. More specifically, the labels used to describe individuals can impact their self-concepts and increase or decrease self-esteem. People's verbal communication practices can also impede or improve their relationships, a topic we will discuss further in Chapter 8. Research by two psychology professors at Emory University supports our claims about the relationship between verbal communication and an individual's identity development and relationship skills. These scholars found that families that converse and eat meals together on a regular basis have children who not only are more familiar with their family histories but also tend to have higher self-esteem, interact better with their peers, and recover more easily from tragedy and negative events (Duke, Fivush, Lazarus & Bohanek, 2003).

In addition, the very language people speak is tied to their identities. Studies of bilingual and multilingual speakers show that their perceptions, behaviors, and even personalities alter when they change languages (Ramírez-Esparza, Gosling, Benet-Martínez, Potter, & Pennebaker, 2006). Why does this occur? The answer is that every language is embedded in a specific cultural context, and when people learn a language, they also learn the beliefs, values, and norms of its culture (Edwards, 2004). So speaking a language evokes its culture as well as who one is within that culture. Thus, the language you use to communicate verbally shapes who you are, as our student explains in *It Happened to Me: Cristina*. This example shows how language use is closely connected to cultural norms, like gender roles. In Mexico, women and men tend to interact in a more flirtatious way, which came naturally to Cristina's students when speaking Spanish. Her experience, then, highlights this connection between language and the very core of our identities.

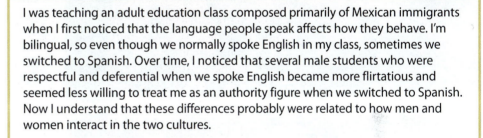

IT HAPPENED TO ME: Cristina

I was teaching an adult education class composed primarily of Mexican immigrants when I first noticed that the language people speak affects how they behave. I'm bilingual, so even though we normally spoke English in my class, sometimes we switched to Spanish. Over time, I noticed that several male students who were respectful and deferential when we spoke English became more flirtatious and seemed less willing to treat me as an authority figure when we switched to Spanish. Now I understand that these differences probably were related to how men and women interact in the two cultures.

VERBAL COMMUNICATION AND THE INDIVIDUAL

Now that we've defined what we mean by verbal communication and noted the important role that language plays in our interactions with others, let's look more closely at the functions and components of language. We will then explore how our various identities (age, ethnicity, and so on) influence our verbal communication and language use.

Functions of Language

You use language so automatically that you probably don't think about the many roles it plays. However, language helps you do everything from ordering lunch to giving directions or writing love poems. Moreover, a single utterance can function in a variety of ways. For example, a simple "thank you" not only expresses gratitude, but it can also increase feelings of intimacy and liking. Consequently, understanding the ways in which language functions can help you communicate more effectively. As we discuss next, language can serve at least seven functions: instrumental, regulatory, **informative**, heuristic, interactional, personal, and **imaginative**.

- The most basic function of language is **instrumental**. This means that you can use it to obtain what you need or desire. For instance, when you invite friends to dinner, the invitation is instrumental in that you want your friends to come to dinner and the invitation helps make that happen.

informative
use of language to communicate information or report facts

imaginative
use of language to express oneself artistically or creatively

instrumental
use of language to obtain what you need or desire

regulatory
use of language to control or regulate the behaviors of others

heuristic
use of language to acquire knowledge and understanding

interactional
use of language to establish and define social relationships

personal language
use of language to express individuality and personality

- A second (and closely related) language function is **regulatory**, meaning that you can use it to control or regulate the behaviors of others. In your invitation, you may ask your friends to bring a bottle of wine or a dessert, as a way of regulating their behavior.

- Another basic function of language is to *inform*—to communicate information or report facts. When you invite your friends to dinner, you usually include the date and time to inform them of when you want them to come.

- You also use language to acquire knowledge and understanding, which is referred to as a **heuristic** use. When you want to invite friends to dinner, you may ask them if they are available at that date and time to learn if your dinner can occur as scheduled or if you need to change the date.

- When language is used in an **interactional** fashion, it establishes and defines social relationships in both interpersonal and group settings. Thus, when you invite your friends to dinner, you engage in a behavior that helps maintain your relationship with them as friends.

- **Personal language** expresses individuality and personality and is more common in private than in public settings. When you invite your friends to dinner, you might jokingly say, "Don't bring that cheap bottle of wine, like you did last time." In this way, you use language to express your sense of humor.

- A final way you can use language is imaginatively. Imaginative language is used to express oneself artistically or creatively, as in drama, poetry, or stories. Thus, if on the cover of your invitation to dinner you wrote, "A loaf of bread, a jug of wine, and thou," you would be using the imaginative function of language. For another example of the imaginative use of language, see *Did You Know? A Little Poem Regarding Computer Spell Checkers.* In addition to showing how language can be used creatively, the poem also illustrates the nature of the relationship between spoken and written English. The fact that one can create

Language plays a central role in communication. For example, it can serve an instrumental function, helping us achieve everyday tasks, like completing a sales transaction.

a poem that makes perfect sense when read orally but has many misspelled words shows how arbitrary English spelling is (when compared to many other languages). That is, different letters can be combined to make the same sound—which is why people learning English as a second language often have great difficulty with spelling!

As our discussion thus far indicates, language has seven basic functions, and speakers use them to accomplish specific goals or tasks. Note that these functions overlap and that one utterance can accomplish more than one function. For example, when inviting your friends to dinner, if you jokingly said, "James, our butler, will be serving dinner promptly at eight, so don't be late!" your utterance would be both imaginative (unless you actually have a butler named James) and regulatory. That is, you would be using language creatively while also attempting to regulate your guests' behavior to ensure that they arrived on time.

DID YOU KNOW?

A Little Poem Regarding Computer Spell Checkers

Eye halve a spell chequer
It came with my pea sea
It plainly marques four my revue
Miss steaks eye kin knot sea.

Eye strike a key and type a word
And weight four it two say
Weather eye am wrong oar write
It shows me strait a weigh.
As soon as a mist ache is maid
It nose bee fore two long
And eye can put the error rite
Its rare lea ever wrong.
Eye have run this poem threw it
I am shore your pleased two no
Its letter perfect awl the weigh
My chequer tolled me sew.

SOURCE: Author unknown. Retrieved March 11, 2009, from http://www.latech.edu/tech/liberal-arts/geography/courses/spellchecker.htm

---

Now that we have summarized the essential functions language can serve, we next examine the basic components that allow us to use language as a flexible and creative tool of communication.

Components of Language

Scholars describe language use as being composed of four components: *phonology* (sounds), *syntax* (structure or rules), *semantics* (meaning), and *pragmatics* (use), as shown in *Visual Summary 3.1: Components of Language*. In this section, we examine the role each plays in the communication process.

Phonology: Sounds

Phonology is the study of the sounds of language and how those sounds communicate meaning in various languages. One way to understand the significance of sounds is to consider how making very small changes in sounds can change the meaning of a word. For example, if you replace the middle sound in *bed*, you can make *bid, bad,* or *bud.* Each change results in a different meaning. One of Yolanda's challenges with her Boston boyfriend was understanding the meaning of his differently accented words. Though these differences in sounds/meaning may seem small, they can lead to serious communication problems, particularly when one is encountering a new accent as was the case with Yolanda, or when learning a new language, as another of our students discusses in *It Happened to Me: Gloria.* Gloria's mistake involved one very small sound (*re* rather than *era*), and yet it resulted in her communicating a nonsensical statement to her friend!

As a student, which functions of language do you use most frequently? Which do you use most often in your professional life? If you use a different function in each of these roles, why do you think this is true?

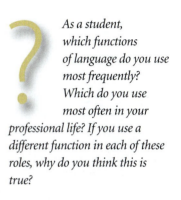

IT HAPPENED TO ME: Gloria

I studied Spanish at a language school in Mexico, and one day I went to a local museum with a Mexican friend, Armando. We were looking at some antique carved tables, and I was trying to tell him about a beautiful oak table that my father had made. I told Armando that it was made "*de madre.*" When he looked confused, I realized that I had said that the table was made of mother (*madre*). I meant to say *madera* (wood). What a difference a few letters can make!

Syntax: Rules

Syntax refers to the rules that govern word order. For example, the sentences "The young boy hit the old man" and "The old man hit the young boy" have very different meanings, even though they contain identical words. You should recall certain rules about combining words—for example, that the verb and the subject in a sentence have to agree, so people say, "the pencil *is* on the table," not "the pencil *are* on the table." Because of these rules, people combine words consistently in ways that make sense and make communication possible.

phonology
the study of the sounds that compose individual languages and how those sounds communicate meaning

syntax
the rules that govern word order

semantics
the study of meaning

denotative meaning
the dictionary, or literal, meaning of a word

connotative meaning
the affective or interpretive meanings attached to a word

pragmatics
field of study that emphasizes how language is used in specific situations to accomplish goals

speech act theory
branch of pragmatics that suggests that when people communicate, they do not just say things, they also do things with their words

Semantics: Meaning

Semantics is the study of meaning, which is an important component of communication.

As you remember from Chapter 1, a central part of our definition of communication is the creation of shared meaning. For any given message, a number of factors create meaning. Perhaps most important are the words speakers choose. For example, what word would you use to describe a friend who always has the answer in class, gets excellent grades, and seems to have a wealth of information at his fingertips? *Smart, intelligent, clever, wise,* or *brilliant*? Because each word has a slightly different meaning, you try to choose the one that most accurately characterizes your friend. However, in choosing the "right" words, you have to consider the two types of meaning that words convey: *denotative* and *connotative*— terms we also discussed in Chapter 1.

The **denotative meaning** refers to the dictionary, or literal, meaning of a word. Referring back to our description of your friend: The dictionary defines *wise* as "Having the ability to discern or judge what is true, right, or lasting; sagacious" and *intelligent* as "Showing sound judgment and rationality" (*American Heritage Dictionary,* 2000). Does either of these words exactly capture how you would describe your friend? If not, which word does?

Words also carry **connotative meanings**, which are the interpretive meanings attached to them. Using the previous example, the connotative meaning of the word *wise* implies an older person with long experience, so it might not be the best choice to describe your young friend.

Pragmatics: Language in Use

Along with phonology, syntax, and semantics, the field of **pragmatics** seeks to identify patterns or rules people follow when they use language appropriately. In the case of pragmatics, however, the emphasis is on how people use language in specific situations to accomplish goals (Nofsinger, 1999). For example, how do rules for communicating appropriately in a sorority vary from those governing a faculty meeting or an evangelical church? The three units of the study of pragmatics are *speech acts, conversational rules*, and *contextual rules*. Let's examine what each contributes to communication.

Speech Acts   One branch of pragmatics, **speech act theory**, looks closely at the seven language functions described previously and suggests that when people communicate, they do not just say things, they also *do* things with their words. For example, when you say, "I bet you ten dollars the Yankees win the World Series," you aren't just saying something, you are actually doing something. That something you are doing is making a bet, or entering into an agreement that will result in an exchange of money.

One common speech act is the request, and a recent study examined one type of request that occurs primarily in U. S. family contexts—the common practice of "nagging" (Boxer, 2002). Nagging (repeated requests by one family member to another) usually concerns household chores and is often a source of conflict. The researcher found that nagging requires several sequential acts: It begins with a first request that is usually in the form of a command ("Please take out the garbage") or a hedged request ("Do you think you could take out the garbage this evening?"). If the request is not granted, it is repeated as a reminder (after some lapse of time), often with an observation about the first request ("Did you hear me? Could you please take out the garbage?"). When a reminder is repeated (the third stage), it becomes nagging and usually involves a scolding or a threat, depending on the relationship—for example whether it is between parent/child ("This is the last time I'm going to ask you. Take out the garbage!") or relational partners ("Never mind. I'll do it myself!").

The researcher found that language use is directly related to relational power; men rarely nagged, because men are perceived as having more power. They can, therefore, successfully request and gain compliance from another family member without resorting to nagging. In addition, children can have power (if they refuse to comply with a request despite lacking status), and parents can lack power despite having status. She concludes

that by nagging, we lose power, but without power, we are forced into nagging, and so it seems a vicious cycle!

Understanding the meaning of various speech acts often requires understanding context and culture (Austin, 1975; Sbisa, 2002). For this reason, people may agree on what is *said* but disagree on what is *meant*. For example, the other day, Katy said to her roommate Hiroshi, "I have been so busy that I haven't even had time to do the dishes." He replied, "Well, I'm sorry, but I have been busy too." What did he think Katy was "doing" with her utterance? When they discussed this interaction, Katy explained that she was making an excuse, while Hiroshi said he heard a criticism—that because *she* hadn't had time to do the dishes, *he* should have. Thus, messages may have different meanings or "do" different things, from different persons' points of view. This difference lies in the sender's and receiver's interpretation of the statement. Most misunderstandings arise not around what was said but what was done or meant.

As we have seen, speech acts may be direct or indirect. That is, utterances can be framed more (or less) clearly and directly. Let's suppose that you want your partner to feed the dog. You may ask directly, "Would you feed the dog?" Or you could state an order: "Feed the dog!" On the other hand, you may communicate the same information indirectly: "Do you know if the dog was fed?" or "I wonder if the dog was fed." Finally, you may make your request very indirectly: "It would be nice if someone fed the dog," or "Do you think the dog looks hungry?"

Which do you think is better—to communicate directly or indirectly? This is actually a trick question. The answer is: It depends—on the situation and the cultural context. Although direct requests and questions may be clearer, they can also be seen as rude and domineering. Recent research shows that compared to Mexicans, U.S. Americans tend to be more indirect in their requests (Pinto & Raschio, 2007), but probably not as indirect as many Asians (Kim, 2002). In addition, when expressing disagreement, most U.S. Americans tend to be more *direct* than most Asians. A recent study investigated how Malaysians handled disagreements in business negotiations and concluded that the Malays' opposition was never direct or on record. Despite their disagreements with the other party, they honored the other, always balancing power with politeness (Paramasivam, 2007). A pragmatic approach reminds us that how language is used always depends on the situation and the cultural context. We'll discuss cross-cultural differences in communication practices further in Chapter 6.

Your use of language varies with the communication situation. For example, you would not discuss the same topics in class as you would in an informal conversational setting such as this.

Conversational Rules Conversational rules govern the ways in which we organize conversation. For example, one rule of conversation in U.S. English is that if someone asks you a question, you should provide an answer. If you do not know the answer, others expect you to at least reply, "I don't know" or "Let me think about it." However, in some cultures and languages, answers to questions are not obligatory. Among the Warm Spring Indians of Oregon, for example, questions may be answered at a later time (with little reference to the previous conversation) or not answered at all (Philips, 1990).

Perhaps the most-researched conversational rules involve turn-taking. The most basic rule for English language speakers, and for many others, is that only one person speaks at a time. People may tolerate some overlap between their talk and another's, but they typically expect to be able to have their say without too much interruption (Schegloff, 2000). Still, as a refinement of this point, Susanna Kohonen (2004) found in her cross-cultural study of

turn-taking that conversationalists were more tolerant of overlaps in social settings such as at parties or when hanging out with friends.

Other rules for turn-taking determine who is allowed to speak (Schegloff, 2006). For example, if you "have the floor," you can generally continue to speak. When you are finished, you can select someone else. You can do this either by asking a question, "So Sue, what is your opinion?" or by looking at another person as you finish talking. If you don't have the floor but wish to speak, you can begin speaking just as the current speaker completes a turn.

The turn-allocation system works amazingly well most of the time. Occasionally, however, people do not follow these implicit rules. For example, the current speaker could select the next speaker by directing a question to her, but someone else could interrupt and "steal" the floor. Also, some speakers are quicker to grab the talk turn, which allows them more opportunities to speak. Then, speakers who are slower to begin a turn or take the floor have fewer opportunities to contribute to the conversation. They may feel left out or resent the other speakers for monopolizing the conversation.

Contextual Rules No matter what language or dialect you speak, your use of language varies depending on the communication situation (Mey, 2001). For example, you probably wouldn't discuss the same topics at a funeral that you would at a bar. What would happen if you did? One challenge for pragmatics scholars, then, is uncovering the implicit communication rules that govern different settings. As noted earlier, communication pragmatics also vary by culture. For example, in some houses of worship, appropriate verbal behavior involves talking very quietly or not all, acting subdued, and listening without responding; in others, people applaud and sing exuberantly. Neither set of communication rules is "right"; each is appropriate to its own setting and cultural context.

With these ideas about the functions and components of language in mind, let's turn our attention to the ways in which our various identities influence our verbal communication.

Influences on Verbal Communication

How is your communication influenced by your identity and the various cultures you belong to? Your age, gender, ethnicity, and other identities all influence your verbal communication; more specifically, they influence language use. Identities can and do influence language sufficiently to produce a distinct **dialect**, a variation of a language distinguished by its **lexical choice** (vocabulary), grammar, and pronunciation. In other instances, the influence of identity is less dramatic, and speakers vary only in some pronunciations or word choices. In this section, we examine how identities related to gender, age, ethnicity, regionality, occupation, and education shape language use. We will also describe how some of these individual influences are related to issues of power and societal hierarchies—a topic that we will address in more detail later in the chapter.

Gender

Growing up male or female may influence the way in which you communicate in some situations, because men and women are socialized to communicate in specific ways. In fact, many people believe that English-speaking men and women in the United States speak different dialects. For example, women's verbal style is often described as supportive, egalitarian, personal, and disclosive, while men's is characterized as instrumental, competitive, and assertive (Mulac, Bradac, & Gibbons, 2001; Wood, 2002). However, some research refutes such claims about gender-based differences in language and communication styles. A recent review of studies revealed very few significant differences (Hyde, 2006). In fact, the differences in men's and women's communication patterns are estimated to be as small as 1 percent, or even less (Canary & Hause, 1993).

How can these contradictory findings be explained? First of all, the media and popular press and even scholarly research tend to focus on and sometimes exaggerate the importance of sex differences. For example, one team of researchers reviewed how journal

dialect
a variation of a language distinguished by its vocabulary, grammar, and pronunciation

lexical choice
vocabulary preference

Components of Language

I LOVE YOU

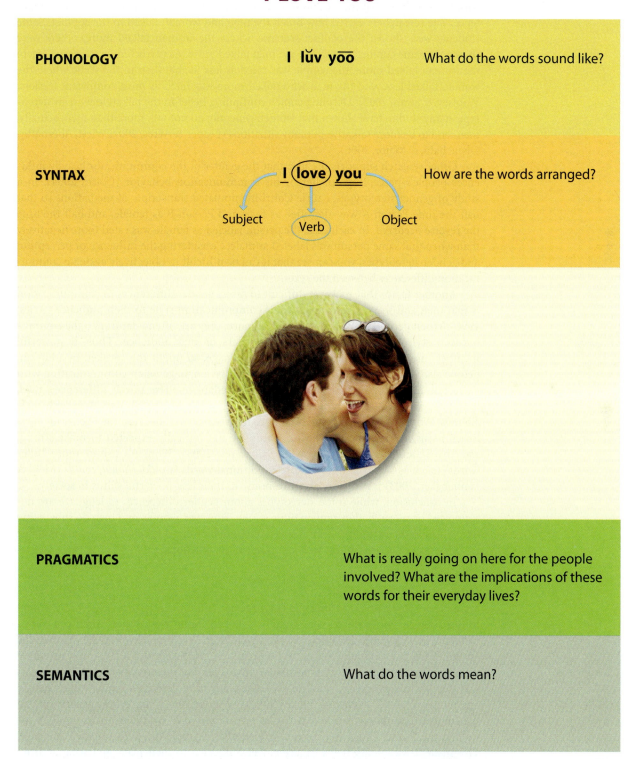

PHONOLOGY   I lŭv yōō   What do the words sound like?

SYNTAX   I love you   How are the words arranged?

Subject   Verb   Object

PRAGMATICS   What is really going on here for the people involved? What are the implications of these words for their everyday lives?

SEMANTICS   What do the words mean?

articles talked about gender differences in the past 50 years and found that because people are more interested in hearing about differences than similarities, television shows, magazines, and books that emphasize these differences tend to sell better and receive wider recognition (Sagrestano, Heavey, & Christiansen, 1998).

Research also shows that gender-based perceptions are hard to change, whether or not the perceptions are true (Rose, 1995). For example, the negative stereotype of the talkative woman is very persistent. In one recent study, students were shown a videotaped conflict between a heterosexual couple and were asked to rate the couple on likeability and competence. The researchers varied how much the man and woman talked in the conflict. Some students were shown the conflict scenario where the woman talked more; others were shown the same conflict, but where the man talked more. As predicted, in the scene where the woman talked more, the couple was rated as less likable than in the scene where the woman talked less. And the man who talked more was rated as most competent (Sellers, Woolsey, & Swan, 2007). Despite people's continuing belief in the talkative-woman stereotype, many studies have shown that women generally do not talk more than men; actually, men tend to be more talkative in many situations (Leaper & Ayres, 2007; Wiest, Abernathy, Obenchain, & Major, 2006).

Other research supports the idea that the gender of the communicator heavily influences people's perceptions of her or his communication behavior (Coltri, 2004). In a study of gender stereotypes, Laurie Coltri manipulated transcripts of mediations so that half the time Person A was identified as male and Person B as female, and half the time the reverse occurred. In each case, the person labeled as female was rated more negatively than when that same person was labeled as male. Considering the influence of perception and gender stereotypes, you can see that it can be difficult to objectively evaluate communication differences between the sexes.

Another factor that makes it difficult to assess gender differences in communication is that men and women may adapt their communication style to their audience (Aries, 1996). When people adapt to a specific audience, they are often adapting to the communication style of the more powerful members of that audience. Thus, if powerful members use more direct or task-focused language, so might the speaker. In addition, people also often use more deferential or tentative language when communicating with more powerful people. Both men and women adapt to these power differences; thus, both groups are more likely to use tentative language with their bosses than with their siblings. Women use language that is more tentative overall because they generally have lower status, and people with lower status are not typically expected to make strong, assertive statements (Reid, Keerie, & Palomares, 2003). Women's use of more "filler words" (such as *like* or *well*) and more conditional words (*would, should, could*) (Mehl & Pennebaker, 2003) is probably also a response to their less-powerful status in society.

In conclusion, while some stereotypes about gender differences in language are not supported by research, they remain quite strong. However, women and men do show some differences in their communication styles, and much of this difference is likely attributable to differences in power, status, and communication situations.

Age

You may not think of age as affecting language use, but it does, particularly when it comes to word choice. For example, you might have talked about "the cooties" when you were a child, but you probably don't now. Moreover, children have a whole vocabulary to describe "naughty topics," especially related to bodily functions. Yet most adults do not use those words. Adolescents also develop vocabulary that they use throughout their teenage years and then drop during early adulthood. Adolescents have described highly valued people and things as "cool," "righteous," "bad," "hot," and "phat" depending on the generation and the context. The abbreviated words in text messaging—e.g., B4N (Bye for now), BRB (be right back), XOXO (hugs and kisses)—are another example of youth-oriented language. This distinct vocabulary helps teenagers feel connected to their peers and separate from their parents and other adults. See *Did You Know? No Slang* for other examples of teen slang terms.

DID YOU KNOW?

No Slang

Here are some examples of contemporary slang used by various groups in the United States. Which do you recognize or use?

BF/GF: Boyfriend/Girlfriend
BRB: Be Right Back
GTG: Got to Go
IDK: I don't know
(L)MIRL: (Lets) meet in real life
MorF: Male or Female
MOS: Mom Over Shoulder
Noob: Newbie—often an insult to somebody who doesn't know much about something
PIR: Parent In Room
POS: Parent Over Shoulder
PRW: Parents Are Watching
Warez: Pirated Software
W/E: Whatever

SOURCE: "25 Internet Slang Terms All Parents Should Know." Retrieved July 29, 2010 from http://www.noslang.com/top20.php

The era in which you grew up also influences your vocabulary. As you age, you continue to use certain words that were common when you were growing up, even if they have fallen out of use. This is called the **cohort effect** and refers to common denominators of a group that was born and reared in the same general period. For example, your grandparents and their contemporaries may refer to dancing as "cutting a rug," while younger speakers rarely use this term. However, research suggests that in one case, young girls set trends in language use both for their own and other cohorts. This research focused on girls in Southern California and their "northern California vowel shift." For example: "Like, what dew you mean, tha-yt I ha-yvee an accent?" At a meeting of a high school club in Southern California called Girls for a Change, teenage girls discussed ways to fix cultural ills as "something important to dew." Among different approaches, they considered "tew-toring." Evidence indicates that some young men and older women adopted some of the sounds started by these teenage girls. Thus, as new ways of saying things found their way into the general language, a regional—or even statewide—dialect emerged (Krieger, 2004).

People's communication skills and the meanings they attribute to concepts also vary due to their age. Why? Older people are more cognitively developed and have had more experiences; therefore, they tend to view concepts differently than do younger people, especially children (Pennebaker & Stone, 2003). For example, children typically engage in egocentric speech patterns (Piaget, 1952). This means that they cannot yet adapt their communication to their conversational partners or understand that others may feel or view the world differently. Children lack the number of constructs adults have. For example, very young children have little concept of future or past time, so understanding what might happen next week or month is difficult for them. Consequently, parents usually adapt their communication when trying to help children understand some event in the future.

Regionality

Geographical location also strongly influences people's language use. The most common influence is on pronunciation, as Yolanda discovered—in our opening example. For example, how do you pronounce the word "oil"? In parts of New York it is pronounced somewhat like "earl," while in areas of the South it is pronounced more like "awl," and in the West it is often pronounced "oyl" as in "Olive Oyl." Along with age and gender, the geographic region is often associated with particular dialects. Why do these differences arise?

cohort effect
the influence of shared characteristics of a group that was born and reared in the same general period

Historically, wherever a geographical boundary separated people—whether it was mountains, lakes, rivers, deserts, oceans, or some social boundary such as race, class, or religion—verbal differences developed (Fromkin & Rodman, 1983). Moreover, people tend to speak similarly to those around them. For example, in the eighteenth century, residents of Australia, North America, and England had relatively little contact with one another; consequently, they developed recognizably different dialects even though they all spoke the same language. Typically, the more isolated a group, the more distinctive their dialect.

In the United States, dialectical differences in English originally arose because two groups of English colonists settled along the East Coast. The colonists who settled in the South, near present-day Virginia, primarily came from Somerset and Gloucestershire—both western counties in England—and they brought with them an accent with strongly voiced *s* sounds and with the *r* strongly pronounced after vowels. In contrast, the colonists who settled in the North, what we now call New England, came from midland counties such as Essex, Kent, and London, and they possessed a dialect that did not pronounce the *r* after vowels—a feature still common to many New England dialects, including the Boston area—which probably accounted for some of Yolanda's difficulty in understanding her Boston boyfriends' family and friends (Crystal, 2003).

Other waves of immigration have occurred over the past four hundred years, increasing dialectical diversity in the United States. Each group of immigrants brings a distinctive way of speaking and culture-specific communication rules. Some groups, especially those who have remained somewhat isolated since their arrival, maintain much of their original dialect, such as the inhabitants of Tangier Island in the Chesapeake Bay (Crystal, 2003). Other groups' dialects have assimilated with the dialects of their neighbors to form new dialects. Thus, the seventeenth-century "western" English dialect of Virginia has become the southern drawl of the twenty-first century.

Today, the world is a global village, so people from all over the country and the world are in contact with one another or have access to similar media. Nonetheless, according to one comprehensive study, local dialects are stronger than ever (Labov, 2005; Preston, 2003). This is due in large part to the fact that people tend to talk similarly to the people they live around and hear every day. Thus, dialectic differences originally occurred because of patterns of isolation, but they persist because of exposure. As people have increasing contact and access to a range of language models, dialectic differences may become less pronounced, but it will be a long time—if ever—before they completely disappear.

Ethnicity and Race

One's ethnicity can influence one's verbal style in a number of ways. In the United States, English is a second or co-language for many citizens. Speaking English as a second language, of course, influences syntax, accent, and word choice. For example, if one is Latino/Latina and learns Spanish either before or at the same time as English, the same syntax may be used for both. Thus, Spanish speakers may place adjectives after nouns (*the house little*) when they speak English because that is the rule for Spanish. The reverse can also occur: When English speakers speak Spanish, they tend to place adjectives before nouns, which is the rule for English but not for Spanish.

Speakers' ethnicity can also influence their general verbal style. For example, Jewish Americans may engage in a style of talking about problems that non-Jews perceive as complaining (Bowen, 2003); some Native American tribes use teasing as a type of public reprimand (Shutiva, 2004); and some Chinese Americans who live in the southern United States are particularly likely to let other speakers choose conversational topics (Gong, 2004). When two ethnic or racial groups speak the same language but use different syntax, lexical items, or verbal style, one or both groups may view the other's verbal style as incorrect or as a failed attempt at proper speech rather than as a dialect with its own rules (Ellis & Beattie, 1986).

These views can have important real-life implications—political and monetary. Take the controversy about **Ebonics**, a version of English which has its roots in West African, Caribbean, and U.S. slave languages. Some linguists emphasize the international nature of the language (as a linguistic consequence of the African slave trade); others stress that it is a

Ebonics
a version of English that has its roots in West African, Caribbean, and U.S. slave languages

variety of English (e.g., the equivalent of Black English) or is different from English and viewed as an independent language. The controversy over definition has had important real-life consequences. A few years ago, the Oakland, California, school board passed a resolution that recognized Ebonics as a separate language, not just a dialect. The resolution instructed teachers to "respect and embrace the language richness of Ebonics." But more important, the school board required schools to provide English-as-a-second-language instruction to students who spoke Ebonics as their first "language." A number of teachers and policymakers viewed Ebonics as simply substandard English, not even a dialect, and were not willing to recognize it as a legitimate language or provide funds for English-language instruction (Wolfram, Adger, & Christian, 1999). This language controversy had far-reaching implications—involving not only the teachers and parents, but linguists and policymakers.

jargon
technical terminology associated with a specific topic

Education and Occupation

We discuss education and occupation together because they are often mutually influencing. For example, medical doctors speak a similar language because they share a profession, but also because they were educated similarly. Typically, the more educated people are, the more similarly they speak (Hudson, 1983). Thus, larger dialect differences occur between easterners and midwesterners if they have not been to college than if they have doctoral degrees. This does not mean that all lawyers speak the same or that all professors speak similarly; rather, it suggests that differences become less pronounced as people receive more education.

Education affects dialect in part because any given university or college attracts people from different parts of the country. Therefore, college students have contact with a variety of dialects. At the same time, as students attend college, they develop similar vocabularies from their shared experiences and learn similar terms in their classes. For example, you may never have used the term *dyad* to refer to two people before you went to college, but this is a term you might encounter in a range of courses, including psychology, sociology, anthropology, and communication.

Your occupation also influences the specialized terms you use to communicate. The specialized terms that develop in many professions are called **jargon**. Professors routinely speak of *tenure, refereed journals*, and *student credit hours*. Physicians speak of *contusions* (bruises), *sequelae* (results), and *hemorrhagic stroke* (a stroke where a blood vessel bursts). In fact, most occupations have their own jargon. In addition to influencing your lexical choices, your occupation may also influence your overall communication style—including tone of voice and some nonverbal behaviors. For example, nursery school teachers are often recognizable not only by their vocabulary but also by the rhythm, volume, and expressivity of their communication style.

To sum up, then, various features of language—phonology, syntax, semantics, and pragmatics—contribute to the development of meaning in verbal communication. These features combine with individual influences in language use, such as gender, age, race, ethnicity, and level of education, to create one's specific communication style. These influences are often also related to variations in status and power within society. In this next section, we explore further how these societal forces operate, to explain their consequences for everyday communicators.

THE INDIVIDUAL, VERBAL COMMUNICATION, AND SOCIETY

How do societal forces influence verbal communication? Culture and power are two of the most important influences. Culture impacts verbal communication primarily through its influence on language and perception. As we have already mentioned, power is connected to verbal communication because within society, some language styles are viewed as more powerful, with consequences for both the powerful and the powerless.

Language and Perception

Does the specific language you speak influence your perception—how you see the world? Let's consider this question by looking at a couple of examples. The English language expresses action in the past, present, and future. English speakers may say "Alan went to the library" (past), "Alan is at the library" (present), or "Alan will be going to the library" (future). In contrast, Japanese makes no distinction between the present and future. The question, then, is: Do English speakers and Japanese speakers think about present and future actions in different ways? Some experts would answer yes, that language serves not only as a way for us to voice our ideas but itself shapes ideas (Hoijer, 1994, p. 194).

This concept is the basis for the **Sapir-Whorf hypothesis**. It argues that the language people speak determines the way they see the world. According to this hypothesis, the distinction between the present and the future is not as clear-cut for Japanese speakers as it is for English speakers. As another example, surfers have many more words for the types of waves in the ocean than do nonsurfers (Scheibel, 1995); the Sapir-Whorf hypothesis argues that, because of this, surfers actually perceive more types of waves than do others.

So, how much does language influence perception? A number of experts have challenged the Sapir-Whorf hypothesis position (Kenneally, 2008), and now most agree that while the language we speak can influence how we perceive the world around us, it is more of a tool than a prison (Pinker, 2007). Even though this interpretation suggests that we are not entirely bound by the language we speak, it does allow for the central proposition of the Sapir-Whorf hypothesis, that language is a powerful tool. Spoken (or written) words can have powerful impacts on us and others. Consider how the words "I pronounce you husband and wife" can influence lives, or "I confer on you the degree of Bachelor of Arts." However, we need to note that these words are powerful only when spoken by someone with authority, with designated power. In the next section, we explore the relationship between language use and power that is based in informal social hierarchies; we will also discuss the consequences for powerful and powerless communicators.

Language and Power

In many ways, language and power are inextricably connected. As we discussed earlier, individual influences on verbal communication (e.g., gender, ethnicity, and regionality) are often linked to power and status differences. These power differences, while individual, stem from societal forces such as social hierarchies. Let's look at how societal forces create these individual influences.

People in power get to define what languages and communication styles are appropriate, as we showed in our earlier discussions. In addition, people who use language and communication according to the rules of the powerful may be able to increase their own power. This view of the relationship between language and power is explained by *cocultural theory*. **Cocultural theory** explores the role of power in daily interactions, using the five following assumptions:

1. In each society, a hierarchy exists that privileges certain groups of people; in the United States, these groups include men, European Americans, heterosexuals, the able bodied, and middle- and upper-class people.
2. Part of the privilege these groups enjoy, often subconsciously, is being able to set norms for what types of communication are acceptable (Orbe, 1998). Consequently, the communication patterns of the dominant groups (in the United States: rich, male, White, educated, straight) tend to be more highly valued. For example, the preferred communication practice in many large corporations is still that used by White males: direct, to-the-point, task oriented, and unemotional (Kikoski & Kikoski, 1999).
3. Language maintains and reinforces the power of these dominant groups—again, mostly subconsciously. Thus, people whose speech does not conform to what is valued in society may be excluded and/or negatively stereotyped. As we noted earlier, commentators sometimes characterize women's speech as sounding more tentative than male speech. Because society values male speech styles at work,

Sapir-Whorf hypothesis
the idea that the language people speak determines the way they see the world (a relativist perspective)

cocultural theory
explores the role of power in daily interactions

women in corporate leadership positions are often criticized for not being direct or tough enough, or for being too cooperative or nurturing in their communication practices.

4. In the relationship realm, as we described earlier, society tends to value a more-female communication style, and men may be critiqued for failing to communicate appropriately with their intimates. Similarly, society tends to value a British accent over a southern drawl, and "standard" English over Ebonics. Remember that none of these language variations is inherently good or bad, powerful or powerless; *it is the societal hierarchies that teach us how to view particular communication practices.* Of course, not every White male is direct, to the point, and task oriented, nor does every woman speak tentatively at work. Nor is every woman supportive and self-disclosive, and every man distant and terse in close relationships. These generalizations can help explain communication practices, but they should not solidify into stereotypes.

5. These dominant communication structures impede the progress of persons whose communication practices do not conform to the norms. For example, what are the consequences for women who do not conform to "male" communication norms in a corporation? Or for African Americans who do not conform to the "White" communication norms of the organizations in which they work? Or for students who do not conform to the "middle class" communication norms at a university? Most likely, they will be labeled negatively ("not serious enough," "soft," "doesn't have what it takes") and marginalized.

We explore these ideas further in Chapter 6. Now, let's look at how these societal hierarchies affect attitudes toward words, accents, and dialects, and how they impact identity labels.

Power and Words

Attitudes about power can be built into language by certain roots or by the very structure of the language. Consider words like *chairman* or *fireman*, or the use of "he" as the generic to mean *human*. While people used to think that it didn't matter whether we used masculine pronouns or words to mean human, researchers discovered that people didn't think *human* when someone mentioned the word *man;* they thought about a man. Similarly, new awareness of terms such as *Mr.* (not designating marital state) and *Mrs.* (which does) has resulted in changes—like *Ms.* and *he/she.*

While some languages like Japanese or Korean are highly gendered—that is, traditionally, men and women used almost separate languages—English is only somewhat gendered, or *androcentric.* Androcentrism is the pairing of maleness with humanity and the consequent implication that females are in some separate category—often to women's disadvantage. Scholars recently reviewed 50 years of psychology articles for androcentric bias. While they found few uses of *he* for *human,* information was still portrayed in a way that emphasized the male as the norm. For example, women's communication style is described as being "different" (from men's), whereas male style is rarely described comparatively. Researchers point out that being different is not necessarily harmful but probably reflects some of the underlying stereotypes (and societal hierarchies) we have discussed earlier (Hegarty & Buechel, 2006).

What are the implication of this discussion—power and language use—for students? We do not mention these kinds of gender differences in language to interfere with your freedom of speech or to be politically correct. Instead, our objective is to point out the importance of adapting one's language to one's audiences. Gender-neutral language has gained support from most major textbook publishers, and from professional and academic groups, as well as major newspapers and law journals. As one English professor suggests, "If you anticipate working within any of these contexts, you will need to be able to express yourself according to their guidelines, and if you wish to write or speak convincingly to people who are influenced by the conventions of these contexts, you need to be conscious of their expectations" (Jacobson, 2008).

Specific suggestions for using gender-neutral language, as well as avoiding heterosexist bias are presented in *Building your Communication Skills: Avoiding Bias in Language*.

Power and Accent

Where did people learn that an English accent sounds upper crust and educated? Or that English as spoken with an Asian Indian accent is hard to understand? In addition, as discussed earlier, communicators often stereotype Black English as sounding uneducated.

Building Your Communication SKILLS

Avoiding Bias in Language

Two professors give suggestions for avoiding gender and heterosexual bias in writing. What are the reasons for or against following these suggestions? Which groups of people do you think would be more in favor of these changes—those with or without power in U.S. society? What do you think of the "further alternatives"? Would you use them?

Using Gender-Neutral Language

- Use *They* As Singular—Most people, when writing and speaking informally, rely on singular *they* as a matter of course: "If you love someone, set them free" (Sting). If you pay attention to your own speech, you'll probably catch yourself using the same construction. Some people are annoyed by the incorrect grammar that this solution necessitates, but this construction is used more and more frequently.

- Use *He or She*—Despite the charge of clumsiness, double-pronoun constructions have made a comeback: "To be Black in this country is simply too pervasive an experience for any writer to omit from her or his work," wrote Samuel R. Delany. Overuse of this solution can be awkward, however.

- Use Pluralizing—A writer can often recast material in the plural. For instance, instead of "As he advances in his program, the medical student has increasing opportunities for clinical work," try "As they advance in their program, medical students have increasing opportunities for clinical work."

- Eliminate Pronouns—Avoid having to use pronouns at all; instead of "a first grader can feed and dress himself," you could write, "a first grader can eat and get dressed without assistance."

- Try Further Alternatives—use *he/she* or *s/he* instead of *he*, or use a new generic pronoun (*thon, co, E, tey, hesh, hir*).

Avoiding Heterosexual Bias in Language

- Use *sexual orientation* rather than *sexual preference*. The word *preference* suggests a degree of voluntary choice that is not necessarily reported by lesbians and gay men; neither has it been demonstrated in psychological research.

- Use *lesbian* and *gay male* rather than *homosexual* as adjectives referring to specific persons or groups; use *lesbians* and *gay men* as nouns. The word *homosexual* perpetuates negative stereotypes with its history of pathology and criminal behavior.

- The term *bisexual* as an adjective refers to people who relate sexually and affectionally to both women and men. This term is often omitted in discussions of sexual orientation and thus give the erroneous impression that all people relate exclusively to one gender or another.

SOURCES: "Some notes on gender-neutral language." Retrieved May 23, 2008 from http://www.english.upenn.edu/~cjacobso/gender.html. "Avoiding heterosexual bias in language." Retrieved May 23, 2008, from http://www.apastyle.org/sexuality.html

While these associations come from many sources, they are certainly prevalent in the media. People have become so accustomed to seeing and hearing these associations that they probably don't even question them. In fact, William Labov, a noted sociolinguist, refers to the practice of associating a dialect with the cultural attitudes toward it as "a borrowed prestige model." For example, until the 1950s, most Americans thought that British English was the correct way to speak English (Labov, 1980). Even today, people continue to attribute status (or lack thereof) based on a speaker's accent, as reported by our student in *It Happened to Me: Bart*.

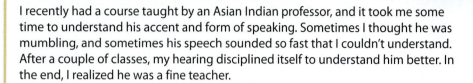

IT HAPPENED TO ME: Bart

I recently had a course taught by an Asian Indian professor, and it took me some time to understand his accent and form of speaking. Sometimes I thought he was mumbling, and sometimes his speech sounded so fast that I couldn't understand. After a couple of classes, my hearing disciplined itself to understand him better. In the end, I realized he was a fine teacher.

Such language stereotypes can be "set off" in one's head before a person even speaks, when one *thinks*—generally because of the person's appearance—that she or he will not speak standard English (Ruben, 2003). This is probably what happened to our student, Bart. On first seeing the professor and then hearing his accent, Bart thought that the professor might not be a qualified teacher. Once he adjusted to the Indian English accent, he found he could understand his Indian professor just fine and realized the depth of knowledge and experience the professor had to offer.

How does one group's language and accent become elevated and another denigrated? The answer lies partly in understanding the social forces of history and politics. The positive and negative associations about African American, White, and British English developed during the nineteenth and twentieth centuries when European Americans were establishing themselves as the powerful majority in the United States, and as they were passing legislation that subjugated African Americans and other minority groups. Thus, it is not surprising that the languages of these groups were viewed so differently. Similarly, in India, the English spoken by people from India was negatively stereotyped as the aberrant language of the colonized, because England was the colonial power in India until the mid-twentieth century. Similar attitudes can be seen toward immigrant groups today; their accented English is often stigmatized, sometimes leading to language discrimination and lawsuits, as illustrated in *Did You Know? Language Discrimination*.

DID YOU KNOW?

Language Discrimination

The American Civil Liberties Union provides the following legal explanation of language discrimination:

What is language discrimination?

Language discrimination occurs when a person is treated differently because of that person's native language or other characteristics of that person's speech. In an employment situation, for example, an employee may be being subjected to language discrimination if he or she is treated less favorably than other employees because he or she speaks English with an accent, or if the employee is told he or she does not qualify for a position because of a lack of English proficiency. Outside the employment context, language discrimination may also occur if a person is denied access to businesses or government services because he or she does not speak English.

Is language discrimination illegal?

Although the law in this area is still developing, many courts and governmental agencies consider language discrimination to be a form of discrimination on the basis of

(continued)

DID YOU KNOW? *(continued)*

race or national origin, which are prohibited by well-established civil rights laws such as Titles VI and VII of the Civil Rights Act of 1964 (a federal law), and the California Fair Employment and Housing Act (a state law). Other laws, such as the federal Civil Rights Act of 1866, may also apply to such discrimination.

Why is language discrimination illegal?

The laws mentioned above make it illegal for employers to discriminate against an employee because of his or her national origin. ("National origin" refers to the country that a person, or that person's ancestors, came from.) But because the primary language a person speaks is closely related to the place that person came from, or the place that person's family came from, being discriminated against for using that language, or because of characteristics having to do with that language, is essentially the same as that person being discriminated against because of his or her national origin.

SOURCE: American Civil Liberties Union Web site. Retrieved March 11, 2009, from http://www.aclunc.org/library/publications/asset_upload_file489_3538.pdf

Power and Identity Labels

The language labels that refer to particular identities also communicate important messages about power relations. Members of more-powerful groups frequently apply labels to members of other groups without input from members of those less-powerful groups. For example, straight people label gays, but rarely refer to themselves as straight. White people use ethnic and racial labels to refer to others (*people of color, African American*, or *Black*), but rarely refer to themselves as White. This power to label seems "normal," so most people don't think twice about specifying that a physician is a "woman doctor" while never describing another as a "male doctor." Or they might identify someone as a gay teacher, but not a White teacher (even if this teacher is both). People usually don't think about the assumptions that reflect societal power relations; in sum, individuals feel the need to mark minority differences, but they tend not to identify majority group membership.

The more powerful not only get to label the less powerful; they may also use language labels to stigmatize them. However, the stigma comes from the power relations, not from the words themselves. For example, *Polack* simply means "a man from Poland" in the Polish language, but the stigma associated with the term comes from the severe discrimination practiced against Eastern Europeans in the early twentieth century, which led to jokes and stereotypes that exist to this day. The term *Oriental* originated when Western countries were attempting to colonize, and were at war with, Asian countries—and the connotative meaning was *exotic* and *foreign*. Today, many Asians and Asian Americans, like our student, Hiroko, resent this label. See *It Happened to Me: Hiroko.*

IT HAPPENED TO ME: Hiroko

I get really tired of people referring to me as "Oriental." It makes me sound like a rug or a cuisine. I refer to myself as Asian American or Japanese American. I know people probably don't mean anything negative when they use it, but it makes me uncomfortable. If it's somebody I know well, I might ask them not to use that word, but usually I just don't say anything.

This resentment can make communication more difficult for Hiroko and for those who use this term to refer to her. As this example reveals, the dictionary meanings of words do not always reveal the impact of identity labels. Members of minority communities are the best informants on the communicative power of specific labels.

Not everyone in an identity group has the same denotative meaning for a particular label. For example, some young women do not like to be called "girl"; they find it demeaning. Others are comfortable with this term and view these calls for sensitivity in language as nothing more than unnecessary political correctness.

In summary, language, power, and societal forces are closely linked. The societal environment profoundly influences the way people perceive the world and the language choices available to them. Those in power set the language and communication norms, often determining what verbal communication style is appropriate or inappropriate, elegant or uneducated. The privileged also frequently get to choose and use identity labels for those who are less powerful. Those whose language does not fit the standard, or who are the recipients of negative labels, may feel marginalized and resentful, leading to difficult communication interactions.

Think about labels and terms we have for males and females. Why do you think so many more negative terms exist for females than for males?

ETHICS AND VERBAL COMMUNICATION

We have already discussed a number of ethical issues related to verbal communication in this book. In Chapter 1, we argued that ethical communicators consider the benefit and/or harm associated with their messages. In this section, we give two suggestions for communicating more ethically: becoming more aware of the power of language and becoming more conscious of how you use it.

Become Aware of the Power of Language

As we noted in Chapter 1, language is a powerful force that has consequences and ethical implications. Wars have been started, relationships have been ruined, and much anger and unhappiness have resulted from intentional and unintentional verbal messages. The old adage "Sticks and stones can break my bones, but words will never hurt me" is not always true. Words *can* hurt, as shown in *Communication In Society: Mind Your (Terror) Language.*

When a speaker refers to others by negative or offensive identity terms, the speaker not only causes harm, he or she also denies those labeled individuals their identities—even if it isn't intentional. Earlier, we described Hiroko's rejection of the word *Oriental* as a label. One of our students told us how bad she felt when she realized that the term *Oriental* is potentially offensive and that she had been using it to refer to an international student, like Hiroko, in her work group. Using her embarrassment as a learning experience, she initiated an enlightening discussion with the international student. She learned that often the best

Communication in SOCIETY

Mind Your (Terror) Language

In the article summarized below, author Khody Akhavi describes an attempt (when George W. Bush was president) by the U.S. government to use language that is not offensive to Arabs and Muslims when discussing political issues. How important is the language we use in political discourse? What are the reasons for changing our language in the way the author suggests?

Author Khody Akhavi explains that members of the US government have been advised by the National Counterterrorism Center (NCTC) to avoid the use of potentially offensive phrases or jargon that could reflect poorly on Muslim and Arab communities. In Arabic, *jihad* does not, by definition, involve warfare but rather refers to someone who "striv[es] in the path of God." Thus, instead of religiously charged words like "*jihad*," the NCTC advocates more generalized terms such as "terrorist" or "violent extremist." As the NCTC points out, government representatives may unwittingly lend religious credence to terrorists and acts of terrorism by employing theological terminology like "*jihadis*" or "a global *jihad.*"

According to Akhavi, the NCTC also cautioned against utilizing the political characterization of "moderate" to refer to adherents of a particular religion. In this case, "moderate" is inaccurate, implying that someone is operating at a lower level of piety than others of the same faith. Instead, the NCTC suggests phrases like "majority" or "mainstream" because such terms contextualize the adherent's beliefs by comparing them to those beliefs held by others within the same faith. Many U.S.-based Muslim advocacy groups welcome these changes, noting that they disconnect religious identity from terrorist activity. As Ibrahim Cooper, a spokesman for the Council on Islamic American Relations noted, "It is a good step that they at least take these terms into consideration. . . . we should all be thinking about this."

SOURCE: Akhavi, K. (2008, May 21). "Mind your (terror) language." *Asia Times Online.* Retrieved November 28, 2009, from http://www.atimes.com/atimes/Middle_East/JE21Ak04.html

way to discover what someone "wants to be called" is to ask. However, a conversation of this nature can only occur in the context of a mutually respectful relationship—one reason to have a diverse group of friends and acquaintances.

Become Conscious of Your Language Use

A second suggestion for communicating more ethically is to become more conscious of how you use language. Most of the time, people are on automatic pilot when communicating. Thus, try asking yourself: Am I sending the messages I think I am sending? Are people interpreting messages the way I intend? One way to check is to ask others what they understood. If they didn't get your point, try paraphrasing or saying the same message in a different way. By doing this, you increase the possibility that they will understand your meaning and that they know you sincerely want them to understand.

IMPROVING YOUR VERBAL COMMUNICATION SKILLS

While there are no easy recipes for improving your verbal communication skills, we can offer three suggestions for communicating in a way that is both ethical and effective: The first involves supportive versus defensive communication behaviors, the second concerns confirming versus disconfirming communication; and the final has to do with the uses of "I" statements.

Supportive Versus Defensive Communication

Communication scholars have discovered that one of the best strategies for being effective in interpersonal and group situations is to use supportive, rather than defensive language (Becker, Halbesleben & O'Hair, 2005; Garvin-Doxas & Barker, 2004). What do we mean by supportive and defensive language? Defensive behavior occurs when an individual perceives threat from another. For example, if your friend says to you "you know I've noticed that you never really pay your share of the bill when we go out with other friends" you are likely to perceive this as a threat to your self-image and thus react defensively (see Table 3.1).

One of the main problems with defensive communication is that it tends to prevent the listener from concentrating on the message and thus elicits more defensive communication, creating circular responses that are increasingly defensive. In the above example, you are likely to ignore the core of your friend's message (that he thinks you should contribute more) and react to the threat with more defensive communication, e.g. "you're not so generous yourself. You still haven't paid me for the time I lent you $5 to pay for parking."

Fortunately, the converse is also true, using more supportive language ensures that the listener is able to concentrate on the message rather than their own anxieties and resistance provoked by defensive communication Let's look more closely at 6 contrasting characteristics of supportive and defensive language behaviors, shown in the Table below (Gibb, 1961; Eadie, 1982). Let's see how you might use supportive rather than defensive language in a conversation you might have with your roommate about sharing the household chores.

Evaluation vs description. Messages that seem **evaluative** are likely to increase defensiveness in the listener compared to more descriptive messages. For example, saying to your roommate "I've noticed that the kitchen area seems to get cluttered more quickly than other areas of the house" is a more supportive message than "you just don't clean as well as I do"—which is much more evaluative.

Problem Orientation vs control. Statements that seem to control the listener tend to cause resistance and defensiveness whereas taking a more problem oriented approach is more supportive. "Keeping the kitchen clean is really a challenge for us since we both have such hectic work schedules" reflects a problem orientation whereas "You have got to do better with keeping the house clean" reflects a more **controlling** approach. Likewise, messages that appear to be strategic (manipulative) are more likely to cause defensiveness than a more spontaneous message. No one likes to feel like they are being manipulated. So it

evaluative communication
messages that carry judgments of right and wrong, good or bad

controlling communication
messages that attempt to impose one's will on another, perhaps with coercion

TABLE 3.1 Supportive Versus Defensive Communication	
Supportive Communication is:	**Defensive Communication is:**
Descriptive	Evaluative
Problem Oriented	Controlling
Spontaneous	Strategic
Empathic	Neutral
Equality-oriented	Superiority focused
Provisional	Certainty focused

would be better to approach your roommate more spontaneously than to use language that conveys a message that you've decided a long time ago that the untidy house is their fault and you've strategized how you can get him or her to see your point of view.

Expressing a neutral (indifferent) message is much more likely to cause defensive reactions as compared to an **empathic** one. For example, you might say "You're really working long hours these days, it must be tough to spend all that time at work and you probably don't feel like you have time to do anything for yourself, let alone cleaning the house!" which is much more supportive than a more indifferent "you work a lot, you don't have time for anything."

Expressing superiority would obviously cause more defensiveness (as in "we both know I'm a better organized person and always manage to get my work done") vs a more **equality-oriented** message: "we are both really busy and just need to figure out a way to get this work done."

Finally, messages that are expressed in more provisional language are more supportive than statements of certainty, which tend to cause more defensive reactions "Do you think we can figure out some way to keep the house clean by equally sharing the chores" is more provisional than the statement of certainty, like "I've got it figured out—I've prepared a schedule for us that I'll post in the kitchen and we should both follow it."

We have all been in situations where we've reacted defensively perhaps as the recipient of messages that are evaluative, manipulative, and controlling. As you can see, by striving to use language that is more descriptive, provisional, and empathic, we can reduce others' defensiveness and thus improve our communication effectiveness in many situations.

Confirming and Disconfirming Communication

One type of communication that can provoke **defensive communication** and is often unethical (because of the harm it can cause) is *disconfirming communication*. **Disconfirming communication** occurs when people make comments that reject or invalidate a self-image, positive or negative, of their conversational partners (Dance & Larson, 1976). You will see how this specific type of communication can combine several characteristics of defensive language discussed above. Consider the following conversation:

Tracey: Guess what? I earned an A on my midterm.
Lou: Gee, it must have been an easy test.

Lou's response (if said in a serious tone) is an example of disconfirming communication; it suggests that Tracey could not have earned her A because of competence or ability. Consequently, his message disconfirms Tracey's image of herself. You can disconfirm people either explicitly ("I've never really thought of you as being smart") or implicitly (as Lou did).

How can messages such as these cause harm? Imagine that you received numerous disconfirming messages from people who are important to you. How might these messages affect you? They can negatively influence your self-image and also impair your relationships.

equality-oriented communication
messages that convey sense of worth in others and their ideas, viewpoints

empathic communication
messages that convey sympathy and caring

defensive communication
comments that threaten others self image or persona

disconfirming communication
comments that reject or invalidate a positive or negative self-image of our conversational partners

confirming communication
comments that validate positive self-images of others

For example, when couples engage in disconfirming behavior, their marital dissatisfaction increases (Caughlin, 2002; Weger, 2005).

If you want to learn to replace disconfirming messages with confirming ones, what should you do instead? First, you can remind yourself that **confirming communication** validates the positive self-images of others, so you can respond as in the following example.

> *Tracey:*   Guess what? I earned an A on my midterm.
> *Lou:*   That's great. I know it's a tough class; you deserve to be proud.

Confirming messages are not only more ethical, they are usually more effective. Most people enjoy communicating with those who encourage them to feel good about themselves. Although engaging in confirming communication will not guarantee that you will instantly be popular, if you are sincere, your communication will be more effective and you will know that you are communicating ethically. If using confirming communication does not come naturally to you, you can practice until it does.

But no one can always be confirming, so you might be wondering how you can provide negative feedback to people when a situation calls for it. We discuss how to do this next.

Confirming messages are not only more ethical, they are usually more effective. Most people enjoy communicating with those who encourage them to feel good about themselves.

"I" Statements

One type of disconfirming message involves making negative generalizations about others. Although you likely recognize that your friends and family members are complex and variable, have you nevertheless found yourself making negative generalizations such as those listed here?

"You are so thoughtless."
"You are never on time."

As you can see, negative generalizations (which also are called "you" statements) are typically disconfirming. But in the real world, some people *are* thoughtless and some *are* consistently late. So is there an ethical and effective way to make your dissatisfaction known? Yes. You can use "I" statements. "I" statements allow you to express your feelings (even negative ones) by focusing on your own experiences rather than making negative generalizations (or "you" statements) about others.

"I" statements are conveyed through a three-part message that describes

1. the other person's behavior,
2. your feelings about that behavior, and
3. the consequences the other's behavior has for you.

Taking the examples just given and rewriting them as "I" statements, you could come up with:

"When you criticize my appearance (behavior), I feel unloved (feeling), and I respond by withdrawing from you (consequence)."

"I think I must be unimportant to you (feeling) when you arrive late for dinner (behavior), so I don't feel like cooking for you (consequence)."

"You" statements often lead recipients to feel defensive and/or angry because of the negative evaluation contained in the message and because the listener resents the speaker's position of passing judgment. "I" statements arouse less defensiveness, but they

also force speakers to explore exactly what they are dissatisfied with, how it makes them feel, and the consequences of the other person's behavior. "I" statements prevent speakers from attacking others in order to vent their feelings. They are also more effective than "you" statements because the receiver is more likely to listen and respond to them (Kubany, Bauer, Muraoka, Richard, & Read, 1995).

While many communication scholars believe in the value of "I" statements, a recent study found that people reacted similarly to *both* "I" and "you" statements involving negative emotions. However, the authors of the study point out that their study involved written hypothetical conflict situations. They admit that their results might have been different if they had studied real-life conflict situations (Bippus & Young, 2005).

Although "I" statements can be effective in a variety of contexts, this does not mean they are *always* appropriate. Situations may arise where others' behavior so violates what you believe is decent or appropriate that you wish to state your opinions strongly. Thus, if your friend abuses alcohol or takes illicit drugs, you may need to say "You should not drive a car tonight" or "You need to get help for your addiction." The effectiveness of one's verbal communication must always be evaluated in the context of the situation, the relationships one has with others, and one's goal.

SUMMARY

Language is the foundation of verbal processes and plays a significant role in people's lives, assisting in relationship development, creating identities, and accomplishing everyday tasks. Language functions in at least seven ways: instrumental, regulatory, informative, heuristic, interactional, personal, and imaginative. The four components of language study are phonology, the study of sounds; syntax, the grammar and rules for arranging units of meaning; semantics, the meaning of words; and pragmatics, the rules for appropriate use of language.

Individual influences on language include speakers' memberships in various identity groups (gender, age, regionality, ethnicity and race, education and occupation). When identities influence several aspects of language (vocabulary, grammar, and punctuation), speakers have distinct dialects. In other instances, identity groups' language variations may be minor, involving only some pronunciation and word choices.

Societal forces affect verbal processes because they shape our perceptions and the power relationships that surround us. The language used in a given society influences its members' perceptions of social reality, while power relationships affect how its members' verbal patterns are evaluated.

Communicating more ethically involves recognizing the power of language and becoming more conscious of how you use language; improving verbal communication skills involves using supportive and confirming language and "I" language when expressing dissatisfaction.

KEY TERMS

cocultural theory 64	dialect 58	imaginative 53
cohort effect 61	disconfirming communication 71	informative 53
confirming communication 72	Ebonics 62	instrumental 53
connotative meaning 56	empathic communication 71	interactional 54
controlling communication 70	equality-oriented communication 71	jargon 63
defensive communication 71	evaluative communication 70	lexical choice 58
denotative meaning 56	heuristic 54	personal language 54

phonology 55
pragmatics 56
regulatory 54

Sapir-Whorf hypothesis 64
semantics 56

speech act theory 56
syntax 55

CHAPTER REVIEW QUESTIONS

1. What are the seven functions of language? Give an example that illustrates how each works.

2. What is phonology? Syntax? Semantics? How do they work together to facilitate effective communication?

3. What do pragmatics scholars study? How do they determine pragmatics in specific communication contexts?

4. What is the difference between connotative and denotative meaning?

5. How do regional dialects develop?

6. How do our gender, age, ethnicity, and race influence the way we speak?

7. What role does power play in our everyday communication?

ACTIVITIES

1. For each of the following scenarios, write a paragraph describing a typical communication exchange. For each, think about the various elements of verbal communication: sounds, grammar, meaning (word choice), conversational rules, and contextual rules.

   - an informal family outing
   - a meeting with your advisor
   - a bar, where you are trying to impress potential partners

   HINT: Working in a small group, see whether you and your classmates can come up with some shared contextual rules for communication in these various situations. Give some reasons why you can or cannot come up with shared rules.

2. Take three sheets of paper and write one of the following words on each sheet: *garbage, milk, mother*. Take the first piece of paper and crumple it up and then stomp on it. Do the same with the second and third pieces. How did you feel crumpling up and stomping on the first piece of paper? The second? The third? What does this say perhaps about the difference between denotative and connotative meanings?

3. Think about two accents or dialects you've heard, either in a personal encounter or on radio or television. For each one, answer the following questions:

   - Do you have a negative or positive association for this dialect/accent?
   - Where did these associations (negative or positive) come from?
   - How might these associations (negative or positive) influence the way in which you communicate with a person who uses this accent or dialect?

   Share your answers with your classmates. Do you have similar reactions and associations for the same accent or dialect? What does this say about the power of society in influencing perceptions about communication and language use?

4. For each of the examples that follow, create an "I" statement that expresses your feelings about the situation:

   - Once again, your roommate has borrowed some of your clothes without asking and has returned them dirty and/or damaged.
   - For the third time this semester, your instructor has changed the date of an exam.
   - Your good friend has developed a habit of canceling plans at the last moment.
   - Your romantic partner embarrasses you by teasing you about personal habits in front of friends.

   Form a group with two or three of your classmates. Take turns reading your "I" statement for each situation. Discuss the strengths and weaknesses of each statement. As a group, develop an "I" statement for each situation above that best expresses the group's feelings without encouraging defensiveness in the receiver.

5. Locate five people who either grew up in different parts of the United States or who grew up in different countries. Try to include both men and women and people of different ages in your sample. Ask each person to answer the following questions:

   - What do you call a carbonated beverage?
   - How do you pronounce *roof*?
   - What expressions do you use that some other people have had trouble understanding?
   - What does the term *feminist* mean?
   - Who do you think talks "different"?

WEB ACTIVITIES

1. Go to: http://classweb.gmu.edu/accent/ where you can listen to people from many different language backgrounds and accents, reading the same paragraph. Listen to several recordings. For each recording, answer these questions: What impressions do you have of the speaker? Educated? Uneducated? Clever? Interesting? Someone you'd like to get to know? Think about where your impressions and meanings came from. How might these impressions affect the way you communicate with someone who has this accent?

2. Go to: http://linguistlist.org/topics/ebonics/ This Web site provides an overview of the California Ebonics controversy. It has links to the original and amended resolution passed by the Oakland Unified School district and to a discussion board on this topic. Think about communication between teacher and students in the classroom. How might a teacher communicate with a child who speaks Ebonics if the teacher considers Ebonics (1) a language, or (2) a substandard version of English?

3. Go to: http://www.arches.uga.edu/~bryan/AAVE/ This is a Web site that provides information on the origin of Ebonics and the distinction between a dialect and a language. After reading this material, do you think Ebonics is a dialect or a language—or neither? How might your view on this influence how you communicate with someone who speaks Ebonics to you?

4

NONVERBAL COMMUNICATION

*R*ecently, a colleague took her four-year-old daughter with her to a business meeting. After observing the interaction for a few minutes, her daughter Anna whispered, "When it's your turn to talk, you have to make your mad face."

Even though Anna is only four years old, she is sensitive to nonverbal cues. Already, she is able to read others' facial expressions and assigns meaning to them. But Anna is not unique; from a very early age, all children learn the basics of nonverbal communication. In fact, infants routinely rely on nonverbals to learn from and communicate with their parents, and some even learn to use nonverbal signs to communicate their desires before they learn to talk (Murphy, 2004).

In this chapter, we take a close look at the intricacies of nonverbal communication and the many factors that shape nonverbal messages and their interpretation. First, we provide a definition of nonverbal communication and describe its importance. We then give you an overview of the types of nonverbal codes and examine the functions that nonverbal messages serve. We next explore how societal forces intersect with individuals' nonverbal communication. We conclude the chapter by discussing ethical issues in nonverbal communication and providing you with suggestions for improving your nonverbal communication skills.

Once you have read this chapter, you will be able to:

● Define nonverbal communication.
● Explain the important role nonverbals play in the communication process.
● Identify four factors that influence the interpretation of nonverbal communication.
● Define five nonverbal codes.
● Discuss the five functions of nonverbal messages.
● Recognize the role power plays in nonverbal communication.
● Understand how prejudice and discrimination are triggered by nonverbal communication and are expressed through it.
● Discuss six guidelines for ethical nonverbal communication.
● Delineate five ways to better interpret nonverbal behavior.

CHAPTER OUTLINE

WHAT IS NONVERBAL COMMUNICATION?

THE IMPORTANCE OF NONVERBAL COMMUNICATION

NONVERBAL COMMUNICATION AND THE INDIVIDUAL
Influences on Nonverbal Communication
Nonverbal Codes

THE FUNCTIONS OF NONVERBAL MESSAGES
Communicating Information
Regulating Interaction
Expressing and Managing Intimacy
Establishing Social Control
Signaling Service-Task Functions

THE INDIVIDUAL, NONVERBAL COMMUNICATION, AND SOCIETY
Nonverbal Communication and Power
Nonverbal Communication, Prejudice, and Discrimination

ETHICS AND NONVERBAL COMMUNICATION

IMPROVING YOUR NONVERBAL COMMUNICATION SKILLS
Summary
Key Terms
Chapter Review Questions
Activities
Web Activities

nonverbal communication
nonverbal behavior that has
symbolic meaning

WHAT IS NONVERBAL COMMUNICATION?

Nonverbal communication occurs when people use nonverbal cues such as facial expression, gestures, and movement symbolically—that is, to create meaning. More specifically, the nonverbal components of communication include all the ways in which people transmit messages through means other than words. Nonverbals communicate messages in and of themselves, as when you wave hello, blow a kiss, or, as the students at Hangzhou University in China do, wear a sacred flame Olympics T-shirt. Nonverbals help us express and interpret the verbal aspects of communication—such as when individuals indicate anger by turning their backs and saying, "I don't want to talk with you right now."

As the last example illustrates, nonverbal communication is integral to communication interactions because the verbal and nonverbal aspects of communication work together to create messages. The nonverbal aspects of an interaction are also important because they can significantly influence how individuals interpret messages, especially those related to feelings, moods, and attitudes. Nonverbal cues are central to the expression of emotion because communicators are often more comfortable expressing their feelings nonverbally (such as by smiling or glaring) than they are stating them more explicitly through words (Mehrabian, 2007). For example, how often do you flat-out state, "I am mad at you" to a friend or colleague? If you are like most people, this is a relatively rare event; instead, you probably rely on some type of nonverbal cue to indicate your dissatisfaction.

How much do the nonverbal aspects of communication contribute to the interpretation of messages? This is a topic that scholars have debated for the past thirty years, with some claiming that the contribution is quite large and others arguing that such is not the case. To read a brief review of this debate, see *Did You Know: How Much Does Nonverbal Communication Contribute to Meaning?*

? *How effective do you believe you are in interpreting others' nonverbal communication? What makes you think you are either skilled or unskilled in this regard?*

DID YOU KNOW?

How Much Does Nonverbal Communication Contribute to Meaning?

How much of the meaning of a message do you think is conveyed by its nonverbal components? Fifty percent? Seventy-five percent? Ninety percent? Have you ever tried to convey a complex message nonverbally? If so, how successful were you?

One of the most common beliefs about communication is that over 90 percent of the meaning of a message is transmitted by its nonverbal elements. However, most scholars agree that this number significantly overstates the true contribution of nonverbal messages (Argyle, 1970; Birdwhistle, 1970; Hsee, Hatfield, & Chemtob, 1992). Then where did the belief come from? It is based on work conducted by Albert Mehrabian (1971), a researcher who argued that 38 percent of meaning is derived from vocally produced sounds such as pitch and volume and 55 percent from facial expressions, leaving only 7 percent of meaning to be provided by the verbal message.

Mehrabian's analysis, however, exhibited several problems. First, he did not consider the contributions to meaning made by gestures and posture. Second, he tried to estimate the contribution of particular nonverbal behaviors—for example, vocal features versus facial expression. In practice, however, no one behavior is particularly useful in determining how people interpret meaning. So many factors influence each person's body movements that we cannot accurately distinguish which is the most meaningful. As another researcher, M. L. Patterson (1982, 1983) suggests, only correlated groups of behaviors—stance, posture, facial patterns, and arm movements—can provide us with an accurate hypothesis about a person's meaning. In other words, although nonverbal cues clearly contribute to how people interpret the meaning of a message, it is

impossible to determine exactly to what extent verbal and nonverbal components each contribute to the meanings people ascribe.

For more information on this topic, see "Busting the myth of communication is 93 percent nonverbal" at http://www.spring.org.uk/2007/05/busting-myth-93-of-communication-is.php

THE IMPORTANCE OF NONVERBAL COMMUNICATION

We devote an entire chapter to nonverbal communication because of the important role it plays in interaction. We also do so because nonverbal communication can be complex and ambiguous—both to convey and to interpret. If, as we stated above, people begin learning nonverbal communication as children, why, then, do they often have difficulty interpreting others' nonverbal communication? Likely, it is due to the fact that humans express a wide array of nonverbal cues, many of which can be quite subtle. Consequently, understanding nonverbal communication requires knowledge and skill. However, don't rush out to buy a paperback that promises to teach you to "read a person like a book." Unfortunately, no book, not even this one, can give you the ability to interpret every nonverbal behavior in every context.

Why not? Because understanding nonverbal communication requires that you interpret behavior and assign meaning to it, and you don't always have the information you need for that. If you notice a stranger staring at you, what does it mean? Does the person think he knows you? Is he interested in you? Is he being aggressive? Or is the person simply lost in thought and only *appears* to be looking at you?

As you can see, a communicator's nonverbal cues can be unclear. Because a variety of factors, including context, culture, and even intentionality, determine the meaning of a specific nonverbal behavior, interpreting an individual's signals can be tricky. In addition, nonverbal cues are continuous, meaning that people exhibit nonverbal behaviors virtually all the time they are conscious. Therefore, it can be difficult to decide what behaviors are acting in concert to create a given message. For example, Joan was talking to her husband about their need to strengthen their marriage. Just when her husband asked what she wanted to do about this problem, she happened to look over at her computer screen and saw it go blank. In frustration, she threw up her hands and sighed heavily. Even though she was responding to her computer failure, her husband thought she was responding to his question, and his feelings were hurt.

Nonverbal communication can also be difficult to interpret because nonverbal cues are multichanneled; that is, they can be transmitted in a variety of ways simultaneously. Speakers can convey nonverbal messages through their facial expressions, voice qualities, gaze, posture, gestures, and other channels we will discuss throughout this chapter. Moreover, because a variety of cues may occur at the same time, it can be difficult and confusing to keep up with everything (Schwartz, Foa, & Foa, 1983). If, for example, you are focusing on someone's face, you may miss important messages conveyed by the body.

Popular books on nonverbal communication typically assume that each behavior has one meaning regardless of the context or who is performing it. Such explanations don't consider context, culture, or individual variations in behavior, nor do they account for the relationships that exist among the people being observed. All these factors, and more, can influence the meaning of a nonverbal behavior in a specific instance. So don't believe that just because someone has her arms crossed over her body, it means she is closed off to you. It may just mean she needs a sweater.

Nonetheless, understanding nonverbal communication can make you a better communicator and help you navigate everyday life. For example, humans rely on nonverbal signals to determine if other humans are a threat. In the television show *Going Tribal*, journalist Bruce Parry visited the remote Suri tribe in Ethiopia. As Parry encountered his first tribal member, he carefully observed the tribesman, who thrust his bow and arrow at Bruce and paced quickly back and forth while averting his gaze. Although many of the

Suri's nonverbal behaviors communicated belligerence, the fact that he did not stare aggressively influenced Bruce to approach him slowly with a gift of tobacco—which was accepted.

We need to make similar assessments of nonverbal behaviors on a daily basis. This may be especially true for individuals whose identities are less valued culturally or whose societal positions make them more vulnerable. Because of this vulnerability, such individuals tend to become quite adept at reading and interpreting nonverbal communication. In a study that compared African Americans and White Americans, researchers found that African Americans were far better at detecting prejudicial attitudes as expressed in subtle nonverbal behavior than were Whites (Richeson & Shelton, 2005). Similarly, another study found that compared with heterosexual men, gay men were better able to identify the sexual orientation of unfamiliar men when watching videos of them (Shelp, 2002).

Nonverbal communication can also affect public policy decisions. For example, more and more schools have begun to institute dress codes. The supporters of this policy argue that school uniforms "help erase cultural and economic differences among students" (Isaacson, 1998) and improve student performance and attendance. This claim rests on the assumption that one form of nonverbal communication, attire, should be regulated because it provides a distraction and disruption. Efforts to ban flag burning in the United States and France's ban on the wearing of headscarves in school by Muslim girls are other examples of public policy attempts to regulate nonverbal expression. Countries would not engage in efforts to control nonverbal expression if it were not so important.

School dress codes attempt to regulate one form of nonverbal communication, attire.

NONVERBAL COMMUNICATION AND THE INDIVIDUAL

In popular books on nonverbal communication, you are likely to read that if someone leans toward you (called a *forward body lean*), they are interested in you or involved in their interaction with you. Although sometimes this is true, we caution you against believing that this or any other nonverbal behavior has a single meaning. Why? Assigning one simple meaning to a nonverbal behavior ignores the multiple meanings that may exist, depending on the context in which the behavior occurs. Forward body lean is, in fact, often a sign of interest or involvement; however, does it *always* indicate interest? Absolutely not! A person might lean forward for a variety of reasons: her stomach hurts, the back of her chair is hot, or her lower back needs to be stretched.

To understand the meaning of a nonverbal behavior, you have to consider the entire behavioral context, including what the person might be communicating verbally (Jones & LeBaron, 2002). Therefore, interpreting others' nonverbal behavior requires that you consider a variety of factors that can influence meaning. To interpret nonverbals, you also need to know the codes—or symbols and rules—that signal various messages. These are the topics we take up next.

Influences on Nonverbal Communication

Culture is one of the more important factors that influences the meaning of nonverbal communication. In the United States, the "thumbs-up" signals success, and the "hitchhiker's thumb" asks for a ride, but these nonverbal signs carry potentially vulgar meanings in a variety of other cultures. In East Africa, instead of pointing with fingers, people often point with their lips—a gesture that is completely unfamiliar to most people in the United States. Thus, the meaning of any nonverbal behavior is defined by the cultures of those

interacting (Axtell, 1993; Segerstrale & Molnár, 1997), as our student explains in *It Happened to Me: Abbad*.

Although Abbad's experience may seem extreme, the increasing levels of contact between people from varying cultures in the twenty-first century means that more opportunities currently exist for misunderstandings based on nonverbal cues. To assist you in developing greater sensitivity to cultural differences in nonverbal communication, see *Building Your Communication Skills: Developing Sensitivity to Cross-Cultural Nonverbal Communication*. In Chapter 6, we discuss in more detail how culture influences communication.

In addition to culture, the relationship between the people interacting affects how people interpret the meaning of nonverbal behaviors (Manusov, 1995). If a husband takes his wife's hand as they are crossing the street, the meaning is some mixture of care and affection; however, if a boss were to do the same with a subordinate, the meaning is more complex and potentially confusing or troubling.

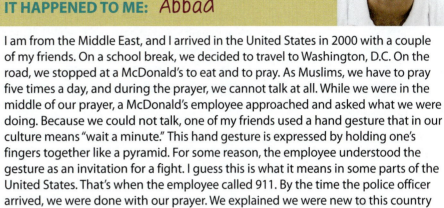

IT HAPPENED TO ME: Abbad

I am from the Middle East, and I arrived in the United States in 2000 with a couple of my friends. On a school break, we decided to travel to Washington, D.C. On the road, we stopped at a McDonald's to eat and to pray. As Muslims, we have to pray five times a day, and during the prayer, we cannot talk at all. While we were in the middle of our prayer, a McDonald's employee approached and asked what we were doing. Because we could not talk, one of my friends used a hand gesture that in our culture means "wait a minute." This hand gesture is expressed by holding one's fingers together like a pyramid. For some reason, the employee understood the gesture as an invitation for a fight. I guess this is what it means in some parts of the United States. That's when the employee called 911. By the time the police officer arrived, we were done with our prayer. We explained we were new to this country and that the hand gesture we used means something else in our culture. We apologized to the employee for the misunderstanding and continued on our trip.

Building Your Communication **SKILLS**

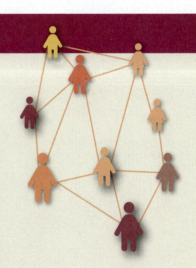

Developing Sensitivity to Cross-Cultural Nonverbal Communication

Most people expect that verbal communication will vary across cultures and anticipate that they will have difficulty communicating in a non-native language. However, fewer people recognize that nonverbal communication can differ considerably across cultures and that they need to be careful when interpreting nonverbal communication cross-culturally. Below we offer you five strategies to help you communicate nonverbally and interpret others' nonverbal communication in unfamiliar cultures.

1. **Observe Closely**. When entering a new culture, set aside your normal understanding of nonverbal signals and anticipate the unexpected. Assume that you do not know the rules, and observe people in the culture carefully to determine patterns of behavior. For example, you may assume that individuals from Japan are happy or amused if they giggle or laugh quietly; however, if you observe their behavior over time and across contexts, you will likely become aware that this behavior often reflects feelings of embarrassment or anxiety. In addition, be sensitive to subtle differences in behavior within a culture. For instance, you may find the tendency to giggle or laugh when embarrassed to be more pronounced among Japanese females than among males.

2. **Mirror Others' Behavior**. If you are uncertain, mirror the behaviors you see others in the culture displaying. If people take off their shoes before entering a home or eat only with their right hands, then you should do the same. However, once again, you want to be aware of contextual cues that suggest whether the behavior is specific to people of a certain sex, age, or status. For example, when Michelle Obama met the

(continued)

(*continued*)

Queen of England, she was criticized for touching the Queen—even though the Queen had touched her first. In England, no one is supposed to touch the Queen without permission, even if she touches them.

3. **Appreciate Differences in Time and Space**. Be aware that cultures vary in how people use time and space. This is especially important for the business traveler. Before visiting a new culture, determine what constitutes being "on time." In the United States, if people arrive within five minutes of an event's beginning, they are usually thought to be on time. However, in Germany or Switzerland, they might be judged as late, and in Algeria or Brazil, they are likely to be considered early. Similarly, cultures differ in how close people stand to each other while talking or whether it is more appropriate to sit facing a colleague (as in the United States) or side by side (as is typical in China).

4. **Use Nonverbal Emblems Cautiously**. Some nonverbal gestures used to convey messages in one country have very different meanings in another. For example, during his wife's delivery, one man saw the obstetrician hold up all five fingers on one hand and the thumb of the other. He interpreted it to mean that his wife had birthed five children and all were okay; however, it actually meant that he was now the father of six children! (In the United States, the thumb is rarely used to indicate the number one; rather, the index figure is used.) More serious misunderstandings can arise when an innocuous nonverbal emblem in one country carries a vulgar meaning in another—as is true of the U.S. okay sign in Brazil, the V for victory in England, and the thumbs-up in Australia and West Africa.

5. **Confirm Interpretations and Attributions**. When possible, ask a cultural native to confirm or correct your interpretations of others' nonverbal communication and the attributions you make about them. If you clearly demonstrate that you are nonjudgmental and desire to learn, most people will respond positively.

Third, the meaning individuals attribute to others' nonverbal behavior varies based on how well they know the communicators. For example, if you know that your best friend tends to smile when she is angry, you will be better at interpreting her nonverbals than will a stranger. Once you know people, you can interpret their nonverbal cues more accurately.

Finally, observers tend to interpret individuals' nonverbal behavior based on their sex. For example, when women toss their hair, the behavior is often read as flirtatious. However, if a man does the same, one is more likely to believe that he is just trying to get his hair out of his eyes. As we discussed in Chapter 2, sex differences in nonverbal and verbal communication are due to both biological, social, and cultural influences.

Nonverbal Codes

Nonverbal codes or signals are distinct, organized means of expression that consist of both symbols and rules for their use (Cicca, Step, & Turkstra, 2003). Although we describe a range of such codes in this section, we do not mean to imply that any one code occurs in isolation. Generally, a *set* of behaviors and codes together determines the meaning or significance of an action.

For our purposes, we isolate a specific kind of behavior for analysis; however, in the real world, without knowing the context, interpretations about any behavior may be questionable or even wrong (Patterson, 1983). In this section, we'll look at the five aspects of nonverbal codes—*kinesics, paralinguistics, time and space, haptics,* and *appearance and artifacts*—to see how this system of coding works.

Kinesics

Kinesics is the term for a system of studying nonverbal communication sent by the body, including gestures, posture, movement, facial expressions, and eye behavior. For clarity, we group kinesic communication into two general categories: those behaviors involving the body and those involving the face.

nonverbal codes
distinct, organized means of expression that consist of symbols and rules for their use

kinesics
nonverbal communication sent by the body, including gestures, posture, movement, facial expressions, and eye behavior

The Body Our bodies convey many nonverbal messages. For example, people use **gestures** such as pointing, waving, and holding up their hands to direct others' attention, signal hello, and indicate that they want to be recognized. Communicators use four types of nonverbal gestures: *illustrators, emblems, adaptors*, and *regulators*. **Illustrators** are signals that accompany speech to clarify or emphasize the verbal messages. Thus, when people come back from a fishing trip, they hold their hands far apart to indicate the size of the fish that got away. **Emblems** are gestures that stand for a specific verbal meaning; for example, in the United States, forming an *O* with the thumb and forefinger while raising the other three fingers communicates that everything is "OK." **Adaptors** are gestures we use to manage our emotions. Many adaptors are nervous gestures such as tapping a pencil, jiggling a leg, or twirling one's hair. Finally, people use **regulators** to control conversation; for example, if you want to prevent someone from interrupting you, you might hold up your hand to indicate that the other person should wait. In contrast, if you wish to interrupt and take the floor, you might raise a finger to signal your desire.

Gestures contribute a lot to our communication efforts; even their frequency can signal meaning. For instance, people who are excited indicate their involvement by using many and varied gestures; those who have little involvement may indicate their lack of interest by failing to gesture. For an example of how differences in nonverbal gestures can affect communication, see *Communication in Society: Etiquette for the World Traveler*.

People also use their bodies to convey meaning through posture and movement. In general, posture is evaluated in two ways: by how "immediate" it is and by how relaxed it appears (Mehrabian, 1971; Richards, Rollersor, & Phillips, 1991). **Immediacy** refers to how close or involved people appear to be with each other. For example, when individuals like someone, they tend to orient their bodies in the other person's direction, lean toward them, and look at them directly when they speak. How do people act when they wish to avoid someone? Typically, they engage in the opposite behavior. They turn their backs or refuse to look at them, and if they are forced to stand or sit near the person they dislike, they lean away from them. To understand this, imagine how you would behave if you were attempting to reject an unwanted amorous advance.

Relaxation refers to the degree of tension one's body displays. When you are at home watching TV, for instance, you probably display a relaxed posture, lounging in a chair with your legs stretched out in front of you and your arms resting loosely on the chair's arms. However, if you are waiting at the dentist's office, you may sit hunched forward, your legs pressed tightly together, and your hands tightly grasping the chair arms.

gestures
nonverbal communication made with part of the body, including actions such as pointing, waving, or holding up a hand to direct people's attention

illustrators
signals that accompany speech to clarify or emphasize verbal messages

emblems
gestures that stand for a specific verbal meaning

adaptors
gestures used to manage emotions

regulators
gestures used to control conversation

immediacy
how close or involved people appear to be with each other

relaxation
the degree of tension displayed by one's body

Communication in SOCIETY

Etiquette for the World Traveler

Have you observed travelers from abroad violating a nonverbal norm while visiting the United States? What did they do? How did you respond? Now that you know more about nonverbal communication practices around the world, what would be your response if you observed a similar violation?

To help you prepare for using appropriate nonverbal communication when you travel, the travel Web site Vayama.com offers etiquette tips.

1. In Brazil, don't make the OK sign with your hand. It's considered a very rude gesture.
2. In China, don't take the last bit of food on a serving plate. It's considered impolite. Also, leave a little bit of food on your plate when you're full so the hosts know you are done; otherwise they'll bring out even more food!
3. In Denmark, don't be too touchy-feely. It's not appreciated.
4. In Italy, don't pull away or get offended if an Italian associate wishes to hug you. Embrace him or her in return.
5. In Egypt, don't use your left hand to eat.
6. In India, *do* make sure your head is covered when entering a mosque or a Sikh gurdwara.
7. In Iran, do arrive on time. Lateness could be considered rude.
8. In Thailand, don't talk with your hands or put your hands in your pocket while talking to someone.
9. In Nigeria, understand that Nigerians communicate with a lot of gestures and body language, so you may have to pay attention to nonverbal cues when conversing.
10. In Greece, be aware of how to indicate yes or no with body language, as it's different in Greece than in the United States. Yes is a slight downward nod of the head, and No is a slight upward nod of the head.

SOURCE: "Etiquette for the world traveler." Retrieved March 21, 2009 from www.vayama.com/jsp/destination

The way you walk or move can also communicate messages to others, particularly about your moods or emotional states. Sometimes you use movement deliberately to communicate a message—such as when you stomp around the apartment to indicate your anger. Even when your movement is not intentional, observers can and do make judgments about you. One study found that observers could identify when pedestrians were sad, angry, happy, or proud, just from the way they walked (Montepare, Goldstein, & Clausen, 1987). However, some emotional states (anger) were easier to identify than others (pride), and some individuals were easier to classify than were others. So although people consciously communicate a great deal with their body movements and gestures, and observers interpret others' movements, some messages are more clearly transmitted than others. Many of the same factors discussed earlier—such as culture, context, background knowledge, and gender—affect one's ability to interpret kinesic behavior.

The Face Facial expressions communicate more than perhaps any other nonverbal behavior. They are the primary channels for transmitting emotion, and the eyes in particular convey important messages regarding attraction and attention. Some research suggests that facial expressions of happiness, sadness, anger, surprise, fear, and disgust are the same across cultures and, in fact, are innate (Ekman & Friesen, 1969, 1986), although not all scholars agree. Moreover, through observations of deaf, blind, and brain-damaged children, researchers have concluded that the commonality of facial expressions that does exist among humans is not due to observation and learning but rather to genetic programming (Eibl-Eibesfeld, 1972; Ekman, 2003).

The ability to accurately recognize others' emotions gives individuals an edge in their interactions. For example, people who are adept in this respect tend to achieve more favorable outcomes in negotiations (Effenbein, Foo, White, Tan, & Aik, 2007). However, a variety of studies shows that individuals can be trained in emotion recognition and thus improve their ability to recognize others' emotional expressions, especially if their targets are from different cultures than their own (Elfenbein, 2006).

Of course, people don't display every emotion they feel. People learn through experience and observation to manage their facial expressions, and they learn which expressions are appropriate to reveal in what circumstances. In the United States, expectations of appropriateness differ for men and women. Males are often discouraged from showing sadness, while females frequently are criticized for showing anger. In addition, women are routinely instructed to smile, no matter how they feel, while relatively few men receive the same message. Consequently, people learn to manage their facial expressions so they don't reveal emotions that they believe they shouldn't feel or that they don't want others to see.

As mentioned earlier, eye behavior is especially important in conveying messages—for humans as well as animals. For example, both humans and dogs use prolonged gaze (a stare) to communicate aggression, and they avert their gaze when they want to avoid contact. Furthermore, eye behavior interacts with facial expressions to convey meaning. Thus, most people believe that a smile is genuine only when the eyes "smile" as well as the lips. Actors such as Julia Roberts and Tom Cruise are particularly gifted at this; they can, at will, express what appears to be a genuine smile.

As with other types of nonverbal communication, context and culture shape the meanings people attach to eye behavior. For example, cultures differ significantly in how long one is supposed to engage in eye contact and how frequently. Many Native Americans such as the Cherokee, Navajo, and Hopi engage in minimal eye contact compared to most White U.S. Americans (Chiang, 1993). Swedes tend to gaze infrequently but for longer periods of time, while southern Europeans gaze frequently and extensively (Knapp & Hall, 1992, 2001). Your relationship with others also affects how you interpret their eye behavior. Thus, you may like a romantic partner to gaze into your eyes but find the same behavior threatening when exhibited by the mail carrier.

Paralinguistics

paralinguistics
all aspects of spoken language except the words themselves; includes rate, volume, pitch, stress

The vocal aspects of nonverbal communication are referred to as **paralinguistics**, which include rate, volume, pitch, and stress, among others. Paralinguistics are those aspects of language that are *oral* but not *verbal*. That is, paralinguistics describe all aspects of spoken

language except the words themselves. Typically, you recognize other speakers' voices in large part through their paralinguistics, or how they sound rather than the specific words they say. Thus, callers often expect relatives and friends to recognize them just from hearing their voices on the telephone. If a receiver doesn't recognize a caller, the caller may feel hurt or offended, which can turn a simple phone call into an anxiety-producing quiz. Paralinguistics are composed of two types of vocal behavior: *voice qualities* and *vocalizations*.

Voice Qualities **Voice qualities** include speed, pitch, rhythm, vocal range, and artic- ulation; these qualities make up the "music" of the human voice. We all know people whose voice qualities are widely recognized. For example, during the 2008 presidential campaign, the vocal qualities of the two candidates were remarked upon frequently. President Obama's vocal style was seen as more effective; his pitch, volume, and deliberate rate of speech were viewed as inspiring calm and confidence. Senator McCain varied his tempo and tone, especially when he appeared angry or excited; this quality is believed to have reinforced the Obama campaign's characterization of him as "erratic" (Miller, 2008). To compare the vocal qualities of various presidents, go to http://www.presidentsusa.net/au- diovideo.html which provides audio and video recordings.

Speakers whose voices vary in pitch and rhythm seem more expressive than those whose voices do not. For example, people, such as the late Billy Mays, who sell products during infomercials typically vary their volume as well as pitch and rhythm to convey excitement and engage listeners in their messages. Speakers also vary in how they articulate sounds, some pronouncing each word distinctly, and others blurring them. We tend not to notice this paralinguistic feature unless someone articulates very precisely or very imprecisely. If you have difficulty understanding a speaker, the fault usually lies not with how fast the person talks but with how clearly he or she articulates. When combined, these paralinguistic qualities make one's voice distinctive and recognizable.

Vocalizations The sounds we utter that do not have the structure of language are referred to as **vocalizations**. Tarzan's yell is one famous example. Vocalizations include cues such as laughing, crying, whining, and moaning as well as the intensity or volume of one's speech. Also included are sounds that aren't actual words but that serve as fillers, such as "uh-huh," "uh," "ah," and "er."

The paralinguistic aspects of speech serve a variety of communicative functions. They reveal mood and emotion; they also allow us to emphasize or stress a word or idea, create a distinctive identity, and (along with gestures) regulate conversation.

Time and Space

How people use time and space is so important to communication that researchers have studied this and developed specialized terms to describe the uses. **Chronemics**, from the Greek word *chronos* meaning "time," is the study of the way people use time as a message. It includes issues such as punctuality and the amount of time people spend with each other. **Proxemics** refers to the study of how people use spatial cues, including interpersonal dis- tance, territoriality, and other space relationships. Let's see how these factors influence communication and relationships.

Chronemics People often interpret others' use of time as conveying a message, which places it in the realm of communication. For example, if your friend consistently arrives more than an hour late, how do you interpret her behavior? Culture strongly influences how most people answer this question (Hall & Hall, 1987). In the United States, time is typically highly valued; we even have an expression that "time is money." Because of this, most people own numerous clocks and watches, events are scheduled at specific times, and functions typically begin "on time." Therefore, in the United States, lateness can communi- cate thoughtlessness, irresponsibility, or selfishness. A more positive or tolerant view might be that the perpetually late person is carefree.

Not all cultures value time in the same way, however. In some Latin American and Arab cultures, if one arrives thirty minutes or even an hour after an event is scheduled to begin, one is "on time." When people come together from cultures that value time differently, it can lead

voice qualities
qualities such as speed, pitch, rhythm, vocal range, and articulation that make up the "music" of the human voice

vocalizations
uttered sounds that do not have the structure of language

chronemics
the study of the way in which people use time as a message

proxemics
the study of how people use spatial cues—including interpersonal distance, territoriality, and other space relationships—to communicate

to conflict and a sense of displacement. This happened when one of our colleagues taught a class in Mexico. On the first class day, she showed up at the school shortly before the class was scheduled to begin. She found the building locked and no one around. And even though she knew that Mexicans respond to time differently than she does, she never got comfortable arriving "late" during her stay and routinely had to wait outside the building until someone showed up to let her in.

The timing and sequencing of events convey a variety of messages. For example, being asked to lunch carries a different meaning than being asked to dinner, and being asked to dinner on a Monday conveys a different message than being asked to dinner on a Saturday. Also, events tend to unfold in a particular order; so we expect first dates to precede first kisses and small talk to precede task talk. When these expectations are violated, we often attribute meaning to the violations. For example, if you expect a stranger to shake your hand upon being introduced, you will likely search for an explanation if she or he hugs you instead (Burgoon & Hale, 1988; Burgoon & LePoire, 1993).

In addition, some people use time **monochronically**, while others use it **polychronically**, and the difference can be perceived as transmitting a message (Hall, 1983; Wolburg, 2001). Individuals who use time monochronically engage in one task or behavior at a time—reading *or* participating in a conversation *or* watching a movie. If you engage in multiple activities at the same time, you are using time polychronically. Historically in the United States, people have used time monochronically; however, now that technology is so pervasive, more people are using time polychronically as they listen to their iPods, talk on cell phones, and send text messages while they interact with others. Unfortunately, people who use time monochronically may be insulted by those who use it polychronically, leading to comments such as "Put down that Gameboy and pay attention to me when I talk to you!"

Whenever an individual's use of time differs from that of others, miscommunication is possible. If you tend to value punctuality more than others do, you may arrive at events earlier than expected and irritate your hosts, or you may be perceived as too eager. Similarly, if you don't value punctuality, you may discover that others won't schedule activities with you or are frequently angry at you. Relationships and communication benefit when the people involved understand how the others value and use time.

Proxemics   Earlier, we touched on *proxemics*, the study of how one uses space and how this use of space can serve a communicative function. The distance people stand or sit from one another often symbolizes physical and/or psychological closeness. If a longtime friend or partner chooses not to sit next to you at a movie theater, for example, you will probably be perplexed—perhaps even hurt or angry. Research by Edward T. Hall, a well-known anthropologist, has delineated four spheres or categories of space that humans use (Hall, 1966). Let's take a look at each.

Intimate distance (0 to 18 inches) tends to be reserved for those one knows very well. Typically, this distance is used for displaying physical and psychological intimacy, such as lovemaking, cuddling children, comforting someone, or telling secrets. **Personal distance** (18 inches to 4 feet) describes the space we use when interacting with friends and acquaintances. People in the United States often use the nearer distance for friends and the farther one for acquaintances, but culture and personal preference strongly influence this choice. When others prefer closer distances than you do, you may find their closeness psychologically distressing. Jerry Seinfeld has referred to these people as "close talkers."

Social distance (4 to 12 feet) is the distance most U.S. Americans use when they interact with unfamiliar others. Impersonal business with grocery clerks, sales clerks, and coworkers occurs at about 4 to 7 feet, while the greatest distance is used in formal situations such as job interviews. **Public distance** (12 to 25 feet) is most appropriate for public ceremonies such as lectures and performances, although an even greater distance may be maintained between public figures (such as politicians and celebrities) and their audiences. (See *Visual Summary 4.1: Proxemics*.)

One's culture, gender, relationship to others, and personality all influence whether one feels most comfortable at the near or far range of each of these spheres. In the United States,

monochronically
engaging in one task or behavior at a time

polychronically
engaging in multiple activities simultaneously

intimate distance
(0 to 18 inches) the space used when interacting with those with whom one is very close

personal distance
(18 inches to 4 feet) the space used when interacting with friends and acquaintances

social distance
(4 to 12 feet) the distance most U.S. Americans use when they interact with unfamiliar others

public distance
(12 to 25 feet) the distance used for public ceremonies such as lectures and performances

Proxemics

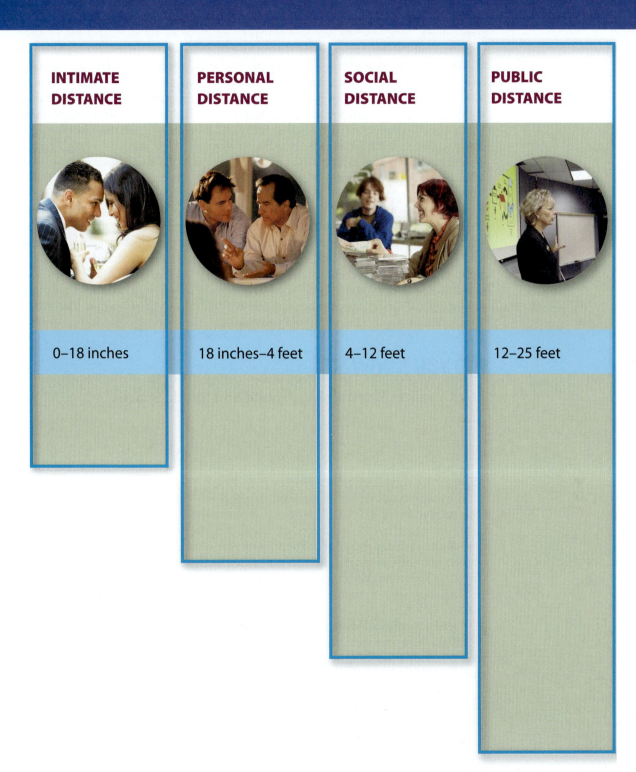

INTIMATE DISTANCE	PERSONAL DISTANCE	SOCIAL DISTANCE	PUBLIC DISTANCE
0–18 inches	18 inches–4 feet	4–12 feet	12–25 feet

two unacquainted women typically sit or stand closer to each other than they do to unfamiliar males, while many males are more comfortable sitting or standing closer to unknown females than they are even to men they know (Burgoon & Guerrero, 1994). However, people in other cultures may prefer the closer ranges. Cultural disparities can result in a comedic cross-cultural "dance," where one person tries to get closer to the other, and that person, made uncomfortable by the closeness, moves away.

What does the space between interactants in a given culture reveal? It can communicate intimacy or the lack of it; it can also communicate power and dominance. If person A feels free to enter person B's space without permission but refuses to allow B the same privilege, this lack of reciprocity communicates that A is dominant in the relationship. This situation is common between supervisors and subordinates and may exist in some parent–child relationships as well.

All humans, as well as animals, have strong feelings of territoriality, or ownership of space. Just as dogs bark or growl when they perceive that someone has invaded their space, humans become agitated or upset when others intrude on space they think of as "theirs." A primary way in which we attempt to claim and maintain control of a space is by personalizing or marking it, especially with artifacts. Thus, we alter spaces to make them distinctly our own—putting up a fence around a residence, placing a purse in a chair, or displaying family photos in an office. These markers are a form of nonverbal communication that specifies territorial ownership or legitimate occupancy (Becker, 1973). Markers function mainly to keep people away, thereby preventing confrontational social encounters. To better understand the relationship between markers and territoriality, see *Did You Know: Territoriality: Maintaining Private and Public Spaces*.

DID YOU KNOW?

Territoriality: Maintaining Private and Public Spaces

Do you have bumper stickers or decals on your car? If so, do you think the research findings below describe you or people you know? How do you mark your other personal and public territories? What do you think your markers say about you?

Watch out for cars with bumper stickers.

That's the surprising conclusion of a recent study by social psychologist William Szlemko. Drivers of cars with bumper stickers, window decals, personalized license plates, and other "territorial markers" not only get mad when someone cuts in their lane or is slow to respond to a changed traffic light, but they are far more likely than those who do not personalize their cars to use their vehicles to express rage—by honking, tailgating, and using other aggressive behavior.

It does not seem to matter whether the messages on the stickers are about peace and love (Visualize World Peace, My Kid Is an Honor Student) or angry and in your face (Don't Mess With Texas, My Kid Beat Up Your Honor Student).

Szlemko and his colleagues found that people who personalize their cars acknowledge that they are aggressive drivers, but usually do not realize that they are reporting much higher levels of aggression than people whose cars do not have visible markers.

"The more markers a car has, the more aggressively the person tends to drive when provoked," Szlemko said. "Just the presence of territory markers predicts the tendency to be an aggressive driver."

The key to the phenomenon apparently lies in the idea of territoriality. Drivers with road rage tend to think of public streets and highways as "my street" and "my lane"—in other words, they think they "own the road." Why would bumper stickers predict which people are likely to view public roadways as private property?

Social scientists such as Szlemko say that people carry around three kinds of territorial spaces in their heads. One is personal territory—like a home, or a bedroom. The second kind involves space that is temporarily yours—an office cubicle or a gym locker. The third kind is public territory: park benches, walking trails—and roads.

Drivers who individualize their cars using bumper stickers, window decals, and personalized license plates, the researchers hypothesized, see their cars in the same way as they see their homes and bedrooms—as deeply personal space, or primary territory.

"If you are in a vehicle that you identify as a primary territory, you would defend that against other people whom you perceive as being disrespectful of your space," Bell added. "What you ignore is that you are on a public roadway—you lose sight of the fact you are in a public area and you don't own the road."

Haptics

Although researchers in communication know that touch, or **haptics**, is important, it is among the least-studied forms of nonverbal communication. Nonetheless, research does indicate that infants and children need to be touched in order to be physically and psychologically healthy (Field, 2002). Also, although people vary considerably in how much or what type of touch they prefer, most enjoy being touched by those they care about.

Touch can be categorized into several general types (Givens, 2005), but people rarely notice the types unless a discrepancy occurs between their expectations and their experience. **Professional**, or **functional touch**, is the least intimate; people who must touch others as part of their livelihood, such as dentists, hairstylists, and hospice workers, use this type of touch. Because touch often conveys intimacy, people who must use professional touch have to be careful of their interaction style; for example, they may adopt a formal or distant verbal communication style to counteract the intimacy of their touch. **Social-polite touch** is part of daily interaction. In the United States, this form of touch is more intimate than professional touch but is still impersonal. For example, many U.S. Americans shake hands when greeting acquaintances and casual friends, though in many European countries (such as France and Italy), hugging and kissing are appropriate forms of social touch. Even within the United States, people have different ideas about what types of touch are appropriate socially.

Friendship touch is more intimate than social touch and usually conveys warmth, closeness, and caring. Although considerable variation in touch may exist among friends, people typically use touch that is more intimate with close friends than with acquaintances or strangers. Examples include brief hugs, a hand on the shoulder, or putting one's arm loosely around another's waist or shoulders. **Love-intimate touch** is most often used with one's romantic partners and family. Examples are the long kisses and extended hugs we tend to reserve for those with whom we are closest. However, the types of behaviors that constitute friendship or love-intimate touch may differ based on an individual's culture, sex, and/or social position, as our student discovered in *It Happened to Me: Beth*.

Beth's experience is not uncommon. When people from different cultures—even regional cultures—come together, they often discover that not only do some of their verbal expressions differ, so do their nonverbal ones. What could Beth have done in this situation? It would have been both appropriate and useful for her to mention her discomfort with what she perceived as personal touch in the workplace. She wouldn't have to be unpleasant; she could simply reveal that she uses this type of touch exclusively for her intimates and that she prefers her coworker not touch her this way. The interaction might be a bit awkward for a moment, but this is better than tolerating unwanted nonverbal behavior.

haptics
the study of the communicative function of touch

professional touch
type of touch used by certain workers, such as dentists, hairstylists, and hospice workers, as part of their livelihood; also known as *functional touch*

functional touch
the least intimate type of touch; used by certain workers such as dentists, hairstylists, and hospice workers, as part of their livelihood; also known as *professional touch*

social-polite touch
touch that is part of daily interaction in the United States; it is more intimate than professional touch but is still impersonal

friendship touch
touch that is more intimate than social touch and usually conveys warmth, closeness, and caring

love-intimate touch
touch most often used with one's romantic partners and family

IT HAPPENED TO ME: Beth

I grew up in upper Michigan, where people rarely touch unless they know each other very well. Then I started working with a guy from the South. From the beginning, he touched me whenever we talked; he touched my arm, put his hand on my shoulder, or even put his arm on the back of my chair. This infuriated me! I thought he was being condescending and too familiar. Later, I realized that he does this with everybody. I understand that he doesn't mean anything by it, but I still don't like it.

In the United States, sex strongly influences patterns of touch. Heterosexual males, for example, are more likely to reserve hand-holding for their romantic partners and small children, while females touch other women more frequently and hold hands with older children, their close female relatives, and even female friends. In general, women tend to touch other women more frequently than men touch other men, and in cross-sex interactions, men are more likely to initiate touch than are women (Hall & Hall, 1990). However, in cross-sex interactions, the nature of the relationship influences touch behavior more than does the sex of the participants. Across all stages of heterosexual romantic relationships, partners reciprocate touch, so they do not differ in the amount of touch (Guerrero & Andersen, 1991); however, men respond more positively to their partners' touch than do women (Hanzal, Segrin, & Dorros, 2008). In addition, men initiate touch more in casual romantic relationships, while women do so more often in married relationships (Guerrero & Andersen, 1994).

You may have noticed that each form of touch we have discussed has a "positive" quality. Of course, people also use touch to convey negative messages. For example, one study revealed that individuals use aggressive touch and withdrawal of affectionate touch with children to signal their displeasure (Guerrero & Ebesu, 1993). Aggressive touch includes hitting, kicking, and pinching, while withdrawal of affection involves rejecting the touch attempts of others, as when one pushes another's arm away or refuses to hold hands.

Another type of touch that can be perceived negatively is **demand touching**, a type of touch used to establish dominance and power. Demand touching increases in hierarchical settings, such as at work. One significant characteristic of demand touching is that touchers typically have higher status and have more control over encounters than do receivers; this allows them more freedom of movement and more visual contact. An everyday example of demand touch is when a supervisor stands behind a subordinate and leans over to provide directions, placing his or her hand on the subordinate's shoulder. The subordinate can't easily move or look directly at the supervisor, and the subordinate may feel both physically and psychologically constrained (Kemmer, 1992).

Appearance and Artifacts

In all cultures, individuals' appearance matters, as do their **artifacts**, or the clothing and other accessories they choose. Let's first consider appearance and how it operates as a nonverbal code. In general, people's looks are believed to communicate something about them, and people develop expectations based on how others look. Hairstyle, skin color, height, weight, clothing, accessories such as jewelry, and other aspects of appearance all influence how we are perceived and how we perceive others. And in the United States, appearance is seen as especially important (Newport, 1999).

What is considered attractive, however, is influenced by one's culture and the time period in which one lives (Grammer, Fink, Joller, & Thornhill, 2003). Many people find it hard to believe that the Mona Lisa was considered a great beauty in her day, and even more people wonder who could ever have liked the clothes and hairstyles their parents sported in their youth. Although the global village we now live in means that the media transmit images that can be seen all over the world, cultures still vary in what they consider most attractive. The current ideal body type for women in the United States, as portrayed in the media, for example, is considered too thin and unfeminine by many African Americans (Duke, 2002). And while some American women get collagen injections to achieve full lips, our Japanese students tell us that such thick lips are not considered attractive in Japan. Some Europeans dislike the defined musculature favored for males in magazines and television ads in the United States.

In the United States, people invest considerable time, money, and energy adapting their appearance to cultural ideals. They diet, color and style their hair, frequent gyms and tanning booths, and even undergo surgery to be more attractive. People engage in all these efforts because the U.S. culture generally equates beauty with happiness, success, goodness, and desirability.

While people face certain limits in reshaping their bodies and other physical attributes, they have great flexibility in using clothing and other artifacts to convey important messages about themselves. This is especially true of men; evaluations of their status and wealth are

demand touching
a type of touch used to establish dominance and power

artifacts
clothing and other accessories

typically based on their appearance and artifacts (Crane, 2000). However, the (mostly) male bankers and brokers on Wall Street are learning the downside of this association. Because expensive—and somewhat boxy—business suits became strongly associated with these professions (which fell out of favor during the recent recession and collapse of important financial institutions), many bankers and brokers began to purchase more informal and close-fitting business attire to disassociate themselves from these careers.

Clothing is used to convey other messages as well. For example, nurses, flight attendants, and police officers wear uniforms to help others identify them and to send specific messages about their jobs (Gundersen, 1990). Thus, police officers wear paramilitary uniforms not only to allow us to easily identify them but also to reinforce their role in maintaining social order.

Individuals also choose their accessories and artifacts—such as purses, watches, jewelry, sunglasses, and even cars—to communicate specific messages about status, personality, success, and/or group membership. A student who carries a leather briefcase on campus creates a different image than one who carries a canvas backpack, and a person who drives a hybrid car conveys a different identity than one who drives an SUV. In these ways, people can use artifacts to make announcements about who they are and what they value without having to say a word. We might argue that people in the United States, where it is not considered polite to announce one's status or success, often use artifacts to make those announcements (Fussell, 1992).

Integrating all of these various nonverbal codes to create clear and effective messages can be a challenge. To help you improve your ability to communicate your nonverbal messages successfully, see *Building Your Communication Skills: Five Tips for Enhancing Nonverbal Communication Skills*.

Building Your Communication SKILLS

Five Tips for Enhancing Nonverbal Communication Skills

Because you probably learned most of your nonverbal cues implicitly and received little direct instruction on how to communicate them effectively, you may not be aware of how successfully you convey your nonverbal messages. However, if you practice these five tips, you can not only become aware of your abilities, you can actually improve them.

First, monitor your nonverbal behavior. That is, pay attention to your posture, vocal tones, use of space and time, and the other codes we have discussed in this chapter to assess when you are the most, and least, effective in conveying the messages you intend to communicate.

Second, monitor others' reactions to you. This is a corollary to the recommendation above. You want to pay attention to whether others' understand you as well as to how they react to your nonverbal cues. For example, when you are upset, do others' responses indicate that they understand your emotional state?

Third, ask friends and relatives to give you feedback on your nonverbal behavior. Ask them to tell you when your nonverbal cues are clearest and least clear. You might discover, for instance, that when you are uncomfortable with a message you are communicating, you send mixed signals regarding your emotions or intentions.

Fourth, videotape your informal interactions with others, and observe your own behavior and how others react to you. This may be more informative than any other strategy you try.

Fifth, and finally, once you have collected all the available information on your nonverbal behavior, make a conscious effort to improve it. Then, after you have worked on improving your nonverbal communication style, repeat steps one through four to determine if you have been successful.

Which nonverbal code or codes do you rely on most when interpreting others' nonverbal messages? Which do you rely on least? How do these choices influence the way in which you interpret others' nonverbal cues?

As you can see from our discussion thus far, multiple categories of nonverbal behavior influence communication. These categories are, in turn, influenced by multiple individual and cultural factors. In the next section, we explore how these categories work together to influence how we send and interpret messages.

THE FUNCTIONS OF NONVERBAL MESSAGES

Earlier, we discussed the codes or categories of nonverbal behavior such as proxemics that individuals use to express themselves. Here, we address the functions or purposes these behaviors can serve when they are performed independently or, more frequently, in concert with one another.

Understanding the function of nonverbal cues often requires you to examine all the nonverbal codes that are being enacted. For example, when you use or interpret nonverbal behaviors, you don't isolate kinesics from haptics or proxemics; rather, you enact or observe an integrated set of behaviors, consider the context and the individual, and then attribute meaning. If you see two people standing closely together in a public place, you wouldn't necessarily assume that they were being intimate (intimacy being one function of nonverbal messages). Rather, you would examine how relaxed or tense their bodies appeared, evaluate their facial expressions and gaze, and consider the appropriateness of intimate displays in this public space (for example, a bar versus a church). Only then might you make an attribution about the meaning or function of the couple's behavior.

In general, scholars have determined that nonverbal behaviors serve five functions during interaction (Patterson, 1982, 2003): *communicating information, regulating interaction, expressing and managing intimacy, establishing social control*, and *signaling service-task functions*. The most basic function is to communicate information, and this is the one we examine first.

Communicating Information

From the receiver's point of view, much of a sender's behavior is **communicating information**. For example, when you meet someone for the first time, you evaluate the pattern of the sender's behavior to assess a variety of factors. First, you might evaluate the sender's general disposition to determine if it is warm and friendly or cool and distant. You will likely also assess her more-fleeting nonverbal reactions to help you decide if the person seems pleased to meet you or is just being polite. Finally, of course, you evaluate the person's verbal message. For example, does the speaker say, "I've been looking forward to meeting you," or does she say, "I'd love to chat, but I've got to run." You then combine all these pieces of information to ascribe meaning to the encounter.

Nonverbal communication helps individuals convey and interpret verbal messages. They can do this in five ways:

- by repeating a message (winking while saying, "I'm just kidding")
- by highlighting or emphasizing a message (pointing at the door while saying, "Get out!")
- by complementing or reinforcing a message (whispering while telling a secret)
- by contradicting a message (rolling one's eyes and speaking in a hostile tone while saying, "I love your haircut")
- by substituting for a message (shaking one's head to indicate disagreement)

communicating information
using nonverbal behaviors to help clarify verbal messages and reveal attitudes and moods

Thus, understanding nonverbal communication can make you a better *verbal* communicator.

Regulating Interaction

regulating interaction
using nonverbal behaviors to help manage turn-taking during conversation

Nonverbal communication is also used as a way of **regulating interaction**. That is, people use nonverbal behaviors to manage turn-taking during conversation. Thus, if you want to start talking, you might lean forward, look at the current speaker, and even raise one finger. To reveal that you are finished with your turn, you may drop your volume and pitch, lean back,

and look away from and then back toward the person you are "giving" your turn to. The regulating function tends to be the most automatic of the five, and most of us rarely think about it. The behaviors you use in this way include the more stable ones—such as interpersonal distance, body orientation, and posture—as well as more fluid behaviors like gaze, facial expression, volume, and pitch that are important in the smooth sequencing of conversational turns (Capella, 1985).

Expressing and Managing Intimacy

A third function of nonverbal communication, and the most studied, involves **expressing and managing intimacy**. The degree of your nonverbal involvement with another usually reflects the level of intimacy you desire with that person. If you are on a date and notice that your partner is leaning toward you, gazing into your eyes, nodding his head, and providing many paralinguistic cues such as "uh huh" as you talk, your date is revealing a high degree of nonverbal involvement, which often signals attraction and interest. Of course, people can manipulate these behaviors to suggest attraction and involvement even if they are not experiencing these feelings. For example, when subordinates talk with their supervisors, they often display fairly high levels of nonverbal involvement, regardless of their true feelings for their bosses.

Nonverbal communication can be used to manage turn-taking during interaction.

Establishing Social Control

People also use nonverbal communication as way of **establishing social control**, or exercising influence over other people. Individuals engage in the social-control function when they smile at someone they want to do them a favor or when they glare at noisy patrons in a theater to encourage them to be quiet. You can use either positive or negative behaviors (or both) in your efforts to control others. People who are "charming" or very persuasive are typically extremely gifted at using nonverbal behavior to influence others.

When expressing and managing intimacy, people tend to respond in similar, or reciprocal, ways to one another's nonverbals. On the other hand, when engaging in social control, people tend to respond in complementary ways to one another's nonverbals.

Signaling Service-Task Functions

Finally, nonverbal communication has a **service-task function**. Behaviors of this kind typically signal close involvement between people in impersonal relationships and contexts. For example, physicians frequently engage in very intimate touch as a part of their profession, as do manicurists, tailors, and massage therapists. In each of these cases, however, the behavior is appropriate, necessary, and merely a means to a (professional) end.

Clearly, accurately interpreting nonverbal messages is complex, requiring awareness of a number of elements—factors that influence individuals' communication patterns, nonverbal communication codes and signals, and the communicative functions of nonverbals. However, in some senses, we have only shown you one piece of the picture, as we have thus far focused primarily on nonverbal communication as performed by individuals. In the next section, we expand the frame to explore how societal forces influence both performance and interpretation of nonverbal messages and behavior.

expressing and managing intimacy
using nonverbal behaviors to help convey attraction and closeness

establishing social control
using nonverbal behavior to exercise influence over other people

service-task functions
using nonverbal behavior to signal close involvement between people in impersonal relationships and contexts

THE INDIVIDUAL, NONVERBAL COMMUNICATION, AND SOCIETY

Nonverbal communication, like all communication, is heavily influenced by societal forces and occurs within a hierarchical system of meanings. One's status and position within the societal hierarchy, as well as one's identity, are all expressed nonverbally. However, the more powerful elements in society often regulate these expressions. In addition, nonverbal communication can trigger and express prejudice and discrimination. Let's see how this operates.

Nonverbal Communication and Power

Nonverbal communication and power are intricately related—especially via the nonverbal codes of appearance and artifacts. In the United States, power is primarily based on an individual's access to economic resources and the freedom to make decisions that affect others. Economic resources are typically revealed or expressed through nonverbal codes. Thus, people display wealth through the clothing they wear, the quality of their haircuts, and the value of their homes and cars. Whether one has the money to pay $100 for a haircut or goes regularly to Great Clips clearly communicates one's social class and power. English professor Paul Fussell (1992) provides an extensive description of how nonverbal messages communicated in our everyday lives reveal class standing. Consider, for example, the messages communicated by one's home. Fussell notes that the longer the driveway, the less obvious the garage, and the more manicured the grounds, the higher is one's socioeconomic class.

In addition to using nonverbals to communicate their own status and identities, people use them to evaluate and interpret others' status and identities. Based on these interpretations, people—consciously and unconsciously—include and exclude others, and approve or disapprove of others. For example, in wealthy communities, people who don't "look" affluent may be stopped and questioned about their presence or even be asked to leave. More overtly, gated communities offer clear nonverbal messages about who belongs and who does not. Of course, it isn't just the wealthy that use artifacts to convey their identity and belonging. Gang members, NASCAR fans, football fans, and many others use attire as well as gestures to signal their individual and group identities.

Although all groups use nonverbal communication to convey identity, more-powerful segments of society typically define what is allowed. Many corporations, for example, regulate the nonverbal expression of employees' identity through dress codes and policies on tattoos or body piercings, and some even regulate men's facial hair. Often, these policies are enacted to communicate a particular image to the public. For this reason, the military and many police organizations have policies on tattoos as well, and they enforce them (Zezima, 2005). Because these organizations are hierarchical, the decisions made by those in power must be followed by those who wish employment there.

Many individuals, such as football fans, use attire as well as gestures to signal their group identities.

Why do you think businesses institute policies regarding customers' attire? Do you think they should? Why or why not?

Businesses even develop policies that attempt to regulate nonverbal aspects of their *customers'* identities. Some restaurants require a coat and jacket for men, stores and other businesses implement "no shoes, no shirt, no service" policies, and some entertainment venues prohibit patrons from wearing ball caps or other types of informal wear (Walker, 2004). Mother's, a nightclub in Chicago, recently refused entrance to six Black college students on a school trip because they were wearing baggy jeans, which was a violation of the club's "baggy-jean policy." In this case, however, customers fought back and sued the club for discrimination. They did so because it is against the law to enact dress codes that have the effect of targeting a specific sex or cultural or racial group, and some believe that this is the intention of Mother's dress code (EOC, 2009; Kumar, 2009). Thus, organizations can control the ways in which employees and customers portray their identities, but there are limits to their doing so.

The more-powerful segments of society also define what is most desirable and attractive in our culture. For example, cosmetic corporations spend $231 billion annually to develop

beauty products in order to persuade consumers to buy them. The largest cosmetic companies have recently expanded to China, where the nation's 451 million women are of great interest to the cosmetic market—which was valued at $8 billion in 2006 (Carvajal, 2006). As discussed earlier, the media broadly communicate to us the definitions of beauty. This is why many U.S. Americans believe that blonde hair is better than brown, thin is better than fat, large breasts are better than small, and young is better than old—beliefs that are not universally shared. Messages promoting a specific type of youth and beauty might seem rather harmless, until one considers the consequences for those who are not thin and blonde, and especially those who have no possibility of meeting the dominant standards of beauty. How does this hierarchy of attractiveness affect their communication with others? Do people respond to them negatively because of their appearance? Might they feel marginalized and resentful—even before they interact with others who more clearly meet the dominant standards?

Nonverbal expressions are also an important part of cultural rituals involving societal expectations. In U.S. culture, it is not acceptable to wear white to a wedding, unless one is the bride; and typically only black or another dark color is considered appropriate for funerals. Aspects of dress are very important in the United States at other cultural events as well, particularly for women. The outfits worn to the Academy Awards and Golden Globe ceremonies are reviewed and evaluated and are a topic of great interest for many people. Similarly, what the president's wife wears on Inauguration Day and at subsequent parties is a subject of conversation; the media have frequently commented on Michelle Obama's attire, starting from when her husband was a presidential candidate and she appeared on television wearing a JCrew sweater. Societal forces drive this interest in particular nonverbal expressions. In all these cases, women know that their nonverbal messages will be carefully scrutinized and evaluated.

Nonverbal Communication, Prejudice, and Discrimination

At the intersection of societal forces and nonverbal communication are prejudice and discrimination. Both can be triggered by nonverbal behavior and are also expressed through nonverbal behavior. Let's look at how this works. First, one's race and ethnicity, body shape, age, or style of dress—all of which are communicated nonverbally—can prompt prejudgment or negative stereotyping. How often do people make a snap judgment or generalization based on appearance? Second, prejudice and discrimination are expressed nonverbally. In some extreme cases, nonverbal signals have even triggered and perpetrated hate crimes. For example, one night in Phoenix, Arizona, Avtar (Singh) Chiera, a small-business owner and a Sikh, waited outside his business for his son to pick him up. Two White men pulled up in a small red pickup truck, yelled at him, and then opened fire on him. Because of anger over the events of 9/11, the two men likely targeted him as an Arab because of his turban and beard, even though Sikhs are neither Arab nor Muslim (Parasuram, 2003). In this encounter, nonverbal messages were the most important; the words spoken (if any) were of minimal impact.

While the example given above is extreme, there are many other, more subtle ways that prejudice can be communicated nonverbally—for example, averting one's gaze or withholding a smile. It can be as subtle as leaning your body away or editing your speech. Sociologist A. G. Johnson (2001, pp. 58–59) gives a list of nonverbal behaviors that can be interpreted as prejudicial. These are mostly noticed only by the person experiencing them, and the person sending these messages often does so unconsciously and unintentionally:

- Not looking at people when we talk with them
- Not smiling at people when they walk into the room; staring as if to say, "What are you doing here?"; or stopping the conversation with a hush the newcomer has to wade through to be included in the smallest way
- Not acknowledging people's presence or making them wait as if they weren't there
- Not touching their skin when we give them something
- Watching them closely to see what they're up to
- Avoiding someone walking down the street, giving them a wide berth or even crossing to the other side

Given the power of nonverbal communication, you may find it helpful to consider how your nonverbal communication reflects your own ethical stance. To guide you in making appropriate choices, we explore the ethics of nonverbal communication in the next section.

ETHICS AND NONVERBAL COMMUNICATION

The ethics of nonverbal communication are actually quite similar to the ethics of communication in general. When people engage in unethical behavior, such as deceiving or threatening or name-calling, their nonverbal behavior typically plays a central role in their messages. For instance, liars use nonverbal behavior to avoid "leaking" the deception, and they may also use it to convey the deceptive message. Moreover, deceivers may feel that lying nonverbally—for example, by remaining silent—is less "wrong" than lying with words. In the Old Testament, Joseph's brothers were jealous of their father's affection for him, so they sold Joseph into slavery. When they returned without him, however, they didn't "tell" their father what happened; instead, they gave him Joseph's bloody coat and let their father draw the conclusion that an animal had killed Joseph. In this way, they deceived their father without actually speaking a lie—behavior that was just as unethical as if they had lied verbally.

Communicators can also behave unethically when they use nonverbals that ridicule, derogate, or otherwise demean. If you speak in a patronizing vocal tone, if you scream at the less powerful, or if you touch people inappropriately, you are engaging in unethical nonverbal communication. Similarly, if you respond to others' communication in a way that misrepresents how you actually feel, you are being unethical. Thus, if you laugh at a racist or sexist joke even though you dislike it, your behavior is unethical both because it derogates others and because it misrepresents your true reaction to the joke.

Here are some guidelines for making ethical choices regarding nonverbal communication: Consider whether

- your nonverbal behaviors reflect your real attitudes, beliefs, and feelings;
- your nonverbal behaviors contradict the verbal message you are sending;
- your nonverbal behaviors insult, ridicule, or demean others;
- you are using your nonverbal behavior to intimidate, coerce, or silence someone;
- you would want anyone to observe your nonverbal behavior;
- you would want this nonverbal behavior directed to you or a loved one.

Remember that you are just as responsible for your nonverbal communication as you are for your verbal communication. And resolve to approach both realms with the same degree of ethical concern.

IMPROVING YOUR NONVERBAL COMMUNICATION SKILLS

By now, you may be wondering how you've managed to negotiate the world of nonverbals at all. How do you decide, for example, if a masseuse's touch is appropriately (service-task) or inappropriately intimate? How can you determine if your subordinate genuinely likes you and your ideas (nonverbal involvement) or is trying to flatter you (social control)? To help you make such decisions more effectively, we offer the following suggestions for improving your ability to interpret others' nonverbal communication.

First, recognize that *cues can be misinterpreted*. If you tell a joke and a listener fails to laugh, don't assume that the person is disapproving or lacks a sense of humor. He or she may not have heard the joke, may not have understood it, or simply may be someone who does not laugh out loud when amused. It can be easy to misread a single nonverbal signal. The person's *overall* demeanor is far more telling than a single gesture viewed in isolation.

Because signals can be misread, it is important that you *read* **nonverbal behaviors** *as a group*. As we discussed earlier, a single gesture can be interpreted multiple ways. To more accurately interpret nonverbal behaviors, look at a variety of cues, from voice tone to body

nonverbal behavior
all the nonverbal actions people perform

tension to gaze. If you focus too much on a single cue, you might overlook others that contribute to or clarify the message.

In addition, you should *evaluate the context* in which the message occurs. You can improve your comprehension of nonverbal messages by analyzing the context, your knowledge of the other person, and your own experiences. For example, if you are playing basketball and a teammate slaps you on the rear and says "good job," the message may be clear. Given the context, you may read it as a compliment and perhaps a sign of affection or intimacy. But what if the slap on the rear occurs at work after an effective presentation? Given that such behavior is generally inappropriate in a business context, you will (and should) probably assess its meaning more closely. You might ask yourself whether this person simply lacks social skills and frequently engages in inappropriate behavior. If so, the message may be inappropriate but still be meant in a positive fashion. In contrast, if the person knows better and has touched you inappropriately at other times, the behavior may be intentionally designed to express inappropriate intimacy or social control.

It is also helpful to *look for congruency of behaviors.* One important way of assessing nonverbal communication is to examine how it interacts with the verbal messages you receive (Jones & LeBaron, 2002). That is, how congruent (similar) are the two sets of messages? When the two types of messages are **congruent**, you can be more confident that they are "real." For example, a positive verbal message (I like you) combined with a positive nonverbal message (smile, forward body lean, relaxed posture) conveys a more convincing positive message. Of course, verbal and nonverbal messages can also be **contradicting**. When using sarcasm, people intentionally combine a positive verbal message (I like your new hairstyle) with a contradictory or negative nonverbal message (a hostile tone). However, at other times, people offer contradictory messages unintentionally or carelessly. Caretakers often confuse children (and encourage misbehavior) by telling a child to stop a particular behavior while smiling or laughing. How does a child interpret this message? Most will accept the nonverbal aspect of the message and ignore the verbal (Eskritt & Lee, 2003).

If you have tried all of these strategies but you are still unsure, don't make an assumption; instead, *ask questions about nonverbal signals.* If you are confused, you can offer an interpretation and ask if you are correct. Thus, you could say, "So I understand you to be saying that you are ready to move forward on the contract. Is this correct?" Or you can ask a direct question, such as "You say you are happy to go to the party with me, but you don't really look happy. Can you tell me why?"

Finally, to improve your nonverbal communication interpretive skills, you need to *be mindful and practice.* Some people have a gift for interpreting nonverbal messages and seem capable of reading others "like a book." However, you can build this skill by paying careful attention to nonverbal behavior and practicing these tips.

congruent
verbal and nonverbal messages that express the same meaning

contradicting
verbal and nonverbal messages that send conflicting messages

SUMMARY

Nonverbals are an important component of communication. They help you interpret and understand verbal messages and, in doing so, help you more effectively navigate your everyday life. Studying nonverbals is particularly important because they are complex and ambiguous. Without sufficient understanding of how the various nonverbal codes work together in specific contexts, cultures, and relationships, one can easily misunderstand others' nonverbal messages or assume meaning where none exists.

Nonverbal communication is defined as all the messages that people transmit through means other than words, and it occurs when nonverbal behavior has symbolic meaning. To understand the meaning of a nonverbal behavior, you have to consider the entire behavioral context, including culture, relationship type, background knowledge, and gender. Nonverbal communication occurs through five codes or types of signals: kinesics, paralinguistics (vocal qualities), chronemics (time) and proxemics (space), haptics (touch), and appearance and artifacts. These codes can combine to serve one of five functions: communicating information,

regulating interaction, expressing and managing intimacy, exerting social control, and performing service-task functions.

As we've shown, nonverbal communication is not performed in a vacuum; rather, power relationships as well as societal norms and rules influence the range of nonverbal behaviors we are allowed to perform and how those behaviors are interpreted. In addition, everyone needs to be aware that nonverbal communication can trigger and express prejudice and discrimination. Thus, nonverbal communication has ethical aspects. Ethical considerations for nonverbal communication involve nonverbal "deception" and nonverbal behaviors that ridicule, derogate, or otherwise demean others.

You can become more effective in interpreting others' nonverbal communication by assessing the congruence of the verbal and nonverbal components of a message; analyzing the context, your knowledge of the other person, and your own experiences; and remembering that not every nonverbal behavior is intended to be communicative.

KEY TERMS

adaptors 83	gestures 83	polychronically 86
artifacts 90	haptics 89	professional touch 89
chronemics 85	illustrators 83	proxemics 85
communicating information 92	immediacy 83	public distance 86
congruent 97	intimate distance 86	regulating interaction 92
contradicting 97	kinesics 82	regulators 83
demand touching 90	love-intimate touch 89	relaxation 83
emblems 83	monochronically 86	service-task functions 93
establishing social control 93	nonverbal behavior 96	social distance 86
expressing and managing intimacy 93	nonverbal codes 82	social-polite touch 89
	nonverbal communication 78	vocalizations 85
friendship touch 89	paralinguistics 84	voice qualities 85
functional touch 89	personal distance 86	

REVIEW QUESTIONS

1. How does nonverbal communication differ from nonverbal behavior that is not communicative? Provide an example of each.

2. How does one's relationship with another person influence one's interpretation of that person's nonverbal communication?

3. What is kinesics? What are two general categories of kinesics?

4. What is nonverbal immediacy? How does liking typically affect one's nonverbal immediacy behaviors?

5. What is the difference between using time monochronically and polychronically?

6. What are artifacts, and how do they communicate status or class?

ACTIVITIES

1. **Waiting Times**
   How long is the "appropriate" amount of time you should wait in each of the following situations? Specifically, after how long a period would you begin to feel angry or put out?
   Estimate waiting times for:

   a. your dentist
   b. a checkout line in a department store
   c. a movie line
   d. a friend at lunch
   e. a friend at dinner
   f. being on hold on the telephone
   g. your professor to arrive at class
   h. a stop light
   i. your romantic partner at a bar
   j. your professor during office hours

   Do you see any patterns in your expectations for waiting times? What influences your expectations most? Your relationship with the other party? The comfort of the

waiting area? Your ability to control events? Compare your waiting times with others' to see how similar or different they are.

2. **Violating Norms for Proximity**. For this exercise, we would like you to violate some of the norms for spacing in your culture. Try standing slightly closer to a friend or family member than you normally would, then note how they react. If you have a romantic partner or very close friend, sit much farther from them than you normally would. For example, in a theater, sit one seat away from him or her, or sit at the opposite end of the couch if you would typically sit closer. Pay attention to the reactions you elicit. Finally, when talking with an acquaintance, increase the distance between you each time the other person tries to decrease it, and see how the other person responds. What do these responses to space violations reveal to you regarding the importance of spacing norms in the United States?

NOTE: Be careful in your selection of people with whom you violate norms of space, and be prepared to explain why you are behaving so "oddly".

WEB ACTIVITIES

1. http://www.presidentsusa.net/audiovideo.html Go to this Web site and compare the vocal qualities of four presidents—two presidents who served prior to the widespread use of television and two who have served since. What role do you think vocal versus visual cues played in the popularity of each president? Are there presidents whose appearance you find more appealing than their vocal qualities? Are there presidents whose vocal qualities you find more appealing than their appearance?

2. http://www.cio.com/article/facial-expressions-test The study of facial expressions of emotion is complex. However, we do typically associate some general features with particular emotions. Go to this Web site and perform the exercise described there. How accurate were you? Did you find one or more of the expressions easier to identify than the others?

3. **Cultural Differences in Nonverbal Communication**. Go to a search engine such as Google, and look for a Web site that explains the rules for nonverbal communication and behavior in a culture outside the United States with which you are not familiar. What rules surprised you? What rules were similar to the ones you use? What do you think would happen if you used your "normal" rules for nonverbal behavior in this culture?

5
LISTENING

I come from a family where we enjoy arguing about things like politics and religion. In my first college class, however, I found that people did not respond well to my comments. I felt like people weren't listening to what I said, and sometimes they looked away and wouldn't respond. After taking a class in communication and learning about bad listening habits and effective strategies, I realized that many of my fellow students didn't have very good listening skills, and that I, too, often don't listen to what others are saying because I'm always thinking of the next thing I'm going to say. It's hard, and it has taken conscious effort, but I've been trying to listen to what others say and acknowledge their thoughts before I respond. I think it's helped me a lot, because now I find the discussion in my classes more productive and interesting.

Listening may be the single most important skill in the communication process, but most of us, like our student Aisha, don't really think about it all that much. Why is this? Perhaps because it seems like a passive skill, unlike speaking or writing. Or perhaps we think that listening can't be taught or learned. After all, very few college courses teach listening theory and practice. However, as we'll discover in this chapter, a great deal of academic research focuses on the listening process, and communication experts have shown that being aware of the dynamics of listening and working on it can lead to much better communication overall.

In this chapter, we will first describe the process of listening. Then we'll identify five important reasons for improving our listening skills as well as some of the influences and barriers to effective listening. Finally, we'll discuss the role of societal forces in listening, ethical issues related to listening, and suggestions for becoming a more effective listener.

Once you have read this chapter, you will be able to:

- Describe the listening process.
- Identify reasons for learning about listening.
- Describe four listening styles.
- Describe three sets of listening skills.
- Analyze the influences on listening.
- Identify and describe barriers to effective listening.
- Understand the role of societal forces (power and privilege) in listening.
- Describe ethical challenges in listening.
- Discuss three ways to improve your own listening behavior.

CHAPTER OUTLINE

WHAT IS LISTENING?

THE IMPORTANCE OF LISTENING

LISTENING AND THE INDIVIDUAL
Influences on Listening
Barriers to Listening

THE INDIVIDUAL, LISTENING, AND SOCIETY
Social Hierarchy
Listening in Context
Listening and Community

ETHICS AND LISTENING

IMPROVING YOUR LISTENING SKILLS
Become Aware
Identify Poor Habits
Strive for Mindful Listening

Summary

Key Terms

Chapter Review Questions

Activities

Web Activities

listening
the process of receiving, constructing meaning from, and responding to spoken and/or nonverbal messages

sensing
the stage of listening most people refer to as "hearing"; when listeners pick up the sound waves directed toward them

understanding
interpreting the messages associated with sounds or what the sounds mean

evaluating
assessing your reaction to a message

responding
showing others how you regard their message

WHAT IS LISTENING?

The first step in striving to improve listening skills is to understand exactly what we mean when we talk about listening. Thus, we first provide a definition and then describe the process of listening.

While there are probably many definitions for **listening**, the one we'll use is provided by the International Listening Association. Listening is "the process of receiving, constructing meaning from, and responding to spoken and/or nonverbal messages" (An ILA Definition of Listening, 1995, p. 4). As you can see, this definition includes the concept described in Chapter 1 as the decoding phase of the communication process, and it involves four stages: *sensing, understanding, evaluating,* and *responding* (Rosenfeld & Berko, 1990). (See *Visual Summary 5.1: Stages of Listening.*) **Sensing** is the stage most people refer to as "hearing"; it occurs when listeners pick up the sound waves directed toward them. For example, even a "quiet" room has many sounds, such as the hum of heating or ventilation, quiet conversations, or the sounds of a radio. For communication to occur, you must first become aware that information is being directed at you. In other words, you have to hear the sounds. But of course, sensing or hearing something is not the same as understanding or evaluating the information—the next steps. This means that hearing is not the same as listening. Hearing is really only the first step.

Once you sense that sounds are occurring, you have to interpret the messages associated with the sounds—that is, you have to **understand** what the sounds mean. For example, you are alone watching a horror movie when you hear a knocking sound. What meaning do you assign it? Is it a friend dropping by to say hello, or a stranger trying to break into your house? The meaning you assign affects how you will respond—both physiologically and communicatively.

After you understand (or at least believe you understand) the message you have received, you **evaluate** the information. When you evaluate a message, you assess your reaction to it. For example: Do you believe the story Josie just told? Are you happy your boss recommended you for a promotion? Was the compliment you received sincere? Evaluation is an essential part of the listening process—and your evaluations influence your responses.

Finally, you **respond** to messages. Your response provides the most significant evidence that you are listening to others. Responding means that you show others how you regard their messages. For example, you might respond to a funny story by laughing, to a complaint with an apology, to an apology with forgiveness. Even failing to respond is a type of response! You can respond in numerous ways; however, your response may be influenced by *how* you listen.

Even though you might now understand the process of listening, like our student Aisha, you might not initially understand why it is important to learn about it. After all, listening seems rather automatic—something we don't think about very often. The next section shows, however, that improving our listening skills can lead to many personal and professional benefits.

THE IMPORTANCE OF LISTENING

The most important reason for learning more about listening is that we spend so much time doing it! Experts estimate that college students spend 55 percent of their total average communication day listening. About half that time is spent in interpersonal listening (class, face-to-face conversations, phone, listening to voice messages) and the other half in media listening. The rest of students' communication time is distributed in the following way: 16 percent speaking, 17 percent reading, and 11 percent writing (Emanuel, Adams, Baker, Daufin, Ellington et al., 2008). In addition to the pervasiveness of listening in our daily communication, there are five other important reasons for learning about listening: Better listening skills can lead to improved cognition, improved academic performance, enhanced personal relationships, enhanced professional performance, and even better health. Let's look at each of these in turn.

First, having better listening skills can improve your memory and give you a broader knowledge base and an increased attention span (Diamond, 2007, p. 18). The brain is like any other muscle; you have to use it to improve it. The more you work it, the better you'll

Stages of Listening

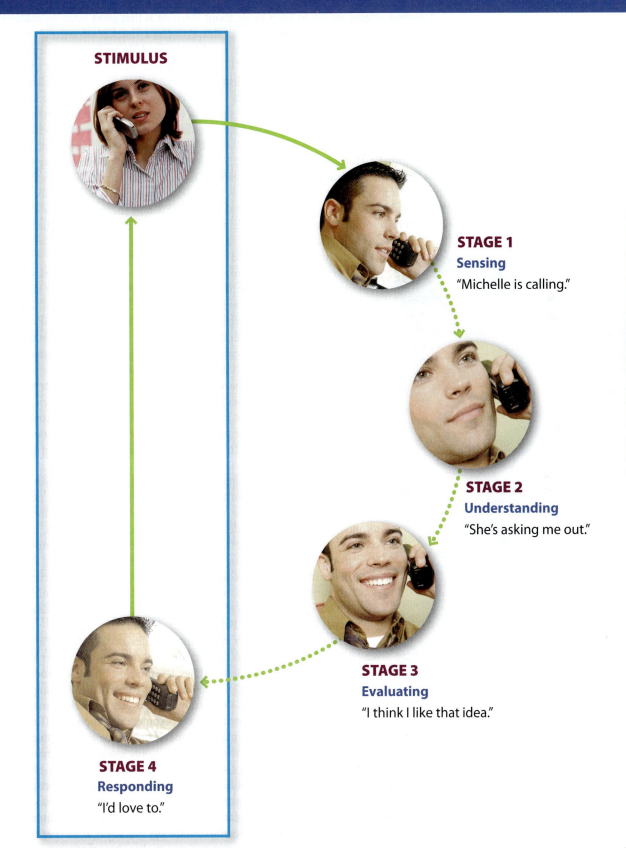

STIMULUS

STAGE 1
Sensing
"Michelle is calling."

STAGE 2
Understanding
"She's asking me out."

STAGE 3
Evaluating
"I think I like that idea."

STAGE 4
Responding
"I'd love to."

listening style
a set of attitudes, beliefs, and predispositions about the how, where, when, who, and what of the information receiving and encoding process

action-oriented listening style
listening style that reflects a preference for error-free and well-organized speaking

informational listening
listening skills that are useful in situations requiring attention to content

content-oriented listening style
a listening style that reflects an interest in detailed and complex information, simply for the content itself

critical listening
listening skills that are useful in a wide variety of situations—particularly those involving persuasive speaking

Influences on Listening

Not everyone listens in the same way; our personal listening habits may be influenced by gender, age, ethnicity, or even certain idiosyncratic patterns. Let's look first at the various listening styles and then turn to other characteristics that may influence how we listen.

Listening Styles

According to experts, a **listening style** is a set of "attitudes, beliefs, and predispositions about the how, where, when, who, and what of the information reception and encoding process" (Watson, Barker, & Weaver, 1995, p. 2). To put it more simply, it is "the way people prefer to receive oral information" (Watson et al., 1995, p. 9). Researchers have identified four listening styles used in various situations and find that individuals tend to prefer to use one (or two) of the styles over the others (Barker & Watson, 2000; Watson et al., 1995).

Each listening style emphasizes a particular set of skills, which are useful for particular situations. The point of this is not that you should strive to develop a particular style or that having a particular style ensures that you will be a good listener, but that your listening style should vary somewhat by context or situation. And, indeed, studies have shown that most people do vary their listening style from situation to situation (Imhof, 2004).

As you read the descriptions below, think about which style(s) you prefer. Which are you less likely to use? Which sets of skills might you need to work on to become a more effective listener?

Action-oriented listening style The **action-oriented listening style** reflects a preference for error-free and well-organized speaking. People using this style focus more on the content of the message than the person delivering it, and they want not only to hear the message, but to do something with it. They may get impatient if a speaker is not direct or concise enough.

The action-oriented style requires **informational listening** skills, useful in situations requiring attention to content. For example, at work, you probably listen primarily for content, to make sure you understand the instructions of your boss, supervisor, or coworkers. Informational listening skills are also useful at school, during course lectures or when professors give detailed instructions about assignments. How can you improve your informational listening skills? Here are some suggestions:

1. Attend to what the speaker is saying: Maintain eye contact; face the person, and lean toward them. Show the speaker that you *want* to understand what they are saying.
2. Don't judge the speaker prematurely. Making mental judgments can prevent you from understanding the content of the speaker's message.
3. Paraphrase: Reflect the speaker's words back to them to make sure you understand and to let the speaker know you are listening—for example, if your professor is describing instructions for an assignment, you might say, "You're saying that the 5-page paper is due tomorrow."
4. Clarify: Asking questions can clear up any confusion on your part or get you more information. For example, if you don't completely understand your professor's instructions, you might ask, "How should we submit the paper? Can we e-mail it to you, or do you want us to hand it in to you in class?"
5. Review and Summarize: Periodically review and summarize to make sure you understand the information. Summarizing captures the overall meaning of what has been said and puts it into a logical and coherent order, but summaries should not add any new information. After your summary, you might also ask, "Is that correct?" so that the speaker still has control. For example, you might say, "So we hand in a five-page paper to you in class tomorrow on the topics we discussed today? Is this correct?"

Content-oriented listening style The **content-oriented listening style** reflects an interest in detailed and complex information, simply for the content itself. People using this style prefer debate or argument content over simpler speech; they attend to details and are interested in the quality of the speech.

This style involves the informational listening skills detailed above and an additional set of **critical listening** skills (Mooney, 1996). These skills are useful in a wide variety of

Communication in SOCIETY

Effective Listening Skills of Managers

In the article summarized below, journalist Martin Kornacki describes the results of recent research emphasizing the importance of line (factory) managers' communication skills. Do you think these findings can be generalized to other work contexts? For example, supervisors in fast food restaurants? Supervisors of departments in white-collar professions?

According to new research findings, line managers' communication skills—especially listening skills—are particularly important during periods of economic downturns.

In a recent news article, journalist Martin Kornacki describes a research study that found that employees who believe that their managers listen to them and answer questions honestly have greater confidence in their organization's future, which then translates into commitment to the organization, and greater productivity—even if the economic outlook is uncertain.

The key seems to be good relationships between managers and workers—fostered by listening skills. Kornacki also interviewed clinical psychologist Dr Amy Silver, who has worked with organizations in turbulent situations. She emphasizes the role of active listening in establishing solid trusting relationships between line managers and line workers. According to Dr. Silver, the best relationships—characterized by genuineness, empathy and rapport—are built from "active listening by both parties, with slightly more emphasis on the more powerful party to do so." She goes on to say that it's called active listening "because it is easy to listen, but not so easy to truly listen." She also points to many research studies that demonstrate that the quality of the relationship is crucial in determining productivity in business contexts.

Kornacki concludes that companies who do not invest in improving managers' communication skills are generally less productive and these differences between good and poor business practices are highlighted during economic recessions.

SOURCE: Kornacki, M. (2009, April 20). "Managers' communication skills put under scrutiny by new research." *TJ online*. Retrieved January 21, 2010 from http://www.trainingjournal.com/news/2069.html#

attentively, heart rate and oxygen consumption are reduced, which leads to increased blood and oxygen to the brain—a healthy cardiovascular condition (Diamond, 2007, p. 17). James J. Lynch (1985), a renowned psychologist, conducted pioneering research showing that human interaction (or the lack of it) can dramatically affect cardiovascular systems. He described an experiment where patients with hypertension were hooked up to a computerized blood-pressure-monitoring system and then conversed with the experimenter. The result was that when the patients talked about their own problems, their blood pressure increased to high levels. However, when the experimenter distracted the patients by telling them a nonthreatening personal story or reading a passage from a book, the patients' blood pressure dropped to much-lower levels. Lynch explains that these drops in blood pressure occurred because the patients momentarily focused on something outside themselves—listening to and interacting with the experimenter (cited by Shafir, 2000, p. 241). These results seem to show that listening—an important aspect of personal connectedness—can play a part in human health.

Now that we've described the listening process and the importance of learning about listening, the next section shows how an individual's personal characteristics influence the listening process. We also describe how different situations require different types of listening skills.

LISTENING AND THE INDIVIDUAL

Perhaps you can think of some people you know to be good listeners and others who are not so good. Perhaps you find it easier to listen in some situations and not others. In the next section, we describe factors that influence whether listening in any particular situation is easier or more difficult, including such factors as individual listening styles and individual characteristics such as gender, age, and nationality. Finally, we discuss physical and psychological listening barriers.

listening style
a set of attitudes, beliefs, and predispositions about the how, where, when, who, and what of the information receiving and encoding process

action-oriented listening style
listening style that reflects a preference for error-free and well-organized speaking

informational listening
listening skills that are useful in situations requiring attention to content

content-oriented listening style
a listening style that reflects an interest in detailed and complex information, simply for the content itself

critical listening
listening skills that are useful in a wide variety of situations—particularly those involving persuasive speaking

Influences on Listening

Not everyone listens in the same way; our personal listening habits may be influenced by gender, age, ethnicity, or even certain idiosyncratic patterns. Let's look first at the various listening styles and then turn to other characteristics that may influence how we listen.

Listening Styles

According to experts, a **listening style** is a set of "attitudes, beliefs, and predispositions about the how, where, when, who, and what of the information reception and encoding process" (Watson, Barker, & Weaver, 1995, p. 2). To put it more simply, it is "the way people prefer to receive oral information" (Watson et al., 1995, p. 9). Researchers have identified four listening styles used in various situations and find that individuals tend to prefer to use one (or two) of the styles over the others (Barker & Watson, 2000; Watson et al., 1995).

Each listening style emphasizes a particular set of skills, which are useful for particular situations. The point of this is not that you should strive to develop a particular style or that having a particular style ensures that you will be a good listener, but that your listening style should vary somewhat by context or situation. And, indeed, studies have shown that most people do vary their listening style from situation to situation (Imhof, 2004).

As you read the descriptions below, think about which style(s) you prefer. Which are you less likely to use? Which sets of skills might you need to work on to become a more effective listener?

Action-oriented listening style The **action-oriented listening style** reflects a preference for error-free and well-organized speaking. People using this style focus more on the content of the message than the person delivering it, and they want not only to hear the message, but to do something with it. They may get impatient if a speaker is not direct or concise enough.

The action-oriented style requires **informational listening** skills, useful in situations requiring attention to content. For example, at work, you probably listen primarily for content, to make sure you understand the instructions of your boss, supervisor, or coworkers. Informational listening skills are also useful at school, during course lectures or when professors give detailed instructions about assignments. How can you improve your informational listening skills? Here are some suggestions:

1. Attend to what the speaker is saying: Maintain eye contact; face the person, and lean toward them. Show the speaker that you *want* to understand what they are saying.
2. Don't judge the speaker prematurely. Making mental judgments can prevent you from understanding the content of the speaker's message.
3. Paraphrase: Reflect the speaker's words back to them to make sure you understand and to let the speaker know you are listening—for example, if your professor is describing instructions for an assignment, you might say, "You're saying that the 5-page paper is due tomorrow."
4. Clarify: Asking questions can clear up any confusion on your part or get you more information. For example, if you don't completely understand your professor's instructions, you might ask, "How should we submit the paper? Can we e-mail it to you, or do you want us to hand it in to you in class?"
5. Review and Summarize: Periodically review and summarize to make sure you understand the information. Summarizing captures the overall meaning of what has been said and puts it into a logical and coherent order, but summaries should not add any new information. After your summary, you might also ask, "Is that correct?" so that the speaker still has control. For example, you might say, "So we hand in a five-page paper to you in class tomorrow on the topics we discussed today? Is this correct?"

Content-oriented listening style The **content-oriented listening style** reflects an interest in detailed and complex information, simply for the content itself. People using this style prefer debate or argument content over simpler speech; they attend to details and are interested in the quality of the speech.

This style involves the informational listening skills detailed above and an additional set of **critical listening** skills (Mooney, 1996). These skills are useful in a wide variety of

Stages of Listening

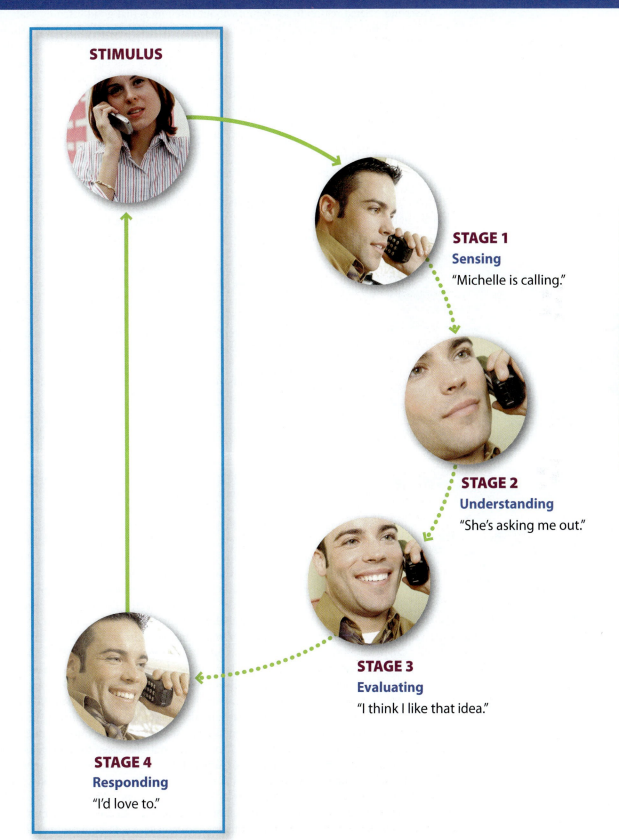

STIMULUS

STAGE 1
Sensing
"Michelle is calling."

STAGE 2
Understanding
"She's asking me out."

STAGE 3
Evaluating
"I think I like that idea."

STAGE 4
Responding
"I'd love to."

be able to process and remember information (Janusik, 2005b). The first step in working the brain, as Aisha discovered, is to pay better attention when others are speaking. You can't remember something if you've never learned it, and you can't learn something—that is, encode it into your brain—if you don't pay enough attention to it.

A second, related reason to learn more about listening is that good listening skills can enhance academic performance. Perhaps not surprisingly, a number of research studies have shown that college students who have good listening skills are better students than those who are less effective listeners (Beall, Gill-Rosier, Tate, & Matten, 2008). For example, in one study, college students were given a listening test after their first year of college. The results showed that almost half the students (49 percent) who scored low on the listening test were on academic probation, while only 4 percent of those who scored high were in that situation. Conversely, 69 percent of those who scored high on the listening test were in the honors program, while only 4 percent of the low scorers had achieved academic honors status (Bommelje, Houston, & Smither, 2003). With these figures in mind, you may wonder whether someone can learn to be a good listener. The most recent research shows that one of the most important outcomes of classes on listening is that students become more aware of what constitutes good listening (Beall et al., 2008). This may mean that while a college course can help you identify the skills needed to be a good listener, like Aisha—the student in the chapter opening—you may need a lot of practice and attention to skill building on your own to become an effective listener.

Better listening is also linked to enhanced personal relationships—a third reason to learn more about listening. In earlier chapters, we have discussed how effective communication skills can lead to enhanced personal relationships. This is also true for listening skills (Imhof & Janusik, 2006). It's easy to understand how better listening could lead to fewer misunderstandings, which in turn can lead to greater satisfaction, happiness, and a sense of well-being for us and those we care about (Diamond, 2007, p. 14).

Business professionals have long emphasized that effective listening is a highly desirable workplace skill; in fact, the *Harvard Business Review*, one of the most respected business journals, has published 43 articles containing "listen" as a key word in the past 50 years (Flynn, Valikoski, & Grau, 2008, p. 142). Effective listening in the workplace starts in the hiring process. Employers place high importance on oral communication skills (including listening) and look for listening skills when hiring potential employees. Once on the job, listening skills are an important part of effective work performance; studies show that for many professionals—including information technology professionals, safety managers, manufacturing agents, business coaches, and change managers, to name a few—effective work performance is positively related to listening ability (Flynn et al., 2008). Listening skills are particularly important in medical contexts (Holmes, 2007). Physicians with good listening skills have more satisfied patients, and better listening skills can even have monetary value; doctors with better listening skills have fewer malpractice lawsuits (Davis, Foley, Crigger, & Brannigan, 2008).

What makes listening so important in professional contexts? Part of the reason may lie in the fact that (as with personal relationships) better listening at work means fewer misunderstandings, less time lost on the job, and greater productivity (Diamond, 2007). Listening seems to play an interesting role in career advancement as well. One study showed that as workers move into senior-level management, listening skills become more important (Brownell, 1994). This may be because managers spend more time listening than other employees, and in addition, they need to not only listen for information but

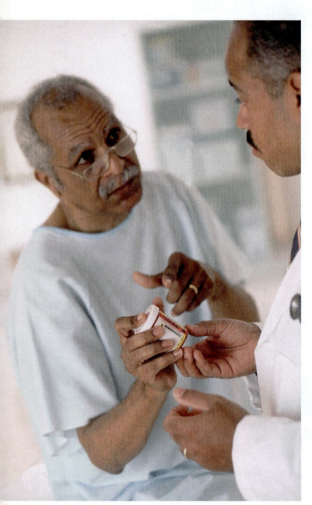

Good listening skills are particularly important in medical contexts. Better listening means fewer misunderstandings and ultimately better health outcomes.

also demonstrate empathy in their listening (Kotter, 1982; Nichols, 1995; Sypher, 1984). As shown in *Communication in Society: Effective Listening Skills of Managers*, when managers use effective listening skills, they are not only likely to develop good relationships with their employees, they also encourage productivity—particularly important during economic downturns.

Finally, you may not know that good listening can actually lead to improved health—our final reason for learning how to be a better listener. Some studies show that when we listen

situations—particularly those involving persuasive speaking—for example, when you are listening to a political speech, a sales pitch, or even in more informal settings, such as when friends or acquaintances try to persuade you to see their point of view about an issue or activity. Consider these suggestions for developing critical listening skills:

1. Consider the speaker's credibility: Is this speaker qualified to make these arguments? Is this speaker trustworthy?
2. Listen between the lines. Are the words and the body language consistent? Are the content and the emotion in harmony?
3. Evaluate the messages being sent and their implications. Ask yourself, "What conclusions can be drawn from what is being said? Where is this leading?"
4. Weigh the evidence. Does what is being said make sense? Are the speaker's opinions logical? Are they supported by fact?
5. Periodically review and summarize. As with informational listening, you need to periodically check to make sure you understand the message. Ask yourself, "Do I have it straight? Do I understand the speakers' arguments and main points?"

People-oriented listening style People using a **people-oriented listening style** are interested in hearing about others' experiences, thoughts, and feelings, and finding areas of common interest. This style is often associated with friendly, open communication and an interest in establishing ties with others rather than in controlling them (Villaume & Bodie, 2007). The people-oriented style is particularly useful in informal personal situations, when listening to friends and/or relational partners. People-oriented listening involves **supportive listening** skills, focused not only on understanding information but also "listening" to others' feelings—which they may communicate nonverbally, as we've seen in Chapter 4. Consider the following suggestions for effective supportive listening (Fowler, 2005; Salem, 2003). Notice also how many of them involve nonverbal behaviors on the listener's part, and also the overlap with informational listening skills:

1. Put the other person at ease. Give them space and time and "permission to speak." Do this by showing them that you *want* to hear them. Look at them. Nod when you can agree. Encourage them to talk.
2. Remove distractions. Be willing to turn off the TV, close a door, stop texting on your cell phone, or stop reading your mail. Let them know that they have your full attention.
3. Empathize with the other person. Especially if they are telling you something personal or painful, take a moment to stand in their shoes, to look at the situation from their point of view. Empathy can be expressed by (a) being a sounding board, which means allowing the person to talk, while maintaining a nonjudgmental, noncritical manner; (b) resisting the impulse to discount the person's feelings with stock phrases like "it's not really that bad" or "you'll feel better tomorrow"; and (c) paraphrasing what you think the person really means or feels. This can help the person clarify his/her thoughts and/or feelings—for example, "It sounds like you're saying you feel overwhelmed with the new project"—and communicates that you understand the emotions/feelings involved.
4. Be patient. Some people take longer to find the right word, make a point, or clarify an issue.
5. Watch your own emotions. As we'll discuss later in the chapter, emotions can be a barrier to effective listening. If what the speaker is saying creates an emotional response in you, listen very carefully to get the full meaning of the words.

Time-oriented listening style The **time-oriented listening style** prefers brief, concise speech. Time-oriented listeners don't want to waste time on complex details; they just want the bullet points. They may check their watches when they think someone is taking too long to get to the point. They may also state how much time they have for an interaction in order to keep the interaction concise and to the point. No specific set of skills accompanies this style; in fact, this style seems to involve rather ineffective listening behavior, except in situations where time is of the essence and concise information is imperative (e.g., emergency situations). If

people-oriented listening style
a listening style that is associated with friendly, open communication and an interest in establishing ties with others

supportive listening
listening skills focused not only on understanding information but also "listening" to others' feelings

time-oriented listening style
a listening style that prefers brief, concise speech

you tend to prefer this style in many situations, you may want to consider which of the other three styles may be more effective.

In conclusion, to become a more effective listener in a variety of personal and professional contexts, identify your preferred style(s) and then work on developing the skill sets that accompany the other styles. For example, if you tend to be a people-oriented listener, you might improve your informational and critical listening skills. On the other hand, if you tend to prefer the content-oriented style, you might work to develop your supportive listening skills.

In the next section, we turn to other individual influences on listening behaviors. How do individual identity characteristics such as gender, age, and ethnicity affect listening behaviors? Do males and females tend to listen differently? Do older people listen in a different way than do younger people? And a related set of questions: Should we adapt our listening behaviors depending on who we are listening to? For example, should we listen to children differently from adults? Let's look at how the experts weigh in on answers to these questions.

Gender

Some scholars think that, in general, men and women not only differ in their listening styles, but that women tend to be better listeners than men. Other researchers have found no gender differences in listening behavior (Imhof, 2004; Pearce, Johnson, & Barker, 2003). Before looking at the research on this topic, let's discuss the issue of gender stereotypes—the common perceptions people have concerning gender and listening.

Two communication scholars have identified common gender-based listening stereotypes: Men, they say, are supposedly logical, judgmental, interrupting, inattentive, self-centered, and impatient, whereas women are emotional, noninterrupting, attentive, empathetic, other-centered, responsive, and patient (Barker & Watson, 2000). Just by reading these stereotypes, you may think that women are better listeners than men, and many people do seem to hold this belief (Brownell, 1994; Pearce et al., 2003). Nevertheless, researchers have only documented three areas of gender differences in listening behavior: Women are more accommodating and focused on the speaker, men focus on facts and handle distractions better, and men interrupt more than women.

Apparently, some of these differences have roots in biological characteristics of males and females. Take the findings that women tend to be more other-oriented, empathetic, and responsive listeners (focused on relationships and people) and that men focus on facts when listening (Johnston, Weaver, Watson, & Barker, 2000; Silverman, 1970; Villaume & Bodie, 2007). The explanations for these differences may lie in the brain. Some scientists suggest that, in processing language, men use the left hemisphere, while women use both the left and right hemispheres. Scientists also know that data can move easily between the right and left hemispheres. Because of this, women may connect words and feelings more easily than men, which may lead to the perception that they are more feeling oriented and responsive than men in their listening behavior.

In addition, this biological difference may also lead to the stereotype that men focus on facts and women on relationships. Because men use one brain hemisphere to process information and women use two, men can more easily tune out some messages and focus on one message at a time, recalling general ideas and paying little attention to details (Barker & Watson, 2000). Here's an example of these differences (Barker & Watson, 2000, p. 131):

What Gustavo might tell his good friend Natalie:

G: I saw your aunt today.
N: Where did you see her?
G: At the grocery store.
N: Oh, really. What did she say?
G: Not much, just asked if you and I were going to stop by during our school vacation and something about stocking up for the holidays.

What Natalie would relate to her good friend Gustavo:

I saw my aunt at the grocery store today. She was shopping to beat the holiday rush and wanted to make sure she bought the grandchildren's favorite foods. She reminded me to prepare my special chocolate decadence dessert to bring when we stop to see them. She

told me she's cooking a standing rib roast and doesn't want it to take as long to cook as it did the last time we had a family gathering.

> *G:* What did you tell her?
>
> *N:* I said I'd have to call her because I still have a term paper to write, and I know you're working on Saturday, and I was thinking of going to the movies with a friend on Sunday.

Do these conversations sound typical? While it is possible that Natalie asked more questions or the aunt was more willing to talk with Natalie than with Gustavo, these conversations seem to demonstrate the conventional notion that females listen for relational details, and males recall general ideas and pay little attention to details—particularly in a relational context. As we've discussed in earlier chapters, most behavioral scientists believe that, while some innate gender differences may exist, most behavioral differences between men and women are more influenced by cultural norms than biology (Janusik, 2005a). Thus, even though biology might account for some differences in listening behavior, most adult behaviors are a complex combination of biology and societal influences. In many cultures, women are socialized to be more considerate, cooperative, helpful, and sympathetic, as Natalie may be demonstrating in the examples above. It is easy to see why—with the biological differences in brain and cognitive processes as a starting point, and cultural encouragement to reinforce these differences—women are regarded as more effective listeners.

To sum it up, there do seem to be a few gender differences in listening behaviors, but both men and women can demonstrate feminine *and* masculine listening behaviors. Remember, too, that gender differences are not fixed; people of both genders can learn to be effective listeners (Barker & Watson, 2000; Nichols, 1995). For a discussion on improving your listening skills across genders, see *Building Your Communication Skills: Do's and Don'ts for Improving Listening between Men and Women.*

Building Your Communication **SKILLS**

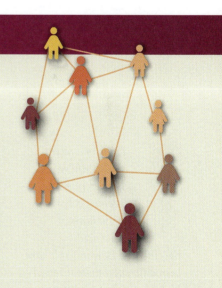

Do's and Don'ts for Improving Listening between Men and Women

1. DON'T automatically assume that men and women listen differently. Holding onto rigid assumptions and stereotypes about gender can prevent you from focusing on and understanding others' messages.

2. DO accept that there may be some gender differences in listening. As we've noted, there may be some biological and societal bases for some gender behaviors. So, don't get annoyed if a woman seems to respond emotionally, and don't get annoyed when a male listener focuses mostly on task details. The bottom line is to be open to variation in listening behaviors.

3. DO examine whether you demonstrate ineffective behaviors that reinforce gender stereotypes and try to eliminate these behaviors. For example, women should try to not be inappropriately emotional; men should try to not interrupt, etc.

4. DO practice good listening skills, regardless of their association with gender. For example, good listening skills include empathy. While empathy is usually associated with women, it's one of the most effective ways to improve a relationship, and everyone can practice putting themselves "in the speaker's shoes" and trying to see things from the speaker's perspective. By the same token, listening for details, a behavior associated with males, can be a very useful for both male and female listeners in many situations.

SOURCES: http://www.associatedcontent.com/article/54347/gender_differences_in_communication.html?cat= 41; http://books.google.com/books?id=hMNUzO_L6MgC&pg=PA138&lpg=PA138&dq=improving+listening+ between+men+and+women&source=bl&ots=aZU2aEz-9_&sig=yJLfRusPp8bj3c9O46x4mBdmb_s&hl=en&ei= BKd_TL7oAYH7lwemg4iqDg&sa=X&oi=book_result&ct=result&resnum=10&ved=0CDsQ6AEwCQ#v=onepage& q=improving%20listening%20between%20men%20and%20women&f=false; http://www.simmalieberman.com/ articles/genderstrategies.html.

Age

Do you listen differently to your parents than you do to your younger siblings? The fact is that people have different communication capacities and skill levels during various life stages, which means that we often adapt our listening behaviors depending on the age of the speaker (Nichols, 1995). For example, because young children are in the process of developing their communication skills, they sometimes struggle to interpret the meanings of others and to follow adult conversational norms—that is, to listen when others are speaking, not to interrupt, and to respond to instructions. So, yes, we can and should adapt our listening behaviors for children (Barker & Watson, 2000). First, be patient when they are struggling to say something; children have more to say than they can express. You can demonstrate patience and involvement by maintaining eye contact when they're speaking and asking questions. As one communication expert says, "A listened-to child is a confident child" (Nichols, 1995, p. 32). Second, be aware of the impact your feedback and responses have; children tend to think literally. If you tell them that a big bad witch is going to come and take them away if they misbehave, they may believe you.

Teenagers may also require some special listening behaviors. In many cultures, including that of the United States, teenagers are in a crucial stage of learning to be independent. Part of this process may involve closing off channels of communication or being critical of parents and other adults (Nichols, 1995). As with children, listening effectively to teenagers involves patience and restraint—not asking too many questions or giving too much criticism, being available to listen when the teen wants to talk, and acknowledging when the teenager acts responsibly (Barker & Watson, 2000; Nichols, 1995).

Our potential for effective listening seems to increase as we grow into adulthood; for example, college seniors are better listeners than college freshmen (Aurand, Ridnour, Timm & Kaminski, 2000). But these capacities may also diminish as we grow even older. At least one study found that younger managers (under age 45) were better listeners than older managers (Brownell, 2002). And as we get older, listening may become more difficult if hearing ability is an issue (we'll discuss hearing disability in the next section, under barriers to listening). However, not everyone who is old is deaf. Assuming that they are—that is, yelling and treating the listener like a child—can be hurtful and insulting.

Nationality

Do people in other countries listen differently? If so, one difference may lie in what people consider appropriate nonverbal expressions of listening (Pearce et al., 2003; Thomlison, 1996). In most Western cultures, good listening is demonstrated by eye contact, head nods, and some back-channeling vocalizations (hmmm, oh, etc.). However, in some countries, like Vietnam and Thailand, good listening behavior (listening respectfully) involves avoiding eye contact. In yet other countries, like Japan, good listening may involve lots of head nods, back channeling and even saying "yes, yes," which actually means "I hear you," not "I agree with you" (Fujii, 2008). We'll explore more cross-cultural differences in communication patterns in the following chapter.

However, to summarize, factors that can influence an individual's listening behavior include gender, age, ethnicity, and/or nationality, as well as one's own listening-style preferences and the particular situation. Still, one cannot assume that an individual will listen in a particular way just because she or he belongs to a certain gender, age, or nationality group. Listening is a complex behavior, and numerous factors beyond these kinds of identity characteristics can serve as barriers—the topic we turn to next.

Barriers to Listening

Like our student in the opening vignette, people have many reasons for not listening to others, but some typical ones include physical and physiological barriers, psychological barriers, conflicting objectives, and poor listening habits (Active Listening, 1999; Nichols, 1995). Let's explore in more detail how these factors can interfere with effective listening.

Physical and Physiological Barriers

Physical barriers to listening include a noisy environment or physical discomforts that make it difficult to concentrate. We have all had the experience of trying to listen to someone in a noisy bar or in a room with a loud television or while standing outside with traffic

Think of a recent conflict you've had. and describe how listening behaviors might have influenced the outcome. How might it have been different if those involved had spent more time listening instead of talking?

whizzing by on a busy highway. Physical barriers are the most elemental; if we can't hear because of the noise around us, it doesn't matter how refined our listening skills are.

Another physical barrier is tiredness. Whether one's tiredness is caused by lack of sleep or high stress, it can be a barrier to good listening. For example, it's difficult for students to listen effectively in class when they're exhausted; and it's difficult for parents to listen to children when they are stressed out from working hard and managing their many responsibilities. As we hope you understand by now, listening well takes effort and requires alertness and focus—both of which may be absent when one is tired.

A second type of listening barrier is physiological—for example, a hearing disability. While we often assume that good listening is a skill, listening is also impacted strongly by a person's physical ability to hear. The American Speech and Hearing Association estimates that over 30 million people in the U. S. have a hearing loss that could be treated (see *Did You Know? Statistically Speaking, How Many People Are Deaf or Hard of Hearing?*). Unfortunately, many people with hearing loss do not have it treated—whether because of vanity (not wanting to wear a hearing aid), lack of funds, or ignorance

Noise is a common physical barrier to listening; if we can't hear because of the noise around us, it doesn't matter how refined our listening skills are.

DID YOU KNOW?

Statistically Speaking, How Many People Are Deaf or Hard of Hearing?

While listening is generally viewed as a skill, an alternative view is that listening is also impacted strongly by a person's physical ability to hear. This author addresses the question What is the biggest statistical mystery in the deaf and hard-of-hearing community of the United States (and the world)? and tells us that there is little agreement on the answer. How often do you assume that the person listening to you has no hearing impairment? How might this assumption influence the outcomes of your communication encounters?

How many of us there are? No one really knows. There are some demographic statistics available, but they are either outdated or unreliable because some people may not wish to identify themselves as having a hearing loss, or the question forms may not ask directly if a person has a hearing loss. The estimated demographic figure has ranged from 22 million deaf and hard of hearing to as high as 36 million deaf and hard of hearing. Of these, only a few million are considered "deaf" and the remainder are hard of hearing. Further muddying statistics is the fact that some "deaf" people may actually be hard of hearing, and some "hard of hearing" people may actually be deaf. There are certainly enough of us with hearing losses that companies recognize the potential purchasing power of such a large segment of society . . .

While most people with hearing loss are older folks who have lost hearing with age, approximately 12 out of every 1,000 persons with hearing impairment is under 18 years of age, based on the most recently available NCHS statistics. That means that the chances are excellent that at least one student in your child's school will have a hearing loss.

The Census Bureau offers demographical statistics on disability and employment, taken from a Survey of Income and Program Participation (participation in public assistance programs). That data has numbers only in the thousands, rather than the millions. One interesting pattern that emerges from this statistical data set is that people with less severe hearing loss are more likely to be employed than those with more severe hearing impairments.

SOURCE: Berke, J. (2007, December 2). "Statistically, how many deaf or hard of hearing?" Retrieved May 21, 2009 from http://deafness.about.com/cs/earbasics/a/demographics.htm

about the disability. Getting over this barrier may mean recognizing and treating the disability, or, in the case of mild impairment, asking people to speak up.

Psychological Barriers

Common psychological barriers that prevent us from listening effectively are boredom and preoccupation. The human mind can process information at a rate of about 600 words per minute, while people speak an average of about 100 to 140 words per minute. Consequently, your mind has plenty of time to wander, and you can easily become distracted or bored, which will certainly undermine the amount that you listen to and retain.

A second, related psychological barrier is preoccupation. During an interaction, people often think of other things and, thus, do not listen to what is being said. Preoccupation can be caused by having an extensive to-do list and feeling stressed about getting it all done, for example. Three other common sources of preoccupation include having a personal agenda in a conversation (Shafir, 2000, p. 62), being emotional, and having conflicting objectives. How can having a personal agenda in a conversation lead to preoccupation and inattentive listening? As one example, let's say you've just met someone in a social setting who is the head of a corporation where you would like to work. During your conversation, you do your best to impress her as she talks about her professional activities and ideas; you smile, nod enthusiastically, and try to act in a professional manner. However, when you finally get to speak, you repeat ideas that she has just expressed or ask questions that she has already answered. Why? Because you weren't listening; you were too preoccupied with your own agenda to hear what she was saying. In this case, you probably didn't do the one thing you wanted to do—impress her. These kinds of listening failures can lead to frustration and maybe even feelings of low self-worth. What is the lesson, then? Listeners do better to put their own goals aside during a conversation and focus on the priorities and concerns of their conversational partner.

A second source of preoccupation comes from strong emotions. Anger or fear or even joy, for example, can make a person too preoccupied to listen and can also influence how he or she understands and reacts to messages (Nichols, 1995). If you are frustrated or irritable, you are more likely to interpret casual comments as criticism. On the other hand, if something wonderful has just happened to you, you may be concentrating on your good news and how you are going to celebrate, rather than focusing on the speaker. Thus, a wide variety of emotions can distract you and influence how you listen and respond in communicative interactions.

Emotions can also make people defensive and thus impair their listening abilities. Defensive listening occurs when someone perceives, anticipates, or experiences a threat (Eadie, 1982; Gibb, 1961). In such cases, the listener often puts up a "wall" for protection. These walls can distort incoming messages, leading to misinterpretation. For example, one of our colleagues described how her emotional reactions to her father hindered her ability to listen to him: "We had such a rotten relationship that every time he even opened his mouth to speak, I was so defensive, so sure he was going to criticize me or yell at me that I never even heard a word he said." Some people are more defensive than others; their personalities and experiences have influenced them to respond defensively to many messages. However, certain types of messages are more likely to elicit defensive listening. As we discussed in Chapter 3, messages that are evaluative, controlling, superior, or dogmatic tend to prompt a defensive reaction.

Preconceived ideas about issues or participants can also trigger strong emotions. For example, sometimes we allow a negative past experience with a person to interfere; that is, if you expect your sibling (or father) to be angry at you, you will likely interpret any comment as hostile—as was the case with our colleague and her father, described above. For another example, if you are usually sarcastic, then others are likely to hear even your compliments as insults. Unfortunately, people often find it difficult to acknowledge their own preconceptions, let alone recognize those of others. Good advice here is to use your past experience to help you learn about the world, but do not rely on it as your only source for evaluating a present situation.

The psychological barriers discussed here can act as "filters that allow only selected words and ideas into our consciousness . . . [they can also] screen out the less comfortable and uncomfortable messages, [so that] only pieces of messages are received—the comfortable pieces" (Shafir, 2000, p. 47). The end result is that these barriers can stifle the potential for developing meaningful relationships and new ideas. Later in the chapter, we'll see how some barriers, reinforced by societal hierarchies, are so impenetrable that they totally restrict certain

Review the listening barriers described here. Which do you most commonly experience? Which do you think are the most difficult to overcome?

persons from entering our ear space—for example, people who differ from us in race, physical ability, or social class.

Conflicting Objectives

A third barrier to listening involves conflicting objectives. How people understand and react to others' communicative attempts depends in part on their objective(s) for the conversation. For example, how do you listen to a lecture when your instructor announces, "This will be on the midterm"? How do you listen when told the material will not be on a test? Your different objectives for these situations likely influence how well you listen.

Sometimes participants in a conversation differ in their objectives for an interaction. For example, during a business meeting, Hank's objective was to explain a new procedure for evaluating employees, while Roberta's objective was to get a raise. Consequently, they focused on different aspects of their conversation, assigned different meanings to what occurred, and remembered different aspects of the meeting. Of course, people may have multiple objectives for an interaction, each of which will influence how they listen and respond.

Poor Listening Habits

As it turns out, people can more easily define poor listening than effective listening. Similarly, people can more easily identify the listening habits and flaws of others than they can their own, as was the case for Aisha in our opening story; she saw other students' poor listening behaviors before she recognized her own. The same is true for the subjects in the study described in *Building Your Communication Skills: Are You an Ineffective Listener?* Can you think of other annoying habits you would like to add to this top-ten list? Are you guilty of any of these? Most of us are.

As Aisha learned, the most important way to avoid these bad habits is to first become more aware of our own listening behavior and to really focus on the other speaker rather than on our own thoughts, feelings, and what *we're* going to say next. As we've mentioned, however, societal factors can have an important impact on one's ability to listen effectively, and this is the subject we turn to next.

Building Your Communication **SKILLS**

Are You an Ineffective Listener?

Five common ineffective listening behaviors can prevent you from getting a speaker's message. Look at each one and ask yourself: (1) Am I ever guilty of doing this? If yes, (2) think about situations in which you're most likely to engage in this particular behavior, and (3) identify ways you might correct the behavior. For example, perhaps you tend to mentally second-guess, predict what the speaker is going to say in social situations when you are hanging out with your friends. You may even interrupt or finish the other's sentences. One way to correct this habit is to resolve not to say anything until the speaker has finished talking. What about the other poor habits?

1. Wandering: Probably the most common, the listener's mind wanders from time to time, not really focused on what the speaker is saying. The words go in one ear and out the other.

2. Rejecting: The listener "tunes out" the speaker at the very beginning of the message, most often because of a lack of respect or dislike for the speaker.

3. Judging: Here, the listener focuses on what the speaker says, but makes a hasty evaluation of the speaker's message, thereby not attending to the remainder of the message.

4. Predicting: So common-the listener gets ahead of the speaker and finishes her thoughts; again, missing at least some of the speaker's message.

5. Rehearsing: The listener is thinking about what she is going to say next.

SOURCES: http://www.earthlingcommunication.com/a/listening/seven-deadly-sins-of-not-listening.php; http://ezinearticles.com/?Poor-Listening-Skills—A-Major-Barrier-To-Effective-Communication&id=950245; http://www.managementhelp.org/commskls/listen/gd_vs_pr.htm.

THE INDIVIDUAL, LISTENING, AND SOCIETY

As emphasized throughout this textbook, communication behaviors do not exist solely on the individual level, but are a complex interaction of individual and societal factors. Let's examine listening as it's affected by three levels of societal forces: social hierarchy, context, and community.

Social Hierarchy

Societal norms and social hierarchy influence much of our communication behaviors, and listening is no exception (Dillon & McKenzie, 1998). Let's look more closely at how this works. Every society transmits messages about who is most powerful and important, and these are the people who set the communication norms. How do these messages affect our listening?

Each time we meet someone for the first time, we immediately evaluate whether that person is worth listening to. We mentally go through our personal (influenced by society's) criteria. If the person doesn't meet the criteria, the person's words "become fainter and fainter until only our thoughts fill our attention" (Shafir, 2000, p. 58). Some of the most crucial information to be gained as listeners—like people's names—gets lost while we process acceptability checklists. Two important "filters" are social status and physical appearance.

Social Status

One criterion on many people's acceptability checklist is social status. We ask ourselves, "Is this person worthy of my time and attention?" Most of us are more attentive and listen more closely to those we consider equal to us or higher in society's hierarchy. For example, we listen closely to the words of physicians, teachers, successful business people, and celebrities. Rebecca Z. Shafir (2000), a renowned speech pathologist and listening expert, recounts the story of a manager of a large department who, as part of his power trip, ordered his staff to follow him down the hall as they asked questions or presented ideas (like the scheming boss, Wilhelmina, in the TV sitcom *Ugly Betty*):

> He rarely made eye contact with his subordinates and walked past them as they spoke. Yet, when conversing with his peers or those higher on the administrative ladder, a dramatic change in his voice and body language took place. He looked them in the eye and smiled, nodding his head at any comment or suggestion. He laughed uproariously at their jokes and thanked them profusely for their unique insights (p. 53).

Shafir goes on to say that this manager's attention to status overrode his ability to gain the voluntary cooperation of his staff and resulted in ineffective management, low staff morale, and high turnover. Regardless of the positions we hold, most of us are similarly influenced by systems of hierarchy, and these systems are sometimes tinged with prejudice. For example, do we listen with as much attention to people who have less education? As our student explains in *It Happened to Me: Danny,* he sometimes finds himself tempted to disregard his noncollege friends and even family members, and he has to remind himself that formal education does not determine the value of a person.

IT HAPPENED TO ME: Danny

Being in college, I'm a part of a culture that's very different from the culture where I grew up. In college, people value talking about ideas, learning new information, and working toward becoming more "educated." When I go home, however, I have to remember that not everyone in my family, and even some of my friends, went to college; they do not understand a lot of the jargon I use, and they don't know about the things I've studied. I try to be mindful of this when I visit; I don't want to sound condescending. I also try to remember that their opinions are equally valid and that I need to listen as attentively to them as I do to my college friends.

Physical Appearance

One of the most common obstacles to listening relates to physical appearance. Societal forces set the norms for physical attractiveness, which include being physically able-bodied, having symmetrical features, and displaying certain weight and height norms. This means that many people hold stereotypes about people with disabilities or physical challenges (e.g., people who are extremely overweight or small), and they often find it difficult to

listen to them, avoiding eye contact or ignoring the person entirely. One of our colleagues, Tanya, had a stroke as a young adult and uses a walker or wheelchair. She describes a common situation she encounters:

> It really irritates me sometimes when I'm in public and people avoid looking at me, look at my husband instead and ask him what I want. Why can't they listen to what *I'm saying* and respond to *me*?

In sum, social hierarchies can act as a filter that, in turn, influences people's listening behaviors.

Listening in Context

As discussed earlier, different contexts may call for different listening styles and behaviors. For example, in professional contexts, we generally focus on content or action listening, while in social contexts, we generally focus more on people and relationship affirmation. With friends, we are often called on to listen sympathetically and with little judgment, establishing empathy (Nichols, 1995) and communicating a recognizable "*feeling* of being heard" (Shotter, 2009, p. 21).

In professional contexts, too, whether one is working on an assembly line or as a manager, listening with empathy is important because it enables people to understand each other and get the job done (Imhof, 2001; Nichols, 1995). At the same time, employees must be cautious about letting their work relationships get too personal. For example, Donna was happy when her new boss, Lena, confided details about her divorce and her problems with her children. However, she soon found that Lena's confidences were taking lots of time and keeping her from getting work done. In addition, she discovered that her coworkers were critical of her for being unable to keep things on a professional level. The lesson, then, is that colleagues need to balance task and relational listening skills (Nichols, 1995).

Societal forces may affect listening behavior in any context. For example, if, due to gender, age, race/ethnicity, or sexual orientation, individuals are the victims of prejudice, discrimination, or even bullying in social or workplace contexts, they may not be able to easily adapt their listening behavior. Others' bullying or discriminatory reactions to them may completely undermine their attempts to demonstrate good communication skills. For example, a disabled person may display good listening skills in a conversation by making eye contact, leaning forward, and paying close attention, but if the speaker expresses prejudice toward the disabled person by *not* making eye contact, then the disabled person's good communication skills have little impact. We'll address the role of prejudice and discrimination in communication further in Chapter 6 (Communication Across Cultures).

Listening and Community

Communication scholar David Beard (2009) reminds us that in addition to all the voices in various hierarchies and contexts that we listen to everyday, we also listen to **soundscapes**—the everyday sounds in our environments. Together, these sounds establish a community identity. For example, in many small towns, church bells—or in some countries, the imam calling Muslims to prayer five times daily—help define the boundaries of regional or religious communities and shape a community identity.

For a historical example, Beard contrasts the soundscapes of the North and South around the time of the Civil War and demonstrates their relation to northern and southern identity. The North was loud and industrial, whereas the South had a quiet, rural ambience. Beard argues that these soundscapes played an important part in the regional identities of both groups. Northerners felt comforted and "at home" hearing trains whistle, engines roar, and horns beep in busy traffic, along with the noises of factories. They might have felt out of place in the quiet of a country scene.

For a more contemporary example of community-specific soundscapes, consider generational differences. That is, contrast the technological soundscapes of your parents' and grandparents' generations—the hiss of the needle on a record player, the screech of dial-up access, the sound of a rotary phone dialing, the chimes of the NBC logo—with your own soundscapes. What were the soundscapes of the neighborhood where you grew up? What sounds do you hear every day that may represent your generational identity and communities?

soundscape
the everyday sounds in our environments

Although, as you've seen, the quality of one's listening is subject to powerful social forces as well as individual factors such as listening style, gender, and age, we do have some latitude for making choices about our own behavior. In other words, we make ethical decisions about listening—the topic we turn to next.

ETHICS AND LISTENING

People have several ethical decisions to make about listening. These ethical choices include choosing what you will listen to and when, as well as how you will respond when listening to other people or to the soundscapes that surround you.

To begin with, choosing to listen or not is an ethical decision. Just because someone wants to tell you something doesn't mean you have to listen. And sometimes the very act of listening—or refusing to—means taking a moral stand. For example, let's say a friend of yours is passing along a vicious rumor about another person or telling a racist joke. You have an ethical decision to make. Are you going to listen? How are you going to respond?

As discussed in Chapter 1, you also have an ethical choice about offering feedback. You can tell your friend you don't want to listen, or even gently explain why you don't want to. Or you can say nothing, sacrificing honesty to avoid making yourself (and others) feel uncomfortable. In certain situations (e.g., public settings), offering negative feedback may cause great embarrassment, and you may decide to wait until you are in a more private setting. What are the consequences of each of these decisions? If you listen to something offensive, you are in effect agreeing with the remark. If you tell your friend (either at the moment or later) that you don't want to listen to such remarks, there may be a moment of awkwardness, but the friend may think twice before making similar comments in the future. Obviously, there are no easy answers; you need to consider the consequences and possible outcomes in each situation as you make these ethical decisions.

In a public setting, we can decide to listen (or not listen). Listening or not listening has a potential impact on us and our thinking; listening may open us up to ideas previously unexplored or may reinforce our own beliefs.

Mediated communication contexts can also pose ethical issues with regard to listening. For example, the more you use communication technologies (computers, PDAs, mobile phones), the more likely you are to have access to personal information through e-mail, voice, and text messages that may not be intended for you. You choose what private information to listen to, and also what to do with the information. Many of these choices hold consequences for yourself and others and, thus, constitute ethical decisions (Brownell, 2002).

What are some guidelines for dealing with private information? As we suggested in Chapter 1, you might first consider the privacy expectations of the individual who sent the message. Perhaps this person has made it clear that he or she wants this information kept private. Or you might consider that if you were in this person's position, you would want the information to be kept private. Or perhaps you know that the sender does not care if the information is shared more widely. Depending on the privacy expectation, the ethical decision might be to listen to/read or not listen to/read the messages. You might also consider the consequent benefit and harm of listening. Would the individuals sending the messages feel harmed? Would any benefit result from your listening to the messages? The answer to these questions probably depends a great deal on your relationship with the sender. A very close friend may not mind your listening in on his/her messages; someone you don't know very well may strenuously object.

What other kinds of choices do we make, as listeners, to become more or less ethical beings? Here are some you might not have considered:

1. The choice to cut ourselves off from listening to our immediate environments: We can choose to listen alone (putting on the headset/earphones), which sometimes might be a positive, self-constructive act. At other times, however (that is, when our relational partner wants to talk), doing so can be isolating and damaging to relationships.

2. The choice to listen selectively: For example, we can choose to listen to media "candy" or to media that enhance and inspire us as people. We can choose to listen to a friend's choice of media so that we can discuss it together, or we can listen only to our own choices.

3. The choice not to listen: For example, in the public arena, we can decide to listen (or not listen) to a political speaker who espouses ideas we oppose. Listening or not listening has a potential impact on us and our thinking; listening implies the possibility of change in attitudes and behavior. Listening to a political speaker (or even a friend) promoting ideas/beliefs that we disagree with may open us up to ideas previously unexplored or may reinforce our own beliefs. Choosing never to listen to opposing views ensures that we won't alter our beliefs or learn to defend them in a logical and constructive way.

4. The choice to listen together. For example, when we attend a music concert or a political rally, we open ourselves to being part of a community of music fans or political sympathizers (Beard, 2009). The consequences of the decision to listen with a particular community may open up opportunities for new experiences that may alter our future thinking and/or behavior.

The point is that all these choices are just that—choices. While we don't usually consider these types of choices when we think of listening, the decisions we make regarding them do influence our communication life—influencing our communication identity and our relationships with those important to us.

IMPROVING YOUR LISTENING SKILLS

A recent study asked, "If you could improve one thing about your husband, what would it be?" Out of all the possibilities, the number-one change—heard from almost 60 percent of respondents—was that women wanted their husbands to be better listeners. In contrast, 46 percent wanted a husband who helped out more around the house, and 40 percent wished their husband made more money (The husband makeover, 1998, p. 87). Clearly, people value being listened to. As is the case with all communication skills, however, there are no surefire, easy recipes for becoming a more effective listener. Still, three guidelines might help you improve.

Become Aware

Most of us think of ourselves as better listeners than we really are. In fact, we don't think much about our personal listening behaviors until something bad happens as a result of poor listening—for example, we show up at the wrong location for an important meeting, we forget to return an important call, or we miss an important social event, or in Aisha's case, she became frustrated because others didn't seem to be listening to her. While Aisha seemed to discover this on her own, it might happen that friends or colleagues draw attention to our poor listening habits. Our first reaction might be to get defensive or make excuses. Perhaps a better response would be to take inventory of our listening behaviors; only then can we identify any poor listening habits.

Identify Poor Habits

As noted, most people have some poor listening habits, particularly in our close and intimate relationships, where partners often develop irritating practices such as finishing the other person's sentences, interrupting, and not even listening at all. These irritating behaviors crop up especially if you are an action- or time-oriented listener. Ask yourself, then: What keeps me from really listening? Which filters block my ability to hear and understand

what others are saying? Overcoming listening barriers—especially those that are reinforced by social hierarchies—can be very challenging.

Perhaps one way to overcome those societal messages is through awareness that our listening behaviors play an important role in the outcome of communication encounters. A number of research studies have shown that when people listen attentively to one another, the speaker is more likely to speak coherently. On the other hand, when listeners do not pay careful attention, speakers tend to be less coherent. Put another way, regardless of who they are or their social location, when speakers feel they are listened to with respect and attentiveness, they become better communicators and vice versa.

Strive for Mindful Listening

Applying the concept of mindful listening, described by renowned listening expert Rebecca Z. Shafir (2000), can help. We defined mindfulness in Chapter 2. Mindful listening, a specific kind of mindfulness, is based on Eastern philosophy and Zen Buddhism; it is defined by focus, concentration, and compassion, and it can bring health, peace, and productivity to our everyday lives. This very holistic approach requires that we listen with the heart, body, and mind; and for most of us, that means a major change in attitude. Mindful listening focuses on the *process* of listening versus the *payoff*. Thus, Shafir suggests that in order to be a better listener to each of our friends, family members, and acquaintances, we need to understand their "movie."

Shafir compares listening to movies with listening to others. Most of us don't have trouble focusing on and paying attention while watching a movie; we get caught up in the plot, the emotion, and the characters. Why, she asks, should listening to others be any different? To continue the comparison, if we approach a listening opportunity with the same self-abandonment as we do the movies, think how much more we might gain from those encounters (Shafir, p. 95). After all, listening is not just taking in information; it is also "bearing witness" to, validating, and affirming another's expression (Nichols, 1995, p. 15).

Being a mindful listener requires three elements:

1. the desire to get the whole message
2. the ability to eliminate the noisy barriers discussed earlier
3. the willingness to place your agenda lower on the priority list than the speaker's

Mindful listening is related to empathy, the ability to identify with and understand someone else's feelings. As listening expert Michael Nichols states it, the core of listening is "to pay attention, take an interest in, care about, validate, acknowledge, be moved . . . appreciate" (1995, p. 13).

SUMMARY

Listening is defined as "the process of receiving, constructing meaning from, and responding to spoken and/or nonverbal messages" and occurs in four stages: sensing, understanding, evaluating, and responding. Listening is considered to be one of the most important communication skills, partly because we spend so much time doing it! In addition to the pervasiveness of listening, there are five other important reasons for learning about listening: Better listening skills can lead to improved cognition and also improved academic performance, enhanced personal relationships, enhanced professional performance, and even better health.

Not everyone listens in the same way; our personal listening habits may be influenced by our gender, age, ethnicity, or even our own predominant listening style, which can be people-, action-, content-, or time-oriented. Action-oriented style involves informational listening skills; content-oriented style involves informational and critical listening skills; people-oriented style involves supportive listening skills. People have many reasons for not listening to others, but some typical ones include physical or physiological barriers, psychological barriers, conflicting objectives, and poor listening habits.

Finally, listening habits and preferences are influenced by societal forces: contexts and hierarchies. Moreover, ethical considerations come into play with respect to listening behavior. Ethical decisions include choosing what to listen to and when, how to respond when listening to other people or to the soundscapes around us, including media. While we can offer no surefire, easy recipes for becoming a more effective listener, three guidelines might help: Become aware of your personal listening patterns, identify your poor listening habits or barriers, and practice mindful listening.

KEY TERMS

action-oriented listening style 106
content-oriented listening style 106
critical listening 106
evaluating 102
informational listening 106

listening 102
listening style 106
people-oriented listening style 107
responding 102
sensing 102

soundscape 115
supportive listening 107
time-oriented listening style 107
understanding 102

CHAPTER REVIEW QUESTIONS

1. What is listening and what processes are involved in it?

2. Why is it important to listen?

3. How do gender, age, and culture affect listening?

4. How can one become a more effective listener? If you had to pick one strategy to work on, which would you pick and why?

ACTIVITIES

1. When you are in class or in a large group, notice how people listen to each other and respond. Reflect on what you think is more or less effective about others' listening skills. Then apply what you observed to your own listening skills.

2. Ask someone to observe your listening skills over a period of time. This person can be a parent, friend, teacher, or romantic partner; just ask someone who will give you constructive feedback on how you can improve your listening skills. Try to implement those suggestions.

WEB ACTIVITIES

1. Go to http://www.d.umn.edu/kmc/student/loon/acad/strat/ss_listening.html According to the information in this Web site, the average college student spends about 14 hours per week in class listening to lectures—or at least "hearing" them. The Web site identifies seven strategies for improving listening skills in lecture classes. Which of these do you consistently practice? Which do you sometimes practice? Which are strategies you never thought about before?

2. Go to http://www.youtube.com/watch?v=NRjAokddf9I&feature=related In this YouTube video, Professor Earl presents reasons for listening and ways to improve your listening skills. Watch it to see if the information presented complements or contradicts what you have learned in this chapter. Which do you think is the most important of her four "keys" to improved listening?

3. Go to http://www.listen.org/ Visit the homepage of the International Listening association, an organization that "promotes the study, development, and teaching of listening and the practice of effective listening skills and techniques." Click on the "Quotations" and "Listening Facts" buttons on the left to read interesting information about listening activities. For example, did you know that elementary school students reported themselves as having better attention spans than all other age groups? Did you know that when entering new locations, the early Jesuit missionaries made it a point not to speak for approximately six months? Instead, they listened.

6
COMMUNICATION ACROSS CULTURES

*I*n my first semester in the United States, I lived in the dorm and made many friends from different countries. One day, I was eating lunch when my Korean and Turkish friends started arguing loudly. The issue was the value of our school. The Turkish girl didn't like our school and was thinking of transferring. The Korean student defended our school vehemently.

The Korean and Turkish students wouldn't talk to each other after the argument, and the conflict created a very uncomfortable climate. I was concerned about both of them because we were all friends. So I asked some of my American friends what they thought about the issue. They said, "It's not your problem, Kaori. It's their problem. Stay away from it." I was shocked that my American friends didn't seem to care about the conflict and its negative influence, and it took me a while to understand what the phrase "it's their problem" means in this highly individualistic American society. I've been in the States 7 years, and now I use the phrase myself. Do I think it's good? I don't know. At least I know I'm adapting better to American culture. Do I like it? I don't know. It's just how it is here. But I know that I would never ever say that to my family or friends in Japan.

Kaori's story illustrates a number of points about intercultural communication. First, intercultural contact is a fact of life in today's world, and second, as Kaori's story shows, while intercultural contact can be enriching, it can also bring conflict and misunderstandings. In Kaori's case, the clash between her American friends' individualistic belief and her more collectivistic orientation led her to believe that Americans did not value friendships as much as she did. Finally, the story illustrates that it is very common now for individuals, like Kaori, to live "on the border" between two cultures and, like Kaori, to have to negotiate conflicting sets of cultural values.

Also like Kaori, you have many opportunities to meet people from different cultures. You may sit in classes with students who are culturally different from you in many ways—in nationality, ethnicity, race, gender, age, religion, and sexual orientation. In addition, via travel and communication technology, you have many opportunities for intercultural encounters beyond the classroom. Given the current global political situation, however, you might be skeptical about the ability of people from different cultures to coexist peacefully. Interethnic violence in the Darfur region of Sudan in Africa and in the former Yugoslavia, clashes between Buddhists and Hindus in India and between Catholics and Protestants in Northern Ireland, and tension in the United States between African Americans and Whites may lead people to believe that cultural differences necessarily lead to insurmountable problems. However, we believe that increased awareness of intercultural communication can help prevent or reduce the severity of problems that arise due to cultural differences.

In this chapter, we'll first define what we mean by *intercultural communication* and then explore its importance. Next, we will describe the increasingly common experience of individuals who must negotiate different cultural realities in their everyday lives. Then we'll examine how culture influences our communication and present a dialectical perspective on intercultural communication. Finally, we'll discuss how society affects communication outcomes in intercultural interactions and provide suggestions for how one can become a more ethical and effective intercultural communicator.

CHAPTER OUTLINE

WHAT IS INTERCULTURAL COMMUNICATION?

THE IMPORTANCE OF INTERCULTURAL COMMUNICATION

Increased Opportunities for Intercultural Contact

Enhanced Business Effectiveness

Improved Intergroup Relations

Enhanced Self-Awareness

INTERCULTURAL COMMUNICATION AND THE INDIVIDUAL

Intercultural Communication on the Borders

The Influence of Cultural Values on Communication

A Dialectic Approach

THE INDIVIDUAL, INTERCULTURAL COMMUNICATION, AND SOCIETY

Political, Historical, and Social Forces

Intercultural Communication and Power

ETHICS AND INTERCULTURAL COMMUNICATION

IMPROVING YOUR INTERCULTURAL COMMUNICATION SKILLS

Increase Motivation

Increase Your Knowledge of Self and Others

Avoid Stereotypes

Summary

Key Terms

Chapter Review Questions

Activities

Web Activities

Once you have read this chapter, you will be able to:

- Define intercultural communication.
- Identify four reasons for learning about intercultural communication.
- Give an example of each of six cultural values that influence communication.
- Describe the dialectical approach to intercultural communication.
- Understand the role of power and privilege in communication among people from different cultural backgrounds.
- Give three guidelines for communicating more ethically with people whose cultural backgrounds differ from your own.
- Discuss three ways to improve your own intercultural communication skills.

WHAT IS INTERCULTURAL COMMUNICATION?

Generally speaking, **intercultural communication** refers to communication that occurs in interactions between people who are culturally different. This contrasts with most communication studies, which focuses on communicators in the same culture. Still, in practice, intercultural communication occurs on a continuum with communication between people who are relatively similar in cultural backgrounds on one end and people who are extremely different culturally on the other. For example, your conversations with your parents would represent a low degree of "interculturalness" because, while you and your parents belong to two different cultural (age) groups, you probably have much in common—nationality, religion, and language. On the other hand, an interaction with a foreign teaching assistant who has a different nationality, language, religion, age, socioeconomic status, and gender would represent a high degree of interculturalness. While these two examples represent different ends on the continuum, they are both intercultural interactions. So you can see that many, if not most, of your daily interactions are intercultural in nature.

The two essential components of intercultural communication are, of course, culture and communication. Having read this far in your text, you should have a good understanding of communication. However, we think it is worthwhile to review our definition of **culture**. In Chapter 1, we defined culture as *learned patterns of perceptions, values, and behaviors shared by a group of people*. As we also mentioned, culture is dynamic (it changes), **heterogeneous** (diverse), and operates within societal power structures (Martin & Nakayama, 2008, p. 28). The next section explores reasons why we should study the topic of intercultural communication.

THE IMPORTANCE OF INTERCULTURAL COMMUNICATION

You can probably think of many reasons for studying intercultural communication. For one, you probably have more opportunities than ever before for intercultural contact, both domestically and internationally, and you are likely to communicate better in these situations if you know something about intercultural communication. In addition, increased knowledge and skill in intercultural communication can improve your business effectiveness, intergroup relations, and self-awareness. Let's look at each of these reasons more closely.

Increased Opportunities for Intercultural Contact

Experts estimate that 25 people cross national borders every second—one billion journeys per year (Numbers, 2008). Increasing numbers of people travel for pleasure—some 900 million in 2008 (*Tourism Highlights*, 2009). Many people, as our student Kaori mentioned above, also travel for study. According to the Institute of International Education, almost 700,000 international students study in the United States each year and

intercultural communication
communication that occurs in interactions between people who are culturally different

culture
learned patterns of perceptions, values, and behaviors shared by a group of people

heterogeneous
diverse

more than 250,000 U.S. students study overseas (IIE, 2009a, 2009b). Many students study abroad because of the exciting opportunities that exist for intercultural encounters, as exchange student Allison explains in *Did You Know? Meeting Other Travelers Adds Depth to Argentina Visit.*

DID YOU KNOW?

Meeting Other Travelers Adds Depth to Argentina Visit

Allison, from the United States, is an exchange student in Argentina. Here's an excerpt from her travel blog:

Argentina has absolutely EVERYTHING—huge national glacier parks with penguins and walruses and skiing, deserts and mountains and beautiful plains, and they've even got the east coast beach! We went to the northwest last week; four of us stayed in a youth hostel there. It was absolutely one of the most fun experiences of my life. I felt like I discovered a secret that had been hidden from me all my life. I IMMEDIATELY felt at home. It was just a bunch of kids traveling from all parts of the world, just hanging out and meeting people and sharing all their stories.

Our first friends we met were two Canadian kids who had been backpacking through South America the past two months. We spent a lot of time with them drinking *mate* (the traditional Argentine tea) and chatting. There was also a Venezuelan girl and a Japanese girl. It was a pleasure sharing a room with them. In talking to everyone, I became even more aware of how misinformed about international news we are in America and how uncommon it is for us to be concerned about what's going on in the rest of the world.

I had an intriguing conversation with an Israeli soldier who had been traveling through South America during his time off. Hearing his stories was absolutely heartbreaking. No one of any age should have to endure those things, and he's been doing it since he was 18. I guess that's how it is for people who live in countries where that's just their reality. They become accustomed to falling asleep with gunshots outside their windows and getting up to go to work not having any idea whether or not they'll die. It's awful and such a foreign concept to us; maybe we should make it more of a reality…

Another source of increased opportunity for intercultural contact exists because of the increasing cultural diversity in the United States. The 2000 census revealed a dramatic increase in ethnic/racial diversity, and this trend is expected to continue, as shown in Table 6.1 (Passel & Cohn, 2008). The Hispanic population will triple in size and constitute approximately 30 percent of the population by 2050; in the same time period, the Asian American population will double in size and will represent about 10 percent of the total population. African Americans will remain approximately the same in numbers and comprise 13 percent of the population; Whites will continue to be a smaller and smaller majority as minority populations increase.

In addition, the nation's elderly population will more than double in size from 2005 through 2050, as the baby-boom generation enters the traditional retirement years. The number of working-age Americans and children will grow more slowly than the elderly population and will shrink as a share of the total population (Passel & Cohn, 2008).

And of course the Internet also provides increased opportunity for intercultural encounters. You could play chess with someone in Russia through the Internet, discuss the fine points of mountain climbing with people anywhere in the world on a sports listserv, or collaborate with students from around the country on a virtual team project in one of your classes. The opportunities that these contacts offer, discussed in the next sections of the chapter, should motivate us all to learn more about the intricacies of intercultural communication.

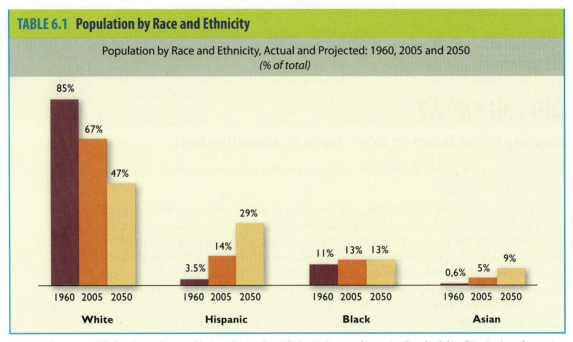

TABLE 6.1 Population by Race and Ethnicity

Population by Race and Ethnicity, Actual and Projected: 1960, 2005 and 2050
(% of total)

Note: All races modified and not Hispanic (*); American Indian/Alaska Native not shown. See "Methodology." Projections for 2050 indicated by light brown bars.

SOURCE: Pew Research Center, 2008

Enhanced Business Effectiveness

Studying intercultural communication can also lead to greater success in both domestic and international business contexts. In the domestic context, the U.S. workforce is becoming increasingly diverse. Furthermore, businesses the world over are expanding beyond national borders—often to former colonies where the colonizer's language is firmly established but wages are lower. For example, British and U.S. businesses are outsourcing services to the former English colonies of Ireland and India. Likewise, French businesses send jobs to Tunisia and Morocco (Blanco, Farrell, & Labaye, 2005).

Despite this trend toward outsourcing, a primary cause for international business failures is lack of attention to cultural factors (Riddle, 2000). For example, when Disney Corporation established its "Euro Disney" outside Paris in the early 1990s, the venture almost failed, in part because Disney executives mistakenly assumed that they could transfer their U.S. cultural practices directly to the French context. However, the French workers rebelled at the Disney dress code that mandated their hair and fingernail length; they also rebelled at being told they had to smile and act enthusiastic (also part of the Disney code), and they eventually took their displeasure to court (Schneider & Barsoux, 2003).

What cultural differences prompted this displeasure? According to intercultural communication experts, the Disney policies went against French people's fundamental distrust of conformity and disrespect for mandated procedure (Hall & Hall, 1990, p. 106). In addition, the notion of smiling constantly at work offended the French—contrary to the U.S. service industry's expectation for workers. Also, the French resented the idea that management and workers could be friends—reflecting a distrust of an egalitarian approach to management (Jarvis, 1995). While the company overcame many of its cross-cultural difficulties, including becoming more multilingual, it continues to struggle financially (Norris, 2007).

Improved Intergroup Relations

While we cannot reduce all the political problems of the world to ineffective intercultural communication, the need for better communication and understanding between countries and ethnic groups is clear. A case that is particularly important to U.S. citizens is the anti-American sentiment in the Middle East. Many experts think that to reverse this tide, the United States should establish meaningful contact with the silent majority in the Muslim world, in ways other than through military force or traditional diplomacy. One way to do

this is to acquire intercultural knowledge and skills through learning the language, culture, and history of a country or region and being able to listen (Finn, 2003). U.S.-sponsored programs such as the Peace Corps and the Fulbright scholarship were designed with this kind of intercultural exchange and understanding in mind.

mediation
peaceful third-party intervention

Intercultural communication expertise can also facilitate interethnic relations, which have increasingly involved conflict. Consider the ethnic/religious strife between Muslims and the Western world, the ethnic struggles in Bosnia and the former Soviet Union; the war between Hutus and Tutsis in Rwanda (Africa); the continued unrest in the Middle East; and the racial and ethnic struggles and tensions in neighborhoods in Boston, Los Angeles, and other U.S. cities. These conflicts often call for sophisticated skills of intercultural communication and **mediation** or peaceful third-party intervention (Bercovitch & Derouen, 2004). For example, communication scholar Benjamin Broome (2004) has successfully facilitated interethnic relations in Cyprus, one of the most heavily fortified regions in the world. Through his efforts, small groups of Greek and Turkish Cypriots have worked together to identify communication barriers and propose suggestions for improved relations between their two groups. Even with mediation, however, miscommunication and intercultural conflicts can persist. Witness the long-standing conflicts in the Middle East, as well as the historical rifts between the world's largest religious groups. In some cases, people are not motivated to resolve intergroup conflict. We must admit that there is no easy cure-all for intercultural tensions and misunderstandings.

Enhanced Self-Awareness

The final reason for studying intercultural communication is to increase self-awareness. This may seem like a contradiction, but it is not. Psychologist Peter Adler (1975) says that intercultural exploration begins as a journey into the cultures of others but often results in increased self-knowledge and understanding. People often learn more about themselves and their own cultural background and identities by coming into contact with people whose cultural backgrounds differ from their own, as our student discovered during her stay in South Africa (see *It Happened to Me: Susan*). It was only when she became a racial minority in South Africa that she realized how privileged she was as a member of the cultural majority (White) in the United States and came to understand some of what it means to be a cultural minority in any society.

IT HAPPENED TO ME: Susan

I rarely ever thought about being White or an American until my family and I spent a year in South Africa. Then, I thought about both every day, especially about my being White. The official language of South Africa is English, but even though we technically spoke the same language as the South Africans, my family and I had problems. It started when we were to be picked up from the airport in a *combie*, but I didn't know what that was. It turned out to be a van! Small pickup trucks were *bakkies*, traffic signals were *robots*, and friends wanted to collect my *contact details*, which meant that they simply wanted the number of my *mobile*, better known as a cell phone, and our address. I felt that every time I opened my mouth, everyone *knew* I was American. The Black/White thing was even more pronounced. When we went down to the flea market or to the Zulu mass at the church we attended, we stood out like "five white golf balls on a black fairway," as my husband liked to say. I wondered if the self-consciousness I felt being White was the same as an African American feels walking down the street in America.

With these reasons for studying intercultural communication in mind, let's explore some of the cultural differences that affect individuals' interactions with one another.

INTERCULTURAL COMMUNICATION AND THE INDIVIDUAL

While almost everyone communicates daily with people who are different from themselves in some ways, not all cultural differences have equal impact on one's interactions. For example, age differences would be less likely to impact one's interactions with others than would ethnic and/or national differences. Here we will examine some of the cultural differences that affect individuals' interactions with one another. We begin by exploring three

border dwellers
people who live between cultures and often experience contradictory cultural patterns

voluntary short-term travelers
people who are border dwellers by choice and for a limited time, such as study-abroad students or corporate personnel

voluntary long-term travelers
people who are border dwellers by choice and for an extended time, such as immigrants

involuntary short-term travelers
people who are border dwellers not by choice and only for a limited time, such as refugees forced to move

involuntary long-term travelers
people who are border dwellers permanently but not by choice, such as those who relocate to escape war

culture shock
a feeling of disorientation and discomfort due to the lack of familiar environmental cues

reverse culture shock/ reentry shock
culture shock experienced by travelers upon returning to their home countries

types of intercultural interactions that can occur when individuals from different cultures coexist. We then explore specific cultural values that shape individuals' communication experiences, and we conclude this section by examining the ways in which individuals within a culture can be both similar to and different from one another.

Intercultural Communication on the Borders

Because of increased opportunities for cultural contact, more people find themselves living a multicultural life. Travelers, racial/ethnic groups that live in proximity, immigrants, and people whose intimate partners come from other cultural backgrounds are only some of the groups that live between cultures, or as **border dwellers**. Here we refer to people who live on cultural borders as *border dwellers* because they often experience contradictory cultural patterns; thus, they may have to move between ethnicities, races, religions, languages, socioeconomic classes, or sexual orientations. One can become a border dweller in one of three ways: through travel, through socialization (cocultural groups), and through participation in an intercultural relationship. Let's look at each in turn.

Border Dwellers Through Travel

Individuals travel between cultures both voluntarily and involuntarily, and for both long and short periods. **Voluntary short-term travelers** include study-abroad students, corporate personnel, missionaries, and military people. **Voluntary long-term travelers** include immigrants who settle in other locations, usually seeking what they perceive is a better life, as is the case for many immigrants who come to the United States. **Involuntary short-term travelers** include refugees forced into cultural migration because of war, famine, or unbearable economic hardship. For example, many people fled Iraq during Saddam Hussein's rule. **Involuntary long-term travelers** are those who are forced to permanently immigrate to a new location, including many who fled Kosovo during the war in the 1990s. (For an illustration, see *Visual Summary 6.1: Border Dwellers Through Travel*.)

When people think of traveling or living in a new culture, they tend to think that learning the language is key to effective intercultural interaction; however, intercultural communication involves much more than language issues. People must also adapt to a new environment and deal with an entirely new way of thinking and living.

Travelers who enter another culture voluntarily for a defined period usually experience culture shock. **Culture shock** is a feeling of disorientation and discomfort due to the unfamiliarity of surroundings and the lack of familiar cues in the environment. When short-term travelers return home to their own country, they may experience similar feelings, known as **reverse culture shock**, or **reentry shock**—a sort of culture shock in one's own country. After being gone for a significant time, aspects of one's own culture may seem foreign, as our student Maham discovered on his return home to Pakistan after living in the United States. Later, when he returned to the United States, he probably experienced another (probably slight) culture shock (see *It Happened to Me: Maham*). As we'll see, border dwellers like our student experience some form of culture or reentry shock with each border crossing.

Most travelers, like Maham, eventually adapt to the foreign culture to some extent if they stay long enough and if the hosts are welcoming. This is often the case for northern Europeans who visit or settle in the United States. On the other hand, if the environment is hostile or the move is involuntary, adaptation may be especially difficult and the culture shock especially intense. For example, many evacuees from Hurricane Katrina were forced to relocate. In some instances, they were greeted with great sympathy and hospitality in the new locations; in other instances, they were subjected to considerable

IT HAPPENED TO ME: *Maham*

I would say that I experienced culture (reentry) shock when I visited Pakistan after I had been away from there for 4 years. In those 4 years, I had basically forgotten the language and become very unfamiliar with the culture. Even though I enjoyed my visit to Pakistan a lot, I had problems adjusting to some of the ways of life. I no longer felt familiar with the bargaining system… where people can go to the store and bargain for prices. I felt very out of place…. As I spent more time there, however, I adjusted and got used to how people did things there.

Border Dwellers Through Travel

	VOLUNTARY	**INVOLUNTARY**
SHORT TERM	 **Tourists, Missionaries, Study Abroad Students**	 **Temporary Refugees from War, Famine, or Economic Hardship**
LONG TERM	 **Immigrants**	 **Permanent Refugees from War, Famine, or Economic Hardship**

racism (Rabbi, 2005). Asian, African, and Latino students in the United States tend to have a difficult adaptation due to experiences of discrimination and hostility based on their race/ethnicity (Jung, Hecht, & Wadsworth, 2007; Lee & Rice, 2007).

Sometimes people even experience culture shock when they move from one region of the United States to another, such as someone who moves from Boston to Birmingham or from Honolulu to Minneapolis. Again, we can see this in the evacuation of tens of thousands of African American southerners from New Orleans after Hurricane Katrina, some of whom were sent to stay in the mostly White state of Utah. A number of these evacuees said that Utah was so different from what they were used to that the experience seemed unreal.

For most travelers, the most stressful time in their sojourn is the beginning, though they may experience anxiety even before leaving their home. International students may worry about finding a place to live, navigating a foreign university, surviving without the support of family and loved ones, and having enough money; tourists may be anxious about transportation and negotiating a new language (Lin, 2006). Once in the new culture, most sojourners encounter two types of challenges: (1) dealing with the psychological stress of being in an unfamiliar environment (feeling somewhat uncertain and anxious) and (2) learning how to behave appropriately in the new culture, both verbally (e.g., learning a new language) as well as nonverbally (e.g., bowing instead of shaking hands in Japan) (Kim, 2005). Some immigrants find learning the language too daunting and never learn it, although their children and grandchildren do. For example, recent surveys by the Pew Hispanic Center of more than 14,000 Latinos found that while only about 25 percent of Latino immigrants say they are fluent in English, 88 percent of their children and 94 percent of their grandchildren say they are (Hakimzadeh & Cohn, 2007).

Many factors determine why an individual may be more or less successful at adapting to a new culture. For example, younger people who have had some previous traveling experience seem to be more successful than older travelers. Those who have a social support network also seem to more easily manage culture shock and cultural adaptation. This social support can come from organizations like an international students' office or a tourist bureau that assists with housing or transportation. Close relationships with other sojourners or host-country people can also provide support in the form of a sympathetic ear; through these relationships, sojourners can relieve stress, discuss, problem-solve, acquire new knowledge, or just have fun (Kashima & Loh, 2006; Lin, 2006).

The role of social support is even more crucial for long-term travelers such as immigrants. If there is little social support or the receiving environment is hostile, immigrants may choose to separate from the majority or host culture, or they may be forced into separation (Berry, 2005). Another option for immigrants is to accept *some* aspects of the new culture, such as dress and outward behavior, while retaining aspects of the home culture. For many recent immigrants to the United States, this has been a preferred option and seems to lead to less stress. For example, Asian Indians constitute one of the largest immigrant groups in the United States. Many have successfully adapted to U.S. life both professionally and socially. Still, many retain aspects of their Indian culture in their personal and family lives—continuing to celebrate ethnic or religious holidays and adhering to traditional values and beliefs (Hegde, 2000). The same is true for many Latino immigrants. However, this integration of two cultures is not always easy, as we'll see in the next section. Families can be divided on the issues of how much to adapt, with children often wanting to be more "American" and parents wanting to hold on to their native languages and cultural practices (Ward, 2008).

Most immigrants eventually adapt to the foreign culture to some extent if they stay long enough, and if the hosts are welcoming.

Border Dwellers Through Socialization

The second group of border dwellers is composed of people who grow up living on the borders between cultural groups. Examples include ethnic groups, such as Latinos, Asian Americans,

and African Americans, who live in the predominantly White United States, as well as people who grow up negotiating multiple sexual orientations or religions. In addition to those who must negotiate the two cultures they live in, the United States has increasing numbers of multiracial people who often grow up negotiating *multiple* cultural realities. The 2000 census form was the first that allowed people to designate more than two races, and since then, the group of people that chooses to be categorized as multiracial has grown faster than any other (Jones & Smith, 2001). Probably the best-known multiracial American is President Barack Obama; his father was an exchange student from Kenya and his mother a U.S. American student. Other famous multiracial Americans include Vin Diesel who is Black and Italian; American singer Mariah Carey, who is Black, Irish, and Venezuelan; Dwayne Johnson, also known as "The Rock," who is Black and Samoan; and news anchor Soledad O'Brien, whose parents are Irish-Australian and Cuban.

Typically, cultural minorities are socialized to the norms and values of both the dominant culture and their own; nonetheless, they often prefer to enact those of their own. They may be pressured to assimilate to the dominant culture and embrace its values, yet those in the dominant culture may still be reluctant to accept them as they try to do so (Berry, 2005). For example, a German woman whose family came from Turkey encountered teachers in Germany who perceived her to be part of a Turkish minority and thus had low expectations for her performance (Ewing, 2004). And members of minority groups sometimes find themselves in a kind of cultural limbo—not "gay" enough for gay friends and not "straight" enough for the majority, not Black enough or White enough, etc.

All of the multiracial Americans we identified above have had to, at some point, respond to criticism that they had not sufficiently aligned themselves with one or another of their racial groups. During the 2008 presidential campaign, President Obama was criticized for being "too White." Vin Diesel and Mariah Carey have both been criticized for refusing to emphasize their Black racial heritage, and Dwayne "The Rock" Johnson was originally condemned for not recognizing his Black heritage but was later praised for attending the Black Entertainment Television awards.

Border Dwellers Through Relationships

Finally, many people live on cultural borders because they have intimate partners whose cultural background differs from their own. Within the United States, increasing numbers of people cross borders of nationality, race, and ethnicity in this way, creating a "quiet revolution" (Root, 2001). Overall, partners in interethnic and interracial romantic relationships have traditionally faced greater challenges than those establishing relationships across religions, nationalities, and class groups. Many people do not realize that, until 1967, it was illegal for African Americans and Whites to marry within the United States (Root, 2001). However, attitudes toward intercultural relationships have changed significantly in the past decades—particularly attitudes toward interracial relations (Taylor, Funk, & Craighill, 2006). According to the most recent census information, interracial marriages have increased tenfold from 1970 to 2000. In fact, experts estimate that more than 7 percent of America's 59 million married couples in 2005 were interracial, compared to less than 2 percent in 1970. Latinos, American Indians, and Hawaiians are most likely to enter interracial marriages, while African Americans and Whites have the lowest rates (Crary, 2007; Lee & Edmonston, 2005).

Such relationships are not without their challenges, as described in *Building Your Communication Skills: Sobering Advice for Anyone Contemplating a Cross-Cultural Marriage.* The most common challenges involve negotiating how to live on the border between two religions, ethnicities, races, languages, and sometimes, value systems. For example, Whites in close relationships with African Americans learn firsthand about racism from their partners and must learn to function in both White and Black social circles—which often do not overlap (Rosenblatt, Karis, & Powell, 1996).

The balancing act between cultures can be especially challenging when friends, family, and society disapprove (Fiebert, Nugent, Hershberger, & Kasdan, 2004). A Jewish man (also a professor) who married a Muslim woman reflects on how people would react if he

Building Your Communication SKILLS

Sobering Advice for Anyone Contemplating a Cross-Cultural Marriage

This hard-won advice is intended only for those couples who are truly considering entering into a cross-cultural marital situation. Simply marrying someone whose ancestry is different from your own is not quite the same thing. My personal experience centers around the relationship between a Japanese female and an American male, although I'd like to think that the basic ideas could be applied to any cross-cultural situation.

Rule#1: *Don't assume that your interest in your partner's culture will last, or that it will somehow prevent conflicts from occurring.* Never underestimate the depth of the roots of your own upbringing. Your beliefs, your emotions, your priorities, in short, your whole approach to life, are shaped by the culture in which you were brought up.

Rule#2: *Don't assume that the other person will change significantly just because of the relationship or because of your charming influence.* The best thing you can do for each other is to acknowledge the fact that conflicts will occur and will often occur for the simplest and most unexpected reasons.

Rule#3: *Don't assume anything. Make sure you discuss with your partner every aspect of your future life together.* Also, don't assume that when your partner says something is unimportant that it does not have to be discussed. Those areas are often the *most* important things to discuss.

Rule#4: *Make it a point to talk about some tough topics (like money, raising children, where to live, etc.) before making those wedding arrangements.* Start an argument or two. Find out what it's like to fight by your partner's rules. You might as well know whether you will be able to work together toward a solution when the inevitable crisis comes up.

Rule#5: *Make sure that between the two of you, there is at least one language in which you are both fluent.* As a test, try taking some very subtle feeling or belief and explain it to your potential mate. Have him or her explain it back. If there is not a substantial understanding of what you explained, wait a while until one or the other of you is able to achieve a good degree of fluency in the other's language.

Rule#6: *Examine your own motives.* Is this someone you would hook up with even if you were safe and happy in your own country? If you are the partner who is trying to live in another culture, remember this: Culture shock can do funny things to a normally rational mind. First get yourself comfortable with your surroundings. Disarm the "convenience" in the relationship and then see what you think. Learn more about the subtle parts of your partner's culture and then decide if you can tolerate, work with, and actually love that person because they are different and not *despite* those differences.

Rule#7: *Don't underestimate the importance of keeping good relations with your partner's parents.* This is especially true if your partner is the one from Japan (or some other non-Western culture). It seems that we in the U.S. (and I can hardly speak for any other Western cultures) have developed a great deal of independence from our families. However, the same is not true in Japan. There is still a great deal of synergy between parent and offspring, even well after they have left the nest and formed families of their own. If you can't get their active support, then at least settle for passive acceptance. Anything less should be a sign of trouble ahead.

Rule#8: *Be ready to help your partner through the inevitable rough spots.* Well, okay, this is sound advice for any couple. But just remember that you both will be setting out on an adventure—a full-time firsthand learning experience in the other person's

cultural labyrinth. None of us, I am convinced, ever really appreciates how many things we learn about life when we are young and that we take for granted every day. We consider many of these things just plain "common sense" but they're only common if you and your partner have common backgrounds.

SOURCE: From Larabell, J. (2003). "Sobering advice for anyone contemplating a cross-cultural marriage." Retrieved October 16, 2005, from www.larabell.org/cross.html. Reprinted by permission of Joe Larabell. Found at http://larabell.org/cross.html

decided to convert to Islam—something his family seemed to expect that his wife would press for:

> What a scandalous action! My family would be outraged and my friends startled. What would they say? How would I be treated? What would colleagues at the university do if I brought a prayer rug to the office and, say, during a committee meeting, or at a reception for a visiting scholar, insisted on taking a break to do my ritual prayers? (Rosenstone, 2005, p. 235)

These challenges can be even more pronounced for women, because parents often play an important role in whom they date and marry. A recent study found that women were much more likely than men to mention pressure from family members as a reason that interethnic dating would be difficult (Clark-Ibáñez & Felmlee, 2004).

Negotiating Cultural Tensions on the Borders

How do people negotiate the tensions between often-contradictory systems of values, language, and nonverbal behavior of two or more cultures? The answer depends on many factors, such as one's reason for being on the border, length of stay or involvement, receptivity of the dominant culture, and personality characteristics of the individuals (Kim, 2005).

In most cases, people in such situations feel caught between two systems; this experience has been described as feeling as if one were swinging on a trapeze, a metaphor that captures the immigrant's experience of vacillating between the cultural patterns of the homeland and the new country (Hegde, 1998). Writer Gloria Anzaldúa (1999), who is Chicana, gay, and female, stresses that living successfully on the border requires significant flexibility and an active approach to negotiating multiple cultural backgrounds. She struggles to balance her Indian and Spanish heritage, as well as her patriarchal Catholic upbringing, with her spiritual and sexual identity. The result, she says, is the *mestiza*—a person who has actively confronted and managed the negative aspects of living on the border. Similarly, communication scholar Lisa Flores (1996) speaks of how some Chicana feminist writers and artists acknowledge negative stereotypes that portray Mexican and Mexican American women as uneducated Spanglish-speaking laborers, passive sex objects, and servants of men and children. And through their work, they transform these negative images into images of Chicanas as strong, clever bilinguals who are proud of their dual Anglo-Mexican heritage. In addition, they reach out to other women (women of color and immigrant women) so that they can work together to achieve more justice and recognition for women who live "in the middle" between cultural worlds.

As you can see, managing these tensions while living on the border and being multicultural can be both rewarding and challenging. Based on data from interviews she conducted, Janet Bennett (1998) described two types of border dwellers, or as she labeled them, "marginal individuals": *encapsulated marginal people* and *constructive marginal people*.

Encapsulated marginal people feel disintegrated by having to shift cultures. They have difficulty making decisions and feel extreme pressure from both groups. They try to assimilate but never feel comfortable or at home.

In contrast, **constructive marginal people** thrive in their "border" life and at the same time recognize its tremendous challenges, as Gloria Anzaldúa described. They see themselves as choice-makers. They recognize the significance of being "in between," and they continuously negotiate and explore this identity.

encapsulated marginal people
people who feel disintegrated by having to shift cultures

constructive marginal people
people who thrive in a border-dweller life, while recognizing its tremendous challenges

To summarize, people can find themselves living on cultural borders for many reasons: travel, socialization, or entering an intercultural relationship. While border dwelling can be challenging and frustrating, it can also lead to cultural insights and agility in navigating intercultural encounters.

The Influence of Cultural Values on Communication

In Chapters 3 and 4, we described how culture influences verbal and nonverbal communication. You might think that these differences would be key to understanding intercultural communication. Just as important is understanding **cultural values**, which are the beliefs that are so central to a cultural group that they are never questioned. Cultural values prescribe what *should* be. Understanding cultural values is essential because they so powerfully influence people's behavior, including their communication. Intercultural interaction often involves confronting and responding to an entirely different set of cultural values than one's own. Let's see how this works.

About 50 years ago, anthropologists Florence Kluckhohn and Fred Strodtbeck (1961) conducted a study that identified the contrasting values of three cultural groups in the United States: Latinos, Anglos, and American Indians. Later, social psychologist Geert Hofstede (1997, 1998, 2001) and his colleagues extended this analysis in a massive study, collecting 116,000 surveys about people's value preferences in approximately 80 countries around the world. Psychologist Michael Bond and his colleagues conducted a similar, though smaller, study in Asia (Chinese Culture Connection, 1987). Together, these studies identified cultural values preferred by people in a number of countries, six of which are discussed in the following sections. While these value preferences may apply most directly to national cultural groups, they can also apply to ethnic/racial groups, socioeconomic class groups, and gender groups.

As you read about these cultural-value orientations, please keep the following three points in mind. These guidelines reflect a common dilemma of intercultural communication scholars—the desire to describe and understand communication and behavior patterns within a cultural group and the fear of making rigid categories that can lead to stereotyping.

1. The following discussion describes the *predominant* values preferred by various cultural groups, not the values held by *every person* in the cultural group. Think of cultural values as occurring on a bell curve: Most people may be in the middle, holding a particular value orientation, but many people can be found on each end of the curve (these are the people who *do not go along* with the majority).
2. The following discussion refers to values on the cultural level, not on the individual level. Thus, if you read that most Chinese tend to prefer an indirect way of speaking, you cannot assume that every Chinese person you meet will speak in an indirect way in *every* situation.
3. The only way to understand what a particular individual believes is to get to know the person. You can't predict how any one person will communicate. The real challenge is to understand the full range of cultural values and then learn to communicate effectively with others who hold differing value orientations, regardless of their cultural background.

Now that we've laid the basic ground rules, let's look at six key aspects of cultural values.

Individualism and Collectivism

One of the most central value orientations identified in this research addresses whether a culture emphasizes the rights and needs of the individual or those of the group. For example, many North American and northern European cultural groups, particularly U.S. Whites, value individualism and independence, believing that one's primary responsibility is to one's self (Bellah, Madsen, Sullivan, Swidler, & Tipton, 1996; Hofstede, 2001; Kikoski & Kikoski, 1999). In relationships, as Kaori discovered in our opening vignette, those with this **individualist orientation** respect autonomy and independence, and they do not meddle in another's problems unless invited. In cultures where individualism prevails, many children are raised to be autonomous and to live on their own by late adolescence (although they may return home for short periods after this). Their parents are expected to take care of themselves and not "be a burden" on their children when they age (Triandis, 1995).

---

cultural values
beliefs that are so central to a cultural group that they are never questioned

individualist orientation
a value orientation that respects the autonomy and independence of individuals

contaminated in any way. For example, the Creek and Cherokee have an Eagle Dance. According to the American Eagle Foundation, "If for any reason an eagle feather is dropped, it needs to be cleansed." One individual is charged with guarding the eagle feather and ensuring that the proper cleansing ceremony is performed.

Golden also describes the consternation of many Indians when the U.S. Fish & Wildlife Service recently raided Indian residences and arrested several Indians in three states, including her home state of Oklahoma, for illegal possession of eagle feathers. Congress has passed laws to protect the Bald Eagle and Golden Eagle, and now a permit is required to possess the feathers. While there is an exemption for American Indians, as Golden explains, many Indians have received their feathers from family members or in traditional ceremonies and do not have the required permit.

SOURCE: From Golden, B. (2010, April 5). "Soaring with Eagles." *Native American Community Examiner*. Retrieved July 26, 2010 from www.examiner.com/x-4316-Native-American-Community-Examiner~ y2009m4d5-Soaring-With-the-Eagles American Eagle Foundation website. Retrieved July 26, 2010 from http://www.eagles.org /native_american.htm

---

In the United States, differences arise between real estate developers, who believe that humans take precedence over nature, and environmentalists and many Native American groups, who believe that nature is as important as humans. This conflict has surfaced in disagreements over water rights in Oregon (Hemmingsen, 2002) and over the proposed eight-million-acre habitat for the endangered spotted owl in the southwestern United States (McKinnon, 2004).

Power Distance

Power distance, the fifth value orientation, refers to the extent to which less-powerful members of institutions and organizations within a culture expect and accept an unequal distribution of power (Hofstede, 2001). In Denmark, Israel, and New Zealand, the predominant cultural value is to favor small power distances, meaning a belief that inequality, while inevitable, should be minimized and that the best leaders emphasize equality and informality in interactions with subordinates. In many situations, subordinates are expected to speak up and contribute.

Societies that value large power distance—for example, Mexico, the Philippines, and India—are structured more around a hierarchy in which each person has a rightful place and interactions between supervisors and subordinates are more formal (Hofstede, 2001). Seniority, age, rank, and titles are emphasized more in these societies than in small-power-distance societies.

People who are used to large power distances may be uncomfortable in settings where hierarchy is unclear or ambiguous. For example, international students who come from countries where a large-power-distance value predominates may initially be very uncomfortable in U.S. college classrooms, where relations between students and teachers are informal and characterized by equality—a situation described by our student from India in *It Happened to Me: Nagesh*.

Like most international students, Nagesh probably eventually adapted to the American classroom norms of informality and relative equality and found it easier to speak up in class. In contrast, U.S. Americans abroad often offend locals when they treat subordinates at work or home too informally—calling them by first names, treating them as if they were friends. For example, when President Bush visited Europe, he referred to the Belgian Prime Minister by his first name, Guy, which surprised and amused many Belgians—who are accustomed to more formality.

power distance
a value orientation that refers to the extent to which less powerful members of institutions and organizations within a culture expect and accept an unequal distribution of power

IT HAPPENED TO ME: Nagesh

I was amazed when I first saw American classrooms. The students seemed very disrespectful toward the teacher. They had their feet on the desks and interrupted the teacher while he was talking if they didn't understand something. In my country, students would never behave this way toward a teacher. I found it difficult to speak up in this kind of classroom situation.

long-term versus short-term orientation
the dimension of a society's value orientation that reflects its attitude toward virtue or truth

short-term orientation
a value orientation that stresses the importance of possessing one fundamental truth

monotheistic
belief in one god

long-term orientation
a value orientation in which people stress the importance of virtue

polytheistic
belief in more than one god

dialectic approach
recognizes that things need not be perceived as either/or, but may be seen as both/and

dichotomous thinking
thinking in which things are perceived as "either/or"—for example, good or bad, big or small, right or wrong

What kinds of communication problems do you think occur when members of a diverse work team hold different value orientations toward being and doing? How might someone who prefers a being orientation view someone with a doing orientation and vice versa?

Note that value orientations represent what *should be*, not what *is*. While many Americans say they desire small power distance, the truth is that rigid social and economic hierarchies exist and that most people are born into and live within the same socio-economic class for their whole lives (Herbert, 2005).

Long-Term Versus Short-Term Orientation

The research identifying the five values we've described has been criticized for its predominately Western European bias. In response to this criticism, a group of Chinese researchers developed and administered a similar, but more Asian-oriented, questionnaire to people in twenty-two countries around the world (Chinese Culture Connection, 1987). They then compared their findings to previous research on value orientations and found considerable overlap, especially on the dimensions of individualism versus collectivism and power distance. These researchers also identified one additional value dimension that earlier researchers hadn't seen: **long-term versus short-term orientation**.

This dimension reflects a society's attitude toward virtue or truth. A **short-term orientation** characterizes cultures in which people are concerned with possessing one fundamental truth, as reflected in the **monotheistic** (belief in one god) religions of Judaism, Christianity, and Islam. Other qualities identified in the research and associated with a short-term orientation include an emphasis on quick results, individualism, and personal security and safety (Hofstede, 1997).

In contrast, a **long-term orientation** tends to respect the demands of virtue, reflected in Eastern religions such as Confucianism, Hinduism, Buddhism, and Shintoism, which are all **polytheistic** religions (belief in more than one god). Other qualities associated with a long-term orientation include thrift, perseverance and tenacity in whatever one attempts, and a willingness to subordinate oneself for a purpose (Bond, 1991, 1996).

While knowing about these value differences can help you identify and understand problems that arise in intercultural interactions, you might be concerned that this approach to the study of intercultural communication leads to generalizing and stereotyping. The next section presents an approach that helps counteract this tendency to think in simplistic terms about intercultural communication.

A Dialectic Approach

Dialectics has long existed as a concept in philosophical thought and logic. In this book we introduce it as a way to emphasize simultaneous contradictory truths. Thus, a **dialectic approach** helps people respond to the complexities of intercultural communication and override any tendencies to stereotype people based on cultural patterns. The notion is difficult to understand because it is contrary to most formal education in the United States, which emphasizes **dichotomous thinking**, where things are "either/or"—good or bad, big or small, right or wrong. However, a dialectic approach recognizes that things may be "both/and." For example, a palm tree may be weak *and* strong. Its branches look fragile and weak, and yet in a hurricane it remains strong because the "weak" fronds can bend without breaking. Similar dialectics exist in intercultural communication; for example, Didier may be a Frenchman who shares many cultural characteristics with other French people, but he also is an individual who possesses characteristics that make him unique. So, he is both similar to and different from other French people. A dialectic approach emphasizes the fluid, complex, and contradictory nature of intercultural interactions. Dialectics exist in other communication contexts such as relationships, which we explore in Chapter 8. Six dialectics that can assist you in communicating more effectively in intercultural interactions are discussed next.

Cultural–Individual

This dialectic emphasizes that some behaviors, such as ways of relating to others, are determined by our culture, while others are simply idiosyncratic, or particular to us as individuals. For example, Robin twists her hair while she talks. This idiosyncratic personal preference should not be mistaken for a cultural norm. She doesn't do it because she is

female, or young, or Protestant, or African American. Although it isn't always easy to tell whether a behavior is culturally or individually based, taking a dialectic approach means that one does not immediately assume that someone's behavior is culturally based.

Personal–Contextual

This dialectic focuses on the importance of context or situation in intercultural communication. In any intercultural encounter, both the individual and the situation are simultaneously important. Let's take the example of a French student and an American student striking up a conversation in a bar. The immediate situation has an important impact on their communication, so their conversation would probably differ dramatically if it occurred at a synagogue, mosque, or church. The larger situation, including political and historical forces, also plays a role. In the build-up to the Iraq War of 2003, for example, some French students encountered anti-French sentiment in the United States. At the same time, the characteristics of the specific individuals also affected the exchange. Some students would ignore the immediate or larger situation and reject the anti-French sentiment—especially if they were opposed to the war themselves. Others would attach great importance to the larger context and view the French students negatively. The point is that reducing an interaction to a mere meeting of two individuals means viewing intercultural communication too simplistically.

Political contexts, like the anti-French attitudes during the build up to the Iraq war influenced interactions between ordinary French people and U. S. Americans.

Differences–Similarities

Real, important differences exist between cultural groups; we've identified some of these in this chapter. However, emphasizing only differences can lead to stereotyping; it is important to recognize that commonalities exist as well.

Static–Dynamic

While some cultural patterns remain relatively stable and static for years, they can also undergo dynamic change. For example, most people get their information about American Indians from popular films like *Pocahontas* or *The Indian in the Cupboard*, which portray Indians living the rural life they lived centuries ago, even though the majority of Indians today live in urban areas (Alexie, 2003). A static–dynamic dialectic requires that you recognize both the traditional and contemporary realities of a culture.

History/Past–Present/Future

An additional dialectic in intercultural communication focuses on the present and the past. For example, one cannot fully understand contemporary relations between Arabs and Jews or Muslims and Christians without knowing something of their history. At the same time, people cannot ignore current events. For example, the conflict over where Yasser Arafat was to be buried in the autumn of 2004 flowed from a complex of historical and contemporary relations. His family had resided for generations in Jerusalem and wanted him laid to rest there. Israel, having current control of Jerusalem and viewing Arafat as a terrorist leader of attacks against Israel, refused.

Privilege–Disadvantage

In intercultural interactions, people can be simultaneously privileged and disadvantaged (Johnson, 2001). This can become quite clear when one travels to developing countries. While U.S. Americans may be privileged in having more money and the luxury of travel, they can also feel vulnerable in foreign countries if they are ignorant of the local

languages and customs. Poor Whites in the United States can be simultaneously privileged because they are White and disadvantaged due to their economic plight. As a student, you may feel privileged (compared to others) in that you are acquiring a high level of education, but you may also feel economically disadvantaged because of the high cost of education.

This dialectic approach helps us resist making quick, stereotypical judgments about others and their communication behavior. A single person can have individualistic and collectivistic tendencies, can be both culturally similar and different from us, and can be culturally privileged in some situations and culturally disadvantaged in others. All these elements affect communication in both business and personal relationships.

THE INDIVIDUAL, INTERCULTURAL COMMUNICATION, AND SOCIETY

As you likely have gathered by now, intercultural communication must be understood in the context of larger societal influences. In this section, we first focus on social, political, and historical forces; second, we turn our attention to the role of power in intercultural communication.

Political, Historical, and Social Forces

That societal forces can affect intercultural encounters is exemplified by the varying reactions toward some immigrant groups after the attacks of September 11. Scholar Sunil Bhatia (2008) found, through interviews with Asian Indian Americans, that these immigrants experienced reactions from others that caused them to question their "American" identity. Before 9/11, they considered themselves well adapted to American culture. However, after 9/11, people treated them differently. Their neighbors, who knew them well, were much friendlier and sympathetic. However, some strangers were more hostile (sometimes mistaking them for Arab Muslims). Thus, they were reminded that they were different; they were not completely accepted as Americans by the American majority. One of our students recounts how the events of 9/11 influenced her relationship with a college friend from Jordan in *It Happened to Me: Monica*.

IT HAPPENED TO ME: Monica

I had a roommate in college. We shared many interests. I even planned on taking a trip to visit her in Jordan, but after 9/11, she didn't mention the trip again. Also, for a month or two after 9/11, when others asked where her accent was from, she lied and replied "Turkey" to protect herself from people perhaps blaming her for the attacks. These events really put a strain on our relationship.

Monica was sorry for her friend's discomfort—even feeling she had to lie—but she might have reacted more sympathetically. For example, Monica could have made it clear that she did not blame her friend for the attacks and asked her friend to explain her experience living as a Muslim in the post-9/11 United States. She might also have explained the source of her friend's fear to their mutual friends and acquaintances, to help them understand how she felt as a target of stereotyping and prejudice.

Historical forces can also influence contemporary intercultural interaction, as we noted earlier in our discussion of dialectics. For example, while slavery is long gone in the United States, one could not understand contemporary Black–White relations in this country without acknowledging its effect. Author James Loewen (1995) describes the twin legacies of slavery that are still with us: (1) social and economic inferiority for Blacks brought on by specific economic and political policies from 1885 to 1965 that led to inferior educational institutions and exclusion from labor unions, voting rights, and the advantage of government mortgages; (2) cultural racism instilled in Whites. These legacies, in turn, affect interracial

dialogues, which some have characterized as uneasy, unequal encounters with few authentic conversations (Houston, 2004; Kivel, 1996).

As a society, which institutions or contexts now promote the best opportunities for interracial contact? Neighborhoods? Educational institutions? Churches, synagogues, and other places of worship? The workplace? Neighborhoods and workplaces do not seem to provide opportunities for the *type* of contact (intimate, friendly, equal-status interaction) that facilitates intercultural relationships (Johnson & Jacobson, 2005). On the other hand, it appears that *integrated* religious institutions and educational institutions provide the best opportunities for intercultural friendships and the best environment to improve interracial attitudes (Johnson & Jacobson, 2005). For example, a study of six California State University campuses found that the students on these campuses had equal numbers of inter- and intra-racial encounters (Cowan, 2005). These campuses are very diverse, and no one ethnic or racial group is a majority, which may facilitate such interactions among students. However, a more recent study cautions that students in multicultural campuses sometimes assume that they have intercultural relationships just by virtue of being surrounded by cultural diversity, and while they may have many inter-cultural *encounters*, they may not make the effort to actually pursue intercultural *friendships* (Halualani, 2008).

Intercultural Communication and Power

As we have noted in previous chapters, power is a pervasive theme in societal impacts on communication. For example, in Chapter 3 (Verbal Communication), we described how the more powerful groups in society establish the rules for communication and how others usually follow these rules or violate them at their peril (Orbe, 1998). A number of factors influence who is considered powerful in a culture. For example, being White in the United States has more privilege attached to it than being Latino (Bahk & Jandt, 2004). While most Whites do not notice this privilege and dominance, most minority group members do (Bahk & Jandt, 2004). Being male has also been more valued historically than being female (Johnson, 2001), and being wealthy is more valued than being poor. Further, being able-bodied is traditionally more valued than being physically disabled (Allen, 2003; Johnson, 2001). Every society, regardless of power-distance values, has these kinds of traditional hierarchies of power. While the hierarchy is never entirely fixed, it does constrain and influence communication among cultural groups.

How do power differences affect intercultural interaction? They do so primarily by determining whose cultural values will be respected and followed. For example, faculty, staff, and students in most U.S. universities adhere to the values and communication norms set by the White, male-dominant groups. These values and communication norms emphasize individualism (Kikoski & Kikoski, 1999). Thus, while group work is common in many courses, professors usually try to figure out how to give individual grades for it, and most students are encouraged to be responsible for their own work. Moreover, the university is run on monochronic time (see Chapter 4), with great emphasis placed on keeping schedules and meeting deadlines—and these deadlines sometimes take precedence over family and other personal responsibilities (Blair, Brown, & Baxter, 1994). The communication style most valued in this culture is also very individual-oriented, direct and to the point, and extremely task oriented, as is the case in many organizations in the United States (Kikoski & Kikoski, 1999).

What is the impact for those who come from other cultural backgrounds and do not fit into this mold—say, for those who have collectivistic backgrounds and value personal relationships over tasks and homework assignments? Or for those whose preferred communication style is more indirect? They may experience culture shock; they may also be sanctioned or marginalized—for example, with bad grades for not participating more in class, for not completing tasks on time, or for getting too much help from others on assignments. These kinds of clashes and misunderstandings play out in multiple contexts, including reality television and the corporate world, as described in *Communication in Society: TV Reality Not Often Spoken of: Race.*

Communication in SOCIETY

TV Reality Not Often Spoken of: Race

According to media critic Eric Deggans, reality television shows like *The Apprentice* and *Survivor* reveal a harsh racial reality in America that is played out in many sectors of society: the saga of the assimilated minority individual (one who gets along easily with White people) versus the nonassimilated minority who sticks out like a "burr on a silk bed," often clashing with the majority group. In a recent article, he notes that on *Survivor* and *The Apprentice*, there are often two persons of color—one assimilated and one unassimilated. The unassimilated person separates from the larger group quickly, usually as a result of personal clashes that lead to hard feelings, increased isolation, and eventual ejection from the show. There are harsh assumptions on both sides: The unassimilated person thinks the group is overacting to their difference and suspects racism; the group thinks the isolated person is overreacting to personality differences and using race to justify personal reactions.

Deggans goes on to say that this is a sad-but-common pattern in the minority struggle to fit in to corporate culture and White society: "The minority can be 'hypervisible,' basking in the way their differences may set them apart from the crowd. Or they can be 'invisible,' minimizing their differences with the majority to the point that they blend in. Both approaches present dangers: The hypervisible person tends to spark conflicts with the majority group, which often doesn't understand why the minority member holds himself apart. And the invisible person has so little impact on the group, she might as well actually be transparent."

In concluding his article, Deggans describes a recent research study of Black executives that found that "assimilated" Black executives often formed friendships with their White coworkers and were rewarded by the corporation, but these same executives were sometimes mistrusted by other minority workers. In contrast, the unassimilated were less trusting of White coworkers. Exhausted by the effort of navigating White culture at work, they remained certain that most White people in their lives would eventually betray them.

SOURCE: From Deggans, E. (2004, October 24). *St. Petersburg Times*. Retrieved March 20, 2009, from www.sptimes.com/2004/10/22/Floridian/TV_reality_not_often_.shtml

ETHICS AND INTERCULTURAL COMMUNICATION

How can you communicate more ethically across cultures? Unfortunately, no easy answers exist, but a few guidelines may be helpful.

First, remember that everyone, including you, is enmeshed in a culture and thus communicating through a cultural lens. Recognizing your own cultural attitudes, values, and beliefs will make you more sensitive to others' cultures and less likely to impose your own cultural attitudes on their communication patterns. While you may feel most comfortable living in your own culture and following its communication patterns, you should not conclude that your culture and communication style are best or should be the standard for all other cultures. Such a position is called **ethnocentrism**.

Second, as you learn about other cultural groups, be aware of their humanity and avoid the temptation to view them as an exotic "other." Communication scholar Bradford Hall has cautioned about this tendency, which is called the *zoo approach*:

> When using such an approach we view the study of culture as if we were walking through a zoo admiring, gasping and chuckling at the various exotic animals we observe. One may discover amazing, interesting and valuable information by using such a perspective and even develop a real fondness of these exotic people, but miss the point that we are as culturally "caged" as others and that they are culturally as "free" as we are (1997, p. 14).

From an ethical perspective, the zoo approach denies the humanity of other cultural groups. For example, the view of African cultures as primitive and incapable led Whites to justify colonizing Africa and exploiting its rich resources in the nineteenth century.

Third, you will be more ethical in your intercultural interactions if you are open to other ways of viewing the world. What you were taught about the world and history may not be the same as what others were taught. People cannot engage in meaningful

ethnocentrism
the tendency to view one's own group as the standard against which all other groups are judged

communication if they are unwilling to suspend or reexamine their assumptions about the world. For example, some Europeans believe that the United States became involved in the Middle East so it could control its oil interests, while many U.S. Americans believe that concern over weapons of mass destruction and human rights was the motivation. If neither group will consider the opinion of the other, they will be unlikely to sustain a mutually satisfying conversation on the topic.

IMPROVING YOUR INTERCULTURAL COMMUNICATION SKILLS

How can you communicate more effectively across cultures? As with ethics, no magic formula exists, but here are several suggestions.

Increase Motivation

Perhaps the most important component is *motivation*. Without the motivation to be an effective communicator, no other skills will be relevant. Part of the problem in long-standing interethnic or interreligious conflicts—for example, between the Israelis and the Palestinians—is the lack of interest, on both sides, in communicating more effectively. Some parties on both sides may even have an interest in prolonging conflict. Therefore, a strong desire to improve one's skills is necessary.

Increase Your Knowledge of Self and Others

In addition to being motivated, you become a more effective intercultural communicator if you educate yourself about intercultural communication. Having some knowledge about the history, background, and values of people from other cultures can help you communicate better. When you demonstrate this type of knowledge to people from other cultures, you communicate that you're interested in them and you affirm their sense of identity. Obviously, no one can know everything about all cultures; nonetheless, some general information can be helpful, as can an awareness of the importance of context and a dialectical perspective.

Self-knowledge is also very important. If you were socialized to be very individualistic, you may initially have a hard time understanding collectivistic tendencies. Once you become aware of these differences, however, you can more easily communicate with someone who holds a different perspective. Growing up in a middle-class family may also influence your perceptions. Many middle-class people assume that anyone can become middle class through hard work. But this view overlooks the discrimination faced by people of color and gays and lesbians. How can you increase your cultural self-awareness? Perhaps the best way is to cultivate intercultural encounters and relationships.

Developing facility in intercultural communication occurs through a cyclical process. The more one interacts across cultures, the more one learns about oneself, and then the more prepared one is to interact interculturally, and so on. However, increased exposure and understanding do not happen automatically. Being aware of the influence of culture on oneself and others is essential to increasing one's intercultural experience and competence (Ting-Toomey, 1999).

Where should you start? You can begin by examining your current friendships and reach out from there. Research shows that individuals generally become friends with people with whom they live, work, and worship. So your opportunities for intercultural interaction and self-awareness are largely determined by the type of people and contexts you encounter in your daily routine.

Avoid Stereotypes

Cultural differences may lead to stereotyping and prejudices. As we discussed in Chapter 2, normal cognitive patterns of generalizing make our world more manageable. However, when these generalizations become rigid, they lead to stereotyping and prejudices. Furthermore, stereotyping can become self-fulfilling (Snyder, 2001). That is, if you stereotype

people and treat them in a prejudiced or negative manner, they may react in ways that reinforce your stereotype.

On the other hand, we must note, overreacting by being very "sweet" can be equally off-putting. African Americans sometimes complain about being "niced" to death by White people (Yamato, 2001). The guideline here is to be mindful that you might be stereotyping. For example, if you are White, do you only notice bad behavior when exhibited by a person of color? Communicating effectively across cultural boundaries is a challenge—but one we hope you will take up.

SUMMARY

Intercultural communication is defined as communication between people from different cultural backgrounds, and culture is defined as learned patterns of perceptions, values, and behaviors shared by a group of people. Four reasons for learning about intercultural communication are increased opportunity, increased business effectiveness, improved intergroup relations, and enhanced self-awareness.

Culture is dynamic and heterogeneous, and it operates largely out of our awareness within power structures. Increasing numbers of individuals today live on cultural borders— through travel, socialization, or relationships. Being a "border dweller" involves both benefits and challenges.

Six core cultural values differentiate various cultural groups, and these value differences have implications for intercultural communication. A dialectical approach to intercultural communication can help individuals avoid quick generalizations and stereotyping. There are at least six intercultural communication dialectics: cultural–individual, personal–contextual, differences–similarities, static–dynamic, history/past–present/future, and privilege–disadvantage.

Society plays an important role in intercultural communication because intercultural encounters never occur in a vacuum. Societal forces, including political, historical, and social structures, always influence communication. Power is often an important element, in that those who hold more powerful positions in society set the rules and norms for communication. Those individuals who do not conform to the rules because of differing cultural backgrounds and preferences may be marginalized. To ensure that you are communicating ethically during intercultural interactions, avoid ethnocentric thinking, recognize the humanity of others, and remain open to other ways of understanding the world. Finally, you can become a more effective intercultural communicator in at least three ways: by increasing your motivation, acquiring knowledge about self and others, and avoiding stereotyping.

KEY TERMS

border dwellers 126
collectivistic orientation 133
constructive marginal people 131
cultural values 132
culture 122
culture shock 126
dialectic approach 136
dichotomous thinking 136
encapsulated marginal people 131
ethnocentrism 140

heterogeneous 122
human–nature value orientation 134
individualist orientation 132
intercultural communication 122
involuntary long-term travelers 126
involuntary short-term travelers 126
long-term orientation 136
long-term versus short-term
    orientation 136
mediation 125

monotheistic 136
polytheistic 136
power distance 135
preferred personality 133
reverse culture shock/reentry
    shock 126
short-term orientation 136
view of human nature 133
voluntary long-term travelers 126
voluntary short-term travelers 126

CHAPTER REVIEW QUESTIONS

1. What are the reasons for studying intercultural communication? Which do you think are most important?

2. How do individuals come to live on cultural borders? What are some benefits and challenges to border dwelling?

3. Identify six common core values that differentiate various cultural groups. How might these values influence intercultural communication?

4. How does adopting a dialectical perspective help us avoid stereotyping and prejudice?

5. What are three suggestions for communicating more effectively across cultures? Which do you think is the most important? Why?

ACTIVITIES

1. **Cultural Profile**
List all the cultural groups you belong to. Which groups are most important to you when you're at college? When you're at home? Which groups would be easiest to leave? Why?

2. **Intercultural Conflict Analysis**
Identify a current intercultural conflict in the media. It can be conflict between nations, ethnic groups, or genders. Read at least three sources that give background and information about the conflict. Conduct an analysis of this conflict, answering the following questions:
   - What do you think are the sources of the conflict?
   - Are there value differences?
   - Are there power differences?
   - What role do you think various contexts (historical, social, political) play in the conflict?

3. **Intercultural-Relationship Exercise**
Make a list of people you consider to be your close friends. For each, identify ways in which they are culturally similar and different from you. Then form groups of four-to-six students and answer the following questions. Select a recorder for your discussion so that you can share your answers with the rest of the class.
   - Do people generally have more friends who are culturally similar or different from themselves?
   - What are some of the benefits of forming intercultural friendships?
   - In what ways are intercultural friendships different or similar to friendships with people from the same cultures?
   - What are some reasons people might have for not forming intercultural friendships?

WEB ACTIVITIES

1. Go to: http://www.census.gov/population/cen2000/atlas/censr01-1.pdf This Web site is a U.S. government report on demographic diversity in the United States taken from the 2000 census. On page 21 of this report, a U.S. map shows the country's racial and ethnic diversity. How diverse are the areas you've lived in? Did the diversity of the population influence your opportunities for intercultural encounters?

2. How high is your intercultural intelligence? Take the "Intercultural Competence Self-Assessment" at http://racerelations.about.com/od/skillsbuildingresources/a/selfassessment.htm to find out.

3. Go to: http://www.online-communicator.com/maskinfo.html The designer of this Web site describes why he removed an image of a Native American mask from his Web site. He had been contacted by an Iroquois Indian who requested that he remove the image because it is sacred and not to be reproduced by non–Indians. According to this Web site, what other popular images of Native Americans are offensive or inaccurate?

7

COMMUNICATION AND NEW TECHNOLOGIES

veryday I check Facebook—either on my laptop or on my smart phone—to see if anything new has happened with my friends. First, I look at people's statuses to see what they are doing at that moment; maybe they are studying for an exam or maybe they are at work. I also look to see if my friends have added any new photos, especially from events such as this weekend's camping trip or Matt's birthday party. I hope no one posts any embarrassing pictures of me—I have family members new to Facebook! Today, I also changed my profile picture since I just got a new haircut, and I updated my favorite music to include the Black Eyed Peas. That concert was the best!

Our student Danielle's social networking practices illustrate a number of issues that we will address in this chapter. For example, how do people present themselves online, and how do they communicate as a result of their choices? How has the prevalence of social networking sites like Facebook changed the way people communicate? And how does computer-mediated communication affect individuals' identities and their relationships with others?

In this chapter, we focus on *computer-mediated* communication (CMC), which plays an increasingly important role in most of our lives. First, we define what we mean by CMC; then we explore its importance. Next, we examine individuals' use of CMC, including the identity issues it raises. We then examine the impact of societal forces on CMC—including how gender, race, and ethnicity influence it, and who does (and does not) have access to it. Finally, we discuss the future of CMC and some of the ethical issues related to it. We conclude with suggestions for improving your own use of computer-mediated communication.

Once you have read this chapter, you will be able to:

- Define computer-mediated communication (CMC).
- Identify reasons for learning about CMC.
- Explain the differences between face-to-face communication and CMC.
- Recognize the types of issues that can arise in identity and relationship development when using CMC.
- Understand the role of power and privilege in CMC.
- Describe the digital divide and its possible solutions.
- Analyze ethical challenges in CMC.
- Discuss three ways to improve your own mediated communication skills.

CHAPTER OUTLINE

WHAT IS COMPUTER-MEDIATED COMMUNICATION?

THE IMPORTANCE OF COMPUTER-MEDIATED COMMUNICATION

HOW DOES COMPUTER-MEDIATED COMMUNICATION IMPACT OUR COMMUNICATION CHOICES?
  Media Deficit Approach
  Media Augmentation Approach
  Social Network Theory

COMPUTER-MEDIATED COMMUNICATION AND THE INDIVIDUAL
  Managing Identity
  Relationship Development

THE INDIVIDUAL, COMMUNICATION TECHNOLOGY, AND SOCIETY
  Gender, Age, Ethnicity, and Technology Use
  Power, Access, and the Digital Divide
  Globalization and the Digital Divide
  Closing the Digital Divide

ETHICS AND COMPUTER-MEDIATED COMMUNICATION
  Ethics and Online Identity
  Building Relationships Online

IMPROVING YOUR COMPUTER-MEDIATED COMMUNICATION SKILLS
  E-mail Etiquette
  Cell Phone Etiquette
  Evaluating Internet Information

Summary

Key Terms

Chapter Review Questions

Activities

Web Activities

computer-mediated communication (CMC)

the exchange of messages carried through an intervening system of digital electronic storage and transmitted between two or more people

digital

information that is transmitted in a numerical format based on only two values (0 and 1)

Internet

a system of networks that connects millions of computers around the world

World Wide Web (WWW)

one of a number of services that moves over the Internet; it uses HTML (Hypertext Markup Language) as its document format

Massively Multiplayer Online Games (MMOGs)

text-based "virtual reality" games in which participants interact with environments, objects, and other participants.

cyberspace

synonymous with the Internet or online world

WHAT IS COMPUTER-MEDIATED COMMUNICATION?

Computer-mediated communication (CMC), which developed alongside computer technology, is the exchange of messages carried through an *intervening* system of **digital** electronic storage and transmitted between two or more people. CMC differs from face-to-face (FtF) communication because with FtF, messages are transmitted more-or-less directly, without the aid of exterior technology (Wood & Smith, 2005, p. 6)—a difference with significant implications, as you will soon see. In contrast, most CMC involves communicating online, using the Internet and the Web. While cell phones are not technically speaking *computer*-mediated communication, they allow us access to the Internet and are now an important form of mediated communication around the world (Goggin, 2006).

Key channels of CMC are the **Internet**, a system of networks that connects millions of computers around the world, and the **World Wide Web (WWW)**, a system of interlinked hypertext documents contained on the Internet. Using a browser on your computer, the WWW allows you to view pages containing text, images, videos, and other multimedia, and to navigate between them using hyperlinks. Online CMC encompasses a wide range of communication possibilities, from personal and commercial Web page to the more interactive e-mail, text messages, tweets, social networking sites (SNS), chats, and **MMOGs (Massively Multiplayer Online Games)**—all accessed on a variety of devices, from desktop and laptop computers, Personal Digital Assistants (PDAs), smart phones, and other mobile devices (see Table 7.1).

The integration of these technologies affords us convenience and allows us to be connected to the Internet practically wherever we go. Portable devices like phones and laptops now use wireless technology. You can talk on the phone while walking the dog, take notes on your computer during class, access MapQuest or phone directories while traveling, answer work e-mail while sitting in the doctor's office (Rainie, 2010). Most CMC scholars, including the authors of this book, are particularly interested in these interactive possibilities, where the "real give and take of social life" in **cyberspace** occurs (Walther & Parks, 2002, p. 3).

TABLE 7.1 Common Computer-Mediated Communication Technologies	
E-mail	Exchange of textual (word-based) messages between two or more parties.
Blog ("Web log")	Web site, like a journal, maintained by an individual with regular entries of commentary, descriptions of events, or other material such as graphics or video. Entries are commonly displayed in reverse-chronological order.
Bulletin board systems	A form of e-mail that communicates to a larger audience. Messages are sent to a single computer address, where they are "posted" for others to read and respond to.
Chats	A type of real-time discussion. Text-based messages sent to and simultaneously read by a group of people.
MMOGS: (Massively Multiplayer Online games)	Text-based "virtual reality" game. Real-time interaction. Participants interact with environment, objects, and other participants.
Instant messages	Text-based message system that allows two people to exchange real-time messages—like private chat.
Short-messaging service (SMS) or text messages	Very brief text messages exchanged on mobile phones.
SNS (social networking sites)	Web-based service where people construct their profiles, identify others with whom they share a connection, and interact with their lists of connections and others within the system.
Twitter	Social networking and micro-blogging service that allows its users to send and read other users' updates (otherwise known as *tweets*), which are text-based posts of up to 140 characters in length.

SOURCE: Adapted from Thurlow et al. (2004, pp. 28–29); Wood & Smith (2005, pp. 10–15).

THE IMPORTANCE OF COMPUTER-MEDIATED COMMUNICATION

You should learn more about CMC for at least three reasons: It is a pervasive form of communication, it has been adopted more rapidly than any other communication technology, and it changes how we communicate with others in multiple ways. First, we say that CMC is pervasive because most of us now engage in it almost constantly. In fact, a recent study showed that children 8 to 18 years old spend almost 8 hours (every waking minute except for time in school) on some electronic communication device (smart phone, computer, television, etc.) (Rideout, Foehr, & Roberts, 2010). On any one day, you may communicate with a professor through e-mail; with other students in an online discussion board; with friends via text messages, Twitter, and Facebook (as our student Danielle did); and with your parents via cell phone. As of December 2009, about 74 percent of adults and 93 percent of young people in the United States were using the Internet (Rainie, 2010).

Second, in addition to their pervasiveness, recent communication technologies are important because they have been adopted so quickly. In 20 years, the Internet has changed the way we inform ourselves, educate ourselves, work, shop, bank, and stay in touch with others. Wireless and cell phone technology has spread even faster. Since 1983 when cellular service first began, mobile phone use has grown to about 4.6 billion (out of 6.7 billion) people worldwide (Castells, Qiu, & Fernández-Ardevol, 2006; The Apparatgeist calls, 2010). What's more, 56 percent of Americans have accessed the Internet by wireless devices—laptops, cell phones, game consoles, etc. In fact, when asked how hard it would be to give up a specific technology, those surveyed said that the cell phone would be the most difficult to do without, followed by the Internet, TV, and landline telephone (Horrigan, 2008a).

Third, CMC impacts multiple daily activities. For example, most people use CMC in four basic ways: (1) exchanging e-mail and instant messages, (2) seeking and exchanging information, (3) entertaining themselves, and (4) completing financial transactions (Daily Internet Activities, 2009).

A 2009 survey revealed that about 89 percent of Internet use involves the exchange of messages, and 88 percent involves seeking information—by far the two most common uses of the Internet. E-mail is used much less by teens (ages 12 to 17) than other generations. They prefer sending text messages from their phone or keeping in touch through social networking sites (SNSs), as our student Danielle does (Jones & Fox, 2009). Online you can find the best margarita recipe; locate phone numbers, addresses, and directions; seek information about unfamiliar illnesses; check the weather; and explore an endless array of other topics.

You can also follow news on commercial Web sites or **blogs** (short for *weblogs*). About 70 million blogs now exist worldwide, and bloggers collectively create almost one million posts every day (*State of the blogosphere* 2008). Blogging activity has increased exponentially since 1999, partly because mainstream media have increasingly recognized blog content as legitimate news sources and because blogging software, especially connected to Twitter, allows users the ability to update rapidly and easily—seen most dramatically in the coverage of the election protests in Iran (Mclean, 2009; Sussman, 2009). People blog for many reasons: to document their lives; to express opinions or commentary; as an outlet for thoughts and feelings; to test ideas or "muse"; and for community forums (Sussman, 2009).

One of the most common information-gathering uses of CMC for college students, however, is doing course research. Some of your online research may involve **podcasts**, as colleges and universities now provide podcasts of various lecture series and important speakers on campus. Currently, 19 percent of all Internet users say they have downloaded a podcast to listen to or view at a later time (Jones & Fox, 2009). Newspapers and magazines like *The Wall Street Journal* and *The Economist* and radio and TV networks like NPR and PBS even offer daily podcasts of their publications and shows.

Some experts worry about our overreliance on the Internet for information; they say that we only "skim" on the Internet and that we don't have to remember information anymore because it's always at our fingertips. As a result, they speculate, we are becoming less able to concentrate and recall information (Carr, 2008). The importance of Internet

blogs
short for "Web logs"; a Web site, like a journal, maintained by an individual with regular entries of commentary, descriptions of events, or other material such as graphics or video

podcast
a prerecorded audio program that's posted to a website and is made available for download so people can listen to it on personal computers or mobile devices.

search activities in our lives may be seen in the fact that *google* is now a verb. If we need information, we google it!

CMC is also used for entertainment—and this third use is most popular among adolescents and college students and those with high-speed connections at home (Jones & Fox, 2009). Three popular online activities are watching and downloading videos, playing video games, and downloading music. For example, 53 percent of American adults age 18 and older play video games—often on the Internet—and about 20 percent play every day or almost every day (Lenhart, Jones, & MacGill, 2008).

The fourth common use of the Internet is centered around financial transactions, including shopping, paying bills, checking bank accounts, and managing stock portfolios. This activity also varies by generation. Although most of us have used the Internet in this way, members of Generation X (ages 33 to 44) lead in online shopping and are more likely than any other generation to do their banking online (Jones & Fox, 2009).

It's easy to see that many everyday activities and transactions that used to be conducted face-to-face are now being carried out in cyberspace using computer-mediated communication. How do these changing patterns affect our everyday communication, our identity, and our relationships?

HOW DOES COMPUTER-MEDIATED COMMUNICATION IMPACT OUR COMMUNICATION CHOICES?

Because CMC is a relatively recent and rapidly changing form of communication, it is difficult to arrive at definitive conclusions about its exact role in everyday life. Researching this aspect of communication can be like trying to hit a moving target. Still, with a basic understanding of what CMC is and the ways in which it can differ from FtF communication, we can get some sense of its increasingly important role.

To begin, consider this question: Have you ever tried to decide whether to communicate a message by e-mail, by text message, or in person? Perhaps you had a difficult issue to discuss and were unsure what the most effective mode of communication would be. If so, you had good reason to feel unsure. CMC and face-to-face communication differ in several ways, and these differences can impact the outcome of your conversation.

When it comes to determining whether FtF is more useful than CMC (or vice versa), even scholars disagree. Early researchers proposed the **media deficit approach**, which suggests that mediated communication is less useful than face-to-face communication. More recently, however, many CMC experts have emphasized the **media augmentation approach**, which suggests that mediated communication can play a complementing or augmenting role in our face-to-face communication. We'll consider each of these approaches.

Media Deficit Approach

The media deficit approach is based on two characteristics of early mediated communication. First, it is a **filtered** form of communication—which means it lacks nonverbal cues. Second, it is asynchronous in nature—which means a delay may occur between the time the message is sent and when it is responded to.

Filtered Communication

As you learned in Chapter 4, nonverbal cues play an important role in understanding the totality of a person's message. When you speak to someone face-to-face, you see their gestures, facial expressions, and attire; you hear their sighs, accent, or dialect. These are just a few of the many cues that you use to fully understand what a person means. Most communication tools on the Internet, however—like text messages and tweets—are "cues-filtered out" forms of communication. So when you communicate via the Internet, you are no longer able to consider all of those valuable cues that help you determine what is being communicated.

Two "deficit" theories help us understand the impact of filtering on some forms of CMC: social presence theory and media richness theory. **Social presence** refers to the

---

media deficit approach
a theoretical perspective that sees mediated communication as deficient in comparison to face-to-face communication

media augmentation approach
a theoretical perspective that views mediated communication as complementing or augmenting face-to-face communication

filtered
a form of communication that lacks nonverbal cues

social presence
degree of psychological closeness or immediacy engendered by various media

feelings of psychological closeness or immediacy that people experience when they interact with each other (Short, Williams, & Christie, 1976). This closeness is communicated through nonverbal cues, like smiling, leaning forward, and relaxed body posture. **Social presence theory** suggests that face-to-face communication is generally high in this kind of social presence and that media vary in the amount of social presence they convey. For example, talking on the telephone conveys less social presence than face-to-face interaction but more than e-mail communication—where all nonverbal cues are filtered out. The implication is that media low in social presence (like texting, e-mailing, and tweets, for example) seem more impersonal, less sensitive, and less "relationship-focused."

Media richness theory describes the potential information-carrying capacity of a communication medium (Daft & Lengel, 1984, 1986). According to this theory, face-to-face communication is the richest medium for communicating—because you can see facial expressions and body gestures as well as hear the tone, speed, and quality of a person's voice. (See *Visual Summary 7.1: Media Richness Theory.*) All these factors relay a tremendous amount of information and allow you to interpret messages more accurately. You not only hear the words, or the content of the message, but you also receive the relational messages that are being sent nonverbally and that reveal how that person feels about you. If the other person is smiling, leaning toward you, and maintaining eye contact, you probably infer that the person is happy or glad to talk with you. If the person is scowling and avoiding eye contact, you might infer that she or he is angry or unhappy with you.

According to media richness theory, some types of mediated communication do allow for a certain amount of richness. Consider video/audio communication or Skype, an Internet-based video chat service. When you communicate using a webcam, you might miss some immediate context cues, such as body posture or gestures, but you have the benefit of seeing some of the nonverbal behaviors of the person you're communicating with. The telephone is a less rich medium. Conversation partners can process the audio information and discern some paralinguistic cues, but they don't see facial expression, eye gaze, or gestures.

The least-rich media—according to media richness theory—are e-mail, text messaging, and tweets. But nonverbal cues aren't completely absent here either. Some relational/nonverbal information *can* be communicated in CMC. For example, some people convey relational information by **emoticons**, or pictographs, such as the smiley face—:)—or they use abbreviations like LOL (laughing out loud) or H&K (hugs and kisses).

Of course, writing (including writing e-mails and text messages) is a form of communication that includes many techniques for expressing mood and feelings. For example, moods can be expressed by punctuation, by the length of sentences, and by various adjectives and adverbs. You can also communicate intonation by emphasizing particular words in a sentence or by repetition. Using capital letters counts as shouting, as you can see in the following message (and some people avoid this to keep from offending others). Is there any question about its tone?

I just DON'T understand you; it just doesn't MAKE ANY SENSE. Why would you not want to spend the weekend here? WHY? I worked overtime for three weeks in a row so I could have the weekend off, told all my friends that you were coming to visit, and NOW you tell me you can't make it. I JUST DON'T BELIEVE IT!!!!!

Asynchronous Interaction

Another difference between face-to-face communication and some types of CMC is the degree to which the exchange of messages is synchronous or asynchronous. Face-to-face communication and media like the telephone and CMC chats are **synchronous**; that is, messages are sent and received at the same time. However, e-mail, bulletin board messages, and video recordings are **asynchronous**; that is, messages may be received at a later time. Text messaging may be synchronous or not, depending on how quickly the other person acknowledges and/or responds to the message.

When you send a computer-mediated message through an asynchronous medium, it is almost impossible to know if the other person has received your message—because you

social presence theory
theory that suggests that face-to-face communication is generally high in social presence and that media vary in the amount of social presence they convey

media richness theory
describes the potential information-carrying capacity of a communication medium

emoticons
pictographs used in e-mail to convey relational information

synchronous
communication in which messages are sent and received at the same time

asynchronous
communication in which messages are sent and then received at a later time

Media Richness Theory

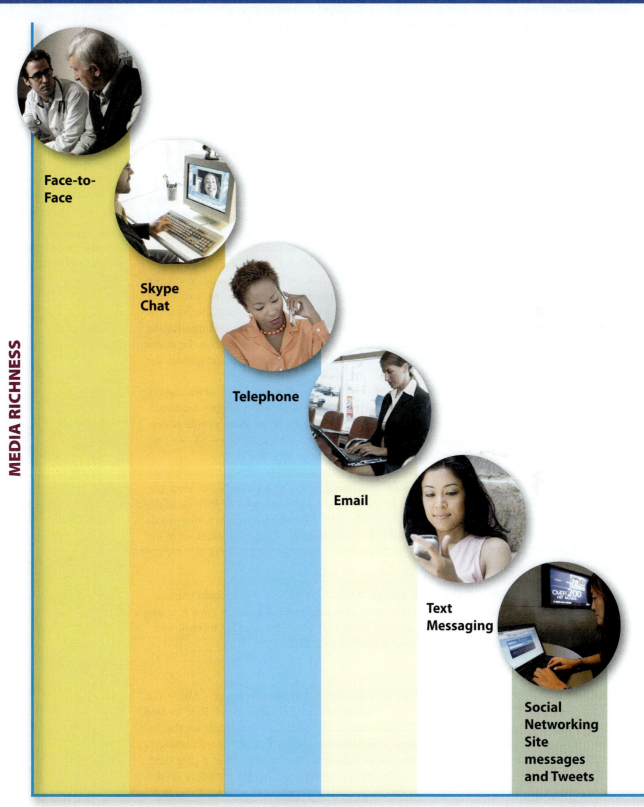

MEDIA RICHNESS

Face-to-Face

Skype Chat

Telephone

Email

Text Messaging

Social Networking Site messages and Tweets

MEDIA TYPE

don't receive any "in the moment" response. Such silences or nonresponses can be problematic. In face-to-face interaction, silences can be meaningful and are usually interpreted by nonverbal cues to mean hesitation, reflection, or perhaps anger. But silence after posting a new Facebook status or sending a text message might mean anything, ranging from lack of interest to a technology glitch. Yet the implications for relationships can be severe.

According to media deficit theorists, asynchronicity may also create a lack of shared reality. That is, asynchronicity in CMC may impact personal relationships because the notion of friendship includes shared experiences, feelings, and activities. So, when you receive terrific news that you want to share with your best friend, telling him or her through an e-mail message or delayed text message (if your friend does not immediately respond to your message) does not have the same impact that a face-to-face conversation does. See *Communication in Society: Love in the Age of Social Networking* to read how constant texting and lack of face-to-face contact can make relationships seem more distant—and certainly more complicated.

While there are few distinct differences between face-to-face and mediated communication when it comes to social presence and media richness, how do the characteristics of filtering and asynchronicity in CMC affect communication in everyday life? Deficit scholars suggest that the answer partly depends on the purpose of the conversation and the context. In contexts where messages communicate basic information—such as getting an Evite or driving directions from a friend—the filtering of nonverbal cues and the leanness of the medium may not be a problem. However, communicating feelings—for example, breaking up with someone by text messaging—may be a different story. Personal preferences may also come into play. Some shy people prefer mediated communication over face-to-face meetings (Auter, 2007). Also, age makes a difference; your grandmother probably prefers to talk with you face-to-face or on the telephone rather than by text messages. In the end, deficit theorists emphasize the deficiencies of some CMC—that is, their lack of social presence and information-carrying richness compared with face-to-face communication—and that their impact varies based on context, working well for some and not for others.

Think of a recent conflict you had and describe how it might have been different if the communication media had been different. How might it have gone over the telephone? Face-to-face? Text messaging?

Communication in SOCIETY

Love in the Age of Social Networking

In a recent article, reporter Nicole Rosenleaf Ritter writes about the good and not-so-good sides of technology. According to Ritter, "When it comes to technology, young people and relationships, the interplay can perhaps best be summarized by a phrase familiar to Facebook users: 'It's complicated.'"

Ritter reports that most young people love the convenience of social networking sites like Facebook, MySpace, and Twitter and the ease of cell phone texting. It provides opportunities to make new friends, reconnect with old friends, and stay in constant contact with those we love.

However, according to the people Ritter interviewed, there are some downsides. Some young people say that all the CMC makes dating harder. That is, people are texting more than talking, and after all the texting, relationships seem more distant and less personal.

Others mentioned "the speed of gossip" on social networking sites as a downside, explaining that there is no such thing as a private relationship or breakup on Facebook. When someone changes their 'relationship status,' it's there for everyone to see.

According to one college counselor who Ritter interviewed, while the constant contact gives young people an important sense of belonging, something might be lost in all the texting and CMC: human contact. "I think that some people are bypassing face-to-face bonding and missing the clues that they would get from sitting down with someone," he said. "There are no inflections and they are getting no feedback. That can cause misunderstandings."

All of this, Ritter concludes, points to just why teens and 20-somethings find technology and relationships "complicated." "While the technology is necessary and omnipresent, it can be difficult to navigate, especially when the rules still are being written."

SOURCE: Ritter, N. R. (2010, January 8). "Love in the age of social networking too much text and not enough talk?" *The Great Falls Tribune*. Retrieved January 8, 2010, from http://www.greatfallstribune.com/article/20100108/LIFESTYLE/1080324/Love-in-the-age-of-social-networking-too-much-text-and-not-enough-talk

Media Augmentation Approach

Most current CMC experts emphasize the media augmentation approach, which suggests that CMC complements or augments face-to face encounters. Scholars who support this view note that having prior information about a person can be helpful when you are interpreting their CMC relational messages. In this way, e-mail and text messages are rendered less "lean." For example, suppose you and a classmate have been texting each other about a recent assignment:

> *Your Classmate:* I bombed that last assignment. Most of the class did too. Maybe he'll grade on a curve. How'd u do?
> *You:* Did okay. B+, i think.
> *Your Classmate:* That's just great for u.

Interpreting the phrase "that's just great for u" is easier if you know something about the way your classmate usually communicates. Otherwise, her text response could mean anything from supportive of you ("That's just *great* for u!"), to hostile that you succeeded when the rest of the class didn't ("That's just great for *u*.")—potentially ruining the curve for everyone else—to sarcastic ("That's *just great* for *you*.") (Rooksby, 2002).

At the same time, several media augmentation scholars point out that the asynchronicity of CMC messages can also have positive effects. For example, it can give people time to formulate a message, which might be especially important in a conflict situation or when communicating in a foreign language (Osman & Herring, 2007; Thompson & Ku, 2005). In the same way, they point out, the lack of physical data that may trigger stereotypes and prejudice is also a potential benefit of the cue-filtering characteristics of CMC. For example, on the Internet, we may not be able to determine someone's race/gender/age/ability-disability and so are less likely to show prejudice or discrimination in online communication (Merryfield, 2003; Postmes, Spears, & Lea, 1998).

Further, according to media augmentation scholars, mediated and face-to-face communication are not necessarily two different realities. People simply use multiple media with varying degrees of social presence and media richness, in addition to face-to-face interaction, to fit their social needs and lifestyles (Boase, 2008; Sawhney, 2007). For example, in a series of research studies, college students were asked to rate the quality of their interpersonal interaction online as compared with their face-to-face and telephone interactions. The majority of students rated the quality of all three forms about the same. Thus, the authors of the study concluded, people do not perceive face-to-face communication as vastly superior to online communication. Moreover, they wrote, "instead of a trade-off between high quality FtF conversations and lower quality internet interaction, students are supplementing high quality FtF conversations and telephone calls with really good internet interactions" (Baym, Zhang, & Lin, 2004, p. 316). A more recent study of Americans of all ages found that face-to-face contact "still trumps" all other means of communication—that is, people still spend more time in FtF communication than they do using cell phone, landline phone, text messaging, e-mail, and instant messaging and visiting social networking sites (Hampton, Sessions, Her, & Rainie, 2009).

Media augmentation experts acknowledge that some skepticism about the impact of new communication technologies is understandable. Still, they caution, we should not assume that online communication is inferior to FtF communication.

Social Network Theory

Social network theory proposes that the patterns of connections among people affect their social behavior and communication. In short, the more that people are socially connected to each other, the more intensely they are likely to communicate using various media available to them. Indeed, one study found that people who had more frequent FtF social contacts also had more frequent online contacts—compared to those who had fewer FtF contacts. These findings suggest that, as with previous advances in communication technology (for example, the telephone), CMC enhances the process of connecting people rather than isolating them (Bimie & Horvath, 2002).

social network theory
proposes that the patterns of connections among people affect their social behavior and communication

More recent research has considered cell phone use too. These studies come to similar conclusions—that is, that cell phones and the Internet have not weakened relationships, nor do they act as poor substitutes for FtF contact. Instead, the research shows that individuals use various media to connect with different social networks. For example, people tend to use mobile phones to stay in contact with people they already know well, and they use the Internet to expand their social network—getting to know or staying in touch with people who are geographically distant. So, a person may get to know someone on the Internet, and as these ties develop, the Internet friends may contact each other through other means—either in person or by phone (Boase, 2007; Hampton et al., 2009; Katz, 2007; Kim, Kim, Park, & Rice, 2007; Ling, 2004). At least one expert suggests that mobile phones can even restore the comfort and intimacy that was degraded by twentieth-century technologies, especially the television (Gergen, 2002).

As you can see, then, while the social presence and richness (or lack thereof) of various communication media are important, the differences between face-to-face and mediated communication are not distinct, and the jury is still somewhat out on exactly how CMC affects our lives and relationships. What is clear is that CMC is an important part of our lives, and people use multiple media in addition to face-to-face interaction to fit their social needs and lifestyles. Whether it undermines or enhances our connections and communications with others is yet to be seen. And this should not be a surprise, considering the pace of its development and how much we still have to learn about its capacities. With these thoughts in mind, let's look at a related topic: how personal identity is performed and managed in CMC.

COMPUTER-MEDIATED COMMUNICATION AND THE INDIVIDUAL

Clearly, CMC's unique properties can powerfully impact communication between individuals. The combined effects of filtering and asynchronicity have important implications for identity and, in turn, for personal relationships. Let's examine the way this works.

Managing Identity

The same characteristics that filter out nonverbal cues and make some CMC a "leaner" form of communication add an interesting dimension to how communicators present themselves online. For example, in some types of CMC—for example, when posting on an Internet forum—we can control the amount of information we disclose about ourselves, providing a fluidity to our identities that we don't have in face-to-face communication. Think back to Danielle in the opening vignette. She made several decisions about the identity she wanted to communicate through Facebook.

As we noted in Chapter 2, one's identity (or self-concept) is developed and expressed through communication with others. Early CMC researchers thought that online identities differed significantly from offline identities. However, as CMC has become the norm in our lives, researchers have begun to suggest that some CMC provides us the opportunity to express identities in ways not possible in face-to-face communication (Zywica & Danowski, 2008, p. 7). Three identity issues are discussed below. Two extreme possibilities are (1) being anonymous or (2) presenting yourself as someone you are not in real life (psuedoidentity). A third, more common issue in CMC involves deciding what information to present to others online—related to impression management, discussed further in Chapter 9.

Anonymity and Psuedoanonymity

As we discussed earlier in this chapter, when you communicate with someone over e-mail or in an online course-discussion forum—unless they infer information from your name—they would not know your age, gender, race, nationality, or many of the other cues that affect our perceptions of individuals. So CMC offers the possibility of withholding more aspects of your identity from public consideration than has ever before been possible.

spoofing
misrepresenting oneself online

spam
unwanted commercial messages
and advertisements sent
through e-mail

phishing
e-mail messages that try
(fraudulently) to get consumer
banking and credit card
information

cyberbullying
the deliberate and repeated misuse
of communication technology
by an individual or group to
threaten or harm others

pseudoanonymity
projecting a false identity

This anonymity may be beneficial or detrimental, depending on your viewpoint. Communication researchers Andrew F. Wood and Matthew J. Smith (2005) identify three issues in the complex relationship between anonymity and identity in online communication. The first has to do with the informative aspect of the identity. On the one hand, knowing something about the person sending information gives a context for judging his or her messages. If you know, for example, that the person answering your medical question online is a doctor, that person seems more credible than a person without a medical degree. On the other hand, information on age, gender, and race can form the basis for stereotyping and prejudice.

A second issue regarding anonymity is its capacity to liberate speech. For example, without knowing who has issued a statement, the legal restrictions on speech are difficult to enforce. So if someone, while **spoofing**, or misrepresenting oneself online, makes racist or libelous statements, it is almost impossible to implement legal sanctions. On the other hand, anonymity can give some people courage to express unpopular opinions or question conventional wisdom, which they might be afraid to do in face-to-face interaction.

The third issue related to CMC and anonymity is that the combination has generated a new set of group norms. In some ways, the freedom that people feel as a result of their anonymity may lead them to be less responsible communicators. For example, one professor noted that in online courses, "students are sometimes aggressive . . . something that never happened in face-to-face classes" (Smith, Ferguson, & Caris, 2001, p. 25). Anonymity can also lead to bad behavior in virtual worlds. Recently, two players were banned from *Second Life* for depicting sexual activity between an adult and a child (Serious trouble, 2007). In addition, anonymity facilitates e-mail rumors and hoaxes—e.g., warnings that canola oil can cause cancer; claims that companies like Microsoft will give away free money to people who forward the e-mail message to five additional people. (For information about evaluating these types of messages, go to http://urbanlegends.about.com/od/internet/a/current_netlore.htm).

Additional detrimental issues are the millions of **spam** messages (unwanted commercial messages and advertisements sent through e-mail), which might be greatly reduced if addresses or spammers' identities were easier to trace. **Phishing**—the practice of fraudulently trying to get consumer banking and credit card information—is another problem for Internet users. Increasing numbers of fake e-mails are showing up in e-mail inboxes, "warning" users that their account information needs to be checked and then pointing to Web sites that ask the user to enter financial information. Technology companies and banks are aggressively pursuing those who send spam and phishing messages (Seagraves, 2004).

Another form of bad behavior online is **cyberbullying**—"the deliberate and repeated misuse of communication technology by an individual or group to threaten or harm others" (Roberto & Eden, in press). Cyberbullying differs from traditional bullying partly because it can be anonymous, it can occur anywhere (through voice, text, picture, or video messages on cell phones, and through social networking sites, chat rooms, bulletin boards, etc.), and an infinite number of viewers can observe or participate. Research shows that cyberbullying can have many negative consequences for victims, ranging from psychological problems like depression, anxiety, and low self-esteem to disastrous consequences, as in the most famous case of Megan Meier who committed suicide after being harassed on MySpace by a schoolmate's parent (posing as a 16 year old boy). Some experts report that 25 to 30 percent of minors are involved in cyberbullying, leading many schools to implement cyberbullying prevention programs.

The final form of online bad behavior related to anonymity that we'll discuss is deception. If you have represented yourself as something you are not on a discussion board or on your Facebook or MySpace profile, you are not alone. Forty-nine percent of young people say they have put false information on their social networking sites, and they give many reasons for doing so. Fabricating data on these sites may protect you from unwanted advances from strangers, or it can shield you from the watchful eye of your parents (boyd, 2007).

Beyond anonymity is a phenomenon made possible by CMC: **pseudoanonymity**, or projecting a false identity. For example, people can invent identities through very acceptable means in MMOGs like *World of Warcraft, EverQuest II,* and *Karaoke Revolution,* or in virtual worlds like *Second Life* and *Entropia Universe.* The original

multiplayer game was *Dungeons & Dragons,* but hundreds of MMOGS now exist on the Internet—some for gaming and others, like *Second Life,* for socializing, pedagogical purposes, or commercial ventures. In these virtual worlds, as many as 10,000 people or their **avatars**—digital alter-egos/versions of themselves—can be present at the same time, engaged in activities from hanging out, to holding charity fundraisers, to operating sex clubs (Siklos, 2006). Some universities have developed sites on *Second Life* where professors and students can interact, and a big American bank is using PIXELLearning's simulator for "diversity and inclusion training" (Serious trouble, 2007).

avatar
a computer user's representation of himself/herself, or alter ego

Even though some of these communities are based on false identities, deception can still occur. For example, in one MMOG called *Bluesky,* a player and her boyfriend decided to take turns playing a character to see if other players would notice. When they decided to "confess" to the other players, some felt betrayed, even though identities in this game were understood to be assumed or false (Kendall, 2002). In this case, the outcome was relatively benign. In other cases, however, people have misrepresented themselves with far more significant results. Vivian, one of our students, recounted a troubling Internet-related incident involving a teacher (see *It Happened to Me: Vivian*). In this case, both individuals used anonymity in deceptive ways, allowing the police officer to perform her job and resulting in an arrest for the teacher who had committed a crime.

You may remember a few years ago that sites like MySpace were implicated in a series of sexual interactions between adults and minors, although some researchers say that concerns about sexual predators on SNSs were greatly exaggerated (boyd & Ellison, 2007).

In virtual worlds like this, people, through their avatars, can participate in various activities—from hanging out, to playing games, to attending virtual pedagogical functions such as lectures or academic courses.

Impression Management Online

You may never have taken advantage of online anonymity, and with the rise of SNSs, the whole point is to be seen and known. But like our student Danielle, you have probably made decisions about what kind of information to reveal about yourself on these sites. But how do you decide? Researchers have discovered that some decisions about what to reveal on SNSs are related to a person's age, their self-esteem, and their popularity. As it turns out, younger adolescents experiment more with online identities than young adults do (Valkenburg & Peter, 2007a). Perhaps not surprisingly, people with low self-esteem tend to reveal more and present exaggerated information about themselves online. For example, someone might say that he is an avid skier and scuba diver when, in reality, he likes these sports but hasn't actually done either in the past ten years (Zywica & Danowski, 2008). In contrast, popular users tend to make strategic moves to enhance their popularity—for example, changing their profile picture in order to appear more popular and changing their Facebook profiles, noting new activities or interests, and adding friends (Zywica & Danowski, 2008).

Another aspect of self-presentation is listing friendship links, because "You are who you know." Unlike "friends" in the everyday sense, "friends" on SNSs can be used to provide context and to offer users a kind of imagined audience to interact with (boyd & Ellison, 2007). But adding too many friends can have the opposite effect, raising doubts about one's popularity and desirability (Tong, Van Der Heide, Langwell, & Walther, 2008). How much personal information to include in an SNS profile may also be determined by privacy and security concerns.

IT HAPPENED TO ME: *Vivian*

At my high school, my math teacher was arrested and fired for communicating over the Internet with a 13-year-old girl. They formed a relationship, and when he went to meet her, he found a female police officer. So both participants were lying. The police officer told my teacher she was a young girl, and my math teacher told her he was a 16-year-old boy.

Unfortunately, young people are not always aware of the public nature of the Internet, and they disclose too much information on SNSs. For example, spammers have used freely accessible profile data from SNSs to craft phishing schemes that appear to originate from a friend on the network. Targets were much more likely to give away information to this "friend" than to a perceived "stranger" (boyd & Ellison, 2007). As we noted in Chapter 1, potential employers can also access profile information. According to one study, 34 percent of employers surveyed admit to dismissing a candidate from consideration because of what they found on social networking sites (see *Did You Know? Employers Admit to Disqualifying Candidates Due to Facebook Content*).

To summarize, the anonymity of CMC affords many possibilities for performing and managing identities, but it also brings with it ethical challenges, which we discuss later in the chapter. Let's now turn our attention to how relationships develop and are maintained through CMC.

DID YOU KNOW?

Employers Admit to Disqualifying Candidates Due to Facebook Content

My conversations with dozens, and perhaps even hundreds, of employers who hire college students for internships and recent graduates for entry-level jobs have led me to believe that about 75 percent are searching social networking sites such as Facebook and MySpace as part of their background-checking process. But one question that was harder to answer was how many of those employers have declined to hire a candidate because of content on those sites.

Careerbuilder recently surveyed hiring managers and found that of those who admit to screening job candidates using Facebook, MySpace, and other social networking sites, 34 percent admit to dismissing a candidate from consideration because of what they found on the social networking sites. The top areas for concern among these hiring managers were:

- 41% – candidate posted information about themselves drinking or using drugs
- 40% – candidate posted provocative or inappropriate photographs or information
- 29% – candidate had poor communication skills
- 28% – candidate bad-mouthed their previous company or fellow employee
- 27% – candidate lied about qualifications
- 22% – candidate used discriminatory remarks related to race, gender, religion, etc.
- 22% – candidate's screen name was unprofessional
- 21% – candidate was linked to criminal behavior
- 19% – candidate shared confidential information from previous employers

I've said it before and I'll say it again: Don't put anything online on any site unless you would feel comfortable sharing that information with your favorite grandmother. Posting information online is like getting a tattoo; there's nothing inherently wrong with it, but you have to understand that it is permanent and that people who you may not want to see it will at times see it.

SOURCE: CollegeRecruiter Web site. Retrieved December 11, 2008, from http://www.collegerecruiter.com/weblog/2008/09/employers_admit.php

Relationship Development

Today, most of us carry on relationships through CMC. In fact, you probably have some relationships that exist only online, such as with acquaintances you met in an online course or on a bulletin board. You may have other friends with whom you interact both on and offline. So before we go any further in this discussion, we want to reiterate two

points we made earlier, in the section about the media augmentation approach. First, people who spend a lot of time online are not necessarily introverted, nor do they prefer the filtered CMC because they can't establish "real" relationships. Some early research indicated that when *some* people increase online interaction, they do decrease contact with their "real" friends and acquaintances (Kraut et al., 1998). And young people who suffered from depression were more likely than others to use the Internet to make friends (Hwang, Cheong, & Feeley, 2008). However, most researchers have argued that Internet socializing complements rather than replaces traditional socializing (Finn & Korukonda, 2004).

Second, offline relationships are not necessarily more "real" than Internet relationships. As we noted earlier, many relationships are maintained through multiple media—Internet, telephone, and face-to-face encounters—depending on geographical and other circumstances (Baym et al., 2005; Beer, 2008). With these thoughts in mind, let's consider the impact of CMC on three types of relationships: friendships, romantic relationships, and relationships in the workplace.

Friendships

While online and offline relationships have much in common, CMC impacts our relational development in several ways: Online relationships offer a larger field of availables, and they overcome limits of time and space.

The phrase **field of availables** describes the fact that the field of potential partners and friends accessible through CMC is much larger than in face-to-face relationships. This is true for two reasons. First, you can come into contact with many more people online than you ever would in person. Moreover, when online, you have fewer reasons to dismiss someone as a potential friend/partner, because initial physical cues are not present. The fact that you engage with someone in a chat room, over e-mail, or on a discussion board means that you already have something in common, which is a powerful means of attraction.

The nature of online friendships can have both positive and negative implications. On the positive side, online relationships may be more durable. For example, if you have a relationship that is strictly online and you relocate to another region of the country (or even overseas), the relationship may not be affected. As people are increasingly mobile, CMC affords more continuity than was possible before (Kendall, 2002).

On the other hand, online relationships can be somewhat more fragile, partly because they require some skepticism; as discussed above, deception frequently occurs in initial stages of online relationships. How can you effectively navigate social networking Web sites, for example, where online relationships are developed? Because the information you post on SNSs is potentially accessed by hundreds of thousands of people, you should carefully consider how much and what type of information you post. For example, would you tell a complete stranger who you were with last night and what you did? Probably not, but if you post this information on a social networking site, you would be doing just that, unless you take some precautions. Therefore, when you go on Facebook or MySpace, it's useful to ask yourself: Do I know who has access to the information? Do I know how it will be used? How much information do I want to share with others? For some guidelines, see *Building Your Communication Skills: Guidelines for Using Social Networking Sites.*

When you do develop friendship online with people you like, more trust is required than in face-to-face relationships (Boyd, 2003; Carter, 2004; Rooksby, 2002). As one MMOGer said:

> You have these friends, but maybe the worst thing is knowing that the last time you "see" somebody may be the last time you ever see them. There's no guarantee that they're ever coming back. This happened last year. [One of our players] just disappeared (Kendall, 2002, p. 149).

For this reason, many people who develop friendships on discussion boards or in chat rooms also exchange e-mail addresses or phone numbers—or even meet offline—in order

field of availables
the field of potential partners and friends accessible through CMC that is much larger than in face-to-face relationships

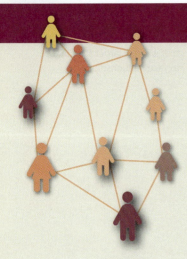

Building Your Communication **SKILLS**

Guidelines for Using Social Networking Sites

Southampton Solent University offers the following guidelines to their students for using Social Networking Sites (SNS):

1. Know whether a site is secure or not. If it has a yellow padlock symbol at the bottom, it is secure. But know that even if the padlock symbol is displayed, be cautious. Clever programmers can insert spoof symbols.

2. Protect your identity. Know that networking sites make money by selling information to marketing companies who use it to try to sell things to you and your friends. Check the site's privacy policy to see what they do with your information.

3. Be careful what you say or show about yourself or anyone else. Don't post info or photos that you or anyone else might find embarrassing or that you don't what family, professors, or potential employers to see or know about.

4. Know that "there are no erasers on the Internet." Once you post information on a site, it can be very difficult to remove it because of file sharing, archiving, and other considerations. Even if you unsubscribe to a site, the info may remain visible for a long time.

5. Use SNS safely. Facebook, for example has a number of options that will restrict who can see what's in your account. Spend some time with the settings if you don't want all your info visible to potentially several hundred thousand people. For example, when you register, enter only very basic info about yourself. Then click on the Privacy option at the top right-hand corner of the screen and adjust settings. Set profile privacy settings to "only my friends." Then click on Search privacy setting. Under the "Who can find me?" the default is "all my networks and all of my friends." Only choose "everyone" if you are willing to let anyone see that you are in Facebook. It's probably a good idea to deselect the "allow my public search listing to be indexed by external search engines."

SOURCE: "Guidelines for Using Social Networking Sites" (2006). Southampton Solent University. Retrieved January 26, 2010, from http://portal-live.solent.ac.uk/university/stay_safe/internet.aspx

---

to establish more trust (Kendall, 2002). As noted early, many friendships are maintained through both online and offline interaction. Most SNSs primarily support preexisting social relations rather than offering opportunities to initiate new ones (boyd & Ellison, 2007; Ellison, Steinfeld, & Lampe, 2007).

Communication researcher Joseph Walther (1996) suggests that those in Internet relationships can develop intimacy more quickly than those in FtF relationships. Perhaps this is because in communication carried out via e-mail, participants place great importance on the few cues that aren't filtered out. In fact, those receiving messages seem to "fill in the blanks" about the personality of the sender (Rosen, Cheever, Cummings, & Felt, 2008). They can also take time to carefully craft their own messages. For example, when people sit at the computer replying to a newfound friend, they tend to give the written words great meaning and to disclose more rapidly than they might in face-to-face interaction (McKenna, Green, & Gleason, 2002). However, when moving a CMC-only relationship offline, the timing may be important; some experts suggest that it is better to move a relationship offline fairly soon after an initial meeting, before people develop an idealized notion of their online partner and have unrealistic expectations (Ramirez & Zhang, 2007, p. 306).

Romantic Relationships

Who becomes involved in online romantic relationships, and how does online romance differ from in-person romance? According to one survey, 37 percent of single U.S. American Internet users who are looking for a romantic partner have gone to a dating Web site (Madden & Lenhart, 2006). Many of these Web sites feature a scientific approach, which often includes compatibility and personality testing. Others focus on niche marketing, including Spark Networks. Spark's online dating sites include JDate for Jewish singles, as well as CatholicMingle.com, InterracialSingles.net, BlackSingles.com, LatinSinglesConnection.com, and Chemistry.com, and the company promotes itself as more inclusive than other sites such as eHarmony.com (Facenda, 2008).

Online dating sites seem to be used by people across all income and educational levels, and by both males and females. Sites like lavalifePRIME, BOOMj.com, and PrimeSingles.net are among those offering social networking for older singles (Jayson, 2008). In one study, people around 40 years of age were the most active online daters, probably because it is relatively difficult for people of this age group to find a romantic partner using more traditional strategies. Singles in this age group are often divorced and may have to combine taking care of children with a busy career (Valkenburg & Peter, 2007b). Younger people are increasingly using Facebook and Facebook's new online dating sites—Are You Interested? and Meet New People—to find romantic partners (Krauss, 2008).

Psychologists have identified three qualities of Internet communication that are particularly relevant to romantic relationships: The ease of finding similar others, of "getting past the gates," and of achieving intimate exchanges (McKenna et al., 2002).

It's easy to see how one can meet people with similar interests via online bulletin boards, discussions boards, or singles' chat rooms, where people gather precisely because they share an interest. In contrast, finding people with similar interests offline may be more difficult.

Second, and perhaps even more important, when meeting online, it's easier to "get past the gates" that people sometimes close to each other because of features such as physical appearance, visible shyness, or lack of strong social skills. Getting past the initial barriers can increase self-esteem and confidence, which in turn can lead to more ease in initiating relationships.

Third, CMC may give rise to easier, quicker self-disclosure and intimacy (as we have noted). For example, on Internet dating sites, profiles are set up to reveal extensive information about potential partners—describing their personalities, interests (what they read, music they listen to, and so forth), ideal dates, and political persuasion. It is easy to see how CMC in this context may lead to relationships in which people develop intimacy more quickly (Henderson & Gilding, 2004; Whitty, 2007).

However, developing online relationships poses dangers and can provide opportunities for deception and fraud (as described earlier in *It Happened to Me: Vivian*). In one study of online dating practices, researchers found that 50 percent of the participants admitted to lying about their looks, relationship status, age, weight, socioeconomic status, or interests (Whitty, 2007). Furthermore, many people have been swindled out of money by criminals who pose as potential suitors and ask for money after gaining the trust and interest of dating partners (Mangla, 2008). It pays to be careful online; for suggestions on staying safe, see *Building Your Communication Skills: Safety Tips for Dating Online* (Madden & Lenhart, 2006).

Even in the face of potential dangers, people can and do form close, lasting relationships on the Internet. Many of the same things that make offline romantic relationships work are important in online relationships, like intimacy, trust, and communication satisfaction (Anderson & Emmers-Sommer, 2006). But can these relationships survive face-to-face meetings? The answer depends on whether one has engaged in honest self-disclosure, communicated one's "true self," and established solid commonality (McKenna et al., p. 24).

Work Relationships

While most workers report that communication technologies have improved their ability to do their jobs, share ideas with coworkers, and work in a flexible way, there are some

Building Your Communication SKILLS

Safety Tips for Online Dating

1. Avoid giving out personal information such as your home address or telephone number to people you meet on the Internet; not everyone is what they seem. There are predators out there, but they won't look like wolves; they'll be disguised as sheep.

2. Exercise caution when agreeing to meet anyone in person whom you've met online. Before you arrange any such meeting, at least try to address the following:
   a. Can you verify through a third party whom you know and trust the true identity of this person?
   b. Is there a way to verify the information provided by this person?

3. If you choose to arrange a meeting, make it on *your* terms:
   a. Meet in as public a place as possible.
   b. Arrange your own transportation to and from the meeting.
   c. Bring a friend along for security; consider a "double date" the first time.
   d. Set your conditions for the encounter, and don't let your new friend change them.
   e. Stay near other people and in lighted areas throughout the meeting.
   f. If things go awry, can you positively identify the person to the police?

4. Limit meetings to public places until you are comfortable with the other person and certain of who they are and what they want from the relationship.

SOURCE: Richard M. Hamilton. *The Police Notebook.* Copyright © 1997, University of Oklahoma. All rights reserved. Retrieved March 30, 2009, from http://www.ou.edu/oupd/kidsafe/websafe.htm

concerns. According to a recent report, almost half the workers surveyed said that these technologies result in longer hours and increased stress levels, because many continue their work after they get home and are expected to read e-mail and be available for cell phone calls after work (Madden & Jones, 2008).

In any case, CMC has had a huge impact on work relationships. The impact varies, however, depending on the type of relationship—whether it is a superior–subordinate relationship, a peer relationship, or a team relationship.

Superior–Subordinate Communication A major impact of online communication in the workplace is its status-leveling effect. Before CMC, gatekeepers like receptionists and secretaries controlled access to the boss. However, with e-mail, anyone can have instant access to superiors. In addition, communicating by e-mail gives subordinates the opportunity to think carefully about their communication before sending it.

CMC also gives superiors a way of checking up on subordinates. For example, the messages sent through e-mail may be stored forever on company servers, so management can monitor employees' correspondence (Thurlow, Lengel, & Tomic, 2004). Many companies now monitor employee e-mail and Internet usage, and Web-based security cameras are increasingly common. Also, technologies such as GPS and employee badges with radio frequency identification (RFID) tags provide an even higher level of employee monitoring. These tracking systems can record, display, and archive the exact location of any employee, both inside and outside the office, at any time—an extension of in-house security measures such as the monitoring of e-mail and the control of access to corporate computing resources (James, 2003).

Another issue raised by CMC between superiors and subordinates concerns decisions about what should be handled over e-mail versus face-to-face. For more on

the type of workplace misunderstandings that can occur using e-mail, read *It Happened to Me: Cruzita.*

Peer Communication While the field of availables may increase through CMC in work contexts, access to certain kinds of information often decreases when one relies on CMC.

For example, in face-to-face work contexts, you can observe the person in the next office during meetings and talk with them in the halls or mailroom. However, if you are using CMC to communicate with a coworker who is based at a different location than you are, you have little information about

IT HAPPENED TO ME: *Cruzita*

I sent my manager an e-mail requesting some time off, but she didn't receive it. When I found out that I did not get the weekend off, I was mad at her, but she had no idea I had sent her an e-mail. If my manager and I had communicated face-to-face, we would not have had a mix-up of this kind.

them. This lack of information increases uncertainty as well as the potential for disagreements and misunderstandings, as one of our students describes in *It Happened to Me: Mei-Lin.*

To summarize, online relationships have unique characteristics that distinguish them from in-person relationships. While these characteristics expand opportunities for

relationship development, they also present challenges, and each type of relationship—whether a friendship, a romance, or a work relationship—has unique challenges. When we expand the frame of reference beyond individuals, as we do in the next section, you will encounter a new set of CMC-related issues and challenges—those posed by societal forces.

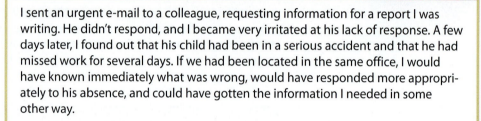

IT HAPPENED TO ME: *Mei-Lin*

I sent an urgent e-mail to a colleague, requesting information for a report I was writing. He didn't respond, and I became very irritated at his lack of response. A few days later, I found out that his child had been in a serious accident and that he had missed work for several days. If we had been located in the same office, I would have known immediately what was wrong, would have responded more appropriately to his absence, and could have gotten the information I needed in some other way.

THE INDIVIDUAL, COMMUNICATION TECHNOLOGY, AND SOCIETY

All online activities—whether for fun, socializing, or information seeking—are enacted by humans within a social context and the larger society. These activities both reflect and influence larger societal norms. For example, some of the same social hierarchies that exist in the larger society also exist in the realm of CMC. When we sort people out by various identities (for example, gender, ethnicity, or race), we find differences in how many of them use communication technologies (see Tables 7.2 and 7.3), and also in how they are perceived to use the Internet. In this section, we'll first look at how various identities influence technology use and then examine causes and remedies for the digital divide.

Gender, Age, Ethnicity, and Technology Use

Let's consider gender first. In one study, college students were asked to identify various computer activities as either "masculine," "feminine," or "neutral." Not surprisingly, they identified arcade-style computer games as the most masculine activity, followed by high-tech peripherals (PDAs, digital cameras), banking, and downloading music. In contrast, they identified e-mailing, Internet chat rooms, studying online, and shopping as feminine activities (Selwyn, 2007). These perceptions seem to represent traditional gender roles—men being more oriented toward action and females more interpersonally oriented (Jackson, Ervin, Gardner, & Schmitt, 2001). The authors conclude that "it is erroneous to

presume that gender stereotyping of new technologies—and in particular the computer—has ceased to exist" (Selwyn, 2007, p. 534). How accurate are these stereotypes?

As it turns out, some of the perceptions are accurate. Males tend to use the Internet to search more than females (Fallows, 2008), are more likely to play online games and to play a larger variety of games (Lenhart et al., 2008), and are more likely to download podcasts (Madden & Jones, 2008). Women tend to e-mail more than men and visit SNSs more frequently (boyd, 2007), and they tend to communicate more in online discussions than men (Caspi, Chajut, & Saporta, 2008). Some evidence indicates that women are a bit more anxious about relatively advanced and complex computer technology and so are less likely to play complicated online games than men (Wang & Wang, 2008), although other evidence shows males and females having equal levels of computer skills (Cheong, Halavais, & Kwon, 2008). Nevertheless, some of the stereotypes are unfounded. For example, women are not more likely to shop online; males and females participate in online shopping equally (Horrigan, 2008b). Taken together, then, this evidence suggests that the use of communication technologies only partially reinforces gender stereotypes.

How do other identities—such as age—interact with CMC? As one might expect, young Americans are much more comfortable with new technologies than older folks, and they tend to use communication technologies in different ways. As described at the beginning of the chapter, the younger you are, the more likely you are to play online games (Lenhart et al., 2008), download music and podcasts (Madden & Jones, 2008), create your own blog or personal Web page, and share your own artistic creations online (Lenhart, Madden, Macgill, & Smith, 2007). The same patterns extend to mobile phones; young people are more likely to text and tweet than are older people (Lenhart, 2009). However, the stereotype of older people avoiding technology is quickly changing. In fact, the fastest-growing group of Internet users is older people (age 70-plus). A few online activities that were previously dominated by younger generations are now practiced more equally across all generations under 73 years old—activities such as searching for information and downloading videos (Jones & Fox, 2009).

Stereotypes of ethnic groups also persist online. Studies show that characters in video games are overwhelmingly White and male. Outside sports video games, only a few Black characters exist, and they are often portrayed as gangsters or street people. And typical of popular media, Latinos and Native Americans are extremely underrepresented as video game characters. While there are many White male game players, many of the gamers worldwide are female, people of different racial and ethnic backgrounds, and of varying ages. The typical gamer is not a White male adolescent, which seems to be the assumption of video game creators (Sinclair, 2009; Williams, Martins, Consalvo, & Ivory, 2009).

As you can see, not everyone is equally represented in the communication technology revolution. Nor does everyone have access to digital life and cyberspace. The issue of access is perhaps the most important way in which societal forces affect computer-mediated communication.

Power, Access, and the Digital Divide

According to a recent Pew Report on Internet and American Life, about 25 percent of Americans are not online (Rainie, 2010), and in many countries, only a tiny fraction of the population has access to computers and the Internet. While there is high Internet usage in Asia, Western Europe, North America, and hi-tech economies such as South Korea, China, and Japan, usage in developing countries and especially in Africa is scarce. Many of these emerging economies still lack landline telephone services (Wray, 2007). In Africa, Internet penetration is 7 percent, compared to 19 percent in Asia, 28 percent in the Middle East, almost 30 percent in Central and South America, 52 percent in Europe, 60 percent in Oceania (Australia, New Zealand), and almost 75 percent in North America. As you can see in Table 7.2, there are pockets of low Internet use in many parts of the world (http://www.internetworldstats.com/stats.htm).

This inequity of access between the technology "haves" and the "have nots" has been called the **digital divide**, and it exists within the United States and also on a global

digital divide
the inequity of access between the technology "haves" and the "have nots"

TABLE 7.2 The Global Digital Divide Percentage of Internet Users as of 2008

Country	% of population
Iceland	93
Norway	90
S. Korea	77
Japan	76
Canada	75
U.S.A.	74
Spain	72
Germany	66
Chile	56
China	27
Tunisia	26
Mexico	25
Egypt	16
Nigeria	7
India	7
Nicaragua	3
Laos	2
Somalia	1

SOURCE: http://www.internetworldstats.com/stats.htm

scale. Why do differences in access matter? In a global information society, information is an important commodity that everyone needs in order to function. In addition, to function effectively in society, people need **cultural capital** (Bourdieu, 1986), or certain bodies of cultural knowledge and cultural competencies. Those with the most power in a society decide what constitutes cultural capital, and it is passed down from parents to children, just as economic capital is.

In the United States and much of the world, cultural capital includes the ability to gain access to and use CMC in appropriate ways. This ability is especially important in an increasingly "networked" society. Without these skills and knowledge, one can feel disconnected from the center of society (van Dijk, 2004; Rojas, Straubhaar, Roychowdhury, & Okur, 2004). For example, a researcher told of a man who had no experience with computers. When the man went for a haircut, he was told to check in at the computer terminal at the counter. He was too embarrassed to admit not knowing how to use the keyboard or cursor, so he left the shop without getting a haircut. Why is this man on the far side of the digital divide? What factors keep him and so many others from having access to the Internet?

In Africa, only about 7 percent of the population has Internet access, compared to 19 percent in Asia, and South America, and almost 75 percent in North America. Why do these differences matter?

cultural capital
cultural knowledge and cultural competencies that people need for functioning effectively in society

Who Is Online?

One of the most recent and popular communication technologies via the Internet—Twitter—seems to have almost no digital divide. A very recent survey of online users shows that the largest differences are between urban (20%) and rural (10%) Twitter users and

younger and older users (20% of 18 to 34 year olds, 10% of 35 to 44 year olds, and 5% of 45 to 65 year olds). However, there are no income or racial/ethnic differences and only slightly more women (21%) than men (17%) users (Lenhart, 2009).

While there is little digital divide among Twitter users, the same cannot be said of Internet users. Many studies show that in the United States, the people most likely to have access to and use the Internet:

- are young or middle age;
- have college degrees or are currently students;
- have comfortable incomes.

Gender differences in terms of access—once a feature underlying the digital divide in the United States—have all but disappeared, as researchers now find little difference in how often men versus women use the Internet (Fallows, 2008).

Racial and ethnic disparities are also shrinking rapidly, especially among adolescents— the fastest growing group of Internet users—but socioeconomic status and education level make a tremendous difference in Internet access (See Table 7.3). People who make more than $75,000 a year are much more likely to be online than those making less than $30,000 (94% vs. 60%). Those with some college training are more than twice as likely to be online (87%) than those without a high school diploma (39%). In the United States overall, 75 percent of Whites, 70 percent of African American, and 64 percent of Latinos are online. However, when you look more closely, you see that only about 41 percent of Latinos without a high school education use the Internet compared to 94 percent of those with a college education. For those Latinos making less than $30,000 a year, only 56 percent use the Internet, while among those making $75,000 or more, 88 percent use the Internet (Livingston, Parker, & Fox, 2009).

As we've mentioned, age also keep some people offline: 93 percent of young people (ages 18 to 29) are online, compared to 77 percent of people ages 50 to 64 and only 43 percent of those over age 65.

What Keeps People Offline?

While the digital divide is shrinking for some population groups, others continue to lag— Americans 65 and older, those with low incomes and less education, and people with physical disabilities. In all, 21 percent of Americans have never been online and are categorized as the "truly disconnected"; this number has remained constant for five years (Horrigan, 2009). About 16 percent of these nonusers say they have no access, 10 percent say it is too expensive, and 4 percent say they have no computer. About 22 percent said they have no desire to go online—even if they live in a home with Internet access. Some say that going online is not a good use of their time (4%). Others are reluctant because they say it is too difficult to use (7%) (Horrigan, 2009).

Some of these reasons may flow from the lack of a specific type of cultural capital— **technocapital**, or access to technological skills and resources. What hinders people from acquiring technocapital? One reason might be competing social and cultural influences.

According to one study, the factors that turned people away from computer use were family attitudes and resources, the educational system, peer pressure, and institutional factors (Jackson et al., 2004). This study investigated computer use in a poor neighborhood in Austin, Texas, a technologically progressive city with a number of programs to ensure public access to CMC and innovative training programs. Via interviews and surveys, researchers discovered that many of the poorest families in Austin—even though they had radios, cell phones, and televisions—did not own computers or have access to the Internet. Further, while some parents understood the importance of computer skills, they did not feel that they had the time or energy to communicate this to their children. Moreover, although they owned other electronic devices, they did not feel that they had the funds needed for computers. In addition, the neighborhood school, like most schools in poor neighborhoods, lacked sufficient computer facilities and adequate computer training (Jackson et al., 2004).

technocapital
access to technological skills and resources

TABLE 7.3 Demographics of internet users

Below is the percentage of each group who use the internet, according to our December 2009 survey. As an example, 74% of adult women use the intenet.

	Internet users
Total adults	**74%**
Men	74
Women	74
Race/ethnicity	
White, Non-Hispanic	76%
Black, Non-Hispanic	70
Hispanic (English- and Spanish-speaking)	64
Age	
18–29	93%
30–49	81
50–64	70
65+	38
Household income	
Less than $30,000/yr	60%
$30,000–$49,999	76
$50,000–$74,999	83
$75,000+	94
Educational attainment	
Less than High School	39%
High School	63
Some College	87
College+	94
Community type	
Urban	74%
Suburban	77
Rural	70

SOURCE: The Pew Reseach Center's Internet & American Life Project, November 30-December 27, 2009 Tracking Survey, N=2,258 adults, 18 and older, including 565 cell phone interviews. Interviews were conducted in English and Spanish. Margin of errors is 20%.

These inequities in educational resources, combined with parental attitudes, reinforce students' notion that computers and computer skills are not for them, and so they acquire a negative attitude toward computer technology. A more recent study found similar results. This study tried to identify what determined people's "Internet connectedness" and found that, even more important than socioeconomic status, ethnicity, or access to

diffusion of innovations
theory that explains why some innovations, like computers and Internet technology, are accepted by some people and rejected by others

home computers were (1) the social environment—that is, whether people have family and friends who use the Internet and who can help them resolve Internet-related problems—and (2) whether they see the Internet as central to important activities (Jung, 2008). Just like the earlier study, this study showed that even though people may be avid video game players, they may still see computer skills as being for others and as irrelevant to their lives.

One theory that explains why some people accept new technologies and others don't is the **diffusion of innovations**, developed by communication scholar Everett Rogers (2003). The theory suggests that in order for people to accept a new technology like the computer, they have to see it as useful and compatible with their values and lifestyles. Moreover, if people important to the individual (for example, an adolescent's peers) adopt the innovation first, then the individual is more likely to adopt it. So, while giving people access to computers and the Internet is an important first step, it is not enough to close the digital divide.

Institutional structures also reinforce the social environment. Many of the very poor say that TV and billboard Internet ads are irrelevant to them. Indeed, most of these ads—often showing White middle-class people (professionals or college students) touting the advantages of getting "connected"— are probably not directed at them. They also don't use the free computers in the public libraries, because they regard libraries as unfriendly places (Rojas, Straubhaar, Rochowdhury, & Okur, 2004). Thus, the digital divide has deep societal and cultural roots—and arises from far more than a lack of access to computers.

Globalization and the Digital Divide

Compared with the United States, even larger digital inequities exist on a global scale, as illustrated in Table 7.2. The issue of who does and does not have technocapital, and whose culture dominates it, are relevant in our current global economy. Why? Some activists and policy makers hope that, facilitated by CMC, economic globalization—meaning increased mobility of goods, services, labor, and capital—can lead to a more democratic and equitable world. And some evidence supports this hope. For example, outsourcing American jobs to overseas locations has provided income opportunities for many in English-speaking countries such as Ireland and India. And, in spite of some governments' attempts to limit their citizens' access to CMC, the Internet provides information, world news, and possibilities for interpersonal communication that were not previously available (Scanlon, 2003; Wheeler, 2001).

However, other evidence suggests that globalization primarily benefits wealthy Western nations, promoting their cultural values and technology and enriching their countries. Evidence here includes the fact that Western countries control and profit from the majority of CMC hardware and software. Furthermore, English has become the dominant language of the Internet, and most software is developed in English, even though only a small percentage of the world's population speaks English (Herring, 2004; Keniston, 2001).

After examining Western domination of communication technology and media products (music, film, television), researcher Fernando Delgado (2002) makes the case that this domination enhances the digital divide and impacts interpersonal communication across cultures. Specifically, he argues that people in poorer countries are left behind by the CMC revolution, and they resent the control wielded by Western technology.

Closing the Digital Divide

One recent theory—which is similar to the diffusions of innovations theory described above—is proposed by Dutch sociologist Jan van Dijk (2004) and addresses strategies for lessening the digital divide. Van Dijk emphasizes that access to computer hardware is only one part of the exclusion from the digital world. To cross the digital divide, people must have access to four levels of technocapital: mental, material, skills, and usage. Furthermore, each level builds on the previous one.

Mental access—the first and perhaps most important level of technocapital—relates to motivation and acceptance of CMC as meaningful. In other words, to cross the digital divide, people must be convinced that computer and Internet skills are important. As we noted earlier regarding many older people and some poorer people, however, they often do not see the benefit for themselves. Thus, those concerned with minimizing the digital divide recommend that more attention and effort be directed to overcoming these mental-access barriers (Lenhart et al., 2003).

The second level of technocapital—material access to computer hardware—is where most public policy currently focuses. For example, one U.S. federal program uses telephone taxes to pay for Internet connections in elementary schools; state and local funds are used to pay for Internet connections at public libraries; and companies donating computer and technical training are given tax incentives (Lenhart et al., 2003; Marriot, 2006). On a global scale, engineers have developed a $100 laptop featuring a seven-inch color screen, wireless Internet connectivity, and a hand-crank that supplies 10 minutes of power for every minute of cranking (Hutchinson, 2006). Clearly, without access to hardware and Internet connections, acquiring technocapital can be very difficult.

The third level of technocapital—skills access—is also critical. Many nonusers view lack of training and lack of user-friendly technology as barriers, and frustration levels can be significant. In order to facilitate skills access, hardware and software developers must better understand the minds of users, taking into consideration their diverse cultural communication norms and practices. In other words, we need "technology that can think like the user" and that can think like users from many cultural backgrounds (Jackson et al., (2004), p. 180).

Finally, usage access means knowing how to use a variety of computer applications. For example, learning to use the Internet or build a Web site takes more know-how than using the computer to play games or send e-mail. Even if people have computers, their lack of technological proficiency and social resources may frustrate them, leading to what some experts call a "secondary digital divide" (inequalities in Internet skills, problem-solving behaviors, and Internet-usage patterns) in high-tech societies (Cheong, 2008).

People's computer-usage knowledge is often related to their educational levels. One study showed that even when people have the same access to computers, those with more education tend to have more usage knowledge and use the Internet for more varied applications. More important, they use the computer in ways that ultimately enhance themselves professionally and personally; for example, they visit sites that provide useful information about national and international news, health and finances, government services, and products (Hargittai & Hinnant, 2008). Knowing how to use a broad range of applications would provide less-educated and lower-income people with more technocapital and the social and economic opportunities that come with participation in the "connected" life (Jackson et al., 2004).

ETHICS AND COMPUTER-MEDIATED COMMUNICATION

One message we hope you take from this chapter is that CMC, in itself, is neither better nor worse than face-to-face communication. It is simply different. However, these differences allow for irresponsible, thoughtless, or even unethical communication online. How can you become an ethical user of CMC? There are at least two areas of ethical consideration. The first concerns the presentation of identity online, and the second involves building online relationships.

Ethics and Online Identity

As we discussed earlier, the issue of identity and ethics online is complex, and one can take various positions on these issues. An extreme position would be that one should never misrepresent oneself. On the other hand, CMC clearly offers legitimate opportunities (like MMOGs), where one can take on an entirely new identity. As we discuss in the

Did You Know? Ten Commandments of Computer Ethics box below, a guiding principle is that one should "do no harm." In our earlier MMOG example, while some players felt betrayed, one could argue that the harm done to players was minimal. In the example of Vivian's teacher, who pretended to be a young boy on the Internet, the behavior was clearly deceitful in addition to being criminal.

DID YOU KNOW?

The Ten Commandments of Computer Ethics

1. Thou shalt not use a computer to harm other people.
2. Thou shalt not interfere with other people's computer work.
3. Thou shalt not snoop around in other people's computer files.
4. Thou shalt not use a computer to steal.
5. Thou shalt not use a computer to bear false witness.
6. Thou shalt not copy or use proprietary software for which you have not paid.
7. Thou shalt not use other people's computer resources without authorization or proper compensation.
8. Thou shalt not appropriate other people's intellectual output.
9. Thou shalt think about the social consequences of the program you are writing or the system you are designing.
10. Thou shalt always use a computer in ways that ensure consideration and respect for your fellow humans.

SOURCE: Retrieved March 30, 2009, from http://cpsr.org/issues/ethics/cei/

An increasing problem is the incivility of messages on bulletin boards and blogs. When bloggers disclose their feelings and opinions, they become vulnerable to personal attacks via comments left by readers. Women, who host more personal blogs than do men, are often targets of vulgar or insulting comments—from death threats to manipulated photos (Stone, 2007). Some Web site and software developers have suggested that a set of guidelines for conduct be created and implemented to "bring civility to the Web" (Stone, 2007). They suggest that bloggers control if and when they will allow anonymous comments by strangers, and they also recommend that bloggers make it known on their pages which behaviors they will tolerate. Incorporating these standards is a difficult project considering the size of the community and how some users consider any standards regarding Web conduct to violate free speech.

Communication, of course, is interactive and reciprocal; it takes two people to engage in any interaction, and both have responsibility. As we discussed in Chapter 1, the receiver is responsible for being somewhat skeptical of others' communication. In the case of CMC, skepticism should focus on how people present their identity—particularly in certain contexts (for example in SNS, discussion forums, chat rooms, or other online venues).

One idea under discussion for addressing identity problems is a mandatory Internet ID. This fixed identity would "travel" with a user from site to site. While the benefits include decreasing some crime (particularly the exploitation of children) and some unethical behavior, it raises the issue of basic privacy rights. Moreover, for some people, as noted earlier, anonymity is part of the "fun" of the Internet. In addition, finding a way to implement an effective ID that would protect everyone and not be susceptible to fraud or identity theft would be challenging.

One possible solution would be to tailor the ID requirements to the context. For example, some sites could require ID, while others would not, and the users at those sites would follow a "buyer beware" guideline. Internet users could then choose their sites based on their own comfort levels.

What do you think about a mandatory identity that would be required for Internet users? What would be the advantages? Disadvantages?

Building Relationships Online

The first step in building ethical relationships online is to remember how CMC differs from face-to-face communication. First, because nonverbal cues are filtered in CMC, you need to provide as much information as you can to help the receiver discern the "tone" of your message. For example, you may have to explain in words (or emoticons) the humorous tone that in person you would communicate with facial expressions or gestures.

A second step is to consider whether an online communication is appropriate for your message, and here, the relevant factors are your relationship with the receiver and the purpose of the message. For example, in a work context, a lean e-mail message can convey essential information. However, personal messages may be better delivered in person, especially if miscommunication is likely and you need immediate feedback to make sure you are understood.

Twitter, one of the most recent social networking technologies, seems to have almost no digital divide—no income or racial/ethnic differences and only slightly more female than male users.

IMPROVING YOUR COMPUTER-MEDIATED COMMUNICATION SKILLS

What should you take from this chapter that can help you be a better CMC communicator? First, you can strive to communicate more politely, especially via e-mail and cell phone. Second, you can learn to evaluate CMC information more carefully.

E-mail Etiquette

Because e-mail is still prevalent in work and some social contexts, it is worth considering how to increase its effectiveness. The most important guideline is to think before writing a message and hitting the send button. Remember that what you put in writing can never be unwritten and that others besides the intended recipient may see it. Here are a few specific suggestions:

- Send e-mail only to those who will want or need to use it. Don't forward the joke about the pope, the rabbi, and the e-business consultant to everyone. Those who don't share your sense of humor—or are too busy to laugh—might lose respect for you.
- Give your e-mail a context. That is, don't just say "FYI" or "Hi" in the subject area of the e-mail; let the recipient know specifically what you're writing about. This is especially important in work contexts. Because of the status-leveling effects of e-mail, people get many more messages now than they ever did by telephone, so they want to know the subject of those messages.
- Check your spelling carefully. While the standards for spelling and grammar have been lowered a little for e-mail, sending e-mails full of typos and grammar mistakes communicates a lack of respect for yourself and the recipient.

Cell Phone Etiquette

As a society, we are in the process of inventing rules for polite ways to use new communication technologies. E-mail messaging has been around for a while, but cell phones are a relatively new technology, and we're still figuring out how to use them in ways that promote smooth and effective relational communication. For some suggestions for using cell phones, both voice and texting, see *Building Your Communication Skills: Guidelines for Voice and Text Messaging*.

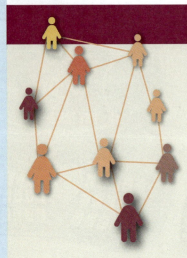

Guidelines for Voice and Text Messaging

The overall guideline for both voice and text messaging is that common courtesy still rules! Be polite and respectful of others in public areas as well as in social situations with friends. Here are some general guidelines for cell phone use:

- Know when to turn off your phone (e.g., meetings, movies, worship, seminars). Put it in vibrate mode when in places where you can take a call but don't want to disturb others.

- Be respectful of others' schedules. Don't assume that because you are awake, working, or not busy that the person you're calling or texting is as well. Many a pleasant slumber has been interrupted by the recurring ringtone or "beep" of messages.

- Ask permission to use the phone when appropriate. For example, if you are expecting a call or text message during a meeting, inform others at the beginning of the meeting that you are expecting an important message, and get their permission to take it or respond to a text message.

- In public places, avoid talking where you may be distracting to others—for example, in places of business (waiting rooms, banks) where people may be concentrating or reading.

- When talking on the phone, in most situations, speak in a lower-than-normal voice. You will be heard by the caller and not by others in the room. According to a new survey, speaking too loudly on mobile phones is the most irritating thing about people using cell phones in public. More than half of those questioned said that loud talking was even more annoying than ringtones or even taking calls while at the dinner table (http://www.textually.org/textually/archives/cat_cell_phone_etiquette.htm)

- When you're with friends, keep the voice conversations short and limit your use of your PDA or smartphone. Contrary to popular belief, composing a text message or surfing the Internet while in a face-to-face conversation with someone is as rude as taking a voice call.

- Be careful when using phones (voice or texting) while driving: It is not only very dangerous but also unlawful in many states in the United States and in most countries (including India).

Here are some additional guidelines that apply specifically to text messaging:

- Remember that text messages are informal. They shouldn't be used for formal invitations or to dump your girlfriend or boyfriend—the casualness reduces the impact and meaning of the message.

- Don't get upset if you don't get a reply. Before you text someone and get frustrated at the lack of a response, consider reasons for their nonresponse: Maybe they don't have text capability, they may be out of range, their phone may not be working, they may be busy and not able to text, etc.

- Be aware of your tone. Same as with e-mail, what seems to you to be a completely inoffensive message may be grossly misinterpreted by the recipient, causing possible discomfort or even irreparable harm to your relationship.

- Consider whether to use slang. Don't expect your stodgy superiors at work to know text messaging lingo. And don't expect to win points with your kids by trying to be cool either.

- Remember that text messages can be traced. Anonymous messages—if you must send them—are still best sent from Web sites.

SOURCES: Adapted from "Cell Phone Etiquette, Mobile Phone Manners, Mobile phone Etiquette." 2000Indianchild.com. Retrieved March 30, 2009, from http://www.indianchild.com/cell_phone_etiquette.htm Also from "Top 10 list of SMS etiquette, The Wireless Developer Network." Retrieved January 26, 2010, from http://www.wirelessdevnet.com/newswire-less/thefeature04.html

Evaluating Internet Information

While the Internet provides a wealth of information, it is not all equally credible. Thus, perhaps the most important question to ask when reviewing information is where it came from. Is it one person's opinion, or is it based on solid research? For example, when you are gathering information for a course research project, academic journal articles accessed through EBSCO, Lexis/Nexis, or another online database are preferable to student papers posted on the Internet or Web sites that do not identify the source of the information.

A second question to ask yourself concerns the motivation behind the information source. Is the Web site sponsored by an organization that has a particular political viewpoint? For example, if you are searching for information about the abortion debate or globalization, most Web sites you access are likely to have a particular viewpoint. This does not mean that they don't provide useful information, just that you need to recognize the biases and use the information accordingly.

Recognize also that many search engines, like Yahoo and Google, are becoming increasingly commercialized. Businesses pay these search engines to post their Web sites first. Therefore, if you are trying to find information on the top-ten computer companies in the United States, you will most likely get Web addresses of companies trying to sell you computer hardware and software rather than an objective rating.

As we move forward, CMC will inevitably be a part of our lives. It is deeply embedded in the way we do business and research, and in the ways we socialize and connect with others. Clearly, we have much to think about as we use this tool to communicate responsibly, ethically, equitably, and with social awareness in every context.

SUMMARY

The most frequently used computer-mediated communication (CMC), and the focus of this chapter, is *interactive* communication technologies such as e-mail, instant messaging, and text messages. While cell phones are not technically speaking *computer*-mediated communication, they allow us access to the Internet (CMC) and are now an important form of mediated communication around the world.

Computer-mediated communication is worthy of study because of its pervasiveness, the rapidity with which it has been adopted, and its influences on the ways in which we search and exchange information and develop relationships.

Communication scholars offer two views of the relationship between CMC and face-to-face communication: The deficit approach and the media augmentation/ approach. Specifically, some CMC filters out most nonverbal cues used in face-to-face communication, and it can be conducted asynchronously—leading early CMC experts to propose a media deficit approach. However, now the lines between face-to-face and CMC are rather blurred, leading scholars to emphasize the media augmentation approach.

Compared with face-to-face communication, some CMC affords more control over how people present themselves. Specifically, online one can perform multiple identities, be rather anonymous, or even assume a false identity (pseudoanonymity). In addition,

CMC relationships differ from in-person relationships in that CMC affords access to many more potential relationships, and these relationships are not bound by time or space. These characteristics make CMC relationships somewhat more durable but also somewhat more fragile.

CMC uses are also affected by societal forces and especially in terms of who has access to it. The digital divide—the differential access to CMC by various income, age, and national groups—separates those who have access from those who do not. Power also comes into play in the digital divide, as it does in other parts of society, where the most powerful are the ones who develop and define computer literacy and expertise—sometimes excluding those from less-powerful groups.

Communicating ethically using CMC is especially important in the presentation of identity online and in building online relationships. Suggestions for communicating effectively using CMC include following e-mail and cell phone etiquette and carefully evaluating Internet information.

KEY TERMS

asynchronous 149
avatar 155
blogs 147
computer-mediated communication (CMC) 146
cultural capital 163
cyberbullying 154
cyberspace 146
diffusion of innovations 166
digital 146
digital divide 162

emoticons 149
field of availables 157
filtered 148
Internet 146
Massively Multiplayer Online Games (MMOGs) 146
media augmentation approach 148
media deficit approach 148
media richness theory 149
phishing 154
podcast 147

pseudoanonymity 154
social network theory 152
social presence 148
social presence theory 149
spam 154
spoofing 154
synchronous 149
technocapital 164
World Wide Web (WWW) 146

CHAPTER REVIEW QUESTIONS

1. What are the key differences between CMC and face-to-face communication?

2. Why is it so easy to misrepresent one's identity online? What ethical guidelines should people follow when managing identities online?

3. What are some differences in how Internet relationships develop compared to offline relationships?

4. Why is trust much more important when working together online than it is when working face-to-face? What can we do to build trust in online working relationships?

5. What is the digital divide? What are the most important factors that determine whether one has access to computers and the Internet? What might be done to decrease or eliminate this divide?

ACTIVITIES

1. Don't use any CMC for two days and then answer the following questions. To what extent did you miss this form of communication? What did you miss most/least? What might you conclude about the role that CMC plays in *your* everyday life and relationships? How do you view those who have limited access to CMC?

2. Select any personal Web page from the Internet and describe the identity you think the person is trying to project. Describe the elements that contribute to this identity. What kind of information is presented? What information is missing?

3. Visit an MMOG (go to http://www.mudconnector.com/ for a list and access to many MMOGs). Log in and participate for a while. Then answer the following questions: Did you enjoy the experience? Why or why not? Did you try to project a different identity than you usually do? Describe your interaction with other players. How did your communication with them differ from CMC in other contexts—for example, bulletin boards, e-mail? Why?

WEB ACTIVITIES

1. Go to http://www.computeruser.com/resources/dictionary/index.html This website offers a high-tech dictionary, definitions and meanings for the latest computer terminology and acronyms, meanings for emoticons, domain names, and chat stuff. How much of this information are you familiar with? Imagine someone who knows none of this information. In what ways might their day-to-day CMC activity be limited?

2. Go to http://www.pbs.org/wgbh/amex/telephone/index.html This PBS Web site has a timeline of many inventions as well as a bibliography for each one. Look at it for information about the invention of the telephone, radio, television, Internet, etc. If you had to give up one of these inventions, which would it be? How would your day-to-day communication be different without it? How would you compensate for the lack of it?

3. Go to http://www.zakon.org/robert/Internet/timeline/ This is a very interesting, detailed, and up-to-date "timeline of the Internet" maintained by Robert H. Zakon, of the Hobbes Group, with all-important dates in the development of the Internet—up to the present time. At what point on this timeline did you begin using the Internet? Has the rapidly increasing number of Web sites affected your CMC use? If so, how?

8

INTERPERSONAL COMMUNICATION AND RELATIONSHIP DEVELOPMENT

*J*ulia and her friend Cristina were at a club one weekend when Julia spotted a man who had hit on her earlier in the evening. As he walked toward the two women, Julia leaned over and said, "There's that jerk I was telling you about." Eighteen months later, Cristina and the "jerk" were married.

How is it that one person's jerk is another person's ideal mate? And why do people become friends with one person but not another? Perhaps you have also questioned why some relationships seem to end before they even begin. Though researchers haven't unraveled all the mysteries of interpersonal relationships, they have made considerable progress in explaining how and why relationships develop, are maintained, and sometimes fail—and the role communication plays at each stage. To help you understand communication in interpersonal relationships, we begin by providing a definition for the communication that occurs within them. We then describe the importance of these relationships. Next, we address the role of the individual in interpersonal relationships and explore the factors that increase the likelihood that you will become involved with another person. We next examine four approaches that explain how communication influences relationship development between friends and romantic partners. Finally, we explore the societal forces that influence interpersonal communication and relationships, as well as present you with guidelines for communicating more ethically and effectively in your own relationships.

Once you have read this chapter, you will be able to:

- Identify the three factors that influence a person to initiate a relationship.
- Describe four approaches to relationship development.
- Identify tactics for initiating friendships and romantic relationships.
- Articulate the strategies romantic couples and friends use to maintain their relationships.
- Explain the reasons why individuals terminate romantic relationships and friendships, as well as the communication strategies they use to terminate them.
- Understand the role that society plays in the formation and maintenance of interpersonal relationships.
- Describe ethical interpersonal communication.
- Explain four tactics for maintaining long-distance friendships.

CHAPTER OUTLINE

WHAT IS INTERPERSONAL COMMUNICATION?
Interpersonal Communication Involves Interdependent Parties
Interpersonal Communication Exists on a Continuum
Interpersonal Communication Is Relational

THE IMPORTANCE OF INTERPERSONAL COMMUNICATION AND RELATIONSHIPS

INTERPERSONAL COMMUNICATION, RELATIONSHIPS, AND THE INDIVIDUAL
Influences on Relationship Development
Models of Relationship Development
Communicating in Friendships and Romantic Relationships

SOCIETY, POWER, COURTSHIP, AND MARRIAGE
Society, Power, and Romantic Relationships
Society, Power, and Friendship

ETHICS AND INTERPERSONAL COMMUNICATION

IMPROVING YOUR MAINTENANCE SKILLS IN LONG-DISTANCE FRIENDSHIPS
Maintain Frequent Contact
Encourage Openness
Engage in Positivity
Offer Social Support

Summary

Key Terms

Chapter Review Questions

Activities

Web Activities

dyad
two people

WHAT IS INTERPERSONAL COMMUNICATION?

Most definitions of interpersonal communication fit into one of two types: those that define interpersonal communication based on the *number of people* involved in the interaction (quantitative) and those that define interpersonal communication based on the *type of interaction* that occurs among the parties (qualitative). Many of the quantitative definitions suggest that interpersonal communication is that which occurs within a **dyad**, or between two people (Knapp & Daly, 2002). A few scholars suggest that the number can be larger—perhaps as many as five or six—especially if the parties share a close relationship, such as families do. On the other hand, qualitative definitions suggest that interpersonal communication is interaction that occurs between people who are interdependent, see each other as unique, and/or have an established relationship (Capella, 1987; Miller & Steinberg, 1975). Our definition stems from this second perspective. As we explain below, we view interpersonal communication as interaction that occurs between interdependent parties, exists on a continuum and is inherently relational.

Interpersonal Communication Involves Interdependent Parties

Interpersonal communication occurs between parties who are interdependent in that each person's behavior affects the other. According to this basic definition, you can have interpersonal communication and relationships with a wide range of people—wait staff, sales clerks, physicians, friends and romantic partners. You are interdependent with these people because you rely on them in various ways—to sell you goods and services, to help heal you when ill, or to provide love and affection. In turn, they rely on you to purchase or use their services, to pay your bills, and to offer support and acceptance. However, as these examples suggest, not every relationship is equal.

Interpersonal Communication Exists on a Continuum

Relationships with wait staff, physicians, and sales clerks are not interpersonal in the same sense as those with friends, family, and romantic partners (LaFollette, 1996). With clerks, doctors, and wait staff, you have "role relationships," that is, relationships that exist only in the context of the roles the individuals play for one another—as doctor/patient, clerk/customer, and waiter/diner. These relationships tend to be functional, temporary, and/or casual (DeVito, 2009).

The connections you develop with friends, family, and romantic partners are qualitatively different from these more-temporary or functional relationships (Kelley et al., 1983). Close relationships are distinguished from more casual ones by their level of intimacy, importance, and satisfaction (Berg & Piner, 1990), as well as by the fact that the people in them see each other as unique and irreplaceable (Janz, 2000). Also, people in close relationships expect their relationships to endure over time because they are committed to them (Wright, 1999). On the other hand, casual relationships are perceived as interchangeable and less enduring (Janz, 2000). So, although you might like your mail carrier and would miss seeing her if she quit, you would likely be content to receive your mail from someone new. But if your fiancé or best friend terminated your relationship, you would probably not be content with a substitute.

Interpersonal Communication Is Relational

Saying that interpersonal communication is relational means that the type of interactions that occur between the participants is influenced to a large extent by the kind of relationship they have. For example, in casual or temporary relationships, conversations typically involve little disclosure or affection (Janz, 2000), while in close relationships, they usually involve high disclosure and considerable openness (Janz, 2000). Interpersonal communication is also relational in the sense that relationships are created and defined by the communication that takes place within them. Thus, the shift from a casual to a close relationship occurs because the individuals move from engaging in low-intimacy and low-disclosure interaction toward communication that is more disclosive and personal. Similarly, close relationships can become more casual and less intimate as the participants engage in less-open and more-distant communication.

THE IMPORTANCE OF INTERPERSONAL COMMUNICATION AND RELATIONSHIPS

Close relationships are essential for most people's happiness; their presence (or lack thereof) is also associated with a person's physical and mental health. In fact, when people don't have these types of relationships in their lives, they are more likely to experience depression and anxiety (Miller, 2002). People with even a few close relationships experience greater well-being than those who have none (Gierveld & Tilburg, 1995). People with satisfying relationships also experience greater physical health. For example, studies of marital relationships reveal that compared with people in unhappy marriages, people in happy ones are less likely to experience high blood pressure and serious heart episodes (Holt-Lunstad, Birmingham, & Jones, 2008).

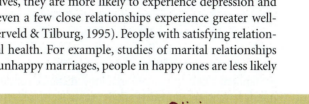

IT HAPPENED TO ME: *Olivia*

I was at a friend's house, eating junk food and watching TV when someone knocked on the door. Standing there in the rain, with tears running down her face and sobbing, was one of our friends. She told us that her mom had hit her and thrown her things out her bedroom window. We sat with her for ages until she calmed down; then we asked her to stay the night.

Interpersonal relationships also offer a sense of belonging as well as provide emotional and physical support, as illustrated in *It Happened to Me: Olivia*.

Olivia's example demonstrates that although relationships supply love and acceptance, sometimes they are also a source of distress. For this reason, having a variety of relationships can be fundamental to life satisfaction.

To help you understand how you can develop rewarding relationships with friends as well as romantic partners, let's explore the factors that influence whether you are likely to initiate a relationship, how relationships unfold over time, and communication choices that lead to satisfying relationships.

INTERPERSONAL COMMUNICATION, RELATIONSHIPS, AND THE INDIVIDUAL

For any romantic or platonic relationship to develop, you must first notice that a particular person exists and be interested enough to initiate contact with him or her. Sara still remembers meeting her husband, Luis, fifteen years ago when she was a doctoral student. A mutual friend introduced them, and she became very interested when she saw him (tall, good looking, and muscular!) and learned that he was finishing his doctorate. She spent most of the evening talking to him, even though thirty other people attended the party. At first, Sara thought they were just lucky to have fallen for one another, but later she learned that social scientists would argue that their relationship wasn't a matter of luck at all.

Influences on Relationship Development

According to relationship researchers, the three factors that most influence one's attraction to another—*proximity*, *physical attractiveness*, and *similarity*—were all operating the evening Sara and Luis met. They were students at the same university (proximity), they found each other physically attractive (physical attractiveness), and they discovered that they had similar career goals (similarity). Consequently, one could argue, Sara and Luis' relationship was more than a happy accident. Of course, proximity, physical attractiveness, and similarity don't guarantee that a friendship or romance will occur, but they do set the stage for relationships to develop. Let's explore how these three factors influence relational development and the role that communication plays in each.

Proximity

Most people are not aware of it, but **proximity**—how close you are to others—plays an important role in relationship development. Historically, proximity referred to physical closeness between people. People typically became friends with or dated those who lived in

proximity
how close one is to others

their apartment complexes, neighborhoods, or dorms; those who were in their classes; or those with whom they worked (Sias & Cahill, 1998; Sprecher, 1998). Now, however, technologies such as email, text messaging, and cell phones have made it easier for people to create the feeling of proximity even with individuals who are not physically nearby.

Proximity has a strong impact on your interactions and relationships. It provides the opportunity for you to notice others' attractive qualities, learn about your similarities, and develop a relationship (Berscheid & Reis, 1998). Usually, the easier it is to interact with someone, the easier it will be to develop and sustain a relationship. Of course, some people do develop and maintain long-distance relationships, but they may need to make more effort to sustain their relationships than those in more proximate relationships (Rindfuss & Stephen, 1990). If you are in a long-distance romantic relationship and want to understand how you can successfully sustain it, see *Building Your Communication Skills: Strategies for Maintaining Long-Distance Romantic Relationships.*

Building Your Communication SKILLS

Strategies for Maintaining Long-Distance Romantic Relationships

Long-distance romantic relationships are common among college students and are becoming common even for working adults. Although long-distance relationships can succeed, they typically require more conscious effort than those that are proximate. However, if you use the following strategies, you can increase the likelihood that your relationship will endure.

Define the "rules" of the relationship

If you want your long-distance relationship to last, early in the relationship you and your partner need to determine what is acceptable and unacceptable in your relationship. For example, you need to determine whether your relationship will be exclusive or not (that is, whether you will or won't date others). Eventually, you will also need to discuss whether you see yourselves together in the future and, if so, how you will decide who will relocate so that you can be together.

Be open and honest

Jealousy and insecurity pose significant threats to long-distance relationships. Because partners have less information about each others' behavior, they often experience uncertainty regarding the others' feelings and fidelity. Sharing your feelings of commitment and being open and truthful with your partner about what you are doing and who you are seeing can help maintain trust in the relationship and help ensure its longevity.

Communicate with each other frequently

To a great extent, relationships are created and maintained through the communication interactions couples share. This is even truer for couples separated by distance. Consequently, talking with each other frequently is important. Fortunately, text messaging, emailing, calling, and Skyping with one another are easy and relatively inexpensive strategies for staying in contact. It is also important that you vary the ways in which you communicate with one another. Texting can be great for saying hello, expressing affection or asking and giving simple information, but if you have an important or controversial topic to discuss, you will find it more useful to call on your cell or, better yet, use Skype so that you can capture the nuances of your conversation.

Listen to each other

One of the more significant roles partners play in relationships is as an audience for each others' expression of thoughts and experiences. Listening to your partner talk

about the mundane experiences of his or her day is central to understanding, feeling connected and making him or her feel cared for and valued.

Engage in activities together—even while you are apart

An important part of relationships is doing things together so that you can talk and reminisce about them. Consequently, it is helpful if you can find ways to participate in activities together. For instance, you can watch a TV show or movie together while you are on the phone so that both of you can comment on it as you would if you were in the same room. Alternatively you can play a game together while you are on Skype or you can both visit *Second Life* and build a home or engage in another activity. You can also listen to music, take an online quiz together, or cook the same meal and eat it simultaneously.

For more ideas on activities you can share, go to http://www.lovingfromadistance.com/thingstodo5.html.

Attractiveness

Obviously, proximity is not enough to launch a relationship. Most of us have daily contact with dozens of people. How is it that you connect with some and not others? One of the more obvious answers is **attractiveness**. While most of us are attracted to those we find physically appealing (Buss, Shackelford, Kirkpatrick, & Larsen, 2001), we also tend to develop relationships with people who are approximately as attractive as we are. This tendency is called the **matching hypothesis**. Interestingly, the matching hypothesis applies to friendships (Cash & Derlega, 1978), romantic relationships (White, 1980), marriage (Hinsz, 1989), and even roommates (Kurt & Sherker, 2003).

Fortunately, attractiveness is a broad concept. People are attracted to others not only because of their physical appearance but also for their wonderful personalities and/or charming ways. Most of these qualities are revealed through communication; thus individuals with good communication skills are often perceived as more attractive than they might be otherwise (Burleson & Samter, 1996). Therefore, improving your communication skills can increase others' desire to form relationships with you.

Similarity

It may be equally obvious that most people are attracted by **similarity**; they like people who are like them, enjoy the things they enjoy, value what they value, and with whom they share a similar background (Byrne, 1997). In many cases opposites *do* attract, but when it comes to background, values, and attitudes, "birds of a feather more often flock together." For example, evolutionary psychologist Davis Buss found that the more similar the participants in his study were, the more likely they were to report increased levels of attraction (1985). This makes sense. If you like to socialize, enjoy the outdoors, and are involved in a religious community, you may find it difficult to develop a relationship with someone who is introverted, prefers to stay home to read and listen to music, and avoids organized religion. However open-minded you are, you probably view your orientation to the world as preferable, especially concerning values such as religion, politics, and morals. (To read about one area where *differences* are considered ideal, see *Did You Know? DNA Dating Site Predicts Chemical Romance*.)

attractiveness
the appeal one person has for another, based on physical appearance, personality, and/or behavior

matching hypothesis
the tendency to develop relationships with people who are approximately as attractive as we are

similarity
degree to which people share the same values, interests, and background

DID YOU KNOW?

DNA Dating Site Predicts Chemical Romance

The first dating service to use lab-based genetic profiling launched online last week. Scientific Match promises to pair up people who will be physically attracted to each other because their DNA is different.

Well-matched couples will like each others' natural scents, have more fun in bed, and bear healthier children than those who are genetically similar, the company claims.

The service, available only in the Boston area, charges $1,995 for a year-long subscription.

(continued)

DID YOU KNOW? *(continued)*

"I strongly believe this will dominate the future of dating services," said founder Eric Holzle, a mechanical engineer.

Members swab their cheeks and send in saliva samples. A lab spends two weeks analyzing the immune system genes, and then the company matches individuals with genetic profiles that are unalike.

"We look at six specific genetic reference points on DNA, and none of those six can match to make a match," Holzle explained.

He was inspired by a well-known "sweaty T-shirt" study of a dozen years ago, in which biologists found that women liked the smell of dirty shirts worn by men who were immunologically dissimilar to themselves.

As with other online dating sites, Scientific Match's users can fill out written profiles and upload photographs. Genetic details are not displayed, except to indicate a match. The service runs criminal background checks to exclude anyone who has committed crimes involving violence or identity theft.

Scientific Match is open to straight and gay people. However, women taking the birth control pill are turned away because some studies show they are more attracted to men with similar immune system genes.

SOURCE: Adapted from Wenzel, E. (2007, December 17). "DNA dating site predicts chemical romance." *NewsBlog*. http://news.cnet.com/8301-107843-9834683-7.html. Retrieved June 26, 2009.

You may wonder how individuals determine whether they are similar in values, attitudes, and background. Generally, they discover this during the early stages of conversational interaction (Berger & Calabrese, 1975; Berger & Kellerman, 1994). According to a communication theory called **uncertainty reduction theory** (Berger & Calabrese, 1975), much early interaction is dedicated to reducing uncertainty about others and determining if one wishes to interact with them again. Communication, then, is the foundation on which all relationships are built. With this in mind, let's look next at how researchers view the development of relationships.

Models of Relationship Development

Because relationship development is an important aspect of life and because the process sometimes goes awry—for example, 43 percent of first marriages end within 15 years (Bramlett & Mosher, 2002)—scholars have devoted considerable effort toward creating models to explain it. Although no model can exactly represent how human relationships evolve, four approaches offer insight into how relationships develop and change over time as people communicate with one another: social penetration theory, stage models, the turning point model, and dialectical theory.

Social Penetration Theory

Social penetration theory (Altman & Taylor, 1973; 1987) is based on the premise that communication—specifically self-disclosure—is key to relationship development. According to this theory, people gradually increase their self-disclosure as they get to know one another and, through a process of reciprocal disclosure, strangers become friends or lovers. The authors propose that self-disclosure occurs across three dimensions: breadth, depth, and frequency. **Breadth** describes the number of topics dyads willingly discuss. For example, you probably discuss only a few general topics with strangers, such as movies, what you do for a living, or hobbies; however, as you become more intimate with others you likely discuss a wider range of topics, including how you feel about the people in your life or dreams you have for the future. At the same time, the depth of your conversations also increases as the two of you learn more about each other. **Depth** refers to how profound or personal communication exchanges are; people tend to provide superficial disclosures to strangers (for example, I like Thai food) and reserve more personal revelations for their intimates (for example, I am disgusted if the different foods on my plate touch each other). **Frequency** is

uncertainty reduction theory
theory that argues that much early interaction is dedicated to reducing uncertainty about others and determining if one wishes to interact with them again

social penetration theory
a theory that proposes that relationships develop through increases in self-disclosure

breadth
the number of topics dyads willingly discuss

depth
how profound or personal communication exchanges are

frequency
how often self-disclosure occurs

how often self-disclosure occurs; individuals usually share more disclosures with people with whom they are close.

Psychologists Altman and Taylor propose that through increases in communication breadth, depth, and frequency, people become more familiar with and trusting of one another; and as they become closer, they feel comfortable revealing more of themselves. Through this circular process, relationships of increasing intimacy develop. However, not all dyads engage in increasingly intimate disclosure and closeness. Some, such as romantic couples who repeatedly break up and reconcile, move back and forth between stages of increasing and decreasing disclosure and intimacy.

Based on their social penetration theory, Altman Taylor developed a four-stage model to explain how relationships develop based on the depth, breadth and frequency of people's communication with one another. These four stages—orientation, exploratory affective exchange, affective exchange, and stable exchange—are described below in Table 8.1

Communication, especially self-disclosure, is key to relationship development.

initiating
stage of romantic relational development in which both people behave so as to appear pleasant and likeable

experimenting
stage of romantic relational development in which both people seek to learn about each other

intensifying
stage of romantic relational development in which both people seek to increase intimacy and connectedness

integrating
stage of romantic relational development in which both people portray themselves as a couple

Knapp's Stage Model

The best-known stage model was developed in 1978 by Mark Knapp, a communication scholar (Knapp, 1978; Knapp & Vangelisti, 1997). As shown in Figure 8.1, Knapp's stage model conceptualizes relationship development as a staircase composed of five steps that lead upward toward commitment: **initiating**, **experimenting**, **intensifying**, **integrating**, and **bonding**. It also portrays relationship dissolution as occurring in five steps that lead downward: **differentiating**, **circumscribing**, **stagnating**, **avoiding**, and **terminating**. In this model, couples at the relationship-maintenance level of development move up and down the staircase as they move toward and away from commitment due to the fluctuation of their relationships (see Figure 8.1).

Knapp's stage model is a *communication* model because it explores how individuals' communication practices affect relationship development and decline. For example, *circumscribing* is identified by the fact that couples' conversations focus mostly on "safe" topics, such as household tasks, while experimenting is defined by couples' communication efforts to learn more about one another. This stage model assumes that one can determine what stage a dyad is in by observing what they say and do. For example, if couples spend most of their communication interactions discussing the ways in which they are

TABLE 8.1 Altman and Taylor's Four Stages of Relationship Development		
Stage	**Description**	**Type of Interaction**
Orientation	The dyad's first meeting	Low breadth of topics and depth of disclosure
Exploratory Affective Exchange	Encounters between people in casual friendship or dating relationships	Increased breath of topics but relatively low depth of disclosure
Affective Exchange	Encounters between good friends or dating partners	Considerable breadth of topics and depth of disclosure, but some topics may be off limits and some disclosure not shared
Stable Exchange	Best friends and committed relational partners	Breadth of topics and levels of disclosure are very high, though some information may still be concealed

bonding
stage of romantic relational development characterized by public commitment

differentiating
stage of romantic relational dissolution in which couples increase their interpersonal distance

circumscribing
stage of romantic relational dissolution in which couples discuss safe topics

stagnating
stage of romantic relational dissolution in which couples try to prevent change

avoiding
stage of romantic relational dissolution in which couples try not to interact with each other

terminating
stage of romantic relational dissolution in which couples end the relationship

stage model
a type of model that conceptualizes relationship development as occurring in a stair-step fashion, with some stages leading toward commitment and other stages leading toward dissolution

FIGURE 8.1 Knapp and Vangelisti's Stages of Relational Development

Stage models conceptualize relationship development as occurring in a stair-step fashion, with some stages leading toward commitment and other stages leading toward dissolution.

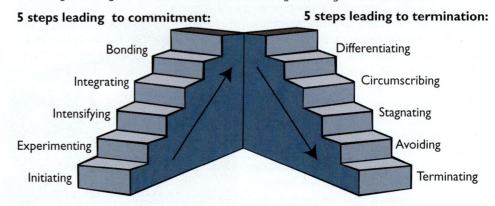

5 steps leading to commitment:
Bonding
Integrating
Intensifying
Experimenting
Initiating

5 steps leading to termination:
Differentiating
Circumscribing
Stagnating
Avoiding
Terminating

different, they are at the *differentiating* stage. As Table 8.2 reveals, each stage is based on the types of communication couples perform within it.

As you might have noticed, Knapp's model includes a *termination* stage. This does not suggest that all relationships end, but it does recognize that many relationships do (Weber, 1998). Relationships that end are often treated as "failures," and the people who experience them often feel that they have done something wrong. But, in fact, as people grow and mature, they often change their social networks (Dainton, Zelley, & Langan, 2003). This is not to suggest that you won't have long-lasting or permanent relationships, but not every relationship termination should be viewed as a mistake.

The models we have discussed thus far are **stage models**. They help us organize events so we can better understand how relationships develop; however, stage models tend to be linear. They assume that people move from one stage to another in a fairly orderly progression. Knapp has responded to this critique by arguing that dyads can skip stages but that they have to go back at some point and move through the skipped stages. For example, when a couple engages in a "one-night stand," they may move from initiation to integration in a matter of hours. However, if they stay together, they will have to go back and experience the experimenting and intensifying stages. Knapp also argues

TABLE 8.2 Knapp's Stages of Romantic Relational Development

Stage	Goal	Example
Initiating	Appear pleasant, likeable	"Hi! I sure like your car."
Experimenting	Learn about each other	"Do you like to travel?"
Intensifying	Increase intimacy, connectedness	"I can't imagine being with anyone else."
Integrating	Establish dyad as a couple	"I love you. I feel like you are a part of me."
Bonding	Public commitment	"Will you marry me?"
Differentiating	Increase interpersonal distance	"I'm going; you can come if you want to."
Circumscribing	Discuss safe topics	"Did you pick up the dry cleaning?"
Stagnating	Prevent change	"Let's not talk about it right now, okay?"
Avoiding	Decline to interact with partner	"I'm too busy now. I'll get back to you later."
Terminating	Ending the relationship	"It's over."

SOURCE: Mark L. Knapp, & Anita L. Vangelisti. (1992). *Interpersonal communication and relationships* (2nd ed.) Boston, MA: Allyn & Bacon, Boston, MA.

that over the course of a relationship, dyads move up and down the staircase as people and events change.

As you read about the stage models of relationship development, you may have thought that these models don't describe your own experiences very well. If so, you are not alone. A number of researchers questioned whether all dyads follow sequentially organized stages. Instead, they believed that relationships can follow a number of paths: Some may be fairly straight like a sidewalk, while others may be like winding mountain paths. **Relational trajectory models** view relationship development as more variable than previously thought (Baxter & Bullis, 1986; Surra, 1987).

Relational Trajectory Models

The most popular model that emerged from this research is referred to as the **turning point model** (Baxter & Bullis, 1986). It is a nonlinear model that best captures the fact that relationship development can be bidirectional—that is, that couples move both toward and away from commitment over the course of their relationship, as shown in Table 8.3. This model proposes that couples engage in approximately fourteen types of "turning points" that influence the direction of their relationship trajectory. For example, the turning point "passion" (first kiss or saying "I love you") tends to be an event that increases couples' commitment to their relationship, while the turning point "external competition" (such as a rival lover) decreases commitment to the relationship.

A turning point model of friendship has also been developed, with different turning points from the romance-based model (Baxter & Bullis, 1986). For example, turning points most often associated with increased closeness between friends include participating in activities together, taking a trip together, sharing living quarters, self-disclosing, hanging out with mutual friends, and sharing common interests. Decreased closeness most often occurs when friends stop living together, have conflicts, experience interference from one person's romantic partner, move so that they no longer lived near one another, or undergo change (Johnson, Wittenberg, Haigh, & Wigley, 2004).

Communication professor Leslie Baxter and her colleagues have also examined relationship dialectics to explain how dyads develop relationships. As you may remember from Chapter 7, *dialectic* is a term that is used in many areas of study, such as philosophy, psychology, and communication (Altman, Vinsel, & Brown, 1981; Baxter, 1988). It refers to

relational trajectory models
relationship development models that view relationship development as more variable than do stage models

turning point model
a model of relationship development in which couples move both toward and away from commitment over the course of their relationship

TABLE 8.3 Turning Points in Developing Relationships

Turning Point	Description	Effect on Relationship
Get-to-know time	Events and time spent together learning about one another	Increases commitment
Quality time	Special occasions for appreciating the other and/or the relationship	Increases commitment
Physical separation	Time apart due to school breaks, etc.	Little effect on commitment
External competition	Competing for partner's time/attention due to others or events	Decreases commitment
Reunion	Coming back together after physical separation	Increases commitment
Passion	Physical/emotional expression of affection	Increases commitment
Disengagement	Ending the relationship	Decreases commitment
Positive psychic change	Acquiring a more positive outlook on partner/relationship	Increases commitment
Exclusivity	Decision to date only each other	Increases commitment
Negative psychic change	Acquiring a more negative outlook on partner/relationship	Decreases commitment
Making up	Getting back together after a breakup	Increases commitment
Serious commitment	Moving in with one's partner or getting married	Increases commitment
Sacrifice	Providing support or gifts to one's partner	Increases commitment

SOURCE: Baxter, L.A., & Bullis, C. (1986). "Turning points in developing romantic relationships." *Human Communication Research, 12,* 469–493.

the tension people experience when they have two seemingly contradictory but connected needs. As you will see, developing close relationships is associated with the ability to manage these contradictory but connected desires.

A Dialectical Model of Relationship Development

Have you experienced any of the following: You feel lonely when you are separated from your romantic partner, but you sometimes feel suffocated when you're together? You want to be able to tell your best friend anything, but you sometimes feel the need for privacy? You want your friends to be predictable, but not so predictable that they're boring? These types of feelings arise when you experience a dialectical tension, and they are common in all types of relationships. How you respond to and manage these tensions impacts how successfully you can develop and maintain relationships.

Three primary dialectical tensions exist in relationships: *autonomy/connection, expressiveness/privacy,* and *change/predictability* (Baxter, 1988). (See *Visual Summary 8.1: The Dialectical Model of Relationship Development.*) **Autonomy/connection** refers to one's need to connect with others and the simultaneous need to feel independent or autonomous. For example, early in relationships people typically have a high need to feel connected to their romantic partners and can barely tolerate being separated. But as the relationship develops, most people need time away from their partners so that they don't feel stifled or overwhelmed. This tension is more common during the early stages of relationship development, and the success with which people effectively manage it influences their ability to develop a relationship. If they insist on too much autonomy, the relationship may end; if they have too much connection, one person may feel overwhelmed and withdraw. Read more about the dialectical tension between autonomy and connection in *It Happened to Me: Laurel.*

IT HAPPENED TO ME: *Laurel*

I started seeing this guy a few weeks ago, and I finally understand why I've been feeling the way I do. Although I enjoy being with him, I have started to feel smothered. He wants to talk on the phone several times a day, he e-mails me little notes, and he wants to spend more evenings together than I do. I enjoy hanging out with my friends and being alone; he wants to be with me all the time. I was beginning to think there was something wrong with him: then I read Baxter's article on relationship dialectics. Now I think we just have different needs for autonomy. However, I don't know if we will be able to manage this so that we'll both be happy.

Like Laurel, many dyads have different needs for autonomy and connection in their relationships. If you find yourself in this situation, what can you do? First, if your relationship is somewhat established, have a discussion with your partner about your different requirements for connection and explore ways in which each of your needs can be met. On the other hand, if your relationship is new and you are the one feeling smothered, you might find that if you wait a while, your partner will feel more secure in the relationship and will need less direct contact with you. However, if you are the partner who wants more contact, you could initiate more contact then evaluate how your partner responds.

The second tension—**expressiveness/privacy**—describes the need to be open and to self-disclose while also maintaining some sense of privacy. For example, while Warren may reveal his feelings about his romantic partner to his closest friend, he may not disclose that he was fired from his first job. To maintain their relationships, dyads need to manage this tension effectively. If you reveal too much information too early, others may find your communication behavior inappropriate and shy away from you. On the other hand, if you fail to open up and express yourself, others may perceive you as aloof or cold and may not continue a relationship with you. As you can see, the tension between expressiveness/privacy is important in the initiating stage of relationship development, as well as during the development and maintenance stages.

Finally, the **change/predictability** tension explains the human desire for events that are new, spontaneous, and unplanned, while simultaneously needing some aspects of life to be stable and predictable. For example, you probably want your partner's affection for you to be stable and predictable, but you might like your partner to surprise you occasionally with a new activity or self-disclosure. This tension exists at all stages of relationship

autonomy/connection
a dialectical tension in relationships that refers to one's need to connect with others and the simultaneous need to feel independent or autonomous

expressiveness/privacy
a dialectical tension in relationships that describes the need to be open and to self-disclose while also maintaining some sense of privacy

change/predictability
a dialectical tension in relationships that describes the human desire for events that are new, spontaneous, and unplanned while simultaneously needing some aspects of life to be stable and predictable

development, but may be most prevalent during the maintenance phase. Relationships that are completely predictable may become boring, but those that are totally spontaneous are unsettling; either extreme may render the relationship difficult to sustain.

Dialectics are constantly in process. Each day, couples and friends manage their individual and relationship needs for autonomy/connection, expressiveness/privacy, and change/predictability. Keep in mind, however, that it is the manner in which they manage these tensions that influences the continuance of their relationships. Understanding how these dialectical tensions work will help you respond to the competing feelings you may experience in your own relationships.

While we know more about heterosexual relationships than we do about gay and lesbian relationships, what we do know suggests that these two types of relationships may follow different paths. In heterosexual relationships, friendship and romantic involvement have traditionally been mutually exclusive; in other words, people whose romantically intimate relationship has ended don't usually remain friends afterward (Baccman, Folkesson, & Norlander, 1999; Nardi, 1992). In contrast, gay friendships often start with sexual attraction and involvement but evolve into friendship with no sexual/romantic involvement (Baccman, Folkesson, & Norlander, 1999; Nardi, 1992). However, this difference appears to be less true than it once was, as more heterosexual young people appear to be combining the categories of friendship and sexual involvement.

Communicating in Friendships and Romantic Relationships

Friendships can differ markedly from romances in how much we reveal, especially in the early stages. But other differences exist as well. For example, we typically expect exclusivity from our romantic partners, but not from our friends. Also, people often have higher expectations about romantic partners, especially with regard to physical attractiveness, social status, and a pleasing personality (Sprecher & Regan, 2002). And we may require greater expressions of commitment and caring from romantic partners than from friends (Goodwin & Tang, 1991). In the following sections we explore in more detail the similarities and differences between friendships and romances.

Initiating Relationships

A person's ability to begin a conversation is essential to the development of any relationship. While many people disparage small talk, there can be no "big talk" if small talk does not precede it. But even before you engage in small talk, you need to be able to signal your interest to others.

Initiating Romantic Relationships Meeting romantic partners and establishing relationships can be a problem for many people. Dating anxiety is pervasive among adolescents and young adults (Essau, Conradt, & Petermann, 1999) and even among adults who have previously been married (Segrin & Givertz, 2003). Recent research suggests that locating sexual partners may be easier for young adults than initiating and developing long-term relationships (Mongeau, Ramirez, & Vorell, 2003). Although men in heterosexual relationships traditionally initiate romantic relationships, waiting for a man to make the first move does not seem to be an effective strategy for women. When asked if they would pursue a relationship with a woman who didn't at least hint at her interest and availability, most men said no (Muehlenhard & McFalls, 1981; Muehlenhard & Miller, 1988). Thus, in order for men to initiate interaction, they need women to send cues that they are interested and available. How does one do this? Frequently, potential romantic partners "test the water" by flirting. Considerable research has been conducted on flirting in heterosexual relationships, both because of its crucial role in the initiation of romantic relationships and because of its ambiguity. Unfortunately, we know much less about flirting during gay and lesbian courtship, so the discussion that follows refers primarily to heterosexual relationships.

Much flirting (though not all) is nonverbal, because nonverbal communication entails less risk. For example, if the other person does not respond, you can pretend you weren't flirting after all. When initiating a potential romantic/sexual relationship, women are more active than men. In fact, women use more eye contact, smiles, brief touches, and grooming behavior to signal interest and attraction. Although men do use gazing, smiling, and

Which of the four approaches to relationship development best describes the development of your most recent romantic relationship or friendship? In what ways did your relationship follow or deviate from this approach?

Think back to the last time you were aware that someone was interested in you romantically. How did you know? What verbal and nonverbal behaviors suggested that romance was a possibility?

The Dialectical Model of Relationship Development

AUTONOMY/ CONNECTION

The need to connect with others and the simultaneous need to feel independent or autonomous

Autonomy

Connection

EXPRESSIVENESS/ PRIVACY

The need to be open and to self-disclose while also maintaining some sense of privacy

Expressiveness

Privacy

CHANGE/ PREDICTABILITY

The need for events that are new, spontaneous, and unplanned—while simultaneously needing some aspects of life to be stable and predictable

Change

Predictability

grooming behaviors, the only behavior they engage in more than women do is intimate touching (hugging, hand holding). Thus, women engage in more flirtation at the onset of the interaction; then, men tend to escalate the relationship through touch (McCormick & Jones, 1989). To learn more about how women's behavior in this context differs from men's, see *Did You Know? Women's and Men's Flirtation Behaviors Differ*. You can also visit the Web site for the Social Issues Research Center at **www.sirc.org/publik/flirt.html** if you would like to learn more about the "science of flirting."

DID YOU KNOW?

Women's and Men's Flirtation Behaviors Differ

Although both men and women are active during flirtatious interactions, women and men do not behave the same. In fact, communication researchers Melanie Trost and Jess Alberts (2006) have identified a number of ways in which men and women vary with regard to their flirtatious behavior. Here are some of the differences they have identified:

- Women tend to be more skillful than men at delivering and detecting nonverbal cues of interest during an initial flirting interaction, whether interacting with a stranger an acquaintance.
- Women possess a larger repertoire of flirting strategies to signal interest than do men. Women have been identified as displaying as many as 52 different flirting behaviors!
- Women's signals are more likely to initiate a successful flirting interaction.
- Women have a larger repertoire of strategies for rejecting unwanted flirtations—and more frequently use them.
- Women who use flirtatious behaviors are more likely to be approached by men. Women who display few flirtatious signals are approached less than 0.5 times per hour. Women who emit a high number of flirtation behaviors are 8 times more likely to be approached by men (that is, they are approached four times per hour on average).

Once couples successfully convey their interest and initiate a conversation, if their interest continues, they may begin dating. Unfortunately, this is not always easy. People often lack confidence in their social and communication skills (Essau, Conradt, & Petermann, 1999). In general, however, successful dating appears to be related to effective communication skills. For example, individuals who self-disclose a little as they initiate relationships are more successful than those who disclose a lot or none at all. Competent daters know that one should disclose primarily positive information early in relationships. They also act interested in what others have to say, help others out, and are polite and positive. Finally, those who successfully initiate relationships are more able to plan and ask for dates. Unfortunately, many individuals haven't learned the skills needed to initiate dating relationships (Essau, Conradt, & Petermann, 1999; Galassi & Galassi, 1979). Some people even display conversational

Successful dating is related to effective communication skills.

behaviors that have been found to be *unsuccessful* in dating situations. These behaviors include trying too hard to make an impression, disclosing too much information too soon, being passive (waiting for the other person to initiate conversation and activities), and acting too self-effacing (or modest) (Young, 1981).

At times, initiating a dating relationship may seem like a rather complicated dance. Each person has a part, but the dance steps vary from one couple to the next. Fortunately, initiating friendship can seem a bit more straightforward.

Initiating Friendships Initiating a conversation is perhaps the most crucial communication skill in developing friendships. However, saying hello and initiating conversation can be difficult. Why? As in courtship situations, people may fear rejection. In fact, many people assume that the other person's failure to initiate a conversation is due to lack of interest (Vorauer & Ratner, 1996). If everyone felt this way, however, no relationship would ever begin. Remember: If you wish to meet new people, you may need to be the one who begins the conversation!

What is the best way to approach a new person? Typically, a nonthreatening comment works, such as, "This sure is an interesting class," as does an impersonal question, such as, "Are you a communication major?" For more suggestions, see *Building Your Communication Skills: Initiating a Conversation.*

If the other person is receptive, you can continue the conversation, and if the person isn't responsive, you can walk away. Once you begin the conversation, you can keep it going by asking a broad, open-ended question. For example, you could ask, "Why did you choose this university?" or "What do you enjoy doing when you're not working?" You want to be

Building Your Communication SKILLS

Initiating a Conversation

How do you respond when you walk into a party, class or meeting and you don't know a single person in the room? Do you strike up a conversation with someone who appears interesting, or do you sit by yourself waiting for someone to talk to you? If you tend to wait for others, you may be cheating yourself out of the opportunity to expand your network of friends and potential romantic partners. To help you become more skillful at initiating conversations, we offer you the following suggestions.

- Say a simple hello and offer a friendly smile; this can be very effective. You probably aren't the only person who feels a little uncomfortable or shy.

- Stand or sit near someone you are interested in getting to know, then comment on something in the environment that affects you both – such as the room temperature, how difficult it was to get into the class, or how loud the music is.

- Ask a question or comment on something the person has or is that interests you. You could indicate that you find his/her accent intriguing and ask where they are from, or you could say that you like an item they are wearing and ask where you might purchase one like it.

- Make a comment about the event you're attending and follow up with a question such as how they heard about it or why they chose to come.

- Offer an opinion and then engage the other person by asking her or his opinion. You might say "I am really looking forward to this class; how about you?"

- Ask a favor. You could ask if the person would hand you something, if it is okay to sit at his/her table, or if they can tell you what time it is. Even if they say no, you have begun interacting.

sure to ask questions that can't be answered with a yes or no or with only a brief response. Your goal is to get the other person talking and to learn more about him or her.

Maintaining Relationships

Effective communication is, of course, essential to developing and maintaining relationships. In fact, a strong association exists between peoples' communication skills and their satisfaction with their relationships—particularly romantic ones (Emmers-Sommers, 2004; Noller & Fitzpatrick, 1990). As romantic relationships become more intimate and move toward greater commitment, couples' ratings of their communication satisfaction increases. In contrast, as dating relationships move toward dissolution, couples' satisfaction with their communication decreases (Guerrero, Eloy, & Wabnik, 1993). It appears that effective communication and relationship satisfaction operate in a circular process; that is, effective communication increases couples' happiness with their relationships and that satisfaction leads to more effective communication. Communication is also essential to developing friendships. Most of the important functions that friends serve—providing companionship and a sense of belonging, offering emotional and physical support as well as reassurance, and giving feedback on self-disclosures—are communication based (Duck, 1991).

Though initiating friendships and romances can be anxiety producing, it can also be exhilarating and fun. When relationships are new, we tend to focus on their more positive aspects. However, as relationships endure, we have a harder time ignoring their shortcomings. Consequently, maintaining relationships over time can be challenging.

Maintaining Romantic Relationships Through Communication Communication researchers Dan Canary and Laura Stafford conducted some of the earliest studies of how couples keep their relationships satisfying. Based on their research, they created a typology of **relational maintenance** behaviors that heterosexual, gay, and lesbian couples use (Canary & Stafford, 1994; Haas & Stafford, 1998) (see Table 8.4).

More recently, scholars have examined the nonstrategic, routine communication behaviors heterosexual and gay couples perform that help maintain their relationships (Alberts, Yoshimura, Rabby, & Loschiavo, 2005). They determined that couples use twelve types of conversational behaviors as they live their lives together, including humor/joking, self-report (or self-disclosure), positivity (attempts to make interactions pleasant), and talking about television. Moreover, they found that, on weekends, couples tend to engage in more conflict, humor, household-task talk, and planning.

relational maintenance
behaviors that couples perform that help maintain their relationships

TABLE 8.4 Couples' Maintenance Behaviors

Behavior	Examples
Positivity	Act nice and cheerful; make interactions enjoyable
Openness	Encourage partner to disclose thoughts and feelings; discuss relationship
Assurances	Stress commitment to partner; imply relationship has a future
Social networks	Spend time with the other's friends; focus on common friends; show willingness to spend time with the other's friends and family
Sharing tasks	Help equally with tasks; perform household tasks
Joint activities	Spend time hanging out; engage in activities together
Mediated communication	Write letters; use e-mail or phone to keep in touch
Avoidance/antisocial	Be less than completely honest; avoid the other; act badly
Humor	Tease; be sarcastic in a funny way; use funny nicknames

SOURCE: Adapted from Stafford L. (2003). "Maintaining romantic relationships: Summary and analysis of one research program." In D. Canary & M. Dainton (Eds.), *Maintaining relationships through communication* (pp. 51–78). Mahwah, NJ: Erlbaum.

In general, studies indicate that specific communication patterns such as joking, spending time talking about one's day, encouraging self-disclosure, and expressing commitment to the relationship help couples maintain their relationships.

Maintaining Friendships Through Communication Conversation plays an important role in friendship as well. One study determined that many conversations with friends last only about three minutes and that these conversations were mostly small talk. Nonetheless, people rated these conversations as highly significant (Duck, 1991). Thus, intimate disclosures may be important, but so are the daily, routine interactions that connect friends and reaffirm or maintain their relationships.

Interestingly, scholars have found that friends are most satisfied with each other when they possess similar levels of communication skills (Burleson & Samter, 1996). That is, it is not how skillful friends are overall that predicts their satisfaction with each other but whether they possess "similar or different degrees of communication skill (or lack of skill)" (Dainton et al., 2003, p. 85).

Scholars have also studied the maintenance behaviors friends use to keep their relationships alive. For example, one study found that friends use assurances (indicating the importance of the friendship), positivity, open discussion, and listening, though less often than do romantic partners (Canary, Stafford, Hause, & Wallace, 1993). Several researchers have found that simply spending time together is an important maintenance strategy for friends (Fehr, 2000; Messman, Canary, & Hause, 2000). More specifically, they discovered that shared activities and ongoing interaction sustain a relationship and that absence of interaction is often given as the reason for a friendship ending (Dainton et al., 2003). Other communication researchers argue that good conflict-management skills are vital for enduring friendships (Burleson & Samter, 1996), and several point out that the use of telephone calls and email are essential to long-distance ones (Johnson, 2000). To learn more about how you can maintain your long-distance friendships, see the section called *Improving Your Maintenance Skills in Long-Distance Friendships* on page 196 of this chapter.

As you can see, communication is essential to both friendship and romantic relationship maintenance. However, sometimes we find ourselves unable, or unwilling, to invest energy in maintaining previously valued friendships or romances.

Ending Relationships

Not all relationships endure. When couples are consistently dissatisfied, one or both partners will likely exit the relationship. Some courtship relationships end after the first date, while others end after months or years. Friendships end as well. Relatively few people retain all the friends they make over the course of their lives (Rawlins, 1992). Despite this, relationship termination can be an awkward stage—both to experience and to study. People are generally much more willing to answer questionnaires and speak with researchers about developing or maintaining a relationship than about ending one. Studying this process is also difficult because relationship de-escalation and termination typically occur over an extended period, with no easy way to say exactly when the process began. Some relationships do end abruptly and decisively, however. The two basic trajectories for ending romantic relationships as well as friendships are called *sudden death* and *passing away* (Duck, 1982; Hays, 1988).

Sudden death refers to relationships that end without prior warning (at least for one participant). Some people are shocked to discover that their partners are leaving. Though unexpected for the one partner, the other may have been thinking about his or her departure for some time. Regardless of who has been thinking what and for how long, occasionally an event occurs—such as infidelity or betrayal—that so damages the relationship that the partners terminate the relationship relatively quickly.

More typically, relationships **pass away**, or decline over time, and the partners are aware that problems remain unresolved. During this period, the partners may vacillate between attempts to improve the relationship and efforts to de-escalate it. Over months or even years, romantic couples may seek counseling, take trips together, or try other methods to improve the relationship, while friends may sporadically try to renew their friendship.

sudden death
the process by which relationships end without prior warning for at least one participant

passing away
the process by which relationships decline over time

At the same time, they may develop outside interests or friends as they withdraw from the relationship. It can be a difficult period, especially for romantic couples.

To help you understand this often-confusing stage of relationship development, we next explore the reasons why relationships end and the strategies people use to terminate them.

Reasons for Courtship Dissolution When asked why their relationships terminated, gay and heterosexual couples provide very similar reasons (Baxter, 1991; Kurdek, 1991). The most frequent explanations were lack of autonomy, lack of similarity/compatibility, lack of supportiveness, and infidelity. Heterosexual couples also indicated that insufficient shared time, inequity, and the absence of romance contributed to the demise of their relationships. People also terminate relationships because characteristics they thought they liked in a partner become less appealing over time. One study determined that in almost one-third of the courtship relationships examined, the qualities individuals initially found attractive became the qualities that led to the end of the relationship (Felmlee, 1995)—a concept called *fatal attractions*. For example, one woman liked her relational partner because he had a "don't-care" attitude and liked to have fun, but she later found him immature (Felmlee, 1995).

When relationships end, everyone looks for explanations. People blame themselves, they blame the other person, or they may even blame people outside the relationship. Sometimes no one is to blame (Duck, 1991). For example, relationships may end because the partners live too far apart or the timing is wrong. You might meet Ms. or Mr. Right, but if you meet immediately following a painful breakup or just as you are beginning a new and demanding job, you won't have the emotional stability or time needed to develop a successful relationship. In sum, relationship termination is normal, though it can be difficult.

Romance Termination Strategies Researchers have identified five general categories of disengagement strategies for dissolving romantic relationships (Cody, 1982). Surprisingly (or perhaps not), the most frequent strategy romantic couples use to end their relationships is **negative identity management**, which means communicating in ways that arouse negative emotions in order to make the other person upset enough to agree to break off the relationship. A person using this strategy might criticize his or her romantic partner or convey indifference to his or her feelings and desires.

De-escalation is the second most used of the disengagement strategies. It covers a broad range of strategies—from promising some continued closeness (we can still be friends) to suggesting that the couple might reconcile in the future. When using de-escalation, one partner attempts to reframe or change the definition of the relationship.

Justification is the strategy that is used third most frequently. As the label implies, justification strategies attempt to provide a reason or excuse for why the relationship has failed and should end. In this case, one partner might explain the positive consequences of ending the relationship (we can devote more time to our careers) or the negative consequences of not ending the relationship (we will come to hate each other).

Positive-tone strategies, on the other hand, address the feelings and concerns of the partner and try to make her or him feel better; for example, a partner might say, "I care for you, but you deserve someone who can commit to you." To read about one student's experience with this termination strategy, see *It Happened to Me: Akira*.

Behavioral de-escalation strategies occur least frequently. These strategies involve avoiding the partner. Behavioral de-escalation strategies are likely the least common because it is difficult to avoid a person with whom you have a romantic relationship. If Richard doesn't return Rob's phone calls or avoids the classes they have together, Rob will most likely track him down to find out why.

---

negative identity management
communicating in ways that arouse negative emotions in order to make the other person upset enough to agree to break off the relationship

de-escalation
attempts to reframe or change the definition of the relationship

justification
providing a reason or excuse for why the relationship should end

positive-tone strategies
address the feelings and concerns of the partner

behavioral de-escalation
avoiding the partner

IT HAPPENED TO ME: Akira

Last year my girlfriend decided that we should start seeing other people. She used what I now understand is a positive-tone strategy. She tried making me feel better by saying that we were too young to be tied down, that she still cared for me and that we could stay friends. She even said "It isn't you; it's me." But I knew the truth—it was me.

Reasons for Friendship Dissolution   Why do friendships end? Friendships are particularly vulnerable to termination because few societal pressures encourage their continuance (Blieszner & Adams, 1992) and because friends may not expect to have consistent contact. Some friendships decline without either person being aware of it. Once the friends recognize the decline, their relationship may be beyond recovery (Rose, 1984). Thus friendships, unlike romantic relationships, can end without either person being dissatisfied with the relationship.

Friendships end for a range of reasons, based on how close the friendship was. Casual friends are more likely to report that their relationships ended due to lack of proximity, while close and best friends more often state that their relationships terminated because of decreased affection. In addition, best and close friends report that their friendships dissolved due to interference from other relationships, such as one person's romantic partner (Johnson et al., 2004).

Scholars have identified five specific factors that can contribute to the termination of a friendship: lack of communication skills, rule breaking, deception, boredom, and other reasons (Duck, 1988). With regard to the first factor, we know that poor conversationalists tend to be lonely (Duck, 1988) and that lonely people are not perceived to be competent communicators (Canary & Spitzberg, 1985). The lesson is that if you wish to maintain relationships, you must display appropriate communication skills. The quantitative definitions suggest that interpersonal communication is that which occurs within a dyad—or between two people (Knapp & Daly, 2002)—the skills we discuss throughout this book.

Friendships also end because one or both members violate fundamental, often unspoken rules of the relationship that have been established over the course of the friendship (Argyle & Henderson, 1984; Bowker, 2004). For example, most friends believe that good friends don't gossip about each other, flirt with each other's romantic partners, or lie to each other. Successful relationship partners discern the rules of the relationship and adhere to them.

Friends' Termination Strategies   Because friendships are less formal, their endings may be more subtle and less obvious than those endured by romantic couples (Hays, 1988). For example, a friend's permission is not required to end a friendship, and one can simply cut off contact abruptly, which happens only rarely in romantic relationships.

When friends desire relationship dissolution, they are likely to use one or more of the following disengagement strategies: withdrawal/avoidance, Machiavellian tactics, positive tone, and openness (Baxter, 1982). As with behavioral de-escalation among romantic couples, when friends engage in **withdrawal/avoidance**, they spend less time together, don't return phone calls, and avoid places where they are likely to see the other. **Machiavellian tactics** involve having a third party convey your unhappiness about the relationship and your desire to de-escalate or end it. Positive-tone strategies, like those used by romantic couples, express concern for the rejected friend and try to make the person feel better. Thus, you might tell a friend that you wish to end your friendship because school and work take up too much time, rather than admitting that you do not enjoy his company any more. Finally, **openness** means that you straightforwardly explain to your friend why the relationship is ending.

Which termination strategy is best for ending a friendship? Most often, your strategy selection will depend on how close you are to your friend. In close friendships, especially those in which you see each other often, openness or positive-tone strategies are most appropriate. Even if you are very angry with your friend, your previous intimacy requires that you confront her or him and not rely on avoidance or third parties to do your "dirty work." For less intimate friendships or friends you see infrequently, you may find that withdrawing from the relationship or avoidance works well because you are not dependent on each other's companionship. However, if you are not close to a person who hurt you deeply and cannot avoid him or her, using a third party to convey your desire to end the friendship might be appropriate.

What rules do you have for close friendships? That is, what could a friend do that would be such a significant violation of your expectations that you would terminate your friendship?

withdrawal/avoidance
a friendship-termination strategy in which friends spend less time together, don't return phone calls, and avoid places where they are likely to see each other

Machiavellian tactics
having a third party convey one's unhappiness about a relationship

openness
a state in which communicators are willing to share their ideas as well as listen to others in a way that avoids conveying negative or disconfirming feedback

SOCIETY, POWER, COURTSHIP, AND MARRIAGE

Many people think that relationships depend solely on the individuals involved, that our decision to befriend or become intimate with another person is a matter of choice, and that how we communicate and behave within relationships is strictly a matter of preference. However, society wields strong influences on our choices and behavior. Sometimes these influences are explicit and a matter of law, as in restrictions against marriage between underage teenagers. Other societal influences are more subtle. For example, why is it that 95 percent of all marriages are racially homogenous (United States Bureau of the Census, 1998)? Similarly, why do most couples who marry have a wedding ceremony, and why are people expected to tell their romantic partners "I love you"? The reasons lie in powerful, sometimes unrecognized societal norms. These laws and norms determine to a large extent whom we find desirable as romantic partners and friends and how we communicate with them.

Society, Power, and Romantic Relationships

Most heterosexuals are unaware of the effect cultural norms have on their romance choices (O'Brien & Foley, 1999) or on how they express affection and commitment. For example, not only are most marriages in the United States racially homogenous (as we have noted), they also tend to occur between people of similar religious backgrounds (Shehan, Bock, & Lee, 1990), economic status (Kalmijin, 1994), age (Atkinson & Glass, 1985), education (Mare, 1991), weight (Schafer & Keith, 1990), and appearance (Chambers, Christiansen, & Kunz, 1983). Such a high degree of similarity, or **homogeneity**, suggests that individual preference is not the only factor influencing our choices. To learn how this pattern of racial homogeneity may be changing, see *Communication in Society: Race and Romantic Relationships in the United States.*

Commonly held stereotypes also influence choices about whom one should or should not date and marry. In intercultural couples, certain combinations are more common than others. In 75 percent of Black–White marriages, the husband is Black and the wife is White, and in 75 percent of White–Asian couples the husband is White and the wife of Asian (Sailer, 2003). The frequency of these pairings reflects strong societal norms about who is

Communication in SOCIETY

Race and Romantic Relationships in the United States

Have you dated or married someone from a different ethnic or racial group? If not, might you be likely to do so in the future? Do you think these relationships face more problems than those between people of the same racial or ethnic group?

Over the past 50 years, the prevalence and perceptions of interracial romantic relationships have changed dramatically in the United States. Many states prohibited Black-White interracial marriages prior 1967, and the last state to remove such a law was Alabama, doing so in November 2000 (Hartill, 2001). Consequently, in 1970, only about 1 out of 1000 marriages (1/10 of 1 percent) in the United States was interracial (Troy, Lewis-Smith, & Laurenceau, 2006). Just thirty years later, however, 5.4 percent of all marriages were interracial relationships (Lee & Edmonston, 2005).

The prevalence of interdating (dating across racial and ethnic groups) is even more common. In one survey, over half of Whites, African American, and Hispanic teenagers reported dating someone of another ethnicity (Troy, Lewis-Smith, & Laurenceau,

2006) while another found that 35.7 percent of White Americans had interdated, along with 56.5 percent of African Americans, 55.4 percent of Hispanic Americans, and 57.1 percent of Asian Americans (Yancey, 2002).

Perceptions of the quality of interethnic and interracial romantic relationships have lagged behind their prevalence. Even today, these relationships are often believed to be burdened with more problems than intraracial ones. They are often believed to be less satisfying, more conflictual, and less successful. However, psychology professors Troy, Lewis-Smith, and Laurenceau (2006) determined that romantic partners in interracial relationships reported significantly higher relationship satisfaction compared to those in intraracial relationships. They also found no differences between interracial and intraracial relationships in relationship quality and conflict patterns.

As these studies suggest, the percentage of interracial marriages today may be less than 6 percent, but changing attitudes and dating patterns among young adults mean that in the coming years this percentage is likely to be much higher.

attractive (and who is not) as well as common stereotypes about what type of woman makes a good wife.

Just as societies have norms for mate selection and behavior, they also have norms for communication in the context of romantic relationships. For example, who do you think should say "I love you" first or propose marriage? Many people believe that males in heterosexual relationships should take the lead (Owen, 1987). In some cultures, however, romantic couples rarely express their feelings or only express them in private. In Japan, couples rarely touch or express emotion in public. Although young couples may hold hands, spouses virtually never kiss in public (Times Square Travels, 2004). Other cultures prohibit public expressions of affection, as in Indonesia, where it is illegal to kiss in public (MSNBC News, 2004), or in Kuwait, where homosexuality is illegal, as is any public display of affection between men and women (World Travels, 2004). Thus, every relationship is situated within a set of societal and cultural norms and expectations, and what occurs within that relationship is likely to be affected by those norms.

Because of the national debate concerning gay and lesbian marriage, most people recognize that through laws, society in most parts of the United States limits the sex of the person one can choose to marry. However, many heterosexuals fail to consider how strongly social norms and laws affect the ways in which gays and lesbians can communicate with and about their romantic partners. Regardless of one's position on the desirability of gay and lesbian romances and marriage, the impact of legal and normative restrictions on gay relationships merits consideration. Gay people often can't express affection in public without fear of negative, even violent, responses. In many instances they don't even feel safe recognizing their partners or referring to them. For this reason they may refer to their lovers as "friends" or "roommates" or attempt to conceal their romantic partner's sex by never using pronouns such as *him* or *her*. Having to alter one's verbal and nonverbal behavior to conform to society's norms may seem a small matter if you are heterosexual. But imagine what life would be like if in many contexts you could never acknowledge your partner, you had to pretend that you were "just friends," and you had to continuously be on guard to avoid revealing this "secret." Not only would this be exhausting, it would significantly inhibit your ability to be close to others. Unfortunately, this is the life that many gays and lesbians live.

In addition to the social norms that affect how we develop and communicate within romantic and courtship relationships, the practices of specific institutions impact our communication and relationships. For example, many faiths have long prescribed whom their members should marry, how many spouses they could have, and even if they should date. For example, the Mormon faith once permitted men to have more than one wife (although it no longer does); Muslim men are instructed to marry Muslim women; and Hindus often discourage young people from dating and selecting their own marital partners.

Although over time religions can and do alter their positions on these issues (for example, the Church of Jesus Christ of Latter-Day Saints' position on polygamy), they may be slower to change than other social institutions. For example, Penny Edgell (2003) surveyed 125 churches and discovered that 83 percent of them still maintained an organization and theology based on the idea of the nuclear family in which the father works, the mother stays at home, and the couple has children. She further points out that a number of churches are not receptive to gay and lesbian couples, who then have difficulty practicing their faith. In these ways, religious institutions influence how we view relationships as well as how we act within them and communicate about our relationships.

Similarly, business organizations create policies and practices that affect the types of relationships and communication practices their employees can have. Many organizations prohibit coworkers from establishing "affectional relationships" while others (such as the military) ban fraternization—relationships that cross the organizational hierarchy. Corporations also develop policies to limit nepotism—hiring one's family members—or express their views on same-sex relationships by providing, or not providing, domestic-partner benefits. Organizations often also create rules that attempt to control and influence employees' communication, through sexual harassment policies, secrecy clauses, and dictates on what can be communicated to others outside the organization.

Society, Power, and Friendship

Unlike marriage, friendships are not governed by laws and institutions. However, social norms still affect our choice of friends or our behavior within friendships. Take a moment to think about your closest friends over the past five years. How similar are they to you? Do you have any friends who are decades older than you? How many of your friends are from a different ethnic group than you are? Clearly some people do have friends who differ from themselves on demographic factors such as race, age, income, and education, but this is more often the exception than the rule (Aboud & Mendelson, 1996). As we discussed in Chapter 6, these multicultural relationships, though potentially very rewarding, sometimes take more "care and feeding" than relationships in which two people are very similar. Intercultural friends may receive pressure from others, particularly from majority group members, to stick with people who are similar to them (Pogrebin, 1992).

Thus friendship is not only an individual matter; it is also a social event that occurs in contexts that exert a powerful influence on its development (Allan, 1977). In the United States, friendships play an extremely important role in the lives of adolescents. In this culture, then, parents are encouraged to understand that their adolescent children will turn away from talking and spending time with them (Rawlins, 1992). On the other hand, married adults are expected to place their romance partners and families before their friends (Dainton et al., 2003).

ETHICS AND INTERPERSONAL COMMUNICATION

Although communicating ethically is important in all contexts and relationships, nowhere is it more important than in the context of close relationships. If you communicate unethically with your friends, family, and romantic partner, the consequences may be severe. Certainly relationships have ended due to deception, secrecy, and even the truth too harshly expressed. All of the ethical considerations we have discussed throughout this book are important in close relationships, but here we will focus on authentic communication.

As you may recall from Chapter 1, authentic communication refers to communication that is open and free from pretense. **Inauthentic communication** refers to attempts to manipulate an interaction or person for personal goals; it denies the right to communicate to those with a legitimate interest in the issue. Authentic communication is particularly important in close relationships for two reasons: We expect our closest friends and family members to be authentic, or "real," with us, and authentic communication is connected to intimacy.

For most people, intimacy is based on the feeling that one knows and is known by another. When we feel intimate with others we believe that we are connecting with their "true" selves and that we can be our truest selves in the relationship. However, when people are not authentic in their communication with those close to them or deny them the right to communicate authentically, it can decrease intimacy and even lead to termination of the relationship. And if we discover that an intimate friend or partner has been inauthentic and manipulative, we will not only feel deceived but betrayed. For example, if you discover that your friend has been pretending to like your romantic partner while making negative remarks about her on the sly, you will probably feel angry and betrayed. In addition, if you want to continue the relationship, you now have to deal not only with your friend's feelings about your romantic partner but also with your friend's deceit.

How can you ensure that your interactions with close others are authentic? You can do so by being open to others' communication efforts, being open in your own communication, taking responsibility for what you say, and respecting the rights of others to speak. In effect, we are suggesting that you need to avoid the three "pitfalls" of inauthentic communication: topic avoidance, meaning denial, and disqualification.

To maintain an authentic relationship with another you need to confront issues that are important to the relationship and to the other party. If one or both of you prohibit the other from discussing issues that are important to either of you, you are engaging in inauthentic communication. For example, if your good friend wishes to discuss his or her sexual identity and you refuse to do so, you are shutting down communication and likely damaging your intimacy with the other person.

inauthentic communication attempts to manipulate an interaction or person for personal goals

In addition, authentic relationships require that you take responsibility for what you say and mean. If you are angry and tease your friend harshly because of it, it is inauthentic to deny that you are angry and trying to be hurtful. Even worse, if you put the onus on your friend for being "too sensitive," you are compounding the problem of your inauthenticity. Repeated interactions such as this can undermine trust and intimacy.

Finally, authentic communicators allow others to speak regardless of their own position or experience. If your single friend attempts to give you relationship support and advice, you disqualify him or her if you refuse to listen because your friend isn't married. You can also disqualify a romantic partner by denying him or her the right to speak on a topic because of his or her sex or because you perceive yourself to be more expert on the topic. If you find yourself saying, "What could you know about this?" then chances are you are disqualifying the other party and you are engaging in inauthentic communication.

Engaging in authentic communication can help you develop and maintain your relationships more effectively. To help you begin the process, we conclude this chapter with suggestions for how you can more effectively engage in one fundamental type of relationship communication.

IMPROVING YOUR MAINTENANCE SKILLS IN LONG-DISTANCE FRIENDSHIPS

Because people are more mobile now than ever before, you are likely to find yourself confronted with the need to maintain friendships across physical distances. If you are confronted with this situation, know that long-distance relationships that are high in communication are also typically high in satisfaction and commitment (Oswald & Clark, 2003). Therefore, developing appropriate communication skills for long-distance friendships can help you sustain these relationships even when you are apart.

The strategies you use to maintain long-distance relationships are similar to those needed for face-to-face ones, but they may differ in their importance and frequency.

The four strategies that are most important in long-distance relationships are: frequency of interaction, openness, positivity, and social support (Oswald & Clark, 2003).

Maintaining frequent contact is essential to maintaining long-distance relationships.

Maintain Frequent Contact

Making the effort to maintain *frequent contact* with your long-distance friend is essential. Although you can typically rely on seeing local friends through planned events, accidental encounters and your social network, if you don't invest time and energy in contacting long-distance friends, you are likely to drift apart. This frequent contact can occur through a mixture of email, social network sites such as Facebook, phone calls and visits to one another. These interactions need not be lengthy or require a specific reason to occur. In fact, in many ways the quantity of your interactions is just as important, if not more so, than their quality.

Encourage Openness

Successful long-distance friendships are also marked by their *openness*. People who disclose their thoughts and feelings on important and commonplace issues—and who encourage their friends to do the same—have more satisfying and enduring relationships. As we mentioned

in our discussion of long-distance romances, relationships are created and maintained by the conversations we have within them, so talking about the mundane events in friends' lives helps them feel connected and understood.

Engage in Positivity

Successful long-distance friendships are also those in which the participants engage in *positivity*. People who are perceived as upbeat and cheerful during interactions are also seen as being more attractive and fun. Almost everyone finds interactions with happy and optimistic people more enjoyable than those with the perpetually depressed and down-trodden. Positive people also tend to be more interested in others as well as more accepting and affirming. This does not mean that you can never be sad, depressed or in need with long-distance friends; however, if you constantly display these behaviors in interactions with your long-distance friends, they may invest less energy in maintaining your friendship.

Offer Social Support

Finally, individuals who offer social support to their long-distance friends tend to find that their relationships are longer lasting. *Social Support* refers to the instrumental and emotional comfort friends provide to each other. *Instrumental support* describes concrete behaviors that help friends manage their problems, such as providing advice, information, or material goods such as money. *Emotional support* is composed of the things people say and do that make others feel loved and cared for and that bolster their sense of self-worth. You offer emotional support when you talk with your friend about her or his problems, provide encouragement and positive feedback, and express your caring and commitment to the friend and friendship.

SUMMARY

Interpersonal communication is worth studying because of the significant impact it has on one's ability to develop satisfying relationships. Interpersonal communication refers to interaction that takes place between interdependent parties, occurs on a continuum and is inherently relational. In addition, although interpersonal communication can occur in both casual/temporary and close/intimate relationships, it differs markedly between them.

Close relationships are those in which the participants see each other as unique and irreplaceable and in which the communication is marked by high disclosure and openness. Also, people in close relationships are committed to their relationships and expect them to endure.

The three factors that most influence the likelihood that one will be attracted to another are proximity, physical attractiveness, and similarity. Once people are attracted to one another, they use communication to engage in a process of relational development. This process has been explained using two types of models: stage models, which divide the process of relationship development into phases leading to growth and decline; and trajectory models, which examine the events that lead individuals to move toward and away from commitment.

Communication behaviors are connected with the three basic stages of relationship development: initiation, maintenance, and termination. Strategies for initiating relationships include opening with impersonal questions, listening attentively, being polite, expressing approval, and asking open-ended follow-up questions. Strategies and routine behaviors that friends and lovers use to maintain their relationships include being open, expressing positivity, and offering assurances, among others. Because many relationships end, researchers have examined the reasons individuals give for ending them and the strategies they use to do so, which include negative identity management, positive-tone strategies, justification, and de-escalation strategies.

In addition to the behaviors individuals perform, societal laws and norms also influence the development of friendships and romances and the communication that occurs within them. These societal elements may determine whom we marry and/or befriend, how we communicate with relational partners, and how we communicate with the rest of the world about these relationships.

Finally, you can improve the relationships you develop by engaging in authentic communication and improving your communication skills in long-distance friendships. Authentic communication involves being open to others' communication efforts, being open in your own communication, taking responsibility for what you say, and respecting the rights of others to speak. Enhancing your friendship skills in long-distance relationships entails engaging in frequent interactions, being open and expressive, presenting yourself positively, and offering social support.

KEY TERMS

attractiveness 179
autonomy/connection 184
avoiding 182
behavioral de-escalation 191
bonding 182
breadth 180
change/predictability 184
circumscribing 182
de-escalation 191
depth 180
differentiating 182
dyad 176
experimenting 181

expressiveness/privacy 184
frequency 180
inauthentic communication 195
integrating 181
intensifying 181
initiating 181
justification 191
Machiavellian tactics 192
matching hypothesis 179
negative identity management 191
openness 192
passing away 190
positive-tone strategies 191

proximity 177
relational maintenance 189
relational trajectory models 183
similarity 179
social penetration theory 180
stage model 182
stagnating 182
sudden death 190
terminating 182
turning point model 183
uncertainty reduction theory 180
withdrawal/avoidance tactics 192

CHAPTER REVIEW QUESTIONS

1. What are the two general models of relationship development? Which ones include, or have been adapted to include, both romantic and friendship relationships?

2. What strategies do women use to initiate a relationship through flirting? What behaviors do men use?

3. What is a dialectic? What are the three most common dialectics in close relationships?

4. What strategies do romantic partners use to terminate their relationships? Which strategies do friends also use to end their relationships?

ACTIVITIES

1. **Evaluating Strategies for Initiating Conversations**
Go out to a variety of public places (library, grocery store, bank) and initiate conversations with five people you don't know. Be sure to interact with a variety of people—male, female, older, younger, White, Black, Hispanic. Each time you initiate a conversation, try different strategies listed in "Communicating More Effectively." Which strategies did you feel most comfortable using? Which strategies were most effective? Was your choice of strategy dependent on the person with whom you initiated the conversation? What seemed to influence how successful a given strategy was?

2. **Maintaining Friendships and Romantic Relationships**
Interview two people and ask them how they maintain their closest friendship. What conscious, deliberate strategies do they use to ensure that they will stay close with their good friends? Also, what routine behaviors do they use to maintain closeness (for example, using nicknames, e-mailing funny stories)?

Then interview two people and ask them the same questions about how they maintain their current romantic relationship.

Finally, compare the four sets of responses. Do your interviewees use similar or different strategies for maintaining their friendships and their romances?

3. **Societal Influences on Relationships**

Choose six popular magazines from your local grocery store. Be sure to select a wide range of magazines, including those directed toward men and women as well as some focused on political, social, and health issues. Skim through the magazines first looking at the advertisements. What can you tell about the way in which friendships and romances are viewed in the United States? As you look through the magazines, ask yourself these questions:

a. To what degree do the people in the ads "match" as to ethnicity, age, attractiveness, height and weight, and other factors?

b. How many of the romantic couples are gay or lesbian?

c. How many of the friendship pairs depicted are female? Male?

d. In the ads depicting friends, what are female friends doing? What are male friends doing?

e. How many ads picture people who are "overweight"? Physically unattractive? What products are they advertising?

f. What population of readers does the magazine target?

After answering these questions, look for patterns that exist within magazines according to their target audience. What does this reveal about society's views of friendships and romantic relationships?

WEB ACTIVITIES

1. Go to www.onlinedatingmagazine.com/articles/howtobreakup.html and read the ten tips for how to effectively end a relationship. Which of the strategies seem like good advice to you? Which strategies seem unrealistic or ineffective? What strategies would you add to the list?

2. Go to www.gottman.com/qz2/BidsForConnection.html, a Web site for the Gottman Institute. Dr. Gottman is the foremost researcher on marital and relationship stability. While thinking of a close friend or your most recent romantic partner, take the quiz "Bid for Connection." What does the quiz reveal about your emotional connection in this relationship? What can you do to improve your ability to make bids for emotional connection in this relationship?

9
MANAGING CHALLENGES IN INTERPERSONAL RELATIONSHIPS

*H*ank: I can't believe you lied to me. You said you were going to hang out at home, and now I discover you went to the library to "study" with Steve. What's going on between you two? Rosa: Steve and I are just friends! I didn't tell you about our study session because you always jump to the wrong conclusions. You don't trust me, so I can't tell you the truth. Hank: Oh, so it's my fault that you're a liar. Is it my fault that you're a cheater too? Rosa: That's it! I can't talk to you when you're being such a jerk.

Although relationships provide love, companionship, and joy, they can also be the source of some of our greatest suffering. Once we open ourselves to intimacy and commitment, like Hank and Rosa, we also open ourselves to the possibility of hurt and betrayal. All relationships face challenges to their continued existence, so it is not a question of whether problems will arise—it is a question of how individuals respond to those challenges.

To help you create more satisfying and enduring relationships, in this chapter we begin by defining what we mean by interpersonal *relationship challenges*; then we describe the importance of managing these challenges. Next, we address how individuals can address such challenges by developing social influence skills, managing aversive communication interactions such as deception and hurtful messages, and responding to threats to their relationships, including infidelity. We then explore how the societal forces of power, culture, and emotion influence the occurrence of and responses to relationship challenges. We conclude the chapter with a discussion of the role ethical communication plays in managing relationship challenges and how you can more effectively apologize when you have injured someone.

Once you have read this chapter, you will be able to:

- Differentiate primary from secondary influence goals.
- Identify the four weapons of influence and the resistance strategies for each.
- Describe the truth bias and how it impacts individuals' ability to detect deception.
- Articulate the communication strategies that escalate conflict related to jealousy.
- Understand how to deliver potentially hurtful messages more effectively.
- Explain strategies individuals can use to protect their romantic relationships from temptations.
- Explicate the differences between battering and situational couple violence.
- Describe five strategies for preventing sexual coercion.
- Discuss the influence of culture and power on the expression of emotion.

CHAPTER OUTLINE

WHAT ARE RELATIONSHIP CHALLENGES?

THE IMPORTANCE OF MANAGING RELATIONSHIP CHALLENGES

THE INDIVIDUAL AND RELATIONSHIP CHALLENGES

Developing Social Influence Skills

Managing Aversive Communication Interactions

Relationship Threats

THE INDIVIDUAL, RELATIONSHIP CHALLENGES, AND SOCIETY

Society, Sex Roles, and Relationship Challenges

Society, Emotion, and Relationship Challenges

ETHICS AND RELATIONSHIP CHALLENGES

IMPROVING YOUR INTERPERSONAL COMMUNICATION SKILLS

Summary

Key Terms

Chapter Review Questions

Activities

Web Activities

relationship challenges
a wide range of interactional problems and situations that can threaten the continuance of a relationship

social influence
the ability to influence others

WHAT ARE RELATIONSHIP CHALLENGES?

Relationships challenges include a wide range of interactional problems and situations that can threaten the continuance of a relationship. In Chapter 8, we discussed one type of relationship challenge—the dialectical tensions that arise in relationships. As we indicated there, when the autonomy/connection, expressiveness/privacy, and change/predictability tensions are managed effectively, relationship may improve; but when these contradictions are poorly handled, they can lead to the termination of a relationship.

In addition to these dialectical tensions, people in relationships may experience partners who deceive them, betray their confidences, express jealousy, attempt to persuade or control them, and commit acts of infidelity, among many other things.

THE IMPORTANCE OF MANAGING RELATIONSHIP CHALLENGES

When people first fall in love or become friends, they find it difficult to imagine that their relationships will include problems and disappointments. The new lover is their soul mate; the new friend is just like them! However, any relationship that persists for more than a few weeks is likely to encounter problems, and research suggests that many relationships are not able to survive these challenges. For example, two studies of dating relationships among high school students found that, on average, these relationships lasted between 4 months (Connally & Johnson, 1996) and 8.6 months (Zimmer-Gembeck, 1998). Friendships can also be fragile; one study determined that approximately 50 percent of high school best friends are no longer best friends after the first year of college (Oswald & Clark, 2003). More distressingly, over 43 percent of first marriages end in divorce within 15 years—and an even higher number of second marriages do so (Bramlett & Mosher, 2001). These high rates of relationship change and failure are due in large part to our inability to respond effectively to the problems we encounter. If you wish to maintain your close relationships, you need the skills necessary to manage and respond to difficulties you might face.

THE INDIVIDUAL AND RELATIONSHIP CHALLENGES

Each interaction between people in a relationship is affected by the communication choices of both partners. While you can only control your own behavior, the choices you make impact how others respond to you and, therefore, how the conversation unfolds. This truth was articulated centuries ago in Proverbs 15:1, which states "A soft answer turns away wrath: but grievous words stir up anger" (Holy Bible, KJV, n.d.). Researchers have scientifically established the truth of this saying; they have found that 96 percent of the time, the likelihood that a relational partner will care how you feel is determined by the attitude with which you begin the conversation. More specifically, people who show vulnerability evoke tenderness and caring from others, while those who are critical are met with defensiveness and hostility (Atkinson, 2005). So even if someone approaches you in anger, you can control the course of the conversation by the tone of your response.

Because we cannot discuss every potential problem you might encounter in your close relationships, in this chapter we will explore three categories of relationship challenges we perceive to be the most pervasive and/or potentially destructive to relationships: social influence, aversive communication behaviors, and relationship threats. Let's take each in turn.

Developing Social Influence Skills

One of the most fundamental challenges that individuals face in their relationships is influencing the people who are important to them. In all types of relationships, people want to have **social influence** over others—to be able to influence others but also to retain the ability to resist others' influence. For example, you want to be able to persuade friends to join you for a night of fun or to help you move into a new apartment. At the same time, you want to be able to occasionally say no to friends' and romantic partners' requests while

maintaining your relationships with them. If you find you can't influence your friends and romantic partners, you may find those relationships dissatisfying and unfulfilling. Similarly, if it is difficult or impossible for you to refuse friends' and romantic partners' unreasonable and unpleasant requests, you will probably find those relationships frustrating or distressing.

Influencing Goals

Every day you engage in attempts to influence the people around you. You might try to persuade a salesperson to give you a discount, your teacher to extend the deadline for a paper, or your friend to join you on a spring break trip. In each case, you have a specific goal or outcome you hope to achieve. However, in many persuasive situations, people have multiple goals. In addition to wanting your teacher to give you an extension, for example, you probably also want to influence her to perceive you as a hardworking student. So when making your request, you will offer justifications that are both convincing and that cast you in a good light. You aren't likely to say that you need an extension because you have been out partying too much with your friends. Rather, you will say that you have a heavy course load this semester, you are working to put yourself through school, and you want more time so that the quality of your work will be higher. In this case, your primary (or most important) goal is to receive an extension on the due date, but your secondary goal is to influence how your teacher perceives you.

Primary Goals People have a range of **primary influence goals**—goals that are related to the outcome you want to take place. These goals include *gaining assistance, sharing an activity, changing behavior,* and *changing the terms of a relationship* (Cody, Canary, & Smith, 1994; Kellerman, 2004). When the goal is to gain assistance, people are seeking families, friends, and colleagues to aid them—for something as simple as help with a project to something as complex as donating a kidney. People often try to entice others to share an activity with them—for example, how many times has a friend tried to persuade you to go out for an evening of fun instead of staying home and studying?

Individuals' goals may include changing another person's behavior. For example, friends try to persuade each other whom to date (or break up with), to be the designated driver, or to share an apartment. Romantic partners try to influence one another to help out more with housework, to spend less money, or to be more thoughtful. Finally, at some point in every relationship, one or both partners try to influence the development of the relationship or some kind of change in the nature of the relationship. Early in their relationship, one romantic partner often wants to influence the other partner to become more serious or exclusive; later on, however, that same partner might to want to slow down or end the relationship.

Secondary Goals In addition to these four primary goals, individuals also possess **secondary influence goals**—goals that constrain or enhance the message they use to accomplish their goals. Such goals help people decide whether to attempt persuasion and, if they do, what type of message to choose (Dillard, Segrin, & Harden, 1989). The five types of secondary goals are *identity goals, interaction goals, relational resource goals, personal resource goals,* and *arousal maintenance goals.*

Identity goals are related to one's self-concept and involve issues, values, and ethics. For example, you may know that you can manipulate others by doing favors for them so that they will feel obligated to do a favor for you. However, whether or not you choose this strategy depends on how you want the other person to view you and/or how you view yourself. If you see yourself (and want others to see you) as an ethical and fair person, you might forgo strategies that could be perceived as manipulative. On the other hand, you may believe that fairness dictates that people repay favors they have received earlier, so you remind people of their obligations when you make requests.

Interaction goals concern rules for how a person should behave when communicating with others. An important interaction goal for many people is to be perceived as socially appropriate. For instance, threatening others in order to influence their behavior can be highly effective, but it is not usually socially appropriate. For this reason, most

primary influence goals
goals that are related to the outcome you want to take place; these goals include *gaining assistance, sharing an activity, changing behavior,* and *changing the terms of a relationship*

secondary influence goals
goals that constrain or enhance the message they use to accomplish their goal

identity goals
goals that are related to one's self-concept and involve issues, values, and ethics

interaction goals
goals related to rules for how a person should behave when communicating with others

relational resource goals
refer to the desire to maintain or increase one's "relational assets"— the emotional support and affection that others provide

personal resource goals
goals related to the desire to maintain material assets

arousal maintenance goals
goals relating to an individual's need to avoid feeling uncomfortable, nervous, or embarrassed when making a request

compliance-gaining messages
communication strategies people use to influence one another

people avoid using threatening messages to persuade others (except, perhaps, parents!). For the same reason, people might avoid strategies that might be perceived as manipulative or aggressive.

Relational resource goals refer to the desire to maintain or increase one's "relational assets"—the emotional support and affection that others provide. If you want to maintain a friendship or romantic relationship, you will probably choose strategies that are polite, indirect, and/or that seem reasonable. However, when you are not concerned with continuing a relationship—such as with a car dealer or a casual acquaintance—you may be willing to use more aggressive and less socially appropriate tactics if you believe that they will help you accomplish your goal.

Personal resource goals are related to the desire to maintain material assets. Most people won't make statements or promises that could result in the loss of a significant amount of their own resources or time. For example, you might be able to persuade your friend to help you move if you let him borrow your car; however, you may hesitate to make the offer because you don't want to lose access to your only mode of transportation. Instead, you might offer pizza and beer as a reward or simply tell her how much you would appreciate her kindness.

Finally, individuals have **arousal maintenance goals.** That is, they don't want to feel uncomfortable, nervous, or embarrassed when making a request. If asking for a favor provokes extreme anxiety and discomfort, you probably won't ask. Instead, you will make the request of someone with whom you feel more comfortable, or you may frame your request as politely and positively as possible. You probably wouldn't feel comfortable threatening your professor with a bad class evaluation if he doesn't review your rough draft, but you might tell him that you appreciate his efforts and really enjoy his class. To learn about one student's efforts to balance his primary and secondary goals, read *It Happened to Me: Tai.* To review the types of primary and secondary influence goals individuals have, see Table 9.1.

For example, consider Kim, who is trying to persuade her sexual partner to use a condom. In this case, Kim's primary goal is to influence her partner's behavior during sex. However, Kim's secondary goals—to be liked, to avoid embarrassment, to maintain the relationship—constrain the strategies she can use to achieve her primary goal. Kim could refuse to engage in sex unless her partner uses a condom, but she may hesitate to use this tactic because she doesn't

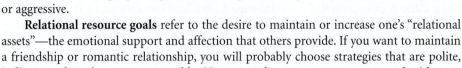

IT HAPPENED TO ME: Tai

Recently, I had a run of bad luck. My car started having engine problems, my hours at work were cut back, and the textbooks for my classes cost more than I had budgeted. I was really short on cash, but I needed to have my car repaired to drive to work, so I thought about asking my parents for a loan. However, I know they don't have a lot of money, and they have made it clear that they have helped as much as they can, so I was really nervous about asking them. For days I went back and forth on whether I should call and ask them. Now that I have studied social influence, I realize that I was torn between wanting to achieve my primary goal (to obtain a loan) and my secondary goal (to minimize my feelings of anxiety). Finally, I decided I really had to achieve my primary goal of getting a loan from my parents, so I called them. They weren't thrilled and I did feel really uncomfortable asking, but they came through for me, so I'm glad I asked.

want to risk jeopardizing her relationship or her partner's feelings for her. Instead, she has to develop a message that will accomplish both her primary and her secondary goals. This may not be possible, however, and Kim's secondary goals may win out—meaning no persuasive message is even attempted. In Kim's case, this might mean setting aside her own safety concerns rather than risking her relationship.

Now that you see the variety of goals you might have when you try to influence others, you're probably wondering exactly how you can accomplish your objectives. In the next section, we explore messages you can use to influence others.

Compliance-Gaining Messages

Compliance-gaining messages are the communication strategies people use to influence one another (Stiff & Mongeau, 2002). What types of compliance-gaining strategies do people use? Perhaps the strategy that first comes to mind is to offer rewards to the person

TABLE 9.1 Primary and Secondary Influence Goals

Type of Goal	Purpose
Primary Influence Goals	
Gaining assistance	To acquire a favor, a loan, help, or support
Sharing an activity	To motivate others to join in a work or social event
Changing another's behavior	To cause another to alter actions, attitudes, beliefs
Changing a relationship	To alter the development or nature of a relationship
Secondary Goals	
Identity	To present a desired self-concept
Interaction	To be perceived as interacting appropriately
Relational resources	To maintain or increase others' affection or support
Personal resource goals	To maintain or minimize losses to one's assets, such as time, money, and property
Arousal maintenance	To minimize feelings of anxiety and discomfort

you are attempting to influence (Dillard, Anderson, & Knobloch, 2002; Marwell & Schmitt, 1967). As we discuss in our examples above, you can be nice to someone or give them something in advance so that they will be more disposed to agree to your request. Or you can make a promise to do something in return. (If you loan me your car, I'll fill it up with gas.) If that doesn't work, you might switch to tactics that are punitive (Dillard et al., 2002; Marwell & Schmitt, 1967). For example, you can threaten to withold something the target wants if they don't comply (e.g., "If you don't stop flirting with other women, I'm ending this relationship!"), or you might become aggressive and call the person stingy for not sharing her car.

Alternatively, you can attempt to persuade people by explaining the consequences of their behavior (Dillard et al., 2002; Marwell & Schmitt, 1967). For example, you could explain the positive outcomes of a behavior: "If you start exercising, you will feel so much better." Or you could articulate the negative consequences of not fulfilling your request: "If you don't start exercising, you are going to become ill."

Other compliance-gaining strategies that we use are claiming that fulfilling the request is for the target's own good—for example, "If you volunteer at the food bank, you'll discover that you actually enjoy it." Alternatively, we can try to gain compliance by stressing how much the requested activity will please us—for example, "I promised that I would recruit one more volunteer for the food bank, and it would mean a lot to me if you would do this." (Dillard et al., 2002; Marwell & Schmitt, 1967).

The strategies people use tend to be based on the type of request they are making and their relationship with the other person. When a person wants to borrow something, for example, he or she typically designs a message that focuses on reducing the cost of the request for the recipient. For example, if you want to borrow your roommate's computer, you could explain that you will only use it when your roommate is not home (Heath & Bryant, 2000).

When people want to ask favors, they again try to minimize cost as well as ask about the target's ability to fulfill the request (Heath & Bryant, 2000). For example, if you want your teacher to write you a letter of recommendation, you might say, "If you aren't too busy, I would really appreciate it if you would write a letter of recommendation for me. I'll give you a stamped, addressed envelope; a copy of my vita; and a brief summary of the major points I'd like for you to address." This request both asks about the target's ability to write the letter and attempts to miminize the target's efforts or costs. (By the way, this is a very successful strategy!)

If people believe they are justified in making a request, they typically use more direct and aggressive verbal messages (Heath & Bryant, 2000). So, if your parents want you to

improve your grades, they may say, "We expect you to maintain a B average, and if you don't, we will have to rethink whether it is worth paying for you to go to college." On the other hand, if the person making the request has a lot to gain from compliance, he or she is likely to use many strategies—for example, messages that offer rewards, that explain the benefits of compliance to the target, and/or that explain why compliance is so important to the requestor.

What can you do to be more effective at making compliance requests? If your relationship is a close one and the request is small, simply asking may be enough. Married couples, for instance, are more likely to make a simple request and just ask their partners to comply (Vangelisti, 2004). Similarly, asking your roommate to carry out the trash may be all that you need to do. If the relationship is not close and/or the request is somewhat larger, you may want to justify your request. Research shows that when making minor requests of strangers or acquaintances, offering a reason can be quite effective (Cialdini, 2001). If you want to cut ahead of people in a checkout line, for instance, you could say, "Do you mind if I go ahead? I only have three items."

For bigger requests, you will want to plan your request more carefully. You should consider your goals, the nature of your request, and your relationship to the other person. If you are haggling with a car dealer, you may not care about maintaining a relationship, and your primary goal of getting a good deal likely significantly outweighs secondary goals such as social appropriateness or identity enhancement. In this case, you may be willing to use more aggressive tactics, such as threatening to take your business elsewhere if you don't get the price you want for your trade-in. Alternatively, when you are communicating with your best friend, you are probably concerned with maintaining the relationship. In this case, identity and social appropriateness goals may be important to you, and you will want to avoid aggressive tactics. If you want to ask a favor, then, you might consider making a promise, cutting the cost of their granting the favor, and stressing how much the favor will mean to you. In each of these instances, adapting your request to the situation will probably increase the likelihood that others will comply.

So far we have focused our discussion on how people attempt to gain compliance from others. However, social influence concerns not only what we can gain from others but also how we can refuse others' requests. In the next section, we will examine how you can resist influence attempts that you do not want to fulfill.

Resisting Others' Influence

Resisting others' influence attempts is easy for some people but challenging for many more. As we grow up, we learn principles of social interaction that make us vulnerable to others' influence—and this can make it difficult to resist influence attempts. Cialdini (2001) calls this the *click, whirr response* (or *automatic response*), because when one person enacts a behavior, it triggers a response in another. Cialdini has identified six ways in which this "click, whirr" response is triggered. He calls these the **weapons of influence.** Here we discuss four of these tactics that are most often used in close interpersonal relationships: reciprocation, consistency, social proof, and liking. By understanding these "weapons" and how they work, you may find it easier to resist others' influence attempts when you want to.

Reciprocation   The first of these weapons of influence is **reciprocation.** This very simple rule states that we should repay others for what they have given us. If I give you a compliment, you should reply in kind. If I share personal information about myself, so should you. This reciprocity rule works so effectively because most of us have an ingrained (learned) response to receiving favors. Because most of us have been taught that not only is it "better to give than to receive," but that a person should not receive without also giving, we generally feel that if we don't return or repay favors, we are not very nice people—that, in fact, we are "moochers" who take but do not give (Cialdini, 2001).

The rule of reciprocity affects us persuasively when a persuader offers a "gift" *with the intention of making a request* in return that he or she hopes we will feel powerless to refuse. Often this involves a relatively even tit for tat, but at other times the request may be for something much greater than the original favor. Yet, because of the rule of reciprocation,

weapons of influence
the six ways in which Cialdini's "click, whirr" response is triggered

reciprocation
a rule that states that we should repay others for what they have given us

you may feel uncomfortable turning down this greater request. For example, a neighbor offers to water your plants several times when you are out of town. Then a month or so later, when he leaves for a trip, he asks that you feed and walk his dogs twice a day. Although taking care of the dogs requires much more effort than watering plants, if you are like many people, you would agree to do so because you feel obligated by the initial favor.

How can you resist this type of influence attempt? First, recognize that if someone does you a favor or gives you a gift, you do not *have to* reciprocate, especially if you believe the other person has done so to be manipulative or if the person is trying to sell you something. If you do feel the need to reciprocate, realize that you don't have to reciprocate in an unbalanced way. If in return for watering your plants, you're asked to watch the neighbor's dogs, you can either decline or you can offer to fulfill a modified version of the request—perhaps agreeing to feed the dogs but not to walk them. Finally, if you find it difficult to say no in such a circumstance, do not accept gifts or favors you don't want to reciprocate. For example, if you know that your coworker routinely takes advantage of others, refuse her initial offer so you don't feel obligated.

Consistency Principle Another automatic response persuaders can manipulate is the human desire to appear **consistent**. Generally, it is in your best interest to behave consistently, and others tend to view you more favorably if you do. How do you judge people who act one way on Monday but another way on Tuesday? In politics, such people are derided as "flip-floppers." Acting consistently also serves as an efficient shortcut. People often order the same dish at a restaurant both because they like it and because doing so is easier than trying to decide among many alternatives.

But your desire to remain consistent can be exploited by others. In this case, people who want to influence you may make a small request in order to obtain compliance with one or more larger requests later. For example, a coworker might periodically ask you to loan him money for lunch, then pay you back right away. Once this pattern has been established, he could then ask to borrow a much larger sum to repair his car. Because you have presented yourself as a person who cares and helps out someone in need, you may feel you need to agree in order to be consistent with the image you have created. The practice of asking for something small then requesting something larger is called the **foot-in-the-door** technique, and it exploits our desire to be consistent with our self-image.

Another strategy that exploits the consistency principle is call **low balling**—the practice of making a request, but once the person agrees to it, the requestor reveals that compliance is more costly than it first seemed. For example, a friend asks if you will drive her to the airport and you agree. She then reveals that she has to be there by 5 AM. In order to appear consistent, you may feel you need to uphold your promise to drive her, even though you would not have agreed if you had known how early you'd have to wake up.

Although consistency is generally a desirable trait, you should protect yourself against people who exploit this tendency. Most important, you can listen to your instincts and say no before the "click, whirr" answer of yes has a chance to take over. Also, being aware of this tendency can make you more thoughtful about how you respond to requests. You might choose to say no to some requests, or you can remind yourself that presenting yourself as a nice or helpful person doesn't mean that you can't say no to requests that make you uncomfortable or that you don't want to fulfill.

Social Proof A third compliance-seeking tactic is called **social proof**. This tactic relies on the tendency we all have to behave in a particular way because others are doing so. For instance, you tend to laugh if you hear other people laughing, even if you aren't really amused. Most commonly, social proof takes the form of someone pointing out that "everybody is doing it" or "nobody else does that." Students often try to persuade professors to believe that no other professor requires a term paper, while professors attempt to convince students that, in fact, every other professor in their departments does so.

When trying to counter social proof as an influence strategy, it's good to keep in mind what your parents probably told you when you argued that you should be allowed to wear makeup, have your own car, or go backpacking in Europe because everyone else was doing

consistency principle
influence tactic that relies on the human desire to appear consistent

foot-in-the-door technique
practice of asking for something small then requesting something larger

low balling
the practice of making a request, but once the person agrees to it, the requestor reveals that compliance is more costly than it first seemed

social proof
influence tactic that relies on the tendency people have to behave in a particular way because others are doing so

it. That is, you can use some variation of "Yes, but if 'everyone' was jumping off the Empire State Building, would you want to do that too?" In other words, just because everyone else is doing it doesn't mean it is right for you—and in reality, not everyone is doing it anyway.

Liking It is probably no surprise that we tend to comply with the requests of people we like. What you may be less aware of is the extent to which others can manipulate your liking in order to influence you. In fact, Cialdini (2001) refers to liking as "the friendly thief." Liking can easily be manipulated because it is linked to qualities such as attractiveness, similarity, and association. It is well documented that physically attractive people experience a "halo effect" and are perceived as intelligent, honest, warm, and friendly (Eagley et al., 1991). This only goes so far, however. Studies have shown that attractiveness is most influential when a small decision is involved. So, an attractive acquaintance might be able to influence you to loan him your class notes but not your car (Stiff & Mongeau, 2002).

People are also more likely to be persuaded by those who are similar to them in values and experiences (Berscheid & Walster, 1969). This is most effective when the characteristics of the speaker are relevant to the topic of the message. For example, you are more likely to purchase clothes from someone who dresses like you than you are to buy a car from someone who dresses like you.

People also like others who are associated with positive experiences and dislike those associated with negative experiences (Lott & Lott, 1965). If you have a good time traveling with a friend, then you will be more easily persuaded to take a trip with him again. On the other hand, if you studied with a classmate but performed poorly on the subsequent test, you may not be open to studying with her again, even if it wasn't her fault.

Without being aware of it, you can be influenced to like someone (because they give you something or you perceive them as attractive or similar to you). Furthermore, once liking is induced, you will be more easily persuaded to comply with their request. Whenever you find yourself liking someone more than the situation warrants, you should ask yourself if you are responding to an influence attempt and if you would be persuaded if you didn't like the person so much.

The best defense against these four weapons of influence is *awareness*. Once you recognize that a person is trying to manipulate you, you can consciously work to avoid falling prey to the "click, whirr" response. It is also helpful to reframe such influence attempts. For example, if someone gives you a gift or does you a favor that seems out of proportion to your relationship, consider whether the behavior is designed to invoke the reciprocity rule and, if so, recognize that you should not feel bound by it (Cialdini, 2001). This does not mean that you should be suspicious every time someone is nice to you but that you should be cautious if you are in a new relationship or the other person's behavior seems extreme. For a quick review of the four weapons of influence and how you can resist them, see Table 9.2.

Although influencing others can pose challenges to a relationship, quite often these challenges are relatively minor. However, some challenges can take a heavier toll on relationships—such as aversive communication behaviors, the topic we take up next.

Managing Aversive Communication Interactions

Close relationships can be marked by the presence of aversive (or negative) behaviors. According to Miller (1997a), 44 percent of us are likely to be annoyed by a relational partner on any given day, and young adults have an average of 8.7 annoying experiences with their romantic partners weekly. In the context of close relationships—among other behaviors—people criticize, nag, betray, deceive, disappoint, ostracize, embarrass, and tease one another. And whatever the intention of the perpetrator, these negative actions are likely to hurt their victims (Kowalski, Valentine, Wilkinson, Queen, & Sharpe, 2003, p. 473). In turn, victims often respond with even-more-negative behaviors, which can lead to a cycle of blame and criticism (Kowalski et al., 2003). Because close relationships tend to be resilient, they can bounce back from these interactions if they don't occur too frequently. But if they do recur and the partners lack effective skills, these behaviors can devastate relationships.

Perhaps one of the most devastating aversive communication behaviors that can occur in close relationships is deception, the topic we discuss next.

Which weapon of influence do you find most difficult to resist? Why? What strategies can you use to respond more effectively when others use this influence tactic?

TABLE 9.2 Resisting the Weapons of Influence

Weapons of Influence	Definition	Resistance Strategy
Reciprocity	An ingrained response based on a belief in the rule that people should repay others for what they have been given	Recognize that one does not have to reciprocate a favor or gift, or reciprocate in an unbalanced way, especially if the favor was not requested. Refuse unrequested gifts or favors from someone trying to sell to you or manipulate you.
Consistency	The human desire to appear consistent so others will think more favorably about them	Listen to your instincts and become more thoughtful of how you respond to requests. Say no to requests that make you uncomfortable and remember that being nice and helpful doesn't mean you can't say no to some requests.
Social Proof	The tendency to behave as others are behaving	Remember that just because others are doing it doesn't mean it is right for you and that many people are not doing it either.
Liking	The inclination to comply with the requests of people one likes	When you find yourself liking someone more than the situation warrants, ask yourself if you are responding to an influence attempt and if you would be persuaded if you didn't like the person so much.

Deception

Deception is far more common than most people realize. Research indicates that concealment and distortion of information is a normal part of many conversations (Turner, Edgley, & Olmstead, 1975). Though some types of **deception** can impair relationships, this is not always the case. For example, a person may withhold information because it is too private to share ("My parents were abusive") or because it might cause pain ("Dinner was wonderful; it didn't taste burned at all"). The effect that the deception has on the relationship can be predicted by how important the lied-about information is. People who discover they've been deceived about an important issue are likely to become resentful, disappointed, and suspicious (Bok, 1978; Sagarin, Rhoads, & Cialdini, 1998).

Even when they recognize that many people lie, married and dating partners usually consider deception to be a rare occurrence in their own relationships. However, one study revealed that 85.7 percent of respondents had deceived their dating partners within the previous two weeks (Tolhuizen, 1990), while in another study, 92 percent of individuals admitted having lied to their romantic partners (Knox, Schacht, Holt, & Turner, 1993). The most frequent issue individuals deceived their partners about was competing relationships.

The findings about deception in dating relationships are especially interesting for two reasons: First, research has established that people are not very good at detecting deception (Burgoon, Buller, Ebesu, & Rockwell, 1994); and second, most people assume that those they love tell the truth (Buller & Burgoon, 1996). This tendency to not suspect our intimates is called the **truth bias**, and it is especially strong in romantic relationships. For example, research shows that people generally do not look for cues that a partner is deceiving them (McCornack & Parks, 1986). However, other research suggests that once suspicion has been introduced, romantic partners' deception detection improves (Stiff, Kim, & Ramesh, 1989). Thus, you probably have a fairly good chance of deceiving your partner *unless* she or he is suspicious; in that case, you are more likely to get caught.

Lying can be just as devastating between friends as between romantic partners. College students have reported being as distressed by a friend's betrayal of their confidences as by a romantic partner's infidelity (Cauffman, Feldman, Jensen, & Arnett, 2000). Some people expect their friends to be even more honest and open with them than their romantic partners are, and, as we mentioned in Chapter 8, deception is one of the primary reasons

deception
concealment, distortion, or lying in communication

truth bias
the tendency to not suspect one's intimates of deception

jealousy
occurs when a person perceives a threat to an existing relationship

hurtful messages
messages that occur when a person criticizes, teases, rejects, or otherwise causes an emotional injury to another

friends give for terminating their friendships. At the end of this chapter, in the section on *Ethical Communication and Relationships,* we offer additional information on deception and its impact on relationships.

Jealousy

Jealousy occurs when a person perceives a threat to an existing relationship. Of course, one can perceive a threat to a relationship and not feel jealous. Jealousy seems to flow from feelings of insecurity about the relationship and/or the ability to cope with a change in it (Cano & O'Leary, 1997). The feeling combines anger, sadness, worry, embarrassment, and disappointment (Guerrero & Andersen, 1998).

Men and women often differ in the ways in which they express and manage jealousy. Men are more likely to consider leaving the relationship and to become involved with other women in an attempt to repair their self-esteem; women are more likely to focus on repairing the relationship (Buss, 1988; White & Mullen, 1989).

The manner in which couples communicate about their jealous feelings can be particularly problematic (Guerrero & Afifi, 1999). Communication researchers have discovered that the way couples deal with and communicate about jealousy has a stronger impact on the relationship than do the jealous feelings themselves (Andersen, Eloy, Guerrero, & Spitzberg, 1995). For example, overt rejection or the expression of disdain by an accused partner during an argument can damage a relationship more than the feelings of jealousy. Thus, if a partner accused of infidelity angrily replies, "I've never been involved with anyone else, but who knows why, since you are such a lousy partner," the hostility of the response can hurt the accuser and even lead to violence (White & Mullen, 1989). In some relationships, an individual can dispel the partner's fears by offering reassurances of love and fidelity, but this requires trust. Unfortunately, jealousy often arises because one partner has little trust in the relationship. Thus, jealous people may reject all assurances and even escalate their accusations (White & Mullen, 1989).

Although jealousy may be more common in romantic relationships, it also exists within friendships (Aune & Comstock, 1991). For example, if a person is becoming close to a second friend and fails to include his first friend in their joint activities, the first may feel jealous. Individuals are often jealous of their friends' romantic partners as well. When people fall in love, they often focus intently on their romantic partners—sometimes to the detriment of their friendships (Roth & Parker, 2001). And friends who communicate their feelings of insecurity and jealousy poorly can damage their friendships. Criticizing the third party, engaging in aggression toward the third party, or complaining repeatedly to the friend can lead to increased conflict and rejection (Grotpeter & Crick, 1996).

Jealousy, which can occur in friendships as well as romantic relationships, arises from feelings of insecurity about the relationship.

Hurtful Messages

The closer people are to one another and the more regularly they interact, the more opportunity they have to hurt one another (Vangelisti, 2007). One way they can harm each other is through hurtful messages. **Hurtful messages** occur when a person criticizes, teases, rejects, or otherwise causes an emotional injury to another (Folkes, 1982). Such messages often involve criticism of another person's sexual behavior, physical appearance, abilities, personality traits, self-worth, or identity, and they suggest that the individual is deficient in some way. They are hurtful because they convey negative feelings and rejection (Vangelisti, 1994). (See *Visual Summary 9.1: Influences on the Perceived Hurtfulness of a Message.*)

Unfortunately, hurtful messages are all too common. A study of romantic partners found that regardless of whether the couple was casually dating, seriously dating, engaged, or married; whether the relationship was long distance or not; the length of the relationship; or the couples' ethnic background, 95 percent of participants could recall a conversation in which their current romantic partners delivered a hurtful message (Zhang, 2005). Although most friends and romantic partners occasionally make hurtful comments, when they occur

frequently, these messages can negatively impact a relationship. In relationships where frequent hurtful messages occur, the members are less satisfied and more distant and less emotionally close (Vangelisti & Young, 2000).

Most hurtful messages focus on relationships, personality, and appearance. However, messages that convey dissatisfaction or lack of regard for the relationship are especially painful. Comments such as "We don't really have anything in common anymore" or "I think we should start seeing other people" are perceived as the most distressing. Relationship messages are probably more upsetting because they signal a fundamental shift in the partner's feelings and because recipients may believe that while they might be able to change their personalities or appearance, they cannot change their partner's feelings.

Hurtful messages don't only include what one *says;* they can also include what one *doesn't say.* If you say "I love you" for the first time and your partner changes the topic, you are likely to be hurt and to perceive this as a rejection or proof that you are unloved. Similarly, if you get a new haircut and your best friend doesn't say anything, you may be upset because you believe your friend doesn't like it—or didn't even notice.

Hurtful messages can be intentional or unintentional. **Intentional messages** are those that are perceived as purposely causing harm to the recipient. When people make hurtful comments to one another when angry, their messages are typically viewed as intentional. Hurtful messages can also be **unintentional**—that is, not intended to hurt the recipient. People can utter unkind comments accidentally, out of thoughtlessness, or from insensitivity, as when a stranger asks a woman who isn't pregnant when her baby is due (Myers, Schrodt, & Rittenour, 2006). Although unintentional hurtful messages may be somewhat less painful than those perceived as intentional (Mills, Nazar, & Farrell, 2002), both can wound the recipient and the relationship.

How hurt you may feel when confronted with a hurtful message depends on a variety of factors. These include how satisfied you are with your relationship, whether you believe the message was intentionally said to hurt you, how the message was delivered, your self-esteem, and how competent you feel to respond to the message as well as the context in which the conversation occurs (Vangelisti, 2007). Partners who are more satisfied with their relationships and those who are in relationships where hurtful messages are infrequent are less likely to believe their partners do not care about the relationship (Vangelisti et al., 2005). Similarly, those who perceive the message as unintentional experience less hurt. Thus, if you confront your best friend to express your concern that his drinking is negatively affecting his grades and his relationships, he is likely to feel less hurt if he perceives that you are doing so because you care about him. To read about one student's experience with hurtful messages, see *It Happened to Me: Lily.*

IT HAPPENED TO ME: Lily

I still can't believe I was so thoughtless, but recently I really hurt my friend Pepper. I was trying to joke with her, but I teased her about something she is really sensitive about—her weight. I was talking about this study I read that said that people's weight tends to be heavily influenced by their friends' weight, and while telling this story, I made a joke that I was going to have to stop hanging out with her. She got really upset, her face turned red, and then she stormed out of the room. I felt terrible. I was just kidding, but I should have known better than to say something so hurtful. Fortunately, later we talked, I apologized, and she forgave me. I don't know what I would have done if she had stayed mad at me.

The way in which a message is framed also influences how it affects the recipient. The intensity of the message impacts the degree to which the recipient feels hurt. **Intensity** refers to the degree of emphasis with which a speaker makes his or her claim (McEwen & Greenburg, 1970). For example, "I am miserable in our relationship" is more intense than "I am not as happy as I once was in our relationship." In addition, the harsher or more negative the language ("I can't stand the sight of you"), the more painful the message is likely to be (Tracy, Van Dusen, & Robinson, 1987). On the other hand, when a hurtful message is framed in a humorous manner, it is perceived as less intentional, and recipients experience less intense feelings and less hurt than when a message is offered seriously (Young and Bippus, 2001).

A person's sense of self also influences how hurt she is likely to feel when receiving a hurtful message. People with higher self-esteem view hurtful messages as more unexpected and less indicative of a lack of caring by their partners. In addition, people who feel able to respond effectively to hurtful messages experience less pain upon receiving them.

Finally, the context in which the message is delivered can impact the recipient's feelings of injury. Hurtful speech that occurs when a couple is alone may be painful, but if it occurs when others are present, the pain and discomfort is often intensified (Miller & Roloff, 2005). Hurtful comments, by definition, are attacks on the recipient's identity, so the presence of an audience can worsen the feeling of being denigrated plus add feelings of embarrassment.

People typically respond to hurtful messages in three primary ways. They can reply actively by attacking back or defending themselves; they might react with acquiescence, such as by crying or apologizing; or they may act invulnerable by being silent or ignoring the comment (Vangelisti, 2007). Research suggests that individuals who are extremely hurt tend to react by acquiescing, while individuals who perceive less hurt react with invulnerability (Vangelisti & Zhang, 2005). In addition, some responses are more productive for a relationship than others. For example, being active and asking questions or seeking clarifications tends to be more helpful than responding actively with sarcasm or verbal attacks. Negative active responses often escalate the negativity of interactions.

Relationship Threats

On occasion, people in long-term friendships and romances need to respond to more serious threats to their relationships. **Relationship threats** describe those challenges that are most likely to negatively impact relationships and to have serious effects. They include the serious—for example, sexual infidelity—and the very serious, such as interpersonal aggression and sexual coercion. These threats are all too common. Approximately 50 percent of all female college students report being sexually coerced at some point (Laumann et al., 1994), and studies of dating and marital relationships suggest that 30 percent to 40 percent of dating relationships and 40 percent to 60 percent of marital relationships are marked by at least one act of infidelity (Guerrero, Andersen, & Afifi, 2007). Because of the prevalence of various threats to one's important relationships, let's take a look at the specific behaviors and interactions that constitute relationship threats and address how you can more effectively respond to them.

Relational Transgressions

Individuals don't always meet their partners' expectations about the way they should behave. Sometimes these misbehaviors are minor—such as when one person stays too late at work or forgets to call when promised. However, when fundamental relationship rules are violated, a person has engaged in a **relational transgression** (Roloff, Soule, & Carey, 2001). In romantic relationships, relational transgressions can include flirting, wanting to date others, forgetting special occasions, or committing infidelity (Metts, 1994). Within friendships, transgressions typically include betraying a confidence, dating a friend's current or ex–romantic partner, deception, and not standing up for a friend (Argyle & Henderson, 1984).

Because we discuss a number of friendship violations elsewhere in this book, here we focus on two serious relationship transgressions that often occur in romantic relationships—romantic/sexual temptations and infidelity. Although these two transgressions are clearly linked (infidelity is generally preceded by temptations), we discuss them separately because both the perpetrator's and the partner's responses to each can differ significantly.

Relational temptations are common, especially during the young-adult years. Even if you are obviously in a relationship, you are likely to be approached, flirted with, or enticed at some point during the course of a lasting romantic relationship. One study found that 93 percent of men and 82 percent of the women in long-term relationships had been approached by someone other than their partner for a romantic relationship—a behavior called "mate poaching" by researchers. In this survey group, 67 percent of men and 41 percent of women had been successfully lured away from an existing relationship, or poached (Schmitt & Buss, 2001).

When do you think it is necessary to convey a hurtful message to others? What do you say to try to reduce the other person's discomfort or pain?

relationship threats challenges that are most likely to negatively impact relationships and have serious effects

relational transgressions takes place when fundamental relationship rules are violated

relational temptations enticements such as flirting and mate poaching from third parties that threaten one's current romantic relationship

Influences on the Perceived Hurtfulness of a Message

Relationship satisfaction—partners who are more satisfied with their relationships experience less distress.

Intentionality—people who perceive a hurtful message as unintentional and offered out of caring suffer less hurt.

Framing—messages that are delivered using less intense (and negative) language cause less hurt.

Self-esteem—people with higher self-esteem view hurtful messages as more unexpected and less indicative of a lack of caring and, therefore, are less upset.

Competence—people who feel able to respond effectively to a hurtful message experience less pain upon receiving one.

Context—hurtful messages that occur when others are present cause more pain and discomfort.

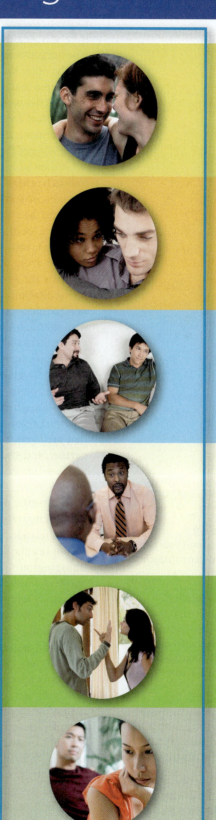

You may have noticed that the results of this study show that men were more than 50 percent as likely to be lured away from their long-term partners as were women. Why? Although you may think that men themselves are completely responsible for this difference, as it turns out, females are more likely than males to attempt to poach someone else's romantic partner. In fact, one study found that single women were more attracted to a man if he was already in a relationship than if he was single. Scholars hypothesize that this is true because a man's presence in a relationship suggests that he is a good romantic partner. On the other hand, women are not entirely responsible for men's straying. Other research discovered that men are more easily lured away from their partners than women are. When an attractive woman flirts with a man, that man is more likely to find his current romantic partner less appealing. On the other hand, when an attractive man flirts with a woman, that woman is more likely to find her current partner even more appealing than she would if she was not flirted with (Gagne & Lydon, 2001).

Given widespread temptations and the tendency for both men and women to attempt to poach others' partners, what can you do to avoid falling victim to temptation? First, you can exercise self-control and recognize when your self-control is weak. For example, if you have just had an argument with your partner, you have been drinking, or you have to exercise a lot of self-control in other areas of your life (such as a rigorous weight reduction program), your self-control will likely be weaker (Gaillilot, 2007). In that case, you may want to avoid putting yourself in temptation's way. Second, it helps if you consciously compare the alternative partner unfavorably to your current partner. That is, if you focus on the attributes and positive qualities your current partner has in comparison to a potential new partner, you will find it easier to remain committed to your partner. Finally, recognize that although the grass may seem greener on the other side of the fence, once you have grazed there awhile, it is likely to be the same old grass you had before.

What can you do to protect your partner from falling victim to poaching (a process called **mate guarding** by researchers)? Most of the research on this topic has found that romantic partners tend to engage in either negative acts (violence, spying, insults) or self-promotional behaviors (improving one's appearance or displaying resources) (Buss, 2002). We don't recommend these! However, we do believe that being aware of the temptations that are likely to confront you and your partner, discussing these temptations with your partner, and strategizing how you might each respond may help the two of you maintain your relationship.

Of course, as difficult as temptations may be, they pale in comparison to being betrayed by a romantic partner through infidelity. **Relational infidelity** is defined as a severe relational transgression in which one or both partners engage in extra-dyadic behaviors that violate relationship rules of monogamy and exclusivity. (If the partners don't have expectations or rules concerning outside partners, then the behavior is not considered a relational transgression.) Although it is difficult to know definitively how many people cheat on their partners, research suggests that such behavior is widespread, at least in dating relationships. One study reported that that 11 percent of women and 21 percent of men reported engaging in sex with someone other than their spouse during their marriage (Greeley, 1994), while another found that 70.9 percent of men and 57.4 percent of women reported being unfaithful to a dating partner (Hansen, 1987).

Partners can commit two types of infidelity—emotional and physical. **Emotional infidelity** refers to behaviors such as flirting, dating, spending time together, and falling in love with someone other than one's partner (Roscoe et al., 1988). **Physical infidelity** is defined as sexual activities that are committed with someone other than one's partner and include acts ranging from kissing to sexual intercourse (Feldman & Cauffman, 2000). Research on sex differences in perceptions of infidelity reveals that men and women may identify different behaviors as acts of infidelity. Women identified dating, spending time with another partner, and keeping secrets from one's partner as unfaithful acts more than men did. At the same time, men reported sexual interactions with another partner as acts of infidelity more so than did women. These findings suggest that more women than men identify acts of emotional betrayal as acts of infidelity, and more men than women identify sexual interactions as acts of infidelity.

mate guarding
attempts to protect your partner from falling victim to "poaching" by others

relational infidelity
a severe relational transgression in which one or both partners engage in extra-dyadic behaviors that violate relationship rules of monogamy and exclusivity

emotional infidelity
refers to behaviors such as flirting, dating, spending time together, and falling in love with someone other than one's partner

physical infidelity
sexual activities that are committed with someone other than one's partner and include acts ranging from kissing to sexual intercourse

Perhaps because men and women perceive infidelity differently, they report engaging in different types of cheating. A study of people in dating relationships found that 38.1 percent of the women and 48.7 percent of men reported having been unfaithful (Boekhout et al., 1999). Of these subgroups, women reported being emotionally but not sexually involved at a higher frequency than did men (33.3 percent vs.12.8 percent), whereas men reported being sexually but not emotionally involved at a higher frequency than did women (61.5 percent vs. 25 percent).

What causes temptations to lead to infidelity? A survey of undergraduate students (Roscoe et al., 1988) indicates that both men and women say that infidelity arises from boredom, geographical distance, a desire for variety/experimentation, attraction to another, and revenge. However, women were more likely than men to give relationship dissatisfaction as a reason, whereas men identified lack of communication/understanding and sexual incompatibility as factors leading to unfaithful behavior.

Once infidelity occurs, many—though not all—relationships end. Approximately two-thirds of marriages and even more dating relationships are terminated after infidelity is discovered. After discovering a partner's infidelity, people who are married are more likely to continue their relationships than are dating partners. Additionally, the longer the couple has been married, the less likely they are to divorce as a result of infidelity (Pittman, 1989). People who stay with their partners tend to be more committed to the relationships (Roscoe et al., 1988), more satisfied with the relationships (Buunk, 1987), and to experience less relational conflict (Buss & Shackelford, 1997).

Relational transgressions occur when fundamental relationship rules, such as fidelity, are violated.

Although you may think that staying with a partner who has cheated is undesirable (or that no one would want to maintain a relationship with you if you cheated), 80 percent of those who divorce as the result of an affair later regret doing so (Staheli, 1995). If you do want to stay in your relationship, you may want to seek support from a friend, a family member, a religious advisor, or a professional counselor. You will likely find it helpful to confide in someone you trust and feel comfortable talking to. Talking to others can help you gain perspective on your experience and sort through how you feel and what you want to do. However, avoid confiding in anyone you believe will take sides and who lacks objectivity (Mending your affair, 2009). To learn more about responding effectively to partner infidelity, see *Building Your Communication Skills: Responding to a Partner's Infidelity.*

As painful and devastating as relational transgressions can be to romantic relationships, we address an even more potentially dangerous relationship threat: interpersonal violence.

Interpersonal Violence

Interpersonal violence—physical violence against a partner or child—is a serious problem in the United States. By the most conservative estimates, one million women suffer nonfatal violence by an intimate each year (Bureau of Justice Statistics, 1995); by other estimates, four million American women experience a serious assault by an intimate partner during an average 12-month period (American Psychological Association, 1996). Nearly one-third of American women (31 percent) report being physically or sexually abused by a husband or boyfriend at some point in their lives (Commonwealth Fund, 1998). The statistics on violence against men are less consistent and may be underreported due to men's reluctance to admit being battered by their partners. Current estimates suggest that relational aggression against men comprises 8 to 18 percent of all interpersonal violence (Rennison & Welchans, 2000). Lest you think you are safe because you are not married, know that even in high school, one in five couples reported violence in their relationships.

interpersonal violence
physical violence against a partner or child

Building Your Communication SKILLS

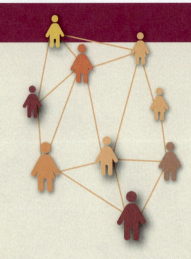

Responding to a Partner's Infidelity

Though a person's initial response to discovering that a partner has been unfaithful (or to having one's own infidelity revealed) may be anger, recrimination, and a desire to terminate the relationship, many people later regret these responses. To ensure that you respond appropriately and make good decisions regarding the future of your relationships, we recommend that you do the following.

When discussing the affair with your partner, take time-outs when emotions run too high or feelings get out of control. It is natural to feel strongly, but you don't want emotional distress to turn into physical violence, and giving vent to your emotions can make you feel worse.

Don't rush to a decision. Your immediate reaction may be to end the relationship—and that might be the right choice. But you don't want to make a choice you will later regret. If your partner is a repeat offender, you may decide that it is time to end the relationship. But if your relationship has been a good one and you are capable of forgiveness (eventually), then you might want to consider trying to repair the relationship.

If you are the offender, you will need to listen to your partner's expressions of hurt and anger, and you must be willing to discuss the affair and what led to it. Your primary job is to help your partner recover from your betrayal and to engage in behaviors that can lead to reestablishing trust. This means that you cannot lie in order to protect yourself or the person with whom you cheated.

Finally, you may find it helpful for you and your partner to discuss your relationship and future with your religious advisor and/or a marital counselor. It can be difficult to determine how to repair a relationship damaged by infidelity, but professionals who have counseled couples will be able to offer you support and advice as you seek to put your relationship back together.

Two types of interpersonal aggression can occur in romantic relationships: battering and situational couple violence. **Battering** describes relationships in which one individual uses violence as a way of controlling or dominating his or her partner (though most batterers are male). During these couples' violent episodes, there is a clear perpetrator and a clear victim. The factors that contribute to battering syndrome are many and complex, and unfortunately, just improving one's communication skills is not enough to change the situation for the better. Therefore, individuals need to recognize the behavioral characteristics of batterers before their relationships solidify. For information on how to recognize a batterer, see *Did You Know? Recognizing a Potential Batterer.*

DID YOU KNOW?

Recognizing a Potential Batterer

A batterer may display any of these symptoms. However, these are warning signs, and you should use judgment before making any sort of accusations or decisions.

Has he or she ever hit you?
Has he or she ever hit former girlfriends/boyfriends or spouses or bragged about previous physical fights with anyone?
What does he or she do when angry?
Is he or she cruel to animals or violent with others?

battering
relationships in which one individual uses violence as a way to control and dominate his or her partner

Does he or she threaten to hurt you or break things, no matter how trivial the disagreement?

Does he or she get angry very fast, very easily, very violently, very often?

Does he or she attempt to keep you and your life under strict control?

Is he or she pathologically jealous?

Does he or she have two personalities?

Does he or she blame you for problems in the relationship—including the violence?

How does he or she react to your success?

Does he or she get violent when drinking?

Is he or she unable to empathize?

Does he or she use sex as a means of apologizing?

Does he or she have trouble with authority figures?

Has he or she had prior trouble with the authorities—been in jail or kicked out of school?

SOURCE: Adapted from Recognizing a potential batterer. *Estronaut: A Forum for Women's Health.* Retrieved October 27, 2008, from www.estronaut.com/a/recognizing_potential_batterer.htm

Situational couple violence is characterized by less-intense forms of violence and tends to be more mutual in its performance, although this does not mean that men and women engage in acts of equal severity. Even in these instances, women usually suffer more serious injuries than men. Among these couples, it may not be clear who is the perpetrator and who is the victim. Ineffective communication patterns are common with these couples, so improving communication skills may reduce interpersonal violence in their relationships.

Research reveals that couples who engage in situational couple violence lack fundamental communication and problem-solving skills. Unfortunately, they also tend to engage in more conflict discussions. They appear unable to let even small matters slide (Lloyd, 1990), and when they do discuss their differences, they are unable to present and defend their positions on issues without becoming hostile (Infante, Chandler, & Rudd, 1989; Lloyd, 1999).

During conflict, these couples are more likely than nonabusive couples to attack each other's character, curse, and threaten (Sabourin, 1996). They also make few attempts to de-escalate the conflict or facilitate their conversations calmly (Córdova, Jacobsen, Gottman, Rushe, & Cox, 1993). In addition, husbands in aggressive relationships attribute hostile intent to their wives' communication and behavior and respond negatively when their wives attempt to influence them (Anglin & Holtzworth-Munroe, 1997).

Situational violence is also present in friendship and peer relationships, although it is a topic that is understudied. Aggressive behavior among friends can be demonstrated in different forms: physical aggression, verbal aggression, and indirect aggression. Physical aggression includes such behaviors as pushing, shoving, or hitting. Verbal aggression includes threatening and intimidating, and engaging in malicious teasing, taunting, and name-calling. Indirect aggression includes behaviors such as gossiping, spreading cruel rumors, and encouraging others to reject or exclude someone. More than one in three high school students say they have been in a physical fight in the past year (Centers for Disease Control, 2002); however, it is not clear how many of these violent conflicts specifically involve friends. What information is available suggests that aggression among friends tends to be more verbal and indirect than physical.

Sexual Coercion

Date rape is another type of negative, possibly violent, interaction in which the participants' communication is of central importance (Willam & Pollard, 2003). People often find it difficult to discuss sexual coercion. Part of the problem arises from lack of clarity on what date rape is. Legally, the definition of **rape** is sexual activity that is "against the victim's will/without the victim's consent" and includes some "degree of force or threat" as well as "penetration" (Spitzberg, 1998, p. 181).

situational couple violence
conflict that is characterized by less-intense forms of violence and tends to be more mutual in its performance, although this does not mean that men and women engage in acts of equal severity

rape
sexual activity that is "against the victim's will/without the victim's consent" and includes some "degree of force or threat" as well as "penetration"

unwanted sex

occurs when one person does not want to have sexual relations but does so without the offender exerting physical force or threats

sexual coercion

physically nonviolent pressure to engage in unwanted sex

Individuals often use the term *date rape* to describe unwanted sex. **Unwanted sex** occurs when one person does not want to have sexual relations but does so without the offender exerting physical force or threats (Spitzberg, 1998). Sometimes people engage in unwanted sex because of concern for the relationship, verbal pressure or harassment, or real concern for personal safety, even though they have not been physically threatened. This situation has been described as **sexual coercion** (Spitzberg, 1998).

One contributor to sexual coercion is the fact that men and women experience cross-sex interaction differently. Behaviors that women call "friendly," men are more likely to label "sexy," and men are more likely than women to believe that women's behavior communicates sexual interest and intent (Abbey, 1987; Muehlenhard, 1989). This difference in perception can lead to differing expectations about sexual contact and misunderstandings regarding sexual consent (Lim & Roloff, 1999). Some research suggests that such misperceptions can contribute to the likelihood of sexual coercion and unwanted sex (Abbey, 1988). Some female college students admit to using *token resistance* (saying no, then giving in) (Muehlenhard & Hollabough, 1988), while some males acknowledge that they have discounted their partners' refusals and persisted in making unwanted sexual advances (Lloyd & Emery, 2000). These patterns can make communicating and interpreting sexual consent more difficult. And if these communication behaviors occur when one or both parties are drinking alcohol—as is frequently the case (Muehlenhard & Linton, 1987)—ambiguity and miscommunication are even more likely. For advice on how to minimize the likelihood that you will become involved in coercive sexual contact, see *Building Your Communication Skills: Preventing Sexual Coercion.*

Individuals are at the center of relationships, and what they say and do affects their relationships at every stage. However, societal norms and pressures shape relationships as well. In the next section, we will examine relationships within this broader framework.

Building Your Communication SKILLS

Preventing Sexual Coercion

The various explanations for date rape and sexual coercion all suggest several cautions. Based on the research concerning date rape and unwanted sex, we recommend the following:

1. Don't drink on a date or in a group unless you are already involved in a positive sexual relationship with your partner. You will not be as effective in communicating your wishes and desires, nor in understanding your partner's, if you are under the influence of alcohol.

2. Do not assume that you know what your partner desires. Instead, ask! Reading another's verbal and nonverbal cues can be difficult, especially if you do not have experience with each other in this area.

3. *Always* assume a no is a "real" no.

4. A corollary of number three: Do not use token resistance. If you do, how can your partner differentiate a "token" no from a "real" one?

5. Communicate your desires and expectations clearly. If you don't want to engage in sexual activity, say so firmly, clearly, and unequivocally. Sometimes in trying to be polite, people end up being indirect and unclear about what they want. For example, instead of saying, "I find you very attractive, but I think I'd rather do this another time," say, "I don't want to have sex with you tonight."

THE INDIVIDUAL, RELATIONSHIP CHALLENGES, AND SOCIETY

Individuals' perceptions of and reactions to relationships largely depend on the social and cultural values and norms they have learned throughout their lives. In this section of the book, then, we examine how relationship challenges are influenced by societal issues such as social expectations regarding sex roles and emotional expression.

Society, Sex Roles, and Relationship Challenges

Societal factors influence negative aspects of romantic relationships, such as relationship violence and sexual coercion. For example, most talk about violence in romantic relationships focuses on the behavior of individual aggressors rather than on the social structures that allow abuse (Lloyd & Emery, 2000). Because of this, society invests considerable money and energy in arresting and punishing perpetrators but very little in making changes to social conditions that would make such behavior less likely—such as decreasing the social acceptance of relationship violence, creating more equal relationships between men and women, and teaching individuals and couples skills that can reduce the occurrence of situational violence.

The ways we talk about romance can encourage acceptance of aggression in relationships. U.S. media frequently portray male aggression as normal and acceptable. For instance, in romance novels, male aggression is often a central, and recurrent, plot point (Kramer & Moore, 2001), and women in these novels often interpret that aggression as a sign of love. Similarly, movies present tension or even overt dislike between men and women as ultimately being responsible for their passionate relationships. This has been true since the beginning of film production, as in the Spencer Tracy and Katherine Hepburn films and *Gone with the Wind.* It remains true today—for example in Julia Roberts movies such as *Runaway Bride, Intolerable Cruelty,* and *Ocean's Eleven.* Perhaps in part because of these media images, many people believe that fighting and arguing is a sign of a passionate love match, though in truth it can be a dangerous one (Galician, 2004). In turn, these beliefs may cause victims of interpersonal violence to believe that they deserve what's being done and that arguing and fighting are signs that "he must really love me."

In addition, although most people assume that men and women experience equity in their relationships (Ferraro, 1996; Lloyd & Emery, 2000) and that men are not abused by their partners, this is not true. The facts are that women typically earn less money than men, are more responsible for children than men, and often are physically weaker than men. These factors seriously compromise how equal women can be in heterosexual relationships, and likely account for the fact that far more women are severely injured and murdered by their partners than vice versa (Ferraro, 1996). At the same time, little conversation occurs about violence against men; in fact, men who are abused are often ridiculed and stigmatized so that they have few places to turn for help and support (Kimmel, 2002). (For more information on how societal views of men affect their experiences as abuse victims, see *Communication in Society: Abused Men: The Silent Victims of Domestic Violence*).

Finally, individuals rarely receive education and training in how to manage conflict and the strong emotions that accompany it. Many colleges and universities offer courses in conflict, but only a small number of students typically take these classes. In addition, most people are exposed to very few models of productive conflict. Instead, children and adolescents observe people screaming and fighting on reality television, in movies such as *The Breakup,* and on talk radio shows. Even within the family, children may not be exposed to effective ways to manage conflict. Cohabitating parents often prefer not to engage in conflict in from of their children, and parents who are separated or divorced frequently engage in hostile and unproductive conflict (Buchanan, Maccoby, & Dornbusch, 1991). Because we know that people who have strong **argumentation skills** (that is, the ability to make an argument) tend to be less verbally aggressive, teaching good argumentation and conflict skills should help reduce the incidence of situational couple violence and other forms of domestic abuse, though few resources have been devoted to doing so.

argumentation skills
the ability to make an argument

Communication in SOCIETY

Abused Men: The Silent Victims of Domestic Violence

Our society commonly views women as victims of domestic violence—rarely as perpetrators. Many men would rather suffer in silence at the hands of their abusive partner than seek protection or legal assistance. When a woman defends herself against her male partner, society will normally support an appropriate defensive response. When a man defends himself against his partner, he is at risk of being labeled as the abuser, not the victim.

Men may also fear being judged by their family and friends, or even professionally, because society has a double standard when it comes to how it views men as victims of abuse compared to women. Often, male victims simply do not know how to cope with the situation because there are few resources available to men who are abused. Men may feel trapped in the relationship because the courts are less likely to believe their testimony or award them custody of the children. There is also the fear that other people will see some personal weakness or low self-image. It is not uncommon for men to have a fear of being perceived as weak in a society that applauds macho-ism over sensitivity.

In court cases, it is hard to discern fact from fiction. While violence perpetrated towards men by women is increasing, more often a man has less of a chance for a fair trial than a woman. Our legal system is still very biased in its view of men as being the perpetrator, not the victim.

SOURCE: Adapted from Lytle, C. (2009, July 21). "Abused men: The silent victims of domestic violence." *Examiner.Com, Phoenix.* Retrieved September 4, 2009, from http://www.examiner.com/x-16919-Virginia-Beach-Abusive-Relationships-Examiner~y2009m7d21-Domestic-abuse-towards-men

In addition, societal responses to sexual aggression tend to perpetuate rather than reduce its occurrence. Today, women are more likely to experience sexual coercion than they were 50 years ago (Koss et al., 1994), and one study found that 50 percent of female respondents had been subjected to sexual coercion (Laumann et al., 1994).

Knowing how to respond appropriately to initiation attempts can be difficult for women because they are frequently judged negatively by third parties if they say yes (Hird & Jackson, 2001). However, they worry that saying no will damage their relationships with romantic partners or friends, and thus, they often have difficulty articulating their own desires. In addition, although many images of male pursuit and female acquiescence are portrayed in books, in films, and on television (Myers, 2007), very few images of nonviolent female resistance are available. This is especially problematic because sexual coercion is typically nonviolent but is based on sexually coercive tactics such as threats to the relationship or appeals to romantic feelings (Hird & Jackson, 2001).

In addition, the popular image that men have urgent and difficult-to-control sexual drives and that women do not implies that women are responsible for controlling sexual contact and male sexuality. Therefore, more attention is paid to how *women* behave during sexual encounters than how men behave. For example, public education campaigns regarding sex are most often directed toward women, because men are assumed to resist any responsible behavior that might interfere with fulfilling their sexual desires (Waldby, Kippax, & Crawford, 1993). These social beliefs and actions create situations in which men feel free to pressure women for sex, and women feel ambivalent about and unable to express their own sexual wishes. As a consequence, coercion has become almost commonplace.

Society, Emotion, and Relationship Challenges

Do you consider yourself unemotional, or are you easily moved to tears? What factors contribute to how often you feel and express emotion? Most people consider emotion an individual experience influenced primarily by the situations people find themselves confronting. What they rarely consider is the degree to which the cultures and societies in which people grow up also affect their emotions. Nonetheless, many of these same people explain the emotional behavior of *other* people by referencing their cultures. For example, many individuals perceive Greeks as being emotionally expressive and the Japanese as emotionally reticent. In truth, everyone's emotional experiences are influenced by their

cultures and families from the time they are very young. For example, Chinese babies react less and express less emotion than do U.S. infants, in part because Chinese parents expect more emotional restraint and reinforce this behavior (Reeve, 2005).

Physiologically, people across cultures tend to react similarly when they experience the same emotion, such as blushing when embarrassed or having cold sweaty hands when fearful (Wallbot & Scherer, 1986). However, the events that provoke these reactions, as well as the duration of the reactions and the frequency of their occurrence, differ across societies. For example, while most young people in the United States blush when they experience embarrassment, the young in Japan appear to experience embarrassment more frequently and intensely than do U.S. young people. (Miller, 1997b).

Societies influence individuals' emotions in several ways. First, each society develops a set of **emotional norms** that suggest which emotions are good or bad to experience. Historically, greed has been considered a bad emotion and, in fact, was listed as one of the seven deadly sins. However, in the United States during the second half of the twentieth century, some of the stigma was lifted; a character in the 1980s film *Wall Street* famously proclaimed that "greed is good." (After the collapse of the stock market in 2008, greed may once again be relegated to its sinful status.) Societies differ in which emotions are considered desirable and which should be suppressed. A study found that Chinese and U.S. citizens evaluated the emotions of anger, sadness, fear, shame, love, and happiness somewhat differently. U.S. respondents described love and happiness as positive emotions, and fear, shame, anger, and sadness as negative ones. On the other hand, Chinese participants only described happiness as a positive emotion, while labeling the remaining ones as negative (Shaver, Wu, & Schwartz, 1992).

Second, societies define **feeling rules** that determine *how* one should feel when experiencing specific events (Pollak & Thoits, 1989). When you are criticized, for instance, how do you feel? If you are like many people in the United States, you probably feel angry and defensive (often mixed with embarrassment and disappointment). In Japan, Korea, and Saudi Arabia, however, people are more likely to experience shame. Scholars suggest that these cultures are "shame" cultures, meaning that they use shame to discourage undesirable behaviors (Gilbert, 1998).

You learn from your parents and society what specific feelings are called and when it is appropriate to express them. In the United States, when toddlers hide behind their parents' legs upon meeting someone new, they often hear their parents say, "Oh, he's feeling shy, but he'll be okay when he gets to know you." Through repeated interactions of this nature, children learn that the feeling they have upon meeting strangers is shyness and that it is something to overcome. Although shyness occurs in many cultures, because of how children are socialized, the incidence of self-reported shyness varies, with Israelis reporting the lowest rates of shyness and Taiwanese and Japanese respondents reporting the highest (Zimbardo, 1989).

Third, societies have **display rules** that govern how people should react when they experience a given emotion. For instance, some cultures permit or encourage aggression as a response to anger, while others promote withdrawal as a response. A study of display rules examined the impact of shame on salespeople in Holland and the Philippines, finding that employees in both cultures felt shame when they had a bad experience with a client. However, their responses were quite different. Dutch salespeople tended to withdraw and therefore performed more poorly at their jobs when they felt shame, while Filipino employees put more energy into building relationships and consequently performed better (Bagozzi, Verbeke, & Gavino, 2003). How we are socialized to respond to emotions, then, affects our behavior in a number of ways.

Other research has examined the degree to which people control the expression of emotion across cultures (Matsumoto, 2006). Russians were found to most tightly control the display of their emotions, closely followed by the Japanese and the South Koreans. On these measures, Americans displayed the least control over their facial expressions. The same study also uncovered significant sex differences. Men were more likely to hide surprise and fear, while women more frequently controlled disgust, contempt, and anger (Henderson & Zimbardo, in press).

Finally, emotional experiences and expressions are influenced by a person's position in society. A female lawyer's emotional experiences are not identical to her male colleague's nor to the experiences of the female custodian who works in her building.

emotional norms
societal rules that suggest which emotions are good or bad to experience

feeling rules
rules defined by society that determine *how* one should feel when experiencing specific events

display rules
societal rules that govern how people should react when they experience a given emotion

TABLE 9.3 Percentage of People Who Feel Fearful Three or More Days Per Week			
Class	Male (%)	Female (%)	Total (%)
Lower	31	31	31
Working	17	17	17
Middle	11	17	14
Upper	5	11	8
TOTAL	15	18	17

For example, a study of emotion, gender, and social class found that lower-class men and women were approximately four times more likely to report feeling fearful on three or more days during the previous week than were upper-class females, and six times more likely than upper-class males (NORC General Social Survey, 1996) (see Table 9.3).

Social position also influences the type of emotions a person is allowed to display in specific contexts. At your job, for example, who is allowed to express anger? Who is allowed to cry? In many organizations, only those with power (especially management) are permitted to show their anger, and only women (and only in specific circumstances) are allowed to cry. A low-level employee may be fired for expressing anger, and a man who cries may find his promotional opportunities affected. If you understand that emotional experiences and expressions differ based on societal expectations and cultural norms, you may find it easier to respond to and understand others' responses to relationship challenges as they arise.

ETHICS AND RELATIONSHIP CHALLENGES

Ethical communication is particularly important in close relationships for two reasons: First, we expect our closest friends and family members to be truthful with us, and second, we relate intimacy with the degree of honesty in a relationship. For most people, intimacy is based on the feeling that one knows and is known by another. When we feel intimate with others, we believe that we are connecting with their "true" selves and that we are able to be our truest selves in the relationship.

However, when people are not honest in their communication with those close to them or deny others the right to communicate openly, it can decrease intimacy and even lead to termination of relationships. And if we discover that an intimate friend or partner is being dishonest, we will feel not only deceived but betrayed. For example, if you discover that your friend has been pretending to like your romantic partner while making negative remarks about her on the sly, you will probably feel angry and betrayed. In addition, if you want to continue the relationship, you now have to deal not only with your friend's feelings about your romantic partner but also with your friend's deceit.

To maintain a close relationship with another, you need to confront issues that are important to the relationship and to the other party. If one or both of you prohibit the other from discussing issues that are important to either of you, you put your relationship at risk. For example, if your good friend wishes to discuss his or her sexual identity and you refuse to do so, you are shutting down communication and likely damaging your intimacy with that friend.

Close relationships require that you confront issues directly and as thoughtfully as you can. If you are upset with your friend and make cutting remarks because of it, you aren't addressing your feelings or solving the problem. In addition, if you deny that you are being hurtful you aren't being fair to your friend or your relationship. Instead when your friend

Close relationships require that you confront issues directly and as thoughtfully as you can.

confronts you for your behavior, you first need to acknowledge the other person's pain and apologize for causing it, and then attempt to address your feelings more directly. If you do not, you may undermine trust and intimacy.

Finally, communicating ethically in your intimate relationships requires that you avoid using manipulation to influence others. As we discussed above, we all desire to influence those close to us, but how we do so is important. Threatening, lying, or using passive aggression to coerce others is dishonest, unfair, unethical, and ultimately likely to fail.

Engaging in ethical communication can help you develop and maintain your relationships more effectively. To begin the process, consider the suggestions presented in the next, and last, section of this chapter.

IMPROVING YOUR INTERPERSONAL COMMUNICATION SKILLS

In a chapter on relationship challenges, we would be remiss if we didn't discuss apologies. Though most people have been apologizing since they were very young (generally insincerely and because their parents forced them to), they still often find it difficult to ask for forgiveness. Apologizing is challenging because it can be uncomfortable to admit one is at fault, and it can be hard to convey that one is truly sorry. Yet a heartfelt apology can go a long way toward repairing a relationship and persuading others to forgive you. Therefore, below we offer some guidelines for apologizing effectively.

- **Don't wait.** Waiting too long can be perceived as negatively as not apologizing at all. It is best to apologize as soon as possible after your transgression. A delayed apology suggests that you are only doing so because you feel coerced, which leads to our next point.
- **Be genuine.** Injured people tend to be very sensitive to any suggestion that you are being insincere. An insincere apology does not repair the damage or your relationship. If you are truly sorry, it will be easier to make a successful apology.
- **Identify what you did wrong.** Make it clear that you know exactly how you injured the other party, and under no circumstance utter the statement, "I am sorry if you feel bad" (got hurt, were disappointed, etc.). This is *not* an apology. Such a statement suggests that somehow the other person is responsible for feeling hurt or injured, and it does not acknowledge what you did wrong.
- **Don't offer justifications/excuses.** As tempting as it may be, do not try to justify your behavior or offer an excuse (e.g., I was drunk or angry or stressed). And certainly do not excuse your behavior by blaming the other person (e.g., If you didn't work all the time, I wouldn't have been so lonely that I cheated on you).
- **Explain how you will ensure that the injury does not occur again.** It is not enough to feel bad about the past; you also need to offer assurances that you have learned your lesson and will not repeat the offense again. Apologies that are not accompanied by a commitment to change are of little value.
- **Accept the other person's anger.** Just because you are now sorry doesn't mean the other person automatically and immediately forgives and forgets. You need to listen to the injured party discuss how your behavior has hurt them, and you need to give them time to get over their pain. It is the least that you owe someone whom you have hurt.

Developing the ability to offer sincere, effective apologies can enhance your life in several ways. First, it can help repair or strengthen relationships that are important to you. Everyone engages in behaviors that hurt or injure those they love, but people who can show that they are truly sorry and will not reoffend can often minimize the long-term effects on their relationships. Second, apologizing shows that you take responsibility for your behavior and that you have integrity, both of which are likely to influence others to forgive you and trust you again. Third, as you gain experience with admitting you are wrong, you will find that—contrary to what many people believe—doing so actually makes you stronger and more respected. Finally, if you follow these suggestions, in time you will find it easier to apologize and perhaps even discover that you have fewer reasons to do so.

SUMMARY

In this chapter, we have addressed relationship challenges and how you can respond to them. In this context, relationship challenges refers to the interactional problems and situations that threaten the continuance of a relationship. Such challenges are pervasive, but one's response can effect whether a relationship thrives or fails when they occur. Throughout this chapter, we have presented you with a range of communication skills that you can use to help you respond effectively when confronted with relationship problems such as influencing others and resisting the influence of others, managing deception and jealousy in close relationships, offering negative feedback through hurtful messages, responding to relationship transgressions, and preventing sexual coercion and couple violence.

One of the most fundamental challenges individuals face is influencing people who are important to them. You can become more effective at influencing others if you understand your own goals and develop compliance-gaining messages to meet them. On the other hand, when you are confronted with others' unwanted influence attempts, you can more successfully resist them if you understand how to counter the "weapons of influence" that communicators often use to elicit others' compliance.

Two other relationship challenges that are less common but potentially more threatening are deception and jealousy. As we discuss in this chapter, individuals in relationships can be under-responsive to deception due to the truth bias, while they may be over-responsive to feelings of jealousy due to insecurity.

Sometimes people are deceptive because they don't want to hurt others. However, as we detailed in our discussion of hurtful messages, it is possible to give negative feedback and/or reveal painful truths if you use appropriate communication strategies such as being specific, framing your messages as kindly and positively as possible, and ensuring that you deliver these messages in private.

Relational transgressions such as relationship temptations and infidelity are closely tied to why people are deceitful and experience jealousy, as well as why they hurt others. Though these transgressions can be extremely painful, relationships can recover from them if partners communicate effectively and take the time to explore the causes and consequences of the transgressions, seek counsel and support from others, and manage their emotions so that they avoid doing further damage to the relationships.

Relational transgressions, jealousy, deception, and even hurtful messages can all contribute to the experience of interpersonal violence. If you are the victim of violence, it is very helpful to be able to distinguish battering, a type of violence that does not usually respond to communication efforts or interventions, and situation couple violence, which does. People who are battered should usually exit the relationship with the support of others, while those who experience situational couple violence can benefit from improving their conflict, social influence, and overall communication skills.

Similarly, not all sexual coercion is responsive to effective communication efforts, though what is termed "date rape" or "unwanted sex" often is. Preventing unwanted sex is more likely when men and women communicate more directly and clearly regarding their desires—and when they realize that their understandings of the event may be quite different.

Finally, differences in social roles and cultural rules regarding emotion influence people's experiences of relationship challenges. Therefore, understanding these differences can help you better respond to the relationship problems you encounter.

KEY TERMS

argumentation skills 219
arousal maintenance goals 204
battering 216
compliance-gaining messages 204
consistency principle 207
deception 209

display rules 221
emotional infidelity 214
emotional norms 221
feeling rules 221
foot-in-the-door technique 207
hurtful messages 210

identity goals 203
intensity 211
intentional messages 211
interaction goals 203
interpersonal violence 215
jealousy 210

low balling 207
mate guarding 214
personal resource goals 204
physical infidelity 214
primary influence goals 203
rape 217
reciprocation 206
relational infidelity 214

relational resource goals 204
relational temptations 212
relational transgressions 212
relationship challenges 202
relationship threats 212
secondary influence goals 203
sexual coercion 218
situational couple violence 217

social influence 202
social proof 207
truth bias 209
unintentional message 211
unwanted sex 218
weapons of influence 206

CHAPTER REVIEW QUESTIONS

1. What are the four weapons of influence discussed in this chapter? How can you protect yourself against them?

2. What factors affect how much pain the recipient of a hurtful message feels? How can you frame a hurtful message to minimize the pain it inflicts?

3. When relational temptations occur, what strategies can you use to resist them? What tactics can you use to prevent them from occurring in the first place?

4. What is the difference between interpersonal violence that is characterized as battering and what is described as situational couple violence? How can you tell if your partner is likely to be a batterer?

ACTIVITIES

1. **Understanding the Role of Deception in Everyday Life**
For this activity, your goal is to be as truthful as possible for one entire day. For example, when asked how you feel, be honest; don't offer an evaluation or opinion unless you feel you can be truthful, and be as nondeceptive as possible in all your interactions. As you do this, note your own and others' reactions to your behavior, the situations where you were temped to lie (and/or did so), as well as how your communication and interactions differed from the norm. Because you may sometimes feel the need to be less than truthful for a variety of reasons, also note when this occurred, with whom, and why you felt compelled to do so. Finally, write a two- to three-page paper in which you describe your experiences on "truth day."

2. **Apologizing Effectively**
Reflect on a recent occasion when you felt you should, or actually did, apologize for something you said or did. If you avoided apologizing, analyze why you were reluctant to do so and what you did instead. If you did apologize, how did you do so? Finally, imagine that you have the opportunity to have the interaction again. Write an apology that you believe would be an effective response to your transgression.

3. **Delivering a Hurtful Message Effectively**
For this activity, your goal is to think of a message that could potentially be hurtful to its recipient and to draft the message following the guidelines for effectively delivering hurtful messages. Imagine that you are really going to make this statement to the recipient, and work to ensure that your message conveys your feelings and concerns but is also sensitive to the feelings of the person to whom you would say it.

WEB ACTIVITIES

1. Go to http://www.psychologytoday.com/tests on the *Psychology Today* Web site, and take the jealousy quiz on the second page. Choose the quiz that describes your sexual orientation and gender (straight female, gay male, etc.) and complete it. Do your results agree with how you view yourself? What scenarios made you feel most jealous? If you rated high in jealousy, what can you do to moderate your feelings?

2. Go to http://www.fox.com/lietome/lightmantests/ and take the lie detection tests provided. How effective were you at detecting deception? When were you most successful? When were you least successful? What did you learn about nonverbal behaviors and deception from the test?

10

MANAGING CONFLICT IN INTERPERSONAL RELATIONSHIPS

*O*livia waited impatiently for her roommate Holly to get dressed so they could drive to campus together. Every morning it was the same thing: Olivia stood by the front door yelling, "Come on! Let's go!" at Holly . . . who completely ignored her. Eventually, Holly would stomp out with wet hair and a sullen look, and they wouldn't be speaking to each other. Olivia was tired of it. It was her car, and if Holly couldn't get ready on time, she could take the bus! Realistically, however, she liked Holly and enjoyed living with her. And she was afraid that if they ever really talked about their morning routine, the conflict would spiral out of control. Consequently, she never said anything, and each morning she became a bit more irritated and dissatisfied.

Although Olivia is unhappy with her roommate, her attitude toward conflict is so negative that she refuses to address their problem. Many people view conflict the same way Olivia does: they fear it, try to avoid it, and see it—at best—as a necessary evil. However, conflict is an essential, important, and potentially creative activity. When addressed skillfully, conflict can lead people to confront important but unresolved issues, to develop innovative solutions to long-standing problems, and to feel more affection and intimacy. However, when conflict is managed poorly, it can lead to dissatisfaction, emotional distance, and worse.

In this chapter, we provide you with the foundation you need to manage your conflicts more effectively. To do so, we begin by defining conflict and explaining why conflict interactions are necessary and useful. We discuss the various strategies individuals use to respond to conflict and we address problematic forms of conflict, negative conflict escalation. We then examine the influence that power, culture, and society exert on conflict and discuss conflict ethics. We conclude the chapter on a high note: providing you with two models for responding more effectively to your conflict experiences.

Once you have read this chapter, you will be able to:

- Define conflict.
- Identify four purposes that conflict serves.
- Describe three causes of conflict.
- Understand the differences between direct and indirect conflict styles and when it is most appropriate to use each.
- Discuss factors that can cause negative conflict to escalate.
- Articulate how power, culture, and society influence conflict interactions.
- Explain the ways in which conflict can be managed competently and strategically.

CHAPTER OUTLINE

WHAT IS CONFLICT?
   Interdependence
   Interests
   Incompatibilities
   Limited Resources

THE IMPORTANCE OF MANAGING CONFLICT EFFECTIVELY

THE INDIVIDUAL AND CONFLICT MANAGEMENT
   What Purposes Does Conflict Serve?
   What Causes Conflict?
   Responding to Conflict: Styles and Strategies
   Choosing a Conflict Response
   Emotion
   Problematic Conflict Interactions

THE INDIVIDUAL, CONFLICT MANAGEMENT, AND SOCIETY
   Power
   Culture
   Gender

ETHICS AND CONFLICT MANAGEMENT
   Be Truthful
   Avoid Name-Calling
   Own Your Messages
   Avoid Coercion

IMPROVING YOUR CONFLICT-MANAGEMENT SKILLS
   A Strategic Approach to Conflict Management
   The Competence Model of Conflict

Summary

Key Terms

Chapter Review Questions

Activities

Web Activities

conflict
occurs when *interdependent* parties perceive that they have *incompatible interests* related to the distribution of *limited resources*

interdependent
when parties have to rely upon each other to achieve their goals

interests
goals, needs, desires, values, and beliefs

WHAT IS CONFLICT?

Although people often think of conflict as being composed of distinct "events" (such as a fight or disagreement), conflict actually is a process: It typically emerges and is enacted over time, and it often has long-term consequences. Moreover, it tends to be ambiguous, chaotic, and confusing (Sillars, 1998). You may begin arguing with your roommate about whether his girlfriend spends too much time at your apartment, for example, only to find the disagreement morphing into a discussion about the girlfriend's personality, how much time the two of you spend together, and whether one of you should move out.

When we say conflict is ambiguous, we mean that conflict participants aren't always clear about its causes, the motivations of the other conflict participants, and even their own feelings about the apparent topic of conflict. Because conflict usually brings out strong emotions in people, it can be chaotic; participants often jump from topic to topic, covering a broad array during just one episode. In addition, people's communication patterns of are often unpredictable, and this can be confusing. People who are normally very calm can become easily frustrated and angry.

How do you know when you are in conflict? Typically, you experience anger or frustration, or you want one thing and your interactional partners want another. However, you may wonder, "Is it conflict when I become angry with the person who cuts in line at the theater? When I want to leave the party early but my friend isn't ready to go? Or when I'd rather eat Chinese food but I go along with my date and agree to eat Italian?" To help you understand when and why you are in conflict, we offer the following definition. **Conflict** occurs when *interdependent* parties perceive that they have *incompatible interests* related to the distribution of *limited resources* (Donohue & Kolt, 1992; Mortenson, 1974). Below, we explain each of these components in more detail.

Interdependence

Parties are **interdependent** when they have to rely upon each other to achieve their goals or fulfill their interests (Putnam, 2006; Putnam & Poole, 1987). For example, runners in a race are interdependent—one runner winning is dependent on other runners losing. Similarly, if you want to pay your bills on time, you are dependent on your roommate giving you his or her share of the payments before the due date. If you need to finish a work project on schedule, you must rely on your work team to complete their tasks. Although you may not realize it, you are interdependent with many other people—including those in the grocery store checkout line who take forever to locate their debit cards, other drivers on the road who cut you off, and your classmates who ask pointless questions. So, people are interdependent—or affected by each other—although we often wish we were not. This interdependence, then, can set the stage for conflict (Roloff & Soule, 2002). To understand how interdependence can increase conflict, read *It Happened to Me: Audria*.

As Audria's story indicates, even good friends who get along well can find themselves in conflict once their interdependence

IT HAPPENED TO ME: *Audria*

Everybody warned us, but we didn't care. We were the best of friends, and nothing could stand between us . . . until we moved into the dorm together. We discovered that we had different expectations (partying vs. studying) and different values (money on fun vs. mandatory expenses). And we had stupid fights that got us to the point where we are no longer on speaking terms. Although it is sad, I know I'm not the only one who is going through this!

increases. Of course, simply being interdependent is not enough to cause conflict; interdependent parties, like Audria and her roommate, must also perceive that their interests are at odds.

Interests

Interests refer to your goals, needs, desires, values, and beliefs (Simons, 1974; Ting-Toomey, 1985). If you want to go skiing over spring break but your father wants you to come home, the two of you are experiencing a conflict in goals. You might have conflict with your dating

partner over your desire for a more (or less) committed relationship or with a friend over your belief that it is okay to break a date with him so you can instead go out with a potential romantic partner. You might also argue with a political adversary over the value of tax cuts for the wealthy or with an airline attendant regarding your need to board a plane when the doors have already closed. As these examples suggest, conflict takes place when you sense that your interests are not compatible with the interests of the people with whom you are interdependent.

Incompatibilities

Incompatibility refers to communicators' *perceptions* that their interests (goals, values, needs, desires, beliefs) are mutually exclusive or in opposition (Putnam, 2006; Ting-Toomey & Oetzel, 2001). We stress the word *perceptions* because conflict arises when people *perceive* that their goals are incompatible with someone else's—even if they are not. For example, coworkers often believe that their managers have favorites, or "pets," and therefore may be in conflict as they attempt to achieve this preferred status. They may believe and act this way even if their manager does not in fact prefer one employee over another. Whether you have actual or simply perceived incompatibilities, conflict is likely to result.

Limited Resources

A primary reason we perceive that our interests are incompatible with others' is our belief that resources are limited. **Limited resources** describe the reality or the perception that sufficient resources do not exist for all parties to achieve their goals or fulfill their interests (Mortenson, 1974; Ting-Toomey & Oetzel, 2001). For example, people are often jealous of their friends' romantic partners because they worry that their friends will only have a certain amount of affection and energy to devote to relationships—whether friendships or romantic relationships.

To recap, interdependent people experience conflict when they believe that another person is preventing them from gaining access to desired, but limited, resources. Remember that these resources can be concrete "things" such as money, jobs, and time, but they can also be more abstract concepts such as respect, affection, and power. And to answer the questions we posed above—yes, you probably do experience conflict when someone cuts in line, when your friend is not ready to leave the party when you are, and when you and your dining companion can't agree where to eat.

THE IMPORTANCE OF MANAGING CONFLICT EFFECTIVELY

Based on our definition, you have probably come to realize that conflict is unavoidable no matter how you feel about it or respond to it. In the course of daily interaction, people "criticize, nag, betray, lie, disappoint, ostracize, and embarrass one another, to name just a few behaviors" (Kowalski, Walker, Wilkinson, Queen, & Sharpe, 2003, p. 473). They also tease, whine, complain, and gripe (Kowalski, 2002). These negative interactions are particularly likely to occur in close relationships. According to Miller (1997), 44 percent of people are likely to be annoyed by a romantic partner on any given day, and young adults report having an average of 8.7 annoying experiences with their dating partners weekly. These displeasing behaviors often lead to conflict. If we develop effective conflict-management skills, however,

Forty-four percent of people are likely to be annoyed by a romantic partner on any given day.

incompatibility
communicators' perceptions that their interests are mutually exclusive or in opposition

limited resources
the reality or the perception that sufficient resources do not exist for all parties to achieve their goals or fulfill their interests

we and our relationships become resilient and can bounce back from these events. Conversely, if conflicts are not managed well, they can devastate our relationships.

Fortunately, developing excellent conflict skills can transform your life for the better. Responding to conflict in a skillful way can improve your work life, your close relationships, and the way you see yourself (Gottman, 1994; Oetzel & Ting-Toomey, 2006). In the following sections, we explain how you can develop these skills if you are willing to devote the time to do so.

THE INDIVIDUAL AND CONFLICT MANAGEMENT

Conflict is typical in relationships, yet most people don't know very much about it. Do you know, for example, what purposes or functions conflict serves or what prompts most individuals' conflict? More important, do you know how to manage your conflicts most productively? If not, do not worry; these are the topics we will explore next.

What Purposes Does Conflict Serve?

If people feel negatively toward conflict, why do they still engage in it? Most obviously, people engage in conflict to get what they want. But sometimes they continue to argue even when the other person has given in or when the issues are trivial. They do so because conflict interactions help people regulate their relationships, their emotions, and their lives.

Conflict is Persuasive

One reason people engage in conflict is that it serves as a type of **persuasive discourse** (Chaiken, Guenfeld, & Judd, 2000; Roloff & Soule, 2002). That is, you have arguments when others interfere with your ability to achieve your goals, and you want to persuade them to stop interfering so that you can fulfill your desires. If your colleague insists on smoking in your office and you don't smoke, you may attempt to persuade him or her to quit. Many conflicts are attempts to influence others, as our student discusses in *It Happened to Me: Shelby*.

Shelby was successful in resolving the conflict with her parents, at least in part because she was able to offer persuasive arguments that influenced her parents to stop interfering with her goal of going to Mexico.

IT HAPPENED TO ME: Shelby

My friends were all going to Mexico, and of course I wanted to go as well. However, my parents were not so excited that four freshman college girls wanted to go to Mexico alone, so we argued for days. They told me multiple times that I couldn't go, due to the fact it wasn't safe enough. I tried and tried to think of ways to make them let me go, but nothing was working, until I remembered that my sister went on a trip alone her freshman year in college. I decided to try to persuade them by reminding them that my sister had gone on a similar trip and had come to no harm; that I was responsible—if not more so—than my sister was at this age, so they could trust me; and that it wasn't fair that my sister got to go on a trip and I didn't. Fortunately, my arguments worked and my parents allowed me to go to Mexico.

Conflict Helps You Regulate Your Relationships

Conflict also helps people manage their relationships (Coser, 1956; Phinney, Kim-Jo, Osorto, & Vilhjalmsdottir, 2005). On a daily basis, family members, friends, lovers, and colleagues have conflicts around issues of power and control, intimacy and distance, and novelty and predictability. Whenever people begin to feel that they have too little power, too much responsibility, too much distance or closeness, or too much predictability (or unpredictability) in their relationships, they experience dissatisfaction. They may attempt to take care of their dissatisfaction by engaging in conflict.

For example, if your supervisor changes your work hours without consulting you, you may resent having no control over the decision, even if the hours work with your schedule. In order to reestablish your control in the relationship, you may decide to engage in conflict. Adolescents typically experience many such conflicts with their parents as a way to establish more independence and control (Adams, Gullotta, & Markstrom, 1994). Similarly, at times

persuasive discourse
arguments offered to persuade others to stop interfering so that you can fulfill your desires

you may feel distant or disconnected from your friends or loved ones, so you initiate conflict as a way to pull them back. Through airing grievances and, more important, making up after the argument, you may begin to feel closer to one another. Unfortunately, sometimes the conflict can spin out of control, and rather than increasing closeness or reestablishing control, it can destroy it.

Conflict is Cathartic

Conflict can also function as a "catharsis" (Coser, 1956; Marcus-Newhall, Pedersen, Carlson, & Miller, 2000). The word **catharsis** comes from a Greek term that means to "cleanse." Occasionally, people try to avoid conflicts only to discover that they have really just been delaying them. They become tense or irritated, and they have to confront whatever is bothering them. After they talk with the other person, they may feel much better just to have "gotten it out in the open," even if the issue itself is not resolved. In this way, they feel cleansed of their bad feelings. But as mentioned above, if the conflict is managed poorly, the participants may end up feeling worse rather than better.

Conflict Can Help You Clarify Issues

Conflict interactions help people clarify how they feel and what they want (Marcus & Gould, 2000). When you enter an argument, you may think you are upset about one issue— like Olivia's issue with Holly's chronic tardiness, for example. Once you begin to discuss the issue, however, you may discover that you are actually upset because you believe your friend does not value you. Similarly, you may engage in a conflict discussion with your romantic partner because you want him or her to cook more often. During the conflict interaction, you may realize that you don't actually mind cooking, but you do want your partner to take more responsibility for planning the meals. In this way, engaging in conflict can help make your concerns and needs clearer—both to you and others.

However, keep in mind that your purposes for engaging in conflict may not always be clear to you (let alone the other person), and any specific argument may serve more than one purpose. The next time you engage in a conflict, think about why you are having the argument and why you are having it at this time. This awareness may help you understand the underlying reasons why you are in conflict, help you determine solutions, and perhaps put the conflict in perspective.

What Causes Conflict?

As you likely realize, people can and do engage in conflict over a wide range of topics. However, the types of issues people fight over can be divided into three broad categories: behaviors, personality characteristics, and relationship rules (Braiker & Kelley, 1979; Canary, Cupach, & Messman, 1995).

Behaviors

Conflicts over behaviors are perhaps the most frequent. **Behavioral conflicts** describe disagreements over specific, concrete behaviors that one performs or fails to perform (Alberts, 1989; Roloff & Soule, 2002). For example, forgetting to lock the front door, arriving late to a party, borrowing a sweater without asking, and losing the cable bill are all behaviors that can cause individuals to feel irritated and to initiate a conflict. In many respects, behavioral conflicts are among the easiest to address because this type of conflict is isolated to a specific behavior, it is usually easy to identify and hard to deny (especially if the person is caught actually wearing the sweater), and because behavioral conflicts focus on what a person has done—not who the person is.

Though behavioral conflicts may be the easiest to resolve, if they occur too often, they can stress a relationship. Thus, we recommend minimizing their occurrence. You can accomplish this in two ways: by learning to accept or tolerate some of your partner's displeasing behaviors and by avoiding behaviors your partner finds particularly disturbing. For example, Jan and Jim experienced recurrent conflicts over Jan's habit of not tightening the lids on bottles sufficiently and Jim's tendency to leave the lights on when

catharsis
the purging of emotions or relieving of emotional tensions; from a Greek term that means *to cleanse*

behavioral conflicts
disagreements over specific, concrete behaviors that one performs or fails to perform

Think of a behavior you find bothersome in a friend or coworker. What could you do to make this behavior more tolerable for you? What behavior of yours do friends or your romantic partner complain about? Is this a behavior you could avoid or modify so others find it less bothersome?

he leaves a room. Because neither of them could remember to change their behavior, they decided that they would accept the other's "bad habit" and become responsible for it. That is, Jan makes sure that lights in the house are turned off when no one is in a room, and Jim avoids shaking bottles until he tightens their lids. By making these choices, they were able to stop fighting about minor issues and each still have their own goals met.

Personality

Personality conflicts can be more difficult to manage because they focus on a global evaluation of the individual and therefore usually constitute an attack upon one's identity (Alberts, 1989; Kurdek, 1994). Where a behavioral conflict might focus on a roommate's failure to take out the garbage, a personal characteristic conflict focuses on the roommate as messy, irresponsible and/or lazy. Because personality conflicts attack a person's sense of self or identity, they often lead to defensiveness, are likely to escalate, and may be more difficult to manage. Because most people cannot or will not change their basic personalities, you will likely find it more productive to frame your conflict around specific behaviors that the other party can change. Therefore, rather than arguing that Holly is thoughtless because she is always late, Olivia could focus on her behavior and discuss strategies for getting her out of the door on time—or strategies that would allow Olivia to be less affected by Holly's lateness.

Relationship Rules

Conflict also arises when partners violate fundamental, often unspoken, rules that have been established over the course of the relationship (Argyle & Henderson, 1984; Bowker, 2004; Roloff, Soule, & Carey, 2001). **Relationship rules** define what is expected and prohibited in specific relationships. For example, most friends believe that good friends don't gossip about each other, flirt with each other's romantic partners, or lie to each other. The most frequently reported relationship rule transgressions among romantic partners are infidelity, wanting to date others, and deception (Metts, 1994). Other commonly broken rules include betraying a confidence, being unsupportive, criticizing, ignoring/avoiding, and gossiping (Jones & Burdette, 1994).

Being aware of the causes of your conflict can help you respond to and manage them better. If you recognize that you are framing a conflict as a personality issue, you can choose to reframe it as a behavior, which may lead your partner to act less defensively and be more willing to accommodate your request for change. If you find yourself accusing a family member of being "meddlesome" (a personality characteristic), you could say instead that you don't want the person to offer unsolicited advice (a behavior). Or, if you realize that your conflict centers on a relationship rule, you can seek to reach agreement with your conflict partner on the relationship rules the two of you will honor.

Perhaps even more important than the topic of your conflicts is the way in which you respond to these disagreements. That is, the conflict styles and strategies you enact significantly impact how your conflicts unfold, how successfully they are managed, and how they affect your relationships.

Responding to Conflict: Styles and Strategies

Although the potential for interpersonal conflict is everywhere—on the freeway when someone cuts you off in traffic, at a party where your best friend drinks and wants to drive, and at school when your teacher assigns you a lower grade than you believe you deserve—not every potential conflict becomes a conflict interaction. On some occasions, you choose to avoid the conflict by not expressing your feelings, or the other party refuses to engage. But sometimes you must engage in conflict.

In such cases, you have to decide how to respond. Your decision will be based on the situation, the issue, the other party, your relationship with that person, and your goals.

personality conflicts
disagreements that focus on a global evaluation of the individual and therefore usually constitute an attack upon one's identity

relationship rules
define what is expected and prohibited in specific relationships

Conflict Styles

To understand the types of responses that are more or less effective in specific contexts, scholars have studied various conflict tactics and styles (Blake & Mouton, 1964; Putnam & Wilson, 1982; Rahim & Buntzman, 1990). A **conflict tactic** is the individual behavior a person uses when engaged in conflict (such as shouting, threatening, persuading, or withdrawing), while **conflict style** describes the pattern of tactics an individual uses repetitively and across parties and contexts (Canary et al., 1995). For example, a threat is a specific *tactic* that might commonly be employed by a person who uses a competitive style.

For the most part, conflict styles differ in the degree to which they are competitive versus cooperative and direct versus indirect (Kilmann & Thomas, 1975; Rahim & Bonoma, 1979; Sillars et al., 2004). **Competitive styles** focus on advancing one's own interests without consideration for the partner's interests. **Cooperative styles** include a focus on the partner's interests as well as one's own. **Direct conflict styles** focus on discussing issues of incompatibility, whereas **indirect conflict styles** avoid direct discussion of these issues. Based on these two dimensions, Guerrero, Andersen, and Afifi (2007) describe six styles of conflict: competitive fighting, collaborating, compromising, indirect fighting, yielding, and avoiding (see Figure 10.1). Let's examine how each is enacted and when it is most effective.

Direct Conflict Styles

Competitive Fighting A **competing or dominating style** represents a high concern for one's own interests and a low concern for the partner's interests (Friedman, Tidd, & Currall, 2000) and is characterized by direct communication. When you compete with others, you focus on your own concerns and interests, and you have little investment in helping the other person achieve his or her goals. People often use a competitive style during car sales and negotiations. The salesperson typically wants the customer to pay as high a price for the car as is feasible, while the customer tries to pay as low a price as possible. This style is most useful when a person is willing to accomplish their own goals at the expense of the other party.

While competing may be an appropriate response on occasion, it can cause problems if you use it frequently or if it becomes your preferred style. Nonetheless, you may need to act competitively if your rights are being violated and the other party is not responsive to more collaborative tactics. For example, in 2007, members of the Writer's Guild of America in Hollywood went on strike (a highly competitive tactic) because the studios refused to

conflict tactic
the individual behavior a person uses when engaged in conflict (such as shouting, threatening, persuading, or withdrawing)

conflict style
describes the pattern of tactics an individual uses repetitively across parties and contexts

competitive style
focuses on advancing one's own interests without consideration for the partner's interests

cooperative style
focuses on the partner's interests as well as one's own

direct conflict style
focuses on discussing issues of incompatibility

indirect conflict style
avoids discussing issues of incompatibility

competing or dominating style
represents a high concern for one's own interests and a low concern for the partner's interests and is characterized by direct communication

FIGURE 10.1 Interpersonal Conflict Styles

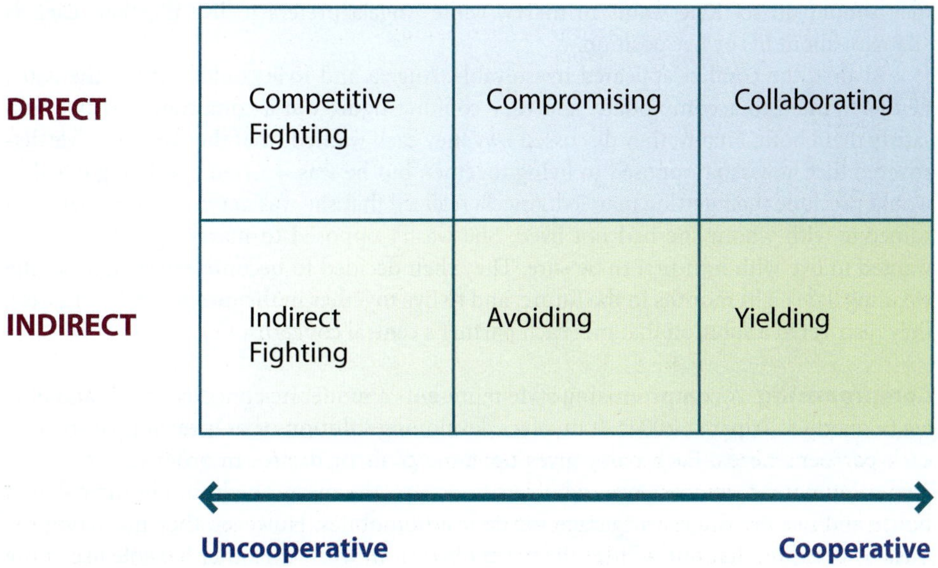

	Uncooperative → Cooperative		
DIRECT	Competitive Fighting	Compromising	Collaborating
INDIRECT	Indirect Fighting	Avoiding	Yielding

SOURCE: Guerrero, Andersen, & Afifi (2007).

give them residuals for Internet content, among other issues, and because they believed that the studios' representatives were not negotiating in good faith.

People often use a competitive style during car sales and negotiations.

Even though a competitive response only focuses on the goals of one person, it's possible to communicate this type of response in a way that will maximize its effectiveness. Competitive responses that are direct and nonaggressive are likely to be more effective and less damaging (Canary & Lakey, 2006). For example, if you want your boss to give you a raise, you are likely to be more effective if you offer a series of arguments for why your performance makes you deserve a pay increase than if you threaten to leave if you are denied one. However, at times you may be tempted to compete directly and aggressively. People are direct and aggressive when they attack others in the attempt to achieve their goals. Sometimes such aggressive attacks are born out of frustration, as appeared to be the case for actor Alec Baldwin in a well-publicized case involving a phone call to his daughter (see *Communication in Society: Actor Makes the Wrong Call*). Personal attacks, such as those used by Baldwin, are rarely effective and usually backfire by escalating conflict and making the attacker look mean or petty.

Collaborating   A **collaborating or problem-solving style** involves a high concern for the self *and* the other party (Ben-Yoav & Pruitt, 1984; Fischer & Ury, 1991). Examples of collaborative/problem-solving strategies include communicating openly and creating solutions that respond to everyone's interests.

Collaboration requires that you look for solutions that satisfy the concerns of all parties. It can be one of the more difficult conflict responses to use, because it requires each person to identify his or her main concerns or issues. Additionally, it can be difficult for people to recognize what is truly important to them, much less to others. For example, Angela and Kyle are a heterosexual couple who have been dating for two years. They both agree it is time to intensify their commitment to one another, but they disagree on how they should do so. Kyle wants to marry, while Angela prefers to live together. Each is adamant about his or her position.

At first, the conflict appeared irresolvable. Angela and Kyle couldn't avoid the issue, neither wanted to accommodate, and they couldn't figure out a compromise that would satisfy them both. Finally, they discussed *why* they each wanted what they wanted. Kyle discovered that he wasn't opposed to living together, but he was worried that living together would preclude their getting married. Angela realized that she was nervous about marrying someone with whom she had not lived. She wasn't opposed to marrying Kyle; she just wanted to live with him first to be sure. They then decided to become engaged, to set the wedding date eight months in the future, and to live together in the meantime. In this case, they discovered a solution that met each partner's central concerns.

collaborating or problem-solving style
involves a high concern for the self *and* the other party

compromising style
represents a moderate concern for self and other

Compromising   A **compromising** style represents a moderate concern for self and others (Conerly & Tripathi, 2004). It involves developing solutions that meet at least some of each partner's needs. Each party gives up some goals or desires in order to get others. Two roommates may argue over who gets to occupy the master bedroom in their shared house and use the single-car garage for their automobiles. However, they may compromise by deciding that one will get the master bedroom while the other has sole use of the garage.

Communication in SOCIETY

Actor Makes the Wrong Call

The following report is an excerpt from an article that appeared in The Washington *Post on April 21, 2007, after a phone call actor Alec Baldwin made to his daughter became public. The article illustrates a variety of issues, including the destructive nature of personal attacks. The story also shows what can happen when private conflicts become public, as well as the role technology can play in making such conflicts public.*

Alec Baldwin Makes the Wrong Call; Actor Berates His Daughter in Voice Mail Leaked to Web

By Frank Ahrens

All parents get angry at their children, but arguments usually remain in the household. If you're Alec Baldwin and you call your 11-year-old daughter a "rude little pig" on voice mail, however, you no longer can expect your outburst to remain in the family.

Baldwin is the latest celebrity to learn the hard lessons of an instantaneous digital world that can turn a private call into a public embarrassment in a matter of days.

The actor is engaged in a custody battle with his former wife, Academy Award–winning actress Kim Basinger, over their 11-year-old daughter, Ireland, following a 2002 divorce that spurred nasty name-calling between the two actors.

On April 11 from New York, Baldwin called his daughter in Los Angeles at an arranged time but found that her phone was turned off. He left a profanity-laced, 2-minute-12-second message, berating her for not answering the phone.

"You don't have the brains or decency as a human being," yells Baldwin, who narrates the beloved "Thomas the Tank Engine" animated children's films. "I don't give a damn that you're 12 years old or 11 years old or a child or your mother is a thoughtless pain . . . who doesn't care what you do as far as I'm concerned!"

A recording of the phone call hit the Internet on Thursday afternoon when it was posted on celebrity news site TMZ.com. By Friday morning, it was Topic A on major talk shows. Baldwin is a noted political liberal, and his voice mail showed up on Rush Limbaugh's program yesterday as the host discoursed on custody battles. Even the hosts on ESPN Radio played the call and devoted extensive airtime to it.

TMZ will not disclose how it got the taped phone call, which spurred Baldwin's lawyer to file a declaration in Los Angeles Superior Court yesterday asking the court to force TMZ to reveal the identity of the source. "If [TMZ] had a tape-recorded message between [Baldwin] and the minor child, it had to have originated from [Basinger] or her employees, agents or attorneys," the filing reads.

Through her publicist, Basinger would say only: "The voice mail speaks for itself."

Aside from its titillation value, Baldwin's rant already has had legal consequences. As a result of the call being made public, a Los Angeles judge has temporarily suspended Baldwin's visitation rights at least until a previously scheduled May 4 custody hearing.

Baldwin apologized yesterday in a statement on his Web site:

"I'm sorry, as everyone who knows me is aware, for losing my temper with my child. I have been driven to the edge by parental alienation for many years now."

The last words heard at the end of Baldwin's voice mail foreshadow the scandal to come, it turns out. A computerized voice can be heard saying: "To replay this message . . ."

People in the United States are often taught the value of compromise. You have probably heard that "you have to give a little to get a little" or that "you can't have everything." These are the basic principles that underlie the compromising response to conflict. If you want a raise and more vacation time while your boss prefers to give you neither, the two of you may compromise with you receiving the vacation time but not the raise. Compromising is often the first response people think of when they are confronted with a conflict.

Compromising can be a useful response to conflict—and more efficient than collaboration. You may be able to quickly decide which issues are most important and work out a deal that lets each conflict participant get what he or she most desires. It also gives the appearance of being fair—that is, everyone has to give up something and everyone gets something. Compromising is effective for conflict situations where the participants' primary goals are different or where the issues are not very complex.

However, compromising is not the best response to every conflict. Some conflicts are too complex to settle with a compromise, or it may not be possible for a compromise to

concessions
giving up something you want

indirect fighting
a conflict style that represents high concern for one's own goals and low concern for one's partner's goals

yielding or accomodating style
a conflict style that entails a low concern for self and a high concern for the other person

Which conflict style do you use most frequently with people who are close to you? Which one do you use with colleagues? If your conflict style changes across these two contexts, why do you think this occurs? In which context do you believe you are most successful?

truly satisfy both partners. If you want children and your partner does not, there really is no effective way to compromise. In addition, when you compromise, you may give up things that are important to you. If you have to give up going to college to maintain your romantic relationship, you may be giving up too much. Finally, people can manipulate the compromising process by pretending to want things they do not actually want. For example, your romantic partner might pretend to want you to attend a party that she or he actually prefers to attend alone. Then, your partner could "compromise" by agreeing to go alone if you let him or her skip your cousin's wedding. Thus, you might be fooled into giving up something important while your conflict partner actually "gives up" something he or she didn't want in the first place.

Many of the tactics used in collaboration also apply to compromise. To be effective at compromising, you must be able to provide information, solicit information, provide support, and accept responsibility, just as you do in collaboration. In addition, you also need to be able to develop and offer **concessions,** which involves giving up something you want. Specifically, you have to determine which issues are of most and least importance to you and articulate what you are giving up.

Although direct conflict styles may seem best because they involve open communication, some people are more comfortable with an indirect style, and at times indirect styles can be useful and appropriate.

Indirect Conflict Styles

Indirect Fighting As with competitive fighting, **indirect fighting** represents a high concern for one's own goals and low concern for one's partner's goals. However, the communication style is indirect (Sillars et al., 2004). One type of indirect fighting is called "passive-aggressiveness." People who are acting passive-aggressively appear to be avoiding or accommodating but then become aggressive in another context, when it isn't expected (Guerrero & La Valley, 2006). For example, if you agree to help your friend move, then "forget" to show up because you'd rather sleep in, or if you work late at your boss's request then deliberately do a poor job on the project to get even, you are behaving passive-aggressively.

Another form of indirect fighting involves ignoring or invalidating your partner's concerns. Whenever Lauro tries to talk to Bryan about his spending habits, for instance, Bryan rolls his eyes and says, "There you go again, being such a downer." Other forms of indirect fighting include whining, holding a grudge, giving the other party the "silent treatment" (Guerrero & La Valley, 2006; Sillars et al., 2004), and being patronizing or sarcastic (Nicotera, 1993). If you say, "I'll go to that stupid party of yours just so you'll stop whining about it," you are engaging in passive aggression. Because you are going to the party grudgingly, you will probably be resentful and conflict could escalate; in the long run, this type of indirect fighting often leads to animosity and damages the relationship.

Yielding A **yielding or accommodating style** entails a low concern for self and a high concern for the other person. Strategies for yielding include giving in to the other person's desires and giving up your own goals (Friedman et al., 2000; Wayne, Liden, Graf, & Ferris, 1997).

On occasion, you may determine that the issues you are arguing about are not important to you, or that your goals are not worth fighting for. You might conclude that you don't care where you and your partner go on vacation, for example, or that you are willing to do more than your share of the housework because you do it better. Consequently, you may decide to accommodate your partner's goals and give up your own. However, you need to be sure that you are truly giving up your own goals. If you are actually just trying to avoid the conflict temporarily, when you feel like resolving it later, the other party may resent that you have changed your position.

When should you use the yielding style? You should yield when you are wrong. For example, because Holly's behavior made Olivia late, she could give in and agree to be ready on time. You should also yield when you have treated someone unfairly or have behaved

inappropriately; in that case, it is probably best to give in to the other person's request. If you break someone's television, you should accommodate his or her request that you pay for the repairs. You might also engage in the yielding style when your own goals are less important than your partner's goals. Although you may not want to attend your partner's office holiday party, it may be more important to your partner that you attend than it is for you to stay away. You might also choose to yield when doing so will strengthen your relationship. Satisfied couples often choose to let their partners have their way (Rusbult, Verette, Whitney, Slovik, & Lipkus, 1991). As long as both partners are perceived as yielding equally over time, it can be an effective response in long-term relationships. However, if you continually give in without good reason, you might begin to feel powerless and start to resent that your partner always gets her or his way.

Avoiding An **avoiding style** is indirect and involves strategies such as withdrawing, joking around, and ignoring. The avoiding style can be cooperative or uncooperative, depending on the situation. For example, two people might agree to disagree as a way of avoiding further conflict. Other times, avoiding conflict leaves problems to fester and become worse. While some people believe that it is important to air all differences if a relationship is to succeed, many happy couples do avoid conflict, at least on some issues (Alberts & Driscoll, 1992) or on some occasions (Caughlin & Vangelisti, 2006). However, if you avoid conflict all the time, you may have difficulty resolving issues that are important to you, and you may find that your rights are trampled on, making it difficult to sustain your relationships.

You may decide however to avoid conflict over issues that are not resolvable. If you do not like your friend's dating partner, what do you gain from engaging in lengthy arguments over the partner's good and bad points? The arguments will not likely change either of your opinions and in fact may generate animosity and weaken your relationship. In such cases, you may choose to engage in long-term avoidance of conflict.

On other occasions, you may feel the need to address an issue, but you decide to wait until a more appropriate time. The night before a final exam is probably not the best time to discuss a family member's poor cleaning habits. You will not be able to communicate as clearly and calmly as you might like. In addition, early in a relationship, you may not want to address some of the conflicts you are feeling. Couples in the first few months of courtship, for example, often experience a "honeymoon" period during which they play down their differences, perhaps because the relationship is too fragile to survive a disagreement. However, as with competing, if avoiding becomes your preferred response to conflict, you will be less likely to achieve your goals and maintain strong, intimate relationships.

Choosing a Conflict Response

Although collaboration represents an "ideal" conflict style in that it attempts to develop win-win solutions, all six conflict styles are appropriate in specific contexts and with specific individuals. For example, compromise is effective when the issue is not too important and you are equally concerned with your own interests *and* the other party's interests; avoidance may be appropriate when the issue is minor or the time is wrong to address a difficult topic; and competitive fighting might be necessary when you are being harassed or otherwise exploited.

How you respond to conflict often depends on how direct or indirect you wish to be and how willing you are to work toward accomplishing your own and others' goals (Canary & Lakey, 2006; Kilmann & Thomas, 1977). If you wish to engage directly in conflict and are most concerned with accomplishing your own goals, you could choose to respond competitively. At other times, you may wish to be indirect and not address either your own or the other person's goals, so you decide to avoid the conflict altogether. Alternatively, you may determine that you don't want to directly confront the issue, and you don't care about your own goals, so you decide to accommodate the other person. To learn more about the conversational tactics you can use to enact each conflict style, see Table 10.1.

avoiding style
is indirect and involves strategies such as withdrawing, joking around, and ignoring; it can be cooperative or uncooperative, depending on the situation

TABLE 10.1 Conflict Tactics

Direct/Nice Tactics

Acknowledges/shows willingness to manage the problem

    Accepts responsibility

    Describes problem as external to the relationship

    Makes concessions; agrees to change behavior

    Offers to compromise

Supports/shows cooperative regard for other

    Expresses approval

    Excuses other

    Engages in cooperative "mind reading" (assumes partner is cooperative)

    Makes supportive remarks

    Shows affection

    Helps elaborate partner's thoughts

Seeks disclosure

    Asks partner to reveal attitudes

    Asks for criticism

Offers disclosure

    Offers benign reports of feelings

    Makes benign observations

    Describes own problems

    Expresses disagreement in a nonhostile manner

Indirect/Nice Tactics

Minimizes personal responsibility

    Implies that conflict is not a problem or does not exist

    Qualifies the extent or nature of the conflict

    Asks general questions

    Offers an excuse for own behavior

    Makes benign statement expressing desire to avoid conflict

Humor/teasing or distraction

    Makes a friendly joke

    Engages in lighthearted humor (not sarcasm)

Direct/Nasty Tactics

Makes accusations about partner

    Attributes negative qualities to partner

    Criticizes partner's behavior or thoughts

    Engages in negative mind reading (assumes partner's mind-set or motives are negative)

    Engages in negative talk

Commands behavioral change
Blames partner or demands change
Threatens partner
Demands immediate compliance
Hostile Questions
Asks question in a hostile manner
Asks leading questions
Put-downs
Rejects personal criticisms or description of the problem in a hostile manner
Uses nonverbal gestures to imply disgust or disapproval
Demeans the other through ridicule or sarcasm
Talks, shouts over, and prevents partner from finishing point
Indirect/Nasty Tactics
Minimizes personal responsibility
Does not acknowledge partner
Makes noncommittal remarks
Expresses negativity, depression, and whining nonverbally
Stonewalls (withdraws from the topic or discussion)
Attempts to change path of discussion
Focuses on procedural issues rather than the discussion at hand
Makes hostile demands to stop discussing the conflict
Makes statements that derail the conversation
Interrupts and disrupts partner's attempts to finish a point
Condescension
Offers hints or statements that reveal a negative attitude, superiority, or arrogance

SOURCE: Adapted from Canary, D. J. (2003).

When conflict erupts, individuals are likely to respond in ways that feel familiar and comfortable—regardless of the issue, the context, or the other person. Therefore, most people must both study and practice before they can develop a wide set of conflict skills and become effective at conflict management. Of course, even the most skillful person isn't always effective or able to choose the "right" or best tactic. Strong emotion can derail any person's ability to make good choices.

Emotion

Conflict is full of emotion; in fact, people rank the seriousness of their conflicts based on the emotions they experience during them (Jones, 2000). For example, when participants feel highly emotional, they are likely to describe their conflicts as "serious," and when they perceive disagreements to be aggressive, they describe their conflicts as "destructive." People become emotional both because their goals are being interfered with and in response to the other person's negativity. People commonly experience emotions like anger, jealousy, hurt, and guilt both during and after conflict interaction. These emotions influence how people communicate and can make it more difficult to manage conflict well (Guerrero & La Valley, 2006).

Anger is the emotion people most commonly associate with conflict, and it is often a central feature of conflict interactions. People become angry when their goals are thwarted.

These may be concrete goals, such as getting a day off from work, or more abstract goals, such as appearing competent at work. Unfortunately, when people feel angry, their first response may be to attack (Lazarus, 1991) through verbally assaulting, hitting, or yelling (Roseman, Wiest, & Swartz, 1994). Of course, people can respond more positively by listening, discussing issues calmly, owning their feelings, avoiding blame, and keeping the conversation on track (Canary, Spitzberg, & Semic, 1998; Guerrero, 1994).

Jealousy is another emotion that occurs during conflict in close relationships (Guerrero & Andersen, 1998). Jealousy may cause competitive and aggressive communication and behavior. In fact, research shows that jealousy is connected with violence and aggression for some people (Dutton, van Ginkel, & Landolt, 1996; Simonelli & Ingram, 1998). In one study, 15 percent of respondents indicated that jealousy had caused violence in their relationships (Mullen & Martin, 1994). However, most people do not respond to jealousy with physical aggression. More commonly, they use competitive strategies (yelling, criticizing, accusing), avoidance (withdrawal), and collaborative strategies (direct, positive, and problem-focused communication) (Guerrero & La Valley, 2006).

Hurt occurs when a person feels psychologically injured by another person (Vangelisti & Sprague, 1998), and it is accompanied by pain, anger, sadness, and suffering. Individuals tend to experience hurt when their personal or relational identities are attacked. Thus, hurt is likely to surface when partners use competitive fighting that includes verbal aggression. If your boss yells at you in front of other coworkers, she attacks your identity as a competent employee. Similarly, if you discover that your best friend has been making negative comments about you, not only is your individual identity assaulted but your understanding of your relationship with your friend has also been undermined.

Finally, and perhaps unexpectedly, guilt also accompanies conflict. Individuals feel guilty when they believe they have hurt or injured someone. Guilt is the flip side of hurt; the same behaviors that cause others to hurt can cause the perpetrators to feel guilty (Baumeister, Stillwell, & Heatherton, 1994). When people feel guilty, they tend to respond by trying to repair the damage by apologizing, admitting guilt, offering justifications, and trying to make the other party feel better (Guerrero, Andersen, & Afifi, 2007). However, sometimes people who feel guilty may respond with defensiveness or justifications because they have difficulty acknowledging that they have erred.

Regardless of the type of emotion experienced, people can become so overwhelmed with emotion during conflict that they act in an irrational or defensive manner. Gottman (1994) used the term **emotional flooding** to describe instances when people become highly aroused and disorganized in response to their partners' negative statements. Rather than focusing on resolving incompatibility, people who are flooded with emotions focus on defending themselves and alleviating the negative feelings they are experiencing.

Problematic Conflict Interactions

As you can see, conflict interactions are affected by the communication patterns and experiences two people develop with one another. You can probably think of people you disagree with calmly and politely, and of others with whom your conflicts escalate beyond civility. Conflict is especially likely to escalate when people use behaviors such as criticism, defensiveness, and aggression. Let's see how this happens.

The Cascade Model of Relational Conflict

John Gottman, a scholar of marital communication, has developed a model that explains how conflict escalates. In his model, dyadic communication behaviors interact to create what he describes as a "cascade" of negativity that, if left unchecked, will lead to relationship dissolution. The term **cascade** refers to the way in which one person's negative conflict behavior can trigger another person's negative behavior in such a way that their conflict patterns escalate and worsen, eventually leading to a decline in relationship satisfaction—similar to a person tumbling down rapids until he falls over the edge of the cliff. To better understand how conflict escalation occurs, see *Did You Know? He Who Cast the First Stone Probably Didn't.*

emotional flooding
instances when people become highly aroused and disorganized in response to their partners' negative statements

Cascade Model of Relational Conflict
John Gottman's model that explains how conflict escalates in a cascade of negativity that, if left unchecked, will lead to relationship dissolution

cascade
the way in which one person's negative conflict behavior can trigger another person's negative behavior in such a way that their conflict patterns escalate and worsen, eventually leading to a decline in relationship satisfaction

DID YOU KNOW?

He Who Cast the First Stone Probably Didn't

Our language has special words, like retaliation, retribution, and revenge, whose common prefix is meant to remind us that a punch thrown second is legally and morally different than a punch thrown first. Legitimate retribution, then, is meant to restore balance. Thus, an eye for an eye is fair, but an eye for an eyelash is not. When the European Union condemned Israel for bombing Lebanon in retaliation for the kidnapping of two Israeli soldiers, it did not question Israel's right to respond, but rather its "disproportionate use of force." It is OK to hit back—just not too hard.

However, research shows that people have trouble applying this principle. In a study conducted at University College London, pairs of volunteers were hooked up to a mechanical device that allowed each of them to exert pressure on the other's finger. Researchers began by exerting a fixed amount of pressure on the first volunteer's finger, who was then asked to exert precisely the same amount of pressure on the second volunteer's finger. Then the second volunteer was asked to exert the same amount of pressure on the first volunteer's finger. And so on. Volunteers took turns applying equal amounts of pressure while researchers measured the actual amount of pressure applied.

The results were striking. Although volunteers tried to respond to each other's touches with equal force, they typically responded with about 40 percent more force than they had just experienced. Each time a volunteer was touched, he touched back harder, which led the other volunteer to touch back even harder. What began as a game of soft touches quickly became a game of moderate pokes and then hard prods, even though both volunteers were doing their best to respond in kind.

Each was convinced that he was responding with equal force and that for some reason the other volunteer was escalating. Neither realized that the escalation was the natural by-product of a neurological quirk that causes the pain we receive to seem more painful than the pain we produce, so we usually give more pain than we have received.

Research teaches us that our reasons and our pains are more palpable, more obvious, and more real than are the reasons and pains of others. This leads to the escalation of mutual harm, to the illusion that others are solely responsible for it, and to the belief that our actions are justifiable responses to theirs.

None of this is to deny the roles that hatred, intolerance, avarice, and deceit play in human conflict. It is simply to say that basic principles of human psychology are important ingredients as well. Thus, we need to learn to stop trusting everything our brains tell us about others and to start trusting others themselves.

In his research, Gottman (1994, 1995) has found that a cascade of four behaviors, which he calls "the four horsemen of the apocalypse"—criticism, defensiveness, contempt, and stonewalling—pose a danger to relationships (see *Visual Summary 10.1: The Four Horsemen of the Apocalypse*).

Criticism According to Gottman, the first "horseman" is **criticism**, which involves attacking the partner's personality or character (rather than a specific behavior). As mentioned in our discussion above, a simple criticism about a behavior might be "I wish you would put your dirty clothes in the hamper instead of throwing them on the floor," while a character-based criticism would be "You are a complete slob." Criticism typically elicits criticism from the partner and, if not managed well, can set the scene for the second horseman, defensiveness.

criticism
attacking the partner's personality or character (rather than a specific behavior); the first of Gottman's "four horsemen"

The Four Horsemen of the Apocalypse

	SOUNDS AND LOOKS LIKE	EXAMPLE
CRITICISM attacking the partner's personality or character	• Making generalizations: "you always…", "you never…" and "you're the type of person who …"	• "You never think about how your behavior is affecting other people. I don't believe you are that forgetful; you just don't think about me"
DEFENSIVENESS attempts by the partner to protect or defend his/her identity	• Making excuses: "It's not my fault…" • Cross-complaining: meeting your partner's complaint, or criticism with a complaint of your own • Ignoring what your partner said • Disagreeing and then cross-complaining: "That's not true, you're the one who …" • Yes-butting: start off agreeing but end up disagreeing. • Repeating yourself without paying attention to what the other person is saying. • Whining: "It's not fair."	• **Sam**: "Why didn't you call the neighbors to let them know that we are not coming tonight as you said you would this morning ?" • **Pat**: "I was just too darn busy today. As a matter of fact you knew how busy my schedule was. Why didn't you just do it?"
CONTEMPT behavior that is designed to insult and psychologically harm the partner	• insults • name calling • sarcasm or mockery • sneering • rolling your eyes • curling your upper lip	• "I've been Mr. Mom to the kids all day, running around like mad to keep this house up and all you do when you come home from work is flop down on the sofa like a couch potato. You are a sorry excuse for a wife."
STONEWALLING one or both partners stop communicating, refuse to respond to each other's communication efforts, and withdraw from interaction. Partners may think they are trying to be "neutral" but stonewalling conveys disapproval, icy distance, separation, disconnection, and/or smugness.	• stony silence • monosyllabic mutterings • changing the subject • removing yourself physically	• **Chris**: You seem to be avoiding me lately. • **Steve**: Will you just leave me alone? • **Chris**: You never want to talk to me about anything. • **Steve**: When I have something to say, I'll let you know.

Defensiveness Defensiveness describes attempts by the partner to protect or defend his/her identity and character through excuses, explanations, denying responsibility for the truth of the attack, whining, and counterattacking. Although defensiveness appears to be a reasonable response to an attack, defensive behavior does not help resolve the conflict and in fact typically escalates it. As one partner defends him or herself, the other partner engages in even more hostile attempts to support his or her claims. People engage in defensiveness when they deny the legitimacy of others' negative claims or complaints about them and when they respond by counterattacking.

Contempt Contempt is harsher than criticism in that it is designed to insult and psychologically harm the partner. Contemptuous behavior treats the partner as if he or she is unimportant or inferior. It is expressed through put-downs, hostile jokes, sarcasm, mocking facial expressions and name-calling. One communicates contempt through statements such as "You are such a pig; it's no wonder nobody wants to live with you." Because contempt is such an assault on one's identity and self-worth, recipients are likely to respond with stonewalling, which is the fourth of Gottman's "horsemen."

Stonewalling If couples do not change their interaction patterns, stonewalling is likely to appear. **Stonewalling** occurs when one or both partners stop communicating, refuse to respond to each other's communication efforts, and withdraw from interaction. Once partners begin to stonewall, they may not be able to repair the relationship because they do not engage in the interactions necessary to do so. You should suspect that your partner is stonewalling if he or she refuses to discuss your relationship or your concerns or if your partner is reluctant to spend time with you.

How can you prevent the four horsemen from visiting your relationships? You can do so by talking about how the two of you talk with one another—that is, through **meta-communication.** One or both parties can attempt to repair negative behavior by pointing it out—such as saying, "Even if we're both angry, let's agree not to call each other names" or "Let's focus on this one issue and not talk about everything in our relationship." Even if these utterances are said in a grumpy and not-altogether-pleasant manner, they can still help couples decrease their negative communication patterns. However, these repair attempts must start as early as possible—before the couple has begun stonewalling one another. For more advice on managing conflict in your romantic relationships, see *Building Your Communication Skills: Tips for Managing and Resolving Conflict.*

defensiveness
attempts by the partner to protect or defend his/her identity and character through excuses, explanations, denying responsibility for the truth of the attack, whining, and counterattacking; the second of Gottman's "four horsemen"

contempt
behavior that is designed to insult and psychologically harm the partner; the third of Gottman's "four horsemen"

stonewalling
occurs when one or both partners stop communicating, refuse to respond to each other's communication efforts, and withdraw from interaction; the fourth of Gottman's "four horsemen"

meta-communication
talking about the ways in which you and your partner communicate with one another

Building Your Communication SKILLS

Tips for Managing and Resolving Conflict

Managing and resolving conflict requires emotional maturity, self-control, and empathy. It can be tricky, frustrating, and even frightening. You can ensure that the process is as positive as possible by sticking to the following conflict resolution guidelines:

Make the relationship your priority.
Maintaining and strengthening the relationship, rather than "winning" the argument, should always be your first priority. Be respectful of the other person and his or her viewpoint.

Focus on the present.
If you're holding on to old hurts and resentments, your ability to see the reality of the current situation will be impaired. Rather than looking to the past and assigning blame, focus on what you can do in the here-and-now to solve the problem.

Pick your battles.
Conflicts can be draining, so it's important to consider whether the issue is really worthy of your time and energy. Maybe you don't want to surrender a parking space if you've been circling for 15 minutes. But if there are dozens of spots, arguing over a single space isn't worth it.

Be willing to forgive.
Resolving conflict is impossible if you're unwilling or unable to forgive. Resolution lies in releasing the urge to punish, which can never compensate for our losses and only adds to our injury by further depleting and draining our lives.

Know when to let something go.
If you can't come to an agreement, agree to disagree. It takes two people to keep an argument going. If a conflict is going nowhere, you can choose to disengage and move on.

SOURCE: Retrieved from *Conflict Resolution Skills*. HELPGUIDE.org. http://www.helpguide.org/mental/eq8_conflict_resolution.htm on August 24, 2010.

Of course, not all conflict is enacted so negatively. To help you increase the likelihood that you will engage in conflict productively, later in this chapter we describe two positive approaches to conflict management. However, first we will examine how society impacts individuals' behavior and relationships.

THE INDIVIDUAL, CONFLICT MANAGEMENT, AND SOCIETY

The discussion thus far presents conflict as a relatively individual and/or dyadic process in which participants' interests, conflict styles, and relationships impact how it unfolds. However, conflict interactions are also influenced by a variety of social factors, including power, culture, and gender socialization.

Power

Power refers to a person's ability to influence the behavior, thoughts, or feelings of another (Impett & Peplau, 2006). As we have discussed throughout this book, a hierarchy exists in societies that grants more power to some people than others. For example, people who have extensive resources or who are connected to people with resources may have more influence or power to make decisions, control activities, and win arguments. Typically, within a dyad or group, the person who is more dependent on the relationship or the other party will have less power, control, and influence (Molm, 1997). For example, employees are often more dependent on their bosses and may, therefore, be reluctant to engage in competitive tactics.

In many relationships, the members perceive themselves as equally influential; the majority of married couples report that power is balanced in their relationships (Blumstein & Schwartz, 1983). However, even if both members of a dyad have equal power overall, each may not have equal power in every context. The person with more financial resources may have more influence regarding expenditures, for instance. Thus, the power dynamics inherent in a specific conflict interaction often affect its outcome.

A person's power in a particular interaction often impacts the way he or she communicates during conflict as well. People who are high in power may be less concerned

power
a person's ability to influence the behavior, thoughts, or feelings of another

with how their conflict partners respond and therefore may be more likely to use direct requests, demands, and competitive behaviors such as insults, threats, and verbal aggression (Davidson, McElwee, & Hannan, 2004; Jae-Yop & Emery, 2003). Your boss may feel free to yell at you when you make a mistake, but you likely don't feel free to do the same to the boss. People who feel that they have little power may be more indirect and less negative and attempt to achieve their goals through tactics such as complaining, hinting, or obliging (Sagrestano, Heavey, & Christensen, 2006). Dyads that are equal in power are likely better positioned to bargain with one another because they each have resources and control.

In addition to power affecting the ways in which a person behaves during conflict interactions, power itself can be an issue that people fight over. For many if not most people in the United States, having and using power is a positive experience; consequently, participants often struggle over access to it (Coleman, 2000). When people fight over minor issues—such as who will pick the movie or who is right about a disputed fact—they are often actually fighting about who is in control or has power. People who feel a need to win at any cost are typically struggling over power issues.

Power is embedded in almost every conflict, and you will find it easier to manage your conflicts if you understand the role power is playing within them. If you have a lot of power in a relationship, for example, you will find it useful to recognize that others may not be as forthcoming or direct with you as you are with them and that you need to avoid venting on those with less power just because you can. In addition, if you find yourself frequently engaging in conflict over which hip-hop artist is better, whether the ending to the final *Harry Potter* book was a disappointment, or other minor issues, you may be struggling over your need for power. Once you recognize this, you may find it easier to avoid conflict over unimportant issues.

Just as a person's power position within a society or relationship influences conflict interactions, the specific cultures of the individuals involved can play a significant role in how people respond or fail to respond to conflict.

Culture

Culture impacts the ways in which people understand, approach, and enact conflict. Individuals' cultural values also influence how they expect conflict to unfold and the types of communication strategies they use. Three cultural values that often influence conflict interactions are individualism-collectivism, low versus high context, and power difference (Ting-Toomey, 1985; Ting-Toomey et al., 2000). **Individualistic cultures** are those that emphasize individual identities, goals, and rights over those of the group, while **collectivistic cultures** emphasize group identity, goals, and concerns over individual desires. **Low-context cultures** prefer communication that is explicit and direct and relatively easy to decode, while **high-context cultures** convey intention or meaning through the communication context (e.g., one's social role) and through nonverbals (tone of voice, silence) (Trubisky, Ting-Toomey, & Lin, 1991). Finally, **power distance** describes the degree to which a culture stresses hierarchy and status differences (Marcus & Gould, 2000). Thus, cultures with **low power distance,** such as the United States, tend to see people as relatively equal and deemphasize status difference, while those with **high power distance,** for instance Japan, emphasize hierarchy, social position, and status differences.

Conflict participants who come from individualistic, low-context cultures that value low power distance (such as the United States and Germany) view conflict quite differently than do those from collectivistic, high-context cultures that value high power distance (such as Thailand) (Garcia, 1996). For example, during conflict, people in the United States and Germany are likely to be more direct, expect to openly address individual goals and interests, prefer efficiency, and focus on the outcomes or results of their conflicts (Ting-Toomey, 1985; Leung, Au, Fernández-Dols, & Iwawaki, 1992). On the

culture
learned patterns of perceptions, values, and behaviors shared by a group of people

individualistic cultures
cultures that emphasize individual identities, goals, and rights over those of the group

collectivistic cultures
cultures that emphasize group identity, goals, and concerns over individual desires

low-context cultures
cultures that prefer communication that is explicit and direct and relatively easy to decode

high-context cultures
cultures that convey intention or meaning through the communication context and through nonverbals

power distance
a value orientation that refers to the extent to which less-powerful members of institutions and organizations within a culture expect and accept an unequal distribution of power

low power distance cultures
cultures that tend to see people as relatively equal and deemphasize status differences

high power distance cultures
cultures that tend to emphasize hierarchy, social position, and status differences

contrary, people in cultures such as Thailand and Denmark place more emphasis on face, or how they are viewed by others, than outcomes; they focus more on the conflict process than its specific outcomes, are likely to be more indirect, and desire and positively evaluate subtlety. Thus, if a German citizen and a Thai citizen engaged in a conflict over who should be next to be waited on at a store, the German citizen would be more likely to say something like "Don't butt in line! I've been waiting the longest; it's my turn." On the other hand, a Thai national might be more likely to suggest, "You may not have seen me waiting here for the past ten minutes; perhaps your view was obscured by the display. But if you desire to go first, then that's okay." However, the Thai may expect that the German would be sensitive to her subtlety and counter with "No, no; you were first, please go ahead."

As you can imagine, when individuals with different cultural orientations engage in conflict, they may find it difficult to manage their disagreements, because they do not even agree on how they should talk about their differences. During intercultural conflicts, for instance, participants from collectivistic cultures may be offended by the other party's disregard of their image, while participants from individualistic cultures may be frustrated by what they perceive as the other party's refusal to speak directly and openly about the issues. Sensitivity to these differences can render cross-cultural conflict interactions more successful.

A third societal factor that can influence conflict interactions—gender—combines aspects of both culture and power. Cultures determine what is gender-appropriate behavior. And in most cultures, men have more power than women. We discuss this topic next.

Gender

According to gender stereotypes, women's conflict strategies are more positive and indirect, while men's are more competitive and direct. However, research indicates that during *actual* conflict, women are more positive in some relationships, while in others they are more negative and competitive.

In interactions with strangers or acquaintances, men and women tend to react in relatively stereotypical ways. When they don't know the other person very well, men are more competitive than women, and women are more likely to accommodate and compromise (Canary & Emmers-Sommer, 1997). Research on conflict in same-sex friendships also suggests that men and women engage in relatively stereotypical conflict behaviors. Females are perceived by their peers to use constructive conflict resolution strategies more frequently than are males (Osterman et al., 1997), and girls are likely to use problem solving, withdrawal, and accommodation more frequently than are boys (de Wied, Branje, & Meeus, 2006).

These findings reflect the fact that in the United States, women are socialized to focus on relationships and to be accommodating and indirect in their interactions with others (La France & Harris, 2004), while men are socialized to be more competitive. Each sex's behavior with strangers, acquaintances, and friends, then, is consistent with their socialization. However, in cross-sex relationships, these stereotypes do not always hold.

In heterosexual romantic relationships, women enact more of several negative behaviors than do men, including demands (Mikolic, Parker, & Pruitt, 1997), overt hostility (Zuroff & Duncan, 1999), criticism (Kelley et al., 1978), and distributive (or competitive) tactics (Messman & Mikesell, 2000). At the same time, men tend to avoid conflict with their romantic partners (Denton, Burleson, Hobb, Von Stein, & Rodriguez, 2001; Gottman & Levenson, 1988).

Why are men more avoidant and women more competitive in heterosexual relationships, contrary to their socialization? Research shows that the person who wants change in a relationship or situation is more likely to confront the other party. In addition, the person who does the confronting is more likely to use competitive, negative messages

(Caughlin & Vangelisti, 2006). In this way, the person who is unhappy is more likely to use negative conflict behaviors, whether it is a woman or a man.

Despite these differences, men and women's behaviors in heterosexual relationships are more similar than different. For example, one study of wives and husbands' conflict interactions revealed that 75 percent of their conflict behaviors were the same (Margolin & Wampold, 1981). In addition, both men and women are more likely to use positive than negative conflict tactics when they disagree.

To sum up, societal expectations and gender socialization have a strong influence on men's and women's conflict behavior. However, structural power differences in heterosexual relationships probably influence the strategies that men and women enact with their romantic partners.

We have discussed a wide range of factors that influence conflict, as well as strategies that may be more or less effective in specific situations and relationships. However, we have not yet addressed an issue that is important to effective conflict management—ethics.

ETHICS AND CONFLICT MANAGEMENT

In the heat of conflict, people say and do things that hurt others, damage their relationships, and lead to regret. How can you prevent this from happening to you? You can do so by remembering some basic rules of ethical conflict communication.

Be Truthful

Truthfulness plays a fundamental role in ethical communication for two reasons: People expect you to be truthful, and communication has consequences. It can be tempting to lie or withhold information to prevent a conflict, but if others discover that you have not revealed important information or that you have overtly deceived them, they may find it difficult to trust or forgive you. However, we must offer an important caveat to being truthful: You should not use honesty as an excuse for being harsh or attacking your partner.

Avoid Name-Calling

Ethical communicators are thoughtful about the types of language they use during conflict—particularly language that refers to others. You may not think about the names you use to describe individuals or groups as an ethical issue. However, calling people names denigrates their humanity and their identities, which *is* an ethical issue. Most people recognize that it is not appropriate to use racial and ethnic slurs or sexist and homophobic references. However, fewer people realize that calling a disagreeable coworker an "idiot," a friend whose politics you disagree with a "fascist," or your roommate a "jerk" is also unethical.

Own Your Messages

Every message contains multiple potential meanings, and ethical communicators "own," or acknowledge, the meanings of their messages. People fail to own their messages when they engage in meaning denial, which occurs when one meaning is "both present in the interaction and denied as meant" (Deetz, 1990). For example, if you are sarcastic and use hostile humor with your friend but deny that you are angry, you have engaged in meaning denial (as we discussed in Chapter 1). If you act this way, you allow yourself to express anger without allowing the other person the same opportunity.

Avoid Coercion

Coercion occurs when people are compelled to behave in a particular way against their wills due to threats of or actual physical or psychological pressure. For example, some individuals use physical violence and threats of violence to control their partners' behavior or

to keep them from leaving the relationship. But coercion can be less obvious. A boss can coerce an employee into not taking a scheduled vacation by hinting at possible repercussions, ex-spouses can threaten to take each other to court if their demands are not met, and one friend can be coercive by ignoring another friend unless their requests are fulfilled.

Based on our discussion of ethics, you may think that effective conflict management involves not doing the "wrong" things. However, you can also use a variety of positive and constructive behaviors to improve your conflict-management skills, as we discuss next.

IMPROVING YOUR CONFLICT-MANAGEMENT SKILLS

Some people are able to manage conflict effectively by being thoughtful and strategic and by using constructive, cooperative styles of communication that reflect competence. Let's look at these effective conflict-management strategies.

People with good conflict skills avoid coercion and hostile attacks.

A Strategic Approach to Conflict Management

The more thoughtful and strategic you are during conflict interactions, the more effective you are likely to be. However, a strategic approach to conflict doesn't begin with the specific tactics you choose; it can (and should) begin much earlier. Before you even initiate a discussion over an issue in conflict, you should know what you want to occur as a result of the interaction. If you wish to confront your roommate about not doing his fair share of the housework, you should first decide what your goal is. Do you want your roommate to do half the chores? To do more than he is currently doing? To appreciate all the efforts you put in? To pay for a housecleaner? Or do you desire some combination of these outcomes? You will be far more successful and satisfied with your conflict interactions if you go into them knowing what you want.

Second, decide if the issue is worth confronting—or worth confronting now. You know what you want, but do you have a reasonable chance of accomplishing your goals? That is, how likely is your roommate to actually participate equally in household chores even if he agrees to do so? Can he afford to help pay for a housecleaner? Will he remember to be appreciative? If the answer truly is no, you may choose not to engage in the conflict. Alternatively, you may decide you do want to have the conversation, but perhaps not right now, because both of you are hungry and tired.

If you decide that the conflict is worth confronting, you next want to try to understand the other party's goals. What, for example, do you think is your roommate's goal? Does he want a clean house without having to do the work? Does he not notice or care when the house is dirty? If he does want a clean house but doesn't want to actually clean it, he may be more amenable to hiring a housekeeper. On the other hand, if he does not notice or even care if the house is dirty, he may be unwilling to contribute financially, is unlikely to do his share of the work, and/or will probably fail to appreciate the efforts that you make. Depending on your understanding of his goals and interests, you will likely suggest different solutions.

You have one more step to complete before you are ready to confront your roommate; you need to plan the interaction. More specifically, you should think about when and

where the conversation should take place and what tactics you believe will be most effective. Typically, you will want to choose a time when neither you nor your roommate is angry, rushed, or stressed. In addition, you should probably have the conversation in private. If others are around, one or both of you may behave more competitively or avoid the interaction entirely because you are embarrassed to be observed by others. Finally, you should think through how you will explain your dissatisfaction with the current state of affairs and how you will frame your suggested solutions. Once you have done all of this, you are ready to engage! But you need to know how to communicate competently so that the conversation can help you accomplish your goals and maintain your relationship, as we discuss next.

The Competence Model of Conflict

Perhaps the best model to guide communicators as they work to improve their conflict-management skills is the **competence model of conflict** developed by communication scholars Dan Canary and Brian Spitzberg (1989). A competence-based approach to managing conflict is valuable both because it works and because it is an ethical approach to conflict management. The competence model is ethical in that it emphasizes the rights of all conflict parties and it presupposes that opposing parties will respect each other and will not exploit, harm, or ignore one another (Canary & Lakey, 2006).

A Definition of Competence

Competence is composed of two elements: **appropriateness,** which is defined as following the relevant rules, norms, and expectations for specific relationships and situations; and **effectiveness,** which involves achieving one's goals successfully. Based on this definition of competence, a conflict behavior is judged to be effective only within specific situations or relationships (Canary, Cupach, & Serpe, 2001; Canary & Lakey, 2006; Spitzberg, Canary, & Cupach, 1994). For example, while competitive strategies may be competent (that is, appropriate and effective) in the context of a sales contest at work, they are not likely to be effective during a discussion with one's parents, for they are not appropriate even if they are effective.

Developing Competence During Conflict

Competence during conflict interactions requires a degree of "mindfulness," or paying attention (Ting-Toomey & Oetzel, 2001), a concept we have touched on throughout this book. Mindfulness during conflict is not as difficult as it may seem, because conflict is not routine behavior, and people tend to pay more attention to nonroutine behavior and interactions (Canary & Lakey, 2006). Thus, people can consciously choose their conflict strategies and tactics, and over time, these choices can become unconscious or mindless (Canary, 2003; Langer, 1989).

A variety of strategies can help people engage in conflict more effectively (Canary & Lakey, 2006). First, individuals should learn to anticipate conflict situations so they can exercise control once the situation arises. For example, if you are in a bad mood, are running late for an appointment, and/or are under a lot of stress, you will be more likely to feel irritable and to engage in a conflict due to these contributing factors. Similarly, you likely know that certain topics, people, or situations can precipitate aggression, irritability, or feelings of powerlessness that are likely to lead to conflict interactions. However, if you can anticipate your negative reactions, you can limit them and control your behavioral choices (Zillman, 1993). Thus, if you have failed an exam, are stuck in traffic, and develop a headache, you should recognize that you are more likely to have a conflict with your roommate or family member once you arrive home. If you take the time to think about your experiences and how you feel, you can become more mindful, calmer, and less likely to vent your frustration on others.

However, if despite your efforts, conflict arises, you can still be mindful of the choices you make (Zillman, 1993). First, you should remind yourself that the outcome of the conflict is determined largely by your own skills and that you can control yourself and the situation. Second, recognize your attitudes about the conflict, yourself, and the other

competence model of conflict
a model developed by communication scholars Dan Canary and Brian Spitzberg that emphasizes appropriateness and effectiveness

appropriateness
following the relevant rules, norms, and expectations for specific relationships and situations

effectiveness
achieving one's goals successfully

During your conflict interactions, are you more appropriate or more effective, or are you both? What changes could you make in your conflict style that would make you more appropriate and/or effective?

conflict strategy
decisions people make based on how direct or indirect they want to be and they how cooperative or competitive they will be

strategy control
behaving mindfully, assessesing information and options, and acquiring increased understanding of the conflict and the partner

party. If you accept responsibility for your own contributions to the conflict, refrain from seeing your conflict partner in a negative way, and consider your own and your partner's goals, you will more effectively manage your emotions, your choice of conflict strategies, and your reactions to your conflict partner (Canary & Lakey, 2006). Still, during the conflict interaction, you need to also be aware of your wish to maintain your relationship and identity.

Communicating Competently During Conflict

Overall, people involved in conflict make two general choices regarding their communication with other conflict parties. People decide how direct or indirect they want to be, and they decide how cooperative or competitive they will be (Sillars et al., 2004). Based on these dimensions, individuals can choose to use any of the **conflict strategies** shown in Figure 10.1. Thus, conflict participants make general strategic choices that then affect the specific conflict tactics they choose.

What does this mean in terms of conflict behavior? It means that individuals should engage in **strategy control.** When behaving mindfully, one assesses more information and options and therefore acquires increased understanding of the conflict and the partner. In turn, these behaviors help people choose conflict behaviors that are responsive to the partner and the self and increase the possibility for cooperation, collaboration, and compromise (Canary & Lakey, 2006). If you become angry with your boss for promoting a coworker instead of you, for example, rather than marching into her office and expressing your extreme displeasure, you should spend time analyzing your feelings, your goals, and the conflict strategies that will help you accomplish your goals. Although ideally you would like your boss to rescind her decision and promote you, a few minutes of reflection will likely help you see that this is improbable. Instead, reflecting may help you understand that you are more likely to persuade your boss to promote you the next time an opportunity arises, especially if you use a collaborative conflict style. To help you become more strategic and competent, review the principles of interpersonal conflict discussed in *Building Your Communication Skills: Principles of Interpersonal Conflict.*

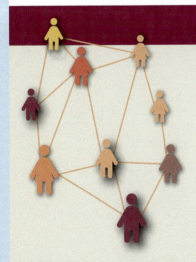

Building Your Communication **SKILLS**

Principles of Interpersonal Conflict

At first, changing your conflict behavior may seem daunting, but effective conflict management involves a concrete set of skills that you can learn and incorporate into your everyday interactions. To help you, we offer five principles by Canary and Lakey (2010) that represent "best practices" for responding to conflict.

Principle 1. Minimize negative interpretations. People respond to others based on how intentional or controllable they believe others' behaviors to be. The more you believe others intend to interfere with your goals, the more negatively you interpret the behavior—and the angrier and more competitive you are likely to be in response (Lindner, 2006). If you minimize negative interpretations of others, you will experience fewer feelings of hurt, anger, and retaliation.

Principle 2. Take others' perspectives. Perspective taking involves recognizing that people perceive the world from different vantage points, depending on their experiences, culture, sex, age, power, and other characteristics (Johnson, Johnson, & Tjosvold, 2006). It requires you to consider how the other person feels about and understands the issue in conflict, based on *their* vantage point. If your roommate consistently fails to do his share of the household chores, you are probably unhappy about it. If you assume that he does so because he is lazy, you may become angry and confrontational. However, if you take his perspective and realize that as a full-time student with a full-time job, he is constantly pressed for time, you are likely to be less angry, more sympathetic, and

better able to discuss your dissatisfaction and how to resolve it. As you probably realize, perspective taking helps minimize negative interpretations.

Principle 3. Balance your relationships. Successful relationships are marked by the partners' ability to balance their negative behaviors with many more-positive behaviors. You should strive to engage in at least five times as many positive as negative behaviors (Gottman, 1994). If your relationship is undergoing difficulty, you will need to focus on creating positive interactions through compliments, hugs, expressions of appreciation, offers of assistance, and other supportive actions. The positive environment you create will help your relationship weather conflicts and negativity.

Principle 4. Focus on interests, not positions. People who understand their own and others' underlying goals (or interests) are better able to generate solutions. Before you approach your boss for a raise, for example, you should understand your own and your boss's interests. In this case, the raise represents your "position." In contrast, your interests are the underlying reasons for your position—for example, wanting to be recognized, to be rewarded for extra effort, or to be able to afford a home. If you understand your interests, you will be able to generate more avenues for meeting them. Thus, if your interest is to receive recognition, then a new title, a new office, a promotion, or some other option may satisfy you. On the other hand, your boss's position may be that she cannot afford to give you a raise; her interests, however, may include a desire to retain you, to prevent your colleagues from also requesting raises, and to balance the department's budget. If each of you focus on your own and the other's interests, you will likely be able to find a solution that satisfies you both. For example, a new title and a bigger office may make you feel appreciated and increase your desire to stay at the company, while it allows your boss to stay within her budget.

Principle 5. Listen actively. Listening actively is a powerful skill (Stone, Patton, & Heen, 1999). Listening carefully and not judgmentally helps you understand others and helps them understand you. When you listen to understand others and not just to persuade them, they are more likely to reveal their interests and goals, to be open to your suggestions, and to listen nonjudgmentally to you. Listening actively requires that you listen both to what is being said and what is not being said, that you ask open-ended questions to help you elicit information and understanding, and that you provide supportive feedback as you listen.

SUMMARY

Last night, Olivia finally approached Holly about their ongoing morning conflict. She explained to Holly that she hated having to rush to campus and that it made her feel stressed every morning. Holly understood but said that she was always running late because Olivia took so long in the bathroom in the morning. Consequently, Olivia agreed to get up earlier and get out of the bathroom quicker so that Holly could get ready and they could leave on time. They also decided to discuss the issue again in two weeks to see if the proposed solution was working for both of them.

The information in this chapter will help you manage your conflicts in a more effective manner, as Olivia and Holly finally did. The chapter has been designed to provide you with the fundamental skills that you need to do so. Toward that end, we encourage you to become more reflective and deliberative in your conflict interactions. That is, we want you to explore your own and others' goals when you engage in conflict and to seek to determine each of your underlying interests so that you can develop solutions that allow each of you to fulfill your most important goals. We also suggest that you strategically select the conflict style that best suits your relationship and goals, such as using more collaborative strategies for important relationships and less-competitive strategies for unimportant issues. If you do so, we believe that you can improve your conflict interactions as well as transform—and enhance—your personal and professional relationships.

KEY TERMS

appropriateness 249
avoiding conflict style 237
behavioral conflicts 231
cascade 240
Cascade Model of Relational Conflict 240
catharsis 231
collaborating or problem-solving
   conflict style 234
collectivistic cultures 245
competence model of conflict 249
competing or dominating
   conflict style 233
competitive conflict style 233
compromising conflict style 234
concessions 236
conflict 228

conflict strategy 250
conflict style 233
conflict tactic 233
contempt 243
cooperative conflict style 233
criticism 241
culture 245
defensiveness 241
direct conflict style 233
effectiveness 249
emotional flooding 240
high-context cultures 245
high power-distance cultures 245
incompatibility 229
indirect conflict style 233
indirect fighting 236

individualistic cultures 245
interdependent 228
interests 228
limited resources 229
low-context cultures 245
low power-distance cultures 245
meta-communication 243
personality conflicts 232
persuasive discourse 230
power 244
power distance 245
relationship rules 232
stonewalling 243
strategy control 250
yielding or accommodating
   conflict style 236

CHAPTER REVIEW QUESTIONS

1. Why is interdependence a central feature of conflict?
2. What are the four functions of conflict?
3. What are the three categories of conflict issues?
4. How do conflict styles and tactics differ?
5. What are the six conflict styles? What are the two underlying dimensions that differentiate the six styles?
6. How does power influence conflict interactions?
7. What are the components of Gottman's Cascade Model of conflict?
8. What are the two primary components of the competence model?
9. What is meant by a strategic approach to conflict management?

ACTIVITIES

1. **Conflict Life-Learning Inventory**
Take a few moments to jot down responses to the following questions. Be prepared to discuss your responses; however, you may choose what information to share and the depth of the disclosure of your life experience with conflict.
   - What impressions of conflict do you recall from your childhood?
   - How did you experience conflict as a child?
   - Did adults and children engage in conflict together, or was conflict reserved for either adults or children?
   - What did you learn from what you experienced?
   - As an adult, what conflict situations are you most comfortable in?
   - As an adult, what conflict situations are you least comfortable in?
   - What conclusions do you draw about the influence your early-life experiences may have on your responses to conflict as an adult?

2. **Understanding Others' Perspectives**
Recall the last time you became angry at someone. Write down what that person did to make you angry. Next, imagine that you had done to someone else exactly what that person did to you. Then, list as many reasonable explanations as you can think of for why you might have done this. Finally, write a one- to two-page analysis. Identify exactly what it was about the behavior that angered you. In your analysis, describe the role that attribution played in your response to the other person's behavior. How can perspective taking alter the way in which you respond to others' behavior? What problems might you encounter in trying to engage in perspective taking during conflict?

3. **Moderating Your Conflicts**
For one week, make every attempt to de-escalate your conflicts with others. To do so, you should listen actively to others, choose effective conflict strategies, take responsibility for your actions and actively seek collaborative solutions. At the end of the week, write a two-to-three page paper wherein you discuss your experiences moderating your conflicts.

WEB ACTIVITIES

1. What is your preferred conflict style? To help you understand your personal conflict style, go to http://findarticles.com/p/articles/mi_qa3616/is_200407/ai_n9425833/ and read the short article "What is Your Conflict Style? Understanding and Dealing With Your Conflict Style." Next, write a one-page paper analyzing which conflict style discussed in the article seems most like your own and why. Then, discuss how the styles discussed in the article are similar to or different from the ones discussed in this chapter.

2. **Friendship Rules**
   One of the primary sources of conflict among friends is breaking often-unstated friendship rules. Go to http://teenadvice.about.com/od/friends/tp/friendship_rules.htm and read the six friendship rules posted on the site. Which of these rules do you think are fundamental rules friends should follow? Can you think of others that should be added to the list?

11

SMALL GROUP COMMUNICATION PROCESSES

*M*y most interesting group experience happened last year in my Family Communication class. We were a group of five students, and each of us was supposed to write one part of the research paper. It was fun because we had the chance to be creative and write about any subject related to family communication. However, one member never e-mailed his work on time, didn't do a good, thoughtful job, and didn't show up for group meetings. The four of us met often, became friends, and always knew what the others were doing. The fifth member never knew what was going on because he never communicated with us. That part was frustrating even though we tried to work around him.

The group experience reported by our student Dawn is typical and illustrates many of the issues we will discuss in this chapter. As she reports, group work can be productive and fun when group members are motivated and get along. However, poor communication or, as in Dawn's case, the lack of participation by one or more group members can diminish the final product.

In this chapter, we begin by explaining what a small group is and then discuss reasons for studying small group communication. After this, we identify the benefits and challenges of small group work and discuss the various communication roles group members can assume. Next, we turn to a discussion of group leadership and a description of the group communication process in decision-making and problem-solving groups. Finally, we discuss the impact of society on small group communication, addressing the issues of power, cultural diversity, and technology. We conclude with suggestions for how you can communicate more effectively and ethically in small groups.

Once you have read this chapter, you will be able to:

- Define small group communication.
- Explain four reasons for learning about small group communication.
- Identify and give an example of each task, relational, and individual role people take in small groups.
- Describe the five steps in the problem-solving agenda.
- Analyze the characteristics of communication that occur during the three phases of small group decision making.
- Identify how diversity influences small group processes.
- Give three guidelines for communicating more ethically in your small group.
- Recognize ways to improve your own small group communication skills.

CHAPTER OUTLINE

WHAT IS SMALL GROUP COMMUNICATION?

A Small Number of People
A Common Purpose
A Connection with Each Other
An Influence on Each Other

THE IMPORTANCE OF SMALL GROUP COMMUNICATION

Reasons to Study Small Group Communication
Advantages and Disadvantages of Group Work

SMALL GROUP COMMUNICATION AND THE INDIVIDUAL

Types of Communication Roles
Effective Small Group Communication

THE INDIVIDUAL, SMALL GROUP COMMUNICATION, AND SOCIETY

Power and Group Communication
Cultural Diversity and Small Group Communication

ETHICS AND SMALL GROUP COMMUNICATION

IMPROVING YOUR SMALL GROUP COMMUNICATION SKILLS

Summary
Key Terms
Chapter Review Questions
Activities
Web Activities

small group communication
communication among a small number of people who share a common purpose or goal, who feel connected to each other, and who coordinate their behavior

WHAT IS SMALL GROUP COMMUNICATION?

You might think that a small group is simply a collection of individuals, but we (and most communication scholars) have a more specific definition. To acquire a clear idea of what we'll be discussing in this chapter, let's consider two types of groups: (1) a group of people waiting in line for a movie and (2) a group of students working on a semester-long research project. The first type of group is not the focus of this chapter, while the second is. We will explain why as we articulate our definition of small group communication.

We define **small group communication** as "communication among a small number of people who share a common purpose or goal, feel connected to each other, and coordinate their behavior" (Arrow, McGrath, & Berdahl, 2000, p. 34). Let's look more closely at who the small group in this definition represents.

A Small Number of People

Most experts agree that three is the fewest number of people that can constitute a small group and that five to seven people is the optimum upper limit for working groups. This general guideline may vary depending on whether the small group is working face-to-face or in virtual teams. In general, small groups of three (whether working face-to-face or virtually) experience better communication in terms of openness and accuracy than larger groups of six. Communication becomes more difficult as group size increases; people may feel more anonymous, and discussions become unwieldy and unfocused as members tend to break into small groups. However, a recent study found that although group size does decrease the quality of communication in face-to-face groups, size has less impact on groups working virtually (Lowry, Roberts, Romano, Cheney, & Hightower, 2006). Under this portion of our definition, people waiting in line for a movie would not likely be considered a small group because any number of people can wait for a movie.

A Common Purpose

While a group of people waiting for a movie fulfills the second requirement of our definition—they share a purpose—that purpose is rather limited. Here we focus on communication in small groups that are working toward a common purpose. Sometimes the purpose may be assigned by an instructor or employer—a semester-long course project, completing a marketing research study for a client, or working together to recommend a candidate for a job. Sometimes groups from many organizations meet to solve a specific problem, such as when a task force is assembled to study the state's disaster preparedness. Having a clear purpose or goal is important and is directly (positively) related to group productivity and increased work performance (Crown, 2007).

A Connection with Each Other

Again, to compare our two kinds of groups, people waiting for the movie need not feel connected to each other. However, work groups need to experience a group identity and recognize their interdependence, because when members do not feel a part of the group, as in Dawn's experience, the group won't function as it should. The challenge for the small group is to find ways to create a sense of group identity for all members, and communication is often key to making this happen.

An Influence on Each Other

Members of small groups need to coordinate their behavior, and in doing so, they may exert influence on each other. People waiting for a movie need not exert influence on each other, whereas members of a work group do. This influence can be positive or negative, and each group member contributes to the success or failure of the whole group. Most groups aren't successful without the positive contribution of all members. In Dawn's experience, for instance, the negative influence of one member undermined the success for all.

In sum, a collection of people waiting in line for a movie rarely constitutes a "small group" because they typically don't influence one another, they don't feel connected to each other or develop a shared identity, and they share a common purpose only in the most limited way. With these features of small groups in mind, let's look at individual communication in small groups.

THE IMPORTANCE OF SMALL GROUP COMMUNICATION

Small groups seem to be an integral part of life. You probably belong to a number of them—social groups, course project groups, work teams at your job, or perhaps support or interest groups in your community. However, you might be surprised to discover that learning how to communicate better in groups can actually enhance your academic and professional achievements. Let's see why this is so.

Reasons to Study Small Group Communication

There are at least four reasons to study small group communication: Small groups are a fact of life, they enhance college performance, they enhance your career success, and they can enhance your personal life.

A Fact of Life

Some people say they hate working in small groups, and they are not alone. A term actually exists, **grouphate**, which describes the distaste and aversion people feel toward working in groups (Sorensen, 1981). As one of our students told us, "I would rather do the whole project myself than try to get together with a group of students I don't know and might not trust to do a good job." A recent study found that students (in a small group communication course) who reported an active dislike for working in groups (grouphate) also reported experiencing less group cohesion, consensus, and relational satisfaction in their group work (Myers & Goodboy, 2005). A person's active aversion to group work, of course, may negatively influence the experience.

Whether you love working in groups or hate it, groups are everywhere. Most of them are either primary or secondary groups (Poole, 1999). **Primary groups** are those that provide us with a sense of belonging and affection, the most common being family or social groups. While these groups are essential, this chapter's focus is on **secondary groups**—those that meet principally to solve problems, as do support groups or work groups. Secondary groups can involve long-term commitments, as in the case of support groups that meet regularly for months or even years or standing committees in an organization. Probably most common are the short-term project groups that students belong to in various classes. Increasingly, this type of group work is supported by technologies such as e-mail, electronic bulletin boards, and chat rooms, which we'll discuss later in the chapter.

Increasing numbers of people join support groups, like this one, to deal with crises, life transitions, or chronic health conditions.

grouphate
the distaste and aversion that people feel toward working in groups

primary groups
groups that provide members with a sense of belonging and affection

secondary groups
groups that meet principally to solve problems

Enhanced College Performance

Learning about small group communication can help you in college and later in your career. Considerable research indicates that college students who study in small groups perform at higher intellectual levels, learn better, and have better attitudes toward subject matter than those who study alone (Allen & Plax, 2002). This is probably because you encounter different interpretations and ideas when studying with others; and, as we'll see in the next section, group work in general leads to higher-quality thinking and decision making. Thus, learning how to interact more effectively in groups and seeking out learning groups to participate in can lead to enhanced college performance.

Enhanced Career Success

Effective communication in small groups is also essential to career success. According to a *Wall Street Journal* survey, when corporate recruiters rate the most important attributes of job candidates for business jobs, "Topping the list are communication, interpersonal skills and the ability to work well in teams" (Alsop, 2003, p. 11). Whether you are in business or another profession, organizations tend to hire those who have proven that they can work well with others (Hughes, 2003). Thus, your career advancement prospects could very well depend on your success in a collaborative work environment.

Enhanced Personal Life

Most people also participate in at least some small groups outside work—e.g., serving on committees in religious, nonprofit, and community organizations. In addition, increasing numbers of people join support groups to deal with crises, life transitions, or chronic health conditions. So learning how to communicate better in small group settings can serve you personally as well as academically and professionally. Despite their prevalence and importance, participation in group work has both advantages and disadvantages, as you'll see in the next section.

Advantages and Disadvantages of Group Work

An advantage of group work is that groups often make higher-quality decisions than do individuals. This occurs for at least two reasons. First, a group can produce more innovative ideas than an individual working alone. The small group discussion itself stimulates creativity (Moore, 2000). This creativity may be due to the aspect of **social facilitation** of group work, meaning that the mere presence of people encourages individuals to productively contribute to the task at hand (Kent, 1994, p. 81). Scholars speculate that the social-facilitation response may be innate because, ultimately, we depend on others to survive; or it may result from awareness that others can reward or punish us. In any case, research shows that people often work harder and do better when others are around, particularly if those others are evaluating their performance (Gagné & Zuckerman, 1999). As one scholar describes it, "Teamwork is an essential ingredient for successful innovation and transformation. Time and time again, studies of successful innovations have emphasized the need for and importance of close cooperation by members of multifunctional groups" (Mensch, 1993, p. 262).

Second, some evidence indicates that small group work can promote critical thinking, leading to better decisions. A group of people offers more collective information, experience, and expertise than any single person can (Propp, 1999; Larson, 2007), and through interaction, all members can benefit from these collective contributions. Also, because group members have to justify their opinions and judgments to other group members, each opinion is subject to careful scrutiny. This scrutiny can lead members to recognize the flaws in their own and others' arguments and encourage the group to think more critically (Gokhale, 1995).

Of course, group work also has disadvantages. For example, groups usually take more time to make decisions than do individuals. Group discussion can be less than satisfying when some group members dominate or withdraw, as happened with Dawn's

social facilitation
the tendency for people to work harder and do better when others are around

group in our opening vignette. Such communication behaviors can cause frustration and conflict, preventing members from working productively (Adams & Galanes, 2003) and cohesively.

Given that most of us need to work in small groups from time to time and that learning how to communicate better in small groups can enhance academic and professional success, what do you need to know to be a successful group member? We begin to answer this question in the following section.

SMALL GROUP COMMUNICATION AND THE INDIVIDUAL

The quality of a group depends on the contributions of members, and one reason for ineffective groups is the poor communication skills of those members (Li, 2007; Oetzel, 2005). Lack of communication can even be disastrous. For example, a British medical journal reported that poor communication among medical-team members resulted in a number of deaths in British hospitals.

As communication scholar Lawrence Frey (1994) states, "Communication is the lifeblood that flows through the veins of groups" (p. x). To better understand communication processes in small groups, consider its two primary dimensions: task communication and relational communication. Task communication is the more obvious of the two. It focuses on getting the job done and solving the problem at hand—for example, requesting information or asking for clarification—whereas relational communication focuses on group maintenance and interpersonal relationships, such as offering encouragement or mediating disagreement. These two types of communication are thoroughly mixed during group interaction; in fact, one statement can fill both functions. Let's see how this might work. When a group is getting bogged down in discussion, one member might encourage the group *and* focus on task by saying something like, "All of these ideas show how creative we are. Which do you think would be the most useful in helping us solve our problem?"

While effective relational communication usually facilitates task accomplishment, too much social talk can have a negative impact; it may reduce the time that should be used to complete the task, and it also distracts from the task focus that is critical for group effectiveness (Li, 2007). Socializing in a group is not the same as relational communication, and effective relational communication could be key in managing excessive social talk. For example, "It's great to hear about the awesome trips everyone took over spring break, but we should probably get back to our task if we want to finish by the end of the class period."

To help you understand how individuals can contribute to (or detract from) task and relationship communication, we next explore the various communication roles that members of small groups perform and the specific communication skills needed to make small groups effective.

Types of Communication Roles

Every group member plays a variety of roles within a group. **Group roles** describe the variety of communication behaviors in the group. These roles can involve either task or relational communication, and of course, they may have elements of both. If you join an established group, you learn the specific group-role expectations through communication with current members. If all members are new to the group, they rely on their perceptions and beliefs as well as their group skills and previous group experience as they work out various role behaviors (Riddle, Anderson, & Martin, 2000).

For example, Mitchell works for a software company. Although the employees of this company are scattered across the country and primarily work at home, they must work together to design software that meets a client's specific needs. Because Mitchell is the expert at writing software programs, he assumes that role. He is careful not to overstep his role, even

group roles
the shared expectations group members have regarding each individual's communication behavior in the group

if he feels that Giuliana, the design person, is not putting the "buttons" where he would put them or the frames where he thinks they would look best. Similarly, Mitchell and Giuliana make sure to follow the advice of the market researcher, who has studied the client's market needs. In this case, each group member knows his or her roles; they have developed this understanding based on their individual and collective experiences in groups. The owner of Mitchell's company flies everyone out to Los Angeles periodically so they can work together and build relationships. Mitchell flies in from Providence, Rhode Island, while others travel from Minneapolis, Atlanta, Miami, Seattle, Phoenix, and Milwaukee. Others simply drive in from nearby Orange County, Santa Barbara, or San Diego. These face-to-face meetings build work relationships and a sense of group cohesion—the members' positive feeling about belonging to the group.

Although group roles often evolve as the team works together, sometimes roles are assigned as part of a job description. For example, LaKresha, the chair of her university's Animal Welfare League, always leads the group's discussions; this is one of her responsibilities as chair. Kristie, as secretary of the organization, always takes notes because that is her role. Effective group members contribute by filling roles that interest them and are compatible with their skills, but they also fill roles that the group needs at a particular time. Thus, successful small group work depends on task and relational communication, which in turn depends on individuals' effective performance of task and relational roles (Benne & Sheats, 1948). In addition, group members may perform a third, less productive type of role, referred to as an individual role. Let's look at these three types of roles and how they contribute to, or detract from, effective group communication.

Task

Task roles are directly related to the accomplishment of group goals; they include behaviors such as leading the discussion and taking notes. These communication roles often involve seeking, processing, and evaluating information.

Let's use a case study to explore how these roles function within a group. Lenore and Jaime are part of a campus task force that is working to improve campus safety. Their small group of seven members met twice a month for several months and discussed the problem and possible solutions. During the discussions, group members filled the various task roles (see Table 11.1), depending on their particular strengths and interests and the needs of the group, changing roles as needed.

For example, Karin tended to serve as initiator-contributor, proposing new ideas and suggesting that the group look at several dimensions of the problem, such as personal security and the protection of private property. Information seekers, in particular John and Ralph, often asked for clarification of facts or information. Opinion seekers, such as Eliza and Wen Shu, asked how other group members felt about various proposals—say, the potential expense that would be incurred by implementing suggested solutions. In addition, opinion givers responded by sharing how they felt about the expense.

As information givers, several members provided statistics about the security problem so that the group could know the extent of the problem. They also provided information on how other campuses had solved similar problems—by increasing numbers of campus police, installing better lighting, and having volunteer "security teams" patrol campus. Serving as elaborator, Lenore told about having her bike stolen and suggested that having an increased number of campus police might have prevented the theft. Jaime often served as coordinator and orienter, showing how various ideas related to each other, while other members filled the role of evaluator-critic, carefully evaluating various ideas. The procedural technician made sure that everyone had paper and pens, while a designated recorder took notes so that at the end of each meeting, members knew what they had covered. One member often served as the energizer, infusing interest into the group when attention and focus lagged.

Not every group has members who can fill each of these roles, and certainly not with the same level of skill. But the more effectively these roles are filled, the better the group will function and the more likely it is that goals will be met.

Think about a small group experience you've had recently. What did other group members say that made you (and others) feel a part of the group? What was said that made you (and others) feel excluded from the group?

task roles
roles that are directly related to the accomplishment of group goals

TABLE 11.1 Small Group Task Roles

Task Role	Description	Example
Initiator-contributor	Proposes new ideas or approaches to group problem solving	"How about if we look at campus safety as issues of personal security *and* protection of private property?"
Information seeker	Asks for information or clarification	"How many instances of theft occur on our campus each year?"
Opinion seeker	Asks for opinions from others	"How do you feel about charging students a fee that would pay for extra police protection?"
Information giver	Provides facts, examples, and other relevant evidence	"My research showed that other campuses have solved similar problems by increasing numbers of campus police and improving lighting."
Opinion giver	Offers beliefs or opinions	"I'm often concerned about my personal safety when I walk to certain campus parking lots at night."
Elaborator	Explains ideas, offers examples to clarify ideas	"If the university had increased security patrols, my bike might not have been stolen last month."
Coordinator	Shows relationships among ideas presented	"Installing new light fixtures might improve personal safety and reduce thefts on campus."
Orienter	Summarizes what has been discussed and keeps group focused	"We've now discussed several aspects of personal safety; maybe it's time to turn our attention to issues of protection of private property."
Evaluator-critic	Judges evidence and conclusions of group	"I think we may be overestimating the problem of theft."
Energizer	Motivates group members to greater productivity	"Wow! We've gotten a lot accomplished this evening, and we only have a few more points to discuss."
Procedural technician	Performs logistical tasks—distributing paper, arranging seating, etc.	
Recorder	Keeps a record of group activities and progress	

SOURCE: Adapted from Benne & Sheets (1948).

Relational

In contrast with task roles, **relational roles** help establish a group's social atmosphere (see Table 11.2). For example, members who encourage others to talk or those who mediate disagreements are filling relational roles. Group members can fill both task and relational roles, depending on the needs of the group. For example, in Lenore and Jaime's group, one member sent out e-mails to get the group organized (task role), and he also sent congratulatory e-mails after the group did a presentation to the student governing council (relational role).

During their discussion of campus safety, some members served as encouragers (praising and accepting others' ideas). Others served as harmonizers (mediating disagreement) or compromisers (attempting to find solutions to disagreements). As communication majors, Lenore and Jaime paid close attention to how the discussion was going. When necessary, they served as gatekeepers, encouraging participation from less-talkative members, or as expediters, gently limiting the contributions of more-talkative members or those who over-socialized (mentioned earlier). One group member served as standard setter, periodically reminding his colleagues of the group's standards, while others served as observers, gathering information that could be used to evaluate group performance. In this group, most members served as followers from time to time, simply listening to others' contributions. Overall, the group met its goal of addressing the problems of campus security partly because members effectively filled both task and relational roles as needed.

relational roles
roles that help establish a group's social atmosphere

TABLE 11.2 Small Group Relational Roles

Role	Description	Example
Encourager	Offers praise and acceptance of others' ideas	"That's a great idea; tell us more about it."
Harmonizer	Mediates disagreement among group members	"I think you and Ron are seeing two sides of the same coin."
Compromiser	Attempts to resolve conflicts by trying to find an acceptable solution to disagreements	"I think both of you have great ideas. Let's see how we can combine them."
Gatekeeper	Encourages less-talkative group members to participate	"Maria, you haven't said much about this idea. How do you feel about it?"
Expediter	Tries to limit lengthy contributions of other group members	"Martin, you've told us what you think about most of the ideas. Why don't we hear from some of the other members?"
Standard setter	Helps to set standards and goals for the group	"I think our goal should be to submit a comprehensive plan for campus safety to the dean by the end of this semester."
Group observer	Keeps records of the group's process and uses the information that is gathered to evaluate the group's procedures	
Follower	Goes along with the suggestions and ideas of group members; serves as an audience in group discussion and decision making	"I like that idea. That's a really good point."

SOURCE: Adapted from Benne & Sheets (1948).

How can you apply this information to improve your own skills as a group member? First, try to keep these roles in mind during your own group work, noting who is playing which role and whether some essential role is missing. Once you've made this assessment, you can try to fill in the missing role behaviors. For example, see if you can identify the roles that are needed in the group situations described in *Building Your Communication Skills: Identifying Roles in Group Situations*.

Building Your Communication **SKILLS**

Identifying Roles in Group Situations

Instructions: Imagine that you are a group member in a communication class project. What would you do as an effective group member in the following situations? What communication roles are needed? (See some suggested answers below)

1. The group seems "stuck" and keeps rehashing the same ideas.

2. One person in the group is dominating the discussion and talking constantly.

3. Two group members are disagreeing strongly in a prolonged discussion, causing frustration for other group members.

4. One group member is providing complex information that seems to confuse other group members.

5. Group members are discouraged at the end of a long and seemingly unproductive meeting.

Possible Role Solutions: (1) initiator-contributor, information giver; (2) expediter, gatekeeper; (3) harmonizer, compromiser; (4) elaborator, coordinator, information giver; (5) energizer, encourager

Individual

The **individual role** tends to be dysfunctional to the group process (see Table 11.3). Group members serving in individual roles focus more on their own interests and needs than on those of the group. Thus, they tend to be uninvolved, negative, aggressive, or constantly joking. A common individual role that blocks effectiveness in student projects is the dominator, who insists on doing things his or her way, as described by our student in *It Happened to Me: James.*

What could James's group members have done to deal with the critical group member? Perhaps they could have tried a relational communication role—for example, they could have complimented the other group members for *their* ideas (e.g., encourager role). When several members note the high quality of an individual contribution, the criticism of one member has less force. Or perhaps someone could have stepped into a task role—for example, acting as an opinion seeker—to solicit other supportive opinions, contradicting the negativity of the dominator group member.

individual roles
roles that focus more on individuals' own interests and needs than on those of the group

IT HAPPENED TO ME: James

I had an experience in one group project where one member acted completely superior to the rest of us. No matter the contributions we made to the project, he always found a way to criticize them. Nothing was good enough for him. Eventually, no one felt they could satisfy him, so we all stopped trying to do our best.

Another common individual role is the joker. When another member contributes, the joker always has to "one up" the comment with a joke or a story, assuming that others will be interested. This member constantly moves the group off task. Here, a member filling the orienter role can help the group refocus on the task at hand.

Other individual roles listed in Table 11.3 are the aggressor, a group member who destroys or deflates the status of other group members, and the blocker, a member who is negative for no apparent reason. Members might limit the negative effects of these group roles by acting as an encourager—countering the negative criticism with positive feedback, such as, "I have to say *I* thought Gene's idea was really intriguing. Let's look at how we might implement it in our project." A gatekeeper can also deal with negativity,

TABLE 11.3 Small Group Individual Roles

Role	Description	Example
Aggressor	Attacks other group members, tries to take credit for someone else's contribution	"That's a stupid idea. It would never work."
Blocker	Is generally negative and stubborn for no apparent reason	"This whole task is pointless. I don't see why we have to do it."
Recognition seeker	Calls excessive attention to his/her personal achievements	"This is how we dealt with campus security when I was at Harvard."
Self-confessor	Uses the group as an audience to report nongroup-related personal feelings	"I'm so upset at my boyfriend. We had a big fight last night."
Joker	Lacks involvement in the group's process, distracts others by telling stories and jokes	"Hey did you hear the one about … ?"
Dominator	Asserts control by manipulating group members or tries to take over group; may use flattery or assertive behavior to dominate the conversation	"I know my plan will work because I was a police officer."
Help seeker	Tries to gain unwarranted sympathy from group; often expresses insecurity or feelings of low self-worth	"You probably won't like this idea either, but I think we should consider contracting out our campus security."
Special-interest pleader	Works to serve an individual need, rather than focusing on group interests	"Since I only have daycare on Wednesdays, can we meet on Wednesday afternoons?"

SOURCE: Adapted from Benne & Sheets (1948).

saying, for example, "It sounds like Denise doesn't think this is a good idea; what do the rest of you think?"

You may also be familiar with recognition seekers, who continuously grabs the spotlight, or with the self-confessor, who uses the group as his or her own personal audience. Other individual roles than can prove disruptive come from the help seeker, who is continuously in need of sympathy and expresses insecurity or feelings of low self-worth, and the special-interest pleader, who places his or her individual needs or biases above the group's goal or focus. Perhaps the best strategies to counteract these individual roles—which take up a lot of air time in unproductive conversation—come from those relational roles that help the group refocus on the task: the gatekeeper or expeditor roles. Several task roles may also prove helpful—for example, the initiator-contributor, who may start a new line of conversation, or the orienter, who helps the group see where they are in accomplishing their task.

As you can see, a group member who consistently assumes negative roles can undermine the group's commitment to goals and its sense of cohesion and ultimately decrease performance and productivity. This is why it's so important for other group members to be aware of effective task and relational behaviors and to demonstrate them (Wellen & Neale, 2006).

Any group member may serve in any of these roles at any time. In a successful group, like Jaime and Lenore's task force, members play various roles as needed, with minimal indulgence in the individual roles. Some group members play only to their strengths and consistently serve in one or two particular roles. This is fine as long as all the needed roles are being filled. *Visual Summary 11.1: Roles in Groups* illustrates several roles that may be at work in a small group setting.

Effective Small Group Communication

Effective groups maintain a balance of task and relational communication, and the sequence of each appears to be more important than the relative amount of each. For example, after an intense period of task talk, group members might defuse their tension with positive social (or relational) talk and then return to task talk (Pavitt, 1999).

What types of communication lead to effective sequencing of task and relational communication? Experts find that the following communication processes lead to task effectiveness and member satisfaction (relational effectiveness) in small groups in many situations—whether a team project in a *Fortune* 500 company, a fundraising committee for a charity organization, or a small group assignment in a communication course (Oetzel, 1998, 2001, 2005):

1. *Equal participation:* All group members contribute at relatively equal levels, taking approximately the same number of turns talking. You might think that it's not important that everyone talks during a group discussion; or perhaps you yourself tend to be quiet and reserved in group meetings. However, the fact is that if everyone participates, the group can consider a wider variety of ideas, attend to more aspects of the situations, and thus make better decisions. Furthermore, group members who do not contribute feel less commitment to the group outcomes and implementation, and may ultimately sabotage the group effort. What can you, as a group member, do to ensure that everyone participates equally? You can monitor the participation of all members, playing the expeditor role to prevent talkative or domineering members from talking too much and the gatekeeper role in drawing out those nonparticipating members. In addition, if you, as a group member, tend to be silent, consider the importance of expressing your views, even if they are primarily expressions of support and agreement.

2. *A consensus decision-making style:* Members participate in and agree with the decisions made by the group. While it is not always possible to have every group member agree with every decision, nonparticipating members and members who disagree with group decisions can have very negative impacts on group outcomes—as described above. Therefore, it is in the best interests of the group to get buy-in from as many members as possible. As a group member, you can facilitate agreement by encouraging participation of all members (described above), by showing how

Think about group experiences you've had. Which task communication roles do you tend to fill? Which relational communication roles? Which communication roles would you like to fill? How flexible have you been in your ability to fill various task and relational roles?

Roles in Groups

LEADING THE DISCUSSION
(Task Role)

PROCESSING INFORMATION
(Relational Role)

RECOGNITION SEEKER
(Individual Role)

BLOCKER
(Individual Role)

RECORDER
(Task Role)

ideas are related (coordinator role), and by encouraging a cooperative conflict style (described below).

3. *A cooperative conflict style:* The group manages conflict by integrating all parties' interests. As we will see later, some conflict is an inevitable part of small group discussion, and when handled well, it can be productive in sharpening issues and getting out various positions. For now, let's just say that effective groups approach conflict in a cooperative, rather than a competitive, divisive manner. This means that the goal in a cooperative approach is to try to turn the conflict into a mutual problem that all members can work on to their mutual benefit. A little later in the chapter, we will provide more specific strategies for dealing with group conflict in a cooperative manner.

4. *A respectful communication style:* Group members demonstrate that other members are valued and important. How is this accomplished? Most often, members show respect by communicating a sense of mutual support and acceptance. This means using the verbal and nonverbal strategies that strengthen interpersonal relationships—described in other chapters in this book. For members of a problem-solving group, it includes being specific and softening messages of criticism; and when promoting a position, it means providing evidence focused primarily on the ideas and tasks and separating the ideas from the person who puts them forward.

In successful groups, all members participate equally in the discussion and problem solving.

How can members best use these skills when the primary goal of a small group is to solve a particular problem? One of the great communication challenges for groups is to pinpoint the problem and all its possible solutions. In this section, we'll first describe a five-stage agenda that problem-solving groups have found useful. Second, we'll examine how decision making occurs in small groups, including a negative group process—groupthink. Finally, we'll describe the characteristics of discussions in small groups whose members are separated geographically and, in particular, the role technology can play in them.

Problem-Solving Agenda

A danger in problem-solving groups is jumping immediately to a solution. One useful tool for avoiding a premature and incomplete solution is an agenda—for the purpose of developing and following a sequence. In fact, early research surveying hundreds of small group participants identified lack of strong procedural guidelines as one of the primary barriers to effective problem solving (Broome & Fulbright, 1995). While many agendas exist, perhaps the best known are variations of educator John Dewey's five-step procedure (Cragan & Wright, 1999, p. 97). Two points are central to using an agenda effectively, and at first they may sound contradictory. First, researchers have found that most problem-solving groups have less conflict and a more consistent focus when they follow formal procedures (Klocke, 2007). Second, successful groups do not necessarily solve all problems in strict sequential order; they may take a variety of paths (Schultz, 1999). In general, then, groups benefit from keeping the agenda in mind, but members may have to cycle back and forth between phases before reaching a solution.

Let's return to our earlier example of the campus security problem and see how that group might follow the five-step problem-solving agenda and the recommendations for effective communication at each step.

Step 1: Define and Delineate the Problem The first step in solving a problem is to make sure that everyone in the group understands it in the same way. After all, the problem can't be solved unless group members know what it is (and is not). On the campus security task-force case study, the group members were successful in part because they agreed on the definition of the problem. They decided that their problem was twofold: (1) the personal security of students in dorms and while walking on campus and (2) the protection of students' personal property. They decided that they would not address the security of class-room and office equipment because they were primarily a student group. This helped them narrow the focus and set limits for the discussion of solutions.

Step 2: Analyze the Problem In some ways, this is the most important phase of the agenda because it determines the direction of potential solutions (Hirokawa & Salazar, 1999). Group members must look at all sides of the problem. To do so, they answer questions like these: Who is affected by the problem? How widespread is it? In the case of the campus security team, the group had to gather data on the exact nature of security problems—the frequency of burglaries, rapes, assaults, and robberies on campus; where and when these incidents were occurring; and what consequences the incidents had.

However, a word of caution is in order: In some cases, too much analysis can result in **analysis paralysis** and prevent a group from moving toward a solution (Rothwell, 1995). Our campus security group, for example, could continue to gather statistics, interview people about the problem, and discuss the problems and never move on to possible solutions.

Step 3: Identify Alternative Solutions As noted earlier, one challenge at this stage is to consider several possibilities and not rush to premature solutions. One way to make sure that many solutions are considered is to **brainstorm**, generating as many ideas as possible without critiquing them. By brainstorming, the campus security group put forth a wide range of possible solutions, including putting up more lighting, increasing the number of campus police, and helping students to register their private property (bikes, computers, stereo equipment, etc.) so that stolen property could be traced. Some solutions were more unusual, including suggestions to eliminate foliage where assailants could hide, to sell wristband tracking devices to students, to place guard dogs in dormitories, and to have 24/7 volunteer security details in the dorms.

Step 4: Evaluate Proposed Solutions Evaluating proposed solutions involves establishing evaluation criteria. The campus security task force, for example, identified three criteria for its solutions: They had to be economically feasible, logistically feasible, and likely to solve the problem of campus security. With these criteria in mind, the task force had a basis for evaluating each solution. This stage is critical, but it can be difficult; if members are tired or frustrated by all the work they've already done, they may jump to conclusions. However, if they keep to the agenda and carefully consider each alternative, they will quickly reject some solutions and find others attractive. According to one study, a strong positive relationship exists between a group's decision-making performance and members' satisfaction with the alternatives chosen (Hirokawa & Salazar, 1999).

Step 5: Choose the Best Solution While this step may seem redundant, choosing the best solution(s) is not the same as evaluating all proposed solutions. Here, it is especially important that everyone participates and buys into the solution, and decision-making procedures are most critical.

The problem-solving agenda is a specific format or set of guidelines that task groups can follow to ensure high-quality solutions. As groups progress through the stages, however, they will need to make multiple decisions. For example, during stage four, the evaluation stage, the group will need to decide what the appropriate criteria are for evaluating proposed solutions, whether they will evaluate all or just some of the proposed solutions, and how they will manage differences of opinion regarding the value of proposed solutions. To help you understand the **decision-making process** that occurs throughout the problem-solving agenda, in the next section we explore the *process* of decision making.

analysis paralysis
potential pitfall in small group interaction; occurs when excessive analysis prevents a group from moving toward a solution

brainstorm
to generate as many ideas as possible without critiquing them

decision-making process
the four-phase process used by a group to evaluate information and arrive at a decision or solution

Decision-Making Phases

How do small groups arrive at good decisions? Are there specific communication processes that can lead to good decisions? What are some warning signs of unproductive decision making? Is conflict a necessary part of the group decision-making process, or should it be avoided? These are questions we'll tackle in this section. As you can imagine, there is no one recipe for effective decision making. However, there are several phases that seem to represent the communication that occurs in effective problem-solving groups: orientation, conflict, emergence, and reinforcement (Bormann, 1975; Fisher, 1980; Fisher & Ellis, 1993; Wheelan, Davidson, & Tilin, 2003).

Before describing these phases, we should note that most groups do not proceed through them in an orderly, linear fashion. Rather, they may cycle through the first phase twice before moving to the next phase, or they may revert back to the conflict phase after reaching the final emergence phase (Poole, 1983). With these thoughts in mind, let's look at the four phases individually.

Phase 1: Orientation During this phase, group members orient themselves to the problem and to each other (if they have just met). Uncertainty at this stage is common and is referred to as **primary tension**. For example, as a group member, you might wonder how the group is going to function. You may have questions about the others in the group: Are you going to like them? Will you all get along, or will you clash? In *It Happened to Me: Kirstin*, one of our students describes a relational problem that emerged at the beginning of her group project, which contributed to the tension the group felt as they began their talk. As you can see, she played an important relational role as a gatekeeper in encouraging the nonparticipating members to communicate and as an harmonizer in helping the group members work through a situation that seemed well on its way to becoming a conflict situation.

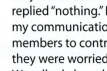

IT HAPPENED TO ME: Kirstin

Being the only communication major in our group, I immediately noticed some problems. The nonverbal cues from two members contradicted their verbal messages. They rolled their eyes or turned their bodies away from the group when they were asked to do a task. When someone asked what was wrong, those two replied "nothing." I knew this did not bode well for the group, so I shared some of my communication skills and knowledge. I encouraged the two nonparticipating members to contribute and asked them again if anything was wrong. They told us they were worried because they'd had a bad experience in an earlier group project. We talked about how we all needed to pull together. I was kind of a cheerleader for the group. So we got through this, and the group arrived at a decision and completed the task without any major conflict.

During phase 1, you may also experience uncertainty about the task you are to undertake: Will everyone contribute equally? Will the work get done efficiently and on time?

Communication at this phase is generally polite, tentative, and focused on reducing uncertainty and ambiguity through clarification and agreement. The importance of the orientation phase is that many relational and task norms are set for the future. Fortunately for Kirstin's group, she realized the importance of equal participation of all group members and was willing to step in and fill the needed role, which got the group off to a good start.

Regardless of the norms that they establish, groups often experience recurring primary tension if they meet over an extended period. For example, at the beginning of each meeting, group members may need to spend time reconnecting and reviewing their views on the task. In response, then, a group member filling the orienter role might summarize what has been accomplished at the most recent meetings, and the recorder could read back minutes or notes from the last meeting.

Phase 2: Conflict The conflict phase in decision making is characterized by **secondary (recurring) tension**. This phase usually occurs after group members become acquainted, after some norms and expectations are set, and when decision alternatives are to be addressed.

As members become more relaxed, they become more animated and honest. Members may interrupt each other, talk loudly, and try on group roles. Some may try to dominate,

primary tension
the uncertainty commonly felt in the beginning phase of decision making

secondary (recurring) tension
the underlying tension group members experience as they struggle over member roles; it generally surfaces in the second stage, but can reoccur throughout the lifetime on the group

push their own agendas, and form coalitions in an effort to increase their influence; others may engage in side conversations as they lose their focus on the decision at hand. It is especially important at this time to follow the suggestions for effective group communication mentioned earlier: equal participation, cooperative conflict style, consensus decision making, and respectful communication (pages 264, 266). Specifically, members should assess the group dynamics and identify which roles are needed. Perhaps an expediter or gatekeeper can ensure equal participation; perhaps a harmonizer and a compromiser can ensure that disagreements are channeled productively. In order to promote consensus decision making, members can step into information- and opinion-seeking roles, and others might become elaborators and coordinators. To promote respectful communication, members can fill encourager and harmonizer roles.

If the group plans to meet frequently over a period of weeks or months, this is the time to discuss expectations and establish group norms—especially norms for handling conflict. For example, in a small group working on a course project, members might tell each other what grade they expect in the course and discuss their strengths and weaknesses with respect to the project. One group member may be very good at conducting Internet research. Another might be skillful at integrating material that others have collected. Someone else might be good at keeping members on task. Articulating these expectations and strengths verbally is more useful than communicating interests or commitment (or lack thereof) nonverbally, by simply not showing up or not participating in discussions or work sessions.

Of course, all groups experience some conflict, and a certain amount of conflict can be both healthy and functional, because it can increase member involvement (Sunwolf & Seibold, 1999). One productive way to handle group conflict is through using a cooperative conflict style that integrates all members' interests (Oetzel, 2005; Poole & Garner, 2006). However, other methods can be used as well, particularly if tensions become very high, including the strategies presented in the box on *Building Your Communication Skills: How to Handle Conflicts in Meetings*.

Building Your Communication SKILLS

How to Handle Conflicts in Meetings

Conflicts in group meetings can be very disruptive, but they can also be helpful. Remember: Conflicts are disagreements. If the person who is disagreeing with you is raising valid questions, the group may benefit by addressing the issues he or she is presenting. In fact, by listening, you may gain valuable insight into what is and is not working within your group. However, if you are the person involved in the conflict, you might not be able to listen well, and the group may need someone else to step in to fill the harmonizer or compromiser role.

When conflict takes precedence over problem solving, here are a few strategies to keep in mind:

- Clarify what the conflict is about.

- Affirm the validity of all viewpoints.

- Frame the conflict in terms of a problem to be solved.

- Set aside a specific time for problem solving to occur.

- Help participants save face.

- Discuss what happens if no agreement is reached.

- Ask if the group can proceed with what they do agree on and hold back on areas of disagreement.

SOURCE: Adapted from Duncan, M. (2009). *Effective meeting facilitation: The sine qua non of planning.* Retrieved July 24, 2009, from http://www.nea.gov/resources/Lessons/DUNCAN1.HTML

Reaching agreement can involve conflict among group members. Recurring and sustained bouts of secondary tension or conflict can be problematic. In response, relational roles may take precedence over task roles. For example, roles that promote trust (assuring members that they can rely on each other to put forward their best effort) and cohesion (expressing a desire to remain in the group) may become crucial. Members can also reduce tension by articulating a positive attitude or feeling about their group, the task, or other members (Carwright, 1968), and by emphasizing group identity and pride in the group's effort. In short, strong relational bonds within a group promote high-quality decisions and problem solving (Keyton, 1999, 2000), and groups with high trust have fewer relationship conflicts (Peterson & Behfar, 2003).

Phase 3: Emergence In the **emergence phase**, the group has worked through the primary and secondary tensions, and members express a cooperative attitude. In successful groups, coalitions dissipate, and group members are less tenacious about holding their positions. Comments become more favorable as members compromise to reach consensus, discuss their problem at length, consider possible alternatives, and eventually generate a group decision (Fisher, 1970, cited in Littlejohn, 2002). This is the longest phase, as group members discuss and attempt to reach agreement. For various procedures that can help groups reach agreement, see *Did You Know? Procedures That Help Groups Agree.*

DID YOU KNOW?

Procedures That Help Groups Agree

- *Voting:* simultaneous (raised hands, vocal), sequential (round robin), or secret (written)
- *Establishing decision rule:* predetermined level of support needed to reach agreement (for example, two-thirds majority, simple majority, or unanimity)
- *Conducting a straw poll:* nonbinding voting method that allows the group to get a sense of members' preferences while still allowing them to change preferences
- *Conceding:* agreement to eventually agree, in spite of individual preferences
- *Using problem-centered leadership:* procedure in which the leader acts as facilitator, guiding group toward agreement
- *Negotiating:* reaching agreement through series of trade-offs

SOURCE: Adapted from Sunwolf & Seibold (1999, p. 401).

Phase 4: Reinforcement During the **reinforcement phase,** members reach consensus, the decision solidifies, and members feel a sense of accomplishment and satisfaction. If a small majority makes the decision, they spend phase 4 convincing other members of its value. In successful groups, members unify and stand behind the solution. Comments are almost uniformly positive.

While coming to a decision easily with lots of group cohesion—meaning that members have positive feelings of belonging—may seem like the ideal situation, it may actually reflect a negative group process: **groupthink.** Groupthink occurs when members arrive at a consensus before all alternatives have been realistically assessed. This occurs when group members feel a pressure to conform; thus, they reject new information and may have a negative perception of individuals outside the group who volunteer information that contradicts the group's decision. In addition, the group members have an illusion of invulnerability and unanimity. These symptoms produce pressure on group members to go along with the favored group position, believing not only that the group preferences will be successful but also that they are just and right (Henningsen & Henningsen, 2006). This phenomenon can have disastrous consequences. The term was coined in an analysis of several foreign policy fiascoes, such as the Bay of Pigs Invasion in 1961 and the escalation of the Vietnam War (Janis, 1982).

emergence phase
the third phase of the decision-making process; occurs when group members express a cooperative attitude

reinforcement phase
the final phase of the decision-making process when group members reach consensus and members feel a sense of accomplishment

groupthink
a negative, and potentially disastrous, group process characterized by excessive concurrence thinking

Another example of the disastrous consequences of groupthink was the *Challenger* space-shuttle explosion 73 seconds into its launch on January 28, 1986. Within days, President Reagan appointed a commission of experts who discovered that the primary cause of the accident was a mechanical failure in one of the joints of the right solid rocket booster. The commission concluded that the contributing cause was a flawed decision-making process at NASA. Several NASA personnel had warned of potential problems with the launch, and numerous opportunities arose to postpone it. However, on each occasion, one or more of the following influences surfaced and reduced the chances for preventing the disaster:

- the unwillingness of individuals to step outside their roles and question those in authority;
- questionable patterns of reasoning by key managers;
- ambiguous and misleading language that minimized the perception of risk;
- failure to ask important questions relevant to the final decision.

In this case, poor communication skills and an unwillingness to explore possible problems and to risk disagreement led to an event that ultimately undermined the respect for and prior achievements of the space agency (Gouran, Hirokawa, & Martz, 1986).

Groupthink does not just occur in high-level organizational groups either. It can occur in any group. For example, Murphy is part of a student advocacy group that works to protest tuition hikes at his college. The group voted quickly to protest tuition hikes, without investigating all the various expenses that could legitimately cause tuition to be increased. They discovered, after organizing a major protest in front of the president's office, that a significant portion of the tuition hikes were related to improving technological services (wireless Internet, more student-access computers) that most students would support. The result of their groupthink was that they had to revisit their initial decision and gather more information, understand exactly the causes of tuition hike, and ultimately decide what, if any, portion of the tuition hike should be protested.

What causes people to engage in groupthink? One reason may be a high level of cohesiveness. While usually viewed as positive, too much group cohesion can lead to premature agreement. Other reasons may be insulation—when groups have very tight boundaries and are not open to new, relevant information (Putnam & Stohl, 1996). Leadership can also promote groupthink: either very strong leadership, where one dominating person promotes only one idea, or the opposite, a lack of leadership, meaning that the group has no direction. Groupthink can also result from a failure to set norms for decision making or, in other words, from a failure to follow a problem-solving agenda. Finally, extreme homogeneity in the backgrounds of group members can also lead to rushed solutions rather than careful examination of alternatives (Henningsen & Henningsen, 2005).

How to avoid groupthink? A group leader can make sure that a problem-solving agenda is followed that encourages full discussion and exploration of issues and solutions. How might you, as a group member, prevent your group from engaging in groupthink? Several task and relational roles would be helpful. For example, by filling information- and opinion-seeker roles, as well as information and opinion giver roles, you could ensure that adequate time is spent in discussion before a decision is reached. In addition, by filling the energizer role, you could encourage the group to continue discussion and not fall into groupthink as a result of fatigue or lack of energy.

Have you ever been in a group that experienced groupthink? If so, what were the causes? What could have been done to avoid the situation?

Technology and Group Communication

As we discussed in Chapter 7, technology is playing an increased role in group work. Some researchers assert that technology enhances positive outcomes in a diverse workforce, as communication technologies reduce the cues that often lead to stereotypes and prejudice. For example, in virtual teams, members cannot see the gender, skin color, or age of their colleagues, which may equalize contributions and facilitate discussion.

Marek, one of our students, works for an international pharmaceutical company and often collaborates on projects with group members he has never met. Members of his team are scattered around the globe in multiple time zones. Thus, he may be online with Luc in

group support software (GSS)
computer-aided program that
supports real-time discussion
between members regardless of
physical location

virtual work team
a group of people identified as a
team by their organization and
responsible for making decisions
important to the organization; it
may be culturally diverse,
geographically dispersed, and have
members who communicate
electronically substantially more
than face-to-face

Montreal, Caroline in London, Liana in Buenos Aires, Ahmed in Riyadh, Setsuko in Osaka, and Giles in Melbourne. Although he may not have met his group's members face-to-face, their tasks are well defined, and thus, the group completes their projects with few problems. Moreover, their diverse cultural backgrounds enhance the group's ideas and produce a stronger product.

A variety of technologies support work for teams like Marek's. Some are immediate and synchronous, like audio and teleconferencing technologies that allow members to see and hear each other from remote locations. Another technology is **Group Support Software (GSS),** a computer-aided program that supports real-time discussion between members regardless of physical location; with GSS, each participant sits at a computer terminal, and the discussion is facilitated by the software program. The best known of these programs is Group Decision Support Software (GDSS).

Recent research has found that to be effective, GDSS users must perceive an advantage to participating in a technology-enabled group over a more traditional group, and the technology used must be compatible with the way the group already works. So in order to conduct a successful meeting, one must first "market" the technology to members, thereby increasing the likelihood of a successful decision-making process. Second, leaders must promote group cohesion, as it is the primary driver of GDSS success (Schwarz & Schwarz, 2007, p. 222).

Some initial research has indicated that GSS can lead to group outcomes that are superior to those relying solely on face-to-face meetings. These advantages appear to flow from its ability to manage and organize simultaneous contributions, leading to improved group performance in brainstorming tasks. However, other research has not found a GSS advantage in group functioning (Dennis & Wixom, 2001-2002; Schwarz & Schwarz, 2007) and suggests that GSS may not be very effective when virtual teams are tackling very complex tasks (Broome & Chen, 1992). At this point, then, it appears that GSS works really well at generating ideas in large groups, but probably less well in decision making. Perhaps the best approach, then, is to have a team use GSS to generate ideas and discuss issues, but then come together for face-to-face or audio- or videoconferencing when they need to make important decisions (Dennis & Wixom, 2001–2002). Although some misunderstandings and conflicts inevitably arise, groups using GSS don't appear to have more conflict overall than face-to-face groups (Hobman, Bordia, Irmer, & Chang, 2002).

An additional trend involves combining several technologies—for example, live videoconferences, text-based document sharing, audio connections, and shared whiteboards on which participants in one location can write, allowing participants in other locations to see their notes. More and more people are working in virtual (or distributed) work teams. In fact, nearly two-thirds of U.S. employees have done so (Connaughton & Shuffler, 2007). A **virtual work team** is a group of people identified as a team by their organization and responsible for making decisions important to the organization; moreover, it may be culturally diverse, geographically dispersed, and have members who communicate electronically substan-

Nearly two-thirds of U.S. employees have worked in virtual teams like this one, reducing travel time and expenses. However, working virtually involves unique communication challenges.

tially more than face-to-face. Additionally, a new kind of virtual-team phenomenon is changing the way people and businesses develop ideas using Internet collaboration—see *Communication in Society: COINs: The Future of Innovation?*

Virtual teams face a number of challenges including distance, geography, and available technology (Poole & Garner, 2006). Some experts say that the communication

Communication in SOCIETY

COINs: The Future of Innovation?

A recent book describes a new kind of virtual team phenomenon that is changing the way people and businesses develop ideas—through collaboration on the Internet.

Peter A. Gloor, a Research Scientist at MIT, along with his colleagues, have been studying a recent Internet phenomenon—Collaborative Innovation Networks or COINs. Gloor defines a COIN as "a cyberteam of self-motivated people with a collective vision, enabled by the Web to collaborate in achieving a common goal by sharing ideas, information and work." (p. 4). These inspired individuals, working together spontaneously as a virtual team, often at great distances, are not motivated by financial gain. Rather they collaborate because of their shared passion for innovation and a commitment to common goals and/or causes. Gloor describes their collaboration as "swarm creativity." As they spontaneously "swarm" together in cyberspace, they create an environment that promotes dynamic and innovative collaborative thinking.

The results of these virtual collaborations have been astounding. As Gloor notes, the Internet itself is an example of a successful COIN. It was started by a group of people working at a physics research lab, then developed and fine-tuned by various groups of students, researchers and computer scientists, crossing conventional organizational structures and hierarchies. The rest, as they say, is history. Other examples of more recent COIN successes are Linux and other Open Source software products, as well as a number of other lesser-known commercial innovations. Gloor point outs that while COINs have existed well before the Internet, the Internet provides instantaneous global accessibility, ensuring a tremendous upsurge in productivity. In addition, Gloor and colleagues stress that for COINs to be successful, the team members not only need to share a passion for the products they're developing but also need a certain level of trust in fellow team members, balanced communication, and a shared code of ethics guiding their collaboration.

SOURCES: Gloor, P. A. (2006). *Swarm creativity: Competitive advantage through collaborative innovative networks.* Oxford: Oxford University Press; Heckman, C. Makedon, F. "Ethical Issues in Virtual Communities of Innovation" https://exchange.asu.edu/exchange/mar22/Drafts/documents/COIN4Ethicomp.pdf. Ethicomp 2004, the 7th International Conference on the Social and Ethical Impacts of Information and Communication Technologies, Syros, Greece, April 14–16. 2004; Paasvaara, M. Schoder, D. Willems, P. "Finding Collaborative Innovation Networks Through Correlating Performance With Social Network Structure" https://exchange.asu.edu/exchange/mar22/Drafts/documents/Gloor_JPR_3.pdf. *Journal of Production Research,* Taylor and Francis, April 2007

problems between virtual team members are related to the number of time zones that separate them (Smith, 2001). If only a few time zones away, members can come to work earlier or later and still have overlapping workdays. If members are separated by many time zones, they face a much bigger challenge, particularly on Fridays and Mondays. However, other experts say that distance is not necessarily a big problem, that teams find a way to work with the geographical distance and time differences (Connaughton & Shuffler, 2007). For example, one company—with team members in the United States and Australia (15 time zones apart)—has a policy that once a month members from each country take turns getting up at 2 AM for videoconferencing with members from the other country. The rest of the time, they rely on voice mail and e-mail.

How can virtual teams work together most effectively? There seem to be two guidelines. One is to engage in frequent communication, which seems to reduce conflict and build trust, and the second is to choose the most appropriate technology for the task at hand (Manzevski & Chudoba, 2000; Schiller & Mandviwalla, 2007). Each technology works best in its niche. Telephone and video conferences provide high-quality and faster communication, but when dealing with large time differences, e-mail is probably better. Some experts suggest that face-to-face communication, particularly at the beginning of a group project, enhances effectiveness (Cannaughton & Shuffler, 2007).

A recent study compared the effectiveness of face-to-face and virtual student groups, all working on the same task—a final class project (Li, 2007). In this project, students were presented with a scenario in which they had to work together to decide what they would need to survive after a plane crash in northern Canada. After the task was completed, the researchers asked the students to assess their group's performance in terms of task and relational procedures and also the quality of their communication. How satisfied were they

with group cohesion? How satisfied were they with the group's process? With its outcomes? Independent observers also rated the groups' interaction and outcomes. Who do you think performed better—the virtual groups or the students who were working face-to-face? Not surprisingly, each type of team was effective in some ways. The virtual teams demonstrated somewhat higher-quality task behaviors but also took more time than did the face-to-face groups to complete tasks. As you might expect, perhaps, the face-to-face groups were better at performing relational role behaviors and completed the task more quickly, but—contrary to the researchers' expectations—did not have significantly better group outcomes. Perhaps this is because some of their relational role behaviors (e.g., too much social talk) did not actually facilitate high-quality task completion. In sum, it seems that virtual teams—whether in business, academic, or social contexts—may be most useful for tasks that do not require quick decisions, but their work can be enhanced by frequent communication and even face-to-face meetings when possible.

THE INDIVIDUAL, SMALL GROUP COMMUNICATION, AND SOCIETY

Small group communication, like all communication, is influenced by societal forces. The world outside influences this form of communication in two important respects: (1) the way in which power is used inside and outside groups, and (2) the role cultural diversity plays.

Power and Group Communication

Small groups function within the influences of the societal forces we have discussed throughout this book: political, economic, and historical. People communicating in small groups bring with them their identities and the hierarchical meanings associated with those identities (see Chapter 2). Those group members who hold the values and follow the communication rules of the dominant group in society may more easily contribute to the group and dominate it, which may cause resentment among those who feel marginalized in society generally (Oetzel, 2005).

Groups also establish a power structure. For example, a group member may be elected or appointed to lead a group, which allows that person to wield *legitimate* power (French & Raven, 1959). Much of an individual's power is derived from her society/ social status and standing. For example, when an individual is appointed to lead a group, this usually occurs because of her position within the social hierarchy of the organization.

These power arrangements come with benefits and drawbacks. On the one hand, productive uses of power can facilitate group processes (Sell, Lovaglia, Mannix, Samuelson, & Wilson, 2004). On the other hand, leaders or group members may turn legitimate power into *coercive* power, or threats, to get others to do what they want. For example, they may threaten to withdraw or undermine the process if group members don't do what they want, as experienced by our student Sarah's group (see *It Happened to Me: Sarah*). In dealing with this dominating member, Sarah's group might have tried some relational roles such as expediter and/or harmonizer to prevent the dominator from derailing the group discussions.

IT HAPPENED TO ME: *Sarah*

We had one girl in our group who was headstrong. She wanted to do the project "her way." She insisted that we follow her suggestions. If we didn't, she refused to participate and made comments that undermined the group work. If we did listen to her, then she was sweet and cooperative, and everything went fine. Some members wanted to try to please her; others resented her manipulation, and this situation caused a lot of conflict in the group.

This use of coercive power is usually unproductive because, as you can see from Sarah's experience, group members resent the threats and may reciprocate by using coercive power when they get the chance. Thus, too much power or a struggle for power

can lead to resentment and poor decision making (Broome & Fulbright, 1995). In contrast, researchers find that groups whose members share power equally have higher-quality communication. When everyone participates and contributes to the discussion equally, power will more likely be distributed equally. In contrast, the unequal power of social hierarchies often occurs in the small group situation because members bring their identities and experiences to the group. Thus, members' cultural identities, which fall along a power hierarchy, can impact small group work. Let's examine how this happens.

Cultural Diversity and Small Group Communication

Given the changing demographics in the United States and abroad, small groups will increasingly include members whose backgrounds differ. As we discussed in Chapter 6, cultural backgrounds influence communication patterns, and small group communication is no exception (Broome & Fulbright, 1995; Poole & Garner, 2006). For example, people from countries where a collectivistic orientation dominates may be most concerned with maintaining harmony in the group, whereas members with an individualistic orientation may be more assertive and competitive (Oetzel, 1998). These differences can pose challenges to accomplishing group goals (Crown, 2007).

How does cultural diversity affect small-group processes? Does it result in poor communication, more conflict, lower productivity, and less satisfaction? Or can diverse groups, with their various viewpoints, make better, more effective, and more creative decisions?

Research indicates that even though interactions might be more complex, especially in the early stages of group work, diversity can lead to positive and productive outcomes. Let's look at how diversity influences four aspects of group communication: innovation, efficacy, group processes, and group enjoyment. We also explore how you, as a group member, can help diverse groups perform more effectively.

Innovation

Several researchers have found that groups with a diverse membership are more innovative than homogeneous groups (King & Anderson, 1990). In one study, ethnically diverse groups produced higher-quality ideas in brainstorming tasks (McLeod, Lobel, & Cox, 1996). In a study of *Fortune* 500 teams, racially diverse groups came up with a greater number of innovative ideas than did homogeneous groups (Cady & Valentine, 1999).

This makes sense, because having different perspectives means also having a variety of information sources to apply to a problem or issue (Salazar, 1997). This variety of information broadens people's views and their ability to evaluate. So, ultimately, a diverse workforce operating in a rapidly changing world can better monitor, identify, and respond quickly and innovatively to external problems than can a homogeneous one (Haslett & Ruebush, 1999). What are the implications for you, as a potential group/team member in professional, academic, or social settings? If the group is a diverse one, know that the potential is there for innovative work. But also remember that for maximum innovation and effectiveness, you and other team members need to encourage equal participation.

Performance (Efficacy)

Some research studies report that diverse groups work more effectively (Bowers, Pharmer, & Salas, 2000), while other studies report the opposite (van Knippenberg, De Dreu, & Homan, 2004). This isn't surprising, given the many types of diversity and the fact that each group develops communication and processes that may help or hinder their performance. Communication in diverse groups may be more challenging at the onset, so that cultural differences in attitudes and communication styles may lead to early conflict (Poole & Garner, 2006). However, if group members handle these differences well, the outcome may be as good as or better than in homogeneous groups (Oetzel, 2005; Larson, 2007; Poole & Garner, 2006). One way to handle differences well is shown in the study described below—by encouraging group cohesion at the onset.

There are several ways to accomplish this. One is by focusing the group's attention on the goal of the group, something shared by all, rather than on individual cultural differences (Crown, 2007; Poole & Garner, 2006). A second strategy is to explore commonalities among group members—for example, shared interests, activities, or experiences. In a college course, group members may discover that they are enrolled in other courses together as well or that they participate in the same extracurricular sport or social activity. In a business setting, the team members may find that they have shared professional experiences or hobbies. Some discussion of these commonalities helps solidify relationships, leading to enhanced group cohesion.

In one study, researchers placed college students in work groups, with some being racially and ethnically diverse and others being more homogeneous. Their task was to complete a class project—to analyze an organization of their choice. The students all completed their projects and then filled out a questionnaire that included four statements about their group's cohesion (for example, "I really like my group") and several about their group's effectiveness (such as how high they expected their project grade to be).

Diverse groups reported higher *efficacy,* or effectiveness, in completing their projects than did less-diverse groups. Not surprisingly, both groups ranked their group cohesion as very important to their performance. The groups reporting the highest effectiveness were those that were highly cohesive and racially and ethnically diverse. The lowest-performing groups were those that were less cohesive and less diverse (Sargent & Sue-Chan, 2001). The researchers concluded that (1) high levels of cohesiveness *and* diversity may weaken barriers that inhibit communication and that (2) "differences and 'otherness' [are] not experienced as a deficiency among groups of university students" (p. 442). It seems that building early group cohesion in diverse groups smoothes the way to managing differences in later discussions (Bantz, 1993; Oetzel, 2005; Polzer, Milton, & Swann, 2002). As a group member, you can help a diverse group perform more productively by facilitating cohesion early on in the team effort.

Group Processes

As we discussed in Chapter 6, one way in which individuals differ across cultures is in their preference for individualism or collectivism, and these preferences impact **group processes.** To understand these preferences, one group of researchers randomly assigned students to task groups so that each group had varying degrees of age, gender, and ethnic diversity. Their group task was a course assignment in which they analyzed conversations using various theories presented in class. The students then filled out questionnaires measuring the communication processes in their group (e.g., participation rate, listening, respect, and conflict management), their own individualistic-collectivist tendencies, and their satisfaction with the group work.

Interestingly, ethnic, gender, and age diversity in this study had very little effect on the communication process, but those who preferred more interdependent or collectivistic interaction participated more and cooperated more in the group. Group members who convey respect and participate in a cooperative manner are also likely to put forth substantial effort toward completing a task and to encourage the contributions of others. Why? Effective communication by some may reduce isolation and encourage effort of all group members. Not surprisingly, those members who participated more were more satisfied with the group outcome (Oetzel, 2001).

A recent related study examined the effect of diversity on group member relationships (Valenti & Rockett, 2008). The researchers hypothesized that when one or more members of a group are demographically different (gender, age, race, ethnicity) from the majority of the group members, they may communicate less with others in their work group and even develop negative feelings about the group. Moreover, they may distance themselves from other group members, not forming any close relationships. In order to test their hypotheses, researchers surveyed employees of a national consulting firm about their communication

group processes
the methods, including communication, by which a group accomplishes a task

practices and attitudes toward work relationships. They were not surprised to find that employees with the same demographic characteristics tended to talk among themselves about personal issues. However, when it came to work-related issues, they were somewhat surprised that the employees' demographic characteristics did not affect how much they communicated with others who were demographically different; this is good news for management.

So what are the implications of these studies? Like the other studies, they show that groups that are diverse in terms of race, age, ethnicity, and gender don't necessarily experience more difficult processes. Moreover, because people are diverse and different in so many ways, one can't make assumptions about any collection of individuals based on physical attributes like age, race, or gender.

Another implication is that team leaders can implement team-building exercises to increase interdependence, promote an open communication climate, and help establish group cohesion (Oetzel, 2001). This kind of leadership, as well as effective group member communication, can enhance cooperation, participation, satisfaction, and effort.

Group Enjoyment

While diverse groups may be more innovative and effective, are they more enjoyable? To explore this question, another study examined the experience of college students who worked in groups that were composed of either (1) mostly Whites or (2) mostly ethnic minorities (Asians, Asian Americans, African Americans, Hispanics, and others of mixed ethnicity). The researchers found that minorities and White students all enjoyed their experiences in minority-dominated teams more than they did in the White-dominated teams. How to explain these findings? The researchers suggest that some level of collectivism may have been working in the minority-dominated groups, and whether or not it was, members of these groups were more attentive to relational harmony (Paletz, Peng, Erez, & Maslach, 2004).

What are the implications of all these studies taken together? First, it seems that there are two types of diversity: (1) demographic diversity (age, gender, ethnicity, and race) and (2) deeper cultural diversity related to attitudes and values—individualism and collectivism preferences—that also play an important role in group functioning (Crown, 2007). Some research shows that demographic differences may influence group processes early in a group's history, while value differences may have more of an impact later on (Ilgen, Hollenbeck, Johnson, & Jundt, 2005).

Second, culturally diverse groups *may* produce more innovative ideas, *may* be more enjoyable, and can be as productive as homogeneous groups. However, enjoyment and productivity do not occur automatically in these groups; they depend largely on the communication skills of the group members, which do not always come naturally. "Many people believe that good communication skills are 'common sense.' Contrary to expectations, the problem with common sense is that it is not all that common" (Oetzel, 2005, p. 366). Thus, leaders and members of culturally diverse groups need to focus on helping all team members, including reticent ones, learn to participate fully and to communicate respectfully in a way that promotes collaboration, group cohesion, and consensus building.

These findings suggest that organizations need to develop policies and programs that allow for and value the unique characteristics of each group (Cady & Valentine, 1999). Further, with proper education and development, diverse teams have the potential of experiencing higher levels of satisfaction and lower turnover (Cox, 1994, cited in Cady & Valentine, 1999). Supporting this idea is the finding that groups with high diversity but without proper education in group process are associated with high turnover and more conflict (Poole & Garner, 2006; Sargent & Sue-Chan, 2001).

To summarize, communicating in groups, as does all other communicating, occurs within societal structures—whether the groups are teams working in a small business,

task forces in a nonprofit organization, or small problem-solving groups in a college course. These social structures establish power relations and status hierarchies that in turn come into play in group interaction. The cultural backgrounds of group members also influence group communication, and, if handled well, cultural diversity can enhance group innovation, performance, communication processes, and enjoyment. At bottom, however, effective group work flows from effective and ethical communication skills, the topic we turn to next.

ETHICS AND SMALL GROUP COMMUNICATION

Ethical communication in small groups is especially important because the success of the group and the task depend on it. One might argue that being in a group carries additional ethical responsibilities because one's individual actions can affect how people think about and react to other members of the group and their ideas. In short, in groups, you are no longer responsible only for yourself but for other members as well.

It might help to think about the ethical guidelines discussed in Chapter 1 and consider how they might apply to a small group context. Being truthful in your communication is particularly important, as you are making contributions that affect larger collective decisions (Hargrove, 1998). Truthfulness also includes being accurate and avoiding exaggeration. For example, if you were reporting facts about crime on campus, you would offer statistics, not just say, "I found out that crime is really a huge problem."

While you should strive for accuracy and honesty in your language, at times you should not say everything you know—for example, to respect the confidentiality of others, including group members. If your friend has been raped and you think this information might help your group discussion about campus security, you should ask for your friend's permission before you say anything to the group. Similarly, group members may disclose personal information in the group discussion that they may not wish repeated outside the group.

Group members should also work toward communicating authentically, as discussed in Chapter 1. As we noted earlier, group cohesion and trust are important to the performance and success of groups. Authentic communication that is open and free from pretense, and language that is inclusive and not hurtful to others, promote the kind of group relationships necessary for group effectiveness.

Finally, as a receiver of information, you must listen with an open mind while also evaluating others' contributions. Doing so will enhance the quality of discussions and help prevent groupthink, in which groups jump to premature conclusions and decisions.

IMPROVING YOUR SMALL GROUP COMMUNICATION SKILLS

While no strategies will work in every group communication situation, two strategies can help you be more effective in many of them.

First, cultivate an interdependent or collectivist attitude. This means that you must sacrifice some of your personal ambition, needs, and wants in favor of the group's needs. People who are extremely individualistic may find this difficult. Yet those with a more collectivist attitude can influence group processes toward more effective communication, more participation, and more satisfaction for all members (Oetzel, 2005).

In addition to cultivating an interdependent attitude, striving for cohesion is very important in successful small group relationships and task accomplishment. Cohesion occurs when team members trust each other. Further, group success depends on the

participation of each member, but members are unlikely to give their best to the group if they can't trust other members to do the same. Trust is particularly important in virtual teams, where members have less face-to-face interaction, and those face-to-face interactions can sometimes provide important cues to the intent or attitude of fellow group members. To build trust and cohesion, try these strategies:

- Focus on the strengths of all group members, and recognize their contributions to group goals. Be sure to acknowledge all group achievements.
- Remind the group of common interests and background experiences. Doing this can help build cohesion, prevent unnecessary conflict, and strengthen group identity.
- Be observant and notice when a member might be feeling unappreciated or uninvolved in the group. Encourage that person to participate. People gain trust and become more trusting as they participate, especially if their participation is encouraged. Fortunately, more trust leads to more cohesion and stronger group identity, which in turn leads to better communication, more satisfaction, and more cohesion.

In sum, the effectiveness of a small group depends in large part on the communication and the relationships established among the members. As a group member, you can promote (or inhibit) the productive communication needed. We believe that using the tools discussed in this chapter will not only make your small group work more effective, but they will make it more enjoyable.

SUMMARY

Small group members share a common purpose, are interdependent, and exert influence on each other. Small group communication is a fact of life, and learning to be a better small group communicator can enhance your academic performance, your career achievement, and your personal success. The primary benefit of small groups is that they are more productive and creative than an individual working alone. The disadvantages are that decisions take longer and relational problems and conflicts can make the experience less than satisfying.

Communication is the "lifeblood that flows through the veins of the small group." Thirteen task and eight relational roles are required for effective group work. In effective groups, individuals fill these roles as needed at any given time during group work. Eight individual roles also exist that group members may fill; these roles, however, tend to be dysfunctional and unproductive. Effective group communication in many types of small groups include: equal participation, a consensus decision-making style, a cooperative conflict style, and a respectful communication style.

The most common type of small group is the problem-solving group, which often follows a five-stage agenda: (1) defining the problem, (2) analyzing the problem, (3) identifying alternative solutions, (4) evaluating the proposed solutions, and (5) choosing the best solution. Related to the five-stage agenda are the four phases of decision making that most groups complete in every stage of the problem-solving agenda: orientation, conflict, emergence, and reinforcement. Technology plays an increasing role in small group work, as we touched on here.

Societal forces impact small group processes via the role of power and cultural diversity in small group work. While cultural diversity can present challenges for group processes, it can also produce innovative, efficient, and enjoyable group experiences if

handled appropriately. Building cohesion and trust in early stages of group work is particularly important in diverse groups. Ethical guidelines for small group communication include being truthful and accurate, respecting confidentiality, and striving for authentic and open communication. Skills for achieving effective group communication include cultivating an interdependent attitude and striving for trust and cohesion.

KEY TERMS

analysis paralysis 267
brainstorm 267
decision-making process 267
emergence phase 270
group processes 276
group roles 259
group support software (GSS) 272

grouphate 257
groupthink 270
individual roles 263
primary groups 257
primary tension 268
reinforcement phase 270
relational roles 261

secondary groups 257
secondary (recurring) tension 268
small group communication 256
social facilitation 258
task roles 260
virtual work team 272

CHAPTER REVIEW QUESTIONS

1. How does a small group, as defined in this chapter, differ from a group of individuals waiting in line at a bank?

2. What is the difference between task and relational role behaviors in small group communication? How are they related to each other?

3. What is groupthink? What are the primary causes of groupthink?

4. Why do many successful problem-solving groups follow an agenda?

5. What are the four phases of decision making? Do most groups follow these phases in a linear or a more circular fashion?

6. How does a collectivist perspective enhance small group work?

ACTIVITIES

1. **Group Roles Activity**
   Think of a recent group experience you've had. Look at the list of task, relational, and individual role behaviors in Tables 11.1 through 11.3. Make a list of all behaviors and roles you filled. Which behaviors (if any) were missing in your group? Which other roles might you have filled?

2. **Group Problem-Solving Activity**
   This activity can be assigned either as an individual or small group experience. Identify a problem you have encountered recently on your campus. Come up with a viable solution to this problem by following the problem-solving agenda. Which steps of the agenda were relatively easy? Which were more difficult? Why?

3. **Groupthink Exercise**
   Consider experiences you've had in group work. Answer the following questions concerning groupthink. After answering the questions, meet with several classmates and compare answers. Then, as a group, come up with suggestions for ensuring against groupthink.

- Have you ever felt so secure about a group decision that you ignored all the warning signs that the decision was wrong? Why?

- Have you ever applied undue pressure to members who disagreed in order to get them to agree with the will of the group?

- Have you ever participated in a "we-versus-they" feeling—that is, depicting those in the group who are opposed to you in simplistic, stereotyped ways?

- Have you ever served as a "mind guard"—that is, have you ever attempted to preserve your group's cohesiveness by preventing disturbing outside ideas or opinions from becoming known to other group members?

- Have you ever assumed that the silence of the other group members implied agreement?

SOURCE: Adapted from Meade, L. (2003). Small group home page. *The Message: A Communication Website.* Retrieved June 19, 2006, from: http://lynn_meade.tripod.com/id62.htm

WEB ACTIVITIES

1. Go to http://www.wilderdom.com/research.html This Web site of the Outdoor Education Research and Evaluation Center contains useful information about group norms, leadership development, and cultural diversity in groups, as well as group games and activities. This section of the Web site lists strategies for providing support in group settings. What role does communication play in each of these strategies?

2. Go to http://www.psysr.org/about/pubs_resources/groupthink%20overview.htm This is another good resource page about group work. It gives examples of groupthink, including several government activities. Read the descriptions of groupthink. In what ways might the search for weapons of mass destruction in Iraq have been a result of groupthink?

12

LEADERSHIP IN GROUPS AND ORGANIZATIONS

I've worked at several different organizations in different sectors, and I have found that the most important thing that leaders, bosses, or supervisors can do is give their subordinates a sense of empowerment. When you're given a task by your boss, you want her to trust that you'll do a good job—you want her to believe in your abilities and give you the space to succeed. I couldn't work for someone who questioned everything I did or watched my every move.

As our student Martha describes it, effective leadership involves more than just giving directions or orders; it can also be about empowerment and sharing power and responsibilities. In this chapter, we will see that there are many ways to provide leadership. We will first define leadership and describe the importance of learning more about this topic. Then we describe leadership communication and several characteristics that may influence one's leadership. We discuss current approaches to understanding and studying leadership, paying close attention to the role of communication. In the second part of the chapter, we address how societal forces interact with individual approaches to leadership and identify ethical issues involved. Finally, we provide suggestions for improving your own leadership potential.

After you read this chapter, you will be able to:

- Define leadership.
- Understand the importance of learning about leadership.
- Describe dimensions of leadership communication.
- Analyze the characteristics that influence leadership.
- Identify and describe five different leadership theories.
- Recognize challenges and make recommendations for virtual team leadership.
- Explain ethical challenges in leadership.
- Discuss ways to improve your own leadership skills.

CHAPTER OUTLINE

WHAT IS LEADERSHIP?

THE IMPORTANCE OF LEADERSHIP

LEADERSHIP AND THE INDIVIDUAL
    The Role of Communication in Leadership
    Influences on Leadership

THEORIES OF LEADERSHIP
    Functional Theory
    Style Theory
    Transformational Leadership Theory
    Servant Leadership Theory
    Toxic Leadership

THE INDIVIDUAL, LEADERSHIP, AND SOCIETY

ETHICS AND LEADERSHIP
    Honesty
    Respect and Service to Others
    Fairness and Justice
    Building Community
    Moral Leadership

BECOMING AN EFFECTIVE LEADER
    Conduct a Leadership Self-Assessment
    Search for Leadership Opportunities
    Improve Your Strategic Communication Skills

Summary

Key Terms

Chapter Review Questions

Activities

Web Activities

leadership
an influence relationship among leaders and followers who intend real changes and outcomes that reflect their shared purposes

WHAT IS LEADERSHIP?

Several definitions of leadership exist, but most include certain basic elements. We define **leadership** as "an influence relationship among leaders and followers who intend real changes and outcomes that reflect their shared purposes" (Daft, 2008, p. 4). Let's look more closely at the key elements in the definition. First, the bottom line is that leadership is an influence relationship and as such can be part of many of our everyday activities (see *Did You Know? Leadership is an Influence Relationship*).

DID YOU KNOW?

Leadership Is an Influence Relationship

Shawn M. Fouts, who works with student leadership training at his university, blogs about his view of leadership as an "influence relationship":

This leadership thing is consuming me. Not that I have always been the consummate leader, mainly due to a lack of knowledge and modeling. But, as I work with this thing called leadership I have come to a few conclusions:

1. Leadership is a philosophy, not a theory.
2. Leadership philosophy is life philosophy, in my mind the two are one.
3. Leadership is nothing more than Relationships + Influence. How can I influence people in my relationships?

Leadership = Relationships + Influence

Profoundly simple really. I wonder why we see such a lack of leadership all around us then? I intentionally choose to be a leader (at the least an active participant) in everything I do, everywhere I go, and in every relationship I currently have and make on a daily basis, no matter how big or how small. But, I have to choose to be an influence and I have to choose what kind of influence I will be, either positive or negative. I wonder if influencing one really is influencing many? I think it's worth a try.

SOURCE: Shawn M. Fouts, *The Student Affairs Blog,* West Texas A & M University. Retrieved August 1, 2009, from http://www.thesablog.org/2007/06/leadership_as_a.html

Second, this influence does not just reside in one person, but rather is a process that involves relationships among people—leaders and followers. In fact, good leaders know how to follow and set an example for others (Daft, 2008; Northouse, 2007; Rost, 2008). Influence is not just top-down but can be reciprocal, multidirectional, and should be noncoercive. In most organizations and groups, superiors influence subordinates, but subordinates also influence superiors. Any leader is a leader as long as there are followers. If followers do not feel that the leader is going where they want to go, many often leave for a different leader. This relationship, then, between the leader and the followers is ongoing and each influences the others. For example, some conservatives are getting involved in the TEA party movement because they are concerned about large federal deficits and large federal spending. Many are paying attention to what Sarah Palin has to say. Other conservatives remain committed to the religious right. They tend to follow Pat Robertson and other leaders. Still others are listening to GOP party officials, such as Michael Steele. The point is that conservatives are interacting with various leaders and other followers and choose which direction they wish to follow.

Third, leadership involves the desire for change. This distinguishes the concept of leadership from management, which is more about order and stability. The people involved in a leadership relationship want substantive changes. A political leader, such as President Obama, was elected as a leader to bring about change. If he does not do so to the satisfaction of the electorate, he may have a difficult time getting reelected.

Fourth, leadership includes attention to goals. The desired changes reflect the shared purposes of leaders and followers. An important aspect of leadership is influencing others to come together around a common vision. This shared vision helps get to a shared goal, as the leader and followers can all take action together to get to this goal For example, Martin Luther King, Jr. built a shared vision around nonviolent protest and mobilized his followers around this shared vision in their engagement with what they felt were unjust legal and social practices. On a more local level, ordinary citizens and students can also rally others around a strongly held idea for change, as we'll see later in the chapter.

This definition covers the full range of leadership levels—from a student chairing a committee in charge of a fraternity fundraiser to a CEO directing a multinational technology company through a difficult merger. At its best, leadership is shared among leaders and followers, with everyone fully engaged and accepting ever-higher levels of responsibility (Daft, 2008).

? Considering the definition of leadership provided here, in which of your relationships and everyday activities do you provide leadership? In which contexts (school, home, extracurricular activities) are you most likely to provide leadership?

THE IMPORTANCE OF LEADERSHIP

There are many reasons to learn more about leadership. First, as we noted in Chapter 11, groups are a part of our everyday life. As a group member in community, church, synagogue, school, or social groups, you may have noticed that most groups and organizations function better with effective leadership. In fact, a group or organization's success is often directly related to the presence of good leadership. For example, one study showed that the most important influence on worker satisfaction and productivity in organizations is the actions of the immediate supervisor (Bock, 2004).

Second, leadership is a concern for all of us because it is not just a quality for those with formal subordinates. Rather, leadership occurs in many forms and contexts; as one expert says, leadership can take place "during a sales call, a customer service response, a family decision or a meeting with friends" (Gollent, 2007). As we'll see later, there is often little difference between leaders and followers; we can be both leaders and followers at different times in the same groups or organization, and in a way, we all share in the responsibility to contribute to smooth and effective functioning of the groups and organizations we belong to (Komives, Lucas, & McMahon, 1998).

Leadership is about relationships, influence, and setting a good example—demonstrated often in community organizations like this Boy Scout troop.

Finally, for the most part, leaders are made—not born—which means that good-quality leadership doesn't just happen. Good leadership (and follower) skills can be learned. This means that we can all benefit from learning something about and practicing good leadership skills. As we describe leadership characteristics and theories throughout this chapter, think about the ways in which you may play leadership roles in the various groups and organizations where you are a member.

LEADERSHIP AND THE INDIVIDUAL

The individual study of leadership includes at least two components: (1) the important role of communication and (2) characteristics that influence leadership (e.g., gender, personality). Let's first address the role of communication in leadership.

The Role of Communication in Leadership

It would be easy to assume that leaders are naturally good communicators, but communication researchers have not confirmed this (Pavitt, 1999); as one leadership expert says, "just because leaders are smart doesn't mean they communicate well. Just because a leader sounds good and has an impressive looking presentation, doesn't mean he or she communicates well. In the end, it's not what you say but what your audience hears—and we argue, what your audience *does*—that counts" (Matha & Boehm, 2008, p. 8).

Most experts agree that communication is key to being an effective leader, regardless of the particular leadership style or the context in which one provides leadership—whether it's providing guidance on a small group project in a communication course, heading up a fundraising project for your sorority, managing the employees at a fast food restaurant, or being CEO of a *Fortune* 500 company. While the responsibilities and skills needed to run a company are more complex than those needed to head up a student organization, regardless of the leadership context, according to Matha and Boehm (2008), "communication is the face of leadership" (p. 20). However, it is easy to take communication for granted and focus on other challenges in the group or organization—a reason that many leaders fail at communication. As one leadership communication consultant puts it, "Communication requires discipline, thought, perseverance and the willingness do it again and again" (Baldoni, 2004, p. 24).

The role of communication in leadership is not just declaring a vision, giving orders, and making sure that the vision is implemented. It is more about building trust and commitment to the vision through communication; it is ultimately about building relationships (Uhl-Bien, 2006) and bringing people together for a common cause. Leadership experts Robert and Janet Denhardt (2004) describe the essence of leadership as the capacity to "energize" potential followers by *connecting* with people at a personal, sometimes emotional level so that they become engaged and active.

Matha and Boehm (2008) give a good example of a CEO of an airline company who recognized the importance of promoting an emotional commitment to a shared vision through effective communication. This particular CEO planned a merger with a rival airline. In an open meeting with his employees, he presented the rationale for the new acquisition: that it would yield new routes, increase market share, and deliver returns to stockholders. However, the employees didn't buy it. For them, the acquisition meant lost seniority and greater competition for the best job assignments, and they hated the airline the CEO wanted to acquire. For years they had been talking about that airline as the dregs of the industry; they couldn't imagine working side by side with employees from the other company. Then the CEO listened to what employees were saying, came to understand the basis for the employees' resistance, and reformulated his communication to make an emotional appeal to the employees. "This acquisition will establish us once again as the most elite airline in the business . . . that's who we are, that's what we deserve." Within six weeks, the employees were not only accepting the acquisition but supporting it (p. 77).

The same principle of connecting with others and energizing them works with leadership in small group work also. Think about the communication that occurs in many small groups brought together to solve a problem or complete a task:

> The conversation will swirl around inconclusively for a while (sometimes a long time) until one person makes a suggestion that others pick up on and begin to act upon. People's reactions may be based on the substance of what was said or on the way in which it was presented, or most likely, some combination of both. But, in any case, we would say that where people react with energy and enthusiasm, leadership has been exercised (Denhardt & Denhardt, 2004, p. 20).

Connecting with potential followers can also be part of a larger strategic communication plan. In this chapter, strategic communication is a positive force, not the negative defensive communication message, referred to in Chapter 5 – also referred to a "strategic communication." What is **strategic communication** in the leadership context? According to leadership experts Matha and Boehm (2008), strategic communication is purpose directed—it directs

strategic communication
communication that is purpose directed—it directs everyone's attention toward the vision, values, and desired outcomes and persuades people to act in a way that helps to achieve the vision

everyone's attention toward the vision, values, and desired outcomes and persuades people to act in a way that helps achieve the vision. This means that a leader must first figure out what motivates people and appeal to that, giving them the information they need to do their job, listening to them, and then getting out of their way, as exemplified by the story our student tells about his boss in *It Happened to Me: Boris*.

Effective leaders are committed to communicating willingly and consistently. As we will see, there is no one way of leading and there is no one way of communication, if leaders are to form meaningful relationships, energize their potential followers, and achieve desired

results (Baldoni, 2004). Later in this chapter, we'll provide clear guidelines that you can use to improve your own strategic communication skills.

Influences on Leadership

What determines whether someone becomes an effective leader? Gender? Personality? Do men and women have different lead-

IT HAPPENED TO ME: Boris

One of the best leaders I had the pleasure of working for was rather quiet and low key, but a good communicator. She often asked us to let her know what we needed that would make us more productive, and if feasible, she supplied it. She had so much confidence in our team that it made us want to work that much harder for her. Whenever she did criticize or step in, she did it in a constructive way, with a collaborative tone. She never made us feel defensive or angry. She was really clear in her expectations for our department and let us run with our work.

ership styles? Do they have equal potential for leadership? Are some people better leaders just because of their personalities? These questions are addressed in the following sections.

Gender and Leadership

Most experts agree that gender plays an important role in perceptions of leadership qualities. More than 15 years ago, a researcher described a dilemma encountered by many women leaders at that time:

> Leadership, as we know it, is steeped in idealized masculine images, our collective fantasy sees leaders as "big, colorful, fast, and assertive." Women attempting to enact this image find themselves caught in a "double bind." If they act like men, they are rejected for being "unfeminine" but if they act like women, they couldn't possibly be a leader. What's a woman to do? (Heifetz, 1994, cited in Ladkin, 2008, p. 65).

Do these stereotypes and the resulting double bind for women leaders still exist today? Before addressing this question, let's look at the current statistics on women in leadership. The fact is that women today occupy few leadership positions within businesses, government, education, and nonprofit organizations (Ladkin, 2008). Although women currently hold more than half of all management and professional positions in *Fortune* 500 companies, they represent only about 5 percent of top earners, 14.7 percent of the board members, 7.9 percent of the highest titles, and less than 2 percent of the CEOs (Catalyst, 2007). In the political realm, while there are a few high-profile women (e.g., Hilary Clinton, Madeleine Albright, Sarah Palin), women currently hold only 90 of the 535 seats (16.83%) in the U.S. Congress (Facts on Women in Congress, 2010). The situation is similar in Europe (Broadbridge & Hearn, 2008; Singh & Vinnecombe, 2006). These statistics reinforce the perception that leadership is a masculine concept (Hoyt, Simon, & Reid, 2009) and that the glass ceiling remains firmly in place. The **glass ceiling** refers to informal barriers, like discrimination and prejudice, that prevent women (and minorities) from advancing in organizations (Hymowitz & Schellhardt, 1986).

Women are underrepresented in leadership positions for many reasons. Some women, perhaps, don't want to choose the leadership route but would prefer to play other roles in an organization. Also, some organizational structures (e.g., hiring procedures, promotional routes, working hours required to demonstrate commitment) may hold women back and contribute to the glass ceiling (Judge & Livingston, 2008; Ladkin, 2008). However, the most frequently cited cause is the negative perception/stereotype of female

glass ceiling
informal barriers, like discrimination and prejudice, that prevent women (and minorities) from advancing in organizations

leaders and women's particular leadership styles. For example, research studies document widespread prejudice against women leaders—even when they perform as well as male leaders (Hoyt et al., 2009).

In one study, students in a large undergraduate class were randomly placed into mixed-sex small groups that were all given a problem to solve. One person (either male or female) in each group was privately given information that would provide an effective solution to the problem and asked to persuade the group to adopt the solution. (The researchers say this is comparable to real-life situations where group members may have critical information that can contribute to effective group problem solving). After the problem was solved in each group, group members were asked to rate each of the participants on a number of dimensions including participation, leadership effectiveness, and likeability. It turns out that the men and women who had the hints were equally effective in persuading their groups to adopt their solution. They were also rated by others as equally influential, competent, and participative. However, the "hint women" (with the prior solutions) were significantly less likely than the "hint men" to be seen as the group's leaders and were rated as less likeable than the "hint men." The researchers note that their results are similar to many other studies and conclude that "women are still not expected to be leaders in problem-solving groups, and will not be evaluated as favorably even when they are as successfully influential as men" (Watson & Hoffman, 2004, p. 679).

A recent survey of 500 upper-level employees seems to support the classroom findings. This survey showed that female employees were less likely to be promoted than males, and if they were promoted, they had stronger performance ratings than males. In addition, performance ratings were more strongly connected to promotions for women than men (Lyness & Heilman, 2006). This suggests that women had to be highly impressive to be considered eligible for leadership roles, whereas this was not the case for men.

Gender stereotypes are not only powerful, they are persistent. Men are stereotypically expected to possess characteristics such as assertiveness, independence, rationality, and decisiveness (attributes considered essential for leadership), whereas women are believed and expected to possess more "communal" characteristics including showing concern for others, warmth, helpfulness, and nurturance—not attributes essential for leadership (Hoyt et al. 2009). Are these stereotypes accurate? Some research has found that, in general, women prefer less-competitive environments than men, tend to be more collaborative and interactive, and are more concerned with relationship building, inclusiveness, participation, and caring. They are also more willing to share power and information and encourage employee development (Daft, 2008, p. 338; Rosener, 1995; Williams, 1995). Other studies found that men's styles were not more task oriented, nor did women seem to lead in a more interpersonal style, but they did find that women's leadership style tended to be more democratic or participative than men's (Eagly & Carli, 2003; Eagly & Johnson, 1990).

Many leadership theories today extol these so-called "feminine" leadership characteristics. That is, values associated with participative leadership such as inclusion, relationship building, and caring—generally considered "feminine" values—are becoming increasingly valuable for both male and female leaders. Today's team-based orientations are looking for more collaborative and inclusive approaches to leadership (Daft, 2008). In addition, women are being increasingly valued as leaders. In fact, a recent Catalyst study

Women are being increasingly valued as leaders. In fact, a recent study found that those with the most women in senior management had a higher return on equities by more than a third.

of 353 *Fortune* 500 companies found that those with the most women in senior management had a higher return on equities by more than a third (Shipman & Kay, 2009).

So, what is the bottom line regarding gender and leadership? One expert suggests a three-pronged approach: (1) Actively work to eliminate negative stereotypes about women leaders, because many are inaccurate. (2) Acknowledge that so-called women's leadership characteristics (collaborative, participative) are included in overall effective leadership styles. If women and men do have different styles, then organizations should celebrate this difference in order to gain the most benefit from unique capabilities (Daft, 2008; Ladkin, 2008). (3) Both men and women should work to achieve diverse leadership strengths. In general, we should focus less on sex-linked skills and traits and ask instead, "Who else is missing from leadership roles?" (Ely, 2003, p. 16, quoted in Ladkin, p. 66).

Personality Traits and Leadership

Another individual characteristic linked to leadership is that of personality traits. Do extroverts make better leaders than introverts? Are effective leaders more open? More intelligent? While thousands of personality dimensions have been examined by psychologists over the years, five overall dimensions seem to emerge in the leadership area (Hogan, Hogan, & Roberts, 1996; Judge, Bono, Ilies, & Gerhardt, 2002; Stogdill, 1974):

- Extraversion: active, assertive, energetic, enthusiastic, outgoing, and talkative
- Agreeableness: appreciative, forgiving, generous, kind, sympathetic, and trusting
- Conscientiousness: efficient, organized, reliable, responsible, and thorough
- Emotional Stability: well-adjusted, calm, and secure
- Open to experience: artistic, curious, introspective, imaginative, insightful, original, with a wide range of interests

One study found that people who score high on four out of five personality dimensions (all but openness) tend to be successful leaders (Hogan, Curphy, & Hogan, 1994). In a later study, historians rated openness to experience as one of the most important personality characteristics of successful U.S. presidents (Schmid, 2000). In a recent study that used comprehensive ratings of leaders (superior, peer, and subordinate), conscientiousness was found to be a significant predictor of leadership ability (Strang & Kuhnert, 2009).

Other studies have found that leaders seem to be smarter than other people as measured by standard IQ tests (Judge, Colbert, & Ilies, 2004). In looking at these research results, remember that researchers found that successful leaders do not necessarily *have to* possess all these personality characteristics, and some may score very low in any one of these dimensions. For example, many successful leaders, including Bill Gates and Steven Spielberg, are **introverts**—people who do not get energy from interaction with others.

The idea that personality or intelligence is related to leadership effectiveness is called **trait theory** (Stogdill, 1974), which suggests that leaders are born. Some of the traits associated with effective leadership are physical and include being male, tall, and good looking. For example, not since 1896 have U.S. citizens elected a president whose height was below average, and even today, people associate height with leadership ability (Judge & Cable, 2004).

Despite the correlation between leaders and particular traits, one cannot ignore the role of society in forming our judgments about who we think makes a good leader. For example, early business writings suggested that the function of the business leader was to "fit in" with others in the workplace. Requirements for fitting in were shared "education, experience, age, sex, race, nationality, faith, politics, and such very specific personal traits as manners, speech, personal appearance" (Barnard, 1938, p. 224). Of course, in 1938, fitting in was only possible for White males of a certain background and education. In addition, the trait approach may reinforce the notion that only people born with certain qualities can achieve leadership, ignoring the fact that only those who have the most status and power in the society also possess these qualities.

Many examples challenge the trait approach to leadership. In recent years, a number of people have developed leadership qualities out of a tragedy or a deep motivation to make the world a better place. Candy Lightner, who founded MADD (Mothers Against Drunk

introverts

people who do not get energy from interaction with others

trait theory

leadership theory that suggests that leaders are born

Driving) when her child was killed by a drunk driver, is one of these. Judy Shepard, mother of Matthew Shepard, a gay student who was severely beaten and murdered, became an outspoken leader and advocate for tolerance and justice (Groutage, 1999). Neither woman was a "born leader," but both took on leadership roles when the situation demanded it.

Perhaps you know of college students who have been motivated to take on similar leadership roles. For instance, undergraduate Sindhura Citineni felt determined to make a difference when confronted by the appalling statistics of world hunger she found while researching on the Internet. Citineni worked out a deal with her university to sell several simple food items in the cafeteria and donate part of the revenue to hunger-relief work—a project called Hunger Lunch. She then led a group of students who expanded that project into Nourish International, now a nonprofit organization that connects college students from universities around the nation to development projects abroad (nourishinternational.org).

Now that we have identified some characteristics associated with leadership but rejected the trait-theory notion that leaders are born not made, what *are* characteristics of a good leader? In the next section, we describe several theories that define and explain effective leadership.

THEORIES OF LEADERSHIP

Most groups and organizations have a leader. Some are designated or appointed, and some emerge during group interaction. In any case, a good leader can be the key to successful communication in a group. Consequently, researchers have attempted to determine the qualities a small group leader should possess. This research has resulted in four theories that explain effective leaders: functional theory, style theory, transformational theory, and servant leadership theory. Additional research focuses on leaders who are particularly ineffective—known as toxic leaders.

Functional Theory

Functional (or situational) theory stands in direct contrast to the notion that leaders are born and that leadership is innate. This theory applies primarily to small group leadership and assumes that leadership behaviors can be learned—even by group members who are not "leadership types." **Functional theory** assumes that whatever the group needs at a particular time can be supplied by a set of behaviors any group member can contribute (Benne & Sheats, 1948; Pavitt, 1999). Thus, this theory argues that the leader can change from time to time, depending on the changing needs of the group.

According to this theory, a group does not need a designated leader; rather, any group member can serve as leader at any particular time by filling the required role. For example, the leader can fill task roles when the group needs direction, whereas she steps into relational roles when group members understand the task but need encouragement. Occasionally, no leadership is needed, such as when the short- and long-term purpose is clear and group members are working well independently.

As we noted in Chapter 11, group success does not depend on the number of task or relational behaviors that group members engage in, but rather on whether they exhibit the required role behavior when needed. For example, too much emphasis on task can lead to negative outcomes if the task is already clearly defined and understood by all group members. Too much relational leadership is distracting if members view it as getting in the way of completing the group task (Rauch & Behling, 1984). Thus, if a group has almost completed its task and discussion is going smoothly, constant encourager behavior may be distracting and unnecessary.

A recent study tried to identify the type of leadership communication needed in functional leadership. The context for the study was a series of simulations in which students needed to make decisions about how to allocate resources in a fictional organization. The researchers analyzed leadership-relevant communication during group discussions and then compared these communication behaviors with group outcomes and with participants' self-reports. They found that groups performed better if their

functional (situational) theory
a theory that assumes that leadership behaviors can be learned

discussion was explicitly directed, if they exchanged relevant and accurate information about the simulation, and if they frequently summed up their decision-making progress. These results suggest an important leadership communication function: ensuring that task roles such as information seeker, information giver, and orienter (discussed in the previous chapter) are effectively enacted in group processes (Pavitt, 1999; Pavitt, High, Tressler, & Winslow, 2007).

A related notion is **shared leadership,** also called **collaborative or distributed leadership** (Pearce & Conger, 2003). Here, the functional leadership approach is extended to an organizational level where team relationships become more of a partnership in an organization (MacNeil & McClanahan, 2005). The requirements for this kind of leadership are: a balance of power where all members are equal partners, a common purpose or goal, a shared responsibility for the work of the group (taking an active role and being accountable for completing individual contributions), respect for the person and skills and ideas that they bring to the team, and working together in complex real-world situations.

Organizations where shared leadership prevails are organizations that are often heavily focused on mentoring and developing leadership potential. A **mentor** is an advocate and guide who nurtures growth, helping the mentee to realize the potential within them. This is usually done through a combination of methods: by modeling new behavior, by having the mentee assist in a new task (such as through an apprenticeship), or by allowing the mentee to work individually with guidance (Omatsu, n.d.).

Recent studies show that shared leadership can work for many types of organizations, including law enforcement, educational, and nonprofit groups. For example, police teams that practice collaborative (shared) leadership (e.g., having an employee steering committee) have much better labor-management relations, better relations with community, and an improvement in police perceptions of their working conditions (Steinheider & Wuestewald, 2008). A similar study found that shared leadership is particularly effective in schools where teachers, administration, and community members need to work together. Under the shared leadership model, the vision for a school is for students, parents, teachers, and principals to all become school leaders in some ways and at some times. The main job of the administrator, then, is to enhance individual skills, promote productive relationships among members, and create a common culture of expectations (MacNeil & McClanahan, 2005). A final study examined leadership of 12 of the most successful nonprofit organizations in the United States and found out that every one of the 12 groups used the shared leadership model throughout their organization (Grant & Crutchfield, 2008).

Style Theory

Style theory asserts that a leader's manner or style of leading a group determines her or his success. Further, this theory describes three common styles of leadership: authoritarian, democratic, and laissezire. (See *Visual Summary 12.1: Leadership Styles.*)

Authoritarian

An **authoritarian** leader takes charge and has a high level of intellect and expertise (Lewin, Lippit, & White, 1939). The authoritarian leader makes all the decisions and dictates strategies and work tasks. This type of leadership is appropriate in military, sports, or crisis situations. For example, military organizations have a highly authoritarian structure, and the chain of command must be rigorously followed. In battle, there is no time for discussion and little room for trial and error. This is also true of sports-team leadership. For example, when 25 seconds are left in a basketball game and the score is tied, only one person—the coach—can tell the team members how to execute the next play.

Authoritarian leadership is also appropriate in crises. Medical teams in an emergency room generally follow authoritarian leadership—one person, the doctor, directs the others in what needs to be done. This style of leadership may also be followed when time for discussion is short or when the stakes are very high (Meade, 1985).

shared (collaborative or distributed) leadership
a type of leadership style where functional leadership is extended to an organizational level; all members are equal partners and share responsibility for the work of the group

mentor
an advocate and guide who nurtures growth, helping the mentee to realize the potential within them—usually through a combination of methods: by modeling new behavior, by having the mentee assist in a new task (such as through an apprenticeship), or by allowing the mentee to work individually with guidance

style theory
theory that asserts that a leader's manner or style determines his or her success

authoritarian leadership style
characterized by a leader who takes charge, makes all the decisions, and dictates strategies and work tasks

democratic leadership style
a leadership style that is characterized by considerable input from group members

laissez-faire leadership style
a leadership style characterized by complete freedom for the group in making decisions

transformational leadership theory
a leadership style that empowers group members to work independently from the leader by encouraging group cohesion

extraversion
the ability to convey positive emotions and project optimism and enthusiasm

Democratic

This is the style we are most familiar with and that seems to work best in many group situations. The **democratic** style is characterized by a great deal of input from group members; the qualities of the leader are best summarized by Lao-Tse (550 BCE): "A good leader is one who talks little; when his work is done, his aim fulfilled, they will all say 'We did this ourselves' " (cited in Foels, Driskell, Mullen, & Salas, 2000, p. 677). In this style, group discussion determines all policies, strategies, and division of labor. Members are free to assume a variety of roles, to contribute when appropriate, and to share leadership. Further, research supports the idea that most groups are more satisfied with a democratic leader than an authoritarian one (Foels et al., 2000; Gastil, 1994). However, as noted in the examples above, different situations call for different leadership styles.

Laissez-faire

Some small group situations call for a **laissez-faire** style, which is characterized by complete freedom for the group in making decisions. The leader participates minimally and may supply materials and information when asked, but she makes no attempt to evaluate or influence the discussion. This style may work when little is at stake, as in some social groups or reading groups (Barge, 1989).

Transformational Leadership Theory

A relatively new theory, **transformational leadership theory,** emphasizes the importance of relationships in leadership. The role of the transformational leader is to empower group members to work independently from the leader by encouraging collaboration between members and group cohesion. This seems to be the leadership style of Martha's boss, described in the vignette at the beginning of this chapter. There are at least four general characteristics shared by transformational leaders. First, they have high moral and ethical standards that engender high regard and loyalty from followers. Second, they have a strong vision for the future that stimulates enthusiasm and builds confidence among followers. Third, they challenge the status quo and encourage innovation in an organization. And finally, they recognize unique strengths and capabilities of followers and coach and consult with them to help them develop their full potential (Bono & Judge, 2004). While researchers have attempted to identify very specific personality traits like agreeableness or conscientiousness or openness that characterize transformational leaders, only one seems to be consistent: **extraversion.** As mentioned earlier, extroversion includes the ability to convey positive emotions and project optimism and enthusiasm (Bono & Judge, 2004). While charisma and extraversion may seem like admirable qualities in a leader, a recent study found that apparently they are not necessary to the bottom-line success of CEOs. In this study, researchers surveyed the top management teams (770 high-level managers) at 128 companies (averaging $6.5 billion in assets and 16,000 employees), asking them to rate their CEOs on perceived charisma and compared these ratings to the companies' actual financial results—before and after the arrival of the CEO. They found no correlation, which the authors report as positive. "Charisma is not necessarily the thing that's going to bring your organization to the top," says Agle. "Experience and competence and regular leadership skills are sufficient" (Agle, Nagarajan, Srinivasan, & Sonnenfeld, 2006).

Transformational leaders are especially effective when they can motivate followers to perform beyond standard expectations, often by inspiring them to put the collective needs of the group above their own individual needs. When this occurs, groups are empowered, cohesive, and effective (Jung & Sosik, 2002).

A recent study of workers in European health care facilities compared different types of leadership (authoritarian, laissez faire, transformational) to discover which, if any, could lead to better employee involvement and better teamwork—shown to reduce stress levels in an often-stressful work environment that of like hospitals. The study found that transformational leadership was the most effective in inspiring individual employee involvement (Savič & Pagon, 2008).

Leadership Styles

DEGREE OF THE CONTROL EXERCISED BY THE LEADER

Authoritarian Leader (César Chávez)

- makes all decisions
- dictates strategies and work tasks

Democratic Leader (Franklin D. Roosevelt)

- seeks input from group members
- determines policies, strategies, and division of labor through discussion
- allows members to assume variety of roles

Laissez-Faire Leader (Thomas Jefferson)

- participates minimally
- makes no attempt to influence decisions

DEGREE OF THE PARTICIPATION OF THE LEADER

charismatic leadership
a leadership style in which extremely self-confident leaders inspire unusual dedication to themselves by relying upon their strong personalities and charm

servant leadership
a leadership style that seeks to ensure that other people's highest-priority needs are being served in order to increase teamwork and personal involvement

TABLE 12.1 Transformational and Charismatic Leaders

Transformational	Charismatic
Strong vision	Strong vision
High expectations for followers	High expectations for followers
Builds relationships	Relies on strong personality
Creates loyalty to organization	Creates loyalty to self
Enduring inspiration	Leadership may be short lived

Transformational leadership is sometimes confused with **charismatic leadership,** a notion from political science and religious studies scholarship (Rowold & Heinitz, 2007). Like transformational leaders, charismatic leaders have a strong belief in their vision. They are also extremely self-confident and able to inspire unusual dedication and loyalty from followers. Followers of charismatic (and transformational) leaders are often willing to set high (sometimes unrealistic) objectives and often make tremendous sacrifices, ultimately achieving more than was expected or deemed possible (Rowold & Heinitz, 2007).

Some scholars have argued that President Obama demonstrates some characteristics of transformational or charismatic leadership. However, others argue that charisma is "in the eye of the beholder" and emphasize the role of context and followers in charismatic leadership phenomena. They point out that, in Obama's case, the uncertainties surrounding the economic crisis just prior to the 2008 election, as well as the complicit media, were significant players in Obama's emergence as a charismatic (or transformational) leader (Bligh & Kohles, 2009). It is probably too early to tell if Obama will emerge/remain as a transformational leader.

As shown in Table 12.1, there are important differences between charismatic and transformational leaders; charismatic leaders rely upon their strong personalities and charm to create loyalty to themselves, while transformational leaders build relationships and strive to create loyalty to the group or organization, not to the individual leader. Thus, when a transformational leader exits the group, the organization is more likely to thrive, because member commitment is to the group. When charismatic leaders leave, the group may falter, because the individuals' commitment is to the leader, not to one another. And unlike transformational leaders who manage to inspire their followers for a long time, charismatic leadership may be relatively short-lived, because these leaders may also be autocratic, self-serving, deceptive, and manipulative, possibly resulting in followers becoming disillusioned (Daft, 2008; Pavitt, 1999). In fact, charismatic leadership can have disastrous results. For example, Hitler and Mussolini were charismatic leaders. While such leaders inspire trust, faith, and belief in themselves, there is no guarantee that their vision or mission will be correct, ethical, or successful.

Servant Leadership Theory

A fourth leadership theory is **servant leadership,** first identified by Robert Greenleaf in 1977 and described as based on a natural feeling that one wants to serve, above all. Greenleaf further describes it as:

> A conscious choice (that) brings one to aspire to lead...The difference manifests itself in the care taken by the servant-first to make sure that other people's highest priority needs are being served. The best test, and difficult to administer, is: do those served grow as persons, do they grow while being served, become healthier, wiser, freer, more autonomous, more likely themselves to become servants? (Greenleaf, 1977, pp. 13–14).

This notion of the servant-leader is actually thousands of years old, based on ideas proposed by famous Indian and Chinese philosophers. For example, Lao Tzu wrote in *The Tao Te Ching,* a guidebook on servant leadership in 600 BCE: "The greatest leader forgets himself and attends to the development of others." Servant leadership was also a core

principle of Jesus, who taught that "whoever wants to become great among you must be your servant" (Holy Bible, NIV, Mark 10:42–45).

According to Greenleaf, a servant-leader must excel at 10 characteristics—mostly communication skills: listening, empathy, healing, awareness, persuasion, conceptualization, foresight, stewardship, commitment to the growth of others, and building community. Servant leadership emphasizes collaboration and the ethical use of power. At heart, the individual is a servant first, making the conscious decision to lead in order to better serve others, not to increase his or her own power. The objective is to enhance the growth of individuals in the organization and increase teamwork and personal involvement (Greenleaf, 1991, 2002).

Many high school, colleges, and universities have service learning programs—founded on the servant leadership model—where students develop leadership skills as they serve others. For example, LaGrange College offers such a program, defining servant leadership as a "philosophy that is an inward journey with self and others to equip a journey outward in committed service to the world. As such, the LaGrange College Servant-Leadership Program aims to help students, staff and faculty grow as individuals in order to enhance the capacity of the college to become a caring and ethical community that challenges the mind and inspires the soul."

Toxic Leadership

A final type of leadership—one that is not effective—is **toxic leadership,** defined as "leadership behavior which poisons, is disruptive, destructive, exploitative, dysfunctional and abusive" (Marturano & Gosling, 2008, p. 160). Toxic leadership is really the deliberative, destructive misuse of power. Perhaps you have encountered leaders who have demonstrated such behaviors, e.g. imposing unrealistic workloads, engaging in workplace bullying and/or harassment, and/or encouraging deceptive or unethical practices.

At first glance, one might question the usefulness of even mentioning such leadership behaviors. However, both the source and display of toxic leadership are very complex, because many toxic leaders also possess productive qualities. For example, Lee Iacocca, as CEO of Chrysler, worked wonders for the ailing car manufacturer but has been severely criticized for his harsh treatment of union employees.

Sometimes toxic behaviors are excused, denied, or even encouraged because they produce results (e.g., financial profits in a company, quick and easy decisions in a small group project) (Lipman-Blumen, 2005). For example, CEO Al Dunlap was admired for his tough-guy image and "slash and burn" strategy at Sunbeam Corporation, not afraid to take on conflict and adversity. However, he was subsequently found guilty of directing a huge accounting fraud and driving Sunbeam into bankruptcy (Lipman-Blumen, 2005).

Toxic leadership behaviors are sometimes associated with excessive charisma, as our student discusses in *It Happened to me: Jeananne.* Such leaders inspire their followers; some even say that followers help create toxic leaders out of complex psychological and social needs. These leaders then take advantage of the privileges of power, are self-aggrandizing and arrogant, and think they have the right to be condescending to and contemptuous of the people who serve them.

Perhaps one reason that toxic leadership behaviors persist is that resisting or exposing them can have serious consequences. In Jeananne's case, the person who challenged Stan might have become the target of his anger and sarcasm; however, in large companies, whistle-blowers often risk isolation or even termination. Coleen Rowley—who spoke out

In your experience, which types of leaders have you encountered? Which were the most effective, in your opinion, and why?

Campus Life
Servant Leadership

Leading Through Serving
Sound like a paradox? At LaGrange College, a servant-leadership initiative reaches across the campus and involves students, faculty and staff in doing just that.

Why Servant-Leadership?
Servant-Leadership involves helping people grow as individuals... helping them to become wiser, healthier, freer, more autonomous—more likely themselves to become servant-leaders. It benefits the least privileged in society so that they will not be further deprived. *(Greenleaf, 1970)*

LaGrange College defines Servant-Leadership as a philosophy that is an inward journey with self and others to equip a journey outward in committed service to the world. As such, the LaGrange College Servant-Leadership Program aims to help students, staff and faculty grow as individuals in order to enhance the capacity of the college to become a caring and ethical community that challenges the mind and inspires the soul.

What You'll Gain
The Servant-Leadership Program focuses on **vocational discernment, ethics,** and **leading through service** in order to cultivate among members of the LaGrange College community:

- The willingness to lead by serving others
- The ability to integrate and balance the characteristics of toughness and tenderness while serving others
- The ability to envision a caring and ethical community in the midst of an individualistic culture
- The courage to act on the vision of creating a caring and ethical community
- The integrity to bring one's whole self to the LaGrange College community
- Compassion to identify with the hurts of others
- Truth-telling and a willingness to hear the truth with out judgment
- Embracing unity by valuing differences and searching out the balancing truths within opposing views
- The courage to be authentic and a willingness to admit and learn from mistakes

LaGrange College Servant Leadership Program webpage.

toxic leadership
leadership behavior that poisons and is disruptive, destructive, exploitative, dysfunctional, and abusive

against the toxicity in the FBI leadership that was partially responsible for not preventing the 9/11 attacks—was stigmatized by her colleagues and supervisor. William Sullivan, a high-ranking FBI employee during Hoover's reign, was terminated after he wrote a letter to then-director J. Edgar Hoover, urging him to resign. Hoover, as we now know, had engaged in various toxic leadership behaviors, including blackmailing people (even U. S. presidents), as well as spying on innocent people and forcing them out of their jobs. Sullivan came to work the day after delivering the letter and found that his name was no longer on his office door and that the locks had been changed (Lipman-Blumen, 2005).

While it can be difficult to resist toxic leadership, some strategies can be successful. Driven by a sense of justice, goodness, or concern for others, some people find it in themselves to confront the toxicity for their own benefit and that of others, to serve as "toxic handlers" (people who absorb, dilute, and somehow deal with the negativity generated by toxic leaders), or to organize group members (to find safety in numbers). Of course, sometimes the most reasonable response is to leave the situation (Lipman-Blumen, 2005).

In the following section, we describe the important role of society in shaping and influencing some of the leadership patterns we have described in this section.

IT HAPPENED TO ME: Jeananne

In my small group class, we had a group leader, Stan, who intimidated everyone. He started out being really charming. He was older than we were, had a rather exotic background with lots of international travel, and had even worked in a big multinational company in Malaysia for a while. I think we were in awe of him at first. He kinda took over the group, and we had to do whatever he told us or risk his wrath. I think I could say he was even abusive—he was very sarcastic and would belittle and make fun of other group members, especially the women. It was a miserable experience. We never really resolved it, just tried to placate him and get through the project, which fortunately only lasted a few weeks.

THE INDIVIDUAL, LEADERSHIP, AND SOCIETY

Ideas about who makes a good leader come from social norms and popular-culture media messages and represent the existing social hierarchies. As noted earlier, a dominant notion even today is that leadership is reserved for White males. How often do we see Asian Americans, American Indians, or women speaking with authority in top leadership positions in government, politics, and *Fortune* 500 companies? Even though we have the first African American U.S. president, you may be surprised to learn that diversity statistics for the boards of the *Fortune* 100 have remained virtually unchanged in the past four years. According to Carl Brooks (2009), president and CEO of the Executive Leadership Council (ELC, an organization of 400 African American senior executives at *Fortune* 500 companies), in 2004, the majority of *Fortune* 100 board members (72 percent) were White men; 28 percent of board seats were held by women and minorities, and there is virtually no change in those figures since 2004 (Behan, 2009).

In higher education, the statistics are similar. For example, in the state of Massachusetts, no minority individual has held a top leadership position (on a permanent basis) in any of the elite schools that give Massachusetts its reputation for quality higher education, or in any of the private colleges in that state, and this finding is similar to the national average (Cooper, 2009). In sports, of 120 teams in the NCAA's Bowl Subdivision, in the top tier of play, only seven have Black head coaches (Dunghy, 2009). And when a minority breaks through the glass or bamboo ceiling, they are more highly qualified than individuals of dominant groups in similar positions (Fisher, 2005). The term **bamboo ceiling** refers to the exclusion of Asian Americans from executive and managerial roles because of prejudice and discrimination.

Ideas about leadership norms and behaviors also come from cultural contexts (Fatahi, 1996; Harris, Moran, & Moran, 2004; Martin, 2005; Schneider & Barsoux, 2003). The same cultural values that we identified in Chapters 6 and 11 (e.g., individualism/collectivism, power distance) play an important role in setting cultural norms for leadership. For example, in many Asian countries, leaders perceive organizations as a large family and emphasize

bamboo ceiling
the exclusion of Asian Americans from executive and managerial roles because of prejudice and discrimination

cooperation through networks of personal relationship. In contrast, leaders in Germany and other central European countries typically strive to run their organizations as impersonal and well-oiled machines (Ardichvili & Kuchinke, 2002; Hofstede, 1997). Similar patterns exist within cultural groups in the United States.

How leaders handle cultural differences and promote minority representation in their groups and organizations can have tremendous impact on the satisfaction and effectiveness of workers and team members. The concept of cultural intelligence, developed by two business scholars, Early and Mosakowski (2004), is a useful measure of leaders' abilities to lead culturally diverse groups (Early & Ang, 2003). **Cultural intelligence (CQ)** refers to a person's ability to interpret unfamiliar gestures and situations and create appropriate behavioral responses. Moreover, people/managers with a high CQ are able to interpret unfamiliar situations and adapt quickly. They are good at picking up cues from others, have self-confidence and motivation, and possess a physical ability to shift speech patterns, expressions, and body language in ways that allow them to be in tune with the people they're around. All these skills allow them to work well with and provide leadership for people from various cultural backgrounds. To enhance your own leadership skills for working with diverse people, see *Building Your Communication Skills: Leading Diverse People.*

cultural intelligence (CQ)
a person's ability to interpret unfamiliar gestures and situations and create appropriate behavioral responses

Building your Communication SKILLS

Leading Diverse People

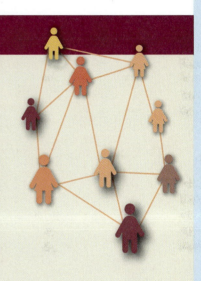

Leadership expert Richard Daft emphasizes that diversity presents challenges and exciting opportunities to leaders who want to build communities in which all people feel encouraged, respected, and committed to common purposes and goals. In addition, he notes, leaders must be committed to the ideals of diversity in order to affect the type of changes that support diversity. He identifies the following personal leadership skills that are essential in supporting diversity in groups and organizations.

- *A personal vision that recognizes and supports a diverse organizational community.* Leaders should have a long-term commitment to include members of various ethnic and cultural groups, races, and ages on all levels of the organization. In addition, they should express that vision through symbols and rituals that reinforce the values of a diverse workforce.

- *A broad knowledge of the dimensions of diversity and awareness of multicultural issues.* Leaders should be familiar with the primary dimensions of diversity, which include age, race, ethnicity, gender, mental or physical abilities, and sexual orientation, as well as the secondary dimensions, which include marital status and religion. Moreover, the leader should put this knowledge into action by using inclusive language and showing respect for differences (see Chapter 6).

- *An openness to change.* Leaders in diverse groups and organizations should encourage feedback from others, be capable of accepting criticism, and be willing to change their own behavior. It is leaders' behavior that has the most impact on whether diversity is truly valued within a group or organization. For example, one CEO includes a section on his family life in his business newsletter, which signals to women and men juggling job and family that the business thinks families are important

- *Mentoring and empowerment of diverse employees or group members.* Leaders should take an active role in creating opportunities for all employees or group members to use their unique abilities. They should also offer honest feedback and coaching as needed and should reward those who show respect to all individuals.

SOURCE: Daft (2008, p. 345).

Another challenge for many of today's leaders is the virtual team context. As we discussed in Chapters 7 and 11, virtual teams are increasingly a way of life for many workers (Connaughton & Shuffler, 2007; Warkentin, Sayeed, & Hightower, 1997). Leadership in virtual teams is more challenging than in face-to-face teams for at least three reasons: First, distances enhance the complexities of communication and make establishing trust and cohesion especially challenging; second, distance and time-zone differences can make on-time task completion especially difficult; finally, global virtual teams often include the challenges of cultural differences (Connaughton & Shuffler, 2007).

A primary role for leaders in virtual teams is to foster interaction—compensating for the lack of "social presence" in mediated communication and drawing out the silent members. Effective leadership may include ensuring periodic face-to-face meetings, or at least some "richer" virtual communication forms—like videoconferencing or Skype—that can facilitate social bonding and relationship building. An effective virtual team leader also needs to keep the team on task, particularly challenging at a distance. This means frequent communication with team members—asking the right questions, tracking contributions and measurable progress, providing constructive feedback, and reinforcing contributions (Connaughton & Daly, 2005; Thompson, 2000).

In sum, societal forces, based on social hierarchies, influence norms and views on leadership, and they also present challenges for heading up diverse workforces. Leadership in virtual global teams requires effective communication skills to overcome the challenges of mediated communication. We now turn our attention to ethical issues involved in leadership.

ETHICS AND LEADERSHIP

The issue of ethical leadership is particularly important today, as we have seen major scandals in the last several years involving unethical behavior of many business and political leaders (Treviño & Brown, 2004). In the current economic climate, corporate leaders who are seen as working hard to build and maintain good reputations in being sincere, transparent, and accurate are viewed positively, and there are examples of ethical leadership (Treviño, Brown, & Hartman, 2003; Treviño, Hartman, & Brown, 2000). One could argue that being an ethical leader is important in itself; however, there are additional reasons for ethical leadership. When a leader is perceived by subordinates as ethical, employees see the leader as more likely to be effective, they are more willing to work harder on the job, and they are more satisfied overall with the leadership (Brown & Treviño, 2006).

Why is ethics such a central issue in leadership? Because of the nature of power and influence. Leadership is a position of influence, and therefore leaders make decisions that implement their visions, and these decisions often impact other people's decisions and lives. Because they have more power than followers, leaders also have more responsibility to be sensitive to the implications of this power and influence (Northouse, 2007). As depicted in the film *Invictus*, Nelson Mandela is an example of an effective and ethical leader who never took the easy way, and he has served as an inspiration to generations of people the world over. For more on Mandela's leadership, see *Communication in Society: Mandela: His Lessons of Leadership.*

What are the characteristics of ethical leadership? Northouse (2007), a leadership expert, identifies four characteristics of ethical leaders: Ethical leaders are honest and just, and they respect others and build community. Let's look at each of these qualities more closely.

Honesty

Honesty and truthfulness are at the core of ethical leadership. If leaders are perceived as dishonest, they are also seen as unreliable and untrustworthy, with dramatic negative consequence for others' satisfaction and loyalty. But being honest is not just about telling the truth; it is also about being open about the difficult situations that can arise in all groups and organizations. An example of unethical behavior related to honesty involved

Communication in SOCIETY

Mandela: His Lessons of Leadership

Richard Stengl of TIME magazine traveled to South Africa to interview Nelson Mandela—"the closest thing the world has to a secular saint"—about his ideas on leadership. He overthrew apartheid, and created a nonracial democratic South Africa by knowing precisely when and how to transition between his roles as warrior, martyr, diplomat and statesman. He is a master tactician. Notice that communication plays a role in many of these lessons. Which do you think might apply to your own leadership experience?

One of the most important of Mandela's leadership lessons is to *Lead from the front, but don't leave your base behind.* Mandela knew the importance of making sure that his supporters were with him, especially when his fight to overthrow apartheid included unpopular strategies—like negotiating with leaders of the apartheid government. Slowly and deliberately, he explained his reasons to his key supporters, and eventually persuaded them. He knew the importance of keeping his coalition strong.

Another important lesson was to *Lead from the back—and let others believe they are in front.* He did this by being a good listener and when he did speak in meetings, he would summarize others' ideas and then gently lay out his own ideas, making others think that it was all their ideas. By doing this he ensured that his followers were strongly committed to the group decisions.

He also so thought it important to *Know your enemy—and learn about his favorite sport.* Because he knew that someday he would be negotiating with Apartheid rulers, he learned their language, Afrikans, and their favorite sport, rugby, so there would be a common topic they could all discuss when they met. As shown in the movie, *Mandela,* he masterfully rallied Black and White South Africans behind the mostly white rugby team which went on to win the World Cup—and brought a joint sense of national pride to a deeply divided country.

Mandela also knew that, in leadership, *Appearances matter and* he always remembered to smile. Like any great leader, he knew that what people saw was as important as what they heard when he was giving campaign speeches. When he was campaigning for president in 1994, he always did a South African village dance that symbolized the struggle against apartheid and flashed a dazzling smile to everyone he came in contact with. It didn't just show friendship, it also symbolized his lack of bitterness and his willingness to forgive and move forward—so important in uniting a bitterly divided country.

Finally, Mandela, the leader, understood that *Nothing is black or white.* He knew that decisions are complex and there are always competing factors and he always communicated this to his followers. His formula for leadership was, what is the goal that I seek and what is the most practical way to get there?

SOURCE: Adapted from Stengel, R. (2008, July 21). "Mandela: His 8 lessons of leadership." *TIME, 173*(3), 42–49.

Ken Lay, the former leader of Enron. When an employee asked whether his job and Enron stock were safe, Lay assured him that his job was safe and that an investment in Enron was a shrewd way to plan for the future. Lay even encouraged employees to sell the rest of their portfolios and put them all in Enron. Meanwhile, Lay was quietly selling his shares and cashing out before the company went bankrupt (Harned, 2009).

Respect and Service to Others

Respect and service to others have been emphasized particularly in the writings on servant leadership and transformational leadership—both situations in which the leader–follower relationship is crucial. When displaying these characteristics, leaders consider the special needs of their followers and sincerely care about them. In practice, they show their concern by mentoring, carrying out team building, and engaging in other activities that empower followers.

Fairness and Justice

When it comes to offering rewards and privileges in a team, the leader plays an important role. Followers must feel that they will be treated equitably and that all will be treated the same unless special circumstances warrant it. For example, Karen's boss always appointed

a rotating committee that advised her during performance evaluation and merit-pay decisions. It was an effective (and ethical) way to ensure that employees felt they were being treated equitably.

Building Community

In helping to move the group/organization members *together* toward a *shared* common vision and goal, the ethical leader attends to the needs and goals of the community of followers (Brown & Treviño, 2006). Lee Child, before becoming a noted author of murder mysteries, worked for 20 years at Granada Television in England. He described the organization as one in which community building was a priority. As a result, he says, it was a place where people loved to work, putting in long hours of overtime because they all believed in the quality products they were producing (e.g., *Brideshead Revisited, Jewel in the Crown*) and were inspired by the shared vision of the company (Child, 2009).

Moral Leadership

This is a relatively recent addition to the list of qualities displayed by ethical leaders (Brown & Treviño, 2006; Daft, 2008; Northouse, 2007). *Moral leadership* means actively influencing followers' ethical and unethical behavior and using the reward system to ensure ethical accountability in the group. The moral leader not only acts ethically but also sets an example, providing the moral compass for the organization and followers. Moreover, an explicit part of the leadership agenda is to use the reward-and-discipline system to hold followers accountable for ethical conduct (Treviño & Brown et al., 2003; Treviño & Hartman et al., 2000).

BECOMING AN EFFECTIVE LEADER

How can you develop skills that will make you a more effective leader in the groups/ organizations to which you belong? Acquiring leadership skills might be compared to learning any new set of skills—like art, music, dance, golf, tennis, or whatever. Leadership experts Robert and Janet Denhardt (2004) suggest that learning the art of leadership is like learning a new dance step in a dance studio. It's all about improvisation, collaboration with others, and self-reflection. First, you can gain some cognitive information (like reading a textbook chapter on leadership!), and then you practice the skill over and over, improvising and working with others to hone your skills. While no magic bullets can make you an effective leader overnight, here are three suggestions: Conduct a self-assessment of your current leadership skills, search out opportunities that will give you experience in developing your leadership skills, and improve your strategic communication skills.

Conduct a Leadership Self-Assessment

Consider your leadership potential. Review the various theories and ideas in this chapter and Chapter 11. Do you consider yourself a leader? Why or why not? What are your main strengths as a leader? Think of leadership in the broad sense. As a leadership expert explained it, if we ask a roomful of college students to raise their hands if they are leaders, perhaps only a few people would respond affirmatively. However, if you asked the same students, "How many of you are able to work well with others and get things done together?" probably most would raise their hands (Omatsu, n.d.).

So think of your abilities to work along with others. Are you able to foster cohesion in a group? Fill task roles in helping to get the task done? Fill relational roles to foster good working relationships? Are you good at seeing the big picture? Setting up a plan? Are you better at following others' plans and getting things done yourself or motivating others to get things done? You might think about strengthening skills you are already good at and developing those leadership communication skills you are lacking. You might even identify

one new facet of leadership that you would like to work on each semester. This assessment should lead you to the next step—searching for leadership opportunities that will help you develop particular leadership skills you want to work on.

Search for Leadership Opportunities

The college experience presents many opportunities for developing leadership skills in a variety of contexts. First, you can gain extensive leadership experience in courses where group work and discussion is part of the class requirement. If classes in your major do not provide these opportunities, choose electives to take classes that do include a group component. You should view these group assignments as opportunities to work on leadership skills, realizing that personnel managers in both small and large companies place importance on leadership skills and working well with others in making their hiring decisions.

On a larger scale, seek opportunities for participation in student organizations, where you can develop leadership skills that could prove essential in your postgraduation career. If possible, find groups that focus on leadership development in a supportive environment.

Improve Your Strategic Communication Skills

As discussed earlier, strategic communication skills are important for most leadership styles. Strategic communication involves establishing an open communication climate, promoting dialogue and facilitating conversations that help move the group or organization forward, and (as mentioned earlier) recognizing the importance of emotion in productive team work.

Create an Open Communication Climate

According to Matha and Boehm (2008), in the highest-performing companies, communication is open, candid, and flowing (p. 18). Open communication really helps to build trust, noted in Chapter 11 as an essential element in effective leader–follower group relationships. This means sharing all types of information throughout the organization or team, using many different methods (newsletter, Internet, meetings, reporting documents, memos, and mail) to keep the focus on the strategy, even welcoming controversial topics in an ongoing conversation (not a monologue) (Baldoni, 2004). Our colleague Miracal recalls her first department meeting as a new social worker, where there was a lack of openness in the communication climate: "The director talked to us about the impending economic problems as if we were children, warning us to stop any unnecessary copying or mailing. It was a total monologue and it felt adversarial. Needless to say, I didn't stay in that job long!" Contrast this to Martha's experience reported in the opening vignette, of a boss who seemed to have an open communication style and worked collaboratively with his or her subordinates. A communication-savvy leader will select rich channels of communication, using stories, metaphors, and informal communication—anything that will break down conventional hierarchical and departmental barriers and encourage open communication. In their communication, the effective leader also helps others understand how their actions interact with and affect others and helps create a shared vision (Daft, 2008).

Promote Dialogue

Promoting dialogue involves being engaged in open communication on a daily basis, asking questions, and listening. Leadership is more about being the person with the *right questions* than the right answers. It's also about listening and getting feedback (Matha & Boehm, 2008). Effective leadership communication involves hearing what others have to say. As one expert says, "if you're not hearing bad news, you have a problem"—meaning that you're probably not *really* listening to others (Baldoni, p. 24). As we learned in Chapter 5, good listening involves the skill of understanding and interpreting a message's genuine meaning. In sum, good leaders are engaged with others, ask lots of questions, and give

others plenty of opportunity to say what's on their mind. In addition, they let others know they've been heard. A good leader can detect messages hidden below the surface of spoken interaction (as we described in Chapter 4, about nonverbal communication)—the messages that employees can't always articulate.

Recognize the Importance of Emotion

Even organizations with authoritarian leadership styles, such as the Marines, know that the rational elements of leadership communication are only one piece of the puzzle. Truly effective leaders seek to understand and leverage the emotional connectedness that employees or organizational members have to the group and their work. For example, the U. S. military leadership stresses the importance of building an emotional commitment to their "team" (Matha & Boehm, 2008). The connectedness results in cohesion and trust. Have you ever felt an emotional connectedness to a work group?

While your leadership opportunities may not include becoming the CEO of a large corporation, the elements of effective communication apply to many leadership contexts: in your family, college or university, or community organizations.

SUMMARY

Leadership communication plays a significant role in many people's lives and can be demonstrated in a variety of ways. Leadership is defined as "an influence relationship among leaders and followers who intend real changes and outcomes that reflect their shared purposes." The individual influences on leadership include gender and personality traits. The reasons why women are underrepresented in leadership positions in business, politics, and government are complex and probably include the prevalence of negative stereotypes regarding women and leadership. However, recent leadership theories place importance on traditional "feminine" leadership qualities and suggest that both men and women should cultivate a variety of leadership skills. While some personality traits are associated with effective leadership, overall leadership is a learned set of skills.

Four theories describe and explain the characteristics and skills that make up effective leadership: functional theory (which includes shared or distributive leadership), style theory, transformational (and charismatic) leadership, and servant leadership. A final theory, toxic leadership, describes ineffective leadership patterns and behaviors that are destructive, disruptive, and dysfunctional.

Societal norms influence notions of leadership because they shape our ideas about who is an effective leader and what an effective leader should look like. The result is that women and minorities are often left out of the leadership equation. There are suggestions in this chapter for providing leadership for culturally diverse groups and organizations.

Ethical considerations in leadership are important, not only for intrinsic reasons but also because ethical leadership can have far-reaching consequences for a group or organization in terms of processes and outcomes. Four qualities characterize ethical leaders: honesty, concern for justice, respect for others, and community building.

Finally, while no magic bullets can make you an effective leader overnight, we offer several suggestions: Conduct a self-assessment of your current leadership skills, search out opportunities that will give you experience in developing your leadership skills, and be a strategic communicator.

KEY TERMS

agreeableness 291	cultural intelligence (CQ) 297	glass ceiling 287
authoritarian leadership style 291	democratic leadership style 292	introverts 289
bamboo ceiling 296	extraversion 292	laissez-faire leadership style 292
charismatic leadership 294	functional theory 290	leadership 284

mentor 291
servant leadership 294
shared or collaborative or distributed
  leadership 291

strategic communication 286
style theory 291
toxic leadership 295

trait theory 289
transformational leadership theory 292

CHAPTER REVIEW QUESTIONS

1. What is the definition of leadership?

2. What does contemporary research have to say about gender and leadership? Do women have a different leadership style than men?

3. What are the theories of leadership? Give an example of each type of leader.

4. Think about various leadership qualities in this chapter. How can some of the "good" traits of leaders also be "bad"?

5. What ethical responsibilities do leaders have to those they lead?

6. What are components of effective leadership communication?

ACTIVITIES

1. Write down the names of three leaders you've encountered in your lifetime and jot down what you think makes them effective/ineffective. Which of the leadership styles identified in this chapter describe their leadership? What was it about their communication that contributed to their effectiveness (or lack thereof) as a leader?

2. Think about some social issues that are of import in today's society, such as the green movement. How would a good leader—whether they be the president, a company CEO, or a nonprofit manager—take these factors into consideration?

3. Conduct an evaluation of yourself as a leader. Ask yourself the following questions:
   a. Do I consider myself a leader? Why or why not?
   b. What is (are) my main strength(s) as a leader? What is my "leadership style"?

   Next, consider how you might develop as a leader. Identify one new facet of leadership that you would like to develop this semester through class projects or other leadership opportunities.

WEB ACTIVITIES

1. Go to https://www.ncslcollege.com/ This is the homepage of the National Conference on Student Leadership (NCSL), which provides leadership development conferences at several locations each year, online leadership training, and student leadership certification courses. They also provide resources for students interested in developing their leadership potential. Click on the Resources section and the article "What matters to you? The Why behind what we do." This article describes the two common traits of student leaders—passion and commitment. Can you identify causes or organizations that you are passionate about and committed to? In what ways could you provide leadership in these areas?

2. Go to http://www.insidehighered.com/layout/set/dialog/news/2009/06/08/work This Web site reports the results of several studies investigating the impact of employment on students' academic and personal lives. One of the findings is that work experience during college can have a positive effect on students' psychological well-being and leadership skills. What are the potential leadership skills you might develop from your past or present employment?

3. Go to http://www.sprintbiz.com/bizpark/markets/smallbiz/newsletters/01spring/mp_index.pdf Take this short assessment to discover useful information about your leadership potential. The results should tell you your leadership strengths and also identify areas you could work on to further develop your leadership skills.

13

SPEAKING IN PUBLIC: TOPIC SELECTION AND SPEECH DEVELOPMENT

I never took a speech class in high school because it didn't fit into my schedule and I wasn't very enthusiastic about public speaking. Then I took it in college and I learned a lot about the basics of public speaking—how to organize and deliver a speech. Although I learned a lot in this course, I learned more after I graduated and my job required a lot of public presentations. I also had public speaking opportunities (e.g., toasts at my friends' weddings and presentations as a volunteer in several local politicians' campaigns). I discovered that, like other skills such as dancing or golf, you develop expertise mainly by doing it over and over again. The public speaking course gave me the foundation, but I later discovered how important actually doing it is.

Like Mitchell, we hope that this chapter will help you take the first steps toward becoming a more confident and capable speaker. Unlike the previous chapters in this book—which are designed primarily to help you understand communication concepts—this chapter focuses on developing communication skills. As you read this chapter, however, you will see how the concepts you encountered in Chapters 3, 4, and 5 can help you in public speaking.

In the following sections, we introduce the basic elements of speech preparation. We'll look at the range of communication events at which people may be called to speak, the importance of understanding audiences, and the basics of constructing, organizing, and delivering a speech. Taken together, these elements supply the foundations for effective public speaking.

One disclaimer: Although this chapter provides you with guidelines for effective public speaking, learning to be an effective speaker is not as simple as following directions on a cake mix box. Following a recipe's instructions typically results in a fairly good cake, but for a really original cake, the baker draws on artistry, practice, and lessons learned from others. In short, public speaking is an *art*. While following a formula may result in a satisfactory speech, adding an artistic element will make you an even better speaker. And, of course, a good speaker needs to practice, practice, practice! Practice may not make you a perfect speaker, but it will give you more confidence and help you become a better speaker.

Once you have read this chapter, you will be able to:

- Explain the importance of public speaking.
- Explain the general and specific purpose of your speech.
- Analyze your audience.
- Develop and organize your speech.
- Understand the ethical issues confronting the public speaker.

CHAPTER OUTLINE

WHAT IS PUBLIC SPEAKING?

THE IMPORTANCE OF SPEAKING IN PUBLIC

ESTABLISHING YOUR REASONS FOR SPEAKING IN PUBLIC
- Identifying Your General Purpose
- Generating and Selecting Your Topic
- Identifying Your Specific Purpose

ANALYZING AND RELATING TO YOUR AUDIENCE
- What Does Your Audience Know About Your Topic?
- Who Is Your Audience?
- What Does Your Audience Know About You?
- What Does Your Audience Expect from You?

DEVELOPING YOUR SPEECH
- Narrowing Your Topic
- Determining Your Main Points
- Identifying Your Thesis Statement
- Finding Supporting Materials

ORGANIZING YOUR SPEECH
- Developing the Body of Your Speech
- Selecting Your Organizational Pattern
- Creating Your Outline

DEVELOPING YOUR TRANSITIONS, INTRODUCTION, AND CONCLUSION
- Developing Effective Transitions
- Developing an Effective Introduction
- Gaining Audience Attention
- Focusing the Audience's Attention on Your Topic by Relating It to Them
- Giving the Audience an Overview of Your Organizational Pattern
- Helping the Audience Understand Your Thesis
- Developing an Effective Conclusion

BECOMING AN ETHICAL PUBLIC SPEAKER

Summary

Key Terms

Chapter Review Questions

Activities

Web Activities

public speaking
the process of speaking with a purpose to a group of people in a relatively formal setting

WHAT IS PUBLIC SPEAKING?

Public speaking is the process of speaking with a purpose to a group of people in a relatively formal setting. As this definition shows, public speaking differs in two fundamental ways from the types of communication we've addressed so far in this book. First, public speaking occurs in a relatively formal setting, similar to some small group communication contexts but more formal than most everyday interpersonal communication. Weddings, graduations, and political rallies are all formal settings that call for deliberate and prepared speeches, which relates to the second important characteristic of public speaking. Namely, it is a manner of speaking that is much more deliberate and purposeful than conversation or small group communication. As such, it usually requires some preparation and even practice to be successful (O'Hair, Stewart, & Rubenstein, 2010).

THE IMPORTANCE OF SPEAKING IN PUBLIC

Speaking in public is a cornerstone of U.S. society that is based upon the civic participation of its citizens. As members of a democratic society, citizens need to become adept public speakers so that they can advocate for what they think is best (Gayle, 2004). In addition, public speaking skills are a requirement for success in most jobs. Increasingly, businesses want employees who can speak well in public and address meetings (Osterman, 2005). This is true for teachers, social workers, bankers, financial planners, and those who work in public relations—but it also applies to those in technical fields, such as engineers, accountants, nurses, medical examiners, police officers, soldiers, and professional athletes.

As we discuss in *Communication in Society: Bill Gates, The Great Communicator?* Microsoft CEO Bill Gates is engaging the issues of world health and education, which stretch beyond

Communication in SOCIETY

Bill Gates, The Great Communicator?

Most people agree that Microsoft cofounder Bill Gates is a brilliant technologist and a generous philanthropist, but he has not been known for his public speaking skills. His Microsoft presentations were usually filled with technical jargon and dull PowerPoint slides. However, his public speaking skills have recently improved, as noted by the summary below of the news coverage of Gates' 2009 presentation on his campaign to eradicate malaria. This shows that even people who have to speak often can work on and improve their public speaking skills . . . and that people notice! What do you think of Bill Gates' attention-getting strategy?

According to news accounts, Gates opened his speech to a gathering of the rich and famous at the TED (Technology, Entertainment and Design) conference by saying, "Malaria is spread by mosquitoes. I brought some. Here, I'll let them roam around. There's no reason that only poor people should be infected." At which point he released a swarm of mosquitoes into the room. As many know, Gates has shifted his passion for technology into a passion for ridding the world of malaria.

By his release of mosquitoes, he did get people's attention and raised awareness about a disease that kills millions worldwide and is spread by mosquitoes.

Gates' attention getter was effective for several reasons, according to Chris Dannen of the FastCompany blog. "For one, Americans are unusually unaware of the danger of mosquito-borne viruses, because many of us live in temperate climates where mosquitoes only breed a few months out of the year. Not only that, we hide from them in climate-controlled, air-conditioned homes and cars, and fend them off with readily-available sprays, candles, and propane-powered things."

Apparently, Gates' speech was effective in many other ways—passionate, concise (20 minutes), interesting, humorous, and engaging—everything that is desired in a speaker" (Gallo, 2009). However, his attention-getter does bring up an ethical issue. Although these particular mosquitoes were disease-free (as he told the audience moments after he released them), is it ethical to create a situation in which people may think, even for a moment, that they are exposed to a potentially deadly danger?

SOURCES: Gallo, C. (2009, February 17). "Bill Gates: The great communicator?" *Businessweek*. Retrieved on August 5, 2009, from http://www.businessweek.com/smallbiz/content/feb2009/sb20090213_774006.htm

Dannen, C. (2009, February 5). "Bill Gates sends mosquitoes into crowd." *FastComparny.com*. Retrieved February 14, 2010, from http://www.fastcompany.com/blog/chris-dannen/techwatch/bill-gates-sicks-mosquitos-crowd-discusses-his-brain

issues in his professional life. Although he is not a public health official, his engagement with larger international concerns is part of his global citizenship. Public speech also remains crucial to the democratic process. Learning to advocate for your interests can be particularly important at the local level, such as when speaking at student organizations or city council meetings, as well as at the national level.

ESTABLISHING YOUR REASONS FOR SPEAKING IN PUBLIC

Understanding the reasons why you will be speaking can help you determine the purpose and objective of your presentation. If you volunteer to speak in public, you probably have an excellent understanding of why you want to speak and what you hope to accomplish. For example, if you want to advocate for building a light rail system in your city, then you already know something about the communication event, your purpose for speaking in front of the city council, and what you want to accomplish.

However, when you are *asked* to speak in a public setting, someone else has (for the most part) already determined the purpose of the speech you will give. For example, if you are asked to make a toast at a friend's wedding, you know why you will be speaking (to celebrate the union of a friend and his or her partner), who your audience will be (the couple's friends, family, coworkers, etc.), when you will be speaking (following the ceremony, perhaps during the reception), and what the expectations are for this kind of speech (lighthearted, sincere, and brief). Often, you know your role—for example, the best man or maid of honor. Other purposes for speaking include introducing someone to an audience, making a presentation to clients, or presenting a petition to your homeowner's association on behalf of your neighbors. Whatever the purpose, refer to *Building Your Communication Skills: Communication Event Checklist* to make sure that you've obtained all the preliminary information you need.

Having complete, accurate information about the communication event will help you prepare your speech in an appropriate way. For example, Josie's academic advisor asked her to make a report on her summer internship in Denmark to the AISEC club—an international organization focused on developing student leadership skills, with chapters on many college campuses. Applying the event checklist, she knew the date and the place where she would speak. She considered her main purpose. She knew that her advisor wanted her to inform the students about international internships, but she also realized that there would be some persuasive elements to her speech, because her experience had had a big impact on her—academically and personally. When she thought about the audience, she knew that she had to find out more about the particular students who would be in attendance: Were they familiar with the purpose of internships? Had they traveled

Building Your Communication **SKILLS**

Communication Event Checklist:

____ 1. Do you know when you are expected to speak (date as well as time)?

____ 2. Do you know where you are to speak?

____ 3. Do you know why you are speaking?

____ 4. What do you know about the audience?

____ 5. Have you requested audiovisual equipment in advance, if you wish to use it?

____ 6. Do you have a name and phone number for a contact person in case a question or emergency arises?

general purpose
whichever of three goals—to inform, persuade, or entertain—dominates a speech

informative speech
a speech that explains, instructs, defines, clarifies, demonstrates, or teaches

persuasive speech
a speech with the aim of convincing the audience

special occasion speech
evocative speeches include presentations given at retirement dinners, award ceremonies, weddings, graduations, and funerals

internationally? What were their majors? She also remembered that she had to order a digital projector because she planned to show a few PowerPoint slides with some of her photos. She knew the e-mail address and office phone number of the professor who was the group's advisor.

How can you begin to prepare an effective, appropriate speech? Based on your understanding of the communication event, like Josie, you should start by focusing on the general purpose of your speech, then carefully select a topic that suits that general purpose. Finally, you should zero in on the specific purpose of your speech. Let's take a look at each of these steps in turn.

Identifying Your General Purpose

Almost every communication message has a purpose, as we described in Chapter 3. For some messages—Let me tell you about Saturday night! Please feed the dog. Did you understand the assignment in history class?—the message is clear. But even in more subtle messages, the speaker has some goal for evoking a response from the listener. The public speaking event is no different. Regardless of topic, your public speech probably has one of three **general purposes**, first identified by the great Roman orator, Cicero, and still taught in public speaking courses today: to inform, to persuade, or to entertain (McKerrow, Gronbeck, Ehninger, & Monroe, 2003; O'Hair, Stewart, & Rubenstein, 2010). However, the objective to entertain has been broadened to evoke feeling, so we will refer to this third type as the *evocative speech*.

The **informative speech**—e.g., Josie's speech to the AISEC club—explains, instructs, defines, clarifies, demonstrates, or teaches. The **persuasive speech** influences, convinces, motivates, sells, preaches, or stimulates action. For example, most political campaign speeches intend to persuade listeners to support the views of the candidate. The evocative speech entertains, inspires, celebrates, commemorates, or builds community (Sprague & Stuart, 2005, p. 65). A common type of evocative speech, including the wedding toast, celebrates aspects of a person or topic. Also known as **special occasion speeches**, evocative speeches include presentations given at retirement dinners, award ceremonies, weddings, graduations, and funerals.

As you might imagine, these three general purposes do not function in isolation. Speakers often persuade others by informing them about something, as in the case of Josie's speech, or they inform audiences by entertaining them. President Barak Obama's speech, "A More Perfect Union," given in Philadelphia on March 18, 2008, was an attempt to inform Americans about his background and the role of race in his family's story and America's story. This speech was not only a response to his critics, but also a call to take race seriously. It was informative, persuasive, and inspiring—all at the same time.

Once you have identified the general purpose of your speech, you are prepared to focus your presentation and achieve your most important communication goals. The next step, then, will be to select a topic that suits your purpose.

Generating and Selecting Your Topic

Coming up with a topic to speak about can be the most interesting *and* the most difficult part of any speech presentation. Assuming that the topic is not already determined for you, here are some guidelines to help you choose:

- **Consider the speaking occasion.** What are the expectations for your presentation? What types of topics would be appropriate to speak about? Be sure your topic matches the speaking occasion. For example, a lawyer was asked to speak at a Chamber of Commerce meeting for people who want to start their own businesses. She knew she was asked to speak because of her expertise in representing business owners. So she decided to prepare an informative speech on the advantages and disadvantages of various business structures—sole proprietorships, partnerships, limited liability companies, and corporations.
- **Consider your interests.** Take an inventory of your interests, passions, and experiences. What are some unusual experiences you've had? What subjects do you know a lot about? What topics do you feel strongly about? What would you like to learn

more about? For example, Aracely had to choose a topic for her informative speech in her public speaking class and decided to present information about ways in which college students could help Haitians after the terrible earthquake killed hundreds of thousands of people there. She's a trained EMT (Emergency Medical Technician) volunteer, has a passion for helping others in need, and thought the speech preparation would give her the opportunity to learn something (and then share this information) about how people can help others in international disasters.

- **Consider your relationship to the speech topic.** Why are you being asked to speak? If you have been chosen because you have a special relationship to someone—for example, the bride or the deceased—consider what topics the audience would consider appropriate and effective from you. If you have been chosen because you are an expert in a particular area, the audience will expect you to demonstrate that expertise and to answer questions effectively. For example, Josie knew that many of the students in the AISEC club would want to know specific details about summer internships and that she should be prepared to answer questions or know where she could direct students to get more information.

In Josie's case, she knew the topic she would talk about. However, if you aren't sure of the topic (e.g., you must give a speech in a public speaking class), you may want to try a thought-listing exercise. Consider the following questions:

- What do I like to do in my free time?
- What am I passionate about?
- What sorts of activities am I involved in?
- If I could be anywhere, where would I be?
- What causes do I care about?

These are just a few questions that might help you develop a list of potential topics. Talk to your friends. Brainstorm with them. Great ideas come out of group discussion!

You may now be considering several topics for your speech, but how do you decide among them? While an almost-infinite number of great speech topics exist, not all topics are equally suited for the circumstances you are going to confront. Public speaking expert Cheryl Hamilton (2009) suggests that for each possible topic, you consider whether it meets the following criteria (pp. 96–98):

The Topic Should Be of Interest to the Speaker

A speech can be especially dry if the speaker is unenthusiastic about the chosen topic. The more you care about your topic, the more likely the audience is to listen. The topic should be one you know well and/or care to learn a great deal about. Enthusiasm makes a difference. Consider the experience of our student in *It Happened to Me: Scott.*

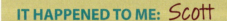

IT HAPPENED TO ME: *Scott*

I am a political science major in my last semester, and instant run-off voting has been my subject of interest since my first year in college. In instant-run-off voting, voters rank-order candidates if no candidate gets a clear majority. The candidate with the least votes is eliminated, and the process is repeated until one candidate obtains a majority of votes. This system is used in some countries and even some states within the United States. It has many advantages, but few people know about it, so I thought it made an excellent choice for my speech topic.

The Topic Should Be of Interest and Relevance to the Audience

An informative speech detailing how to tie one's shoes might not be the most interesting to a class of your college-age classmates. If you were giving this speech to a class of kindergarten students, however, the topic might be of greater interest. Knowing your audience is an essential component of your speech preparation, particularly when it comes to selecting a topic. A speech on how to use Twitter might be of great interest to a class of your peers. However, you might have to reframe the presentation somewhat if you were speaking on the same topic to a less technologically savvy group. We will discuss analyzing and responding to your audience in more detail later in this chapter.

The Topic Can Be Explored Adequately Within the Allotted Time

Timing is everything, and not all topics can be covered in 5 minutes, which may be your allotment. A topic such as the current recession might be of interest to students, yet it would be next to impossible to adequately cover such a large issue within such a short time span. If you are committed to speaking on an expansive topic, scale back the scope of the speech. Narrowing the speech to "how the ailing economy is impacting college students," for instance, might be more feasible given time constraints. We will say more about keeping within a time limit later in this chapter.

The Topic Meets the Criteria of Your Class

This characteristic might not be relevant if you have been given free rein to determine your topic. However, if your instructor gave you specific parameters, be sure to meet them.

The Topic Is Not Too Difficult to Understand

This characteristic is related to understanding your audience. While it is important to select a topic of importance to you and of interest to your audience, it is also important to consider how much previous knowledge your audience already has or will need in order to follow your presentation. If your audience needs to be briefed for at least 3 minutes on a topic before you can get to the issue at hand in a 5-minute speech, the topic might not be best suited for your class. Unique topics can be great, but they shouldn't require you to spend too much time giving background to your audience.

Later in the chapter, we'll discuss topics again, when we guide you through the important process of narrowing a broad topic to an appropriately focused one.

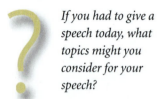

If you had to give a speech today, what topics might you consider for your speech?

Identifying Your Specific Purpose

Once you've established your general purpose and your topic, you can focus on the specific purpose of your speech. Whereas your general purpose may be to inform, persuade, or evoke feeling from your audience, your **specific purpose** focuses on what you would like to inform them or persuade them of, or what types of feelings you want to evoke. You should be able to state this purpose clearly. Look at the following examples:

> **General Purpose:** To inform
> **Specific Purpose:** To inform my audience about how to prevent skin cancer
> **General Purpose:** To persuade
> **Specific Purpose:** To persuade my audience that international summer internships are beneficial
> **General Purpose:** To evoke feelings
> **Specific Purpose:** To evoke positive and warm memories of my Aunt Jutta

Begin by writing down the specific purpose of your speech. Make sure this purpose statement is both clear and focused. Typically, you will need to revise it several times to make it specific enough. For example, if you have written that your specific purpose is: *to inform my audience about cancer,* you have not focused your purpose sufficiently. Like most topics, cancer is a huge subject that could be approached from a wide range of perspectives, including types of cancers, their causes, their treatments, and their cures. Thus, you must be more specific. What about cancer do you want your audience to know? If you live in the southern U. S., you might want to focus on skin cancer. If your audience is relatively young, you might want to focus on what individuals can do to prevent cancer. In speaking to an older audience, you might want to focus on detecting and treating cancer. Consider the following examples:

Josie's general purpose was to inform students about her summer internship experience. She considered telling them about all she learned and saw during her summer in Denmark. Knowing that she only had 10 minutes to talk and considering her audience—students who could benefit from an internship—she narrowed her topic, investigated the most recent requirements and the process for setting up an international summer internship, and decided that her specific purpose was to inform students of the three steps in

specific purpose
what a speaker wants to inform or persuade an audience about, or the type of feelings the speaker wants to evoke

setting up a college student internship experience. But then she thought that maybe she should try to persuade students of the merits of the internship. After all, if they didn't believe that an international internship would benefit them, there was little use in describing how to set up an internship. So her final *general purpose* was to persuade students of the merits of an international summer internship. Her final *specific purpose* was to persuade students that a summer internship could benefit them personally, academically, and professionally.

Unlike Josie, Adan was trying to come up with a speech topic and purpose for his first public speaking assignment. He considered his hobbies—hockey, photography, and plane spotting and decided that the topic that would most interest his fellow classmates would be plane spotting. Plane-spotter hobbyists track different types of aircraft and, like bird watchers, will often travel great distances to record and document the flight of an unusual aircraft. His general purpose was to inform his audience about the hobby of plane spotting, and his specific purpose was to tell students about the different types of plane spotters—those who track powered aircraft and those who track balloons and gliders. Then he considered his audience—students who would probably know little about this hobby and may be not interested in the fine details. He decided that his specific purpose would be to inform his classmates about three interesting plane-spotting experiences: seeing a vintage L1011 on its final flight to an aircraft museum, the flight of the Voyager (the first private plane to fly around the world nonstop), and the 2010 maiden flight of the Boeing 787—the world's first airplane with an all-composite construction.

Suppose you're asked to give a short speech at your Aunt Jutta's memorial service. Your specific purpose might be to tell her friends how wonderful she was. However, you need to narrow the purpose. A general rundown of her good points might not really evoke the fond memories and emotions that you want to elicit from the audience. A better specific purpose would be to evoke memories about two things that people loved about Jutta: her love of people and her generosity of spirit.

demographics
the characteristics of your audience—typically age, gender, race, income, and other qualities that characterize them

ANALYZING AND RELATING TO YOUR AUDIENCE

Understanding and relating to your audience are crucial aspects of public speaking because—regardless of purpose or goals—you cannot have a successful presentation unless you adapt your speech to your audience. In years past, we considered the audience to be the people sitting in front of a speaker. However, given the increasing role of technology, this audience may only be one of several. For example, if your presentation is webcast or recorded for future viewing, you may not have physical contact with the other audiences who will listen to your presentation at a later time. This is a common occurrence in distance-learning classes, where the instructor is in one room and students watch from many locations. It can be difficult—if not impossible—to analyze these remote potential audiences. So for the purposes of our discussion here, we will focus on the audience that will be sitting in the same room with you as you make your presentation.

While you should pay attention to the demographics of your audience, you should also remember that your audience may include others who are not physically present.

This is the time, then, to consider audience **demographics:** the characteristics of your audience—typically age, gender, race, income, and other characteristics that characterize them. Demographic information is not limited to these categories, but you should focus on the attributes that are most important in this speech event. For example, if you are speaking to parents about childhood diseases, then knowing the composition of mothers and fathers in the audience may be helpful. Knowing more about your audience can help you determine your topic as well as the language that may be most effective in your presentation. An audience of a similar age group

audience analysis

the process of determining what an audience already knows or wants to know about a topic, who they are, what they know or need to know about the speaker, and what their expectations might be for the presentation

open-ended questions

questions that give the person being questioned free rein in answering

closed questions

questions that are answerable in a few words

secondary questions

questions that follow up on a previous question

neutral questions

questions that give the person being questioned a chance to respond without any influence from the interviewer

will likely share a set of cultural referents. For example, one student, Kim, concluded her informative speech on whale watching with a reference to a *Saturday Night Live* digital short. The class laughed in response. Kim used this example because she knew that the class would likely be viewers of that particular TV program. Knowing what will resonate with your audience is a critical part of composing an effective speech.

How can you go about gathering information about your audience? At the center of this process is **audience analysis**, which you can begin through discussion with the person who invited you to speak. The information you gather from this discussion, gained by posing questions of various types, can help you adapt to your audience (Lucas, 2005; Yook, 2004). For example, Josie needed to find out the academic level of the students in the AISEC Club whom she would be speaking to. If they were all graduating seniors, there would be no point in persuading them about the merits of a summer internship experience. In this case, she could ask the club's advisor for this information. In addition, she might also consider the students' ages. Younger students might be more interested in internship opportunities than older students who could have family and professional responsibilities. Students' majors would also be important to know. Some majors have highly structured course requirements that permit little flexibility for opportunities like internships.

In preparing his speech about plane spotting, Adan took an informal poll of the students in his class, asking how many had heard of plane spotting and how many liked air travel. He then spoke to several of the students privately to see if they would be more interested in knowing about types of planes or his experiences as a plane spotter.

- **Open-ended questions** are useful in exploring issues, as this type of question lets you give your respondent free rein in answering. For example, ask: How much does the audience know about skin cancer? Summer internship opportunities? Plane spotting as a hobby? For a student audience, what are their majors? Science? Humanities?
- **Closed questions** are answerable in a few words. For example, ask: Are most of the audience males? Females? Under 35? Over 35? Upper class? First- or second-year students? Have any experience with plane spotting?
- **Secondary questions** follow up on a previous question. For example, you might ask, "Is high sun exposure a concern for people in this audience?" or "How many people in the audience would be interested in pursuing an international summer internship?"
- **Neutral questions** give the person being questioned a chance to respond without any influence from the interviewer. For example, "What do you think the audience would like to know about?"

What Does Your Audience Know About Your Topic?

It can be challenging to find out what an audience does or doesn't know about a topic, and you may not be able to know definitively the extent of your audience's knowledge about a particular topic. In the examples described above, speakers used various strategies to discover how much their audience knew about their topics. If you are asked to give a speech about avoiding skin cancer to members of your synagogue, you might pass around a short paper survey prior to your presentation, asking some basic questions about their knowledge of cancer rates. You might ask them which cancers are most common (see if they note skin cancer) and what they personally do—if anything—to prevent getting skin cancer. You could also use one of the common Internet survey services (e.g., SurveyMonkey) if your potential audience is a large one.

In addition, you might ask the synagogue forum organizers about the audience's knowledge about your topic. And you may ask about the typical age range and gender composition of the audience who is expected to attend the forum, which might give you some insight into their knowledge on the topic of skin cancer.

Likewise, Josie used several strategies to discover what her student audience knew about internships. She asked to pass around a short survey at one of the club's meeting, where she got basic demographics on the audience—gender, age, major, student status—and also

elicited information about their past experiences with internships, their desire to know more about international internships, and their professional goals.

Sometimes, it is not possible to survey the audience, as is the case with a eulogy. You may assume that the one thing you all have in common is a friendship or acquaintance with the deceased, and you want to speak respectfully and probably not reveal anything that would reflect poorly on the person (don't tell the story of a wild weekend in Vegas with your Aunt Jutta, when she was much younger).

The more information you have about the audience's knowledge about the topic, the better you will be able to frame your specific purpose appropriately and ultimately tailor the content of your speech to your audience.

Who Is Your Audience?

Another important aspect of the audience analysis involves gathering the information you need about their demographic characteristics—the large social categories that define all of us. When you do a **demographic analysis**, you consider the ages, races, sexes, sexual orientations, religions, and social-class backgrounds of your audience. People who share particular demographic characteristics also often share a set of historical or cultural references, and you might use some of these in your speech. For example, they may be familiar with the same television shows, popular songs, and fashions; hearing these references in your speech can help draw the audience in.

> **demographic analysis**
> the portion of an audience analysis that considers the ages, races, sexes, sexual orientations, religions, and social classes of the audience

You may be familiar with the demographics of your audience—for example, you likely already have this information if you are making a presentation to a group you know well. But if you are unsure of the audience composition, you can ask the person who invited you to speak for further demographic information about your audience.

A question you need to ask yourself as you gather information is: What demographic information do I need to know? Not all demographic information is necessary or helpful in preparing your speech. If you are putting together a presentation for your city council about light rail, for example, you don't need to know if the council members are married, divorced, gay, or straight.

Although it is often helpful, demographic information about your audience can sometimes lead you to make erroneous judgments. For example, knowing that you are speaking to an audience of mostly men can help you tailor your message about the controversies surrounding Title IX and its effects on men's college sports to them. On the other hand, knowing simply that your audience is overwhelmingly female may not help you prepare a speech about fertility and public assistance. U.S. census data show that mothers on public assistance in Texas, Iowa, and Tennessee have higher fertility rates, whereas mothers on public assistance in Delaware, Alabama, and New Jersey have lower fertility rates than the national average (Dyer, 2008). So remember: Use demographic information carefully, and avoid playing into stereotypes about social groups.

> *Have you ever been in an audience when a speaker made an inappropriate assumption about you based on demographics? How did you respond?*

What Does Your Audience Know About You?

As you plan your presentation, in addition to analyzing the characteristics of your audience, also consider what your relationship to them will be—that is, what they know about you and how they will perceive you. For example, will your audience have heard of you? Will they know your qualifications? Will they have met you before? How do they know you? If they do not know you, what will they see when you stand before them? Will they consider you a member of their group?

If your audience knows you in one context but you are speaking in another, you may have to make a special effort to establish your credibility for the occasion. For example, if your audience knows you primarily as a student and you want to speak about skin cancer research, you must establish your expertise by referring to the sources you have consulted or the experts you have interviewed.

What Does Your Audience Expect from You?

To anticipate audience expectations, you need to consider several factors. First, what is the nature of the event? If you are speaking at a wedding, graduation party, or baby shower, for

example, the audience will expect an evocative speech that is brief, upbeat, and optimistic about the honorees.

Second, you need to consider how much the audience members already know about your topic. Knowing this is especially important if the general purpose of your speech is to inform. One author of this textbook, Tom, was invited to speak at a communication conference in Ireland. In accepting this invitation, he asked the conference organizer about the audience and what to expect. Because this was an informative speech in an academic setting, he was told about the academic interests, backgrounds, and theoretical orientations of the audience, which helped him focus his speech preparations.

Third, what cultural factors, if any, may be relevant? For example, Judith, another author of this text, was recently asked to speak at a *quinceañera* party, an event that celebrates the coming of age of Mexican and Mexican American girls. As part of this kind of ceremony, the girl's *padrinos* and *madrinas* (godparents) each give a short evocative speech and present a gift. At a quinceañera, the audience expectation is that the speakers will describe their commitment to nurturing and educating the young lady, and they give her a Bible, a rosary, jewelry, or other gifts to symbolize her transition from girlhood to womanhood. As a madrina, Judith had to educate herself about the audience's expectations before the ceremony.

The cultural backgrounds of an audience may also influence expectations about speech organization. For example, in reporting on public speaking practices in their country, Kenyan students and professors observed that Kenyan speeches did not need to follow the linear format expected in the United States. One described Kenyan speeches as often being circular, resembling a bicycle wheel, with the speaker wandering out repeatedly to the rim to make a point or tell a story and then returning to the center, or thesis (Miller, 2002).

Although audience analysis is crucial to the success of a speech, in today's diverse world, a speaker cannot assume that *everyone* in the audience will share the same expectations regarding content and organization. Nor must you change your opinion to adapt to the audience. That is, after you have educated yourself about your audience and determined that your perspective may not match theirs, you can make important adaptations while still maintaining your position. For example, imagine that you are preparing to argue that the United States should lower the drinking age to 18. If the audience were composed of 18- to 20-year old undergraduate students, you would make a presentation that takes into account that many in your audience might be sympathetic to your proposal. However, if you were speaking to a group of legislators considering such a proposal, your presentation would be quite different—primarily because you might face some resistance to your ideas. In this instance, in addition to making your case, your analysis should include your relationship to the topic. That is, you need to consider how your age might influence the audience's perceptions of you and your interests in advocating this position. For example, if you are 18 and speaking to the legislative audience, you will have to do a lot to convince them that your interest in drinking is not overriding your interest in public safety and public health.

Once you have gathered as much information as possible about your audience, you are now ready for the next step: developing your speech.

DEVELOPING YOUR SPEECH

After you have determined the general and specific purpose of your speech and have selected a topic, you can use the results of your audience analysis to help you locate supporting materials, narrow your topic focus, identify your thesis statement, organize your speech, and, finally, develop effective introductions and conclusions. (See *Visual Summary 13.1: Developing Your Speech* on page 330 for an overview of the speech development process.)

Narrowing Your Topic

It's tempting to try to cover too much in one speech (e.g., how to reform health care in the United States; why war is wrong; the achievements of Bill Gates; Should the government cooperate with China?; how to prevent domestic violence; our generation is different from our parents'). After you select your general topic area, you will probably need to narrow it, based on your audience's interests and expectations, the occasion, and time constraints.

If your general purpose is to inform your audience, you will be most successful if you focus on the aspects of your topic that are most likely to affect them, rather than keeping your topic very broad. For example, if your topic is social unrest in Nigeria, you may more easily engage your audience if you demonstrate how Nigerian social unrest can affect the cost of gasoline at the pump in the United States. For Adan's topic on plane spotting, because the students in his evening class are mostly older students, he narrowed his topic by emphasizing the family-friendly nature of the hobby and its low cost, as young children love a (free) trip to the airport's observation deck for an afternoon of plane spotting. With a younger audience, he might inject some humor into the speech and talk about people's perception of the hobby (that it's as exciting as watching paint dry). With an older crowd, he could stress the important role that plane spotters have played in time of war (because of their expertise in aircraft, they could pass information to the government regarding enemy aircraft they had spotted).

If your general purpose is to persuade your audience to a particular view, you should select and develop your topic with this goal in mind. For example, if you want to persuade your audience that placing limits on executive compensation and bonuses for Wall Street workers is important if these firms received taxpayer funds to bail them out, you should also point to some actions they can take to stop or protest what you consider to be outrageous compensation.

Josie found that she needed to narrow her topic because of time constraints. She only had 10 minutes to persuade her audience of the merits of an internship, so rather than talking about the personal, academic, *and* professional benefits, she decided to concentrate on one area that was most salient to the audience. She considered that for an upper-class-student audience, she should concentrate on how an internship would benefit them professionally— e.g., she could provide statistics/evidence that employers in the students' future professions prefer to hire employees with international work experience. For beginning students, she might stress the academic benefits and focus on how the experience can be integrated into any major. She might also need to address the special concerns of students—the financial aspect—regardless of the student's status or major. She would have to show them that the internship is doable, or the rest of the arguments will be futile.

Finally, if your general purpose is to evoke feeling—say, for giving an award to someone— in considering the audience interests, the occasion, and the time constraints, you would likely highlight the most relevant achievements of the recipient. For example, Karie was asked to present her sorority's annual civic achievement award to a member of the local community. She could have talked about many of the recipients' achievements, but knowing that most of the audience would be university or community members and that there would be other awards given, she focused only on the specific work that the community leader did in connecting students with programs addressing social needs in the community—work with poverty, education, and vocational training.

Determining Your Main Points

As our student Mitchell (mentioned in the chapter opener) learned, the first stop after choosing and narrowing a topic is to develop your main points. In most cases, a speech should be organized around three to five main points. If you have fewer than three points, you may not have broken out your main points sufficiently. Consider, for example, a student who is making an informational presentation comparing and contrasting the war in Iraq with the war in Afghanistan. Her main points are:

Main Point 1: Both Iraq and Afghanistan were viewed as sites of terrorism after 9/11.
Main Point 2: The U.S. did find some allies to back up their military units in both of these places.

Unfortunately, this student hasn't sufficiently touched on some of the major differences and similarities between the wars in Iraq and Afghanistan. In this case, the student realized that her topic was too large for a short presentation, and she decided to adopt a more narrow focus—on the role of the Taliban in the U.S.-Afghanistan situation. If, like the student in this example, you can only come up with two main points, it might

topical pattern
an organizational pattern arranged by main points or topics and presented in the order that seems most suitable

problem-solution or **problem-solution-action pattern**
organizational pattern in which the speaker describes various aspects of a problem and then proposes solutions

the edge to the center) or something large (for example, Ellis Island in New York, moving along a central hallway).

> **Topic:** A tour of Ellis Island
> **General Purpose:** To inform
> **Specific Purpose:** To inform about the four major areas of Ellis Island
> **Thesis Statement:** Ellis Island was an imposing and extensive structure, composed of five primary areas, each playing a specific role in immigrants' processing as they arrived in the U.S.: the Baggage Room, the Registry Room, the Hearing Room, and the Bunk Room.
>
> **Main Points:**
> A. The Baggage Room
> B. The Registry Room
> C. The Hearing Room
> D. The Bunk Room

Topical Organizational Pattern   A **topical** pattern of organization involves dividing a large topic into smaller subtopics. This is the most common pattern of organization, and it covers any pattern than does not lend itself to a chronological or spatial pattern; it is used when your main points have no innate pattern except the one you impose on them. This situation requires more thinking because the points have no predetermined relationship, and you will therefore need to find the scheme that is most logical and will work best for your audience. For example, a presentation on growing a backyard garden (inspired by the Obamas) could be divided organizationally into different types of plants that can be grown or growing techniques. Note that Adan's speech on three most-memorable plane-watching experiences, Josie's persuasive speech on the three ways in which internship can benefit students, and the eulogy for Aunt Jutta on her two best characteristics are all examples of the topical organizational pattern.

For excerpts from two more examples of speeches with topical organizational structures, see: Margaret Chan's "World Now at the Start of the 2009 Influenza Pandemic" in Chapter 15, pages 358–359; Barack Obama's "A More Perfect Union" in Chapter 16, pages 373–374.

> **Topic:** Skin cancer
> **General Purpose:** To inform audience about skin cancer
> **Specific Purpose:** To inform audience steps to prevent skin cancer
> **Thesis Statement:** Skin cancer, a major health problem in the U. S., is preventable by knowing who is at risk and following three suggestions.
>
> **Main Points:**
> A. What is skin cancer?
> B. Who is most at risk?
> C. How can skin cancer be prevented?

Problem-Solution Organizational Pattern   The fourth common pattern is the **problem-solution** organization, in which the speaker describes various aspects of a harmful situation (the problem) and then proposes a plan to solve the problem (the solution). This pattern is frequently used in persuasive speeches. It can be used to persuade on fairly mundane topics, like the problem of and solution to parking on our campus, or to address the something like the lack of courses offered in my major during the summer. It can also be used to structure speeches on more serious, wide-ranging problems. One could construct a speech on the problem of the newly growing rates of teenage pregnancies in the United States, the rising health care costs in the United States, the increased terror attacks worldwide, or the genocide committed in the Darfur region of Sudan, plus the solution to the problem. For another example:

> **Topic:** The legalization of gay marriage
> **General Purpose:** To persuade
> **Specific Purpose:** To persuade my audience that gay marriage should be legalized

a more personal connection to the earthquake. Each type of supporting material gives different kinds of information and evokes different responses from your audience.

After you have narrowed your topic, identified your thesis statement, and gathered supporting materials, you are ready to organize your speech. Like well-written essays, oral presentations need clear structures as well as sound foundations in research—the topic we turn to next.

ORGANIZING YOUR SPEECH

Mitchell, in the chapter opener, discovered in his public speaking course that one of the keys to a successful speech is good organization. If your presentation lacks a clearly organized foundation, your audience may not be able to follow your thinking, and you are likely to lose their attention and interest. Remember: Make sure the audience—which has never before heard the presentation—understands what you are speaking about.

Organizing an effective presentation means choosing and following an organizational pattern that will make sense to your audience. Constructing a presentation also means creating an outline that can serve as the framework for your material. As a final part of organizing your presentation, you should develop your introduction, conclusion, and transitions. While it might seem counterintuitive, we recommend that you work out the introduction and conclusion *after* you have organized the body of your speech. So, let's look first at developing the body of your speech.

Developing the Body of Your Speech

After determining your thesis statement and collecting your supporting materials, you are ready to begin organizing the **body** of your informative speech. The body is where all your evidence and supporting materials are presented. To organize the body, you need to decide on an **organizational pattern**, or *arrangement of main points*, that will best suit your topic and stated objective.

Selecting Your Organizational Pattern

Once you have all your main points and subpoints, you need to consider how to arrange them. Speakers in the United States generally follow one of five organizational patterns: chronological, spatial, topical, problem-solution, or cause-effect.

Organizational Pattern

Chronological organization follows a timeline; for example, how to assemble something, instructions on cooking something, describing a technical procedure, or the steps in a process. For instance, Josie could have given an informative speech on the three steps for setting up an internship program. Also, the speech on the life of a famous person, like Susan B. Anthony, lends itself well to a **chronological** outline.

> **Topic:** The life of Susan B. Anthony
> **General Purpose:** To inform
> **Specific Purpose:** To inform about her advocacy for slaves and women
> **Thesis Statement:** Susan B. Anthony, a 19th-century pioneer, as a result of her family's influence and her own formative experiences, fought for people's civil rights, including the abolition of slavery and voting rights for women.
>
> **Main Points:**
>   A. Her birth and formative years (1820–1840)
>   B. Her fight to end slavery (1840–1860)
>   C. Her fight for women's rights (1860–her death in 1902)

For another example of a chronological organization, see the "Last Lecture" speech in Chapter 15, pages 359–360.

Spatial Organizational Pattern A **spatial organization** arranges points by location and can be used to describe something small (for example, parts of a flower, moving from

body
where all your evidence and supporting materials are presented

organizational pattern
the pattern that structures the material in a speech

chronological pattern
an organizational pattern in which the main points are arranged in a time-order sequence

spatial pattern
pattern that arranges points by location

topical pattern
an organizational pattern arranged by main points or topics and presented in the order that seems most suitable

problem-solution or **problem-solution-action pattern**
organizational pattern in which the speaker describes various aspects of a problem and then proposes solutions

the edge to the center) or something large (for example, Ellis Island in New York, moving along a central hallway).

> **Topic:** A tour of Ellis Island
> **General Purpose:** To inform
> **Specific Purpose:** To inform about the four major areas of Ellis Island
> **Thesis Statement:** Ellis Island was an imposing and extensive structure, composed of five primary areas, each playing a specific role in immigrants' processing as they arrived in the U.S.: the Baggage Room, the Registry Room, the Hearing Room, and the Bunk Room.

> **Main Points:**
> A. The Baggage Room
> B. The Registry Room
> C. The Hearing Room
> D. The Bunk Room

Topical Organizational Pattern A **topical** pattern of organization involves dividing a large topic into smaller subtopics. This is the most common pattern of organization, and it covers any pattern than does not lend itself to a chronological or spatial pattern; it is used when your main points have no innate pattern except the one you impose on them. This situation requires more thinking because the points have no predetermined relationship, and you will therefore need to find the scheme that is most logical and will work best for your audience. For example, a presentation on growing a backyard garden (inspired by the Obamas) could be divided organizationally into different types of plants that can be grown or growing techniques. Note that Adan's speech on three most-memorable plane-watching experiences, Josie's persuasive speech on the three ways in which internship can benefit students, and the eulogy for Aunt Jutta on her two best characteristics are all examples of the topical organizational pattern.

For excerpts from two more examples of speeches with topical organizational structures, see: Margaret Chan's "World Now at the Start of the 2009 Influenza Pandemic" in Chapter 15, pages 358–359; Barack Obama's "A More Perfect Union" in Chapter 16, pages 373–374.

> **Topic:** Skin cancer
> **General Purpose:** To inform audience about skin cancer
> **Specific Purpose:** To inform audience steps to prevent skin cancer
> **Thesis Statement:** Skin cancer, a major health problem in the U. S., is preventable by knowing who is at risk and following three suggestions.

> **Main Points:**
> A. What is skin cancer?
> B. Who is most at risk?
> C. How can skin cancer be prevented?

Problem-Solution Organizational Pattern The fourth common pattern is the **problem-solution** organization, in which the speaker describes various aspects of a harmful situation (the problem) and then proposes a plan to solve the problem (the solution). This pattern is frequently used in persuasive speeches. It can be used to persuade on fairly mundane topics, like the problem of and solution to parking on our campus, or to address the something like the lack of courses offered in my major during the summer. It can also be used to structure speeches on more serious, wide-ranging problems. One could construct a speech on the problem of the newly growing rates of teenage pregnancies in the United States, the rising health care costs in the United States, the increased terror attacks worldwide, or the genocide committed in the Darfur region of Sudan, plus the solution to the problem. For another example:

> **Topic:** The legalization of gay marriage
> **General Purpose:** To persuade
> **Specific Purpose:** To persuade my audience that gay marriage should be legalized

examples

material that provides a concrete and realistic way of thinking about a topic and clarifying it

personal narrative (or lay testimony)

relating an event, incident, or experience in one's own life

expert testimony

the opinion of someone who is an acknowledged expert in some field

same time period, Phoenix was second with a gain of 33,184 new residents (http://www.census.gov/Press-Release/www/releases/archives/population/013960.html). The data source does not tell us *why* over 20,000 more people moved to New York City than to Phoenix. While you might speculate that more job opportunities in New York might have drawn more new residents, the numerical difference might be explained in other ways. Perhaps the intense summer heat in Phoenix was less desirable to many people or the housing-market collapse in Phoenix made New York City more attractive. Thus, you could speculate on a range of reasons for this difference, but the Statistical Abstract does not explain it, so unless you have support for an explanation, you should make it clear that you are merely speculating.

Examples

Examples can also add power to a presentation. A speaker might give a brief example to illustrate a point in passing or use a more extended example that is woven throughout a speech. Examples can be very helpful to your audience, as they provide a concrete and realistic way of thinking about a topic and clarifying it. If you were to speak about nonfiction television programming, for example, your audience might better understand your point if you were to name specific programs, such as *60 Minutes, Nova,* or *Monday Night Football.* Without these examples, some audience members might think you are referring to reality television programs, such as *Survivor, The Bachelor,* or *Big Brother.* Examples also can personalize your points—particularly if you make personal connections to some of the shows you discuss (Lucas, 2005): for example, "When I watch *60 Minutes,* I always . . . " or "My sister, who is a producer on *Nova,* reports that . . . "

Personal Narratives

A third kind of support for your presentation—**personal narrative,** or **lay testimony** (relating an event, incident, or experience in one's own life)—can give your speech a human touch. For example, if you are speaking about non-English languages in the United States and you include your own family's struggle to retain their non-English language, your story (personal narrative) adds a personal insight to the issue. Whether you include your own experiences or the testimony and experiences of others, these stories can be powerful. For example, some immigrants have vivid memories about their experiences learning U.S. English when they arrived. Such stories would give an emotional, personal side to the topic of languages in the United States, as our student explains in *It Happened to Me: Lisa.*

IT HAPPENED TO ME: Lisa

We once had a speaker in class who told us about her family's struggle with diabetes. I had never really thought about diabetes before, and the statistics about diabetes didn't impact me as much as her story. I didn't know that some diabetics had to have their feet amputated, but now that I know, I am much more sensitive to the struggles of diabetics.

Depending on your speech topic, you might include **expert testimony** (the opinion of someone who is an acknowledged expert in some field) as part of your supporting materials. For example, in an informative speech detailing the events of the 2010 Haiti earthquake, you might reference the expert testimony of a geologist explaining why this particular earthquake surprised even geologists. This was due to the fact that they had concentrated on the northern fault and now discovered that a southern fault was also shifting, causing unusual parallel shifting "plates" that created ruptures in the earth's surface:

"The Enriquilla-Plantain Garden Fault may slowly be taking over as the main strain-relief valve for the plate boundary," explains Uri ten Brink, a geophysicist with the US Geological Survey's office in Woods Hole, Mass. In effect, the region has two parallel plate boundaries. "That's quite unusual," he says. Indeed, given the number of people who live on the island, as well as the number who visit, "this was really a wake-up call to me to try and understand this system."

In the same speech, you could also use lay testimony (or personal narrative) of persons who actually experienced the Haitian earthquake, which would provide your listeners with

trade organizations, commercial publishers, independent research organizations, and universities.

America's Historical Newspapers (1690–1922): Provides access to almost three centuries of news from 2,000 newspapers from all 50 states.

America: History and Life: A comprehensive bibliography of articles, book reviews, and dissertations from around the world, focusing on the history and culture of the United States and Canada from prehistory to the present; particularly useful for researchers focused on history, related humanities, and the social sciences.

Genderwatch: Part of the ProQuest collection, provides access to articles from a variety of academic, radical, community, and independent publications on gender-related topics (e.g., sexuality, religion, societal roles, feminism, masculinity, eating disorders, healthcare).

IngentaConnect: Covers academic and professional research articles from 29,500 publications, including 8,000 online. Abstracts are free; full text is available by subscription or pay-per-view.

JSTOR (short for Journal Storage): Provides access to digitized back issues of more than 1,000 journal titles in 18 collections representing 51 disciplines.

PsycArticles: Provides access to full-text articles from 71 journals published by the American Psychological Association, the APA Educational Publishing Foundation, the Canadian Psychological Association, and Hogrefe Publishing Group.

Library of Congress: The largest library in the world, with millions of books, recordings, photographs, maps, and manuscripts in its collections, many available online.

Project EUCLID: Provides access to publications in theoretical and applied mathematics and statistics, covering independent, scholarly, and commercial publishers; jointly managed by Cornell University Library and Duke University Press.

Project MUSE: Provides online access to a comprehensive collection of humanities and social-sciences journals and full-text access to current content from over 400 titles representing nearly 100 not-for-profit publishers.

Now that you've identified a collection of relevant sources, what kinds of material are you looking for within them? Supporting materials include statistics, examples, personal narratives, and testimony by others. Let's look at some of the uses for these support materials.

Statistics

Statistics, or numerical data, can highlight the size of a problem or help when making comparisons. For example, the Pew Global Attitudes Project reported in a 2009 survey that the rise in a positive image of the United States around the world (and specifically in Muslim nations) was due to confidence in Obama as the U.S. president. The survey additionally reported that people in Muslim nations such as Morocco (73%) and Pakistan (52%) felt that Islamic extremism was a threat to their countries. Nearly half of those polled in Turkey (47%) and Indonesia (45%) also felt this threat (**http://pewglobal.org/reports/pdf/248.pdf**). Using statistics like these in a presentation about Islamic extremism can help your audience see that many Muslims have the same fears and concerns as non-Muslims—an important message to convey.

If you are dealing with large numbers, you should consider rounding them off. For example, the U.S. Census Bureau estimates that in 2008, there were 304,059,724 people in the United States (**http://quickfacts.census.gov/qfd/states/00000.html**). Your audience is more likely to remember this statistic if you round it off and say that there were about 300 million (or just over 300 million) people in the United States.

When citing statistics, however, you should be careful about attributing meaning to them. This is because the reasons for statistical differences are not always apparent or reported with the statistical data. For example, the Statistical Abstract of the United States tells us that from 2007 to 2008, New York City gained 53,498 new residents, more than any other U.S. city. In the

statistics
numerical data that highlight the size of a problem or help when making comparisons

with willing participants for your research. When conducting interviews, it is important to craft your questions in advance. First, create a list of topics you intend to cover during your time with your subject, or interviewee. Then, create a list of potential questions. Typically, interviews begin with a few simple questions that gather background information while building rapport. These are often followed by a few general questions that engage the interviewees' interest and encourage them to address the specific interview topic (Schutt, 2001, p. 289). Depending on your topic, the questions you ask may be broader or more focused. Regardless, avoid yes/no questions and instead ask open-ended ones to obtain richer responses. For example, asking student interviewees if they have ever received financial aid may elicit a yes or no response, whereas asking them to describe how they are funding their college education may prompt much more information. You may ask a series of follow-up questions, asking your subject to elaborate or clarify a point.

If the topic is a sensitive one, such as domestic violence or unprotected sex, it is especially important to build rapport and establish trust with the interviewee before initiating the questions. Spending some time in small talk, and thus finding some topics of common interest, is a good way to do this. You also need to think carefully about the sequencing of questions. Start with general, nonthreatening questions and gradually build to the more emotionally challenging questions. Of course, it is important to ensure confidentiality and to tell the interviewee that he or she can terminate the interview at any time (Corbin & Morse, 2003).

Although interviews may be valuable sources and can provide great insight into an issue, they are not representative sources. The opinions of a single person cannot stand in for a group. Because interviews provide only anecdotal evidence, they should not be used as conclusive.

Remember that, as the speaker, you also have a responsibility to present your findings accurately and thoughtfully (see the ethics section of this chapter for more on your responsibilities as a speaker). Additionally, you need to keep careful records of the sources you use as you conduct your research and to cite your sources in your speech. For example, give appropriate credit when you make a claim: e.g., "As the late Michael Jackson once said, 'Just because it's in print doesn't mean it's the gospel.' " (http://www.cbsnews.com/stories/2009/06/25/entertainment/main5115351.shtml)

The same applies when you cite a research study. For example, when giving a speech on global news coverage of the swine flu, public-speaking student Nicole stated, "According to a recent study conducted by the Project for Excellence in Journalism, 'The number of cases of swine flu in a given country had little to do with the volume of coverage around the world. China, for example, had the fewest confirmed cases of any of the countries studied, but the paper studied, *People's Daily*, offered about as much front-page coverage as the average paper in the U.S., which had over 2,000 cases' " (Feldherr & Mitchell, 2009).

Although popular search engines like Google (www.google.com) may yield a range of sources to support your presentation, you will be best served by searching on your university's library Web site. Most university libraries have researching tutorials, and there are many search engines and resources that may help you as you conduct research on your selected topic. (See *Did You Know? Selected Search Engines and Databases.*)

DID YOU KNOW?

Selected Search Engines and Databases

Did you know that a number of search engines and databases are specifically geared to academic research on many topics? The following databases are accessible through most universities and public libraries.

Academic Search Premier (EBSCO): The largest scholarly, multidisciplinary, full-text database in the world, covering almost every category of academic study.

Lexis Academic: Provides the most extensive access to full-text news, business, legal publications, and heavily used databases in higher education.

Statistical Universe: Part of Lexis Nexis, it provides access to statistics produced by federal agencies, states, and intergovernmental organizations, professional and

main points is clearly connected to your thesis statement. Moreover, make sure that the main points develop your thesis statement. For example, consider again the drinking-age argument. This speaker has listed three main points:

Main Point 1: The logic of recognizing 18-year-olds as adults
Main Point 2: The logic of matching the drinking age in other countries
Main Point 3: The need to teach the responsibilities of adulthood

You can tell that these three points develop your thesis statement because they advance reasons for proposing that the drinking age should be lowered.

Finding Supporting Materials

Some topics require extensive research—particularly those on which you are not an expert. However, all speech preparations should include some research to find **supporting materials:** data—audio, visual, and textual—that clarify and provide evidence to support the main ideas.

To give an effective presentation, you must collect a number of solid sources. Quantity, however, should not be valued over quality, nor should you seek to simply pack as much information as possible into your informative speech. More information, regardless of the quality of the sources, does not necessarily translate into a better informative speech. It is your responsibility to select the most compelling sources.

The nature of sources varies greatly. In a presentation, you may use printed, electronic, or oral sources. Examples of printed sources include newspapers, magazines, photographs, and books. Electronic sources include Web sites and blogs. Oral sources include interviews and other forms of interpersonal communication. Regardless of topic, however, some combination of source materials is recommended. Which combination of sources you use is largely dependent upon the nature of your topic. If your topic is a relatively new one, it may be difficult to find printed materials. Instead, Web sites, online newspapers and magazines, and blogs might be your preferred sources. Variation is key, however. Although the *New York Times*, for instance, is a highly credible newspaper, solely using materials published in that publication does not show much depth of research. When giving a speech—particularly in informative and persuasive instances—your credibility rests with the sources you select.

Along these lines, you must remain critical of the sources you seek out. This means two things: 1) taking note of the credibility of the source and 2) noting the source's point of view. First, let us deal with the issue of source credibility. Wikipedia (www.wikipedia.com) is a popular reference tool for quick and direct answers. While Wikipedia may be a useful online tool for a relatively simple search, it lacks the legitimacy of edited and published sources. If you are giving an informative speech on the life of President Thomas Jefferson, for example, you will likely lose credibility as a speaker if your primary source—or even simply one of your sources—is Wikipedia. Not only is Wikipedia inconsistent and unreliable (because wiki pages may be edited indiscriminately by anyone with Internet access), but the topic, Thomas Jefferson, lends itself to a much broader range of readings. Books on Thomas Jefferson abound. Thus, the speaker's lack of wide reading on the topic may suggest lack of rigor. The same may be said for blogs. Like Wikipedia, blogs are the product of individual opinions and should not be taken as fact. This is not to say that you can't use them at all. Rather, blogs, like any source, should be used with caution.

In addition to considering source credibility, the researcher must consider a source's point of view. For instance, if you are giving a presentation about media coverage of the war in Iraq, using a single news source will not give a sense of the breadth of coverage. For example, simply using stories printed in the *National Review,* a conservatively bent magazine, or *The Nation,* a more liberal publication, will undoubtedly skew how you would represent coverage. You need to consider issues of politics (i.e., whether the publication/author is writing from a particular political vantage point) and experience (i.e., does the author have a stake in presenting a story in one way versus another?).

Such concerns should also be present when drawing on oral sources. In your speech, you may use an oral history or interview as a source. You may also conduct your own interviews

supporting materials
information that supports the speaker's ideas

If your general purpose is to inform your audience, you will be most successful if you focus on the aspects of your topic that are most likely to affect them, rather than keeping your topic very broad. For example, if your topic is social unrest in Nigeria, you may more easily engage your audience if you demonstrate how Nigerian social unrest can affect the cost of gasoline at the pump in the United States. For Adan's topic on plane spotting, because the students in his evening class are mostly older students, he narrowed his topic by emphasizing the family-friendly nature of the hobby and its low cost, as young children love a (free) trip to the airport's observation deck for an afternoon of plane spotting. With a younger audience, he might inject some humor into the speech and talk about people's perception of the hobby (that it's as exciting as watching paint dry). With an older crowd, he could stress the important role that plane spotters have played in time of war (because of their expertise in aircraft, they could pass information to the government regarding enemy aircraft they had spotted).

If your general purpose is to persuade your audience to a particular view, you should select and develop your topic with this goal in mind. For example, if you want to persuade your audience that placing limits on executive compensation and bonuses for Wall Street workers is important if these firms received taxpayer funds to bail them out, you should also point to some actions they can take to stop or protest what you consider to be outrageous compensation.

Josie found that she needed to narrow her topic because of time constraints. She only had 10 minutes to persuade her audience of the merits of an internship, so rather than talking about the personal, academic, *and* professional benefits, she decided to concentrate on one area that was most salient to the audience. She considered that for an upper-class-student audience, she should concentrate on how an internship would benefit them professionally—e.g., she could provide statistics/evidence that employers in the students' future professions prefer to hire employees with international work experience. For beginning students, she might stress the academic benefits and focus on how the experience can be integrated into any major. She might also need to address the special concerns of students—the financial aspect—regardless of the student's status or major. She would have to show them that the internship is doable, or the rest of the arguments will be futile.

Finally, if your general purpose is to evoke feeling—say, for giving an award to someone—in considering the audience interests, the occasion, and the time constraints, you would likely highlight the most relevant achievements of the recipient. For example, Karie was asked to present her sorority's annual civic achievement award to a member of the local community. She could have talked about many of the recipients' achievements, but knowing that most of the audience would be university or community members and that there would be other awards given, she focused only on the specific work that the community leader did in connecting students with programs addressing social needs in the community—work with poverty, education, and vocational training.

Determining Your Main Points

As our student Mitchell (mentioned in the chapter opener) learned, the first stop after choosing and narrowing a topic is to develop your main points. In most cases, a speech should be organized around three to five main points. If you have fewer than three points, you may not have broken out your main points sufficiently. Consider, for example, a student who is making an informational presentation comparing and contrasting the war in Iraq with the war in Afghanistan. Her main points are:

Main Point 1: Both Iraq and Afghanistan were viewed as sites of terrorism after 9/11.
Main Point 2: The U.S. did find some allies to back up their military units in both of these places.

Unfortunately, this student hasn't sufficiently touched on some of the major differences and similarities between the wars in Iraq and Afghanistan. In this case, the student realized that her topic was too large for a short presentation, and she decided to adopt a more narrow focus—on the role of the Taliban in the U.S.-Afghanistan situation. If, like the student in this example, you can only come up with two main points, it might

be a sign that you have narrowed your topic *too* much, so that you simply don't have enough to say about it.

A speech about hepatitis D may be an example of a topic that could be too narrowly focused for a nonmedical audience. For example, you could inform your audience about the five kinds of hepatitis, how transmission occurs, and treatment for each kind. This is a much broader discussion, but it offers relevant information for a general audience.

> **Main Point 1:** What is Hepatitis?
> **Main Point 2:** Causes and treatments of hepatitis A
> **Main Point 3:** Causes and treatments of hepatitis B
> **Main Point 4:** Causes and treatments of hepatitis C
> **Main Point 5:** Causes and treatments of hepatitis D
> **Main Point 6:** Causes and treatments of hepatitis E
> **Main Point 7:** How to avoid hepatitis

However, with more than five main points, your audience may find your presentation difficult to follow. In this case, determine if you can combine several points into one larger point, or check to see if you can eliminate any main points. For example, you could combine several of the five main points into fewer points:

> **Main Point 1:** What are the different types of hepatitis?
> **Main Point 2:** What are the causes of the different types of hepatitis?
> **Main Point 3:** What are the treatments for hepatitis?

Once you have identified your main points, divide them into subpoints. These subpoints should all relate to their corresponding main points. Returning to the Afghanistan example, a main point about the role of the Taliban in U.S.-Afghani relations could be divided into the following subpoints:

> **Main Point 1:** The Taliban has played an important role in relations between the U.S. and Afghanistan.
> **Subpoint 1:** Early U.S. support of the Taliban
> **Subpoint 2:** The post-9/11 attacks on the Taliban
> **Subpoint 3:** The current situation with the Taliban in Afghanistan

A well-organized speech helps the audience understand the speaker's message.

Again, limit yourself to three to five subpoints for each main point, as you can lose your audience if you include too many.

Identifying Your Thesis Statement

Your next step is to focus on the specific purpose of your speech and to rephrase that purpose as a **thesis statement**. A thesis statement in a speech functions in the same way as a thesis statement in an essay or a research paper: It tells your audience/reader what your speech/paper is about. As part of your introduction, it gives your audience/reader a central argument that the entire speech is organized around. Thus, having a clear, concise thesis statement is essential to a successful speech. Consider the following example:

> **General Purpose:** To persuade
> **Specific Purpose:** To argue for lowering the drinking age
> **Thesis Statement:** The drinking age should be lowered to 18 years old.

thesis statement
a statement of the topic of a speech and the speaker's position on it

This is an effective thesis statement because it clearly sets out the proposition to be considered.

The thesis statement is the foundation on which you construct your presentation. To do this, list the main points you want to convey, and check to make sure that each of these

Thesis Statement: Gay couples should be allowed to be married and so receive the same benefits as heterosexual married couples in health coverage, hospital visitation rights, and inheritance rights.

Main Points:

    A. Lack of health benefits for gay couples

    B. Hospital visitation problems

    C. Inheritance problems

    D. Benefits and advantages of legalizing gay marriage

For an excerpt from a speech with a problem-solution organization, see Rudy Giuliani's "Speech to the Republican National Convention" in Chapter 16, pages 374–375.

Cause-Effect Organizational Pattern A final organizational pattern is **cause-effect**, a pattern that establishes a relationship among events in order to justify a certain conclusion or course of action. It is often used to create understanding and agreement, rather than to argue for a specific action.

Topic: Global warming
General Purpose: To inform about global warming
Specific Purpose: To inform about the causes and effects of global warming
Thesis Statement: Global warming has complicated causes, ranging from energy consumption and overpopulation to climate patterns. The effects of global warming are equally complex and include higher temperatures, rising sea levels, and melting ice caps.

Main Points:

    A. Causes (technology, energy consumption, and overpopulation)

    B. Effects (higher temperatures, rising sea levels, and melting ice caps)

    C. Slowing global warming

Creating Your Outline

Once you have selected the pattern for your speech, you will have a good idea of the order in which you want to present your points. Thus, you are ready to create your **outline**—the framework that arranges the main points and subpoints of your speech to support your thesis. You are probably already familiar with how to outline. In the past, you may have used outlining chiefly to organize your written compositions. However, outlining is also useful in organizing a public speaking presentation.

Develop your outline using approximately 3 to 5 main points. Fewer than three main points may signal that you have not sufficiently researched your topic or that your topic is too narrow. More than five main points, on the other hand, may suggest that your topic is too broad and is in need of honing.

As shown in Figure 13.1, the outline consists of main points followed by subpoints. Each of your three to five main points should support your thesis statement and be explicitly connected to it. An outline should be considered a working document, and, thus, you shouldn't hesitate to change it again and again. For example, as you work on it, you may see points that you wish to rearrange, ones that you want to emphasize more or less, and new examples that you want to include.

Let's look at some sample outlines—first, for a speech to inform, which uses a topical pattern as its framework. In the following outline, you will see several items in parentheses and brackets. These are meant to show how you can incorporate **transitions**— words, phrases, or sentences that show the connection between the

cause-effect pattern
pattern used to create understanding and agreement, and sometimes to argue for a specific action

outline
the framework that arranges the main points and subpoints of your speech to support your thesis

transitions
words, phrases, or sentences that show the connection between the points in your speech and help your audience understand your organization

FIGURE 13.1 A Sample Outline

Topic Area:
General Purpose:

I. Introduction

    A. Purpose/Topic

    B. Thesis Statement

    C. Brief Preview of Main Points

        1. Main Point 1

        2. Main Point 2

        3. Main Point 3

II. Body of the Presentation

    A. Main Point 1

        1. Subpoint 1

        2. Subpoint 2

    B. Main Point 2

        1. Subpoint 1

        2. Subpoint 2

    C. Main Point 3

        1. Subpoint 1

        2. Subpoint 2

III. Conclusion

signposts
transitions in a speech that help an audience understand the speaker's organization, making it easier for them to follow

points in your speech—that help your audience understand your organization. A **signpost** is a specific transition word like *first, next, finally,* or *similarly* (we'll discuss these transition elements in detail later in this chapter). You may choose to include such notes in your outline. Note that some outline entries are complete sentences, while others are simply fragments. An outline is a flexible form, and you can create it in the way that best captures your ideas but keeps them well structured.

Topic Area: Skin cancer

General Purpose: To inform

I. Introduction

    A. Some basic information can help you to prevent skin cancer.

    B. Skin cancer is a major health problem, but it is preventable.

    C. Skin cancer is the most common form of cancer in the U.S.

    D. Ask the audience: Which half will you be in—those at risk or those who aren't?

(Transition to body)

II. Body

    A. What is skin cancer?

(Signpost: First, let's look at what skin cancer is.)

      1. Two types

        a. highly curable cell carcinomas

        b. more serious malignant melanomas

          i. Malignant melanoma most rapidly increasing form of cancer in U.S. Approximately 70,000 new cases will be diagnosed this year.

(Signpost: Next, I'll discuss how skin cancer affects people.)

    B. Who is most at risk?

      1. Light skin color, hair color, or eye color; family history of skin cancer

      2. History of sunburns early in life

      3. Large numbers of moles, freckles

(Signpost/transition: We should think about what can be done about skin cancer)

    C. How to prevent skin cancer

      1. Wear protective clothing, including a hat with a four-inch brim.

      2. Apply sunscreen all over your body and avoid the sun from 10 AM to 4 PM.

      3. Regularly use a broad-spectrum sunscreen with an SPF of 15 or higher, even on cloudy days.

(Signpost/transition to conclusion: Skin cancer is a disease we should all be aware of.)

III. Conclusion

    A. In this speech, I've discussed what skin cancer is, who it affects, and what we can do to prevent it.

    B. The most important lesson: Act now.

    C. We are all at risk, and we can all act now to prevent skin cancer. (Include a personal story about someone with skin cancer.)

Sources: Skin cancer. Centers for Disease Control. Retrieved February 14, 2010, from http://www.cdc.gov/cancer/skin/

Cancer Facts & Figures 2009, American Cancer Society. (2009). Retrieved February 14, 2010, from http://www.cancer.org/downloads/STT/500809web.pdf

Note that this informative speech also has some elements of persuasion. The outline lays out one strategy for informing the audience about the disease, then moves to steps for prevention and ends with a call for action. As the speaker practices this speech, she or he can fill out both informative and persuasive aspects, but the emphasis will likely remain on informing, as this is the primary purpose of the presentation.

In a persuasive speech, the outline should reflect a slightly different format. The speaker first needs to convince the audience that a problem exists. Then, the speaker moves on to persuading the listeners that something needs to be done about it. Often, the speaker also presents a particular solution that he or she wants the audience to embrace. Therefore, a persuasive outline might look like this:

Topic: The debate over the legalization of gay marriage

General Purpose: To persuade

I. Introduction

    A. Gay marriage should be legalized in the U.S.

    B. Tell Keith and Jeff story. Jeff was a flight attendant on American Airlines Flight 11, which crashed into the World Trade Center on 9/11. Because gay and lesbian couples do not have the same rights and protections under the law that straight married couples do, Keith suffered through an expensive and stressful legal battle to get Jeff's death certificate and settle his legal affairs.

    C. The problems Keith suffered in the wake of Jeff's death are only some of the problems caused by the illegal status of gay marriages in the U.S.

    D. We can solve these and other problems by supporting the legalization of gay marriage in the U.S.

(Signpost/transition to body: The denial of same-sex marriage creates enormous inequalities, the subject we will look at next.)

II. Body

    A. Problem posed by absence of gay marriage

        1. Problems of children with gay or lesbian parents (two unrelated people can't be legal "parents")

        2. Problems for gay/lesbian employees (who aren't eligible for partners' benefits)

        3. Problems of gay/lesbian senior citizens (who can't collect Social Security benefits of their deceased partners)

        4. Denial of rights that married couples have, including hospital visitation, social security benefits, pensions, family leave and immigration rights

(Signpost/transition to solution: There is a solution to this civil rights issue.)

    B. Solution to these problems caused by the absence of gay marriage

        1. Recognize the separation of church and state.

        2. Legalize same-sex marriage.

(Signpost/transition to next main point: Legalizing same-sex marriage has several benefits, as we will see next.)

    C. Benefits and advantages of legalizing gay marriage

        1. Solves civil rights disparities

        2. Creates stronger families for gay parents with children

        3. Creates more equitable situations for gay senior citizens

        4. Creates a more equitable society for all Americans

    D. Encourage audience to sign a petition to legalize gay marriages at dosomething.org (call to action).

III. Conclusion
   A. Summarize main points.
   B. Restate the solution—legalize gay marriage in the U.S.
   C. Return to Keith and Jeff story to provide closure.

Sources: Human Rights Campaign. (2003). Keith & Jeff. Retrieved February 14, 2010, from http:// www. hrc.org/millionformarriage/hrc_adcenter/keith_jeff.html

Action Tips: Sign a petition advocating gay marriage. Retrieved February 14, 2010, from http:// www.dosomething.org/actnow/actionguide/sign-a-petition-advocating-gay-marriage

The persuasive outline differs from the informative outline in that it focuses on persuading the audience that a problem exits that needs a solution. Furthermore, it offers a solution that requires advocacy—signing a petition, for example. Note also that although this is primarily a persuasive speech, it includes both informative elements (what problems gay couples face) and evocative elements (the story of Jeff and Keith, the references to 9/11, and loss).

You can see that an outline can be spare, like the one about skin cancer, or more fleshed out, as is the one about gay marriage. The idea is to create a sound organizational structure and a roadmap from which you can best build your presentation.

DEVELOPING YOUR TRANSITIONS, INTRODUCTION, AND CONCLUSION

After you have developed your outline and arranged your points and subpoints according to the pattern you have chosen, you will need to develop the material from this skeleton into a full-bodied presentation. In doing so, you will want to pay special attention to your transitions and your introduction and conclusion. Let's start with transitions.

Developing Effective Transitions

Each of your main points must connect to your thesis statement, and each must also be tied to the other main points. You can connect ideas and concepts using *transitions*. Transitions are words, phrases, or sentences that show the connection between the points in your speech. Words such as *while, although, so,* and *additionally* are typically used to connect ideas in everyday speech. However, in speeches, they must be used to create engaging transitions. So, for example, after you've mentioned McDonald's, it's not particularly interesting to say, "Burger King is another fast-food restaurant." Doing so sounds like you're simply presenting a list. Instead, link ideas together in more meaningful ways: "While McDonald's remains the dominant fast-food chain in the United States, its competitor, Burger King, also brings something to the fast-food burger market." You want to be sure that your audience remains interested and clear as to how each point relates to the previous one.

While transitions are important when connecting ideas within the body of your speech, you must not lose sight of the larger picture. To keep the audience aware of how your main points connect to your thesis, you will want to be sure to use *signposts*: words and phrases that show how what you've said makes sense within the context of the broader speech (next, we now turn to . . . , finally . . . , let's consider . . . ,).

Developing an Effective Introduction

A strong **introduction** immediately grabs the attention of your audience. It will include your thesis statement, which will alert your audience to what your speech is about and establish the importance of your topic. This is where you set the tone of your presentation; it is also

Can you think of a speaker you've heard who used signposts effectively? If not, pay attention over the next few weeks to all the presentations you hear—in class, on TV, on the radio—and note the effective or ineffective use of signposts.

introduction
opening material of a speech from which the audience members gain a first impression of the speech's content and of the speaker

where you make your first impression and in many cases establish your persona. Therefore, you need to carefully consider what you say (and do) here. An effective introduction achieves four purposes:

attention-getter
strategies speakers use to "get" the attention of the audience

- It gains audience attention.
- It focuses the audience's attention on your topic by relating it to the listeners.
- It gives the audience an overview of your organizational pattern.
- It helps the audience understand your thesis.

Gaining Audience Attention

First, you will want to use an attention-getting device. **Attention-getters** are strategies speakers use, as you might guess, to "get" the attention of the audience. You may accomplish this goal by using one of the following devices:

- *Anecdote or personal narrative.* Telling a story that *directly* relates to your topic helps the audience focus. However, be sure your story relates to your topic. You do not want to go off on a tangent even before beginning! Personal narratives may also enhance your credibility as a speaker. For instance, if you are speaking about the Salvation Army and you are a volunteer there, providing your audience with that information will demonstrate your familiarity with the subject matter. However, don't overemphasize the personal; instead, quickly move on to showcasing your research.

- *Quote.* Quotes can serve as excellent entrées to a topic, if chosen wisely.
- *Humor.* Depending on the nature of the topic, humor may be an ice breaker. However, if you don't feel comfortable with humor, don't feel compelled to try it.
- *Powerful statistic.* A startling statistic can intrigue the audience and encourage attention. For instance, one student's speech began this way: "According to the Centers for Disease Control and Prevention, only one U.S. state had an obesity prevalence less than 20% [in 2008]. Of the remaining 49 states, 32 had a prevalence greater than or equal to 25% of the population. Of those 32, 6 had a prevalence higher than 30%." (Source: **http://www.cdc.gov/obesity/data/trends.html**)
- *Powerful image or other audiovisual aid.* Music or visual images such as photographs or video clips (provided they are not too long) can increase energy and interest at the start of a speech as well as create some suspense. An example of a powerful visual image is Bill Gates' release of (potentially disease-laden) mosquitoes into his audience at the beginning of his speech on eradicating malaria (see page 306). We will discuss audiovisual aids and how to select them later in this chapter.

Use attention-getters to focus your audience's attention on your topic and gain their interest.

While each of these strategies may get the attention of the audience on its own, please avoid using more than one at a time. You do not want to overload your listeners with narratives and statistics. Provide just enough to pique their interest. Consider which strategy might be most effective given your topic and audience. This is another case where knowing your audience can make a great difference in how you shape your speech.

Focusing the Audience's Attention on Your Topic by Relating It to Them

Once you've got the audience's attention, you need to get them focused on your specific topic. For example, why should this statistic about children or a personal story about domestic violence matter to them? You can probably think of a number of reasons, such as concern for problems in their own families, friends' families, or a neighbors' families. Thus, if the topic of your presentation is the warning signs of domestic violence, you have found a connection for the purpose of focusing audience attention on the topic.

Giving the Audience an Overview of Your Organizational Pattern

Previewing the organization will make it easier for your audience to follow your speech. When you preview, you might say, "I'll talk about the four warning signs" and then name them: negative inner feelings, partner's lack of control, partner's controlling behavior, and partner's diminishment of spouse. Then, of course, you need to be sure to follow through on each of these points in the body of the speech (**http://www.helpguide.org/mental/domestic_ violence_abuse_types_signs_causes_effects.htm**).

Helping the Audience Understand Your Thesis

Use your introduction to present your thesis statement so the audience understands the point of the speech. Staying with the domestic violence topic, you might say, "I plan to show you the four warning signs of domestic violence." Consider how the following sample introduction to an informative speech achieves the four goals of an effective introduction.

Sample Informative Introduction:
Topic: The band *Rush*

> For the longest time, it was thought in the United States that Canada was a bad place to visit, and as the classic movie *Canadian Bacon* put it, "Canadians are always dreaming up a lotta ways to ruin our lives. The metric system, for the love of God! Celsius! Neil Young!" But in the case of classic rock and roll, there is one Canadian band that is on an equal playing field with other international greats. This band is of course Rush. With no face time in the Hall of Fame, it has become quite apparent that Rush has suffered an injustice. Today, I am going to talk to you about this distinctive band.

Now consider how this sample introduction to a persuasive speech achieves the four goals:

Sample Persuasive Introduction:
Topic: Gun control
Thesis: Stricter gun-control laws should be instituted in the U.S.
Introduction: Many claim that "guns don't kill people, people kill people." Yet while people may be the ones pulling the triggers, guns make the task much easier. The Second Amendment of the Bill of Rights states, "A well-regulated militia being necessary to the security of a free State, the right of the People to keep and bear arms shall not be infringed." While I have never been one to stomp on the Constitution, I believe that we need a closer examination of this issue. Specifically, we need to reexamine the types of guns and ammunition that can be sold to the public. Further consideration of gun policies should lead us to petition for stricter gun-control laws.

> Rather than take a particularly forceful tone in his introduction, this speaker acknowledged the rights set forth in the Constitution but presented his speech as a challenge to the specifics of gun ownership.

Developing an Effective Conclusion

While the introduction gives your audience a first impression, your **conclusion** determines how they'll view you and your topic as you leave the stage. Thus, your conclusion should be memorable and interesting. Although a summary of what you've stated might help tie your points together, you should move beyond mere summary to draw your speech to a close. As with introductions, several strategies can work well.

- *Quote.* A powerful quote can be a strong way to end a speech. However, if your last words were first uttered by someone else, you must give credit to that individual. The quote should also clearly encapsulate the sentiment you plan to end on. You don't want to confuse your audience with a quotation that does not entirely hit the point you want to make.
- *Anecdote or personal narrative.* An anecdote can effectively draw together several themes discussed in your speech. Make sure, though, that the anecdote is relevant and does not require too much hashing out.
- *Gesture toward the future.* This strategy is often tied to a summary, extending it beyond the present. In some cases, this may mean envisioning an unknown. For example, the conclusion below for the speech about the band Rush uses such a gesture by saying that Cleveland's reputation is related to Rush's place in rock-and-roll history.

The conclusion should accomplish a few goals:

- review the three to five main points in the body of your presentation
- challenge the audience to act (for persuasive speeches)
- state a clear conclusion and leave the audience with a positive view of you and your topic

Whatever closing technique you choose, remember that public speaking is an art that requires artistic judgment. There is no one right or wrong answer, only more-effective and less-effective ones. Consider how the following sample conclusion to an informative speech achieves these three goals.

Sample Informative Conclusion:
Topic: The band *Rush*

> Despite what you may hear via *The Drew Carey Show* and its intro song, "Cleveland Rocks," Cleveland does not rock. In fact, Cleveland is far from rocking. Remember Rush's tremendous contributions to our culture of rock and roll—their place among record-breaking bands like the Beatles, Rolling Stones, and Kiss. As time goes on, we grow further and further away from the classic rock that used to fill our speakers, squandered by acts like Flo Rida and Soulja Boy. Only when this band of multiple gold and platinum albums finally gets to stake its claim in rock-and-roll's Holy Land can the city truly rock.

Now consider how this sample conclusion from an informative speech achieves the same three goals:

Sample Persuasive Conclusion:
Topic: Gun control
Conclusion: Tragedies such as occurred on the campus of Virginia Tech several years ago and more recently in suburban Pittsburgh—where a gunman opened fire at a health club—should lead us to stand up and let our politicians hear our voices, no matter how little we think we matter. In order to release our politicians from the grips of the NRA, we must show them that we notice how they are voting on gun-control measures—because we elect them, and they should be properly representing us. Please contact your local representative. Send a letter to Washington, and tell them of your disappointment with current gun laws. It is our responsibility to act.

conclusion
closing material of a speech where the speaker reviews the main points, may challenge the audience to act, and leaves the audience with a positive view of the speaker and the topic

Developing Your Speech

DEVELOPING YOUR SPEECH

PHASE 1:
Understand the Communication Event

- Identify your general purpose.
- Select your topic.
- Identify your specific purpose.

PHASE 2:
Understand and Relate to the Audience

- Determine what your audience knows.

PHASE 3:
Develop Your Topic

- Narrow your topic.
- Identify your thesis statement.
- Find supporting materials.
- Consider the types of supporting materials.

PHASE 4:
Organize Your Presentation

- Select an organizational pattern.
- Create an outline.
- Develop your introduction, conclusion, and transitions.

PHASE 5:
Deliver Your Presentation

- Determine an appropriate style (type of language and phrasing).
- Consider incorporating visual aids.
- Be aware of the time.
- Consider the means of delivery.
- Develop a persona.

This conclusion reminds the audience of current events as well as pointing to a future where their efforts could change the status quo. The speaker does not rely too heavily on emotions here, but he reinforces the responsibilities of everyday people to create policy change.

BECOMING AN ETHICAL PUBLIC SPEAKER

We have stressed the importance of ethical communication in all contexts in this book, and public speaking is no exception. According to the authors of *The Speaker's Handbook* (Sprague & Stuart, 2005), effective public speaking involves a commitment to ethical communication principles, including at least two specific guidelines: respect for the integrity of your audience and respect for the integrity of ideas.

Respecting your audience's integrity means recognizing that you have a special kind of power in the public speaking situation. "When audience members entrust you with their time and attention, you take on an obligation to treat them with fairness and concern" (Sprague & Stuart, 2005, p. 33). This means that you do not try to manipulate them into making decisions that might endanger their health or safety and that you do not say anything that might deceive them. Your listeners don't have to agree with what you say, but they should be better off—perhaps having more valid options to consider—for having listened to you.

A second and related ethical principle involves respect for the integrity of ideas. An ethical public speaker gives credit for information taken from other sources. If you are using others' ideas or quoting others' words, give them credit. The careers of even prominent scholars and politicians have suffered when they have quoted others' speeches as their own. Respecting the integrity of ideas also means that you have an ethical responsibility to be honest with your audience. For example, if you cite statistics, you have a responsibility to be certain that they are accurate, well-researched numbers. You also have a responsibility to tell the whole truth. For example, you leave a false impression if you say "During my time at Harvard" when you only spent a week there visiting your cousin.

Oversimplifying complex issues is another way in which speakers may undermine the integrity of ideas. It would be wrong, for example, to say that the financiers on Wall Street destroyed the U.S. economy, with reverberations felt around the globe, when the reasons for the recent economic decline are more complex and extend beyond Wall Street: Banks, mortgage brokers, real estate speculators, and many others also played roles.

SUMMARY

The foundations of public speaking include understanding how public speaking differs from other types of communication discussed in this textbook and the important role it plays in our society. The steps to a successful public speech include: establishing your reasons for speaking in public, analyzing and relating to your audience, developing and organizing your presentation, and finally, delivering your speech.

One important lesson of the chapter is that you must understand the larger context for your speech. To do so, understand why you are speaking in public—the general and specific purposes of the event—and your audience. You can understand your audience by analyzing their demographic characteristics as well as their prior knowledge about your speech topic. In order to develop an appropriate and effective speech, you also need to understand what your audience knows about you and what they expect from you as a speaker.

In constructing your speech, you first need to narrow your speech topic, determine your main points, identify a thesis statement, and find your supporting materials. You can then choose an organizational pattern, create an outline for your presentation, and develop the introduction, conclusion, and transitions. Throughout the speech and its delivery, you should work on being an ethical public speaker, which involves having respect for the integrity of your audience and for the integrity of ideas.

KEY TERMS

attention-getter 327
audience analysis 312
body 321
cause-effect pattern 323
chronological pattern 321
closed questions 312
conclusion 329
demographic analysis 313
demographics 311
examples 320
expert testimony 320

general purpose 308
informative speech 308
introduction 326
open-ended questions 312
organizational pattern 321
outline 323
neutral questions 312
personal narrative
    (or lay testimony) 320
persuasive speech 308
problem-solution pattern 322

public speaking 306
secondary questions 312
signposts 324
spatial pattern 321
special occasion speech 308
specific purpose 310
statistics 319
supporting materials 317
thesis statement 316
topical pattern 322
transitions 323

CHAPTER REVIEW QUESTIONS

1. Identify three general purposes for speaking. How is the general purpose different from the specific purpose? Provide some examples.

2. What elements are included in a speech outline?

3. What are the potential benefits and drawbacks of using visual aids?

4. What elements go into a strong introduction and conclusion?

ACTIVITIES

1. **Research the characteristics of a particular kind of speech.**
   Ask your family and friends what they might expect from a speaker who is giving a eulogy, a graduation speech, or a retirement speech. How long would they expect the presentation to be? What level of formality do they expect? Do the people you ask differ in their opinions? What did you learn from this exercise? Compile your findings in a presentation to your class, following the steps outlined in this chapter.

2. **Read a speech by a famous speaker.**
   There is not complete agreement on the most famous speeches, but the top 100 are ranked at: http://www.americanrhetoric.com/top100speechesall.html Read one of these famous speeches and focus on the introduction, conclusion, and transitions. Does the introduction get your attention and tell you what the speech is about?

Are there effective transitions that help you follow the speaker's organization? What kind of lasting impression did the conclusion leave with you? What can you learn from this speech that will help you be a more effective speaker?

3. **Watch a video recording of someone you consider a good speaker**—such as Martin Luther King Jr., John F. Kennedy, Ronald Reagan, Bill Clinton, or Barak Obama. Analyze the speech, the style, and the delivery. How do your favorite speakers organize their speeches? Do they project a particular persona or use a particular style? Take notes as you watch them, and compile your notes into a report that identifies some public speaking skills that you would like to incorporate.

4. **Research some ways in which public speaking functions in other cultures.** How might culture influence how we speak in public?

WEB ACTIVITIES

1. On the March 3, 2009, episode of the *Rachel Ray Show,* Micheline, a business owner, overcomes her fear of public speaking. Go to http://www.rachaelrayshow.com/show/segments/view/conquer-your-biggest-fears/

   Watch this part of the show online and then think about what lessons you have learned about public speaking. What strategies might work for you?

2. Go to the homepage of Toastmasters International at: http://www.toastmasters.org/ Read about this organization, its history, and its purpose. Explore the free resources available. What can you learn about public speaking from this Web site?

3. Explore some of the Web sites about public speaking in the Open Directory at: http://www.dmoz.org/Science/Social_Sciences/Communication/Public_Speaking/ Which ones are more useful and which ones are not as helpful to you? Why?

14

SPEAKING IN PUBLIC: SPEECH DELIVERY

Consider Mia's story:

My sister needed an organ transplant and, as she waited and waited on the organ-transplant waiting list, I learned a lot about the many rules that govern the organ-donation waiting-list system. I decided to give my informative speech on this waiting list, as it is something that I now know a lot about. I practiced my speech and I felt that I was ready. When I delivered my speech, I concluded by telling my audience about my sister. We were very close and she passed away waiting for an organ that never arrived. I started crying; I couldn't help it. I think it upset the audience. I think everyone will remember my speech and the delivery, but I'm not sure what they'll remember about organ donation.

Mia's delivery on the topic of organ-donation waiting lists definitely made an impression on her audience. After her speech, her classmates looked as though they wanted to say something but didn't know what to say. One student hugged Mia, and everyone will remember Mia's speech because it touched them, she had a command of the subject matter, and her delivery demonstrated her strong commitment to the topic. It also left many students feeling awkward.

Many people think of public speaking as all about delivery, but delivery is—as we hope you have seen in the previous chapter—only one aspect of the entire process. Delivery alone will not result in a strong speech. In this chapter, we will discuss important issues surrounding speech delivery, including overcoming anxiety, setting the tone, considering language and style, incorporating visual aids, being aware of the time, choosing a delivery method, projecting a persona, and practicing the speech. Finally, we'll address some ethical issues relevant to speech delivery. But first, we'll learn what delivery is and why it is important.

Once you have read this chapter, you will be able to:

- Explain the importance of speech delivery.
- Identify key issues in speech delivery.
- Connect speech delivery to the three artistic proofs: ethos, pathos and logos.
- Understand the ethical issues in speech delivery.

CHAPTER OUTLINE

WHAT IS SPEECH DELIVERY?

THE IMPORTANCE OF SPEECH DELIVERY

KEY ISSUES IN EFFECTIVE SPEECH DELIVERY

Overcoming Anxiety
Preparing Carefully
Setting the Tone
Considering Language and Style
Incorporating Visual Aids
Being Aware of Time Limits
Choosing a Delivery Method
Projecting a Persona
Practicing Your Speech

THE INDIVIDUAL, SPEECH DELIVERY, AND SOCIETY

Ethos, Pathos, and Logos

SPEECH DELIVERY AND ETHICS

Use Language Sensitively
Use Visual Aids Carefully
Respect Time Limits

Summary
Key Terms
Chapter Review Questions
Activities
Web Activities

delivery
the presentation of the speech you have researched, organized, outlined, and practiced

communication apprehension
feelings of anxiety that accompany public speaking. Commonly referred to as stage fright

WHAT IS SPEECH DELIVERY?

In the context of public speaking, **delivery** refers to the presentation of the speech you have researched, organized, outlined, and practiced. Delivery is important, of course, because it is what is most immediate to the audience. Delivery relies on both verbal communication (see Chapter 3) and nonverbal communication (see Chapter 4). While some rhetoricians separate style from delivery, we have found it useful to discuss the two together, as the style of the speech should be connected to its presentation.

THE IMPORTANCE OF SPEECH DELIVERY

Once you have selected and researched your topic, and prepared and organized your presentation, you will need to work on your delivery. Without diligent work on the initial parts of the speech process, however, even the most impressive delivery has little meaning. On the other hand, combined with a well-prepared and practiced presentation, delivery can be a key to your success as a speaker.

Delivery can communicate your confidence and preparedness to your audience. Effective delivery shows your audience that you have researched your topic and understand what you are speaking about. An effective delivery allows you to pull it all together—to showcase your work and to speak with confidence during your delivery.

Think about some of the brief courtroom speeches you've seen or heard by lawyers on various television shows, such as *Law and Order*. Think about how they communicate confidence and enthusiasm in their arguments when making a case to the jury. If an attorney does not seem confident in his or her delivery, how might it affect the jury's decision?

In the following section, we focus on eight important aspects of delivery: overcoming anxiety, setting the tone, considering language and style, incorporating visual aids, being aware of time, choosing a delivery method, projecting a speaking persona, and finally, practicing and putting your speech into action.

KEY ISSUES IN EFFECTIVE SPEECH DELIVERY

While we often think of delivery as happening at the moment of the speech, the fact is that the foundations of effective delivery should be laid out well before you step up to the podium. Let's look at some of these key issues.

Overcoming Anxiety

If you feel nervous about speaking in public, you should know that it is normal to experience some **communication apprehension**, or "stage fright," when you deliver a speech. Even people you wouldn't expect to experience speech apprehension do. The well-known actor Mel Gibson is reputed to have been so overcome with nervousness in front of other people during his first performance that he had to sit down—his legs were too weak to support him. Other notable celebrities who have experienced similar stage fright include Rod Stewart, Barbra Streisand, Laurence Olivier, and Carly Simon, among others (http://www.msnbc.msn.com/id/20727420/). Mick Book and Michael Edelstein (2009) have even interviewed 40 celebrities about stage fright and how they overcome it, as a guide to helping others overcome their anxiety. Extreme fear of public speaking is the number-one social phobia in the United States (Bruce & Saeed, 1999).

Speakers may express apprehension in a variety of ways—as Mel Gibson experienced when his legs felt weak—but some of the most common symptoms include shaking hands and legs, voice fluctuations, and rapid speech. Moreover, almost all speakers worry that their nervousness is going to be obvious to the audience. Fortunately, many signs of anxiety are not visible. For example, if your hands sweat or your heart pounds when you speak, your audience will probably not notice. Read *It Happened to Me: Jamie* for the story of one of our students, who realized she was the only person who knew she was nervous.

As a speaker, your goal is not to eliminate feelings of apprehension, but to use them to invigorate your presentation. Having some apprehension can motivate you to prepare carefully; it can give you the energy and alertness that make your presentation lively and interesting. Public speaking instructors usually say that they worry more about students who aren't nervous, as it may reflect lack of concern and motivation, than about those who are. Although you may feel that your communication apprehension is too much to overcome, statistics are encouraging. Researchers have found that only "one out of 20 people suffers such serious fear of speaking that he or she is essentially unable to get through a public speech" (Sprague & Stuart, 2000, p. 73). Your own feelings of apprehension will likely be much less than that. Still, several strategies can help you manage (not eliminate!) your fear.

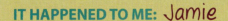

IT HAPPENED TO ME: *Jamie*

When you called on me, my stomach sank. I was ready to run out of the building. When I started my speech, I could feel sweat beading up on my forehead. Then, I thought about all the tools you gave us. In an instant, it seemed, I was done. I stood there, ready for criticism on how bad my speech was. But the class applauded. They had not seen that I was at all nervous. Your comments were that I seemed like a natural speaker.

Preparing Carefully

Experts have discovered that it is not the amount of time you spend preparing, but *how* you prepare. People who are extremely anxious about giving a speech tend to spend most of their time preparing notes. On the other hand, speakers who have less apprehension and are more effective prepare careful notes, but they also spend considerable time analyzing their anticipated audience (Ayres, 1996), a subject we will turn to later in this chapter.

Practice Your Speech Before You Give It

There is no substitute for practice. However, going over the points silently in your head does not count as practice. Practice means giving your speech out loud (possibly in front of a mirror) while timing it and later asking a sympathetic friend (or friends) to listen to it and give you feedback.

Focus on a Friendly Face

Once you are in front of your real audience, find a friendly face in the crowd and focus on that person. The peak anxiety time for most speakers is the first moment of confronting the audience (Behnke & Sawyer, 1999, 2004). Receiving positive reinforcement early on is an excellent way to get over this initial anxiety. When you spot that one person who looks friendly or nods in agreement, keep your eyes on her or him until you feel relaxed.

Finding a friendly face in the audience can be helpful in reducing anxiety.

Try Relaxation Techniques

While the fear may be in your head, it manifests itself in physiological changes in your body; that is, your muscles tense, your breathing becomes shallow, and adrenaline pumps through your system. Effective relaxation techniques for such situations include deep breathing and visualizing a successful speech (Behnke & Sawyer, 2004). Shallow breathing limits your oxygen intake and adds further stress to your body, creating a vicious cycle. Sometimes we're not even aware of these stress indicators. See the *Building Your Communication Skills: Try Relaxing Breathing Exercises* to learn how to break the shallow-breathing cycle.

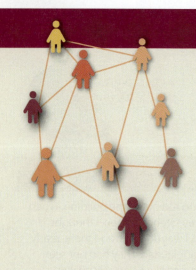

Building Your Communication SKILLS

Try Relaxing Breathing Exercises

By concentrating on our breathing, deep breathing allows the rest of the body to relax itself. Deep breathing is a great way to relax the body and get everything into synchrony. Relaxation breathing is an important part of yoga and martial arts for this reason.

1. Slowly relax your body. You can use the progressive relaxation technique we described above.

2. Begin to inhale slowly through your nose if possible. Fill the lower part of your chest first, then the middle and top part of your chest and lungs. Be sure to do this slowly, over 8 to 10 seconds.

3. Hold your breath for a second or two.

4. Then quietly and easily relax and let the air out.

5. Wait a few seconds and repeat this cycle.

6. If you find yourself getting dizzy, then you are overdoing it. Slow down.

7. You can also imagine yourself in a peaceful situation such as on a warm, gentle ocean. Imagine that you rise on the gentle swells of the water as you inhale and sink down into the waves as you exhale.

SOURCE: http://www.umm.edu/sleep/relax_tech.htm

Do not admit your nervousness. Do not say to yourself or to your audience, "Oh, I'm so nervous up here!" or "I think I'm going to pass out!" These kinds of statements only reinforce your own feelings of apprehension as well as highlighting them for the audience.

Talk Yourself into a Strong Performance

If you watch professional athletes, such as tennis players, you may notice them talking to themselves. Often, these are messages meant for themselves to motivate them to play a better game, hit the ball more accurately, make better backhand returns, and so on. The purpose of this kind of speech is positive motivation. In public speaking, a similar kind of psychological technique can be helpful. As you prepare your speech, practice your speech, and get ready to give your speech, tell yourself that you are going to do very well. Be positive and take a positive and confident approach to the speech.

Consider the Importance of Your Topic to Others

It may be helpful to think about the significance of your topic to others as one way to gain the confidence to give a strong performance. For example, if you are speaking about domestic violence, gun violence, or other important social issues, think about the people who suffer, whose lives are ruined, or whose lives are lost, and your own nervousness will seem insignificant in relation to the point of your speech and the impact you want to have. You don't want your apprehension to become more important than the difference you want to make with your speech. Thinking about others can help you take the focus off of yourself.

Give Speeches

It may seem simple, but this is the strategy most public speaking instructors and students use to overcome anxiety (Levasseur, Dean, & Pfaff, 2004). In short, it becomes easier and easier with each speech. As one seasoned speaker said, "Learning to become a confident speaker is like learning to swim. You can watch people swim, read about it, listen to people talk about it, but if you don't get into the water, you'll never learn" (Sanow, 2005). Take

opportunities to hone your public speaking skills. Volunteer to give speeches, or become a member of Toastmasters International or a local group of public speakers. Take every opportunity that arises to give a speech.

Setting the Tone

Tone refers to the mood or feeling the speaker creates. Sometimes the tone is set by the occasion. For example, speaking at a wedding and speaking at a funeral require different tones, and these tones are determined more by the situation than by the speaker. In other situations—such as speaking in front of a city council to praise them for making a courageous decision about building a new library or park or criticizing them for doing so during a time of tight budgets—the occasion allows the speaker to determine the tone of a part of a meeting. In these kinds of situations, the speaker has the ability to set the tone. When a speaker rallies a crowd at a protest, the speaker has tremendous power to set the tone—as Martin Luther King Jr. often did, so that the crowd was incited not to do violence but to protest nonviolently. In these cases, the speaker may have an ethical obligation to consider the consequences of setting different tones for an audience.

If you are smiling and look happy when you get up to delivery your speech, you will set a tone of warmth and friendliness. If you look serious and tense, you will set a different sort of tone—one of anxiety and discomfort. Remember: You set the tone for your speech long before you begin speaking—in fact, the tone can be set as soon as the audience sees you.

Your tone should be related to the topic of your speech. If you are giving a speech intended to inspire people to take action—such as recycling, participating in a beach clean up, or walking in a fundraiser—an uplifting and positive tone can motivate your audience. For example, when House Speaker Nancy Pelosi spoke about health care reform (see Chapter 16, pages 373–374), she used an uplifting tone: "This is not just about health care for America, it's about a healthier America. This legislation is about innovation. It's about prevention. It's about wellness." If you are telling a tragic personal story, your tone would probably be quite serious. If you are campaigning for one candidate over another, you may want to set a more serious tone for your candidate and a more ridiculing one for the opponent. In Chapter 16, Senator Mitch McConnell set a more aggressive tone as he argued against health care reform and the process it took (page 374). For example, he noted that Americans have "had enough of this year-long effort to get a win for the Democratic Party at any price to the American people. Americans have paid a big enough price already in the time we've lost focusing on this bill." He takes a more partisan tone in his speech than Speaker Pelosi.

Although your tone will run throughout your speech, it can vary as you proceed. For example, you might start out with a serious tone as you point out a problem of some kind, such as cruelty to animals, but you might end with a much more positive tone in moving your audience to address the problem. You may end with a very uplifting tone that invites your audience to envision a future without cruelty to animals and to help make that vision become a reality.

Considering Language and Style

As a speaker, the language you use to give your speech will shape the style of your speech. **Style** refers to the type of language and phrasing a speaker uses, and the effect it creates. Your style can be ornate and indirect; such a style was common in the nineteenth century but is less so today. For example, consider the ornate style used in this selection from Daniel Webster's 1825 "Bunker Hill Monument Oration":

> The great event in the history of the continent, which we are now met here to commemorate, that prodigy of modern times, at once the wonder and the blessing of the world, is the American Revolution. In a day of extraordinary prosperity and happiness, of high national honor, distinction, and power, we are brought together, in this place, by our love of country, by our admiration of exalted character, by our gratitude for signal services and patriotic devotion (Webster, 1989, p. 127).

tone
the mood or feeling the speaker creates

style
the type of language and phrasing a speaker uses and the effect it creates

Alternately, your style can be plain and direct. For example, if Daniel Webster had chosen a plainer style to commemorate the Bunker Hill Monument, he might have said something like this:

> The American Revolution was a great event in our history, and we are here to commemorate its importance by erecting this monument.

These two examples (the first one real, the second one hypothetical) show that an ornate style can stimulate a more emotional response and, in this case, create great pride in the establishment of the United States. The plainer style, on the other hand, gets right to the point and values economy in wording. In his "Last Lecture," Randy Pausch (see Chapter 15, pages 359–360) speaks in a plainer style so that he can communicate clearly and easily with his audience. He uses a plain style with less-wordy language to create a more informal relationship with the audience.

The key is to select a style that is appropriate for the speech you are giving. For example, you may use a plain style if you are giving instructions in a "how-to" sort of speech, but you may use a more eloquent style if you are celebrating someone's accomplishments at a 75th birthday. When choosing a speech style, be aware that the style you use can either enhance or undermine your message. For example, if you speak at a meeting of the local school board using an informal style—maybe referring to the board members as "dudes"—the audience will likely focus more on you than on your topic, because your style would interfere with your ability to convey your message. Or, if you were asked to deliver a speech about college life to a class of fifth graders, you would likely use different words than you would if you were asked to speak to a class of high school seniors. In addition to word choice, you might adjust your sentence length. Overly complex sentences will likely lose younger audiences. Think of telling a story to your friends. How would the way you narrate the story change if you were telling that same story to your parents or coworkers?

The two main elements of style are clarity and appropriateness. Your speech style has the element of **clarity** if listeners are able to grasp the message you intended to communicate. Using **precise language** increases clarity. In everyday conversation, speakers often use words and phrases without much attention to precision. For example, if someone says, "Bob's totally gross," we learn little about Bob; we only know that the speaker has some objection to him or dislikes him for some reason that we do not know. But if the speaker says, "I don't like Bob because he uses vulgar language and ridicules his friends," then we know more specifically how the speaker perceives Bob.

In the interest of clarity, speakers should use their words in precise ways. For example, in describing how someone died, you have many words to choose from: *killed, murdered, terminated, exterminated,* or *assassinated.* Consider the different messages each one conveys. If someone was *killed,* it sounds less intentional than if someone was *murdered.* To say that someone was *terminated* sounds very casual and flippant, like a character in a science fiction or action movie, while *exterminated* communicates a far more sinister death. After all, we call an exterminator if we have a bug infestation, but to exterminate people sounds more closely related to genocide or mass murders. If someone is *assassinated,* it communicates political reasons for this murder. Think carefully about the words you use and what they communicate.

In addition to focusing on the clarity of your language, you also need to consider its **appropriateness**, which generally refers to how formal or informal it should be or how well adapted the language is to the audience's sensitivity and expectations. In general, speakers tend to strive for a more formal style when they are speaking to a larger audience and a less formal style with smaller audiences. Speakers are also apt to use a more formal style during a more formal occasion, such as a big public wedding or funeral, and a less formal style for more casual events, such as a family holiday dinner. Though we can't offer a strict formula for levels of formality or appropriateness, a good rule of thumb is to strive to match your style of presentation to the type of clothing you might wear to the speaking event (see *Building Your Communication Skills: The Importance of Dress*). Just as you wouldn't wear your favorite cut-offs and tank top to a job interview at a bank, you shouldn't use a very informal style of speech if you are making a presentation to your

clarity
the use of language to increase precision and reduce ambiguity

precise language
the use of language to give more specificity and exactness in communicating

appropriateness
following the relevant rules, norms and expectations for specific relationships and situations

Building Your Communication SKILLS

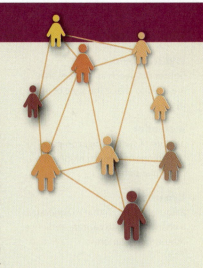

The Importance of Dress

How you dress for a public presentation can influence how others respond to you, as well as how you feel about yourself. Here are some suggestions from the Image Resource Group website at: http://www.professionalimagedress.com/dress-professional-dress.htm This website has suggestions on how professional dress reflects on an organization. As a speaker, these guidelines might be helpful, but you need to pay attention to the occasion as well. While you may not follow all these suggestions, the importance of how we dress cannot be overlooked. Go to the webpage and check out the guidelines. You might take the quizzes as well.

Enhance the image of those who will take your business to the next level

Professional dress is critical in business. It is more than our public skin, it is a language. The way you package yourself sends a message about you, your skills, and your organization. It takes only a few seconds to form a first impression, and more than half of that first impression is based on appearance.

Professional dress for men and women is also a critical component of your organization's brand. Maintaining a competitive edge requires that your staff sustain a consistent visual impression with customers. Your employees are the ambassadors of your organization, and the way they are perceived determines how your organization is perceived by customers, the community, and the marketplace.

company's clients. Similarly, as you may have been told, if you don't know what to wear, it is often better to overdress than to underdress, and the same is true with the appropriateness and formality of your speaking style—that is, it is usually best to speak a little more formally than to speak too informally. Becoming too familiar with an audience (especially one that does not know you) can alienate them and reduce your effectiveness as a speaker.

When you give a public speech, what is the appropriate way to dress? How should you dress for the speeches that you give in class?

The use of very strong language can also impact your audience and gain their attention, although this strategy has to be used very carefully. In August 2009, Treasury Secretary Timothy Geithner is reported to have "blasted top U.S. financial regulators in an expletive-laced critique . . . as [he responded to] frustration . . . over the Obama administration's faltering plan to overhaul U.S. financial regulation" (Paletta & Solomon, 2009, p. A1). Mr. Geithner's fairly aggressive language use could be received in various ways. First, because he is not known for typically using this kind of language, his "repeated use of obscenities" (p. A1) likely made a strong impression. Second, his language choice certainly brought attention to his point, as his rant was covered by the national press. Third, some people saw this language choice as reflective of someone who was losing patience and power. Many observers saw Geithner's approach as a sign that his power was waning, along with the possibility for change in financial regulation. In contrast, however, Stanley Bing, a columnist for *Fortune* magazine, saw something different:

I love it when executives drop the whole statesmanlike thing and get down to what really works: Force. The manipulation of fear. The exercise of power. And nothing establishes who's in charge more than a good display of old-fashioned, fist-in-the-face anger. And what conveys that best? Profanity. Tim Geithner dropped the F-Bomb repeatedly the other day. And I think it's safe to say it's living proof that genuine regulatory reform is now on the way.

(http://stanleybing.blogs.fortune.cnn.com/2009/08/04/geithner-drops-the-f-bomb-or-now-we-know-reform-is-on-the-way/#comments)

What do you think about the use of obscenities in speaking? Is it ever appropriate and effective?

While it may be too early to know the effect of Mr. Geithner's strong language, he certainly gained notoriety for his language choice.

jargon
technical terminology associated with a specific topic

stylistic devices
figures of speech and tropes that are used to shape the style of a message

metaphor
a figure of speech that compares two things or ideas to highlight a particular point

hyperbole
a figure of speech that exaggerates a characteristic to capture audience attention and interest

Giving a clear speech also means avoiding **jargon**, or technical terminology associated with a specific topic. Remember that, while you may know your topic well, your audience may not necessarily be familiar with the words being used. If you were giving a speech to the American Heart Association, it would be fine to assume that your audience is familiar with medical terminology like *stat* (immediately) or *sequelae* (condition due to prior disease). In other cases, it would not be wise to assume that your audience shares your knowledge of such complex language. Similarly, be careful when using acronyms, like *m.i.* (myocardial infarction, or heart attack) or *h.a.*(headache). If you do use an acronym, be sure to clearly define it for your audience. Otherwise, you may lose them before you even begin.

One way to elevate your speaking style is to incorporate **stylistic devices** like **metaphors** or **hyperbole** in your speech. John F. Kennedy was well known for his effective use of rhetorical devices. For example, in a 1961 speech delivered to the Joint Convention of the General Court of Massachusetts, Kennedy used the metaphor *city upon a hill* to emphasize the importance of the role played by Massachusetts' politicians in the national leadership: "Today the eyes of all people are truly upon us—and our governments, in every branch, at every level, national, state and local, must be *as a city upon a hill*—constructed and inhabited by men aware of their great trust and their great responsibilities" (Kennedy, 1961).

Vivid imagery is a crucial part of an effective speech. It is one thing to make your point—it is quite another to make your point through rich imagery and description. A number of stylistic or literary devices are commonly used to aid in such vivid description; for example, alliteration, or the repetition of consonant sounds at the beginnings of words, can be effective. Alliteration can range from the mundane like "bang for the buck" or "high on the hog" to more sophisticated examples such as these article titles: "Science has Spoiled my Supper" and "Kurdish Control of Kirkuk Creates a Powder Keg in Iraq" (Oppel, 2008; Wylie, 1954). For more information on stylistic devices, see *Building Your Communication Skills: Stylistic Devices*.

After considering delivery issues of tone, language, and style, the next step is to think about how best to incorporate visual aids into your speech—the topic we turn to next.

Building Your Communication **SKILLS**

Stylistic Devices

Using rhetorical devices can make your speeches more memorable and give them more style. Some popular rhetorical devices include:

- *Alliteration and Assonance.* Alliteration refers to the repetition of a consonant sound in a series of words. During a commencement address at Knox College in Illinois, then-Senator Obama proclaimed America to be "a place where destiny was not a destination, but a journey to be shared and shaped" (Gallo, March 3, 2008, www.businessweek.com). In this brief phrase, Obama echoed the sound of *destiny* with *destination* and *shared* with *shaped*. Alliteration draws the audience's attention to particular words, thereby reinforcing their rhetorical power. Assonance refers to the repetition of a vowel sound in a string of words. For example, "tilting at windmills" or "high as a kite" are examples of assonance, because the vowel sound *i* repeats.

- *Hyperbole.* Hyperbole refers to an exaggeration intended to capture attention and interest. For instance, when describing her exhaustion, Jackie proclaimed, "I feel like I've walked a million miles today."

- *Metaphor and Simile.* Both devices are types of comparisons. Similes are phrases that compare one thing to another with the use of the words *like* or *as.* For instance, in the film *Forrest Gump,* the title character declared, "Life is like a box of chocolates.

You never know what you're gonna get" (http://www.imdb.com/title/tt0109830/quotes). A metaphor is a comparison that does not use *like* or *as* and analogizes things that would otherwise seem to have little or nothing in common at first glance. John Donne's quote "No man is an island" is a classic example of a metaphor (http://www.poemhunter.com/poem/no-man-is-an-island/).

- *Onomatopoeia.* This refers to the use of words that sound like they mean. For instance, when building tension in a narrative, you may suddenly shout, "Bang! Boom!"

- *Parallelism and Repetition.* Parallelism refers to the repetition of "the same word or expression at the beginning of successive sentences or phrases" (Gallo, March 3, 2008, www.businessweek.com). Dr. Martin Luther King Jr.'s "I Have a Dream" speech is one in which the use of parallelism and repetition was made famous.

- *Personification.* Personification refers to the process of giving an inanimate object human qualities. For instance, when describing the rain, you might say that the sky is crying.

Incorporating Visual Aids

visual aids
audiovisual materials that help a speaker reach intended speech goals

As a student in elementary school, you may have used visual aids in "show and tell" speeches. In these speeches, the visual aid—perhaps a favorite toy, gift, or souvenir—was the central focus of your speech. Now, as part of your college coursework, your instructors may again require that you use visual aids in speeches. Even if you are not required to do so, you may wish to consider incorporating them in your presentations. **Visual aids** are any audiovisual materials that help you reach your speech goals. Some of the most common kinds are video clips, photographs, models, DVD segments, and PowerPoint slides. (For more tips on preparing effective PowerPoint slides, see *Did You Know? PowerPoint Tips*).

To introduce your visual aid during your presentation, follow these general three steps:

1. Introduce the visual aid to your audience by explaining what they will see.
2. Point to the parts of the visual aid that you want them to focus on.
3. Reaffirm the major point of the visual aid, thus pointing the audience to the conclusion you want them to draw.

In a sense, the use of visual aids is a microcosm of your overall speech—that is, it has an introduction, a body, and a conclusion.

DID YOU KNOW?

PowerPoint Tips

When using PowerPoint and other computer-based presentation materials, consider the following tips:

- *Be aware of your font type.* Script fonts are typically difficult to see when projected onto a large screen, so keep to the traditional Serif and Sans Serif fonts. These are easier to read than some of the more playful ones. Your font type should also align with the occasion. If you are giving a presentation for work, stick to a font that communicates professionalism.
- *Be aware of your font size.* Be sure that the audience will be able to read the font. This may require you to check on the size of the room in which you will be presenting.
- *Be aware of your font color.* Keep it simple. When projected onto a large screen, blue letters on a black background, for instance, can be difficult to see.
- *Use animation sparingly, if at all.* While animating fonts can enliven a presentation and make a point more effectively, do not use this computer function to excess. It may be distracting.

Keep in mind that although visual aids can help you reach your speech goals, some can distract the audience from your main points. For example, if you distribute a handout during your speech, audiences will tend to focus on the handout and you will lose their attention. Also, if you finish with a visual aid and leave it up on the screen, the audience will continue to focus on it rather than on you. Finally, speaking to the visual aid instead of your audience is another way to lose audience attention. While it may be tempting to avoid eye contact with the audience, you risk disconnecting with your audience. Let's look at some general guidelines for handling visual aids effectively.

Prepare Your Visual Aids in Advance

If you use the blackboard as a visual aid, for example, you communicate informality and lack of preparation. Your lack of preparation could be insulting to some audiences, who may have made a major effort to come to your presentation. If, on the other hand, you incorporate relevant and well-designed PowerPoint slides, you communicate that you have carefully and thoughtfully prepared your presentation.

Use Visual Aids That Are Easy to See

If your visual aid is too small—for example, if you hold up a 3 × 5 photograph in front of a room full of listeners—it will frustrate your audience. As you speak about something they have difficulty seeing, many audiences will tune you out. Once you have lost your audience, you will have a very hard time recapturing their attention, and you won't reach your speech goals.

Ensure That the Equipment You Need Will Be Available When You Speak

For example, if you want to use a PowerPoint presentation, be sure the room has the appropriate equipment. Today, many classrooms are "smart classrooms" and have this equipment, but it is always best to check. Sometimes classrooms only have overhead projectors, and if you know this, you can prepare overhead transparencies to use in your presentation.

Prepare for Potential Technology Failure

Computers fail, overheads fail, and DVD players are not always correctly connected to LCD projectors. No equipment is foolproof, so you may not be able to show your visual aids. Thus, make sure that your speech can stand on its own and that you are prepared to speak even without the visual aids.

To use visual aids in a way that will help you meet your speech goal, see the *Building Your Communication Skills: Visual Aids Checklist.*

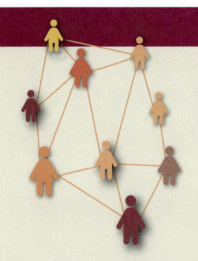

Building Your Communication SKILLS

Visual Aids Checklist

Although you may have carefully prepared your visual aids in advance, it is also important to use them effectively in your presentation. Here are some tips for using visual aids:

☐ Be sure to practice with the visual aids, as speaking and handling visual aids at the same time can be tricky.

☐ Be sure that you are speaking to the audience and maintaining eye contact with them, not looking at the visual aids.

☐ It is a good idea to avoid passing around objects, as the audience will be distracted from you and focus on the object or on passing the object. Try to keep the focus on you.

☐ Explain your visual aid to your audience. Do not simply show it to them and assume that they will know what points you are trying to clarify with the visual aid. Tell them what to focus on and what to notice.

As your own classroom experience has likely demonstrated, when used well, visual aids can be very effective in helping an audience understand a topic. When you use them, be sure that they strengthen your presentation and make your points clearer—not detract from the presentation or fill in as a substitute for content. To determine whether the visual aid is going to enhance or detract from your presentation, ask yourself why you are using it and how it will help to reach your speech goals. For example, in a presentation about types of skin cancer, you could develop a visual aid showing the prevalence of each type and what it looks like.

No matter how dynamic your personality, if your visual aids are not well organized, prepared, and executed effectively, you can lose your audience's interest. Using visual aids that are effectively incorporated will give you confidence in your presentation. If you have prepared an engaging introduction and a clearly organized body with a strong conclusion, all tied together with the artful use of signposts and visual aids, you will have laid the foundation for a successful speech.

After you have selected your style of presentation and incorporated your visual aids, you are ready to consider the presentation of your speech. In the following sections, we will look at several more guidelines for the delivery of your speech.

Being Aware of Time Limits

In the United States, we often think about time as absolute—a phenomenon that can be broken down into clearly measurable units: seconds, minutes, and hours. Yet communication scholars have repeatedly shown that notions of time are relative, as described in Chapter 4 (nonverbal communication). Many public speakers experience this relative nature of time. Some, for example, feel that they have been speaking for a very long time, while their audience may feel that they have heard only a short speech. More often, however, speakers feel that they have not spoken for very long, while their audience is wondering whether the speech will ever end.

Knowing how long to speak is an important aspect of the art of public speaking. The length of any speech should be guided not only by audience expectations and context, but by your content as well. In some instances, the guidelines are rather loose—such as speeches at weddings and retirement celebrations, for example. In other cases, the time limits are very strict, and you may be cut off before you finish. For example, a citizen advocating a position in city council meetings often faces strict time limits. In this case, you should be respectful and adhere to those time guidelines.

On the one hand, if your speech is significantly longer than expected, your audience may become restless, impatient, and even hostile. On the other hand, if your speech is significantly shorter than the time expected, your audience may leave feeling disappointed or shortchanged. After all, they may have made a significant effort to be at your presentation, with expectations that remain unfulfilled. Also, your speech may be part of a larger program, and the planners may be depending on you to fill a particular time slot.

In classroom speech situations, you are often told how long to speak—say, for five minutes. In this situation, your audience expects you to speak for only five minutes—and your instructor expects you to speak for no less than five minutes. One way to make sure you comply is to time yourself when you practice your speech. Doing this will ensure that you know how long your speech runs and whether you need to adjust it. If you have prepared, practiced, and timed your speech, you should have no problem meeting your time requirement.

In non-classroom situations, the goal is to meet the time expectations of the audience. If others are also scheduled to speak, be sure that your speech is not too long. If you speak for much longer than expected, someone else may not have the opportunity to speak. Your long presentation may reflect badly on you, and you could be perceived as inconsiderate of others.

Choosing a Delivery Method

Speakers have several methods for delivering a message—ranging from spontaneous, off-the-cuff remarks to speeches carefully planned, written, revised, and rehearsed. Let's look first at the more spontaneous variety, referred to as impromptu speeches.

Impromptu speeches are those that have not been prepared ahead of the presentation—perhaps because the speaker has been given very little notice or no notice at all. For example, at an event like a business convention, a person may be asked to speak spontaneously as the surprise recipient of an award. Or a person may be asked to make a few comments at a

impromptu speech
a speech that is delivered with little or no preparation

manuscript speech
a speech that is written out word for word and read to the audience

extemporaneous speech
a speech that is written ahead of time but only in outline form

persona
public identity created by a speaker

community or university meeting. Making extensive comments in class can also be thought of as an impromptu speech. This type of speech is often difficult for a beginning speaker. What do you do if you are asked to speak at the last minute? If possible, take a few moments to jot down the major points you wish to make, an interesting way to introduce your topic, and some way of concluding. Organizing your speech in this way will ensure that you make the important points. Be sure to stop when you have made your points.

On some occasions, speakers have their entire speeches written, and they read the speech to the audience. While it may be tempting to take this **manuscript speech** approach, it is not often a good idea. Rarely can a speaker read a speech and manage to make it sound natural. Too many speakers sound like they are reading, rather than speaking naturally to us. Audiences generally prefer to hear from you directly, as if you are speaking from the heart. Engaging your audience with direct address, including direct eye contact, is preferable to the more distanced presentation that results from reading. However, reading a speech can be appropriate if the specific word choices are extremely important and your speech is likely to be quoted directly. Often, the president of the United States reads speeches, as journalists and others are likely to quote him and because lack of attention to word choices can create controversies.

For example, in a question-and-answer session after his speech on September 16, 2001, President George W. Bush referred to the military response to September 11th as a "crusade." His statement resulted in an immediate and strong response from some people in the audience. The Crusades of the medieval period were a significant religious conflict in which Christians left their homes to engage in battles against Muslims in the Middle East. While President Bush may not have intended to frame the military actions against terrorism as a holy war against non-Christians, his word choice—which was spontaneous rather than scripted—pointed to this interpretation. If he had been speaking from a manuscript speech, he could have avoided creating this controversy.

In the middle ground between impromptu and manuscript speech is the **extemporaneous speech**—probably the most common type of delivery. Speaking extemporaneously allows you to be a directly engaged but well-prepared speaker. An extemporaneous speech is written ahead of time, but only in outline form.; then, the speaker uses the outline as a guide. Some extemporaneous speakers may include a few extra notes in the outline to help them remember particularly important points, statistics, or quotations, but the speech is neither written out in its entirety nor memorized. By speaking extemporaneously, you will be able to better engage your audience and adapt your speech to their responses. The sample outlines provided in Chapter 13 are typical of the types of outlines extemporaneous speakers use.

Projecting a Persona

Your **persona**, which includes your personality, is the image you want to convey. If you have seen Ellen DeGeneres on her talk show, you know that she projects a friendly, down-to-earth, almost naïve persona. She dresses informally, she jokes with her audience, and she seems friendly. Ellen's nonverbal communication is very informal and relaxed. She makes direct eye contact with her audience and the television camera; she sometimes slouches in the chair and even does a little "dance" at the beginning of every show. These elements together make up her public persona.

Like talk-show hosts and other television personalities, speakers also adopt personas when they deliver speeches. For example, a speaker who appears to be confident, trustworthy, and calm may have had to create this persona and learn how to project that image. Successful national politicians work to develop personas that are attractive to large groups of people. President Clinton, for example, was described by many—even his detractors—as both affable and engaging in public. While having a

As you think about your own public persona, watch how other public figures create their public personas.

Communication in SOCIETY

Be Cautious with Humor

Many speakers like to use humor in their speeches to keep the audience engaged and the tone more lighthearted. While humor can be a very effective tool for keeping an audience engaged, it can also be problematic, especially when dealing with cultural issues. Here is a list of issues to consider when incorporating humor into a speech.

Some Basic Rules to Remember
- Each culture has its own style of humor.
- Humor is very difficult to export.
- Humor often involves wordplay and very colloquial expressions.
- Humor requires exceptional knowledge of a language.

- Understanding humor requires an in-depth understanding of the culture.
- Ethnic-type humor, stereotyping, and sexist, off-color, cultural, or religious humor should generally be avoided.
- Political humor can be effective in certain circumstances.
- Knowing the type of humor your audience appreciates can guide you.
- When in doubt, the safest approach is to avoid humor.
- Americans in particular begin speeches with a joke. Not all cultures appreciate or respond to this approach.
- Laughing at yourself often diffuses tense situations.

SOURCE: Adapted from Cultural Savvy (2009). "Humor." Retrieved September 28, 2009, from http://www.culturalsavvy.com/humor.htm

---

positive persona can be very helpful in connecting with audiences, be careful about using humor in order to engage your audience. (See *Communication in Society: Be Cautious with Humor* for more on using humor in your speeches.) Humor can be very effective in setting a particular tone with an audience, but it can also ruin a speaker's connection with the audience.

The persona you choose to project should be connected to the communication event and the purpose of the speech, as our student describes in *It Happened to Me: Ted*. If you are speaking at a wedding, you should sound upbeat and positive and project

IT HAPPENED TO ME: Ted

I thought I should always be just 'me' when I spoke. It seemed "fake" to try to pretend to be someone else. But after watching other speakers in various situations and thinking about which 'me' I wanted to speak, I focused on projecting that kind of persona. Establishing a persona has helped me reduce my anxiety. It is only one part of me, but it is the part I want to show the audience. It doesn't feel "fake."

a persona that helps the marital couple, their families, and their friends rejoice in the wedding. Even if you have some concerns that this marriage won't last or that the couple is getting married for all the wrong reasons, the persona you project at the wedding should not broadcast those feelings.

If you have seen videos of Martin Luther King Jr. speaking, you may imagine that he projected a different persona when speaking to his children or a store clerk than he did on the steps of the Washington Monument. At home, he would likely have been more informal and more relaxed with his posture and body movements, and less eloquent in his language. As you can see, creating a public persona is not a matter of falsifying who you are—it is a matter of projecting a more public aspect of yourself. As you know, the self you project varies from context to context, but each reflects the aspects of who you are as a person.

As you create your public persona, consider a few factors that influence others' perceptions of you. First, the speed at which you speak is one aspect of your persona. There is no single, ideal **speaking rate**. Rather, your speaking rate should vary to fit your message. For example, speaking slowly and deliberately can be very effective if you are speaking about the way someone was killed and you want to highlight the gravity of the situation. At other times, you may wish to speak more quickly—particularly for a lighter, more humorous presentation. You may also vary your speed as you move from point to point, to emphasize one item in particular.

Think about the persona and the public image of a great speaker you've heard. Now imagine that person communicating more informally around a dinner table with family, arguing with a coworker, or talking to the cashier in a grocery store. What differences and similarities can you imagine between those two personas? In language use? Body posture? Gestures? Facial expressions?

speaking rate
refers to the speed which someone speaks

vocal variety
the variation in tone, rate, and pauses you use in speaking

vocal projection
the relative strength or weakness of someone's ability to speak loudly enough for an audience in a given context

eye contact
looking at someone or an audience directly, rather than looking away

kinesics
nonverbal communication sent by the body, including gestures, posture, movement, facial expressions, and eye behavior

If you watch television news, you will have noticed that news broadcasters speak quickly. In comparison, people being interviewed often appear to be speaking too slowly, and sometimes the news journalists cut them off. Because of the dominance of television and the fast speech used in that medium, audiences are generally receptive to a speaking rate that is faster than the one used in casual conversation.

You should also pay attention to your **vocal variety**. Vocal variety refers to the variation in tone, rate, and pauses you use in speaking. It is important to vary the way you speak so that you do not sound the same throughout your speech. Vocal variety will keep your audience's interest, and it will help them stay focused on your topic. You can also use vocal variety to bring attention to particular points. If you use strategic pauses, for example, you can guide your audience's attention to specific points you wish to emphasize. Slowing down your speaking rate can also capture your audience's attention and focus them on a particular point.

Keep in mind the importance of vocal volume, or **vocal projection**. You need to speak loudly enough so that your audience can hear you. In large rooms with people sitting far away, you will need to speak louder than if you are speaking in a small room to a small group of people. If there is a microphone available, you will have to decide if you want to or need to use it. If you have difficulty projecting your voice, you may choose the microphone or stand close to your audience. If you have a big booming voice, you may choose to avoid the microphone.

Eye contact is another important element of creating your persona. Making **eye contact** is one of the most direct ways to show your engagement with your audience, and it can lend credibility to your presentation as well. As we saw in Chapter 4, the norm in mainstream U.S. culture is to distrust people who do not look at us directly and to interpret this as a sign of shyness or dishonesty. However, this rule does not apply universally. Some cultures—some Native American and some Asian—do not interpret lack of eye contact this way: They often interpret it as a sign of respect; therefore, you should consider your eye contact and adapt it to the context in which you are speaking.

Gesturing and movement are also a part of your persona. This part of delivery, which we introduced in Chapter 4, is known as **kinesics**. While you may not think that other speakers consider their movements when preparing to speak, the more natural they appear, the more likely it is that they have invested time in practice and deliberate staging. You want your gesturing and movements to look as natural as possible. If they look unnatural and too planned out, these gestures and movements can distract the audience members and focus them on your body movements rather than on your topic. However, it is not very effective to stand stiffly behind a podium. Some very experienced speakers move from behind the podium when it is appropriate to speak more directly to the audience. To ensure that your gestures and movement are effective, practice your speech (we will cover this in the next section).

Remember: You should consider the persona you project even before you begin to speak. Although you may think that your delivery begins when you stand up to speak, you present your persona well before that. In some cases, for example, speakers are part of a panel in front of the audience, or a single speaker is introduced by someone else. In both cases, the speakers are constructing their personas while they wait to speak. Fidgeting, rolling the eyes, yawning, chewing gum, being late, and other nonverbal behaviors mayinfluence how the audi-

Your nonverbal communication is an important aspect of your public persona.

ence perceives you. Assume that you are "on stage" from the moment you walk into the room or come into contact with your audience until the moment you leave.

One of the best ways to ensure that your speaking persona is effective is to practice your speech—the topic we turn to in the next section.

Practicing Your Speech

One of the most effective strategies in public speaking is practice. Once your speech is prepared and once you have considered issues of delivery (anxiety, language, style, tone, visual aids, time limits, delivery methods, and persona), stand up somewhere private and speak *as if* you were in front of an audience. Then do this as many times as you need to in order to be familiar with your speech and feel comfortable delivering it. The bottom line at this stage is that it is essential to practice, practice, practice! Practice in front of a mirror. Practice in front of friends. Sometimes it is helpful to practice the beginning of your speech, as Tamara does in *It Happened to Me: Tamara,* so that you can start off easily and reduce your anxiety. You want to appear confident as you speak, and confidence will come with familiarity. During your delivery, be sure to maintain eye contact with your audience. This will help you connect with them as you speak and will provide you with feedback during your presentation, which may help you adapt accordingly.

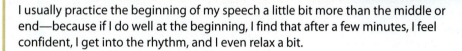

IT HAPPENED TO ME: *Tamara*

I usually practice the beginning of my speech a little bit more than the middle or end—because if I do well at the beginning, I find that after a few minutes, I feel confident, I get into the rhythm, and I even relax a bit.

If your speech is extemporaneous, you may want to change the way that you phrase particular points each time you practice. You can try out different ways of stating or describing some topics. You can see what feels right or which examples should be changed. By practicing, you help to refine your presentation—the language and tone you will use, as well as the fine points of delivery. Practicing your speech can also help you get off to a good start and relax a little as you give your speech.

As we noted earlier, practicing can help you overcome nervousness and make sure that your speech meets the required time limit. It can also help you project natural nonverbal gestures. Typically, the more familiar and comfortable you are with your speech, the more natural will be your gestures; your goal in extemporaneous speaking is to gesture as you would in conversation. When you present your speech to friends or family members, ask them to comment on your gestures and movement as well as your content. Often, new speakers engage in unconscious, repetitive movements, such as rocking back and forth or fiddling with their hair, and they need someone to make them aware of this fact.

By practicing, you can also focus on your signposting, your speech rate, and your eye contact. In other words, you can work on projecting the type of public persona you desire. Each time you practice your speech, you can focus on a different aspect—one time, your gestures, one time, just the content, and so on—until you feel comfortable with the style you have developed.

Be sure to time yourself when you practice your speech. You want to have a sense of the length, in case you need to cut out something or expand on something else. Once you have practiced a number of times, you will have a very good sense of approximately how long the speech will be.

Although you may practice many times, your goal is not to memorize. A memorized speech often sounds memorized, like a recording rather than a real human being. In addition, if you work strictly from memory and you stumble over a word or phrase, you may lose your place and find it difficult to resume your presentation. Instead, during practice, focus on delivering a presentation that is enthusiastic, vibrant, and engaging. Each time you practice, you may come out with different phrasing, different wording, different movements, and so on. When you give your speech, yet another version may appear, but this time, it will likely be a version you are comfortable presenting.

The public speaking process involves a lot of preparation and practice to help you become a good speaker. (See *Visual Summary 14.1: Key Issues in Effective Speech Delivery.*) But clearly, being a good speaker involves more than just speaking. An additional key issue relates to the ethical concerns of speech delivery.

Key Issues in Effective Speech Delivery

OVERCOME ANXIETY

SET THE TONE

CONSIDER LANGUAGE AND STYLE

INCORPORATE VISUAL AIDS

BE AWARE OF TIME LIMITS

CHOOSE A DELIVERY METHOD

PROJECT A PERSONA

PRACTICE YOUR SPEECH

THE INDIVIDUAL, SPEECH DELIVERY, AND SOCIETY

Successful speech delivery is the product of careful negotiation between you (the individual speaker) and society at large. As such, it is important to strive to build ethos, or credibility, and maintain it during your presentation. **Ethos**, according to the ancient Greek philosopher, Aristotle, was one of three **artistic proofs** (means of persuasion that rely on the speaker). The other artistic proofs are **pathos**, or emotion, and **logos**, or rationality.

Ethos, Pathos, and Logos

Your ethos as a speaker is tied to your perceived credibility. Certain speakers may have credibility even before beginning a speech, for ethos is not merely linked to speech content and delivery. Rather, ethos can be connected to an individual's identity and perceived persona (discussed earlier). Family background, for instance, is a source of ethos for some speakers. The Kennedys are a family who derive ethos by virtue of their familial name and longstanding celebrity in the political arena. While you may not necessarily believe the Kennedys to be the most authoritative sources on all topics, members of the family undoubtedly wield credibility because of their name. Many commercials and popular advertisements take advantage of ethos in order to sell products. Gatorade, for example, relies on Peyton Manning's credibility as a champion quarterback in order to promote product sales. By the same token, ethos may also be harmed by public notoriety. In the wake of news of his affair, South Carolina Governor Mark Sanford's ethos was damaged, causing significant fallout following his public apology. In a statement issued on June 24, 2009, Sanford declared, "I apologize to the people of South Carolina. There are many people out there right now who are hurt, angry and disappointed with me, and rightfully so. Over the time that I have left in office, I'm going to devote my energy to building back the trust the people of this state have placed in me" (Gov. Sanford Issues Follow-Up Statement, 2009). In other words, Sanford apologized and was hoping to begin the process of rebuilding his image and his ethos.

Ethos, as previously mentioned, is connected to the concept of persona that we discussed earlier. Because persona is a public identity, it is a social construction. It is a product of communication by individuals and across media. For instance, when Senator John McCain ran for president in 2008, he repeatedly referenced "Joe the Plumber" from Ohio who sought to open a small business. By citing Joe, McCain attempted to create a persona that was accessible and in touch with the needs of working Americans. McCain's running mate, then-Alaska Governor Sarah Palin, who made repeated references to "Joe Six-Pack," similarly attempted to show an interest in and connection to working Americans.

While an individual may strive to present a particular persona, one he/she thinks the audience will find engaging, a persona is subject to the audience's interpretation. It is the interplay between the individual and society that shapes how you, the speaker, are perceived; a disconnect can occur between how you attempt to present yourself and how your audience perceives you. For instance, in response to 2008 Republican vice presidential candidate Sarah Palin's repeated references to "Joe Six-Pack," comedian and writer Tina Fey performed a series of skits for the comedy variety show *Saturday Night Live,* poking fun at the persona Palin sought to convey.

Ethos is also impacted by the way the speaker presents information to the audience—that is, through organization or logos, or rationality. A logos-based approach capitalizes on high-quality information to build a compelling argument. When giving a speech on the dangers of processed foods, Jasmine, a public speaking student, announced that according to the American Heart Association and the Centers for Disease Control, approximately 145 million—almost 35 percent—of adult Americans are overweight (Statistics you need to know, 2009; U.S. Obesity trends 1985–2008, 2009). Using these and other striking statistics that connect diet to the rise in obesity, Jasmine used logos to make her point about the impact of processed foods on health (Processes foods-the cause of obesity, 2006). When an argument is presented in a way that is logical, it becomes accessible to audiences. The use of logos, in conjunction with ethos, can be particularly powerful

ethos
credibility

artistic proofs
artistic skills of a rhetor that influence effectiveness

pathos
the rhetorical use of emotions to affect audience decision making

logos
rational appeals; the use of rhetoric to help the audience see the rationale for a particular conclusion

in an informative speech setting. When used effectively, an audience will develop a deep understanding of the topic.

The third artistic proof, pathos, is typically most effective in persuasive settings and will be discussed in greater depth in Chapter 16.

SPEECH DELIVERY AND ETHICS

Consider the following advice for delivering an ethical speech.

Use Language Sensitively

Avoid language that denigrates, demeans, or devalues other people and other topics. If it is not relevant to your speech topic, you should avoid using pejorative terms that are likely to offend others. This ethical guideline includes words that you know would be offensive in referring to other people by race, gender, sexuality, religion, and so on. Using such terms can turn an audience against you and your ideas rather quickly. Even if no members of a particular group are in your audience, others may find derogatory references offensive. Derogatory language does not only apply to people, but also to cultures, countries, and historical events. As an ethical speaker, be sensitive to your use of language.

Use Visual Aids Carefully

When you use visual aids, consider the ethics of the visual images. What kinds of images might distract the audience from the point of your presentation? Or turn the audience against you? For example, some protesters have used photos of aborted fetuses. Is this ethical? Some photos show President Obama with a Hitler-like moustache. Is this appropriate and acceptable? There is no clear rule regarding appropriateness, but some images may be considered unethical by some audiences. You should consider the ethics of any visual aids you use.

Respect Time Limits

Respect the time limits you are given when you speak. In some situations, this is an ethical concern. For example, at many city council meetings, a number of people may wish to be heard on a particular topic. If you are on a panel of speakers, you should not speak longer than you are expected to speak. If you do go over your time limit, you are taking away time from other speakers. If you take too much time, one or more of the other speakers may not have the opportunity to speak, and you thus undercut the public deliberation at the city council meeting or other venue.

SUMMARY

Delivery is often viewed as synonymous with public speaking itself. Although delivery is only one part of the speech-making process, it is a very important part. As you saw from Mia's personal experience at the beginning of this chapter, delivery can make a big impact on an audience in ways that you may not intend. Also important to delivery are overcoming anxiety and setting the tone of the presentation, which includes thinking carefully about your language use and the style of your presentation. If you use visual aids in your presentation, incorporate them in a way that does not distract from you or from your topic. You will also need to choose a delivery method, determining whether the presentation calls for impromptu, extemporaneous, or manuscript delivery. Also, consider the persona that you want to project by paying attention to your public image, and be aware of the time limits set for the presentation. In order to perform at your best, you must practice, paying attention to your signposting, your delivery, and your overall style. Finally, speakers must uphold a level of ethics in their delivery by not using language that denigrates others, choosing visual aids with care, and respecting time limits.

KEY TERMS

appropriateness 340
artistic proofs 351
clarity 340
communication apprehension 336
delivery 336
ethos 351
extemporaneous speech 346
eye contact 348
hyperbole 342

impromptu speech 345
jargon 342
kinesics 348
logos 351
manuscript speech 346
metaphor 342
pathos 351
persona 346

precise language 340
speaking rate 347
style 339
stylistic devices 342
tone 339
visual aids 343
vocal projection 348
vocal variety 348

CHAPTER REVIEW QUESTIONS

1. What is the appropriate tone for your presentation? How do you know?

2. What style should you strive for in your presentation? How might you craft that kind of style?

3. What are some stylistic devices you might use in a speech?

4. What are the guidelines for using visual aids in a speech?

5. Why should you pay attention to the time limits of a speech?

6. What are some ethical considerations in delivery?

ACTIVITIES

1. Look for an announcement about a speaker on campus. Go to the presentation and focus on the delivery. What did you notice about the speaker's delivery and style? What things did you see that you would like to emulate in your own speeches? What things did you notice that you would like to avoid in giving speeches?

2. Attend a political rally of any kind you like—TEA parties, antiglobalization, health care reform, and so on. Watch the speeches and focus on the delivery of the speakers. In this kind of setting, what do you notice about the delivery and style of the speakers?

3. Learn about techniques for dealing with communication apprehension. Do library research as well as interviews. Find out how others deal with their anxieties. Identify some techniques that will help you deal with communication apprehension.

WEB ACTIVITIES

1. Go to www.youtube.com and type in the name of a speaker. Watch his or her delivery and think about what you might emulate, as well as what you might avoid.

2. Explore a number of rhetorical figures at: http://www.uky.edu/AS/Classics/rhetoric.html. As you look through them, which ones do you find interesting and helpful? Which ones have you heard speakers use?

3. Go to www.whitehouse.gov and watch President Obama's weekly address or any other speeches. What do you notice about his delivery and language use?

15

SPEAKING IN PUBLIC: INFORMATIVE SPEAKING

"*Every once in a while a revolutionary product comes along that changes every-thing. . . . In 1984, we introduced the Macintosh. It didn't just change Apple, it changed the whole computer industry. In 2001, we introduced the first iPod, and it didn't just change the way we all listen to music. It changed the entire music indus-try. Today we're introducing three revolutionary products of this class. The first one is a wide-screen iPod with touch controls. The second is a revolutionary mobile phone. And the third is a breakthrough internet communications device. So three things: a wide screen iPod with touch controls, a revolutionary mobile phone, and a breakthrough communications device. An iPod, a phone, and an Internet communicator. An iPod, a phone, and an Internet communicator. Are you getting it? These are not three separate devices. This is one device and we are calling it iPhone. Today Apple is going to reinvent the phone. . . . " (Macworld, 2007).*

When Apple CEO and cofounder Steve Jobs introduced the company's vaunted iPhone in January 2007, he not only heralded a revolution in mobile technology, he also gave a presentation that became a model for public speakers. In the words of *Businessweek's* Carmine Gallo, Steve Jobs created "a frenzy that gripped every gadget fan in the country" (Gallo, 2007). Jobs's effectiveness as a speaker may be attributed—at least in part—to the unique technology he was presenting. But Jobs not only introduced a product, he also gave a strong informative speech about it. Jobs explained the iPhone's distinctive features and capabilities in a way that was both engaging and stimulating to his audience. Gallo, author and business consult-ant, says: "Jobs conducts a presentation like a symphony, with ebbs and flows, buildups and climaxes. It leaves his listeners wildly excited. The takeaway? Build up something unexpected in your presentations" (Gallo, 2007). Jobs captivated his audience with the introduction of the iPhone. While this is undoubtedly a chal-lenging task for any public speaker, in this chapter we will explore the ways in which you too can capture the attention of your audience in a compelling, informa-tive presentation.

In this chapter, we will first describe informative speaking and address its impor-tance. We will then explore informative speaking's similarities to and differences from persuasive speaking (for more on persuasive speaking, see Chapter 16). We will examine the role of informative speaking in society and its development from the dynamic interplay between the individual and society at large. We will then explore how the speaking occasion and the objective impact how an informative speech is crafted. To this end, we will build upon Chapter 13 by providing sugges-tions for selecting an informative speech topic, conducting research, and organiz-ing presentation materials. We will detail a range of organizational and rhetorical strategies that may be used when developing an informative speech and the possi-bilities for integrating audiovisual equipment into your presentation, building upon Chapter 14. This chapter will conclude with a discussion of ethical concerns arising from informative speaking. First, however, we need to describe what we mean by informative speaking.

CHAPTER OUTLINE

WHAT IS INFORMATIVE SPEAKING?

THE IMPORTANCE OF INFORMATIVE SPEAKING

INFORMATIVE VERSUS PERSUASIVE SPEAKING

TYPES OF INFORMATIVE SPEECHES

Speeches About "Objects"

Speeches About Processes

Speeches About Events

Speeches About Concepts

ORGANIZING INFORMATIVE SPEECHES

Using a Chronological Pattern

Using a Geographical/Spatial Pattern

Using a Topical Pattern

TIPS FOR EFFECTIVE INFORMATIVE SPEAKING

Include Information That Is Accurate and Objective

Include Facts That Are Truthful and Can Be Corroborated

Include Ideas That Are Accessible to Your Audience

Include Visual Aids That Clearly and Accurately Describe Facts

Respect the Ideas of the Audience

SAMPLE INFORMATIVE SPEECH IN OUTLINE FORM

ETHICS AND INFORMATIVE SPEAKING

Summary

Key Terms

Chapter Review Questions

Activities

Web Activities

informative speaking
speaking with the aim of educating the audience

rhetor
a person or institution that addresses a large audience; the originator of a communication message but not necessarily the one delivering it

Once you have read this chapter, you will be able to:

● Explain the nature of informative speaking.

● Understand the role of informative speaking in different areas of public life.

● Differentiate informative from persuasive speaking.

● Describe the four main types of informative speeches.

● Understand the ethical issues confronting the presenter of an informative speech.

WHAT IS INFORMATIVE SPEAKING?

Informative speaking is defined by its objective—to inform or educate the audience. An informative speech may seek to explain or broaden an audience's understanding of a topic, to impart knowledge or information, or to demonstrate. In an informative speech, you—the **rhetor**, or the person addressing the audience—assumes the role of teacher. When cooking and home décor celebrity Martha Stewart appeared on NBC's *Today Show* to explain to audiences at home how to prepare an omelet, she delivered one type of informative speech: the demonstration (How to cook the perfect egg, 2008). Through her narration, Stewart helped her audience navigate the process step by step.

Informative speaking can also be used to help audiences understand important threats to their well-being, whether that is through vital weather information, breaking news alerts, or health information. In 2009, President Obama gave an informative speech on the H1N1 virus, with information on preventing the spread of the flu (see *Communication in Society: Informing the Public About the H1N1 Outbreak*). This use of informative speaking is a key part of everyday life, as we seek out and share information that will help everyone lead healthier and safer lives.

Communication in SOCIETY

Informing the Public About the H1N1 Outbreak

Informative speaking is a part of everyday life and can serve important social functions. In May 2009, President Obama used informative speaking to tell the nation what the federal government was doing to combat the spread of H1N1 flu. He also informed the nation of some steps they could take to help prevent the spread of this flu. President Obama let his audience know that as more information became available, more informative messages would be forthcoming.

"The Centers for Disease Control has recommended that schools and child care facilities with confirmed cases of the virus close for up to fourteen days. It is why we urge employers to allow infected employees to take as many sick days as necessary. If more schools are forced to close, we've also recommended that both parents and businesses think about contingency plans if children do have to stay home. We have asked every American to take the same steps you would take to prevent any other flu: keep your hands washed; cover your mouth when you cough; stay home from work if you're sick; and keep your children home from school if they're sick. And the White House has launched pages in Facebook, MySpace and Twitter to support the ongoing efforts by the CDC to update the public as quickly and effectively as possible.

As our scientists and researchers learn more information about this virus every day, the guidance we offer will likely change. What will not change is the fact that we'll be making every recommendation based on the best science possible."

SOURCE: "Obama outlines U.S. efforts to combat H1N1 flu." *Wall Street Journal.* May 2, 2009. Retrieved February 13, 2010 from: http://blogs.wsj.com/washwire/2009/05/02/obama-outlines-us-efforts-to-combat-h1n1-flu/

THE IMPORTANCE OF INFORMATIVE SPEAKING

When you speak informatively, you impact your audience by explaining an issue, under-scoring its importance, and showing how to accomplish a stated goal. In this way, informative speaking facilitates the functioning of a democracy. As active participants in the democratic process, citizens should be informed and able to hold their representatives accountable for their decisions and actions. For this reason, many political speeches detailing foreign and domestic policies strive to inform the public and open lines of communication.

Informative speaking skills are also beneficial in the workplace—where such speeches aim to share knowledge and information. As you learn how to effectively deliver informative speeches, you will be pre-pared to share information to others in a wide range of situations—like making sales presentations, delivering product demonstrations, giving board meeting presen-tations, and conducting employee training sessions.

INFORMATIVE VERSUS PERSUASIVE SPEAKING

The aim of the informative speech, as we have said, is to inform, or educate. The aim of the **persuasive speech**, however, is to persuade, or convince. While these differences may appear absolute in theory, in practice they are less clearly differentiated. (See *Visual Summary 15.1: Informative Versus Persuasive Speaking.*) For example, as a contributor to the YouTube Reporters' Center, Arianna Huffington, cofounder and editor in chief of *The Huffington Post,* delivered an in-formative speech discussing the place of citizen journalism in the contemporary media landscape. Huffington said:

Informative speeches focus on sharing knowledge and information.

> With the expansion of the web . . . the ability to commit acts of journalism is spreading to everyone, including you. Nothing has demonstrated the power of citizen journalism better than the recent uprising in Iran. People tweeting from demonstrations . . . have been able to tell a story, in real time. One thing is clear: It's time to get out there and report. (Arianna Huffington on Citizen Journalism, 2009)

You may be wondering: Isn't Huffington's conclusion a call to action—an attempt to **persuade**, or convince, the audience to become citizen journalists? Isn't persuasion the objective of an entirely different genre of public address? The simple answer to this question is yes. While Huffington provided a variety of examples of citizen journalism roles in arenas ranging from politics to entertainment—hallmarks of informative speaking—she also at-tempted to persuade her audience to *become* citizen journalists. Huffington sought not only to inform her audience, but also to persuade them to take action. Similarly, when introducing the iPhone, Apple CEO Steve Jobs sought, on the one hand, to inform his audience of the innova-tiveness of his product. At the same time, Jobs was undoubtedly making a *sales pitch*—an at-tempt to convince his audience to *buy* the iPhone rather than the Blackberry, the Sidekick, or another alternative mobile competitor.

As rhetoric scholar Mark Gring argues, "Presentation of partial and/or biased (rather than complete, objective, or neutral) facts is unavoidable, and implicit (at least) claims regarding their presenter's credibility are inescapable. Facts exist but always are interpreted from a perspective; interpreted facts, once presented, become potentially persuasive" (2006, p. 42). For example, if you decide to speak informatively on the topic of school uniforms, you would lay out the debate surrounding the issue and the arguments leveled by different sides. While you may have an opinion, as an informative speaker, you should avoid trying to convince your audience of one argument or another. Rather, your objective should be to provide a guide to understanding the various arguments made with respect to the issue. If

persuasive speech
a speech with the aim of convincing the audience

persuade
to convince

giving a persuasive speech on this same topic, however, your objective *would* be to convince your audience that your side is the one they should support. Thus, while your goal in the informative speech is to broaden your audience's knowledge of this contested issue, your aim in the persuasive version is to compel your audience to take the position from which you are arguing, or at the very least to acknowledge the validity of your stance.

Although a persuasive speech may include explanations or an informative speech may include a call to action, what fundamentally distinguishes these two genres is the specific purpose of the speaker. As the speaker, you must ask yourself: What is my goal? What do I want my audience to know? What do I want my audience to do following my speech, if anything? It is this specific purpose that locates a speech as either predominantly informative or persuasive. What makes a speech topic informative is the manner in which you, the speaker, frame it for your audience.

Consider the following example of a speech that is predominately informative, but with elements of persuasion. In a speech to the House Committee on Energy and Commerce, Jodi Nudelman, Regional Inspector General for Evaluation and Inspections of the Office of Inspector General, U.S. Department of Health & Human Services, painted a clear picture of the lack of inspections to protect the nation's food supply. She reinforced the role of the OIG in overseeing the safety of our food supply, along with other oversight responsibilities. In this sense, her informative speech (note all the facts about the food safety system and the role of the OIG) has persuasive elements.

Good afternoon, Chairman Stupak, Ranking Member Burgess, and other distinguished Members of the Subcommittee. I am Jodi Nudelman, Regional Inspector General for Evaluation and Inspections of the U.S. Department of Health & Human Services (HHS) Office of Inspector General (OIG). I appreciate the opportunity to appear before you to discuss our oversight work as well as the vital role that the Food and Drug Administration (FDA) plays in protecting the Nation's food supply.

Recent high-profile outbreaks of foodborne illness have underscored the importance of food facility inspections. My testimony today will focus on my office's recent review of FDA's inspection program.[1] In short, our report identifies significant weaknesses in FDA's inspections of domestic food facilities. We found that many food facilities went 5 or more years without an FDA inspection. We also found that there was a large decline in the number of food facility inspections conducted by FDA over a 5-year period, as well as a decline in the number of violations identified by FDA inspectors. Further, when violations were identified, FDA did not routinely take swift and effective action to ensure that these violations were remedied.

Our recent report is a part of a larger body of OIG work that demonstrates that more needs to be done to ensure the safety of the Nation's food supply. In a report on food traceability, we found that only 5 of 40 selected products could be traced through each stage of the food supply chain.[2] In addition, more than half of the facilities that handled these food products failed to meet FDA recordkeeping requirements. In another report, we found that 5 percent of selected facilities failed to register their facilities with FDA as required. Of those facilities that did register, almost half failed to provide accurate information in FDA's registry.[3] Finally, we completed a report that found that FDA did not always follow its procedures when overseeing certain pet food recalls and noted that FDA does not have the statutory authority to mandate recalls.[4]

OIG'S MISSION IS TO PROTECT HHS PROGRAMS AND BENEFICIARIES

OIG is an independent, nonpartisan agency committed to protecting the integrity of the more than 300 programs administered by HHS as well as the health and welfare of the people served by them. OIG fights fraud, waste, and abuse through a nationwide network of investigations, audits, and evaluations, as well as enforcement and compliance activities.

OIG's work results in recoveries of misspent or stolen funds and in recommendations for program savings and improvements to program efficiency and effectiveness. In FY 2009, OIG investigations resulted in $4 billion in settlements and court-ordered fines, penalties, and restitution. OIG audits resulted in almost $500 million in expected recoveries. OIG also produced equally important but less quantifiable gains in deterrence and prevention

of fraud, waste, and abuse and in improved program operations. Additionally, OIG has raised awareness of critical issues among policymakers, Government agencies, and other relevant stakeholders. Moving forward, OIG is committed to building on our successes and continuing to protect the integrity of Government programs and their beneficiaries.

Notes: 1. OIG, FDA Inspections of Domestic Food Facilities, OEI-02-08-00080, April 2010; 2. OIG, Traceability in the Food Supply Chain, OEI-02-06-00210, March 2009; 3. The Public Health Security and Bioterrorism Preparedness and Response Act of 2002 requires certain food facilities to register with FDA. The purpose of registration is to provide FDA with reliable information that enables FDA to quickly locate facilities during outbreaks of foodborne illness. See OIG, FDA's Food Facility Registry, OEI-02-08-00060, December 2009; 4. OIG, Review of the Food and Drug Administration's Monitoring of Pet Food Recalls, A-01-07-01503, August 2009.

Now consider the informative speech delivered by Professor Randy Pausch of Carnegie Mellon University in 2007. Pausch died from pancreatic cancer in 2008, and video of the speech known as "The Last Lecture" spread across the Internet, garnering more than 10 million views on YouTube. His words were later published as a book, titled *The Last Lecture* (Pausch & Zaslow, 2008). In the excerpts from his speech, below, you can see how Pausch used personal stories as a way to inform his audience of how to achieve their dreams, no matter how big or small.

So what were my childhood dreams? . . . I wanted to become one of the guys who won the big stuffed animals in the amusement park, and I wanted to be an Imagineer with Disney. . . .

This was the hard one. Believe me, getting to zerogravity is easier than becoming an Imagineer. When I was a kid, I was eight years old and our family took a trip cross-country to see Disneyland. And if you've ever seen the movie National Lampoon's Vacation, it was a lot like that! [laughter] It was a quest. [shows slides of family at Disneyland] And these are real vintage photographs, and there I am in front of the castle. And there I am, and for those of you who are into foreshadowing, this is the Alice ride. [laughter] And I just thought this was just the coolest environment I had ever been in, and instead of saying, gee, I want to experience this, I said, I want to make stuff like this. And so I bided my time and then I graduated with my Ph.D. from Carnegie Mellon, thinking that meant me infinitely qualified to do anything. And I dashed off my letters of applications to Walt Disney Imagineering, and they sent me some of the damned nicest go-to-hell letters I have ever gotten. [laughter] I mean it was just, we have carefully reviewed your application and presently we do not have any positions available which require your particular qualifications. . . . So that was a bit of a setback. But remember, the brick walls are there for a reason. The brick walls are not there to keep us out. The brick walls are there to give us a chance to show how badly we want something. Because the brick walls are there to stop the people who don't want it badly enough. They're there to stop the other people. . . .

All right, . . . so . . . we've talked about my dreams. . . . Somewhere along the way there's got to be some aspect of what lets you get to achieve your dreams. First one is the rule of parents, mentors and students. I was blessed to have been born to two incredible people. This is my mother on her 70th birthday. [shows slide of Randy's mom driving a race car on an amusement park race course] [laughter] I am back here. I have just been lapped. [laughter] This is my dad riding a roller coaster on his 80th birthday. [shows slide of dad] And he points out that he's not only brave, he's talented because he did win that big bear the same day. My dad was so full of life, anything with him was an adventure. [shows picture of his dad holding a brown paper bag] I don't know what's in that bag, but I know it's cool. My dad dressed up as Santa Claus, but he also did very, very significant things to help lots of people. This is a dormitory in Thailand that my mom and dad underwrote. And every year about 30 students get to go to school who wouldn't have otherwise. This is something my wife and I have also been involved in heavily. And these are the kind of things that I think everybody ought to be doing. Helping others.

But the best story I have about my dad—unfortunately my dad passed away a little over a year ago—and when we were going through his things, he had fought in World War II in

the Battle of the Bulge, and when we were going through his things, we found out he had been awarded the Bronze Star for Valor. My mom didn't know it. In 50 years of marriage it had just never come up.

My mom. [shows picture of Randy as a young child, pulling his mom's hair]. Mothers are people who love even when you pull their hair. And I have two great mom stories. When I was here studying to get my Ph.D. and I was taking something called the theory qualifier, which I can definitively say is the second worst thing in my life after chemotherapy. [laughter] And I was complaining to my mother about how hard this test was and how awful it was, and she just leaned over and she patted me on the arm and she said, we know how you feel honey, and remember when your father was your age he was fighting the Germans. [laugher] After I got my Ph.D., my mother took great relish in introducing me as, this is my son, he's a doctor but not the kind that helps people. [laughter] . . .

Other people who help us besides our parents: our teachers, our mentors, our friends, our colleagues. God, what is there to say about Andy Van Dam? When I was a freshman at Brown, he was on leave. And all I heard about was this Andy Van Dam. He was like a mythical creature. Like a centaur, but like a really pissed off centaur. And everybody was like really sad that he was gone, but kind of more relaxed? And I found out why. Because I started working for Andy. I was a teaching assistant for him as a sophomore. And I was quite an arrogant young man. And I came into some office hours, and of course it was nine o'clock at night and Andy was there at office hours, which is your first clue as to what kind of professor he was. And I come bounding in and you know, I'm just I'm going to save the world. There're all these kids waiting for help, da da, da da, da da, da da, da da. And afterwards, Andy . . . put his arm around my shoulders and we went for a little walk and he said, Randy, it's such a shame that people perceive you as so arrogant. Because it's going to limit what you're going to be able to accomplish in life. What a hell of a way to word "you're being a jerk." [laughter] Right? He doesn't say you're a jerk. He says people are perceiving you this way, and he says the downside is it's going to limit what you're going to be able to accomplish. . . .

Remember that regardless of the context or the style of an informative speech—fact based and formal as in Jodi Nudelman's address or informal and personal as in Pausch's—the speaker must be knowledgeable and well-informed. As you can see from these examples, speeches need not be solely informative or persuasive. On some level, *every* speech is persuasive, for no presentation can be entirely devoid of interpretation. Let's turn our attention now to four types of informative speeches.

TYPES OF INFORMATIVE SPEECHES

Informative speech topics typically fall into one of four categories: speeches about objects, processes, events, or concepts (Lucas, 2009, p. 301). See *Did You Know? Four Types of Informative Speeches.*

DID YOU KNOW?

Four Types of Informative Speeches

Type of Informative Speech	What Is It?	Sample Topics
Objects	Person, place, thing	Michael Jackson, Cancún, Guitar Hero, the Beatles
Process	How-to, demonstration	Running a marathon, using a DVR, playing Halo
Event	Festival, holiday, activity	Bastille Day, Pride Week
Concepts	Ideas, issues	Military torture, free speech, school uniforms

SOURCE: Adapted from Stephen E. Lucas, *The Art of Public Speaking*, pg. 301, and Colorado State University's Online Writing Guide, http://writing.colostate.edu/guides/speaking/infomod/pop2b.cfm

Informative Versus Persuasive Speaking

INFORMATIVE SPEAKING

Aims to inform or educate

Martha Stewart's presentation on how to prepare an omelet.

Randy Pausch's Last Lecture.

Arianna Huffington's speech on citizen journalism.

PERSUASIVE SPEAKING

Aims to persuade or convince

Speeches About "Objects"

These informative speeches describe people, places, or things. We have put "objects" in quotation marks as we do not often refer to people or places as objects. The concept here is that an informative speech about people, places, or things attempts to inform the audience about something that exists physically. Because these "objects" are often too large to cover in a single speech, you'll need to decide which of their aspects you want to focus on. For example, if you are going to give an informative speech about Rhode Island, there is too much to cover in a single speech. Even if Rhode Island is the smallest state, there is a lot that a speaker might cover, such as the history of Rhode Island, the geography or economy, or even tourism in Rhode Island. You could even give an entire speech on why the smallest state has the longest name (State of Rhode Island and Providence Plantations).

It is important to focus your speech if you are focusing on an object. Let's look at some examples:

> **Topic:** Michelle Obama
>
> **Specific Purpose:** To inform my audience about Michelle Obama's causes
>
> **Thesis:** Michelle Obama has undertaken three important causes as First Lady.
>
> **Main Points:**
>> A. She supports military families.
>> B. She advocates for organic food.
>> C. She fights against childhood obesity.

Each of these main points would explain some of the activities she has undertaken to draw attention to the issues. Still, they are only one aspect of Michelle Obama's life, and this speech would not attempt to cover other aspects of her life.

Speeches About Processes

These speeches typically are the demonstration, or "how-to," speeches, which seek to take the audience through a practice step by step. By focusing on a process, this type of informative speaking can often be paired with a demonstration. Speeches about processes are often used to show audiences how to do something, whether it is something everyday, like preparing a meal, or something far more technical, such as how to do a particular surgical procedure. As you can see, this type of informative speaking is very helpful in our professional lives as well as our personal lives. Let's look at an example of a speech informing cat owners how to give medicine to their pets.

> **Topic:** Giving medicine to cats
>
> **Specific Purpose:** To inform the audience on how to give medicine to a pet cat
>
> **Thesis:** Cat owners and their friends may need to know how to give medicine to a cat.
>
> **Main Points:**
>> A. Set out the proper amount of the pills or liquid medicine needed.
>> B. Find the cat and wrap him/her in a large towel so that the cat cannot move. The head should be exposed.
>> C. With fingers on both sides of the mouth, open the cat's mouth. Drop the medicine as far back on the tongue as possible.
>> D. Close the cat's mouth and make sure that the medicine is ingested, not spit out.
>> E. Give the cat some water to wash it down and then a treat to associate medicine with treats.

Speeches About Events

These speeches describe incidents, festivals, holidays, activities, and other happenings. People often want to know more about various events, especially if they may go to the event someday. For example, people may want to be informed about Mardi Gras in New Orleans if they are considering going there. Knowing what happens, what to expect, and what to look for can

be helpful information for first-time visitors. It may also be helpful to know if a particular event is one that would be appropriate for young children. If I wanted to go to the Burning Man festival, is it appropriate for children? Informative speeches about these events can help an audience better understand the event and make informed choices about attending.

Speeches about events can also inform audiences about historical events, such as King Philip's War, a war between Native Americans and the English colonists in southern New England. These speeches can include recent events as well, to inform audiences about a current situation, such as the pressure on the euro due to weak EU member states like Greece. Let's look at some other examples.

Topic: Zozobra

Specific Purpose: To inform my audience about the burning of Zozobra

Thesis: The burning of Zozobra is an interesting event that symbolizes the throwing off of the hardships of the past year.

Main Points:

   A. Zozobra is a giant marionette that is burned to dispel the hardships of the past year.

   B. The burning of Zozobra kicks off the Fiestas de Santa Fe in New Mexico.

   C. The event invites flammable items that are no longer wanted, such as photos or divorce papers for a "gloom box" that is burnt with Zozobra.

In this example, audiences learn about this ritual and how it attempts to cleanse bad things from the previous year.

Speeches About Concepts

These speeches entail an explanation of an issue or idea. They often focus on informing an audience about an idea so that they better understand it. For example, the concept of "freedom of speech" does not mean that you can say whatever you want, whenever you want, wherever you want. Someone cannot just walk into your house without your permission to speak about whatever she or he wishes; there are parameters that can be explained in a speech about concepts. Here is a different example:

Topic: Credit default swaps

Specific Purpose: To inform my audience about sovereign credit default swaps

Thesis: Sovereign credit default swaps are like insurance for debt holders against a country defaulting on its loans.

Main Points:

   A. Greek Prime Minister Papandreou recently said that Greece is under attack. Sovereign credit default swaps may be the reason for this claim.

   B. Credit default swaps (CDS) act as insurance for debt holders, to protect them against a country defaulting on its loans.

   C. The weaker a country's economy, the higher the cost of the CDS, which makes it more expensive for that country to borrow funds.

   D. In the context of various economies showing weakness, sovereign CDS may be exacerbating the downward slide of these economies.

Source: Unmack, N. (2010, February 16). A primer on credit default swaps. *Financial Post.* Retrieved February 16, 2010, from **http://www.financialpost.com/opinion/breaking-views/story.html?id=2569093**

ORGANIZING INFORMATIVE SPEECHES

There are three basic organizational patterns that informative speeches typically follow: chronological, geographical/spatial, or topical. We first introduced these patterns in Chapter 13, but in this chapter, we'll look specifically at how they can be used in informative speeches.

chronological pattern
an organizational pattern in which the main points are arranged in a time-order sequence

geographical or spatial pattern
an organizational pattern in which the main points are arranged according to physical location

Using a Chronological Pattern

A **chronological pattern** orders main points in time-order sequence. This organizational structure will be most helpful when giving an informative speech in which the timing of events is critical. For instance, when giving a speech on the solo career of pop singer, artist, and designer Beyonce Knowles, our student Jessica generated the following preliminary outline:

Topic: Beyonce Knowles' artistic growth

General Purpose: To inform

Specific Purpose: To inform my audience about Beyonce Knowles' development as a musical artist

Thesis Statement: Singer Beyonce Knowles' development as a musical artist can be observed in the varied sounds of her progressive albums.

Main Points:

    A. "Dangerously In Love" (2003)

    B. "B'Day" (2007)

    C. "I am . . . Sasha Fierce" (2008)

Source: The Official Beyonce Website, http://www.beyonceonline.com/us/home

Once Jessica determined that her main points would be Beyonce's albums, she had a framework for developing the remainder of the speech.

Chronological organizational patterns are also useful when preparing "how-to," or demonstration, speeches.

Topic: How to use Skype

General Purpose: To inform

Specific Purpose: To inform my audience how to use Skype

Thesis Statement: Using Skype is an easy way to speak with your family and friends around the world.

Main Points:

    A. Install program

    B. Set up profile information

    C. Search for friends and family

    D. Establish speaking time

Source: Skype, http://www.skype.com/

Using a Geographical/Spatial Pattern

A **geographical or spatial pattern** organizes main points according to physical location. As we saw in Chapter 14, this approach to organization can be beneficial when it is easier for an audience to understand and remember your topics from their location. For instance, in his informative speech on the New England Aquarium, John ordered his presentation around the Aquarium's various exhibits and how a visitor might experience those exhibits.

Topic: New England Aquarium

General Purpose: To inform

Specific Purpose: To inform my audience about the diverse species and habitats on display at The New England Aquarium

Thesis Statement: The New England Aquarium is home to a wide variety of animals hailing from diverse habitats.

Main Points: Aquarium Layout:

    A. Amazon Rain Forest

    B. Edge of the Seas

C. Giant Ocean Tank

D. Amazing Jellies

E. Pacific Reef Communities

Source: New England Aquarium. Retrieved July 15, 2009, from http://www.neaq.org/animals_and_exhibits/index.php

Using a Topical Pattern

A **topical pattern** is the most common for informative speakers. In a topical structure, the informational speech is organized by main points, or topics, presented in the order that seems best. These main points, which support the thesis statement, will likely include several subpoints, as in the example below. As you can see, the speaker could have presented his main points in any order—that is, sandwiches did not have to come first. This was simply the speaker's preference.

> **Topic**: Healthy eating on vacation
>
> **General Purpose:** To inform
>
> **Specific Purpose:** To inform my audience about the variety of healthy fast-food options available in our area
>
> **Thesis Statement:** A variety of healthy fast food options exist.
>
> **Main Points and Subpoints:** Healthy fast foods
>
> A. Sandwiches
> 1. Panera
> 2. Au Bon Pain
> B. Burgers
> 1. McDonald's
> C. Mexican food
> 1. Chipotle
> 2. Taco Del Mar
> D. Bakeries
> 1. Corner Bakery
> 2. Au Bon Pain

Source: Minkin, T., & Renaud, B. (2009, July 15, 2009). "America's top 10 healthiest fast food restaurants." Health.com. Retrieved September 27, 2009, from http://living.health.com/2009/02/19/americas-healthiest-fast-food-restaurants/

TIPS FOR EFFECTIVE INFORMATIVE SPEAKING

Now that you have seen the basic foundations of informative speaking, let's take a look at some specific tips for effective informative speaking. These tips are meant to help you as you go through the speech preparation process. Think about these issues as you gather your speech content and create your visual aids.

Include Information That Is Accurate and Objective

Informative speaking includes a lot of information, but that information needs to be accurate and objective. (See *Building Your Communication Skills: Checklist for Fact Finding.*) This means that the information should come from sources that most audience members would see as fair, relatively unbiased, and accurate. The information itself should also be fair and objective. Informative speaking should not emphasize persuading the audience as persuasive speaking does.

---

topical pattern
an organizational pattern arranged by main points or topics and presented in the order that seems most suitable

Building Your Communication SKILLS

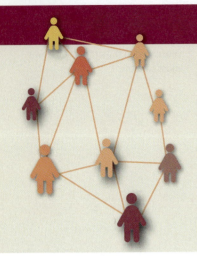

Checklist for Fact Finding

In establishing the facts you will use in your speech, did you:

☐ seek out a variety of sources to confirm the facts?

☐ consider using visual aids to help clarify some facts?

☐ ensure that the facts are understandable to your audience?

☐ explain to your audience why some facts may be in contention?

☐ consider ways to help your audience accept facts that may challenge their current beliefs?

Include Facts That Are Truthful and Can Be Corroborated

Informative speaking relies on information that is truthful and can be corroborated. This means that the information is not opinion, but factual. Factual information is information that can be verified from other sources; opinions cannot. In informative speaking, it is important to rely on factual information. For example, if you say, "I could never live in Vermont—it's too cold!" you are using opinion in making the statement. There is no factual information about what is "too cold"; it is a matter of opinion. Many people live in Vermont and in climates that are even colder. Instead, if you said that the average temperature in Burlington, Vermont, in January is 17.6 F degrees, this information can be verified by going to the National Weather Service (**http://www.erh.noaa.gov/btv/climo/ BTV/monthly_totals/avgtemp.shtml**) or other sources.

Visual aids can be helpful in clarifying information, but be sure the visual aids focus on informing, not persuading, your audience.

Include Ideas That Are Accessible to Your Audience

Informative speaking can involve very complex and technical topics. After all, most audiences do not have the same knowledge about medicine as medical researchers, or legal issues as lawyers, and so on. A key component of successful informative speaking is to adapt the information and the ideas to the audience. This means that it is not always wrong to include a lot of medical terms and concepts; it all depends on the audience. If an audience is comprised of medical doctors and medical researchers, it may be appropriate to use very technical terminology. The ideas and how they are presented should be adapted to the audience's knowledge and background.

Include Visual Aids That Clearly and Accurately Describe Facts

We sometimes say that a picture is worth a thousand words, but images can also be very persuasive and lead an audience away from the focus on information and facts that are the hallmark of an informative speech. If you are using visual aids, be sure that they focus on clarifying

and highlighting the factual information in your speech. In determining if the visual aids are clear and accurate, do not focus only on the words and language used.

Respect the Ideas of the Audience

Avoid language that could be considered offensive or insensitive, and do not present material in a way that might offend your audience. Audiences come to any speech with prior knowledge, beliefs, and attitudes about many topics. At the beginning of the chapter, we saw Steve Jobs introduce the iPhone and he connected it to products that the audience already knew—the iPod, phone and internet. As we suggested in Chapter 13, in order to be effective at informing an audience about something, it is important to understand your audience so that your presentation will acknowledge and respect their current ideas.

Hanover Street in Boston's North End has not always been an Italian American encalve.

SAMPLE INFORMATIVE SPEECH IN OUTLINE FORM

The following is the outline of the body of an informative speech on the history of Boston's North End neighborhood. Within the speech, you can see the student's transitions, main points, and subpoints.

Sample Informative Speech: Boston's North End neighborhood

Purpose: To inform the class of the historical development of the North End and how this development shaped its current landscape

Organizational Pattern: Chronological and topical

Transition: Although today the North End is Boston's answer to New York's Little Italy, it has not always been that way. The neighborhood has experienced several shifts in its ethnic composition since the seventeenth century.

> This student needs to ensure that there is an attention-getting opener, along with a transition into the topic for the audience. The speaker may want to explain to the audience why they may want to know about Boston's North End neighborhood.

Body:

History of the North End

Transition: Because of its relatively isolated location and low cost of living, it was attractive to Irish immigrants with little money.

> The transitions in this speech can be as clear as "first," "second," and so on. This makes the organization clear to the audience.

  A. Irish (1840s–1870s)

   1. By 1855, the Irish constituted approximately half the population of the North End (14,000 of 26,000).

   2. The Irish immigrants took low-paying jobs helping to build Boston's transit system, bridges, and highways to the suburbs.

Transition: After the Irish left the North End for South Boston, Eastern European Jews moved into the neighborhood.

> This student could also include a summary that recaps what has been covered in the main points above, so that the audience remembers the migrations of the three main ethnic groups covered.

  B. Eastern European Jews (mid-to-late nineteenth century)

   1. The Jewish immigrants who moved to the enclave worked predominantly in textile industries.

   2. Additionally, during this period the North End became known not only for textiles but for bakeries, groceries, and other foodstuffs.

If this student wanted to include visual aids, a general map of Boston that shows where the North End is located might have enhanced the speech. Also, some photographs—both historical and contemporary (like the ones below)—might be helpful. The speaker could show the photographs via PowerPoint, in order to avoid passing around photographs or having photos too small to see.

Transition: By the 1920s, Boston's Jewish population had largely moved to the suburbs of the city, leaving the newly arrived Italian immigrants a place to open family businesses and shops.

C. Italians (turn of the twentieth century to present)

   1. Most of the businesses owned by Italian immigrants were family-owned "ma and pa" shops.

      a. Growth of local establishments still in existence today.

Conclusion: When people think of the North End, they usually think just of good Italian food, but there is a lot of history in that part of the city.

Source: Nichols, N. (n.d.). "Your gateway to the North End." Retrieved July 15, 2009, from http://www. northendboston. com/history.htm

A more contemporary view of Hanover Street in Boston's North End. The character of the community will likely continue to change in the future.

ETHICS AND INFORMATIVE SPEAKING

As we have noted in previous sections, being an effective informative speaker entails assuming responsibility for your research and how you communicate your work to your audience. In the context of informative speaking, there are several ethical issues to consider.

The first is research ethics, which we first discussed in Chapter 13. While your ultimate aim is to produce an effective informative speech, you have a responsibility to those whose work you drew from when you conducted your research. In short, you must give credit to your sources and represent their voices accurately and in keeping with their intentions.

It is also important to accurately represent how you gathered your information, aside from using library resources and other research materials. If you visited a particular place to learn more about it, such as a historic site, then you should note that. If you did not, you should not represent yourself as having gathered information in that way, as our student's friend Edra did in *It Happened to Me: Charlotte*. If you interviewed people who survived an experience, such as an earthquake or a tornado, then you should note that as well.

Another issue relates to the ethics of presenting. That is, you must ensure that the language you use is appropriate for the occasion and is accessible to your audience. The ethics of public speaking involves a commitment not only to the factual and accurate representation of information but also to individual honesty and respect for the integrity of research and the audience.

IT HAPPENED TO ME: *Charlotte*

For our informative speech, our teacher asked us to sign up for some place in the city about which it would be interesting to hear an informative speech. By the time my friend Edra signed up, most of the obvious and "good" places were taken, so she took the city zoo. Edra didn't want to actually go to the zoo, so she looked up some stuff online and then gave her speech about the zoo. The speech seemed really good. She had lots of interesting facts about the zoo—all the different types of animals, the number of annual visitors, and so on. It was a good speech that got the audience very interested in Edra's topic. She got lots of questions about the zoo after her speech and, unfortunately, it became clear that she hadn't actually gone to the zoo (which she finally admitted). She lost a lot of credibility. I think that the question-and-answer session after the speech can be considered part of the speech too, as it impacted how the audience thought about the speech.

SUMMARY

Informative speaking is both a requisite component of a deliberative democracy and a fundamental part of communication between individuals and groups. It is also a useful professional skill. The aim of the informative speech is to inform, or educate, and informative speech topics typically fall into one of four categories: speeches about objects, processes, events, or concepts. Preparing an informative speech topic involves several key steps: researching that topic, selecting an organizational pattern (chronological, geographical/spatial, topical), and crafting a detailed outline. Preparing also involves making decisions about including information that is accurate, truthful, accessible, and that respects the ideas of your audience. Finally, a set of ethical challenges confront informative speakers, and these involve appropriate use of research and sources of information, as well as respect for the integrity of the audience.

KEY TERMS

chronological pattern 364

geographical or spatial pattern 364

informative speaking 356

persuasive speech 357

persuade 357

rhetor 356

topical pattern 365

CHAPTER REVIEW QUESTIONS

1. What is the goal of an informative speech?
2. How do informative speeches differ from persuasive speeches?
3. What are some organizational patterns for informative speeches?
4. What are some ways of gathering information for an informative speech?
5. What are two ethical issues that arise in informative speaking?

ACTIVITIES

1. Brainstorm a list of informative speech topics. Using the criteria identified in the chapter, narrow your list based on the premise that you will be speaking in each of the following settings:
   a. Your public speaking class
   b. Your dorm
   c. To your 10-year-old brother's friends at an informal gathering
   d. To your coworkers at your office
2. The following is a list of informative speech topics.
   - Facebook
   - Sonia Sotomayor
   - Rachel Maddow
   - Woodstock
   - *Harry Potter*
   - Sushi

For each of the above topics, consider how your informative speech would change, depending on your audience. Below are your different audiences:
   a. Your public speaking class
   b. A fourth-grade class
   c. Your coworkers at your place of employment
   d. A senior citizens' center

For each of the above scenarios, consider how your word choice, content, and framing would differ.

WEB ACTIVITIES

1. Explore some of the following Web sites to hear oral histories from people with various historical experiences. How might you interview people to gain valuable insights about their experiences? How could you use such information in informative speaking?
   - http://digital.library.louisville.edu/collections/afamoh/
   - http://www.densho.org/
   - http://www.lifestoriesmontreal.ca/

See if you can identify other Web sites with oral histories.

2. *The Statistical Abstract of the United States* is now on the Web at: http://www.census.gov/compendia/statab/ Explore some of the data available through this public source. How might the information contained in this Web site be useful for informative speakers?

16

SPEAKING IN PUBLIC: PERSUASIVE SPEAKING

Even as we end the war in Iraq, even as we welcome home so many of our troops, others are still deployed in Afghanistan. So I want to remind everyone, it was Afghanistan where al Qaeda plotted and trained to murder 3,000 innocent people on 9/11. It is Afghanistan and the tribal regions of Pakistan where terrorists have launched other attacks against us and our allies. And if Afghanistan were to be engulfed by an even wider insurgency, al Qaeda and its terrorist affiliates would have even more space to plan their next attack. And as President of the United States, I refuse to let that happen. (Applause.)

The effort in Afghanistan has been long and been difficult. And that's why after years in which the situation had deteriorated, I announced a new strategy last December—a military effort to break the Taliban's momentum and train Afghan forces so that they can take the lead for their security; and a civilian effort to promote good governance and development that improves the lives of the Afghan people; and deeper cooperation with Pakistan to root out terrorists on both sides of the border.

We will continue to face huge challenges in Afghanistan. But it's important that the American people know that we are making progress and we are focused on goals that are clear and achievable.

[…]

And that sense of purpose that tells us to carry on, not just when it's easy, but when it's hard, even when the odds seem overwhelming—that's what we're about. The confidence that our destiny is never written for us, it's written by us. The faith, that fundamental American faith, that there are always brighter days ahead; and that we not will not simply endure, but we will emerge from our tests and trials and tribulations stronger than before—that is your story. That is America's story. And I'm proud to stand with you as we write the next proud chapter in the life of the country we love.

(President Barak Obama, Disabled Veterans of America conference, 2 August 2010)

When President Obama delivered the above address to the Disabled Veterans of America in August 2010, he exemplified in dramatic fashion, the power of persuasive speaking. Obama's speech, a strong plea to continue to support the war effort in Afghanistan, as well as the troops who are serving or served their country. He used a variety of persuasive speaking strategies—organizational, stylistic, and linguistic—that will be explored in this chapter. For now, we will simply underscore the significance of persuasive speech. Rhetoric, as President Obama demonstrated, can be an intensely powerful tool in attempting to compel us to action or a particular view.

President Obama is a politician who addresses various issues in order to convince legislators, members of the media and the public to support or oppose these issues. Celebrities, and others, have taken on various causes and ask us to take action. Actor Brad Pitt, for example, has taken on the cause of those living in the city of New Orleans and neighboring areas impacted by Hurricane Katrina (2005). Pitt's Make It Right Foundation (www.makeitrightnola.org), which aims to create sustainable housing for families of the devastated Lower 9th Ward left homeless in Katrina's

CHAPTER OUTLINE

WHAT IS PERSUASIVE SPEAKING?

THE IMPORTANCE OF PERSUASIVE SPEAKING

THE POWER TO PERSUADE

    The Power of Ethos

    The Power of Logos

    The Power of Pathos

TYPES OF PERSUASIVE SPEECHES

    Speeches to Impact the Audience's Attitudes

    Speeches to Impact the Audience's Beliefs

    Speeches to Impact the Audience's Values

    Speeches to Impact the Audience's Behavior

ORGANIZING PERSUASIVE SPEECHES

    Using a Problem-Solution or Problem-Solution-Action Pattern

    Using a Claim Pattern

    Using Monroe's Motivated Sequence

TIPS FOR SPEAKING PERSUASIVELY

    Select a Topic Appropriate to Persuasion

    Organize Your Thesis as a Statement of Fact, Value, or Policy

    Establish Credibility Through the Quality of Your Sources

    Avoid Misusing Persuasive Language

PERSUASIVE SPEAKING AND ETHICS

Summary

Key Terms

Chapter Review Questions

Activities

Web Activities

wake, has garnered the attention of popular television programs such as NBC's *Today Show* and CNN's *Larry King Live.* Such shows have given Pitt a platform to speak on behalf of the foundation and its accomplishments, encouraging viewers to become involved in the cause. Pitt is just one celebrity advocate for humanitarian causes. U2 singer Bono has been a vocal advocate in the fight against AIDS/HIV. The list goes on. From stem cell research (Michael J. Fox) to vegetarianism (Alicia Silverstone), there is no shortage of causes requiring our attention, and we hear celebrities address many social issues through persuasive speaking.

The work of Obama, Pitt, and others reminds us why persuasive speaking is so critical. Persuasive speeches not only show us particular problems, they also teach us that we can do something to make a difference and consequently can be empowering. This, as you will recall from Chapter 15, underscores the fundamental difference between informative and persuasive speaking. As communication scholar Mark Gring argues, "Informative speeches are defined by what they do *not* do—they neither actuate nor present disputed information. Persuasive speeches, by implication, *do* something, such as change an attitude or belief, or move to action." (Gring, 2006, p. 44).

This chapter takes on the subject of persuasive speaking—not only its definition but also its role in society. Like informative speeches, persuasive speeches are the product of negotiations between the individual speaker and society. Thus, we will discuss some of the ways in which persuasive speakers negotiate differences between their views and those of society more generally. We will then walk through the process of crafting a persuasive speech, from the selection of the speech topic to the organization of the speech itself. As we move through this process, we will pay careful attention to the use of tone, style, and language. While these three factors contribute to the effectiveness of any speech, in persuasive speaking they assume a somewhat different, and arguably even more vital, significance. Throughout this chapter, we will discuss the ethics of persuasive speaking as well. First, however, we will define persuasive speaking and quickly recap its similarities to and differences from its informative counterpart. Then we will describe in more detail the importance of persuasive speaking.

Once you have read this chapter, you will be able to:

- Define persuasive speaking and its various manifestations.
- Describe the importance of persuasive speaking.
- Explain how ethos, pathos, and logos work together to create persuasive power.
- Recognize and distinguish among the different types of persuasive speeches.
- Select an appropriate organizational pattern for your persuasive speech.
- Make use of key tips specific to building a persuasive speech.
- Understand the ethical issues embedded within the persuasive speaking setting.

WHAT IS PERSUASIVE SPEAKING?

Persuasive speaking is defined by its goal of influencing an audience. Consequently, while you may select the same topic for an informative and a persuasive speech, what will distinguish these two presentations will be your framing of the topic. Say, for instance, that you select the movement to lower the legal drinking age as your speech topic. If you plan to deliver an informative speech on this topic, you might discuss the various arguments made by proponents and opponents. However, if you decide to deliver a persuasive speech on the topic, you would select a position and argue from that side. You might argue that the drinking age *should* be lowered to 18 for a number of

persuasive speaking
speaking with a goal of influencing an audience

reasons. Your speech would be devoted to discussing these reasons and refuting the counter position. At the outset of this chapter, we began with President Obama's urgent and persuasive appeal to support the war effort and troops in Afghanistan. His attempt to get people to see the importance of this effort is clearly persuasive.

While you may never have delivered a formal persuasive speech before, you have, on more than one occasion, attempted to be persuasive. More than likely, you've made more than one persuasive appeal even today.

THE IMPORTANCE OF PERSUASIVE SPEAKING

Persuasive speeches are vital to the functioning of a democratic society. Persuasive speeches may attempt to build coalitions in support of policy initiatives, raise public consciousness of issues, rally support for causes, or compel mass participation. On January 12, 2010, a major earthquake struck Haiti with devastating consequences. In the aftermath of the earthquake, a number of persuasive appeals were made asking for assistance for Haiti. President Obama asked former presidents Bill Clinton and George W. Bush to spearhead a fundraising campaign for Haiti. In their appeal, they note: "Both of us have personally witnessed the tremendous generosity and goodwill of the American people and of our friends around the world to help in times of great need. There is no greater rallying cry for our common humanity than witnessing our neighbors in distress. And, like any good neighbor, we have an obligation and desire to come to their aid" (http://www.clintonbushhaitifund.org/).

This persuasive appeal plays to notions of national identity and what it means to be an American, as well as what it means to be a good neighbor. After one month, the Clinton Bush Haiti Fund had already received 188,000 donations, with some smaller donations and some large, such as Leonardo di Caprio's $1 million donation. (http://www.clintonbushhaiti fund.org/media_item_5.php). Other appeals were made by artists, such as Wyclef Jean, who hosted the "SOS Saving Our Selves—Help for Haiti" concert. The popular "Hope for Haiti Now" telethon was watched by 80 million people and raised $66 million (http://www.msnbc.msn.com/id/35279532).

On March 23, 2010, President Obama signed an important health insurance reform bill that landed on his desk after much persuasive speaking. Many people used persuasive speaking to support health care reform, while many others spoke persuasively against it. Ultimately, those in favor of health insurance reform prevailed. While it is impossible to identify any single persuasive speech as the key event that persuaded legislators to support this reform, we can see how two politicians used persuasive speaking to attempt to persuade other legislators and the public to their perspective.

Former presidents Clinton and Bush spoke persuasively to urge U.S. Americans to contribute to the rebuilding of Haiti after the 2010 earthquake.

In one of the speeches leading up to the vote for health care reform, House Speaker Nancy Pelosi used persuasive appeals to make her case for this reform. She gave a number of reasons why she supported this bill at a bipartisan meeting, on February 25, 2010, hosted by President Obama on health insurance reform:

You have talked about how the present system is unsustainable—for families, for businesses, large, moderate, and small—any size. And it is unsustainable, and you said on March 5 of last year: 'Health care reform is entitlement reform.' Our budget cannot take this upward spiral of cost. We have a moral obligation to reduce the deficit and not heap mountains of debt onto the next generation.

But I want to talk for a moment about what it means to the economy. Imagine an economy where people could change jobs, start businesses, become self-employed,

pursue their artistic aspirations, or be entrepreneurial and start new businesses if they were not job locked because they have a child who is bipolar or a family member who is diabetic with a pre-existing condition. And all of the other constraints that having health care or not having health care places on an entrepreneurial spirit. Think of an economy with that dynamism—of people following their pursuits, taking risks—we want them to take risks and yet we lock them down. And we have an anvil around our businesses because of these increasing costs of health care.

So this bill is not only about the health security of America, it's about jobs. In its life it will create 4 million jobs, 400,000 jobs almost immediately. Jobs, again, in the health care industry but in the entrepreneurial world as well.

Mr. President, with your leadership, we passed the American Reinvestment and Recovery Act last January and got a running start on some of the technology and scientific advancements in this by the investments in biomedical research, health IT, health information technology, a running start by your signing the SCHIP, the children's health bill insuring 11 million children. We got a running start on expanding access, and not only that but doing it in a way that is of the future.

This is not just about health care for America, it's about a healthier America. This legislation is about innovation. It's about prevention. It's about wellness. But most people haven't heard about that, and those people sitting at that kitchen table, they don't want to hear about process. They want to hear about results. They want to know what this means to them. And what it means is a health initiative that is about affordability for the middle class, lowering cost, improving access, accessibility—affordability and accessibility are closely aligned—and accountability for the insurance companies. So it is a very important initiative that we have to take.

She urges her fellow legislators and the public to support health insurance reform. Yet, she is only one of many people who spoke about health insurance reform. One of these speakers was the Senate Republican leader, Senator Mitch McConnell from Kentucky. He used persuasive speaking to oppose passage of this legislation. On the floor of the Senate, on March 3, 2010, he argued:

Well, Americans don't know how else to say it: they don't want this massive bill. They want commonsense, bipartisan reforms that lower costs, and then they want us to refocus our energy on creating jobs and the economy. They've had enough of this year-long effort to get a win for the Democratic Party at any price to the American people. Americans have paid a big enough price already in the time we've lost focusing on this bill.

They don't want it, and they won't tolerate any more back room deals or legislative schemes to force it through Congress on a partisan basis. History is clear: Big legislation always requires big majorities. And this latest scheme to lure Democrats into switching their votes in the House by agreeing to use Reconciliation in the Senate will be met with outrage.

So we respectfully encourage the administration to consider a new approach to reform, one that doesn't cut Medicare to fund a trillion dollar takeover of the health care system or impose job-killing taxes in the middle of a recession, and one that will win the support of broad majorities in both parties. We encourage the administration to join Republicans and Democrats in Congress in listening to what the American people have been telling us for more than a year now.

In contrast to Pelosi's speech which focused on the economic and health benefits of the bill, Senator McConnell focused on the political process which he views as flawed. He also claims that the American people do not want this bill. While some Americans did not want this health insurance reform, other Americans did, and we can see here his persuasive strategy in arguing that the people do not want this reform. Senator McConnell's speech was designed to defeat this bill by arguing that a better process would result in better legislation. There were many speeches given on this legislation, so we cannot know what persuaded legislators to vote for or against this legislation, but we can look at the persuasive strategies used by both sides in their persuasive speeches.

Politics is not the only arena in which persuasion impacts society in an important way. Advertising is an industry that is similarly rooted in persuasive appeals. Companies must, in order to succeed, convince consumers to purchase their products. We must be persuaded of the superiority, or at the very least the comparative advantage, of a particular product in order to consume it. For instance, Bounty, the self-proclaimed "thicker picker upper," uses carefully constructed commercials to convince audiences of its superiority. On their website you can see how they use persuasion for potential consumers at: **http://www. quickerpickerupper.com/en_US/index.shtml.** The commercial is explicitly persuasive, making the case that Bounty is the most effective paper towel.

Besides playing a significant role in politics and advertising, persuasion shapes knowledge, unearths facts, and builds communities (Herrick, 2004, p. 16). While convincing an audience of a candidate's worth or a product's quality, persuasive speech also enables group cohesion by building community of politically like-minded individuals or followers of the same brand. For instance, Mac users constitute a kind of community. As the string of popular Mac-versus-PC ads has shown, the Apple brand carries with it a particular image—one its consumers literally buy into. As one ad shows, Mac users are young and hip, and they don't require the additional (and unnecessary) bells and whistles that characterize PCs. Mac users are devotees of a trendy yet consistent product.

At its base, when an individual acts as an advocate, her or his goal is to convince the audience through a compelling mobilization of evidence. Consequently, in order to be persuasive, one must unearth facts through research and challenge preexisting notions held not only by the audience but in many cases by oneself as well. Collectively, the functions of persuasive speech prove pivotal to the functioning not only of a democracy but also of a consumer culture and society more broadly.

Some experts observe that people now have a renewed interested in public participation because of the anger they feel over the recent economic downturn and their related, growing distrust of political and business leaders. (See *Communication in Society: The Return of Public Deliberation?*) Given these conditions, persuasive speaking is more important than ever.

A primary reason for the importance of persuasive speaking is that it can empower not only the speaker, but the audience as well. By this we mean several things. First, as the speaker, you wield a specific power—the power to influence your audience. As an *advocate,* you are, by definition, speaking *for* someone or something. By speaking to an audience, however, you are also sharing that power by empowering your audience to act in some

Communication in SOCIETY

The Return of Public Deliberation?

Pollster Frank Luntz analyzes his poll data and finds that U.S. Americans are angry but ready to engage in public deliberation. Persuasive speaking is an important part of that civic engagement. Are you ready to participate in this new movement toward more self-government? Can you stand up and speak for your interests?

Americans in the unhappy majority are struggling to keep their jobs as million-dollar bonuses are being awarded at companies their tax dollars bailed out. They're watching Congress showcase the partisan spectacle we now blithely confuse with "government." They have learned (with good reason) to distrust their leaders, their institutions and even their own positive values in a culture that has turned coarse and critical.

The elites under attack complain that rowdy town halls are bad for civic discourse and democracy. But I contend that their empty dismissals of grass-roots anger are much more dangerous. [. . .]

I even spot some green shoots of renewed optimism. First, the town halls themselves, despite their negative tone, are a sign of a healthy desire to engage in political and social discourse. Americans are putting some of the "self" back in self-governance. Competing ideals are actually competing.

SOURCE: Luntz, F. (2009, September 27). "What Americans really want." *Los Angeles Times.* Retrieved September 27, 2009, from http://www.latimes.com/news/opinion/la-oe-luntz27-2009sep27,0,4242608.story

way. In some cases, this may mean that you are enabling your audience to act—in other words, *empowering* them. Or you may be attempting to persuade your audience to use the power they have in a specific way, such as by voting for a particular candidate or purchasing a given object. But the question remains: Where does this power come from? And how can or should it be used in persuasive speaking? These are the questions to which we turn next.

THE POWER TO PERSUADE

In Chapter 14, we discussed the importance of Aristotle's three artistic proofs—ethos, pathos, and logos. These artistic proofs are particularly important in persuasive speaking, as the speaker's ability to build these proofs and connect them to the speech and the speaker can be key to a successful speech (see *Visual Summary 16.1: The Power to Persuade*).

The Power of Ethos

Ethos, or credibility, is especially empowering to speakers—although ethos alone does not ensure persuasive success. When a speaker's ethos is damaged, however, their persuasive power is generally diminished as well.

Upon winning six Olympic medals during the Summer Games in Athens in 2004, U.S. American swimmer Michael Phelps became a marketable commodity to the advertising industry, amassing sponsorship contracts with several large companies, including Visa. Following his stunning eight-gold-medal victory at the Beijing Olympics four years later, Phelps became a marketing magnet, leading some experts to estimate that the swimmer could earn close to $30 million a year in endorsement deals (Goldsmith, 2008).

However, when a photo of the swimmer smoking a marijuana pipe at a party spread across the Internet, some argued that the swimmer's image and his persona, or public image, as a super-human athlete and role model were irreparably damaged. Phelps subsequently issued a public apology, stating, "I engaged in behavior which was regrettable and demonstrated bad judgment. . . . I'm 23 years old, and despite the successes I've had in the pool, I acted in a youthful and inappropriate way, not in a manner people have come to expect from me. For this, I am sorry. I promise my fans and the public it will not happen again" (Crouse, 2009). While Phelps's apology was a clear attempt to reestablish his ethos and revive his tarnished image, several of his sponsors, including cereal company Kellogg's, did not feel that he had succeeded: " 'We originally built the relationship with Michael, as well as the other Olympic athletes, to support our association with the U.S. Olympic team,' a Kellogg spokeswoman said in a statement first obtained by Ad Age. 'Michael's most recent behavior is not consistent with the image of Kellogg's. His contract expires at the end of February and we have made a decision not to extend his contract' " (Rovell, 2009).

The Power of Logos

While ethos is important, it alone can't ensure the success of your persuasive speech. But when your ethos combines with other artistic proofs, you can significantly increase the strength of your persuasive power. For example, **logos**, or rationality, is used alongside ethos in an internet ad for the Honda Insight—the car company's popular green alternative. The ad announces, "more hybrids replacing conventional gas engine vehicles out on the road can only improve things for the environment. To that end, the Insight was designed for excellent fuel economy [1], of course, but the goal was also practicality and affordability." (Honda). For those who are environmentally inclined, the Insight appeals to the logic of protecting the environment—with a car that has "a remarkable new system that helps boost your efficiency and monitor your own driving habits to maximize your mpg for your driving conditions." In this example, the combination of ethos and pathos give the ad's message very strong persuasive power.

ethos
credibility

logos
rational appeals; the use of rhetoric to help the audience see the rationale for a particular conclusion

The Power to Persuade

THE POWER OF ETHOS

Credibility can empower a speaker's persuasiveness.

Damaged credibility can diminish a speaker's persuasive power.

THE POWER OF LOGOS

Particularly when combined with credibility, rationality can increase the strength of your persuasive power.

THE POWER OF PATHOS

Emotion can have immense power in persuading an audience.

pathos
the rhetorical use of emotions to affect audience decision making

boomerang effect
an effect that runs in the opposite direction from the desired effect

The Power of Pathos

While logic can be persuasive in certain settings, **pathos**, or emotion, also can have immense power in persuading an audience. In fact, pathos can in some scenarios be the most persuasive of appeals—especially when the consequences of a cause or issue are particularly serious or severe. Television commercials advertising animal adoption often compellingly use pathos. Singer Sarah McLachlan is associated with many of these ads, in which her slow, sentimental ballads play as a backdrop to images of sad, malnourished, and often poorly treated pets. While you may logically know you can't have a dog or cat, by the end of the commercial, you are likely ready to call and make a monetary donation to this organization (Sarah McLachlan SPCA commercial).

Pity, however, is not the only emotion that holds persuasive power. Anger and fear may also drive a speech. In 2000, MTV launched an antismoking campaign known as the "Truth" ads, which pictured the graphic and potentially fatal effects of cigarette smoking on young and old alike (The Truth—Body Bags TV ad). The campaign, according to reports, led to a decline in youth smoking between 2000 and 2002 and to approximately 300,000 fewer teen smokers. (Tecson, 2005). The power of the ads lay in their unique ability to frighten young people, breaking down the long-held belief (pushed by tobacco companies) that smoking is cool. To read more about the power of fear as a persuasive appeal, see *Did You Know? The Boomerang Effect.*

DID YOU KNOW?

The Boomerang Effect

Researchers at the University of Pennsylvania have found that rather than deter drug use, the National Youth Anti-Drug Media Campaign (http://www.mediacampaign.org/) has produced **boomerang effects**, or effects that run in the opposite direction from those desired. Consequently, the researchers report, the campaign, which cost the federal government upwards of $1 billion, was in some cases encouraging young people to begin using marijuana. In other cases, young people who had been exposed to the media campaign reported pro-marijuana attitudes (Hornik, 2006; Jacobsohn, 2007).

A study published in 2006 by Professor Wolburg of Marquette University found that antismoking appeals to college students also tended to produce boomerang effects by creating anger and defiance. College students who were already smokers were typically not persuaded by the antismoking messages and responded with the opposite effect than what the antismoking campaign desired. She notes that these messages "are counterproductive by triggering boomerang responses" (p. 320).

While the use of pathos in commercials and advertising campaigns is widespread, it has also permeated the political realm, with mixed effects. While on the campaign trail in January 2008, Democratic candidate Hillary Clinton teared up while speaking to an audience. "It's about our country," she said. "It's about our kids' future. It's about all of us together. Some of us put ourselves out there and do this against some difficult odds . . . " (Breslau, 2008). The emotional moment, for some critics, was an inauthentic appeal to pathos—a ploy by Clinton to show a more sensitive side. Others, however, found her emotional response very moving and felt it portrayed an authentic side of her. In contrast, emotion proved to do irreparable damage to Howard Dean in 2004 after what became dubbed his "I Have a Scream" speech. Dean's manic scream in an impromptu show of emotion spurred a host of critiques, concerns about his emotional stability, and late-night lampooning.

Such examples demonstrate how risky appeals to emotion can be. While a moment of vulnerability may be seen as evidence of a softer, more human side, it may also be interpreted as a sign of weakness. How emotional appeals are read is often contingent upon the composition of the audience. Going into a presentation, you may not necessarily know who your

audience will be or whether they will be sympathetic or skeptical. Nor can you predict with assurance how you may react to a question or circumstance, as emotional appeals are not always planned. However, emotion is a powerful component of persuasion. Thus, as the speaker, you must consider your relationship to your audience and anticipate possible reactions to your words. You must consider whether your audience is especially impressionable and what impact fear or anger may have on them. For example, the unethical use of pathos is referred to **demagoguery**, or the attempt "to gain power or control over others by using unethical emotion pleas and appealing to listeners' prejudices" (Beebe & Beebe, 2010, p. 417). Demagogues take advantage of the vulnerability of their audiences—an abuse that should be considered unethical.

We will return to the discussion of ethics later in the chapter. But here, the message is that speakers need to consider the ethics of the appeals they use to draw people to their views. Persuasive speaking plays an important role in a democratic society, but the misuse of this persuasion can create lasting damage from the resulting public policies, court decisions, and other public decisions.

demagoguery
the attempt to gain power or control over others by using unethical emotional pleas and appealing to listeners' prejudices

TYPES OF PERSUASIVE SPEECHES

As communication scholars Beebe and Beebe have argued, the persuasive speech can have one of many goals (Beebe & Beebe, 2010, p. 376). A persuasive speaker may seek to:

- impact the audience's attitudes
- impact the audience's beliefs
- impact the audience's values
- impact the audience's behavior

Let's take a look at each of these types of persuasive speeches.

Speeches to Impact the Audience's Attitudes

Speeches that focus on impacting audience attitudes are focused on changing the likes and dislikes of an audience. If you like something, then you have an attitude about it. If you are a "cat person" and you like cats, then you have an attitude about cats; if you dislike cats, you also have an attitude about cats, but not the same attitude. Some attitudes are easier to change than others. If you like your governor and campaigned for him or her, your attitude about the governor can change from positive to more negative. For example, some South Carolinians have changed their attitudes about Governor Mark Sanford after finding out about his extramarital affair. Other politicians have also seen a change in attitudes toward them for various things they have done, such as former presidential candidate John Edwards, Idaho senator Larry Craig, Louisiana senator David Vitter, among others. Let's look at an example of trying to change an audience attitude:

Topic: Naturism

Specific Purpose: To change the audience's attitude toward naturism and encourage them to have a more positive attitude about it

Thesis: Naturism, or social nudity, is a healthy expression of fitness and connection with nature.

Main Points:

A. Naturism is a political and social movement that emphasizes fitness, healthy living, and healthy food.

B. Naturism emphasizes our connection to nature and environmental issues.

C. Naturism emphasizes social equality, as clothes do not create a hierarchy in naturism.

D. Naturism is not a sexual event or sexual activity.

Persuasive speeches can change attitudes, beliefs, values, and behaviors.

In this speech, the speaker is connecting naturism to ideas that the audience may already have positive attitudes toward, such as health, healthy food, fitness, and environmental issues, as well as social equality. The speech also distances naturism from sexual activities. By connecting with other things that the audience has a positive attitude toward, the speaker invites the audience to have a positive attitude toward naturism.

Speeches to Impact the Audience's Beliefs

Sometimes you may want to influence the audience's beliefs. Our beliefs are those things that we see as true or false. Audiences may believe all kinds of things that impact how we live our everyday lives. People may not understand what "free-range animals" means or what happens in "no-kill animal shelters." In these two cases, the definitions can be misunderstood, and the audience may believe that they are supporting more humane treatment of animals. By using such terms, audiences can hold beliefs that are not accurate, because the federal government, for example, only has guidelines for free-range poultry, but not for other animals. Let's look at another example:

Topic: Mumps, measles, rubella vaccine and autism

Specific Purpose: To inform the audience that there is no connection between the MMR vaccine and autism

Thesis: There is no scientific evidence that the MMR vaccine is linked to autism.

Main Points:

A. The MMR vaccine is used to prevent mumps, measles and rubella. These diseases can cause death, as well as permanent lifelong damage.

B. In 1998, *The Lancet,* a British medical journal, published a study showing a connection between autism and the MMR vaccine.

C. Controversy over study when one author is found to have manipulated the data and ten others retract their study. *The Lancet* formally retracts the article on February 2, 2010.

D. Many people still believe that there is a connection between autism and the MMR vaccine that has led to increased rates of mumps, measles, and rubella.

E. Many additional studies—done by the Centers for Disease Control, the European Union, Swedish researchers, Japanese researchers, etc.—have shown no connection.

Sources: S. Murch, A. Anthony, D. Casson, M. Malik, M. Berelowitz, A. Dhillon, M. Thomson, A. Valentine, S. Davies, J. Walker-Smith. (2004). Retraction of an interpretation. *The Lancet, vol. 363*(9411), p. 750.
Triggle, N. (2010, February 2). Lancet accepts MMR study "false." *BBC News.* Retrieved February 15, 2010, from http://news.bbc.co.uk/2/low/health/8493753.stm

Note how this speech focuses on a specific (fraudulent) scientific study that gave rise to a belief that the MMR vaccine causes autism. This speech is organized both chronologically as well as in a problem-solution format. The problem is the spread of the diseases, and the solution is the vaccine that is not being used because of a misinformed belief.

Speeches to Impact the Audience's Values

Speeches that focus on impacting an audience's values typically focus on those things that people feel are right and good or wrong and bad. Sometimes these values influence people's positions on a range of political issues, and persuasion uses these values to get them to support or oppose various issues. Sometimes, speakers try to juxtapose other competing values to challenge the audience to reconsider the values. Other times, the speaker may try to show how these values are connected to other values so that they are not in competition but work together to form a more consistent value system. Let's look at an example:

Topic: Capital punishment

Specific Purpose: To change the audience's attitudes about capital punishment, or the death penalty

Thesis: Opposing the death penalty is consistent with embracing the sanctity of life.

Main Points:

    A. Life is precious and should be protected at all times.

    B. There are many examples of how we expect people to protect life, whether strangers in accidents, hospital patients, people caught up in a natural disaster, and so on.

    C. Many states with capital punishment also have strong pro-life activists who embrace the value of life.

    D. Valuing life is consistent with opposing the death penalty.

Note how this speech tries to connect other examples of valuing life to opposing the death penalty. It tries to show a consistent use of this value across a number of examples, from helping others in trouble to abortion to the death penalty.

Speeches to Impact the Audience's Behavior

Changing people's behavior is not easy, nor is it always possible. However, there are many times when changing how people live every day is an important and desired goal. At the outset of this chapter, you read about President Obama's speech to the Disabled Veterans of America conference and his attempt to laud them and secure support for the war in Afghanistan and the troops serving their country. Speeches that attempt to change an audience's behavior in some way are often organized in a problem-solution format or a problem-solution-action format. The change in behavior is the solution or action to some problem that the speaker identifies. Let's look at an example:

Topic: Texting while driving

Specific Purpose: To persuade the audience not to text while driving

Thesis: Texting while driving is dangerous, and you should not read or send messages while driving.

Main Points:

    A. Texting while driving is dangerous and has caused many accidents and fatalities.

    B. Some states have outlawed this dangerous practice, but others have not.

    C. The consequences of texting while driving can be life changing for all involved.

    D. It's not worth the risk to your life and the lives of others to text while driving.

Source: Schulte, B. (2008, February 11). "Outlawing Text Messaging While Driving." *US News and World Report.* Retrieved February 15, 2010, from http://www.usnews.com/articles/news/national/2008/02/11/outlawing-text-messaging-while-driving.html

This speech lays out the problem with texting while driving. Then it highlights the fact that it is illegal do in some states. It then argues that it is not worth the danger and consequences to engage in this behavior. If this speech is effective, then hopefully it will impact the behavior (texting while driving).

ORGANIZING PERSUASIVE SPEECHES

You must determine which organizational pattern best meets the specific objective of your persuasive speech. In this section, we will discuss three organizational patterns appropriate for persuasive speeches:

- problem-solution-action
- claim
- Monroe's motivated sequence

While these three organizational patterns overlap somewhat, your objective and line of argumentation will help you determine which pattern best suits your needs. If you intend to rally your audience with a call to action, the problem-solution-action pattern and Monroe's motivated sequence would best fit your objective. If, on the other hand, you intend to influence your audience's beliefs, values, or attitudes, the claim pattern would be more appropriate. You should begin, however, by considering how you want to present your data. Return to your thesis statement to remind yourself of your goals. What will you need to do in order to reach your audience effectively?

As you think about which organizational pattern works best for you, consider the **fallacies of reasoning**—or errors in reasoning—that may impact the effectiveness of your argument or the argument another speaker is making (see *Did You Know? Fallacies of Reasoning*). These common fallacies of reasoning occur frequently.

DID YOU KNOW?

Fallacies of Reasoning

Professor Robert Gass of California State University–Fullerton has assembled a list of common fallacies. Some of these are reproduced below, but his more complete list can be found at his Web site. There are other fallacies as well, and these are very common ones that you should listen for when you encounter persuasive messages.

1. **Faulty cause:** (*post hoc ergo propter hoc*) mistakes correlation or association for causation by assuming that because one thing follows another, it was caused by the first action.
   - **example:** A black cat crossed Babbs' path yesterday and, sure enough, she was involved in an automobile accident later that same afternoon.
   - **example:** The introduction of sex education courses at the high school level has resulted in increased promiscuity among teens. A recent study revealed that the number of reported cases of STDs (sexually transmitted diseases) was significantly higher for high schools that offered courses in sex education than for high schools that did not.

2. **Sweeping generalization:** (*dicto simpliciter*) assumes that what is true of the whole will also be true of the part, or that what is true in most instances will be true in all instances.
   - **example:** Muffin must be rich or have rich parents, because she belongs to ZXQ, and ZXQ is the richest sorority on campus.
   - **example:** I'd like to hire you, but you're an ex-felon, and statistics show that 80% of ex-felons recidivate.

fallacies of reasoning
errors in reasoning

faulty cause
a logical fallacy that mistakes correlation or association for causation, by assuming that because one thing follows another it was caused by the first

sweeping generalization
a logical fallacy that assumes that what is true of the whole will also be true of the part or that what is true in most instances will be true in all instances

3. **Hasty generalization:** bases an inference on too small a sample, or on an unrepresentative sample. Often, a single example or instance is used as the basis for a broader generalization.

   - **example:** All of those movie stars are really rude. I asked Kevin Costner for his autograph in a restaurant in Westwood the other evening, and he told me to get lost.
   - **example:** Pit bulls are actually gentle, sweet dogs. My next door neighbor has one, and his dog loves to romp and play with all the kids in the neighborhood!

4. **Faulty analogy:** (can be literal or figurative) assumes that because two things, events, or situations are alike in some known respects, they are alike in other unknown respects.

   - **example:** What's the big deal about the early pioneers killing a few Indians in order to settle the West? After all, you can't make an omelet without breaking a few eggs.
   - **example:** Banning "head" shops from selling drug paraphernalia in order to curb drug abuse makes about as much sense as banning bikinis to reduce promiscuity.

5. **Bifurcation:** (either-or, black-or-white, all-or-nothing fallacy) assumes that two categories are mutually exclusive and exhaustive; that is, something is either a member of one or the other, but not both or some third category.

   - **example:** Either you favor a strong national defense or you favor allowing other nations to dictate our foreign policy.
   - **example:** It's not TV. It's HBO.

6. **False dilemma:** (a form of bifurcation) implies that one of two outcomes is inevitable, and both have negative consequences.

   - **example:** Either you buy a large car and watch it guzzle away your paycheck, or you buy a small car and take a greater risk of being injured or killed in the event of an accident.
   - **example:** You can put your money in a savings account, in which case the IRS will tax you on the interest, and inflation will erode the value of your money, or you can avoid maintaining a savings account in which case you will have nothing to fall back on in a financial emergency.

7. **Appeal to authority:** (*ipse dixit* also called *ad verecundiam* sometimes) attempts to justify an argument by citing a highly admired or well-known (but not necessarily qualified) figure who supports the conclusion being offered.

   - **example:** If it's good enough for (insert celebrity's name here), it's good enough for me.
   - **example:** Laws against marijuana are plain silly. Why, Thomas Jefferson is known to have raised hemp on his own plantation.

8. **Appeal to tradition:** (don't rock the boat or *ad verecundiam*) based on the principle of "letting sleeping dogs lie." We should continue to do things as they have been done in the past. We shouldn't challenge time-honored customs or traditions.

   - **example:** Of course we have to play "pomp and circumstance" at graduation, because that's *always* been the song that is played.
   - **example:** Why do I make wine this way? Because my father made wine this way, and his father made wine this way.

9. **Appeal to the crowd:** (*ad populum* or playing to the gallery) refers to popular opinion or majority sentiment in order to provide support for a claim. Often the "common man" or "common sense" provides the basis for the claim.

   - **example:** All I can say is that if living together is immoral, then I have plenty of company.
   - **example:** Professor Windplenty's test was extremely unfair. Just ask anyone who took it.

SOURCE: Robert Gass. "Common Fallacies in Reasoning." Retrieved February 14, 2010. from http://commfaculty.fullerton.edu/rgass/fallacy3211.htm

---

hasty generalization
a logical fallacy that bases an inference on too small a sample or on an unrepresentative sample

faulty analogy
a logical fallacy that assumes that because two things, events, or situations are alike in some known respects, they are alike in other unknown respects

bifurcation
a logical fallacy that assumes that two categories are mutually exclusive and exhaustive—that is, that something is either a member of one or the other, but not both or some third category

false dilemma
a logical fallacy which implies that one of two outcomes is inevitable, and both have negative consequences

appeal to authority
a logical fallacy that attempts to justify an argument by citing a highly admired or well-known (but not necessarily qualified) figure who supports the conclusion being offered

appeal to tradition
a logical fallacy based on the principle of not challenging time-honored customs or traditions

appeal to the crowd
a logical fallacy that refers to popular opinion or majority sentiment in order to provide support for a claim

problem-solution or problem-solution-action pattern
organizational pattern in which the speaker describes various aspects of a problem and then proposes solutions

Using a Problem-Solution or Problem-Solution-Action Pattern

The **problem-solution** pattern is also often described as the **problem-solution-action** pattern, depending on whether or not the speaker intends to conclude the presentation with a specific call to action. Either way, here are the steps involved in composing the body of your persuasive speech.

Establish the Problem

This first step entails explaining the situation as a specific problem in need of resolution. It requires you to define the parameters of the speech.

Propose a Solution

The next step is for suggesting a way to resolve the problem you have described. Depending on your ultimate objective, your speech may end here. However, if you seek to encourage your audience to act on your proposed solution, you may need another step.

Call to Action

Get your audience involved directly by offering ways to act. This may entail providing information, a demonstration, or additional suggestions. Below is one sample outline that uses this organizational pattern.

Topic: Meditation

Thesis Statement of Value: Meditation is the key to health and happiness.

Body:

A. Establish a Problem

1. From the moment you wake up in the morning, you're thinking—thinking about getting out of bed, brushing your teeth, brushing your hair, what to wear, how to get to school, what to eat for breakfast, how to stay awake during chemistry class . . .

2. Many thoughts are negative and we don't even realize it. We are subconsciously ruled by fears, thought patterns, and negative emotions.

3. Our stress and tiredness make us unhappy, impatient, and frustrated. It can even affect our health.

B. Solution: Meditation

1. According to Project Meditation and *Time* magazine, meditation is scientifically proven to: decrease stress anxiety, cure depression, increase confidence, improve concentration and focus, increase motivation, heal addictive traits, boost immune system, and increase intelligence-related measures.

2. Meditation lowers blood pressure and heart rate and lowers the amount of stress hormones in the body as well as calming the mind.

3. Meditation can train and even reshape the mind. Tests using the most sophisticated imaging techniques suggest that meditation can actually reset the brain so that someone normally predisposed to stress and anger, for example, can actually rewire their brain to eliminate these and instead cultivate positive emotions.

C. Action

1. Meditation is free and requires only a few minutes. Everyone can do it. Anywhere and anytime.

2. Now I challenge you to try it for a week. Set aside a few minutes and build it into your schedule. See how you feel after a week.

Sources: Project Meditation, http://www.project-meditation.org/; Joel Stein, "Just Say Om." *Time*, 4 August 2003: 48–56.

The above outline clearly defines the problem at hand and proposes a solution (meditation) that will not only reduce the current amount of stress in our lives but allow us to live healthier. As the action, the speaker invited the audience to make meditation a part of their everyday lives.

claim
an argument

Using a Claim Pattern

The claim organizational pattern for persuasive speeches is similar to the topical pattern of the informative speech. As with the topical pattern, there is no one correct way to structure your **claims**, or arguments. However, you will want to carefully consider the order in which you place your claims. While some assert that you should begin with your strongest point and others claim that you should leave it until the end, we strongly recommend placing your strongest points at the beginning of your presentation's body. Remember that you want to make your argument as clearly and persuasively as possible. If you start with a weaker claim, you risk losing the audience's attention altogether—something you hope to avoid at all cost. In short, begin with your most powerful argument at the beginning, follow with the least persuasive argument(s) in the middle, and end with a strong argument. The last argument should be strong, but not as strong as the one you use to begin the speech. Sometimes it is not easy to identify the strongest argument, as we can only guess at how persuasive a particular argument might be. Below is a sample speech outline that uses the claim pattern.

Topic: Post-traumatic stress disorder (PTSD)

Thesis Statement of Policy: The United States military should award the Purple Heart to veterans with PTSD.

A. We already recognize PTSD as a serious combat injury.

1. We treat veterans with PTSD the same way we treat physically wounded veterans in terms of medical evacuation and disability compensation. It is currently possible to be on 100 percent disability compensation as a veteran with PTSD.

2. Opponents will argue that PTSD is not severe enough an injury to recognize. We do not distinguish among degrees of injury when we give out the Purple Heart.

3. Opponents will also argue that people with PTSD are not courageous enough to get the Purple Heart. Today, someone who is shot in the chest running toward a battle will receive the same Purple Heart as someone who is shot in the back while running away.

B. We will change the status of PTSD from something suffered by "crazy people" to an injury suffered by "war heroes."

1. We can anticipate that there will be less discrimination from upper-level officers toward soldiers with PTSD.

2. If veterans seek treatment, we can anticipate less violence and emotional outbursts caused by lack of treatment.

3. Fewer soldiers will feel that they have been wronged by the U.S. military during their time of service.

C. We can fulfill the original purpose of the medal—to award soldiers for making sacrifices for their country in the line of duty.

1. Veterans with PTSD give up more for their country, many of them, than many with a flesh wound. The war doesn't end for them when they go home. Every day is a constant battle with the morally devastating whirlwind of modern warfare.

2. Opponents of awarding the Purple Heart to veterans with PTSD occasionally offer the idea that they could receive a different medal for their injury. While better than the status quo, it is insufficient, as it maintains a dichotomy between greater and lesser sacrifice. It will acknowledge their pain but do nothing to remove the stigma associated with their condition.

Monroe's motivated sequence (MMS)
a five-step organizational pattern based on the notion that in a persuasive speech, the speaker is seeking to fulfill a need of the audience and that in order to fulfill that need, the audience must be moved to act

Sources: Hodge, Charles W., et al. "Combat Duty in Iraq and Afghanistan, Mental Health Problems, and Barriers to Care." *The New England Journal of Medicine.* July 4, 2004.
"Post-Traumatic Stress Disorder." MedicineNet.com. http://www.medicinenet.com/posttraumatic_stress_disorder/article.htm
"PTSD and the Purple Heart." *The New York Times.* January 11, 2009.
"Take Heart." *The Economist.* February 16, 2009.

As with all persuasive speeches, you will need to refute the arguments of your opposition. When using the claim pattern, as in many other persuasive patterns, consider including an argument to counter your opposition with each point you make. If you can effectively neutralize alternative stances before your audience, you will make great strides in persuasion.

Using Monroe's Motivated Sequence

Monroe's motivated sequence (MMS) is a popular organizational strategy for a persuasive speech. Designed by speech professor Alan Monroe, the motivated sequence is based on the notion that in a persuasive speech, the speaker is seeking to fulfill a need of the audience and that in order to fulfill that need, the audience must be moved to act. The motivated sequence entails five steps.

Attention

The attention component of the speech is covered in the introduction. As we mentioned in the previous chapter, a speech's introduction should not only articulate the thesis statement, but it should also grab the attention of the audience with, for example, a shocking statistic, quote, anecdote, or joke.

Need

Once you have piqued the audience's attention, you must establish need. Establishing need entails defining the specific problem to be resolved. This is the step in which you describe the issue at the center of your presentation. It should be compelling. Remember: You want your audience to believe that this problem is important and worthy of their attention.

Satisfaction

Now that your audience can see the problem at hand, you must propose a solution. This step requires you to explain how the problem may be addressed or how the need will be satisfied.

Visualization

Up to this point, your strategy will look similar to the problem-solution organizational pattern. The final two steps of the motivated sequence, however, differentiate it from its alternatives, for once you have laid out a proposed solution to the problem, you must help your audience visualize the benefits of your proposed solution. You want your audience to see what benefits *they* as well as others will reap.

Action

The final step requires you, as the speaker, to call your audience to action. In other words, you must rally your audience, encouraging them to become directly involved.

The following outline exemplifies the motivated sequence at work.

Topic: Reusable bags

Thesis Statement of Fact: Integrating reusable bags into your daily life is an easy and inexpensive way to help save the environment.

Attention. Did you know that . . .

- Americans use 100 billion plastic bags in one year, according to the *Wall Street Journal*? (http://www.reusablebags.com/facts.php?id=4)
- annually 100,000 marine animals are killed by plastic bags?

Need. "Most of the marine debris in the world is comprised of plastic materials. The average proportions vary between 60% and 80% of total marine debris.[1] In many re-

gions, plastic materials constitute as much as 90% to 95% of the total amount of marine debris."[2] (www.plasticdebris.org. Notes: 1. Gregory, M. R., Ryan P. G. 1997. *Pelagic plastics and other seaborne persistent synthetic debris: a review of Southern Hemisphere perspectives.* In Coe, J. M., Rogers, D. B. (eds), Marine Debris—Sources, Impacts, Solutions, New York: Springer-Verlag, pp. 49–66. 2. United Nations Environment Programme: http://www.unep.org/regionalseas/marinelitter/)

Satisfaction. Reusable polypropylene bags use the petroleum resources of 11 plastic grocery bags, but they replace hundreds of plastic bags. Each bag can replace up to 4 plastic bags.

Visualization. If used once a week for two years, a reusable bag will prevent 416 bags from being sent to a landfill, constituting enough petroleum to drive a car 30 miles. (http://www.onebagatatime.com/index.php?page=misc&section=solution_1)

Action. Having just two or three reusable bags and taking them with you when you go shopping or walking around town can save so much energy. You can buy reusable bags from a number of stores and Web sites.

Sources: Plastic Debris Rivers to Sea, http://plasticdebris.org/; 1 Bag at a Time, http://www.onebagatatime.com/; Reusable Bags, http://www.reusablebags.com/facts.php?id=4

TIPS FOR SPEAKING PERSUASIVELY

Selecting a topic for persuasive speaking can be key to a successful speech. If you select a topic that is important to you, that interests you and your audience, and inspires others to engage the topic but has a realistic goal, you are well on your way to success. Then, you want to organize your thesis as a statement of fact, value, or policy so that your audience understands exactly what you are advocating. Build your credibility by using high-quality sources. Finally, avoid misusing persuasive language. Let's take a look at how serious consideration of these issues can lay the groundwork for successful persuasive speaking.

Select a Topic Appropriate to Persuasion

A few factors distinguish a good persuasive speech topic from a good informative speech topic—consider the following persuasive topic tips compiled by public speaking expert Cheryl Hamilton (2009, pp. 292–294). If you keep all these points in mind, you will be sure to choose an engaging persuasive speech topic.

Ensure That Your Topic Fits the Criteria of the Assignment

If you have not been given parameters by your public speaking instructor or whomever is overseeing the speech setting, this is a moot point. However, if you do have an assignment, your speech topic must fit with that assignment. Otherwise, you will begin your presentation at a marked disadvantage.

Select a Topic That Interests You

Typically, when you present on a topic you are interested in, you more easily communicate your enthusiasm to the audience than if you were presenting on a topic of little interest to you. This might seem self-evident, but don't select a topic because it's trendy or you think it's something others might care about. If you don't care about the topic, your audience will notice.

Select a Topic That You Know Well (or care to learn a lot about)

While this point is related to the preceding one, there is a distinction. Because your aim is to persuade your audience, you will be most effective when you show yourself to be an authority on the topic. For audience members to carefully consider your message, they must see you as credible. While credibility, as we have discussed, is tied to a number of factors, your knowledge of the topic is a great part of that ethos. If you don't know much about your topic going in (but are otherwise interested in it), be prepared to invest some time in conducting thorough research!

Select a Topic That Is Interesting and Relevant to Your Audience

Again, we return to audience demographics. Knowing your audience's interests will help you select a topic. Is your audience comprised of classmates? Coworkers? Family members? Each of these situations will likely inspire a different topic. Do not forget your audience! However, as previously mentioned, you must also consider yourself. Choosing a topic purely for the audience may not necessarily be in *your* best interest, so choose wisely.

Select a Topic That Inspires Debate

Although there are lots of persuasive topics out there, the most interesting ones are either controversial or ones that inspire a range of opinions. While your audience may share your perspective, you don't want to simply rehash arguments on an issue that is no longer current. One of the biggest challenges of a persuasive speaker is to present a line of argumentation on a meaty topic in an interesting and compelling way.

Select a Topic That Can Be Argued Within the Time Allotted

To meet this guideline, you need to consider whether your possible topic may either be too broad or overly narrow. For instance, you might be interested in the issue of steroid use in professional sports. However, given the large scale of this topic, you might want to narrow your speech to why major-league baseball player Barry Bonds should be stripped of his various accolades and awards for achievement in the sport. This topic is much more manageable.

Select a Topic with a Reasonable Goal

For instance, vegetarianism is a fine persuasive speech topic. However, you might not want to attempt a task so challenging as converting the carnivores in your class to vegetarians. In all likelihood, the class will not swear off meat by the end of your presentation, no matter how persuasive it is. Instead, you might seek to have the meat eaters in the class concede the benefits of a vegetarian diet. It is undoubtedly a less ambitious goal, but it is one that is easier to accomplish.

In short, topic selection should start with a topic you feel very strongly about. A student of ours found her topic from her own experience with military service and how it changed her life. To read more about her experience, see *It Happened to Me: Susan.*

IT HAPPENED TO ME: *Susan*

My brother was never really good in school. He enjoyed playing sports in high school, but he was pretty average on the field, and he wasn't very interested in his classes. When he graduated, he didn't know what to do next, so he joined the military. My parents were against it. He was severely wounded in Iraq and now needs a lot of help every day. My family has been devastated by all of this, and the burden on my parents has ended their marriage. I know that people want to say my brother is a "hero," but I have pretty strong feelings about the devastation it has left. I think I can make a persuasive case that being a "hero" also means supporting those who have given for the nation, which is what my family is doing—for the rest of our lives.

Organize Your Thesis as a Statement of Fact, Value, or Policy

A thesis statement in a persuasive speech functions similarly to the thesis statement of an informative speech—that is, it tells your audience what your speech is about. However, unlike an informative-speech thesis statement, your persuasive thesis should tell your audience specifically what you intend to argue. Persuasive thesis statements are also often referred to as **propositions**, or "statement[s] with which you want your audience to agree" (Beebe & Beebe, 2010, p. 390). As such, there are three categories of thesis statements, or propositions: *statements of fact, statements of value,* and *statements of policy.*

propositions
statements with which you want your audience to agree

statement of fact
presents something that is either correct or incorrect and can be verified with evidence

Statements of Fact

A **statement of fact** presents something that is either correct or incorrect and can be verified with evidence. Although a statement such as "The War of 1812 began in 1812" is indeed a statement of fact, it might not necessarily make for the most scintillating persuasive speech topic. Rather, a statement such as "The 1969 moon landing broadcast on U.S. national television was a hoax" would make for a more engaging topic, lending itself to several main points and subpoints.

For another example:

Topic: Health benefits of coffee

Thesis Statement of Fact: A daily cup of joe contains greater health benefits than one of tea.

Statements of Value

Statements of value, unlike statements of fact, present something as either right or wrong. These statements attach a worth to the issue being considered. For instance, a statement of value might be "*Gossip Girl* is a more nuanced television show than *The O.C.*"

For example:

Topic: AFI top 100 movies

Thesis Statement of Value: *Willy Wonka and the Chocolate Factory* (1971) should be included on the AFI's list of top 100 movies.

Statements of Policy

Finally, **statements of policy** present a specific action or policy. One example is: "The United States should institute universal health care." Regardless of which type of statement you give in your speech, it should state your fundamental argument in a clear, concise, and engaging way.

For example:

Topic: Marijuana

Thesis Statement of Policy: The United States should legalize the use of marijuana.

The thesis statement tells your audience where you stand with respect to an issue. Remember that it should be a statement that will inspire debate and can be argued. Remember also that you can approach your thesis from any one of the three thesis types. You might first look, then, at the topic from each angle and determine which approach to take in your speech.

Establish Credibility Through the Quality of Your Sources

The quality of your research helps to establish your credibility as a persuasive speaker. Because research is such an important part of your speech, keep these points in mind:

Make Sure Your Sources Are High Quality

As we have said, all sources are not created equal. While your best friend's blog is a source that you may use in your speech, it likely does not wield the same authority as an article printed in the *Wall Street Journal*. If you do decide to use alternative sources that are located outside the mainstream, that is fine, as they can be incredibly rich resources. However, make sure that you are appropriately critical of the source and use other sources alongside this one. Your own credibility as a persuasive speaker rests with the quality of the sources you use.

Ensure That You Are Appropriately Critical of Your Sources

As we said in the previous chapter, your credibility as a speaker is largely contingent on the source materials you use. That said, you should show that you have taken care to be critical of the sources you are dealing with. For instance, certain political commentators hold views that are very conservative. Ann Coulter, for example, is well known as a conservative, so you would not expect her to be a particularly strong advocate for the work of the Obama administration. Her comments, then, should be seen in that light. By the same token, MSNBC's Keith Olbermann, a noted liberal commentator and host of *Countdown with Keith Olbermann,* will be more likely to attack conservatives who oppose a number of issues—such as health care reform and reforms on banks and financial markets—so his comments need to be viewed in the context of his political views. Don't forget to be critical of any interviews you conduct as well. As noted in Chapter 13, interviews can provide a wealth of information, but they can also insert bias in a number of ways. Sometimes it is difficult to separate yourself from a source in order to view it critically. It is nonetheless essential.

statement of value
presents something as either right or wrong

statement of policy
presents a specific action or policy

Take Careful Notes and Keep All Source Citations

Remember that research ethics are just as important as presentation ethics. You have done your work, so show your audience! When you are using the work of another, be sure to appropriately cite your source. Your citations will help you build and maintain ethos. Take care with your research.

Make Sure Your Research is Up to Date

For instance, if you are making an argument regarding the harmful effects of cigarette smoking, you will want to draw on the most recent studies available. This may be challenging (although essential) in a field such as medicine that is constantly developing, but incorporating up-to-date sources will not only show your commitment to your topic but will also enhance your ethos, demonstrating the breadth of your research.

Research a Range of Perspectives

To be an effective persuader, you must consider not only the points you wish to make—the points you want your audience to adopt or believe—but also the arguments that the counter position may launch in an attempt to refute your claims. This means that you must research not only the points that work with your argument but also those that might directly challenge it. For instance, when delivering a persuasive speech on why her class should take up running, Laura cited a 2008 study published in *Skeletal Radiology* that argued that marathoners' knees showed little to no signs of degeneration over a ten year-period of study, refuting long-held beliefs that running destroys the knees (Reynolds, August 11, 2009, http://well.blogs.nytimes.com/2009/08/11/phys-ed-can-running-actually-help-your-knees/). Remember that you want to be well informed and able to refute whatever argument your opponents may throw your way. Sometimes researching a topic can influence what you think about it, as our student describes in *It Happened to Me: Glen.* Glen's earlier beliefs on climate change were put into confusion after he researched the topic. Being a knowledgeable and thoughtful speaker will make a great difference and make you a more persuasive speaker. We will say more about what to do with these counterarguments when we discuss the organization of a persuasive speech.

To determine if you have conducted adequate research on your speech topic, complete the *Building Your Communication Skills: Research Checklist.*

IT HAPPENED TO ME: Glen

I had planned on giving my persuasive speech on climate change. After all, the next big climate-change treaty since the Kyoto Protocol was coming up, and it seemed timely. I wasn't convinced that climate change was that imminent. Every time the topic comes up, it seems like it is our "last chance" to do something, and then we always get another chance. After I began researching climate change, I wasn't sure what I believed anymore. I found some pretty compelling evidence that climate change really is a problem, especially in low-lying islands that are slowly going under with rising ocean levels. I may have to find another topic.

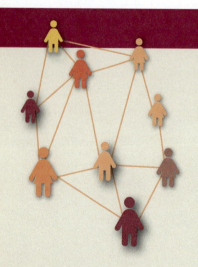

Building Your Communication SKILLS

Research Checklist

In conducting your research, did you

☐ Seek out a variety of sources?

☐ Make sure your sources are high quality?

☐ Ensure that you are appropriately critical of all your sources?

☐ Take careful notes and keep all source citations?

☐ Make sure your research is current and cutting edge?

☐ Research a range of perspectives?

Avoid Misusing Persuasive Language

As we have stressed throughout this text, language is extremely powerful. Thus, be careful not to misuse it in an effort to dramatize. For example, "If you don't recycle your plastics and cans, it's going to lead to the end of the world." Such misuse is unethical and inappropriate. Tone and style are also important. Be especially careful not to belittle or demean those who may not share your perspectives. For example, don't dismiss those who disagree with you as "morons" or "idiots." As we have said, persuasion is difficult. When delivering a speech, if you use a dismissive tone and style, you may create a **hostile audience**, or an audience that turns against you. Regardless of your audience's beliefs, an essential part of the ethics of persuasive speaking is that you respect them.

hostile audience
an audience that turns against the speaker

PERSUASIVE SPEAKING AND ETHICS

The question of ethics haunts persuasive speaking—in part because persuasive speaking plays such a central role in a democratic society. The decisions we make are largely driven by speeches that persuade us about going to war in Iraq, staying in or getting out of Afghanistan, or retaining prisoners in Guantanamo. Persuasive speaking is also important in the courtroom. Juries make decisions about someone's guilt based on persuasive speeches given by prosecuting attorneys and defense attorneys. Precisely because so many decisions are made in the context of persuasive speaking, it is very important to consider the ethics of this kind of speech.

Do not demean those who disagree with you, or you may create a hostile audience.

First, consider the consequences of your persuasive speaking. Although your speech may not end up ruining or saving someone's life, it may still have an impact. If your audiences are persuaded by your speech, who might be helped? Who might be harmed? Thus, when we consider the ethics of persuasive speaking, we often think about the consequences of the speech(es).

Second, consider the ethics of the persuasive strategies you are using. Some people claim that the "ends justify the means," but others disagree about this approach. If you say that it is okay to use any strategy or do anything to get audiences to act, you focus only on strategies and ignore the possible result of your strategies. If, instead, you consider the ethics of the persuasive strategies, you focus on both ends and means. When you're focused on both ends and means, you become concerned with whether your information is accurate, whether your sources are reliable, and whether you are using appropriate emotional appeals. Especially with regard to emotional appeals, you may encounter a range of opinions regarding ethics. For example, some see the use of photos of abused animals, bodies of war victims, or aborted fetuses in persuasive appeals as unethical, but others see their use as appropriate and justifiable.

Third, do not search for a checklist of items in making your ethical decisions. Ethics are complex, and you should consider the ethics of every aspect of your speaking—from the research you do, to the appeals you use, to the effect your speech may have. Sometimes the speaking venue itself can raise ethical questions, such as when the president of Iran, Mahmoud Ahmadinejad, spoke at Columbia University in 2007. Following his speech, many questioned whether the university should even have invited him, as he is known for making controversial and inflammatory claims—for example, denying that the Holocaust occurred. Others, however, insisted that the free exchange of ideas was an important value to be upheld on a college campus. Whatever your speaking task, it should be based on a consideration of the full range of ethical issues.

SUMMARY

Persuasive speaking plays an important role in various arenas throughout society. It is a powerful form that has the capacity to empower audiences. In considering your topic and goal, think about the power of the three artistic proofs: ethos, logos, and pathos. Consider in what way you want to impact your audience's attitudes, beliefs, values, or behavior. The steps in crafting a persuasive speech include selecting a topic; organizing your thesis as a statement of fact, value, or policy; doing high-quality research; and organizing the material into an introduction, body, and conclusion. There are three main organizational patterns of use to persuasive speakers: problem-solution, claim, and Monroe's motivated sequence. Each can be adapted to specific types of speeches, according to the goals of the speech. Additionally, language, tone, and style can impact the goals of a persuasive speaker positively or negatively, as can the selection of audiovisual aids. Finally, numerous ethical concerns arise in a persuasive speech setting, underscoring the importance of careful consideration before delivering such a speech.

KEY TERMS

appeal to authority 383
appeal to the crowd 383
appeal to tradition 383
bifurcation 383
boomerang effect 378
claim 385
demagoguery 379
ethos 376
fallacies of reasoning 382

false dilemma 383
faulty analogy 383
faulty cause 382
hasty generalization 383
hostile audience 391
logos 376
Monroe's motivated sequence (MMS) 386
pathos 378

persuasive speaking 372
problem-solution or problem-solution-action pattern 384
propositions 388
statement of fact 388
statement of policy 389
statement of value 389
sweeping generalization 382

CHAPTER REVIEW QUESTIONS

1. What is the goal of a persuasive speech?

2. Why are persuasive speaking skills so important in today's society?

3. Why is it particularly important to know your audience in preparing a persuasive speech?

4. What are six strategies for researching a persuasive speech?

5. Why are language, tone, and style so important in persuasive speaking?

6. What are two ethical issues that arise in persuasive speaking?

ACTIVITIES

1. Pair off with another student. Ask your partner the following questions. For each question, have your partner recount a specific scenario and describe *how* he/she attempted to be persuasive. Did those strategies succeed? Why or why not? What was the end result?
   - Have you ever asked your parents for money?
   - Have you ever tried to convince your friend to go out with you on a school night?
   - Have you ever tried to convince yourself to sleep past your alarm?
   - Have you ever given a movie review?
   - Have you ever tried to convince your professor that you deserved a higher grade on a paper or exam?

2. In groups of four, brainstorm a list of persuasive speech topics. Which topics would be best suited for:
   a. Your public speaking class?
   b. Your sorority/fraternity?
   c. Your 8-year-old sister's friends?
   d. Your coworkers at Apple?

3. List three potential persuasive speech topics. For each topic, develop a thesis statement of fact, statement of value, and statement of policy. Which is most appealing to you as a speech thesis?

WEB ACTIVITIES

1. Go to http://www.youtube.com/watch?v=BpOvzGiheOM Watch this Mac vs. Bloated PC advertisement. Note how the people are dressed and the appeals made to different audiences. Analyze the persuasive techniques used to sway the viewer to Mac.

2. Go to the homepage of an activist organization, such has PETA or the Birthers, and examine the persuasive strategies they use. Are they more interested in persuading new people to their cause? Or are they focused on reinforcing the beliefs of those who already agree with them? What can you learn about persuasion from examining these appeals? Are there visual images that may raise ethical concerns?

3. Find some commercials on the Internet that rely heavily on emotional appeals (pathos). Analyze these commercials and see if you can distinguish different types of emotional appeals. Which ones are more effective? Why?

GLOSSARY

absolute pertaining to the belief that there is a single correct moral standard that holds for everyone, everywhere, every time

active agents seekers of various media messages and resisters of others

adaptors gestures used to manage emotions

affective exchange stage in which people increase the breadth, depth, and frequency of their self-disclosure

age identity a combination of self-perception of age, along with what others understand that age to mean

agenda-setting capacity the power of media coverage to influence individuals' view of the world

agreeableness a personality dimension describing a person who is: appreciative, forgiving, generous, kind, sympathetic, and trusting

analog information that is transmitted in a continuous numerical format

analysis paralysis potential pitfall in small group interaction; occurs when excessive analysis prevents a group from moving toward a solution

anticipatory socialization activities and experiences that occur before an individual enters an organization but that later assist in the assimilation process

appeal to authority a logical fallacy which attempts to justify an argument by citing a highly admired or well-known (but not necessarily qualified) figure who supports the conclusion being offered

appeal to the crowd a logical fallacy that refers to popular opinion or majority sentiment in order to provide support for a claim

appeal to tradition a logical fallacy based on the principle of not challenging time-honored customs or traditions

appropriateness following the relevant rules, norms and expectations for specific relationships and situations

argumentation skills the ability to make an argument during conflict

artifacts clothing and other accessories

artistic proofs artistic skills of a rhetor that influence effectiveness

arousal maintenance goals goals relating to an individual's need to avoid feeling uncomfortable, nervous, or embarrassed when making a request

assertiveness expressing one's opinions forcefully without offending others

assimilation the communicative, behavioral, and cognitive processes that influence individuals to join, identify with, become integrated into, and (occasionally) exit an organization

asynchronicity occurs when a message is sent and received at different times

asynchronous communication in which messages are sent at a later time

attention-getter strategies speakers use, as you might guess, to "get" the attention of the audience

attractiveness the appeal one person has for another, based on physical appearance, personality, and/or behavior

attribution theory explanation of the processes we use to judge our own and others' behavior

attributional bias the tendency to attribute one's own negative behavior to external causes and one's positive actions to internal states

audience analysis the process of determining what an audience already knows or wants to know about a topic, who they are, what they know or need to know about the speaker, and what their expectations might be for the presentation

authoritarian leadership style characterized by a leader who takes charge, makes all the decisions, and dictates strategies and work tasks

autonomy/connection a dialectical tension in relationships that refers to one's need to connect with others and the simultaneous need to feel independent or autonomous

avatar a computer user's representation of himself/herself, or alter ego

avoiding stage of romantic relational dissolution in which couples try not to interact with each other

avoiding style is indirect and involves strategies such as withdrawing, joking around, and ignoring; it can be cooperative or uncooperative, depending on the situation

bamboo ceiling the exclusion of Asian Americans from executive and managerial roles because of prejudice and discrimination

battering relationships in which one individual uses violence as a way to control and dominate his or her partner

behavioral conflicts disagreements over specific, concrete behaviors that one performs or fails to perform

behaviorism the focus on the study of behavior as a science

bifurcation a logical fallacy that assumes that two categories are mutually exclusive and exhaustive—that is, that something is either a member of one or the other, but not both or some third category

blogs short for "Web logs"; a Web site, like a journal, maintained by an individual with regular entries of commentary, descriptions of events, or other material such as graphics or video

body where all the evidence and supporting materials in your speech are presented

bonding stage of romantic relational development characterized by public commitment

boomerang effect an effect that runs in the opposite direction from the desired effect

border dwellers people who live between cultures and often experience contradictory cultural patterns

brainstorm to generate as many ideas as possible without critiquing them

bullying repeated hostile behaviors that are or appear to be intended to harm parties unable to defend themselves

burnout a chronic condition that results from the accumulation of daily stress, which manifests itself in a very specific set of characteristics, including exhaustion, cynicism, and ineffectiveness

cascade the way in which one person's negative conflict behavior can trigger another person's negative behavior in such a way that their conflict patterns escalate and worsen, eventually leading to a decline in relationship satisfaction

Cascade Model of Relational Conflict John Gottman's model that explains how conflict escalates in a cascade of negativity that, if left unchecked, will lead to relationship dissolution

categorization a cognitive process used to organize information by placing it into larger groupings of information

catharsis the purging of the emotions or relieving of emotional tensions; from a Greek term that means *to cleanse*

cause-effect pattern speech pattern used to create understanding and agreement, and sometimes to argue for a specific action

certainty-focused communication statements that suggest absolute truth and leave no room for differing viewpoints

change/predictability a dialectical tension in relationships that describes the human desire for events that are new, spontaneous, and unplanned while simultaneously needing some aspects of life to be stable and predictable

channel the means through which a message is transmitted

charismatic leadership a leadership style in which extremely self-confident leaders inspire unusual dedication to themselves by relying upon their strong personalities and charm

chronemics the study of the way in which people use time as a message

chronological pattern an organizational pattern in which the main points are arranged in a time-order sequence

circumscribing stage of romantic relational dissolution in which couples discuss safe topics

claim an argument

clarity the use of language to increase precision and reduce ambiguity

closed questions questions that are answerable in a few words

cocultural group a significant minority group within a dominant majority that does not share dominant group values or communication patterns

cocultural theory explores the role of power in daily interactions

cognitive complexity the degree to which a person's constructs are detailed, involved, or numerous

cognitive representation the ability to form mental models of the world

cohort effect the influence of shared characteristics of a group that was born and reared in the same general period

collaborating or problem-solving style involves a high concern for the self *and* the other party

collectivistic cultures cultures that emphasize group identity, goals, and concerns over individual desires

collectivistic orientation a value orientation that stresses the needs of the group

communicating information using nonverbal behaviors to help clarify verbal messages and reveal attitudes and moods

communication apprehension feelings of anxiety that accompany public speaking; commonly referred to as stage fright

communication ethics the standards of right and wrong that one applies to messages that are sent and received

competence model of conflict a model developed by communication scholars Dan Canary and Brian Spitzberg that emphasizes appropriateness and effectiveness

competing or dominating style represents a high concern for one's own interests and a low concern for the partner's interests and is characterized by direct communication

competitive style focuses on advancing one's own interests without consideration for the partner's interests

compliance-gaining messages communication strategies people use to influence one another

compromising style represents a moderate concern for self and others

computer-mediated communication (CMC) the exchange of messages carried through an intervening system of digital electronic storage and transmitted between two or more people

concessions giving up something you want

conclusion closing material of a speech where the speaker reviews the main points, may challenge the audience to act, and leaves the audience with a positive view of the speaker and the topic

confirming communication comments that validate positive self-images of others

conflict occurs when interdependent parties perceive that they have incompatible interests related to the distribution of limited resources

conflict strategy decisions people make based on how direct or indirect they want to be and how cooperative or competitive they will be

conflict style describes the pattern of tactics an individual uses repetitively and across parties and contexts

conflict tactic the individual behavior a person uses when engaged in conflict (such as shouting, threatening, persuading, or withdrawing)

congruent verbal and nonverbal messages that express the same meaning

connotative meaning the affective or interpretive meanings attached to a word

conscientiousness a personality dimension describing a person who is: efficient, organized, reliable, responsible, and thorough

consistency principle influence tactic that relies on the human desire to appear consistent

constructive marginal people people who thrive in a border-dweller life, while recognizing its tremendous challenges

constructs categories people develop to help them organize information

contempt behavior that is designed to insult and psychologically harm the partner; the third of Gottman's "four horsemen"

content analysis approach to understanding media that focuses on specific aspects of the content of a text or group of texts

content meaning the concrete meaning of the message and the meanings suggested by or associated with the message and the emotions triggered by it

content-oriented listening style listening style that reflects an interest in detailed and complex information, simply for the content itself

contingent employees individuals who work in temporary positions, part-time or as subcontractors

contradicting verbal and nonverbal messages that send conflicting messages

controlling communication messages that attempt to impose one's will on another, perhaps with coercion

cooperative style focuses on the partner's interests as well as one's own

critical approach an approach used not only to understand human behavior but ultimately to change society

critical listening listening skills that are useful in a wide variety of situations—particularly those involving persuasive speaking

criticism attacking the partner's personality or character (rather than a specific behavior); the first of Gottman's "four horsemen"

cultivation theory idea that long-term immersion in a media environment leads to "cultivation," or enculturation, into shared beliefs about the world

cultural capital cultural knowledge and cultural competencies that people need for functioning effectively in society

cultural values beliefs that are so central to a cultural group that they are never questioned

culture learned patterns of perceptions, values, and behaviors shared by a group of people

culture industries large organizations in the business of mass communication that produce, distribute, or show various media texts (cultural products) as an industry

cultural intelligence (CQ) a person's ability to interpret unfamiliar gestures and situations and create appropriate behavioral responses

culture shock a feeling of disorientation and discomfort due to the lack of familiar environmental cues

cyberbullying the deliberate and repeated misuse of communication technology by an individual or group to threaten or harm others

cyberspace synonymous with the Internet or online world

deception concealment, distortion, or lying in communication

decision-making process the four-phase process used by a group to evaluate information and arrive at a decision or solution

decoding receiving a message and interpreting its meaning

defensive communication comments that threaten others self image or persona

defensiveness attempts by the partner to protect or defend his/her identity and character; the second of Gottman's "four horsemen"

deliberative rhetoric the type of rhetoric used to argue what a society should do in the future

delivery the presentation of the speech you have researched, organized, outlined, and practiced

demagoguery the attempt to gain power or control over others by using unethical emotional pleas and appealing to listeners' prejudices

demand touching a type of touch used to establish dominance and power

democratic leadership style a leadership style that is characterized by considerable input from group members

demographic analysis the portion of an audience analysis that considers the ages, races, sexes, sexual orientations, religions, and social classes of the audience

demographics the characteristics of your audience—typically age, gender, race, income, and other qualities that characterize them

denotative meaning the dictionary, or literal, meaning of a word

descriptive communication messages that are clear and specific without loaded words or judgmental cues

dialect a variation of a language distinguished by its vocabulary, grammar, and pronunciation

dialectic approach recognizes that things need not be perceived as either/or, but may be seen as both/and

dichotomous thinking thinking in which things are perceived as either/ or—for example, good or bad, big or small, right or wrong

differentiating stage of romantic relational dissolution in which couples increase their interpersonal distance

diffusion of innovations theory that explains why some innovations, like computers and Internet technology, are accepted by some people and rejected by others

digital information that is transmitted in a numerical format based on only two values (0 and 1)

digital divide the inequity of access between the technology "haves" and the "have-nots"

direct conflict style focuses on discussing issues of incompatibility

disconfirming communication comments that reject or invalidate a positive or negative self-image of our conversational partners

display rules societal rules that govern how people should react when they experience a given emotion

downward communication in a traditional conduit model of communication, communication with subordinates

Ebonics a version of English that has its roots in West African, Caribbean, and U.S. slave languages

e-books electronic books read on a computer screen instead of a printed page

economic production role organizational role in which the delivery of products or services maximizes profit

effectiveness achieving one's goals successfully

ego-defensive function the role prejudice plays in protecting individuals' sense of self-worth

elocution the mechanics of public speaking, including proper pronunciation, posture, and grammar

emblems gestures that stand for a specific verbal meaning

emergence phase the third phase of the decision-making process; occurs when group members express a cooperative attitude

emoticons pictographs used in e-mail to convey relational information

emotional flooding instances when people become highly aroused and disorganized in response to their partner's negative statements

emotional infidelity refers to behaviors such as flirting, dating, spending time together, and falling in love with someone other than one's partner

emotional norms societal rules that suggest which emotions are good or bad to experience

emotional stability a personality dimension describing a person who is: well-adjusted, calm and secure

empathic communication messages that convey sympathy and caring

empowerment increasing employees' feelings of self-efficacy

enacting identities performing scripts deemed proper for particular identities

encapsulated marginal people those who feel disintegrated by having to shift cultures

encoding taking ideas and converting them into messages

encounter stage stage in the assimilation process during which individuals learn the norms, expectations, and practices of the organization and begin to accept and adapt to them

Enlightenment eighteenth-century period characterized by the belief that science and reason are the pathways to human knowledge

equality-oriented communication messages that convey a sense of worth of others and their ideas, viewpoints

establishing social control using nonverbal behavior to exercise influence over other people

ethics standards of what is right and wrong, good and bad, moral and immoral

ethnic identity identification with a particular group with which one shares some or all of these characteristics: national or tribal affiliation, religious beliefs, language, and/or cultural and traditional origins and background

ethnocentrism the tendency to view one's own group as the standard against which all other groups are judged

ethnographic relating to studies in which researchers actively engage with participants

ethos credibility

evaluating assessing your reaction to a message

evaluative communication messages that carry judgments of right and wrong, good or bad

examples material that provides a concrete and realistic way of thinking about a topic and clarifying it

experimenting stage of romantic relational development in which both people seek to learn about each other

expert testimony the opinion of someone who is an acknowledged expert in some field

exploratory affective exchange stage in which people increase the breadth of their communication

expressing and managing intimacy using nonverbal behaviors to help convey attraction and closeness

expressiveness/privacy a dialectical tension in relationships that describes the need to be open and to self-disclose while also maintaining some sense of privacy

extemporaneous speech a speech that is written ahead of time but only in outline form

extraversion the ability to convey positive emotions and project optimism and enthusiasm

eye contact looking at someone or an audience directly, rather than looking away

fallacies of reasoning errors in reasoning

false dilemma a logical fallacy that implies that one of two outcomes is inevitable and that both have negative consequences

faulty analogy a logical fallacy that assumes that because two things, events, or situations are alike in some known respects, they are alike in other unknown respects

faulty cause a logical fallacy that mistakes correlation or association for causation, by assuming that because one thing follows another it was caused by the first

feedback the response to a message

feeling rules rules defined by society that determine *how* one should feel when experiencing specific events

field of availables the field of potential partners and friends accessible through CMC that is much larger than in face-to-face relationships

field of experience the education, life events, and cultural background that a communicator possesses

filtered a form of communication that lacks nonverbal cues

foot-in-the-door technique practice of asking for something small then requesting something larger

forensic rhetoric rhetoric that addresses events that happened in the past with the goal of setting things right after an injustice has occurred

formal structure officially designated channels of communication, reflecting explicit or desired patterns of interaction

frame a structure that shapes how people interpret their perceptions

friendship touch touch that is more intimate than social touch and usually conveys warmth, closeness, and caring

function the goals and effects of communication

functional (situational) theory a theory that assumes that leadership behaviors can be learned

functional touch the least intimate type of touch; used by certain workers such as dentists, hairstylists, and hospice workers, as part of their livelihood; also known as *professional touch*

fundamental attribution error the tendency to attribute others' negative behavior to internal causes and their positive behaviors to external causes

gender identity how and to what extent one identifies with the social construction of masculinity and femininity

general purpose whichever of three goals—to inform, persuade, or entertain—that dominates a speech

general systems theory theory that organizations are a system composed of many subsystems and embedded in larger systems and that organizations should develop communication strategies that serve both

generalized other the collection of roles, rules, norms, beliefs, and attitudes endorsed by the community in which a person lives

geographical or **spatial pattern** an organizational pattern in which the main points are arranged according to physical location

gestures nonverbal communication made with part of the body, including actions such as pointing, waving, or holding up a hand to direct people's attention

glass ceiling informal barriers, like discrimination and prejudice, that prevent women (and minorities) from advancing in organizations

globalization the increasing connectedness of the world in economic, political, and cultural realms

group processes the methods, including communication, by which a group accomplishes a task

group roles the shared expectations group members have regarding each individual's communication behavior in the group

group support software (GSS) computer-aided program that supports real-time discussion between members regardless of physical location

grouphate the distaste and aversion that people feel toward working in groups

groupthink a negative, and potentially disastrous, group process characterized by excessive concurrence in thinking

haptics the study of the communicative function of touch

hasty generalization a logical fallacy that bases an inference on too small a sample or on an unrepresentative sample

Hays Code self-imposed rules for Hollywood media content instituted in 1930 with the goal of creating "wholesome entertainment"

healthy feedback the honest and ethical responses receivers provide to the messages of others

hegemony the process by which we consent to social constructions rather than having them imposed on us

heterogeneous diverse

heuristic use of language to acquire knowledge and understanding

hierarchy a power structure in which some members exercise authority over others

high-context cultures cultures that convey intention or meaning through the communication context and through nonverbals

high power-distance cultures cultures that tend to emphasize hierarchy, social position, and status differences

homogeneity a high degree of similarity

horizontal communication in a traditional conduit model of communication, communication with peers

hostile audience an audience that turns against the speaker

hostile work environment an intimidating, hostile, or offensive workplace atmosphere created by unwelcome and inappropriate sexually based behavior; one of two types of sexual harassment recognized by federal law

human communication in society model a transactional process in which people generate meaning through the exchange of verbal and nonverbal messages in specific contexts, influenced by individual and societal forces and embedded in culture

human–nature value orientation the perceived relationship between humans and nature

human relations approach to management that holds that the job of management is actually to educate, interact, and integrate

human resources approach to management that holds that workers are not only economically motivated but that they also bring personal histories and emotional needs to work with them

humanism a system of thought that celebrates human nature and its potential

hurtful messages messages that occur when a person criticizes, teases, rejects, or otherwise causes an emotional injury to another

hyperbole a figure of speech that exaggerates a characteristic to capture audience attention and interest

hyperpersonal relationships Internet relationships that develop intimacy more quickly than do face-to-face relationships

identity who a person is, composed of individual and social categories a person identifies with, as well as the categories that others identify with that person

identity goals goals that are related to one's self-concept and involve issues, values, and ethics

illustrators signals that accompany speech to clarify or emphasize verbal messages

imaginative use of language to express oneself artistically or creatively

immediacy how close or involved people appear to be with each other

impromptu speech a speech that is delivered with little or no preparation

incompatibility communicators' perceptions that their interests are mutually exclusive or in opposition

indirect conflict style avoids discussing issues of incompatibility

indirect fighting a conflict style that represents high concern for one's own goals and low concern for one's partner's goals

individual roles roles that focus more on individuals' own interests and needs than on those of the group

individualistic cultures emphasize individual identities, goals, and rights over those of the group

individualist orientation a value orientation that respects the autonomy and independence of individuals

informal structure unspoken but understood channels of communication, reflecting patterns that develop spontaneously

informational listening listening skills that are useful in situations requiring attention to content

informative use of language to communicate information or report facts

informative speaking speaking with the aim of educating the audience

informative speech a speech that explains, instructs, defines, clarifies, demonstrates, or teaches

ingratiation behavior and communication designed to increase one's likeability

initiating stage of romantic relational development in which both people behave so as to appear pleasant and likeable

innovation a function of organizational communication by means of which systems are changed

instrumental use of language to obtain what you need or desire

integrating stage of romantic relational development in which both people portray themselves as a couple

integration role organizational function in which potentially chaotic social conflicts or problems are managed

intensifying stage of romantic relational development in which both people seek to increase intimacy and connectedness

intensity the degree of emphasis with which a speaker makes his or her claim

intentional messages messages that are perceived as purposely causing harm to the recipient

interaction goals concern rules for how a person should behave when communicating with others

interactional use of language to establish and define social relationships

intercultural communication communication that occurs in interactions between people who are culturally different

interdependent relying upon at least one other party to achieve a goal or fulfill an interest

interests goals, needs, desires, values, and beliefs

Internet a system of networks that connects millions of computers around the world

interpersonal violence physical violence against a partner or child

interpretation the act of assigning meaning to sensory information

interpretive approach contemporary term for humanistic (rhetorical) study

intimate distance (0 to 18 inches) the space used when interacting with those with whom one is very close

intimate terrorism occurs when one partner (usually a male) uses violence to exert control over the partner

introduction opening material of a speech from which the audience members gain a first impression of the speech's content and of the speaker

introverts people who do not get energy from interaction with others

involuntary long-term travelers people who are border dwellers permanently but not by choice, such as those who relocate to escape war

involuntary short-term travelers people who are border dwellers not by choice and only for a limited time, such as refugees forced to move

jargon technical terminology associated with a specific topic

jealousy occurs when a person perceives a threat to an existing relationship

kinesics nonverbal communication sent by the body, including gestures, posture, movement, facial expressions, and eye behavior

Knapp's stage model model of relationship development that views relationships as occurring in "stages" and that focuses on how people communicate as relationships develop and decline

label a name assigned to a category based on one's perception of the category

laissez-faire leadership style a leadership style characterized by complete freedom for the group in making decisions

lexical choice vocabulary preference

leadership an influence relationship among leaders and followers who intend real changes and outcomes that reflect their shared purposes

limited resources the reality or the perception that sufficient resources do not exist for all parties to achieve their goals or fulfill their interests

linear model portrayal of communication as a process occurring largely in one direction

listening the process of receiving, constructing meaning from, and responding to spoken and/or nonverbal messages

listening style a set of attitudes, beliefs, and predispositions about the how, where, when, who, and what of the information receiving and encoding process

logos rational appeals; the use of rhetoric to help the audience see the rationale for a particular conclusion

long-term orientation a value orientation in which people stress the importance of virtue

long-term versus short-term orientation the dimension of a society's value orientation that reflects its attitude toward virtue or truth

looking-glass self the idea that self-image results from the images others reflect back to an individual

love-intimate touch the touch most often used with one's romantic partners and family

low balling the practice of making a request, but once the person agrees to it, the requestor reveals that compliance is more costly than it first seemed

low-context cultures cultures that prefer communication that is explicit and direct and relatively easy to decode

low power-distance cultures cultures that tend to see people as relatively equal and deemphasize status differences

Machiavellian tactics having a third party convey one's unhappiness about a relationship

maintenance a function of organizational communication in which the stability of existing systems is preserved

manuscript speech a speech that is written out word for word and read to the audience

mass-market paperbacks popular books addressed to a large audience and widely distributed

mass-media effects the influence that media have on people's everyday lives

Massively Multiplayer Online Games (MMOGs) Text-based "virtual reality" games in which participants interact with environments, objects, and other participants

matching hypothesis the tendency to develop relationships with people who are approximately as attractive as we are

mate guarding attempts to protect your partner from falling victim to "poaching" by others

media the plural form of *medium*, a channel of communication

media activism the practice of organizing to communicate displeasure with certain media images and messages, as well as to force change in future media texts

media augmentation approach a theoretical perspective that views mediated communication as complementing or augmenting face-to-face communication

media deficit approach a theoretical perspective that sees mediated communication as deficient in comparison to face-to-face communication

media event occasions or catastrophes that interrupt regular programming

media richness the potential information-carrying capacity of a communication medium

media richness theory describes the potential information-carrying capacity of a communication medium

media text a television show, advertisement, movie, or other media event

media violence representations of violent acts in media

mediation peaceful third-party intervention

mentor an advocate and guide who nurtures growth, helping the mentee to realize the potential within them—usually through a combination of methods: by modeling new behavior, by having the mentee assist in a new task (such as through an apprenticeship), or by allowing the mentee to work individually with guidance

messages the building blocks of communication events

meta-communication talking about the ways in which you and your partner communicate with one another

metamorphosis the final stage of the socialization process during which employees come to see themselves as members of the organization and colleagues see them this way as well

metaphor a figure of speech that compares two things or ideas to highlight a particular point

methodology an accepted set of methods for developing new knowledge about a subject

methods the specific ways in which scholars collect and analyze data that they then use to prove or disprove their theories

mindfulness having a clear focus on the activity you are engaged in, with attention to as many specifics of the event as you can

modernism the belief that humans can advance and discover universal truth through rational thinking

monochronically engaging in one task or behavior at a time

monotheistic belief in one god

Monroe's motivated sequence (MMS) a five-step organizational pattern based on the notion that in a persuasive speech, the speaker is seeking to fulfill a need of the audience and that in order to fulfill that need, the audience must be moved to act

motivation feeling personally invested in accomplishing a specific activity or goal

MPAA Motion Picture Association of America

multiracial identity one who self-identifies as having more than one racial identity

mutable subject to change

national identity identification with a particular national group

naturalistic relating to everyday, real-life situations, such as a classroom, café, or shopping mall

neutral questions questions that give the person being questioned a chance to respond without any influence from the interviewer

neutral communication messages that convey indifference, lack of interest

new media refers to the new communication technologies of the late twentieth century and early twenty-first century

new social contract assumes that loyalty is not expected by workers or organizations and that job security is unlikely

noise any stimulus that can interfere with, or degrade, the quality of a message

nominalists those who argue that any idea can be expressed in any language and that the structure and vocabulary of the language do not influence the speaker's perception of the world

nonverbal behavior all the nonverbal actions people perform

nonverbal codes distinct, organized means of expression that consist of symbols and rules for their use

nonverbal communication nonverbal behavior that has symbolic meaning

open to experience personality dimension describing a person who is: artistic, curious, introspective, imaginative, insightful, original, and has a wide range of interests

open-ended questions questions that give the person being questioned free rein in answering

openness a state in which communicators are willing to share their ideas as well as listen to others in a way that avoids conveying negative or disconfirming feedback

orator a public speaker

organization the process by which one recognizes what sensory input represents

organizational culture a pattern of shared beliefs, values, and behaviors

organizational identification the stage of assimilation that occurs when an employee's values overlap with the organization's values

organizational pattern the pattern that structures the material in a speech

orientation the stage in which people first meet and engage in superficial communication

outline the framework that arranges the main points and subpoints of your speech to support your thesis

paradigm belief system that represents a particular worldview

paralinguistics all aspects of spoken language except the words themselves; includes rate, volume, pitch, stress

participants the people interacting during communication

particular others the important people in an individual's life whose opinions and behavior influence the various aspects of identity

passing away the process by which relationships decline over time

pathos the rhetorical use of emotions to affect audience decision making

people-oriented listening style a listening style that is associated with friendly, open communication and an interest in establishing ties with others

perception the processes of selection, organization, and interpretation of the information you collect through your senses: what you see, hear, taste, smell, and touch

perceptual co-orientation a state in which two people share similar perceptions and recognize that their perceptions agree

performance of identity the process or means by which we show the world who we think we are

persona public identity created by a speaker

personal distance (18 inches to 4 feet) the space used when interacting with friends and acquaintances

personal language use of language to express individuality and personality

personal narrative (or lay testimony) relating an event, incident, or experience in one's own life

personal resource goals goals related to the desire to maintain material assets

personality conflicts disagreements that focus on a global evaluation of the individual and therefore usually constitute an attack upon one's identity

persuade to convince

persuasive discourse arguments that take place when others interfere with your ability to achieve your goals and you want to convince them to stop interfering so you can fulfill your desires

persuasive speaking a speech that influences, convinces, motivates, tells, preaches or stimulates action

persuasive speech a speech with the aim of convincing the audience

phishing e-mail messages that try (fraudulently) to get consumer banking and credit card information

phonology the study of the sounds that compose individual languages and how those sounds communicate meaning

physical infidelity sexual activities that are committed with someone other than one's partner and include acts ranging from kissing to sexual intercourse

planning the sequence of actions one develops to attain particular goals

podcast a prerecorded audio program that's posted to a Web site and is made available for download so people can listen to it on personal computers or mobile devices

political economy the ways in which media institutions produce texts in a capitalist system and the legal and regulatory frameworks that shape their options for doing so

political role organizational function in which valued resources and thus power are generated and distributed

polychronically engaging in multiple activities simultaneously

polytheistic belief in more than one god

postmodern approach an approach in which reality is subjective and power is an important issue

postmodernism a broad intellectual and social movement of the late twentieth century

power a person's ability to influence the behavior, thoughts, or feelings of another

power distance a value orientation that refers to the extent to which less-powerful members of institutions and organizations within a culture expect and accept an unequal distribution of power

pragmatics field of study that emphasizes how language is used in specific situations to accomplish goals

precise language the use of language to give more specificity and exactness in communicating

preferred personality a value orientation that expresses whether it is more important for a person to *do* or to *be*

prejudice experiencing aversive or negative feelings toward a group as a whole or toward an individual because she or he belongs to a group

primary groups groups that provide members with a sense of belonging and affection

primary identities identities such as race, ethnicity, and age that have a consistent and enduring impact on your life

primary influence goals goals that are related to the outcome you want to take place

primary tension the uncertainty commonly felt in the beginning phase of decision making

problem-oriented communication messages that convey cooperative spirit, invites others to work together to understand issues

problem-solution or problem-solution-action pattern organizational pattern in which the speaker describes various aspects of a problem and then proposes solutions

production a function of organizational communication in which activity is coordinated toward accomplishing tasks

propositions statements with which you want your audience to agree

professional touch type of touch used by certain workers, such as dentists, hairstylists, and hospice workers, as part of their livelihood; also known as *functional touch*

provisional communication statements that invite alternative views

proxemics the study of how people use spatial cues—including interpersonal distance, territoriality, and other space relationships—to communicate

proximity how close one is to others

pseudoanonymity projecting a false identity

public distance (12 to 25 feet) the distance used for public ceremonies such as lectures and performances

public speaking the process of speaking with a purpose to a group of people in a relatively formal setting

public sphere the arena in which deliberative decision making occurs through the exchange of ideas and arguments

qualitative methods methods in which researchers study naturally occurring communication rather than assembling data and converting it to numbers

quantitative methods methods that convert data to numerical indicators and then analyze these numbers using statistics to establish relationships among the concepts

quid pro quo one of two types of sexual harassment recognized by federal law; requests for sexual favors as a condition of getting or keeping a job or benefit;

racial identity identification with a particular racial group

rape sexual activity that is "against the victim's will/without the victim's consent" and includes some "degree of force or threat" as well as "penetration"

rationality the ability to communicate through reasoning, bargaining, coalition building, and assertiveness

reasoned skepticism the balance of open-mindedness and critical attitude needed when evaluating others' messages

reciprocation a rule that states that we should repay others for what they have given us

reflected appraisals the idea that people's self-images arise primarily from the ways in which others view them and from the many messages they have received from others about who they are

regulating interaction using nonverbal behaviors to help manage turn-taking during conversation

regulators gestures used to control conversation

regulatory use of language to control or regulate the behaviors of others

reinforcement phase the final phase of the decision-making process when group members reach consensus and members feel a sense of accomplishment

relational aggression physical violence against a partner

relational infidelity a severe relational transgression in which one or both partners engage in extra-dyadic behaviors that violate relationship rules of monogamy and exclusivity

relational maintenance behaviors that couples perform that help maintain their relationships

relational resource goals refer to the desire to maintain or increase one's "relational assets"—the emotional support and affection that others provide

relational roles roles that help establish a group's social atmosphere

relational trajectory models relationship development models that view relationship development as more variable than do stage models

relational transgressions takes place when fundamental relationship rules are violated

relational temptations enticements such as flirting and mate poaching from third parties that threaten one's current romantic relationship

relationship challenges a wide range of interactional problems and situations that can threaten the continuance of a relationship

relationship meaning what a message conveys about the relationship between the parties

relationship rules define what is expected and prohibited in specific relationships

relationship threats challenges that are most likely to negatively impact relationships and have serious effects

relative pertaining to the belief that moral behavior varies among individuals, groups, and cultures, as well as across situations

relativists those who argue that language serves not only as a way for us to voice our ideas but "is itself the shaper of ideas, the guide for the individual's mental activity"

relaxation the degree of tension displayed by one's body

religious identity aspect of identity defined by one's spiritual beliefs

Renaissance an era of tremendous intellectual, artistic, and scientific achievements in Europe spanning the fourteenth to the seventeenth centuries

responding showing others how you regard their messages

reverse culture shock/reentry shock culture shock experienced by travelers upon returning to their home countries

rhetor a person or institution that addresses a large audience; the originator of a communication message but not necessarily the one delivering it

rhetoric communication that is used to influence the attitudes or behaviors of others; the art of persuasion

rhetorical analysis used by researchers to examine texts or public speeches as they occur in society, with the aim of interpreting textual meaning

rhetorical audience those people who can take the appropriate action in response to a message

rhetorical critic an informed consumer of rhetorical discourse who is prepared to analyze rhetorical texts

rhetorical event any event that generates a significant amount of public discourse

role expectations the expectation that one will perform in a particular way because of the social role occupied

Sapir-Whorf hypothesis the idea that the language people speak determines the way they see the world (a relativist perspective)

schema cognitive structure that represents an individual's understanding of a concept or person

scientific management approach to management advocated by Frederick Taylor, who believed that there was a best way to complete any task and that rigorous study would help him find it

script a relatively fixed sequence of events that functions as a guide or template for communication or behavior

secondary groups groups that meet principally to solve problems

secondary identities identities such as occupation and marital status that are changeable over the life span and from situation to situation

secondary influence goals goals that constrain or enhance the message individuals use to accomplish their goals

secondary questions questions that follow up on a previous question

secondary (recurring) tension the underlying tension group members experience as they struggle over member roles; it generally surfaces in the second stage, but can reoccur throughout the lifetime on the group

selection the process of choosing which sensory information to focus on

selective attention consciously or unconsciously attending to just a narrow range of the full array of sensory information available

selective exposure the idea that people seek media messages and/or interpret media texts in ways that confirm their beliefs and, conversely, resist or avoid messages that challenge their beliefs

self-concept the understanding of one's unique characteristics as well as the similarities to, and differences from, others

self-esteem part of one's self-concept; arises out of how one perceives and interprets reflected appraisals and social comparisons

self-fulfilling prophecy when an individual expects something to occur, the expectation increases the likelihood that it will

self-respect treating others, and expecting to be treated, with respect and dignity

self-serving bias the tendency to give one's self more credit than is due when good things happen and to accept too little responsibility for those things that go wrong

semantic-information distance describes the gap in information and understanding between supervisors and subordinates on specific issues

semantics the study of meaning

sensing the stage of listening most people refer to as "hearing"; when listeners pick up the sound waves directed toward them

sensory model a model that explains how an individual culture emphasizes a few of the five senses

servant leadership a leadership style that seeks to ensure that other people's highest-priority needs are being served in order to increase teamwork and personal involvement

service-task functions using nonverbal behavior to signal close involvement between people in impersonal relationships and contexts

setting the physical surroundings of a communication event

sexual coercion physically nonviolent pressure to engage in unwanted sex

sexual identity which of the various categories of sexuality one identifies with

shared (collaborative or distributed) leadership a type of leadership style where functional leadership is extended to an organizational level; all members are equal partners and share responsibility for the work of the group

short-term orientation a value orientation that stresses the importance of possessing one fundamental truth

signposts transitions in a speech that help an audience understand the speaker's organization, making it easier for them to follow

similarity degree to which people share the same values, interests, and background

situational couple violence conflict that is characterized by less-intense forms of violence and tends to be more mutual in its performance, although this does not mean that men and women engage in acts of equal severity

small group communication communication among a small number of people who share a common purpose or goal, who feel connected to each other, and who coordinate their behavior

social-class identity an informal ranking of people in a culture based on their income, occupation, education, dwelling, child-rearing habits, and other factors

social distance (4 to 12 feet) the distance most U.S. Americans use when they interact with unfamiliar others

social facilitation the tendency for people to work harder and do better when others are around

social identity the specific identities an individual holds in a society

social influence the ability to influence others, but also to retain the ability to resist others' influence

social movement a large, organized body of people who are attempting to create social change

social network sites (SNSs) Web-based service where people construct their profiles, identify others with whom they share a connection, and interact with people on their lists of connections within the system

social network theory proposes that the patterns of connections among people affect their social behavior and communication

social penetration theory a theory that proposes that relationships develop through increases in self-disclosure

social-polite touch touch that is part of daily interaction in the United States; it is more intimate than professional touch but is still impersonal

social position place in the social hierarchy that comes from the way society is structured

social presence degree of psychological closeness or immediacy engendered by various media

social presence theory theory that suggests that face-to-face communication is generally high in social presence and that media vary in the amount of social presence they convey

social proof influence tactic that relies on the tendency people have to behave in a particular way because others are doing so

social role the specific position or positions one holds in a society

social science approach contemporary term for the behaviorist approach

societal role social function

sophists the people who taught persuasive speaking skills in the Greek city-states

spam unwanted commercial messages and advertisements sent through e-mail

spatial pattern pattern that arranges points by location

speaking rate refers to the speed at which someone speaks

special occasion speech evocative speeches include presentations given at retirement dinners, award ceremonies, weddings, graduations, and funerals

specific purpose what a speaker wants to inform or persuade an audience about, or the type of feelings the speaker wants to evoke

speech act theory branch of pragmatics that suggests that when people communicate, they do not just say things, they also do things with their words

spontaneous communication messages that convey that speaker's talk is unplanned and free of hidden motives

spoofing misrepresenting oneself online

stable exchange stage in which relational partners engage in the greatest breadth and depth of self-disclosure

stage model a type of model that conceptualizes relationship development as occurring in a stair-step fashion, with some stages leading toward commitment and other stages leading toward dissolution

stagnating stage of romantic relational dissolution in which couples try to prevent change

statement of fact presents something that is either correct or incorrect and can be verified with evidence

statement of policy presents a specific action or policy

statement of value presents something as either right or wrong

statistics numerical data that highlight the size of a problem or help when making comparisons

stereotype threat process in which reminding individuals of stereotypical expectations regarding important identities can impact their performance

stereotyping creating schemas that overgeneralize attributes of a specific group

stonewalling occurs when one or both partners stop communicating, refuse to respond to each other's communication efforts, and withdraw from interaction; the fourth of Gottman's "four horsemen"

strategic communication in leadership contexts, positive communication that is purpose directed—it directs everyone's attention toward the vision, values, and desired outcomes and persuades people to act in a way that helps to achieve the leadership vision

strategic (manipulative) communication in interpersonal and small group contexts, negative messages suggesting that speaker is trying to manipulate others

strategy control behaving mindfully, assessesing information and options, and acquiring increased understanding of the conflict and the partner

structure lines of communication, or a system of pathways, through which messages flow

style the type of language and phrasing a speaker uses and the effect it creates

style theory theory that asserts that a leader's manner or style determines his or her success

stylistic devices figures of speech and tropes that are used to shape the style of a message

sudden death the process by which relationships end without prior warning for at least one participant

superiority-focused communication messages conveying that the speaker is superior and the other is inadequate

supportive communication comments that encourage open, honest and constructive interaction

supportive listening listening skills focused not only on understanding information but also on "listening" to others' feelings

supporting materials information that supports the speaker's ideas

sweeping generalization a logical fallacy that assumes that what is true of the whole will also be true of the part or that what is true in most instances will be true in all instances

symbol something that represents something else and conveys meaning

synchronous communication in which messages are sent and received at the same time

syntax the rules that govern word order

task roles roles that are directly related to the accomplishment of group goals

technocapital access to technological skills and resources

terminating stage of romantic relational dissolution in which couples end the relationship

textual analysis similar to rhetorical analysis; used to analyze cultural "products" such as media and public speeches

theory a set of statements that explains a particular phenomenon

thesis statement a statement of the topic of a speech and the speaker's position on it

time and motion studies repeated measurements of detailed task variables to determine their most efficient combination

time-oriented listening style a listening style that prefers brief, concise speech

tone the mood or feeling the speaker creates

topical pattern an organizational pattern arranged by main points or topics and presented in the order that seems most suitable

toxic leadership leadership behavior that poisons and is disruptive, destructive, exploitative, dysfunctional, and abusive

trait theory leadership theory that suggests leaders are born

transformational leadership theory a leadership style that empowers group members to work independently from the leader by encouraging group cohesion

transitions words, phrases, or sentences that show the connection between the points in your speech and help your audience understand your organization

truth bias the tendency to not suspect one's intimates of deception

turning point model a model of relationship development in which couples move both toward and away from commitment over the course of their relationship

TV Parental Guidelines a self-regulating system of the television industry that rates programs in terms of appropriateness for particular age groups

tweets text-based updates of 140 characters or less sent through social networking and microblogging services

uncertainty reduction theory theory that argues that much early interaction is dedicated to reducing uncertainty about others and determining if one wishes to interact with them again

understanding interpreting the messages associated with sounds or what the sounds mean

unintentional messages messages that are not intended to hurt the recipient

unwanted sex occurs when one person does not want to have sexual relations but does so without the offender exerting physical force or threats

upward communication in a traditional conduit model of communication, communication with superiors

upward distortion occurs when subordinates are hesitant to communicate negative news and therefore present information to superiors in a more positive light than is warranted

urgent organizations companies that try to shorten the time it takes to develop new products and respond to customer demands

uses and gratifications the idea that people use media messages and find various types of gratifications in some media texts rather than in others

value-expressive function the role played by prejudice in allowing people to view their own values, norms, and cultural practices as appropriate and correct

V-chip device that identifies television program ratings by content and can block programming designated by the owner

view of human nature a value orientation that expresses whether humans are fundamentally good, evil, or a mixture of both

violent resistance occurs when a partner (most typically a female) fights back against the person terrorizing him or her

virtual work team a group of people identified as a team by their organization and responsible for making decisions important to the organization; it may be culturally diverse, geographically dispersed, and have members who communicate electronically substantially more often than face-to-face

visual aids audiovisual materials that help a speaker reach intended speech goals

vocal variety the variation in tone, rate, and pauses you use in speaking

vocal projection the relative strength or weakness of someone's ability to speak loudly enough for an audience in a given context

vocalizations uttered sounds that do not have the structure of language

voice qualities qualities such as speed, pitch, rhythm, vocal range, and articulation that make up the "music" of the human voice

voluntary long-term travelers people who are border dwellers by choice and for an extended time, such as immigrants

voluntary short-term travelers people who are border dwellers by choice and for a limited time, such as study-abroad students or corporate personnel

weapons of influence the six ways in which Cialdini's "click, whirr" response is triggered

withdrawal/avoidance a friendship-termination strategy in which friends spend less time together, don't return phone calls, and avoid places where they are likely to see each other

World Wide Web (WWW) one of a number of services that moves over the Internet; it uses HTML (hypertext markup language) as its document format

yielding or accomodating style a conflict style that entails a low concern for self and a high concern for the other person

REFERENCES

Chapter 1

Alberts, J. K., Yoshimura, C. G., Rabby, M. K., & Loschiavo, R. (2005). Mapping the topography of couples' daily interaction. *Journal of Social and Personal Relationships, 22,* 299–323.

Andersen, P. A., Lustig, M. W., & Andersen, J. F. (1990). Changes in latitude, changes in attitude: The relationship between climate and interpersonal communication predispositions. *Communication Quarterly, 38,* 291–311.

Barnlund, D. C. (1962). Consistency of emergent leadership in groups with changing tasks and members. *Speech Monographs, 29,* 45–52.

Brewer, M., & Miller, N. (1996). *Intergroup relations.* Pacific Grove, CA: Brooks/Cole.

Buck, R., & VanLear, C. A. (2002). Verbal and nonverbal communication: Distinguishing symbolic, spontaneous and pseudo-spontaneous nonverbal behavior. *Journal of Communication, 52,* 522–541.

Buller, D. B., & Burgoon, J. K. (1996). Interpersonal deception theory. *Communication Theory, 6,* 203–242.

Christians, C., & Traber, M. (Eds.). (1997). *Communication ethics and universal values.* Thousand Oaks, CA: Sage.

Dickens, T. E. (2003). General symbol machines: The first stage in the evolution of symbolic communication. *Evolutionary Psychology, 1,* 192–209.

Diener, M. (2002, January). Fair enough: To be a better negotiator, learn to tell the difference between a lie and a *lie. Entrepreneur Magazine.* Retrieved March 16, 2006, from www.Entrepreneurmagagzine.com

Dixon, M., & Duck, S. W. (1993). Understanding relationship processes: Uncovering the human search for meaning. In S. W. Duck (Ed.), *Understanding relationship processes, Vol. 1: Individuals in relationships* (pp. 175–206). Newbury Park, CA: Sage.

Duck, S. (1994). *Meaningful relationships: Talking, sense and relating.* Newbury Park, CA: Sage.

Eisenberg, E. M., & Goodall, H. L. Jr. (1997). *Organizational communication: Balancing creativity and constraints.* New York: St. Martin's.

Emanuel, R. (2007). Humanities: Communication's core discipline. *American Communication Journal, 9*(2). Retrieved March 11, 2009, from http://www.acjournal.org/holdings/vol9/summer/articles/discipline.html

Gergen, K. J. (1982). *Toward transformation in social knowledge.* New York: Springer.

Holy Bible, King James Version. (n.d.). Exodus 4:14–16. Retrieved December 30, 2009, from http://www.online-literature.com/bible/bible.php

Jaksa, J. A., & Pritchard, M. S. (1994). *Communication ethics: Methods of analysis* (2nd ed.). Belmont, CA: Wadsworth.

Johannesen, R. (1990). *Ethics in human communication.* Prospect Heights, IL: Waveland.

Kant, I. (1949). *Fundamental principles of the metaphysic of morals* (T. K. Abbott, Trans.). Indianapolis, IN: Bobbs-Merrill. (Original work published 1785).

Kruger, P. (1999, June). A leader's journey. *Fast Company,* 116–138.

Laswell, H. D. (1948). The structure and function of communication in society. In L. Bryson (Ed.), *The communication of ideas.* New York: Harper.

Long, R., & Pearson, R. (2009, January 30). Impeached Illinois Governor Rod Blagojevich has been removed from office. *Chicago Tribune Online.* Retrieved March 11, 2009, from http://www.chicagotribune.com/news/local/chi-blagojevich-impeachment-removal,0,5791846.story

Martin, J. N., & Nakayama, T. K. (2005). *Experiencing intercultural communication* (2nd ed.). Boston: McGraw-Hill.

McCabe, D. L., & Trevino, L. K. (1996). What we know about cheating in college: Longitudinal trends and recent developments. *Change, 28,* 28–33.

McCord, L. B., Greenhalgh, K., & Magasin, M. (2004). Businesspersons beware: Lying is a crime. *Graziadio Business Report, 7*(23). Pepperdine University. Retrieved December 30, 2009, from http://gbr.pepperdine.edu/043/lying.html

McCornack, S. A., & Parks, M. R. (1986). Deception detection and relationship development: The other side of trust. In M. L. McLaughlin (Ed.), *Communication Yearbook 9* (pp. 377–389). Newbury Park, CA: Sage. Retrieved March 16, 2006, from www.natcom.org/policies/External/EthicalComm

Mead, G. H. (1934). *Mind, self, and society.* Chicago: University of Chicago Press.

National Communication Association (2003). What is communication? *Pathways.* Retrieved October 24, 2008, from www.natcom.org/nca/Template2.asp?bid=339

Poole, M. S., & Walther, J. B. (2001). *Report of National Communication Association/National Science Foundation funded symposium.* Retrieved March 11, 2009, from www.natcom.org/nca/Template2.asp?bid=394

Robinson-Smith, G. (2004). Verbal indicators of depression in conversations with stroke survivors. *Perspectives in Psychiatric Care, 40,* 61–69.

Roloff, M. E., & Cloven, D. H. (1990). The chilling effect in interpersonal relationships. In D. D. Cahn (Ed.), *Intimates in conflict* (pp. 49–76). Hillsdale, NJ: Erlbaum.

Sartre, J. P. (1973). *Existentialism and humanism* (P. Mairet, Trans.). London: Methuen Ltd. (Original work published 1946).

Schirato, T., & Yell, S. (1996). *Communication & cultural literacy: An introduction.* St. Leonards, Australia: Allen & Unwin.

Shannon, C. E., & Weaver, W. (1949). *A mathematical model of communication.* Urbana, IL: University of Illinois Press.

Tolhuizen, J. H. (1990, November). *Deception in developing dating relationships.* Paper presented at the Speech Communication Association Convention, Chicago, IL.

Verschoor, C. C. (September, 2005). AIG remediation emphasizes compliance but not ethics. *Strategic Finance*. Retrieved March 11, 2009, from www.imanet.org/pdf/3291.pdf

Warren, S. F., & Yoder, P. J. (1998). Facilitating the transition from preintentional to intentional communication. In A. M. Wetherby, S. F. Warren, & J. Reichle (Eds.), *Transitions in prelinguistic communication* (pp. 365–385). Baltimore, MD: Paul H. Brookes.

Watzlawick, P., Beavin, J., & Jackson, D. D. (1967). *Pragmatics of human communication*. New York: W. W. Norton.

Wokutch, R. E., & Carson, T. L. (1981). The ethics and profitability of bluffing in business. In R. J. Lewickis, D. M. Saunders, & J. W. Minton (Eds.), *Negotiation: Readings, exercises, and cases* (pp. 341–353). Boston: Irwin/McGraw-Hill.

Chapter 2

Abrams, J., O'Connor, J., & Giles, H. (2002). Identity and intergroup communication. In W. B. Gudykunst & B. Mody (Eds.), *Handbook of international and intercultural communication* (2nd ed., pp. 225–240). Thousand Oaks, CA: Sage.

Allen, B. (2004). *Difference matters: Communicating social identity*. Long Grove, IL: Waveland.

Azuri, L. (2006, November 3). Public debate in Saudi Arabia on employment opportunities for women. *Inquiry and Analysis, 299*. Retrieved from http://www.memri.org/bin/headlines.cgi?Rank=201&type=ia

Ballen, S. (2007, February 23). The myth of Muslim support for terrorism. *The Christian Science Monitor*. Retrieved December 29, 2009, from http://www.csmonitor.com/2007/0223/p09s01-coop.html

Blumer, H. (1969). *Symbolic interactionism: Perspective and method*. Englewood Cliffs, NJ: Prentice Hall.

Braithwaite, C. (1990). Communicative silence: A cross-cultural study of Basso's hypothesis. In D. Carbaugh (Ed.), *Cultural communication and intercultural contact* (pp. 321–327). Hillsdale, NJ: Lawrence Erlbaum Associates.

Brislin, R. (2000). *Understanding culture's influence on behavior* (2nd ed.). Belmont, CA: Wadsworth.

Bruner, J. S. (1958). Neural mechanisms in perception. *Research Publication of the Association for Research in Nervous and Mental Disease, 36*, 118–143.

Bruner, J. (1991). *Acts of meaning*. Cambridge, MA: Harvard University Press.

Burgoon, J. K., Berger, C. R., & Waldron, V. R. (2000). Mindfulness and interpersonal communication. *Journal of Social Issues, 56*, 105–127.

CBS News. (2009, April 27). *Poll: Blacks see improved race relations*. Retrieved from http://www.cbsnews.com/stories/2009/04/27/opinion/polls/main4972532.shtml

Condon, J. C. (1984). *With respect to the Japanese*. Yarmouth, ME: Intercultural Press.

Cooley, C. H. (1902). *Human nature and the social order*. New York, NY: Scribner's.

Chaiken, S. (1986). Physical appearance and social influence. In C. P. Herman, M. P. Zanna, & E. T. Higgins (Eds.), *Physical appearance, stigma, and social behavior: The Ontario Symposium* (Vol. 3, pp. 143–144). Hillsdale, NJ: Erlbaum.

Classen, C. (1990). Sweet colors, fragrant songs: Sensory models of the Andes and the Amazon. *American Ethnologist, 14*, 722–735.

Classen, C., Howes, D., & Synnott, A. (1994). *Aroma: The cultural history of smell*. London: Routledge.

Croizet, J. C., & Claire, T. (1998). Extending the concept of stereotype threat to social class: The intellectual underperformance of students from low socioeconomic backgrounds. *Personality and Social Psychology Bulletin, 24*, 588–594.

Danghel, E. (1996). The symbolism of smell. *Psychiatria Hungarica, 11*, 683–692.

Davies, R. J., & Ikeno, O. (2002). *The Japanese mind: Understanding contemporary Japanese. Boston, MA: Tuttle Publishing.

De Jong, P. F., Koomen, W., & Mellenbergh, G. J. (1988). Structure of causes for success and failure: A multidimensional scaling analysis of preference judgments. *Journal of Personality and Social Psychology, 55*, 718–725.

Dijk, T. A. van (1977). Context and cognition: Knowledge frames and speech act comprehension. *Journal of Pragmatics, 1*(3), 211–231.

Douglas, W. (1990). Uncertainty, information-seeking, and liking during initial interaction. *Western Journal of Speech Communication, 54*, 66–81.

Douthat, R. (2005). *Privilege: Harvard and the education of the ruling class*. New York, NY: Hyperion

Edwards, R. (1990). Sensitivity to feedback and the development of the self. *Communication Quarterly, 38*, 101–111.

Erickson, A. L. (1993). *Women and property in early modern England*. New York, NY: Routledge.

Estroff, H. (2004, Sep/Oct). Cupid's comeuppance. *Psychology Today*. Retrieved March 15, 2006, from http://www.psychologytoday.com/articles/pto-20040921-000001.html

Fehr, B. (1993). How do I love thee: Let me consult my prototype. In S. W. Duck (Ed.), *Understanding relationship processes 1: Individuals in relationships* (pp. 87–122). Newbury Park, CA: Sage.

Fisher, K. (1997). Locating frames in the discursive universe. *Sociological Research Online*, vol. 2, no. 3. Retrieved from http://www.socresonline.org.uk/socresonline/2/3/4.html

Fiske, S. T., & Taylor, S. E. (1991). *Social cognition* (2nd ed.). New York: McGraw Hill.

Gavetti, G., & Levinthal, D. (2000, March). Looking forward and looking backward: Cognition and experiential search. *Administrative Science Quarterly, 45*, 1–9.

Greenough, W. T., Black, J. E., & Wallace, C. S. (1987). Experience and brain development. *Child Development, 58*, 539–559.

Griffin, E. (1994). *A first look at communication theory*. New York, NY: McGraw-Hill.

Hacker, A. (2003). *Two nations: Black & White, hostile, separate and unequal*. New York, NY: Scribner.

Harwood, J. (2006). Communication as social identity. In G. J. Shepherd, J. St. John, & T. Striphas (Eds.), *Communication as: Perspectives on theory* (pp. 84–90). Thousand Oaks, CA: Sage.

Hecht, M. L. (1993). 2002—A research odyssey. *Communication Monographs, 60*, 76–82.

Hecht, M. L., Jackson, R. L. III, & Ribeau, S. A. (2003). *African American communication: Exploring identity and culture* (2nd ed.). Mahwah, NJ: Lawrence Erlbaum Associates.

Heider, F. (1958). *The psychology of interpersonal relations*. New York, NY: Wiley.

Heine, S. J., & Lehman, D. R. (2004). Move the body, change the self: Acculturative effects on self-concept. In A. Schaller & C. Crandall (Eds.), *The psychological foundations of culture* (pp. 305–31). Hillsdale, NJ: Erlbaum.

Herz, R. S., & Inzlicht, M. (2002). Sex differences in response to physical and social factors involved in human mate selection: The importance of smell for women. *Evolution and Human Behavior, 23,* 359–364.

Imbornoni, M. (2008). Women's rights movement in the U. S. *Timeline of key events in the American women's rights movement, 1848–1920.* Retrieved from http://www.infoplease.com/spot/womenstimeline1.html

Johnson, A. G. (2001). *Privilege, power and difference*. Boston, MA: McGraw-Hill.

Kanizsa, G. (1979). *Organization in vision*. New York, NY: Praeger.

Kelley, H. H. (1973). The processes of causal attribution. *American Psychologist, 28,* 107–128.

Kim, M. S. (2002). *Non-Western perspectives on human communication*. Thousand Oaks, CA: Sage.

Kimmel, M. S. (2005). *The history of men: Essays in the history of American and British masculinities*. Albany, NY: State University of New York Press.

Kirouac, G., & Hess, U. (1999). Group membership and the decoding of nonverbal behavior. In R. S. Feldman, & P. Philippot (Eds.), *The social context of nonverbal behavior* (pp.182–210). New York, NY: Cambridge University Press.

Kraybill, D. B. (1989). *The riddle of Amish culture*. Baltimore, MD: Johns Hopkins University Press.

Krivonos, P. D., & Knapp, M. L. (1975). Initiating communication: What do you say when you say hello? *Central States Speech Journal, 26,* 115–125.

Lakoff, G. (1987). *Women, fire, and dangerous things: What categories reveal about the mind*. Chicago, IL: University of Chicago Press.

Langer, E. J. (1978). Rethinking the role of thought in social interaction. In J. H. Harvey, W. Ickes, & R. F. Kidd (Eds.), *New directions in attribution research* (Vol. 2, pp. 3–58). New York, NY: Wiley.

Link, B. G., & Phelan, J. C. (2001, 5-7 September). *On stigma and its public health implications*. Paper presented at the conference Stigma and Global Health: Developing a Research Agenda, Bethesda, MD. The complete proceedings of the conference are available at: http://www.stigmaconference.nih.gov/

Lupfer, M. B., Weeks, M., & Dupuis, S. (2000). How pervasive is the negativity bias in judgments based on character appraisal? *Personality and Social Psychology Bulletin, 26,* 1353–1366.

Markus, H. R., Mullally, P. R., & Kitayama, S. (1997). Selfways: Diversity in modes of cultural participation. In U. Neisser & D. A. Jopling (Eds.), *The conceptual self in context* (pp. 13–59). Cambridge, UK: Cambridge University Press.

Martin, J. N., & Harrell, T. (1996). Reentry training for intercultural sojourners. In D. Landis & R. S. Bhagat (Eds.). *Handbook of intercultural training* (2nd ed.), (pp. 307–326). Thousand Oaks, CA: Sage.

McGlone, M. S., & Aronson, J. (2006). Stereotype threat, identity salience and spatial reasoning. *Journal of Applied Developmental Psychology, 27*(5), 486–493.

Mead, G. H. (1934). *Mind, self, and society*. Chicago, IL: University of Chicago Press.

Morgan, M. J. (1977). *Molyneux's question: Vision, touch and the philosophy of perception*. Cambridge, UK; New York, NY: Cambridge University Press, 1977.

Neale, M., & Bazerman, M. (1991), *Cognition and rationality in negotiation*. New York, NY, Free Press.

Papalia, D., Gross, D., & Feldman, R. (2002). *Child development*. New York, NY: McGraw Hill.

Pearce, W. B. (1994). *Interpersonal communication: Making social worlds*. New York: HarperCollins.

Putnam, L. L., & Holmer, M.. Framing, reframing and issue development. In L. Putnam & M. Holmer (Eds.) *Communication and Negotiation* (pp. 128–155). Newbury Park: Sage Publications, 1992.

Rosenblith, J. F. (1992). *In the beginning: Development from conception to age two*. Newbury Park, CA: Sage.

Ross, L. (1977). The intuitive psychologist and his shortcomings: Distortions in the attribution process. In L. Berkowitz (Ed.), *Advances in experimental social psychology* (Vol. 10, pp. 173–220). New York, NY: Academic Press.

Roth, M. (2005). *The left stuff: How the left-handed have thrived and survived in a right-handed world*. New York, NY: M. Evans and Co.

Rothenberg, P. S. (1992). *Racism and sexism: An integrated study*. New York, NY: Macmillan.

Sanders, W. B. (1994). *Gangbangs and drive-bys: Grounded culture and juvenile gang violence*. New York, NY: Aldine de Gruyter.

Scollon, R., & Wong-Scollon, S. (1990). Athabaskan-English interethnic communication. In D. Carbaugh (Ed.), *Cultural communication and intercultural contact* (pp. 259–287). Hillsdale, NJ: Erlbaum.

Shih, M., Pittinsky, T. L., & Ambady, N. (1999). Stereotype susceptibility: Identity salience, and shifts in quantitative performance. *Psychological Science, 10*(1), 80–83.

Shore, B. (1996). *Culture in mind: Cognition, culture and the problem of meaning*. New York, NY: Oxford University Press.

Smith, J. L., & White, P. H. (2002). An examination of implicitly activated, explicitly activated and nullified stereotypes on mathematical performance: It's not just a women's issue. *Sex Roles, 47*(3/4), 179–191.

Spitzberg, B. (2001). The status of attribution theory qua theory in personal relationships. In V. Manusov & J. H. Harvey (Eds.), *Attribution, communication behavior and close relationships*. Cambridge, UK: Cambridge University Press.

Steele, C. M., & Aronson, J. (1995). Stereotype threat and the academic performance of African Americans. *Journal of Personality and Social Psychology, 69*(5), 797–811.

Stephan, C., & Stephan, W. (1992). Reducing intercultural anxiety through intercultural contact. *International Journal of Intercultural Relations, 16,* 89–106.

Sullivan, H. S. (1953). *The interpersonal theory of psychology*. New York, NY: Norton.

Ting-Toomey, S. (1999). Face and facework. In J. Mio, J. Trimble, P. Arredondo, H. Cheatham, D. Sue (Eds.), *Key words in multicultural interventions* (pp.125–127). Westport: Greenwood Press.

U. S. Census Bureau (2006, February 22). Facts for features: Women's History Month March 2006. Retrieved March 28, 2010 from http://www.census.gov/Press-Release/www/releases/archives/facts_for_features_special_editions/006232.html

Weick, K. (1995). *Sensemaking in organizations*. Thousand Oaks, CA: Sage.

Wilson, G., & Nias, D. (1999). Beauty can't be beat. In J. A. DeVito & L. Guerrero, (Eds.), *The nonverbal communication reader: Classic and contemporary readings* (2nd ed., pp. 92–132). Prospect Heights, IL: Waveland.

Chapter 3

The American Heritage Dictionary of the English Language (4th ed.). (2000). Boston, MA: Houghton-Mifflin. Retrieved June 12, 2006, from http://www.bartleby.com/cgibin/texis/webinator/ahdsearch?search_type=enty&query=wise&db=ahd&submit=Search

Aries, E. (1996). *Men and women in interaction: Reconsidering the differences*. New York, NY: Oxford University Press.

Austin, J. L. (1975). *How to do things with words* (2nd ed.). Cambridge, MA: Harvard University Press.

Becker, J. A. H., Halbesleben, J. R. B., & O'Hair, H. D. (2005). Defensive communication and burnout in the workplace: The mediating role of leader-member exchange. *Communication Research Reports, 22*(2), 143–150.

Bippus, A. M., & Young, S. L. (2005). Owning your emotions: Reactions to expressions of self-versus other-attributed positive and negative emotions. *Journal of Applied Communication Research, 33*, 26–45.

Bowen, S. P. (2003). Jewish and/or woman: Identity and communicative styles. In A. Gonzalez, M. Houston, & V. Chen (Eds.), *Our voices: Essays in culture, ethnicity, and communication* (4th ed.). Los Angeles, CA: Roxbury.

Boxer, D. (2002). Nagging: The familial conflict arena. *Journal of Pragmatics, 34*, 49–61.

Canary, D. J., & Hause, K. S. (1993). Is there any reason to research sex difference in communication? *Communication Quarterly, 41*, 129–144.

Caughlin, J. P. (2002). The demand/withdraw pattern of communication as a predictor of marital satisfaction over time: Unresolved issues and future directions. *Human Communication Research, 28*, 49–85.

Coltri, L. S. (2004). *Conflict diagnosis and alternative dispute resolution*. Upper Saddle River, NJ: Prentice Hall.

Crystal, D. (2003). *The Cambridge encyclopedia of the English language*. New York, NY: Cambridge University Press.

Dance, F. E. X., & Larson, C. E. (1976). *The functions of human communication*. New York, NY: Holt, Rinehart, & Winston.

Duke, M. P., Fivush, R., Lazarus, A. & Bohanek, J. (2003). *Of ketchup and kin: Dinnertime conversations as a major source of family knowledge, family adjustment, and family resilience*. The Emory Center for Myth and Ritual in American Life. Working Paper No. 26. Retrieved March 25, 2010, from http://www.marial.emory.edu/pdfs/Duke_Fivush027-03.pdf.

Eadie, W. F. (1982). Defensive communication revisited: A critical examination of Gibb's theory. *Southern Speech Communication Journal, 47*, 163–177.

Edwards, J. V. (2004). Foundations of bilingualism. In T. K. Bhatia & W. C. Ritchie (Eds.), *The handbook of bilingualism* (pp. 7–31). Malden, MA: Blackwell.

Ellis, A., & Beattie, G. (1986). The language channel. *The psychology of language* (pp. 53–77). New York, NY: Guilford.

Fromkin, V., & Rodman, R. (1983). *An introduction to language*. New York, NY: Holt, Rinehart, & Winston.

Garvin-Doxas, K. & Barker, L. J. (2004). Communication in computer science classrooms: Understanding defensive climates as a means of creating supportive behaviors. *ACM Journal of Educational Resources in Computing, 4*(1), 1–18.

Gibb, J. R. (1961). Defensive communication. *Journal of Communication 11*(3), 141–148.

Gong, G. (2004). When Mississippi Chinese talk. In A. González, M. Houston, & V. Chen (Eds.), *Our voices: Essays in culture, ethnicity, and communication* (4th ed.). Los Angeles, CA: Roxbury.

Hegarty, P., & Buechel, C. (2006). Androcentric reporting of gender differences in APA journals: 1965–2004. *Review of General Psychology, 10*(4), 377–389.

Hoijer, H. (1994). The Sapir-Whorf hypothesis. In L. Samovar & R. E. Porter (Eds.), *Intercultural communication: A reader* (pp. 194–200). Belmont, CA: Wadsworth.

Hudson, R. A. (1983). *Sociolinguistics*. London, UK: Cambridge University Press.

Hyde, J. S. (2006). Gender similarities still rule. *American Psychologist, 61*(6), 641–642.

Jacobson, C. (2008). Some notes on gender-neutral language. Retrieved May 23, 2008 from http://www.english.upenn.edu/~cjacobso/gender.html

Kenneally, C. (2008, April 22). When language can hold the answer. *The New York Times*, p. F1.

Kikoski, J. F., & Kikoski, C. K. (1999). *Reflexive communication in the culturally diverse workplace*. Westport, CT: Praeger.

Kim, M. S. (2002). *Non-Western perspectives on human communication*. Thousand Oaks, CA: Sage.

Kohonen, S. (2004). Turn-taking in conversation: Overlaps and interruptions in intercultural talk. *Cahiers, 10.1*, 15–32.

Krieger, L. (2004, February 26). Like, what dew you mean, that-ty I hav-yvee an accent? *Detroit Free Press*, p. 16A.

Kubany, E. S., Bauer, G. B., Muraoka, M., Richard, D. C., & Read, P. (1995). Impact of labeled anger and blame in intimate relationships. *Journal of Social and Clinical Psychology, 14*, 53–60.

Labov, W. (1980). The social origins of sound change. In W. Labov (Ed.), *Locating language in time and space* (pp. 251–265). New York, NY: Academic Press.

Labov, W. (Ed.). (2005). *Atlas of North American English*. New York, NY: Walter De Gruyter.

Leaper, C., & Ayres, M. M. (2007). A meta-analytic review of gender variation in adults' language use: Talkativeness, affiliative speech, and assertive speech. *Personality and Social Psychology Review, 11*(4), 328–363.

Mehl, M. R., & Pennebaker, J. W. (2003). The sounds of social life: A psychometric analysis of students' daily social environments and natural conversations. *Journal of Personality and Social Psychology, 84,* 857–70.

Mey, J. L. (2001). *Pragmatics: An introduction* (2nd ed.). Oxford, UK: Blackwell Publishing.

Mulac, A., Bradac. J. J., & Gibbons, P. (2001). Empirical support for the gender-as-culture hypothesis: An intercultural analysis of male/female language differences. *Human Communication Research, 27,* 121–152,

Nofsinger, R. (1999). *Everyday conversation.* Prospect Heights, IL: Waveland.

Orbe, M. P. (1998). *Constructing co-cultural theory: An explication of culture, power, and communication.* Thousand Oaks, CA: Sage.

Paramasivam, S. (2007). Managing disagreement while managing not to disagree: Polite disagreement in negotiation discourse. *Journal of Intercultural Communication Research, 36*(2), 91–116.

Pennebaker, J. W., & Stone, L. D. (2003). Words of wisdom: Language use across the life span. *Journal of Personality and Social Psychology, 82,* 291–301.

Philips, S. U. (1990). Some sources of cultural variability in the regulation of talk. In D. Carbaugh (Ed.), *Cultural communication and intercultural contact* (pp. 329–344). Hillsdale, NJ: Erlbaum.

Piaget, J. (1952). *The origins of intelligence in children.* New York, NY: International Universities Press.

Pinker, S. (2007). *The stuff of thought: Language as a window into human nature.* New York, NY: Viking.

Pinto, D., & Raschio, R. (2007). A comparative study of requests in heritage-speaker Spanish, L1 Spanish, and L1 English. *International Journal of Bilingualism, 11*(2), 135–155.

Preston, D. R. (2003). Where are the dialects of American English at anyhow? *American Speech, 78,* 235–254.

Ramírez-Esparza, N., Gosling, S. D., Benet-Martínez, V., Potter, J. D., & Pennebaker, J. W. (2006). Do bilinguals have two personalities? A special case of cultural frame switching. *Journal of Research in Personality, 40,* 99–120.

Reid, S. A., Keerie, N., & Palomares, N. A. (2003). Language, gender salience, and social influence. *Journal of Language and Social Psychology, 22,* 210–233.

Rose, C. (1995). Bargaining and gender. *Harvard Journal of Law and Public Policy, 18,* 547–65.

Ruben, D. L. (2003). Help! My professor (or doctor or boss) doesn't talk English! In J. N. Martin, T. K. Nakayama, & L. A. Flores (Eds.), *Readings in intercultural communication* (2nd ed., pp. 127–138). Boston, MA: McGraw-Hill.

Sagrestano, L. M., Heavey, C. L., & Christensen, A. (1998). Theoretical approaches to understanding sex differences and similarities in conflict behavior. In D. J. Canary & K. Dindia (Eds.), *Sex differences and similarities in communication: Critical essays and empirical investigations on sex and gender in interaction* (pp. 287–302). Mahwah, NJ: Erlbaum.

Sbisa, M. (2002). Speech act in context. *Language & Communication, 22,* 421–436.

Schegloff, E. A. (2006). Interaction: The infrastructure for social institutions, the natural ecological niche for language, and the arena in which culture is enacted. In N. J. Enfield & S. C. Levinson (Eds.), *Roots of human sociality: Culture, cognition, and interaction* (pp. 70–96). Oxford, UK: Berg.

Schegloff, E. A. (2000). Overlapping talk and the organization of turn-taking for conversation. *Language in Society, 29,* 1–63.

Scheibel, D. (1995). Making waves with Burke: Surf Nazi culture and the rhetoric of localism. *Western Journal of Communication, 59*(4), 253–69.

Shutiva, C. (2004). Native American culture and communication through humor. In A. Gonzalez, M. Houston, & V. Chen (Eds.), *Our voices: Essays in culture, ethnicity, and communication* (4th ed.). Los Angeles, CA: Roxbury.

Sellers, J. G., Woolsey, M. D., & Swann, J. B. (2007). Is silence more golden for women than men? Observers derogate effusive women and their quiet partners. *Sex Roles, 57*(7–8), 477–482. http://www.reuters.com/article/domesticNews/idUSN20435403 20080321

Weger, H. Jr. (2005). Disconfirming communication and self-verification in marriage: Associations among the demand/withdraw interaction pattern, feeling understood, and marital satisfaction. *Journal of Social and Personal Relationships, 22,* 19–31.

Wiest, L. R., Abernathy, T. V., Obenchain, K. M., & Major, E. M. (2006). Researcher study thyself: AERA participants' speaking times and turns by gender. *Equity & Excellence in Education, 39*(4), 313–323.

Wolfram, W., Adger, C. T., & Christian, D. (1999). *Dialects in schools and communities.* Mahwah, NJ: Erlbaum.

Wood, J. T. (2002). *Gendered lives: Communication, gender and cultures.* Belmont, CA: Wadsworth.

Chapter 4

Argyle, M. (1969). *Social interaction.* London: Methuen.

Axtell, R. (1993). *Do's and taboos around the world.* New York, NY: Wiley.

Becker, F. D. (1973). Study of special markers. *Journal of Personality and Social Psychology, 26,* 429–445.

Birdwhistle, R. L. (1970). *Kinesics and context.* Philadelphia, PA: University of Pennsylvania Press.

Burgoon, J. K., Buller, D. B., & Woodall, W. G. (1996). *Nonverbal communication: The unspoken dialogue.* New York, NY: Harper & Row.

Burgoon, J. K., & Guerrero, L. K. (1994). Nonverbal communication. In M. Burgoon, F. G. Hunsaker, & E. J. Dawson (Eds.), *Human communication* (pp. 122–171). Thousand Oaks, CA: Sage.

Burgoon, J. K., & Hale, J. L. (1988). Nonverbal expectancy violations: Model elaboration and application to immediacy behaviors. *Communication Monographs, 55,* 58–79.

Burgoon, J. K., & LePoire, B. A. (1993). Effects of communication expectancies, actual communication, and expectancy

disconfirmation on evaluations of communicators and their communication behavior. *Human Communication Research, 20,* 67–96.

Capella, J. (1985). The management of conversations. In M. L. Knapp & G. R. Miller (Eds.), *Handbook of interpersonal communication* (pp. 393–435). Beverly Hills, CA: Sage.

Carvajal, D. (2006, February 7). Primping for the cameras in the name of research. *The New York Times.* Retrieved, Feb. 23, 2006, from http://www.nytimes.com/2006/02/07/business/07hair.html?ex=1139979600&en=f5f94cb9d81a9fa8&ei=5070&emc=eta1

Chiang, L. H. (1993, October). *Beyond the language: Native Americans' nonverbal communication.* Paper presented at the Annual Meeting of the Midwest Association of Teachers of Educational Psychology, Anderson, IN: October 1–2.

Cicca, A. H., Step, M., & Turkstra, L. (2003, December 16). Show me what you mean: Nonverbal communication theory and application. *ASHA Leader,* pp. 4–5, 34.

Crane, D. (2000). *Fashion and its social agendas: Class, gender and identity in clothing.* Chicago, IL: University of Chicago Press.

Duke, L. (2002). Get real! Cultural relevance and resistance to the mediated feminine ideal. *Psychology and Marketing, 19,* 211–234.

Eibl-Eibesfeld, I. (1972). Similarities and differences between cultures in expressive movement. In R. A. Hinde (Ed.), *Nonverbal communication* (pp. 297–314). Cambridge, MA: Cambridge University Press.

Ekman, P. (2003). *Emotions revealed: Recognizing faces and feelings to improve communication and emotional life.* New York, NY: Times Books.

Ekman, P., & Friesen, W. V. (1969). The repertoire of nonverbal behavior: Categories, origins, usage and coding. *Semiotica, 1,* 49–98.

Ekman, P., & Friesen, W. V. (1986). A new pan-cultural expression of emotion. *Motivation and Emotion, 10*(2), 159–168.

Elfenbein, H. A. (2006). Learning in emotion judgments: Training and the cross-cultural understanding of facial expressions. *Journal of Nonverbal Behavior, 30*(1), 21–36.

Elfenbein, H. A., Foo, M. D., White, J. B., Tan, H. H, & Aik, V. C. (2007). Reading your counterpart: The benefit of emotion recognition ability for effectiveness in negotiation. *Journal of Nonverbal Behavior, 31,* 205–223.

Eskritt, M., & Lee, K. (2003). Do actions speak louder than words? Preschool children's use of the verbal-nonverbal consistency principle during inconsistent communication. *Journal of Nonverbal Behavior, 27,* 25–41.

Equal Opportunity Commission. (2009, February 11). Customer dress codes. Retrieved January 6, 2010, from http://www.eoc.sa.gov.au/site/eo_for_business/shops_and_services/customer_service/customer_dress_codes.jsp

Field, T. (2002). Infants' need for touch. *Human Development, 45,* 100–104.

Fussell, P. (1992). *Class: A guide through the American status system.* New York, NY: Touchstone Books.

Givens, D. B. (2005). *The nonverbal dictionary of gestures, signs, and body language cues.* Spokane, WA: Center for Nonverbal Studies Press.

Grammer, K., Fink, B., Joller, A., & Thornhill, R. (2003). Darwinian aesthetics: Sexual selection and the biology of beauty. *Biological Reviews, 78,* 385–408.

Guerrero, L. K., & Andersen, P. A. (1991). The waxing and waning of relational intimacy: Touch as a function of relational stage, gender, and touch avoidance. *Journal of Social and Personal Relationships, 8,* 147–165.

Guerrero, L. K., & Andersen, P. A. (1994). Patterns of matching and initiation: Touch behavior and touch avoidance across romantic relationship stages. *Journal of Nonverbal Behavior, 18,* 137–153.

Guerrero, L. K., & Ebesu, A. S. (1993, May). *While at play: An observational analysis of children's touch during interpersonal interaction.* Paper presented at the annual conference of the International Communication Association, Washington, DC.

Gundersen, D. F. (1990). Uniforms: Conspicuous invisibility. In J. A. Devito & M. L. Hecht (Eds.), *The nonverbal communication reader* (pp. 172–178). Prospect Heights, IL: Waveland.

Hall, E. T. (1966). *The hidden dimension.* New York, NY: Doubleday.

Hall, E. T. (1983). *The dance of life.* Garden City, NY: Doubleday.

Hall, E. T., & Hall, M. R. (1987). *Hidden differences: Doing business with the Japanese.* Garden City, NY: Anchor.

Hall, E. T., & Hall, M. R. (1990). *Understanding cultural differences: Germans, French and Americans.* Yarmouth, ME: Intercultural Press.

Hanzal, A., Segrin, C., & Dorros, S. M. (2008). The role of marital status and age on men's and women's reaction to touch from a marital partner. *Journal of Nonverbal Behavior, 32*(1), 21–35.

Hsee, C. K., Hatfield, E., & Chemtob, C. (1992). Assessments of the emotional states of others: Conscious judgments versus emotional contagion. *Journal of Social and Clinical Psychology, 11,* 119–128.

Isaacson, L. A. (1998). Student dress codes. *ERIC Digest, 117.* Retrieved June 15, 2006, from http://eric.uoregon.edu/publications/digests/digest117.html

Johnson, A. G. (2001). *Privilege, power, and difference.* Boston, MA: McGraw-Hill.

Jones, S. E., & LeBaron, C. D. (2002). Research on the relationship between verbal and nonverbal communication: Emerging integration. *Journal of Communication, 52,* 499–521.

Kemmer, S. (1992). Are we losing our touch? *Total Health, 14,* 46–49.

Knapp, M. L., & Hall, J. A. (1992). *Nonverbal communication in human interaction* (3rd ed.). New York, NY: Holt, Rinehart & Winston.

Knapp, M. L., & Hall, J. A. (2001). *Nonverbal communication in human interaction.* Belmont, CA: Wadsworth.

Kumar, K. (2009, October 27). Wrighton seeks Chicago inquiry. *St. Louis Post Dispatch.* Retrieved January 6, 2010, from http://www.stltoday.com/stltoday/news/stories.nsf/education/

story/AB0C93A69C9548D38625765C000CF8CA?Open-Document

Manusov, V. (1995). Reacting to changes in nonverbal behaviors: Relational satisfaction and adaptation patterns in romantic dyads. *Human Communication Research, 21,* 456–477.

Mehrabian, A. (1971). *Silent messages.* Belmont, CA: Wadsworth.

Mehrabian, A. (2007). *Nonverbal communication* (2nd ed.). Chicago, IL: Aldine-Atherton.

Miller, E. D. (2008, November 3). Barak Obama and the voice of the president. *Adventures in and out of the mainstream media.* Retrieved January 7, 2010, from http://milleremedia.blogspot.com/2008/11/barack-obama-and-presidential-voice.html

Montepare, J. M., Goldstein, S. B., & Clausen, A. (1987). The identification of emotions from gait information. *Ethology and Sociobiology, 6,* 237–247.

Murphy, J. M. (2004). Nonverbal interventions with infants and their parents. *Journal of Dance Therapy, 20*(1), 37–54.

Newport, F. (1999). Americans agree that being attractive is a plus in American society. *Gallup Poll Monthly, 408,* 45–49.

Parasuram, T. V. (2003, October 23). Sikh shot and injured in Arizona hate crime. *Sikh Times.* Retrieved February 24, 2006, from http://www.sikhtimes.com/news_052103a.html

Patterson, M. L. (1982). A sequential functional model of nonverbal exchange. *Psychological Bulletin, 89,* 231–249.

Patterson, M. L. (1983). *Nonverbal behavior.* New York, NY: Springer.

Patterson, M. L. (2003). Commentary. Evolution and nonverbal behavior: Functions and mediating processes. *Journal of Nonverbal Behavior, 27,* 201–207.

Richards, V., Rollerson, B., & Phillips, J. (1991). Perceptions of submissiveness: Implications for victimization. *Journal of Psychology, 125*(4), 407–411.

Richeson, J. A., & Shelton, J. N. (2005). Brief report: Thin slices of racial bias. *Journal of Nonverbal Behavior, 29,* 75–86.

Schwartz, L. M., Foa, U. G., & Foa, E. B. (1983). Multichannel nonverbal communication: Evidence for combinatory rules. *Journal of Personality and Social Psychology, 45,* 274–281.

Segerstrale, U., & Molnár, P. (1997) (Eds.), *Nonverbal communication: Where nature meets culture* (pp. 27–46). Mahwah, NJ: Erlbaum.

Shelp, S. (2002). Gaydar: Visual detection of sexual orientation among gay and straight men. *Journal of Homosexuality, 44,* 1–14.

Walker, A. K. (2004, July 2). Baltimore-based developer loosens dress code for men. *The Baltimore Sun.* Retrieved January 6, 2010, from http://www.highbeam.com/doc/1G1-118867427.html

Wise, T. (2005, October 23). Opinions on NBA dress code are far from uniform. *Washington Post,* p. A01. Retrieved February 24, 2006, from http://www.washingtonpost.com/wp-dyn/content/article/2005/10/22/AR2005102201386.html

Wolburg, J. M. (2001). Preserving the moment, commodifying time, and improving upon the past: Insights into the depiction of time in American advertising. *Journal of Communication, 51,* 696–720.

Zezima, K. (2005, December 3). Military, police now more strict on tattoos. *The San Diego Union-Tribune.* Retrieved February 22, 2006, from http://www.signonsandiego.com/uniontrib/20051203/news_1n3tattoo.html

Chapter 5

Aurand, T., Ridnour, R., Timm, S. & Kaminski, P. (2000). The listening process: Measuring listening competence. In S. Hall & D. Martin (Eds.), *Proceedings of the American Society of Business and Behavioral Sciences, 7*(4), 391–398.

Barker, L., & Watson, K. (2000). *Listen up: How to improve relationships, reduce stress, and be more productive by using the power of listening.* New York, NY: St. Martin's Press.

Beall, M. L., Gill-Rosier, J., Tate, J., & Matten, A. (2008). State of the context: Listening in education. *The International Journal of Listening, 22,* 123–132.

Beard, D. (2009). A broader understanding of the ethics of listening: Philosophy, cultural studies, media studies and the ethical listening subject. *International Journal of Listening, 23*(1), 7–20.

Bentley, S. C. (2000). Listening in the 21st century. *International Journal of Listening, 14,* 129–142.

Bommelje, R., Houston, J. M., & Smither, R. (2003). Personality characteristics of effective listeners: A five factor perspective. *International Journal of Listening, 17,* 32–46.

Brownell, J. (1994). Managerial listening and career development in the hospitality industry. *The International Journal of Listening, 8,* 31–49.

Brownell, J. (1994). Managerial listening and career development in the hospitality industry. *International Journal of Listening, 8,* 31–49.

Brownell, J. (2002). *Listening: Attitudes, principles and skills.* Boston, MA: Allyn-Bacon.

Davis, J., Foley, A., Crigger, N., & Brannigan, M. C. (2008). Healthcare and listening: A relationship for caring. *International Journal of Listening, 22,* 168–175.

Diamond, L. E. (2007). *Rule#1: Stop talking!: A guide to listening.* Cupertino, CA: Listeners Press.

Dillon, R. K., & McKenzie, N. J. (1998). The influence of ethnicity on listening, communication competence, approach, and avoidance. *International Journal of Listening, 12,* 106–121.

Eadie, W. F. (1982). Defensive communication revisited: A critical examination of Gibb's theory. *Southern Speech Communication Journal, 47,* 163–177.

Emanuel, R., Adams, J., Baker, K., Daufin, E. K., Ellington, C., & Fitts, E. (2008). How college students spend their time communicating. *International Journal of Listening, 22*(1), 13–28.

Flynn, J., Valikoski, T. R., & Grau, J. (2008). Listening in the business context: Reviewing the state of research. *International Journal of Listening, 22,* 141–151.

Fowler, K. (2005). Mind tools on active listening. Retrieved December 7, 2009, from http://www.mindtools.com/CommSkll/Mind%20Tools%20Listening.pdf

Fujii, Y. (2008). You must have a wealth of stories: Cross-linguistic differences between addressee support behaviour in Australian and Japanese. *Multilingua, 27*(4), 325–370.

Gibb, J. R. (1961). Defensive communication. *Journal of Communication, 11*(3), 141–148.

Holmes, F. (2007). If you listen, the patient will tell you the diagnosis. *International Journal of Listening, 21*(2), 156–161.

The husband makeover (September 1998). *Ladies Home Journal*, 146.

International Listening Association (1995, April). An ILA definition of listening. *ILA Listening Post, 53,* 1–4.

Imhof, M. (2001). How to listen more efficiently: Self-monitoring strategies in listening. *International Journal of Listening, 5,* 2–19.

Imhof, M. (2004). Who are we as we listen? Individual listening profiles in varying contexts. *International Journal of Listening, 18,* 36–45.

Imhof, M. & Janusik, L. A. (2006). Development and validation of the Imhof-Janusik listening concepts inventory to measure listening conceptualization differences between cultures. *Journal of Intercultural Communication Research, 35*(2), 79–98.

Janusik, L. (2005a, April). *Teaching listening: A research based approach.* Paper presented at the annual conference of the International Listening Association, Minneapolis, MN.

Janusik, L. (2005b). Conversational listening span: A proposed measure of conversational listening. *The International Journal of Listening, 19,* 12–28.

Johnston, M. K., Weaver, J. B., Watson, K. W., & Barker L. L. (2000). Listening styles: Biological or psychological differences? *International Journal of Listening, 14,* 32–46.

Kotter, J. P. (1982). What do effective managers really do? *Harvard Business Review, 60*(6), 156–167.

Lynch, J. J. (1985). *Language of the heart: The body's response to human dialogue.* New York, NY: Basic Books.

Mooney, D. (1996). Improving your listening skills. Retrieved December 7, 2009, from http://suicideandmentalhealth associationinternational.org/improvlisten.html (copyright by Ken Johnson)

Nichols, M. P. (1995). *The lost art of listening.* New York, NY: The Guilford Press.

Pearce, C. G., Johnson, I. W., & Barker, R. T. (2003). Assessment of the listening styles inventory: Progress in establishing reliability and validity. *Journal of Business and Technical Communication, 17*(1), 84–113.

Rosenfeld, L. B., & Berko, R. (1990). *Communicating with competency.* Glenview, IL: Scott, Foresman/Little.

Salem, R. (2003). Empathic listening. In G. Burgess and H. Burgess (Eds.), *Beyond Intractability.* Conflict Research Consortium, University of Colorado, Boulder. Retrieved December 14, 2009, from http://www.beyondintractability.org/essay/empathic_listening/

Shafir, R. Z. (2000). *The Zen of listening.* Wheaton, IL: Quest Books.

Shotter, J. (2009). Listening in a way that recognizes/realizes the world of "the other." *International Journal of Listening, 23*(1), 21–43.

Silverman, J. (1970). Attentional styles and the study of sex differences. In D. I. Mostofsky (Ed.). *Attention: Contemporary theory and analysis* (pp. 61–79). NewYork, NY: Appleton-Century-Crofts.

Sypher, B. D. (1984). The importance of social cognition abilities in organizations. In R. Bostrom (Ed.), *Competence in communication* (pp. 103–128). Beverly Hills, CA: Sage.

Thomlison, T. D. (1996). Intercultural listening. In D. Borisoff & M. Purdy (Eds.), *Listening in everyday life: A personal and professional approach* (2nd ed., pp. 79–120). New York, NY: University Press of America.

Villaume, W. A., & Bodie, G. D. (2007). Discovering the listener within us: The impact of trait-like personality variables and communicator styles on preferences for listening style. *International Journal of Listening, 21*(2), 102–123.

Watson, K. W., Barker, L. L., & Weaver, J. B. (1995). The Listening styles profile (LSP-16): Development and validation of an instrument to assess four listening styles. *Journal of the International Listening Association, 9,* 1–13.

Chapter 6

Adler, P. (1975). The transitional experience: An alternative view of culture shock. *Journal of Humanistic Psychology, 15,* 13–23.

Alexie, S. (2003). *Ten little Indians.* New York: Grove Press.

Allen, B. (2003). *Difference matters: Communicating social identity.* Waveland Press.

Anzaldúa, G. (1999). *Borderlands/La frontera: The new mestiza.* San Francisco: Aunt Lute Books.

Bahk, M., & Jandt, F. E. (2004). Being white in America: Development of a scale. *Howard Journal of Communications, 15,* 57–68.

Bellah, R. N., Madsen, R., Sullivan, W. M., Swidler, A., & Tipton, S. M. (1996). *Habits of the heart: Individualism and commitment in American life.* Los Angeles: University of California Press.

Bennett, J. M. (1998). Transition shock: Putting culture shock in perspective. In M. J. Bennett (Ed.), *Basic concepts in intercultural communication: Selected readings* (pp. 215–224). Yarmouth, ME: Intercultural Press. First published in 1977, in N. C. Jain (Ed.), *International and Intercultural Communication Annual, 4,* 45–52.

Bercovitch, J., & Derouen, K. (2004). Mediation in internationalized ethnic conflicts. *Armed Forces & Society, 30,* 147–170.

Berry, J. W. (2005). Acculturation: Living successfully in two cultures. *International Journal of Intercultural Relations, 29,* 697–712.

Bhatia, S. (2008). 9/11 and the Indian diaspora: Narratives of race, place and immigrant identity. *Journal of Intercultural Studies, 29*(1), 21–39.

Blair, C., Brown, J. R., & Baxter, L. A. (1994). Disciplining the feminine. *Quarterly Journal of Speech, 80,* 383–409.

Blanco, T., Farrell, D., & Labaye, E. (2005, August 15). How France can win from offshoring. *The McKinsey Quarterly.* Retrieved June 15, 2006, from http://yaleglobal.yale.edu/display.article?id=6144

Bond, M. (1991). *Beyond the Chinese face.* Hong Kong: Oxford University Press.

Bond, M. (Ed.). (1996). *The handbook of Chinese psychology*. Hong Kong: Oxford University Press.

Broome, B. J. (2004). Building a shared future across the divide: Identity and conflict in Cyprus. In M. Fong and R. Chuang (Eds.), *Communicating Ethnic and Cultural Identity* (pp. 275–294). Lanham, MD: Rowman and Littlefield, Publishers.

Budelman, R. *Indian Cultural Tips*. Retrieved June 13, 2006, from http://www.stylusinc.com/business/india/americans_idependant.htm

Chinese Culture Connection. (1987). Chinese values and the search for culture-free dimensions of culture. *Journal of Cross-Cultural Psychology, 18*, 143–164.

Clark-Ibáñez, M. K., & Felmlee, D. (2004). Interethnic relationships: The role of social network diversity. *Journal of Marriage and Family, 66*, 229–245.

Cowan, G. (2005). Interracial interactions of racially diverse university campuses. *The Journal of Social Psychology, 14*, 49–63.

Crary, D. (2007, April 12). Interracial marriages surge across U. S. USAToday.com. Retrieved December 21, 2009, from http://www.usatoday.com/news/health/2007-04-12-interracial-marriage_N.htm

Dunbar, R. A. (1997). Bloody footprints: Reflections on growing up poor white. In M. Wray & A. Newitz (Eds.), *White trash: Race and class in America* (pp. 73–86). New York: Routledge.

Ewing, K. P. (2004). Migration, identity negotiation, and self-experience. In J. Friedman & S. Randeria (Eds.), *Worlds on the move: Globalization, migration, and cultural security* (pp. 117–140). London: I. B. Tauris.

Fiebert, M. S., Nugent, D., Hershberger, S. L., & Kasdan, M. (2004). Dating and commitment choices as a function of ethnicity among American college students in California. *Psychological Reports, 94*, 1293–1300.

Finn, H. K. (2003). The case for cultural diplomacy. *Foreign Affairs, 82*, 15.

Flores, L. A. (1996). Creating discursive space through a rhetoric of difference: Chicana feminists craft a homeland. *Quarterly Journal of Speech, 82*, 142–156.

Gudykunst, W. B., & Lee, C. M. (2002). Cross-cultural communication theories. In W. B. Gudykunst & B. Mody (Eds.), *Handbook of international and intercultural communication* (2nd ed., pp. 25–50). Thousand Oaks, CA: Sage.

Hakimzadeh, S., & Cohn, D. (2007). *English usage among Hispanics in the United States*. Washington, DC: Pew Hispanic Center. Retrieved December 22, 2009, from http://pewhispanic.org/files/reports/82.pdf

Hall, B. J. (1997). Culture, ethics and communication. In F. L. Casmir (Ed.), *Ethics in intercultural and international communication* (pp. 11–41). Mahwah, NJ: Erlbaum.

Hall, E. T., & Hall, M. (1990). *Understanding cultural differences: Germans, French and Americans*. Yarmouth, ME: Intercultural Press.

Halualani, R. T. (2008). How do multicultural university students define and make sense of intercultural contact? A qualitative study. *International Journal of Intercultural Relations, 32*, 1–16.

Hecht, M. L., Jackson R. L. II, & Ribeau, S. (2002). *African American communication: Exploring identity and culture* (2nd ed.). Hillsdale, NJ: Erlbaum.

Hecht, M., Sedano, M., & Ribeau, S. (1993). Understanding culture, communication, and research: Application to Chicanos and Mexican Americans. *International Journal of Intercultural Relations, 17*, 157–165.

Hegde, R. S. (1998). Swinging the trapeze: The negotiation of identity among Asian Indian immigrant women in the United States. In D. V. Tanno & A. González (Eds.), *Communication of identity across cultures* (pp. 34–55). Thousand Oaks, CA: Sage.

Hegde, R. S. (2000). Hybrid revivals: Defining Asian Indian ethnicity through celebration. In A. González, M. Houston, & V. Chen (Eds.), *Our voices: Essays in culture, ethnicity and communication* (pp. 133–138). Los Angeles: Roxbury.

Hemmingsen, J. (2002). Klamath talks begin. *Indian Country Today, 21*, A1.

Herbert, B. (2005, June 6). The mobility myth. *The New York Times*. Retrieved October 7, 2005, from http://www.commondreams.org/views05/0606-27.htm

Ho, M. K. (1987). *Family therapy with ethnic minorities*. Newbury Park, CA: Sage.

Hofstede, G. (1997). *Cultures and organizations: Software of the mind* (rev. ed). New York: McGraw-Hill.

Hofstede, G. (1998). *Masculinity and femininity*. Thousand Oaks, CA: Sage.

Hofstede, G. (2001). *Culture's consequences* (2nd ed.). Thousand Oaks, CA: Sage.

Houston, M. (2004). When black women talk with white women: Why dialogues are difficult. In A. González, M. Houston, & V. Chen (Eds.), *Our voices: Essays in culture, ethnicity and communication* (4th ed.). Los Angeles, CA: Roxbury.

Hulse, E. (1996). Example of the English Puritans. *Reformation Today, 153*. Retrieved June 13, 2006, from http://www.puritansermons.com/banner/hulse1.htm

IIE. (2009a). *Open Doors 2009: International students in the U.S.* Washington, DC: Institute of International Education. Retrieved December 21, 2009, from http://opendoors.iienetwork.org/?p=150649

IIE. (2009b). *Open Doors 2009: U. S. students studying abroad*. Washington, DC: Institute of International Education. Retrieved December 21, 2009, from http://opendoors.iienetwork.org/?p=150651

Jarvis, J. (1995). *Euro Disneyland Paris cultural research project* (Report No. 2). Pittsburgh, PA: Robert Morris College.

Johnson, A. G. (2001). *Privilege, power and difference*. Thousand Oaks, CA: Sage.

Johnson, B. R., & Jacobson, C. K. (2005). Context in contact: An examination of social settings on Whites' attitudes toward interracial marriage, *Journal of Social Psychology, 68*, 387–399.

Jones, N. A., & Smith, A. S. (2001). *The two or more races population. Census 2000 Brief* (U.S. Census Bureau Publication No. C2KBR/01-6). Washington, DC: U.S. Government Printing Office.

Jung, E., Hecht, M. L., & Wadsworth, B. C. (2007). The role of identity in international students' psychological well-being in the United States: A model of depression level, identity gaps, discrimination, and acculturation. *International Journal of Intercultural Relations, 31,* 605–624.

Kashima, E. S., & Loh, E. (2006). International students' acculturation: Effects of international, conational, and local ties and need for closure. *International Journal of Intercultural Relations, 30,* 471–486.

Kikoski, J. F., & Kikoski, C. K. (1999). *Reflexive communication in the culturally diverse workplace.* Westport, CT: Praeger.

Kim, Y. Y. (2005). Adapting to a new culture: An integrative communication theory. In W. B. Gudykunst (Ed.), *Theorizing about intercultural communication* (pp. 375–400). Thousand Oaks, CA: Sage.

Kivel, P. (1996). *Uprooting racism: How white people can work for racial justice.* Gabriola Islands, BC: New Society Publishers.

Kluckhohn, F., and Strodtbeck, F. (1961). *Variations in value orientations.* Chicago: Row, Peterson & Co.

Kohls, R. L. (2001). *Survival kit for overseas living* (4th ed.). Yarmouth, ME: Nicholas Brealey/Intercultural Press.

Lee, J. J., & Rice, C. (2007). Welcome to America? International student perceptions of discrimination, *Higher Education, 53,* 381–409.

Lee, S. M., & Edmonston, B. (2005). New marriages, new families: U.S. racial and Hispanic intermarriage. *Population Bulletin, 60,* 3–36.

Lin, C. (2006). Culture shock and social support: An investigation of a Chinese student organization on a US campus. *Journal of Intercultural Communication Research, 35*(2), 117–137.

Loewen, J. W. (1995). *Lies my teacher told me.* New York: Simon & Schuster.

Martin, J. N., & Nakayama, T. K. (2008). *Experiencing intercultural communication: An introduction* (3rd ed.). Boston: McGraw-Hill.

Matsumoto, D. (2002). *The new Japan: Debunking seven cultural stereotypes.* Yarmouth, ME: Intercultural Press.

McGoldrick, M., Giordano, J., & Pearce, J. K. (Eds.). (1996). *Ethnicity and family therapy* (2nd ed.). New York: Guilford Press.

McKinnon, S. (2004, Sept. 1). Spotted owl habitat plan ruffles feathers. *Arizona Republic,* B1.

Melmer, D. (2004). Buffalo and Lakota are kin. *Indian Country Today, 23,* B1.

Norris, F. (2007, December 3). Euro Disney. *The New York Times.* Retrieved April 7, 2008, from http://norris.blogs.nytimes.com/2007/12/03/euro-disney/

Numbers. (2008, February 4). *Time,* p. 18.

Orbe, M. P. (1998). *Constructing co-cultural theory: An explication of culture, power, and communication.* Thousand Oaks, CA: Sage.

Passel, J. S., & Cohn, D. V. (2008, February 11). U. S. populations projections: 2005–2050.

Porter, T. (2002). The words that come before all else. *Native Americas, 19,* 7–10.

Rabbi: My radio show pulled because of racism. (2005, September 27). *The Associated Press.* Retrieved April 1, 2010, from http://archive.newsmax.com/archives/ic/2005/9/22/173035.shtml

Riddle, D. (2000). Cultural approaches to innovation. *International Trade Forum, 2,* 23–26.

Root, M. P. P. (2001). *Love's revolution: Interracial marriage.* Philadelphia, PA: Temple University Press.

Rosenblatt, P. C., Karis, T. A., & Powell, R. D. (1996). *Multiracial couples: Black and white voices.* Thousand Oaks, CA: Sage.

Rosenstone, R. A. (2005). My wife, the Muslim. *Antioch Review, 63,* 234–246.

Schmidley, D. (2003). *The foreign born population in the U.S., Current Population Reports* (pp. 20–539). Washington, DC: U.S. Census Bureau.

Schneider, S. C., & Barsoux, J. L. (2003). *Managing across cultures.* New York: Prentice Hall.

Shelden, R. G. (2004). The imprisonment crisis in America: An introduction. *Review of Policy Research, 21,* 5–13.

Shim, Y-J., Kim, M-S., & Martin, J. N. (2008). *Changing Korea: Understanding culture and communication.* New York: Peter Lang.

Snyder, M. (2001). Self-fulfilling stereotypes. In. P. S. Rothenberg (Ed.), *Race, class & gender in the U.S.* (5th ed., pp. 511–517). New York: Worth.

Stewart, E. C., & Bennett, M. J. (1991). *American cultural patterns: A cross-cultural perspective.* Yarmouth, ME: Intercultural Press.

Taylor, P., Funk, C., & Craighill, P. (2006). *Guess who's coming to dinner.* Pew Research Center Social Trends Report. Washington, DC: Pew Research Center.

Ting-Toomey, S. (1999). *Communicating across cultures.* New York: Guilford.

Tourism highlights 2009 edition. Retrieved June 23, 2010 from http://www.unwto.org/facts/eng/pdf/highlights/UNWTO_Highlights09_en_HR.pdf

Triandis, H. (1995). *Individualism and collectivism.* Boulder, CO: Westview Press.

Trompenaars, F., & Hampden-Turner, C. (1997). *Riding the waves of culture: Understanding diversity in global business.* Boston: McGraw-Hill.

Ward, C. (2008). Thinking outside the Berry boxes: New perspectives on identity, acculturation and intercultural relations. *International Journal of Intercultural Relations, 32,* 105–114.

Yamato, G. (2001). Something about the subject makes it hard to name. In M. L. Andersen & P. H. Collins (Eds.), *Race, class, and gender: An anthology* (4th ed., pp. 90–94). Belmont, CA: Wadsworth.

Zuni eagle aviary is a beautiful sign. (2002, July 31). Editorial. Retrieved June 13, 2006, from http://indiancountry.com/content.cfm?id=1028047572

Chapter 7

Anderson, T. L., & Emmers-Sommer, T. M. (2006). Predictors of relationship satisfaction in online romantic relationships. *Communication Studies, 57*(2), 153–172.

The Apparatgeist calls. (2010, January 2). *The Economist, 394*(8663), 56–58.

Auter, P. J. (2007). Portable social groups: Willingness to communicate, interpersonal communication gratifications, and cell phone use among young adults. *International Journal of Mobile Communications, 5*(2) 139–156.

Baym, N. K., Zhang, Y. B., & Lin, M-C. (2004). Social interactions across media: Interpersonal communication on the internet, telephone and face to face. *New Media & Society, 6*(3), 299–318.

Beer, D. (2008). Social network(ing) sites…revisiting the story so far: A response to danah boyd & Nicole Ellison. *Journal of Computer-Mediated Communication, 13*, 516–529.

Bimie, S. A., & Horvath, P. (2002). Psychological predictors of Internet social communication. *Journal of Computer-Mediated Communication, 7*, 1–25.

Boase, J. (2008). Personal networks and the personal communication system. *Information, Communication & Society, 11*(4), 490–508.

Bourdieu, P. (1986). The forms of capital. In J. G. Richardson (Ed.), *Handbook of theory and research for the sociology of education* (pp. 241–258). Westport, CT: Greenwood.

boyd, d. m. (2007, June 24). Viewing American class divisions through Facebook and MySpace. *Apophenia Blog Essay*. Retrieved February 18, 2008, from http://www.danah.org/papers/essays/ClassDivisions.html

boyd, d. m. (2007). Why youth (heart) social network sites: The role of networked publics in teenage social life. In D. Buckingham (Ed.), *Youth, identity, and digital media* (MacArthur Foundation Series on Digital Learning). Cambridge, MA: MIT press.

boyd, d. m., & Ellison, N. B. (2007). Social network sites: Definition, history, and scholarship. *Journal of Computer-Mediated Communication, 13*(1), 210–230.

Boyd, J. (2003). The rhetorical construction of trust online. *Communication Theory, 13*, 392–410.

Carr, N. (2008, July/August). Is Google making us stupid?: What the Internet is doing to our brains. *The Atlantic, 302*(1), 56–63.

Carter, D. M. (2004). Living in virtual communities: Making friends online. *Journal of Urban Technology, 11*, 109–125.

Caspi, A., Chajut, E., & Saporta, K. (2008). Participation in class and in online discussions: Gender differences. *Computers & Education, 50*, 718–724.

Castells, M., Qiu, J. L., & Fernandez-Ardevol, M. (2006). *Mobile communication and society: A global perspective*. Cambridge, MA: MIT Press.

Cheong, P. H. (2008).The young and techless? Investigating internet use and problem-solving behaviors of young adults in Singapore. *New Media & Society, 10*(5), 771–791.

Cheong, P. H., Halavais, A., & Kwon, K. (2008). The chronicles of me: Understanding blogging as a religious practice. *Journal of Media and Religion, 7*, 107–131.

Daft, R. L., & Lengel, R. H. (1984). Information richness: A new approach to managerial behavior and organization design. *Research in Organizational Behavior, 6*, 191–233.

Daft, R. L., & Lengel, R. H. (1986). A proposed integration among organizational information requirements, media richness, and structural design. *Management Science, 32*(5), 544–571.

Daily Online Activities. (2009) Pew Internet & American Life Project. Retrieved January 8, 2010, from http://www.pewinternet.org/Trend-Data/Online-Activities-Daily.aspx

Delgado, F. (2002). Mass-mediated communication. In J. N. Martin, T. K. Nakayama, & L. A. Flores (Eds.), *Readings in Intercultural Communication* (2nd ed., pp. 351–360). Boston: McGraw-Hill.

Ellison, N. B., Steinfeld, C., & Lampe, C. (2007). The benefits of Facebook "friends:" Social capital and college students' use of online social network sites. *Journal of Computer-Mediated Communication, 12*(4), 1.

Facenda, V. L. (2008, March 31). Chemistry.com reinforces formula with $40M effort. *Brandweek, 10644318, 49*(13), p. 17.

Fallows, D. (2008). Almost half of all internet users now use search engines on a typical day. Pew Internet & American Life Project Data Memo. Retrieved March 30, 2009, from http://www.pewinternet.org/Reports/2008/Search-Engine-Use.aspx

Finn, S., & Korukonda, A. R. (2004). Avoiding computers: Does personality play a role? In E. P. Bucy & J. E. Newhagen (Eds.), *Media access: Social and psychological dimensions of new technology use* (pp. 73–90). Mahwah, NJ: Erlbaum.

Gergen, K. J. (2002). The challenge of absent-presence. In J. Katz & M. Aakhus (Eds.), *Perpetual contact: Mobile communication, private talk, public performance* (pp. 223–227). Cambridge, UK: Cambridge University Press.

Goggin, G. (2006). *Cell phone culture*. New York: Routledge.

Hampton, K. N., Sessions, L. F., Her, E. J., & Rainie, L. (2009). Social isolation and new technology. Retrieved December 13, 2009, from http://www.pewinternet.org/~/media//Files/Reports/2009/PIP_Tech_and_Social_Isolation.pdf

Hargittai, W., & Hinnant, A. (2008). Digital inequality: Differences in young adults' use of the Internet. *Communication Research, 35*(5), 602–621.

Henderson, S., & Gilding, M. (2004). "I've never clicked this much with anyone in my life": Trust and hyperpersonal communication in online friendships. *New Media & Society, 6*, 487–506.

Herring, S. C. (2004). Slouching toward the ordinary: Current trends in computer-mediated communication. *New Media & Society, 6*, 26–36.

Horrigan, J. C. (2008a). Info on the go: Mobile access to data and information. Pew Internet & American Life Project. Retrieved December 8, 2008, from http://www.pewinternet.org/pdfs/PIP_Mobile.Data.Access.pdf

Horrigan, J. C. (2008b). The Internet and consumer choice. Pew Internet & American Life Project. Retrieved December 15, 2008, from http://www.pewinternet.org/pdfs/PIP_Online%20Shopping.pdf

Horrigan, J. C. (2009). Home broadband adoption 2009. Pew Internet & American Life Project. Retrieved December 13, 2009, from http://www.pewinternet.org/~/media//Files/Reports/2009/Home-Broadband-Adoption-2009.pdf

Hutchinson, A. (2006, February). Mean, green, third world machine. *Popular Mechanics, 183*, p. 20.

Hwang, J. M., Cheong, P. H., & Feeley, T. H. (2009). Being young and feeling blue in Taiwan: Examining adolescent depressive mood and online and offline activities. *New Media & Society, 11*(7), 1101–1121.

Jackson, L. A., Barbatsis, G., Biocca, F. A., von Eye, A., Zhao, Y., & Fitzgerald, H. E. (2004). Home Internet use in low-income families: Is access enough to eliminate the digital divide? In E. P. Bucy & J. E. Newhagen (Eds.), *Media access: Social and psychological dimensions of new technology use* (pp. 155–186). Mahwah, NJ: Erlbaum.

Jackson, L. A., Ervin, K. S., Gardner, P. D., & Schmitt, N. (2001).Gender and the Internet: Women communicating and men searching. *Sex Roles, 44,* 363–379.

James, G. (2003, March 1). Can't hide your prying eyes. *Computerworld, 38,* 35–37.

Jayson, S. (2008, June 2). Singles find love after 45. *USA Today,* Life Section p. 01d. Retrieved March 30, 2009, from http://www.usatoday.com/news/health/2008-06-01-late-life-marriage_N.htm

Jones, S., & Fox, S. (2009). Generations Online in 2009. Pew Internet & American Life Project Data Memo. Retrieved March 29, 2009, from http://www.pewinternet.org/~/media/ /Files/Reports/2009/ PIP_Generations_2009.pdf

Jung, J-Y. (2008). Internet connectedness and its social origins: An ecological approach to postaccess digital divides. *Communication Studies, 59*(4), 322–339.

Katz, J. E. (2007). Mobile media and communication: Some important questions. *Communication Monographs, 74*(3), 389–394.

Kendall, L. (2002). *Hanging out in the virtual pub: Masculinities and relationships online.* Berkeley: University of California Press.

Keniston, K. (2001). Language, power and software. In C. Ess (Ed.), *Culture, technology, communication: Towards an intercultural global village* (pp. 283–306). Albany: State University of New York Press.

Kim, H., Kim, G. J., Park, H. W., & Rice, R. E. (2007). Configurations of relationships in different media: FtF, email, instant messenger, mobile phone, and SMS. *Journal of Computer-Mediated Communication, 12,* 1183–1207.

Krauss, A. (2008, February 20). Piggybacking on Facebook. *The New York Times,* H0, p. 7.

Kraut, R., Kiesler, S., Mukhopadhya, T., & Scherlis, W. (1998). Social impact of the internet: What does it mean? *Communications of the ACM, 41,* 21–22.

Lenhart, A. (2009, October 8). Twitter and status updating: Demographics, mobile access and news consumption. Pew Internet & American Life Project. PowerPoint presentation to AoIR 10.0, Milwaukee, WI. Retrieved December 13, 2009, from http://www.pewinternet.org/Presentations/2009/ 44—Twitter-and-status-updating.aspx#

Lenhart, A., Horrigan, J., Rainie, L., Allen, K., Boyce, A., Madden, M., et al. (2003, April 16). The ever-shifting Internet population: A new look at Internet access and the digital divide. Pew Internet & American Life Project. Retrieved March 30, 2009, from http://www.pewinternet. org/Reports/2003/The-EverShifting-Internet-population-A-new-look-at-Internet-access-and-the-digital-divide.aspx

Lenhart, A., Jones, S., & Macgill, A. R. (2008). Adults and video games. Pew Internet & American Life Project Data Memo. Retrieved March 29, 2009, from http://www.pewinternet.org/ Reports/2008/Adults-and-Video-Games.aspx

Lenhart, A., Madden, M., Macgill, A. R., & Smith, A. (2007). Teens and social media. Pew Internet & American Life Project. Retrieved March 31, 2010 from http://www.pewinternet. org/Reports/2007/Teens-and-Social-Media.aspx?r=1

Ling, R. (2004). *The mobile connection: The cell phone's impact on society.* San Francisco: Morgan Kaufmann.

Livingston, G., Parker, K., & Fox, S. (2009). Latinos online 2006–2008: Narrowing the gap. Pew Hispanic Center. Retrieved January 8, 2010, from http://pewhispanic.org/ files/reports/119.pdf

Madden, M., & Jones, S. (2008). Networked workers. Pew Internet & American Life Project. Retrieved March 29, 2009, from http://www.pewinternet.org/Reports/2008/Networked-Workers.aspx

Madden, M., & Lenhart, A. (2006, March 5). *Online dating.* Pew Internet & American Life Project. Retrieved April 1, 2010, from http://www.pewinternet.org/Reports/2006/Online-Dating.aspx

Mangla, I. S. (2008). Bye-bye love, bye-bye bank account. *Money, 37*(10), p. 18.

Marriot, M. (2006, March 31). Blacks turn to Internet highway, and digital divide starts to close. *The New York Times,* p. A1.

McKenna, K. Y. A., Green, A. S., & Gleason, M. E. J. (2002). Relationship formation on the Internet: What's the big attraction? *Journal of Social Issues, 58,* 9–31.

McLean, J. (2009, October 19). State of the blogosphere 2009 (introduction). *Technorati.com.* Retrieved December 13, 2009, from http://technorati.com/blogging/article/state-of-the-blogosphere-2009-introduction/

Merryfield, M. (2003). Like a veil: Cross-cultural experiential learning online. *Contemporary Issues in Technology and Teacher Education, 3*(2), 146–171.

Osman, G., & Herring, S. (2007). Interaction, facilitation, and deep learning in cross-cultural chat: A case study. *Internet and Higher Education, 10,* 125–141.

Postmes, T., Spears, R., & Lea, M. (1998). Breaching or building the social boundaries: SIDE-effects of computer-mediated communication. *Communication Research, 25,* 689–715.

Rainie, L. (2010, January 5). Internet, broadband, and cell phone statistics. Pew Internet & American Life Project. Retrieved January 7, 2010, from http://www.pewinternet.org/Reports/ 2010/Internet-broadband-and-cell-phone-statistics.aspx

Ramirez, A., & Zhang, S. (2007). When online meets offline: The effect of modality switching on relational communication. *Communication Monographs, 74*(3), 287–310.

Rideout, V. J., Foehr, U. G., & Roberts, D. F. (2010). *Generation M2: Media in the lives of 8- to 18-year-olds* (A Kaiser Family Foundation Study). Menlo Park, CA: Henry J. Kaiser Family Foundation.

Roberto, A. J., & Eden, J. (2010). Cyberbullying: Aggressive communication in the digital age. In T. A. Avtgis & A. S. Rancer (Eds.), *Arguments, aggression, and conflict: New directions in theory and research* (pp. 198–216). New York: Routledge.

Rogers, E. M. (2003). *Diffusion of innovations* (5th ed.). New York: The Free Press.

Rojas, V., Straubhaar, J., Roychowdhury, D., & Okur, O. (2004). Communities, cultural capital, and the digital divide. In E. P. Bucy & J. E. Newhagen (Eds.), *Media access: Social and psychological dimensions of new technology use* (pp. 107–130). Mahwah, NJ: Erlbaum.

Rooksby, E. (2002). *Email and ethics: Style and ethical relations in computer-mediated communication.* New York: Routledge.

Rosen, L. D., Cheever, N. A., Cummings, C., & Felt, J. (2008). The impact of emotionality and self-disclosure on online dating versus traditional dating. *Computers in Human Behavior, 24,* 2124–2157.

Sawhney, H. (2007). Strategies for increasing the conceptual yield of new technologies research. *Communication Monographs, 74*(3), 395–401.

Scanlon, J. (2003, August). 7 ways to squelch the Net. *Wired,* p. 31.

Seagraves, L. (2004, May). Suing the pants off spammers. *Wired,* p. 114.

Selwyn, N. (2007). Guy-tech?: An exploration of undergraduate students' gendered perceptions of information and communication technologies. *Sex Roles, 56,* 525–536.

Serious trouble. (2007, December 8). *The Economist* (Technology Quarterly), pp. 3–4.

Short, J. A., Williams, E., & Christie, B. (1976). *The social psychology of telecommunications.* New York: John Wiley & Sons.

Siklos, R. (2006, October 19). A virtual world but real money. *The New York Times.* Retrieved March 30, 2009, from http://query.nytimes.com/gst/fullpage.html?res=9907E2DA1F30F93AA25753C1A9609C8B63&sec=&spon=&pagewanted=2

Sinclair, B. (2009, September 23). *Study: Minorities underrepresented in games.* Retrieved September 23, 2009, from Gamespot: http://www.gamespot.com/news/6229016.html

Smith, G. G., Ferguson, D., & Caris, M. (2001). Teaching college courses online vs face-to-face. *The Journal, 28,* 18–26.

State of the Blogosphere/2008. (2008). *Technocrati.com.* Retrieved December 13, 2008, from http://technorati.com/blogging/state-of-the-blogosphere/

Stone, B. (2007, April 9). A call for manners in the world of nasty blogs. *The New York Times.* Retrieved March 30, 2009, from http://www.nytimes.com/2007/04/09/technology/09blog.html

Sussman, M. (2009). Day 5: Twitter, global impact and the future of blogging – SOTB 2009. *Technocrati.com.* Retrieved December 13, 2009, from http://technorati.com/blogging/article/day-5-twitter-global-impact-and/

Thompson, L., & Ku, H-Y. (2005). Chinese graduate students' experiences and attitudes toward online learning. *Educational Media International, 42*(1), 33–47.

Thurlow, C., Lengel, L., & Tomic, A. (2004). *Computer mediated communication: Social interaction and the Internet.* Thousand Oaks, CA: Sage.

Tong, S. T., Van Der Heide, B., Langwell L., & Walther, J. B. (2008). Too much of a good thing? The relationship between number of friends and interpersonal impressions on Facebook. *Journal of Computer-Mediated Communication, 13,* 531–549.

Valkenburg, P. M., & Peter, J. (2007a). Online communication and adolescent well-being: Testing the stimulation versus the displacement hypothesis. *Journal of Computer-Mediated Communication, 12*(4), Article 2.

Valkenburg, P. M., & Peter, J. (2007b). Who visits online dating sites? Exploring some characteristics of online daters. *Cyberpsychology & Behavior, 10*(6), 849–852.

van Dijk, J. (2004). Divides in succession: Possession, skills, and use of new media for societal participation. In E. P. Bucy & J. E. Newhagen (Eds.), *Media access: Social and psychological dimensions of new technology use* (pp. 233–254). Mahwah, NJ: Erlbaum.

Walther, J. B. (1996). Computer-mediated communication: Impersonal, interpersonal, and hyper-personal interaction. *Communication Research, 23,* 3–43.

Walther, J. B., & Parks, M. R. (2002). Cues filtered out, cues filtered in: Computer-mediated communication and relationships. In M. L. Knapp & J. A. Daly (Eds.), *Handbook of interpersonal communication* (pp. 529–63). Thousand Oaks, CA: Sage.

Wang, H-Y, & Wang, Y-S. (2008). Gender differences in the perception and acceptance of online games. *British Journal of Educational Technology, 39*(5), 787–806.

Wheeler, D. (2001). New technologies, old culture: A look at women, gender and the Internet in Kuwait. In C. Ess (Ed.), *Culture, technology, communication: Towards an intercultural global village* (pp. 187–212). Albany: State University of New York Press.

Whitty, M. T. (2007). Revealing the "real" me, searching for the "actual" you: Presentations of self on an internet dating site. *Computers in Human Behavior, 24,* 1707–1723.

Williams, D., Martins, N., Consalvo, M., & Ivory, J. (2009). The virtual census: representations of gender, race, and age in video games. *New Media & Society, 11*(5), 815–834.

Wood, A. F., & Smith, M. J. (2005). *Online communication: Linking technology, identity and culture* (2nd ed.). Mahwah, NJ: Erlbaum.

Wray, R. (2007, June 14). China overtaking US for fast internet access as Africa gets left behind. *The Guardian,* guardian.co.uk. Retrieved March 30, 2009, from http://www.guardian.co.uk/money/2007/jun/14/internetphonesbroadband.digitalmedia

Zywica, J., & Danowski, J. (2008). The faces of Facebookers: Investigating social enhancement and social compensation hypotheses: Predicting Facebook and offline popularity from sociability and self-esteem, and mapping the meaning of popularity with semantic networks. *Journal of Computer-Mediated Communication, 14,* 1–34.

Chapter 8

Aboud, F. E., & Mendelson, M. J. (1996). Determinants of friendship selection and quality: Developmental perspectives. In W. M. Bukowski, A. F. Newcomb, & W. W. Hartup (Eds.), *The company they keep: Friendship in childhood and adolescence* (pp. 87–112). New York: Cambridge University Press.

Alberts, J., Yoshimura, C., Rabby, M., & Loschiavo, R. (2005). Mapping the topography of couples' everyday interaction. *Journal of Social and Personal Relationships, 22,* 299–322.

Allan, G. (1977). Class variation in friendship patterns. *British Journal of Sociology, 28,* 389–393.

Altman, I., & Taylor, D. A. (1973). *Social penetration: The development of interpersonal relationships.* New York: Holt, Rinehart & Winston.

Altman, I., & Taylor, D. (1987). Communication in interpersonal relationships: Social Penetration Theory. In M. E. Roloff and G. R. Miller (Eds.), *Interpersonal processes: New directions in communication research* (pp. 257–277). Newbury Park, CA: Sage.

Altman, I., Vinsel, A., & Brown, B. B. (1981). Dialectic conceptions in social psychology: An application to social penetration and privacy regulation. In L. Berkowitz (Ed.), *Advances in experimental social psychology* (Vol. 14, pp. 107–160). New York: Academic Press.

Argyle, M., & Henderson, M. (1984). The rules of friendship. *Journal of Social and Personal Relationships, 1,* 211–237.

Atkinson, M. P., & Glass, B. L. (1985). Marital age, heterogamy and homogamy, 1900 to 1980. *Journal of Marriage and the Family, 47*(3), 685–700.

Baccman, C., Per Folkesson, P., & Norlander, T, (1999). Expectations of romantic relationships: A comparison between homosexual and heterosexual men with regard to Baxter's criteria. *Social Behavior and Personality, 27*(4), 364–376.

Baxter, L. A. (1982). Strategies for ending relationships: Two studies. *Western Journal of Speech Communication, 46,* 233–242.

Baxter, L. A. (1988). A dialectical perspective on communication strategies in relationship development. In S. W. Duck, D. F. Hay, S. E. Hobfoll, W. Ickes, & B. Montgomery (Eds.), *Handbook of personal relationships* (pp. 257–273). London: Wiley.

Baxter, L. A. (1991). Gender differences in the heterosexual relationship rules embedded in break-up accounts. *Journal of Social and Personal Relationships, 3,* 289–306.

Baxter, L. A., & Bullis, C. (1986). Turning points in developing romantic relationships. *Human Communication Research, 12,* 469–493. *Relationships, 16,* 547–569.

Berg, J. H., & Piner, K. E. (1990). Social relationships and the lack of social relationships. In S. Duck & R. C. Silver (Eds.), *Personal relationships and social support* (pp. 140–158). London: Sage Publications.

Berger, C. R., & Calabrese, R. J. (1975). Some explorations in initial interaction and beyond: Toward a developmental theory of interpersonal communication. *Human Communication Theory, 1,* 99–112.

Berger, C. R., & Kellerman, N. (1994). Acquiring social information. In J. Daly & J. Wiemann (Eds.), *Strategic interpersonal communication* (pp. 1–31). Hillsdale, NJ: Lawrence Erlbaum.

Berscheid, E., & Reis, H. T. (1998). Attraction and close relationships. In D. Gilbert, S. Fiske, & G. Lindzey (Eds.), *Handbook of social psychology* (Vol. 2., 4th ed., pp. 193–281). New York: McGraw-Hill.

Blieszner, R., & Adams, R. G. (1992). *Adult friendship.* Newbury Park, CA: Sage.

Bowker, A. (2004). Predicting friendship stability during early adolescence. *Journal of Early Adolescence, 24,* 85–112.

Bramlett, M. D., & Mosher, W. D. (2002). Cohabitation, marriage, divorce, and remarriage in the United States. National Center for Health Statistics. *Vital Health Stat, 23* (22), 1–32.

Burleson, B. R., & Samter, W. (1996). Similarity in the communication skills of young adults: Foundations of attraction, friendship, and relationship satisfaction. *Communication Reports, 9,* 127–137.

Buss, D. M., Shackelford, T. K., Kirkpatrick, L. A., & Larsen, R. J. (2001). A half century of mate preferences: The cultural evolution of values. *Journal of Marriage and the Family, 63,* 491–503.

Byrne, D. (1997). An overview (and underview) of research and theory within the attraction paradigm. *Journal of Social and Personal Relationships, 14,* 417–431.

Canary, D. J., & Stafford, L. (1994). Maintaining relationships through strategic and routine interaction. In D. J. Canary & L. Stafford (Eds.), *Communication and relational maintenance* (pp. 3–22). San Diego: Academic Press.

Canary, D. J., & Spitzberg, B. H. (1985). Loneliness and relationally competent communication. *Journal of Social and Personal Relationships, 2,* 387–402.

Canary, D. J., Stafford, L., Hause, K. S., & Wallace, L. A. (1993). An inductive analysis of relational maintenance strategies: Comparisons among lovers, relatives, friends, and others. *Communication Research Reports, 10,* 5–14.

Capella, J. N. (1987). Interpersonal communication: Definitions and fundamental questions. In C. R. Berger & S. H. Chafee (Eds.), *Handbook of communication science* (pp. 184–238). Newbury Park, CA: Sage.

Cash, T. F., & Derlega, V. J. (1978). The matching hypothesis: Physical attractiveness among same-sex friends. *Personality and Social Psychology Bulletin, 4,* 240–243.

Centers for Disease Control and Prevention. (2002). Youth risk behavior surveillance—United States, 2001. In *CDC Surveillance Summaries,* June 28, 2002. *MMWR, 51*(SS-4), 5–6.

Chambers, V. J., Christiansen, J. R., & Kunz, P. R. (1983). Physiognomic homogamy: A test of physical similarity as a factor in mate selection process. *Social Biology, 30,* 151–157.

Cody, M. J. (1982). A typology of disengagement strategies and an examination of the role intimacy, reactions to inequity and relational problems play in strategy selection. *Communication Monographs, 49,* 148–170.

Dainton, M. A., Zelley, E., & Langan, E. (2003). Maintaining friendships throughout the lifespan. In D. J. Canary & M. Dainton (Eds.), *Maintaining relationships through communication* (pp. 79–102). Mahwah, NJ: Erlbaum.

DeVito, J. (2009, March 5). Interpersonal communication: A definition. *The Communication Blog.* Retrieved from http://tcbdevito.blogspot.com/search?q=what+is+interpersonal+communication

Duck, S. W. (1982). Social and cognitive features of the dissolution of commitment to relationships. In S. W. Duck (Ed.), *Personal relationships 4: Dissolving personal relationships* (pp. 51–73). London: Academic Press.

Duck, S. W. (1988). *Relating to others.* Chicago: Dorsey Press.

Duck, S. (1991). *Understanding relationships*. New York: Guilford Press.

Edgell, P. (2003). In rhetoric and practice: Defining the "good family" in local congregations. In M. Dillon (Ed.), *Handbook of the sociology of religion*. New York: Cambridge University Press.

Emmers-Sommers, T. M. (2004). The effect of communication quality and quantity indicators on intimacy and relational satisfaction. *Journal of Social and Personal Relationships, 21*(4), 399–411.

Essau, C. A., Conradt, J., & Petermann, F. (1999). Frequency and comorbidity of social phobia and fears in adolescents. *Behavior Research and Therapy, 37*, 831–843.

Fehr, B. (2000). The life cycle of friendship. In C. Hendrick & S. S. Hendrick (Eds.), *Close relationships: A source book* (pp. 71–82). Thousand Oaks: CA: Sage.

Felmlee, D. H. (1995). Fatal attractions: Affections and disaffections in intimate relationships. *Journal of Social and Personal Relationships, 12*, 295–311.

Galassi, J. P., & Galassi, M. D. (1979). Modifications of heterosexual skills deficits. In A. S. Bellack & M. Hersen (Eds.), *Research and practice in social skills training* (pp. 131–188). New York: Plenum.

Geary, D. C. (2005). *Male, female: The evolution of human sex differences*. Washington DC: American Psychological Association.

Gierveld, J., & Tilburg, T. (1995). Social relationships, integration and loneliness. In C. P. M. Knipscheer, J. Gierveld, T. Tilburg, & P. A. Dykstra (Eds.), *Living arrangements and social networks among older adults*. Amsterdam: VU University Press.

Goodwin, R., & Tang, D. (1991). Preferences for friends and close relationships partners: A cross-cultural comparison. *Journal of Social Psychology, 131*, 579–581.

Guerrero, L. K., Eloy, S. V., & Wabnik, A. I. (1993). Linking maintenance strategies to relationship development and disengagement: A reconceptualization. *Journal of Social and Personal Relationships, 10*, 273–283.

Haas, S. M., & Stafford, L. (1998). An initial examination of relationship maintenance behaviors in gay and lesbian relationships. *Journal of Social and Personal Relationships, 15*, 846–855.

Hartill, L. (2001). A brief history of interracial marriage. *Christian Science Monitor, 93*, 15.

Hays, R. B. (1988). Friendship. In S. W. Duck (Ed.), *Handbook of personal relationships* (pp. 391–408). New York: Wiley.

Hinsz, V. B. (1989). Facial resemblance in engaged and married couples. *Journal of Social and Personal Relationships, 6*, 223–229.

Holt-Lunstad, J., Birmingham, W., & Jones, B. Q. (2008) Is there something unique about marriage? The relative impact of marital status, relationship quality, and network support on ambulatory blood pressure and mental health. *Annals of Behavioral Medicine, 35*, 239–244.

Janz, T. A. (2000). The evolution and diversity of relationships in Canadian families. *Canadian Journal of Higher Education*. Retrieved June 15, 2006, from http://www.lcc.gc.ca/research_project/00_diversity_1-en.asp

Johnson, A. J. (2000, July). A role theory approach to examining the maintenance of geographically close and long-distance friendships. *Paper presented at the International Network on Personal Relationships Conference*, Prescott, AZ.

Johnson, A. J., Wittenberg, E., Haigh, M., & Wigley, S. (2004). The process of relationship development and deterioration: Turning points in friendships that have terminated. *Communication Quarterly, 52*, 54–68.

Kalmijin, M. (1994). Assortative mating by cultural and economic occupational status. *American Journal of Sociology, 100*, 422–452.

Kelley, H. H., et al. (1983). *Close relationships*. New York: W. H. Freeman.

Knapp, M. L. (1978). *Social intercourse: From greeting to goodbye*. Boston: Allyn & Bacon.

Knapp, M. L., & Daly, J. A. (2002). *Handbook of Interpersonal Communication*. Thousand Oaks, CA: Sage.

Knapp, M. L., & Vangelisti, A. (1997). *Interpersonal communication and relationships* (2nd ed.). Boston: Allyn & Bacon.

Kurdek, L. A. (1991). The dissolution of gay and lesbian couples. *Journal of Social and Personal Relationships, 8*, 265–78.

Kurt, J. E., & Sherker, J. L. (2003). Relationship quality, trait similarity, and self-other agreement on personality ratings in college roommates. *Journal of Personality, 71*, 21–40.

LaFollette, H. (1996). *Personal relationships: Love, identity, and morality*. Cambridge, MA: Blackwell Publishers.

Lee S. M., E. B. (2005). *New marriages, new families: U.S. racial and Hispanic intermarriage*. Washington, DC: The Population Reference Bureau. (Population Bulletin, 60, No. 2.).

Mare, R. D. (1991). Five decades of educational assortative mating. *American Sociological Review, 56*, 15–32.

McCormick, N. B., & Jones, J. J. (1989). Gender differences in nonverbal flirtation. *Journal of Sex Education and Therapy, 15*, 271–282.

Messman, S. J., Canary, D. J., & Hause, K. S. (2000). Motives to remain platonic, equity, and the use of maintenance strategies in opposite-sex friendships. *Journal of Social and Personal Relationships, 17*, 67–94.

Miller, R. S. (2002). Suicidal and death ideation in older primary care patients with depression, anxiety, and at-risk. *American Journal of Geriatric Psychiatry, 10*, 417–427.

Miller, G. R., & Steinberg, M. (1975). *Between people: A new analysis of interpersonal communication*. Chicago: Science Research Associates.

Mongeau, P. A., Ramirez, R., & Vorell, M. (2003). *Friends with benefits: An initial exploration of a sexual but not romantic relationship*. Paper presented at the Western States Communication Association.

MSNBC News. (2004, March 8). Lip lock could mean lockup in Indonesia. Retrieved March 8, 2006, from http://www.msnbc.msn.com/id/4478875/

Muehlenhard, C. L., & McFalls, M. C. (1981). Dating initiation from a woman's perspective. *Behavior Therapy, 14*, 626–636.

Mulenhard, C. L., & Miller, E. N. (1988). Traditional and non-traditional men's responses to women's dating initiation. *Behavior Modification 12*(3), 385–403.

Nardi, P. M. (1992). That's what friends are for: Friends as family in the gay and lesbian community. In K. Plummer (Ed.), *Modern homosexualities: Fragments of lesbian and gay experience* (pp. 108–120). New York: Routledge.

Noller, P., & Fitzpatrick, M. A. (1990). Marital communication in the eighties. *Journal of Marriage and the Family, 52*, 832–843.

O'Brien, E., & Foley, L. (1999). The dating game: An exercise illustrating the concepts of homogamy, heterogamy, hyperogamy, and hypogamy. *Teaching Sociology, 27*(2), 145–149.

Oswald, D. L., & Clark, E. M. (2003). Best friends forever: High school best friendships and the transition to college. *Personal Relationships, 10*, 187–196.

Owen, W. F. (1987). The verbal expression of love by women and men as a critical communication event in personal relationships. *Women's Studies in Communication, 10*, 15–24.

Paul, E. L., & Hayes, A. (2002). The causalities of "casual sex": A qualitative exploration of the phenomenology of college students' hookups. *Journal of Social and Personal Relationships, 19*, 639–661.

Pogrebin, L. C. (1992). The same and different: Crossing boundaries of color, culture, sexual preference, disability, and age. In W. B. Gudykunst, & Y. Y. Kim (Eds.), *Readings on communicating with strangers* (pp. 318–336). New York: McGraw-Hill.

Rawlins, W. K. (1992). *Friendship matters*. New York: Aline de Guyter.

Rindfuss, R. R., & Stephen, E. H. (1990). Marital noncohabitation: Separation does not make the heart grow fonder. *Journal of Marriage and the Family, 52*, 259–270.

Rose, S. M. (1984). How friendships end: Patterns among young adults. *Journal of Social and Personal Relationships, 1*, 267–277.

Sailer, S. (2003, March 14). *Interracial marriage gender gap grows.* United Press International (UPI). Retrieved June 28, 2004, from http://www.modelminority.com/article338.html

Schafer, R. B., & Keith, P. M. (1990). Matching by weight in married couples: A life cycle perspective. *Journal of Social Psychology, 130*(5), 657–664.

Segrin, C., & Givertz, M. (2003). Methods of social skills training and development. In J. O. Green & B. R. Burleson (Eds.), *Handbook of communication and social interaction skills* (pp. 135–176). Mahwah, NJ: Erlbaum.

Shehan, C. L., Bock, E. W., & Lee, G. R., (1990). Religious heterogamy, religiosity, and marital happiness: The case of Catholics. *Journal of Marriage and the Family, 52*, 73–79.

Sias, P. M., & Cahill, D. J. (1998). From coworkers to friends: The development of peer friendships in the workplace. *Western Journal of Communication, 62*, 273–299.

Sprecher, S. (1998). Insiders' perspectives on reasons for attraction to a close other. *Social Psychology Quarterly, 61*, 287–300.

Sprecher, S., & Regan, P. (2002). Liking some things (in some people) more than others: Partner preferences in romantic relationships and friendships. *Journal of Social and Personal Relationships, 19*, 463–481.

Surra, C. (1987). Reasons for changes in commitment: Variations by courtship type. *Journal of Social and Personal Relationships, 4*, 17–33.

Times Square Travels. (2004). Travel in Japan. Retrieved June 15, 2006, from http://www.travel&st.ca/ index.php?pageid=52

Trost, M. R., & Alberts, J. K. (2006). An evolutionary view on understanding sex differences in communicating attraction. In D. Canary & K. Dindia (Eds.) *Sex, gender and communication: Similarities and differences.* Mahwah, NJ: Erlbaum.

Troy, A. B., Lewis-Smith, J., & Laurenceau, J. P. (2006). Interracial and intraracial romantic relationships: The search for differences in satisfaction, conflict, and attachment styles. *Journal of Social and Personal Relationships, 23*(1), 65–80.

U.S. Bureau of the Census. (1998, October 10) *Race of wife by race of husband, 1960, 1970, 1980, 1990, 1992.* Retrieved June 28, 2004, from http://www.census.gov/population/ socdemo/race/interractab1.txt

Vorauer, J., & Ratner, R. (1996). Who's going to make the first move? *Journal of Social and Personal Relationships, 13*, 483–506.

Weber, A. L. (1998). Losing, leaving and letting go: Coping with nonmarital breakups. In B. H. Spitzberg & W. R. Cupach (Eds.), *The dark side of close relationships* (pp. 267–306). Mahwah, NJ: Erlbaum.

White, B. (1980). Physical attractiveness and courtship progress. *Journal of Personality and Social Psychology, 39*, 660–668.

White, G. L. (1980). Physical attractiveness and courtship progress. *Personality and Social Psychology, 39*, 660–668.

World Travels. (2004). Kuwait travel guide. Retrieved March 16, 2006, from http://www.wordtravels.com/ Travelguide/ Countries/Kuwait/Basics

Wright, D. E. (1999). *Personal relationships: An interdisciplinary approach.* Mountain View, CA: Mayfield Publishing.

Yancey, G. (2002). Who interracially dates: An examination of the characteristics of those who have interracially dated. *Journal of Comparative Family Studies, 33*(2), 177–190.

Young, J. E. (1981). Cognitive therapy and loneliness. In G. Emery, S. D. Hollon, & R. C. Bedrosian (Eds.), *New directions in cognitive therapy: A casebook* (pp. 139–159). New York: Guilford Press.

Chapter 9

Abbey, A. (1987). Misperceptions of friendly behavior as sexual interest: A survey of naturally occurring incidents. *Psychology of Women Quarterly, 11*, 173–194.

Abbey, A. (1988). Misperceptions as an antecedent of acquaintance rape: A consequence of ambiguity in communication between men and women. In A. Parrot & L. Bechhofer (Eds.), *Acquaintance rape: The hidden crime* (pp. 96–112). NY: John Wiley & Sons.

American Psychological Association. (1996). *Violence and the family: Report of the American Psychological Association presidential task force on violence and the family.* Retrieved June 15, 2006, from http://www.apa.org/pi/ viol&fam.html

Andersen, P., Eloy, S. V., Guerrero, L. K., & Spitzberg, B. H. (1995). Romantic jealousy and relational satisfaction: A look at the impact of jealousy experience and expression. *Communication Reports, 8,* 77–85.

Anglin, K., & Holtzwoth-Munroe, A. (1997). Comparing the responses of martially violent and nonviolent spouses to problematic marital and non-marital situations: Are the skills deficits of physically aggressive husbands and wives global? *Journal of Family Psychology, 11,* 30–313.

Argyle, M., & Henderson, M. (1984). The rules of friendship. *Journal of Social and Personal Relationships, 1*(2), 211–237.

Atkinson, B. J. (2005, January). The love breakthrough. *O, the Oprah Magazine,* pp. 128–131, 163–164.

Aune, K. S., & Comstock, J. (1991) Experience and expression of jealousy: Comparison between friends and romantics. *Psychological Reports, 69,* 315–319.

Bagozzi, R. P., Verbeke, W., & Gavino, J. C. Jr. (2003). Culture moderates the self-regulation of shame and its effects on performance: The case of salespersons in the Netherlands and the Philippines. *Journal of Applied Psychology, 88,* 219–233.

Berscheid, E., & Reis, H. T. (1998). Attraction and close relationships. In D. Gilbert, S. Fiske, & G. Lindzey (Eds.), *Handbook of social psychology* (Vol. 2., 4th ed., pp. 193–281). New York: McGraw-Hill.

Boekhout, B. A., Hendrick, S. S., & Hendrick, C. (1999). Relationship infidelity: A loss perspective. *Journal of Personal and Interpersonal Loss, 4,* 97–124.

Bok, S. *Lying: Moral choice in public and private life.* New York: Random House.

Bramlett, M. D., & Mosher, W. D. (2001). First marriage dissolution, divorce and remarriage: United States. Advance Data, Center for Disease Control No. 323. Retrieved July 19, 2009, from http://www.cdc.gov/nchs/data/ad/ad323.pdf

Buchanan, C. M., Maccoby, E. E., & Dornhusch, S. M. (1991). Caught between parents: Adolescents' experience in divorced homes. *Child Development, 2*(5), 1008–1029.

Buller, D. B., & Burgoon, J. K. (1996). Interpersonal deception theory. *Communication Theory, 6,* 203–242.

Bureau of Justice Statistics. (August, 1995). *Special Report: Violence against women: Estimates from the Redesigned Survey* (NCJ-154348, p. 3). Bureau of Justice Statistics. Retrieved June 15, 2009, http://bjs.ojp.usdoj.gov/

Burgoon, J. K., Buller, D. B., Ebesu, A., & Rockwell, P. (1994). Interpersonal deception: 5. Accuracy in deception detection. *Communication Monographs, 61,* 303–325.

Buss, D. M. (1988). From vigilance to violence: Tactics of mate retention in American undergraduates. *Ethology and Sociobiology, 9,* 291–317.

Buss, D. M. (2002). Human mate guarding. *Neuroendocrinology Letters, 23*(Suppl.4), 23–29.

Buss, D. M., & Shackelford, T. K. (1997). Susceptibility to infidelity in the first year of marriage. *Journal of Research in Personality, 31*(2), 193–221.

Buunk, B. (1987). Conditions that promote breakups as a consequence of extradyadic involvements. *Journal of Social and Clinical Psychology, 5,* 271–284.

Cano, A., & O'Leary, K. D. (1997). Romantic jealousy and affairs: Research and implications for couples' therapy. *Journal of Sex and Marital Therapy, 23,* 249–275.

Cauffman, E., Feldman, S., Jensen, L., & Arnett, J. (2000). The (Un)acceptability of violence against peers and dates. *Journal of Adolescent Research, 15,* 652–673.

Centers for Disease Control. (2002). Violence-related behaviors among high school students—United States 1991–2003. Retrieved March 4, 2010, from http://www.cdc.gov/mmwr/preview/mmwrhtml/mm5329a1.htm

Cialdini, R. (2001). *Influence: Science and Practice* (4th ed.). Needham Heights, MA: Allyn & Bacon.

Cody, M. J., Canary, D. J., & Smith, S. W. (1994). Compliance gaining goals: An inductive analysis of actors' goal types, strategies, and successes. In J. Daly & J. Weimann (Eds.),

Commonwealth Fund. (1998, May). *Health concerns across a woman's lifespan: 1998 survey of women's health.* Retrieved June 15, 2009, http://www.commonwealthfund.org/Content/Publications/Fund-Reports/1999/May/Health-Concerns-Across-a-Womans-Lifespan—The-Common wealth-Fund-1998-Survey-of-Womens-Health.aspx

Communicating strategically (pp. 33–90). Hillsdale, NJ: Erlbaum.

Connally, J. A., & Johnson, A. M. (1996). Adolescents' romantic relationships and the structure and quality of their close interpersonalties. *Personal Relationships, 3*(2), 185–195.

Cordova, J. V., Jacobsen, N. S., Gottman, J. M., Rushe, R., & Cox, G. (1993). Negative reciprocity and communication in couples with a violent husband. *Journal of Abnormal Psychology, 102,* 559–564.

Dillard, J. P., Anderson, J. W., & Knobloch, L. K. (2002). Interpersonal influence. In M. Knapp & J. Daly (Eds.), *Handbook of Interpersonal Communication* (pp. 425–474). Thousand Oaks, CA: Sage.

Dillard, J. P., Segrin, C., & Harden, J. M. (1989). Primary and secondary goals in the production of interpersonal influence messages. *Communication Monographs, 56,* 19–38.

Eagly, A. H., Ashmore, R. D., Makhijani, M. G. and Longo, L. C. (1991) 'What is beautiful is good, but… : A meta-analytic review of research on the physical attractiveness stereotype', *Psychological Bulletin,* 110(1): 109–28.

Feldman, S. S., & Cauffman, E. (2000). Your cheatin' heart: Attitudes, behaviors, and correlates of sexual betrayal in late adolescents. *Journal of research on Adolescence, 9,* 227–253.

Ferraro, K. (1996). The dance of dependency: A genealogy of domestic violence discourse. *Hypattia, 11,* 72–91.

Folkes, V. S. (1982). Communicating the causes of social rejection. *Journal of Experimental Social Psychology, 18,* 235–252.

Gagne, F. M., & Lydon, J. E. (2001). Bias and accuracy in close relationships: An integrative review. *Personality and Social Psychology Review, 8*(4), 322–338.

Gaillilot, M. T. (2007). Self-regulation and sexual restraint: Dispositionally and temporarily poor self-regulatory abilities

contribute to failures at restraining sexual behavior. *Personality and Social Psychology Bulletin, 33*(2), 173–186.

Galician, M. L. (2004). *Sex, love, and romance in mass media: Analysis and criticism of unrealistic portrayals and their influences*. Mawah, NJ: Lawrence Erlbaum.

Gilbert, P. (1998). *Shame, interpersonal behavior, psychopathology and culture*. New York: Oxford University Press.

Greeley, A. (1994). Marital infidelity. *Society, 31*, 9–13.

Grotpeter, J. K., & Crick, N. R. (1996). Relational aggression, overt aggression, and friendship. *Child Development, 67*, 2328–2338.

Guerrero, L. K., & Afifi. W. A. (1999). Toward a goal-centered approach for understanding strategic communicative responses to jealousy. *Western Journal of Communication, 63*, 216–248.

Guerrero, L. K., & Andersen, P. A. (1998). Jealousy experience and expression in romantic relationships. In L. K. Guerrero & P. A. Andersen (Eds.), *Communication and emotion: Theory, research and application* (pp. 155–188). San Diego, CA: Academic Press.

Guerrero, L. K., Andersen, P. A., & Afifi, W. A. (2007). *Close encounters: Communication in relationships*. Thousand Oaks, CA: Sage.

Hansen, G. L. (1987). Extradyadic relations during courtship. *Journal of Sex Research, 23*, 382–390.

Heath, R. L., & Bryant, J. (2000). Human communication theory and research: Concepts, contexts and challenges. Hillsdale, CA: Lawrence Erlbaum.

Henderson, L., & Zimbardo, P. (2010). *Encyclopedia of mental health*? Academic Press. Retrieved August 9, 2009, from http://www
.shyness.com/encyclopedia.html#VI

Hird, M. J., & Jackson, S. (2001). Where "angels" and "wusses" fear to tread. *Journal of Sociology, 37*(1), 27–43.

Holy Bible, King James Version. (n.d.). Proverbs 15:1. Retrieved December 30, 2009, from http://www.online-literature.com/bible/bible.php

Infante, D. A., Chandler, T. A., & Rudd, J. E. (1989). A test of an argumentative skill deficiency model of interspousal violence. *Communication Monographs, 56*, 163–177.

Kellerman, K. (2004). A goal-directed approach to gaining compliance. *Communication Research, 31*(4), 397–445.

Kimmel, M. S. (2002). Male victims of domestic violence: A substantive and methodological research review. *Violence Against Women, 8*(11), 1332–1363.

Knox, D., Schacht, C., Holt, J., & Turner, J. (1993). Sexual lies among university students. *College Student Journal, 27*, 269–272.

Kowalski, R., Valentine, S., Wilkinson, R., Queen, A., & Sharpe, B. (2003). Lying, cheating, complaining, and other aversive interpersonal behaviors: A narrative examination of the dark side of relationships. *Journal of Social and Personal Relationships, 20*, 471–490.

Koss, M. P., et al. (1994). The culture and context of male violence against women. In Koss, M., Goodman, L. Browne, A., et al., Eds. *No safe haven: Male violence against women at home, at

work, and in the community*. (pp. 3–17). Washington, DC, US: American Psychological Association. xviii, 344 pp.

Kramer, D., & Moore, M. (2001). Gender roles, romantic fiction and family therapy. *Family Therapy, 12*(24), 1–8.

Laumann, E. O., Gagnon, J. H., Michael, R. T., & Michaels, S. (1994). *The social organization of sexuality: Sexual practices in the United States*. Chicago, IL: University of Chicago Press.

Lim, G. Y., & Roloff, M. E. (1999). Attributing sexual consent. *Journal of Applied Communication Research, 27*(1), 1–23.

Lloyd, S. A. (1990). Conflict types and strategies in violent marriages. *Journal of Family Violence, 5*, 269–284.

Lloyd, S. A. (1999). The interpersonal and communication dynamics of wife battering. In X. Arriaga & S. Oskamp (Eds.), *Violence in intimate relationships* (pp. 91–111). Thousand Oaks, CA: Sage.

Lloyd, S. A., & Emery, B. C. (2000). The context and dynamics of intimate aggression against women. *Journal of Social and Personal Relationships, 17*, 503–521.

Marwell, G., & Schmitt, D. R. (1967). Dimensions of compliance-gaining behavior: An empirical analysis. *Sociological Quarterly, 9*, 317–328.

Matsumoto, D. (2006). Are cultural differences in emotion regulation mediated by personality traits? *Journal of Cross-Cultural Psychology, 37*(4), 421–437.

McCornack, S. A., & Parks, M. R. (1986). Deception detection and relationship development: The other side of trust. In M. L. McLaughlin (Ed.), *Communication Yearbook 9*. Newbury Park, CA: Sage.

McEwen, W. J., & Greenburg, B. S. (1970). The effects of message intensity on receiver revaluations of source, message, and topic. *Journal of Communication, 20*, 340–350.

Mending your affair. (2009). Mayo Clinic. Retrieved July 30, 2009, from http://www.mayoclinic.com/health/infidelity/MH00110

Metts, S. (1994). Relational transgressions. In W. R. Cupach & B. H. Spitzberg (Eds.), *The dark side of interpersonal relationships* (pp. 217–239). Hillsdale, NJ: Lawrence Erlbaum.

Miller, C. W., & Roloff, M. (2005). Gender and willingness to confront hurtful messages from romantic partners. *Communication Quarterly, 53*(3), 323–337.

Miller, R. S. (1997a). We always hurt the ones we love: Aversive interactions in close relationships. In R. M. Kowalski (Ed.), *Aversive interpersonal behaviors* (pp. 12–29). New York: Plenum.

Miller, R. S. (1997b). *Embarrassment: Poise and peril in everyday life*. New York: Guilford Press.

Mills, R. S. L., Nazar, J., & Farrell, H. M. (2002). Child and parent perceptions of hurtful messages. *Journal of Social and Personal Relationships, 19*, 731–754.

Muehlenhard, C. L. (1989). Misinterpreted dating behaviors and the risk of date rape. In M. A. Pirog-Good & J. E. Stets (Eds.), *Violence in dating relationships: Emerging social issues* (pp. 241–256). New York: Praeger.

Muehlenhard, C. L., & Hollabough, L. C. (1988). Do women sometimes say no when they mean yes?: The prevalence and correlates of women's token resistance to sex. *Journal of Personality and Social Psychology, 54*, 872–879.

Muehlenhard, C. L., & Linton, M. A. (1987). Date rape and sexual aggression in dating: Incidence and risk factors. *Journal of Personality and Social Psychology, 34,* 186–196.

Myers, D. G. (2007). *Exploring psychology* (7th ed.). New York: Worth Publishers.

Myers, S. A., Schrodt, P., & Rittenour, C. E. (2006). The impact of parents' use of hurtful messages on adult children's self-esteem and educational outcomes. In L. H. Turner & R. West (Eds.), *Family communication: A reference of theory and research* (pp. 425–445). Thousand Oaks, CA: Sage.

National Opinion Research Center. *General social survey.* (1996). Retrieved June 16, 2009 http://norc.org/GSS+Website/

Oswald, D. L., & Clark, E. M. (2003). Best friends forever: High school best friends and the transition to college. *Personal Relationships, 10*(2), 187–196

Pollak, L. H., & Thoits, P. A. (1989). Processes in emotional socialization. *Social Psychology Quarterly, 52,* 22–34.

Reeve, J. (2005). *Understanding motivation and emotion* (4th ed.). Hoboken, NJ: John Wiley & Sons.

Rennison, C. M., & Welchans, S. (2000). *Intimate Partner Violence Special Report,* NCJ 178247. Washington, DC: U.S. Department of Justice.

Roloff, M. E., Soule, K. P., & Carey, C. M. (2001). Reasons for remaining in a relationships and responses to relational transgressions. *Journal of Social & Personal Relationships, 18*(3), 362–385.

Roscoe, B., Cavanaugh, L. E., & Kennedy, D. R. (1988). Dating infidelity: Behaviors, reasons, and consequences. *Adolescence, 23,* 35–43.

Roth, M. A., & Parker, J. G. (2001). Affective and behavioral responses to friends who neglect their friends for dating partners: Influences of gender, jealousy, and perspective. *Journal of Adolescence, 24*(3), 281–297.

Sabourin, T. C. (1996). The role of communication in verbal abuse between spouses. In D. D. Cahn & S. A. Lloyd (Eds.), *Family violence from a communication perspective* (pp. 199–217). Thousand Oaks, CA: Sage.

Sagarin, B. J., Rhoads, K. L., & Cialdini, R. B. (1998). Deceiver's distrust: Denigration as a consequence of undiscovered deception. *Personality and Social Psychology Bulletin, 24*(11), 1167–1176.

Schmitt, D. P., & Buss, D. M. (2001). Human mate poaching: Tactics and temptations for infiltrating existing relationships. *Journal of Personality and Social Psychology, 80,* 894–917.

Shaver, P. R., Wu, S., & Schwartz, J. C. (1992). Cross-cultural similarities and differences in emotion and its representations: A prototype approach. In M. S. Clark (Ed.), *Review of Personality and Social Psychology* (Vol. 13, pp. 231–251). Thousand Oaks, CA: Sage.

Spitzberg, B. (1998). Sexual coercion in courtship relationships. In B. Spitzberg & W. Cupach (Eds.), *The dark side of close relationships* (pp. 179–232). Hillsdale, NJ: Erlbaum.

Staheli, L. (1995). *Affair-proof your marriage: Understanding, preventing and surviving an affair.* New York, NY: HarperCollins.

Stiff, J. B., Kim, H. J., & Ramesh, C. N. (1989, May). *Truth biases and aroused suspicion in relational deception.* Paper presented at the annual meeting of the Interpersonal Communication Association, San Francisco, CA.

Stiff, J. B., & Mongeau, P. (2002). *Persuasive communication.* New York: Guilford.

Tolhuizen, J. H. (1990). *Deception in developing dating relationships.* Paper presented at the Speech Communication Association Convention, Chicago, IL.

Tracy, K., Van Dusen, D., & Robinson, S. (1987). "Good" and "bad" criticism: A descriptive analysis. *Journal of Communication, 37*(2), 46–59.

Turner, R. E., Edgley, C., & Olmstead, G. (1975). Information control in conversations: Honesty is not always the best policy. *Kansas Journal of Sociology, 11,* 69–89.

Vangelisti, A. L. (1994). Messages that hurt. In W. R. Cupach, & B. H. Spitzberg (Eds.), *The dark side of interpersonal communication* (pp. 53–82). Hillsdale, NJ: Erlbaum.

Vangelisti, A. (2004). *Feeling hurt in close relationships.* Cambridge: Cambridge University Press.

Vangelisti, A. L. (2007). Communicating hurt. In B. Spitzberg & W. Cupach (Eds.), *The dark side of close relationships* (pp. 121–142). Mawah, NJ: Erlbaum.

Vangelisti, A., L., & Young, S. L. (2000). When words hurt: The effects of perceived intentionality on interpersonal relationships. *Journal of Social and Personal Relationships, 17,* 393–424.

Vangelisti, A. L., Young, S. L., Carpenter, K., & Alexander, A. L. (2005). Why does it hurt? The perceived causes of hurt feelings. *Communication Research, 32,* 443–477.

Waldby, C. S. Kippax, S., & Crawford, J. (1993). Research note: Heterosexual men and "safe sex" practice. *Sociology of Health and Illness, 15,* 246–56.

Wallbot & Scherer (1986). How universal and specific is emotional experience?: Evidence from 27 countries on 5 continents. *Social Science Information, 25*(4), 763–795.

White, G. L., & Mullen, P. E. (1989). *Jealousy.* New York: Guilford Press.

Willam, V. J., & Pollard, P. (2003). Likelihood of acquaintance rape as a function of males' sexual expectations, disappointment, and adherence to rape-conducive attitudes. *Journal of Social and Personal Relationships, 20,* 637–661.

Young, S. L., & Bippus, A. M. (2001). Does it make a difference if they hurt you in a funny way?: Humorously and non-humorously phrased hurtful messages in personal relationships. *Communication Quarterly, 49,* 35–52.

Zhang, S. (2005). *Is honest the best policy? Honest but hurtful evaluative messages in romantic relationships.* Unpublished masters thesis, Ohio State University, Columbus, OH.

Zimbardo, P. G. (1989). *Shyness: What it is; what to do about it.* New York: Perseus Books.

Zimmer-Gembeck, M. J. (1998). *Negotiation and reorganization of peer relationships during adolescence: The emergence of romantic relationships and quality of peer relationships.* Unpublished dissertation, Portland, OR: Portland State University.

Chapter 10

Adams, G. R., Gullotta, T. P., & Markstrom, C. (1994). *Adolescent life experiences* (3rd ed.). Pacific Grove, CA: Brooks/Cole Publishing.

Alberts, J. K. (1989). A descriptive taxonomy of couples' complaints. *Southern Communication Journal, 54,* 125–143.

Alberts, J. K., & Driscoll, G. (1992). Containment versus escalation: The trajectory of couples' conversational complaints. *Western Journal of Communication, 56,* 394–412.

Argyle, M., & Henderson, M. (1984). The rules of friendship. *Journal of Social and Personal Relationships, 1,* 211–237.

Baumeister, R. F., Stillwell, A. M., & Heatherton, T. F. (1994). Guilt: An interpersonal approach. *Psychological Bulletin, 115,* 243–267.

Ben-Yoav, O., & Pruitt, D. G. (1984). Resistance to yielding and expectation of cooperative future interaction in negotiation. *Journal of Experimental and Social Psychology, 34,* 323–335.

Blake, R. R., & Mouton, J. S. (1964). *The managerial grid.* Houston, TX: Gulf.

Blumstein, P., & Schwartz, P. (1983). *American couples: Money, work, sex.* New York: Morrow.

Bowker, A. (2004). Predicting friendship stability during early adolescence. *Journal of Early Adolescence, 24,* 85–112.

Braiker, H. B., & Kelley, H. H. (1979). Conflict in the development of close relationships. In R. L. Burgess & T. L. Huston (Eds.), *Social exchange in developing relationships* (pp. 135–168). New York: Academic Press.

Canary, D. J. (2003). Managing interpersonal conflict: A model of events related to strategic choices. In J. Greene & B. Burleson (Eds.), *Handbook of communication and social interaction skills* (pp. 515–549). Mawah, NJ: Lawrence Erlbaum.

Canary, D. J., Cupach, W. R., & Messman, S. J. (1995). *Relationship conflict.* Thousand Oaks, CA: Sage.

Canary, D. J., Cupach, W. R., & Serpe, R. T. (2001). A competence-based approach to examining interpersonal conflict: Test of a longitudinal model. *Communication Research, 28,* 79–104.

Canary, D. J., & Emmers-Sommer, T. (1997). *Sex and gender differences in personal relationships.* New York: Guildford Press.

Canary, D. J., & Lakey, S. G. (2006). Managing conflict in a competent manner. In J. G. Oetzel & S. Ting-Toomey (Eds.), *The Sage handbook of conflict communication* (pp. 185–210). Thousand Oaks, CA: Sage.

Canary, D., & Lakey, S. (2010). *Strategic conflict.* London: Routledge.

Canary, D. J., & Spitzberg, B. H. (1989). A model of perceived competence of conflict strategies. *Human Communication Research, 15,* 630–649.

Canary, D. J., Spitzberg, B. H., & Semic, B. A. (1998). The experience and expression of anger in interpersonal settings. In P. A. Andersen & L. K. Guerrero (Eds.), *Handbook of communication and emotion: Research, theory, applications and contexts* (pp. 189–213). San Diego, CA: Academic Press.

Caughlin, J. P., & Vangelisti, A. L. (2006). Conflict in dating and marital relationships. In J. Oetzel & S. Ting-Toomey (Eds.), *The Sage handbook of conflict communication* (pp. 129–157). Thousand Oaks, CA: Sage.

Chaiken, S. L., Gruenfeld, D. H., & Judd, C. M. (2000). Persuasion in negotiations and conflict situations. In M. Deutsch & P. Coleman (Eds.), *The handbook of conflict resolution: Theory and practice* (pp. 144–165). San Francisco: Jossey-Bass Publishers.

Coleman, P. T. (2000). Power and conflict. In M. Deutsch & P. T. Coleman (Eds.), *The Handbook of conflict resolution: Theory and practice* (pp. 108–130). San Francisco: Jossey-Bass.

Commonwealth Fund. (1998, May). *Health concerns across a woman's lifespan: 1998 survey of women's health.* Retrieved June 15, 2009, http://www.commonwealthfund.org/Content/Publications/Fund-Reports/1999/May/Health-Concerns-Across-a-Womans-Lifespan–The-Commonwealth-Fund-1998-Survey-of-Womens-Health.aspx

Conerly, K., & Tripathi, A. (2004). What is your conflict style? Understanding and dealing with your conflict style. *Journal of Quality and Participation, 27*(2), 16–21.

Coser, L. A. (1956). *The function of social conflict.* New York: The Free Press.

Davidson, J. A., McElwee, G., & Hannan, G. (2004). Trust and power as determinants of conflict resolutions strategy and outcome satisfaction. *Peace and Conflict: Journal of Peace Psychology, 10*(3), 275–292.

de Wied, M., Branje, S. J. T., & Meeus, W. H. J. (2006). Empathy and conflict resolution in friendship relations among adolescents. *Aggressive Behavior, 33*(1), 48–55.

Deetz, S. (1990). Reclaiming the subject matter as a guide to mutual understanding: Effectiveness and ethics in interpersonal communication. *Communication Quarterly, 38,* 226–243.

Denton, W. H., Burleson, B. R., Hobbs, B. V., Von Stein, M., & Rodriguez, C. P. (2001). Cardiovascular reactivity and initiate/avoid patterns of marital communication: A test of Gottman's psychophysiologic model of marital interaction. *Journal of Behavioral Medicine, 24,* 401.

Donohue, W. A., & Kolt, R. (1992). *Managing interpersonal conflict.* Thousand Oaks, CA: Sage.

Dutton, D. G., van Ginkel, C., & Landolt, M. A. (1996). Jealousy, intimate abusiveness, and intrusiveness. *Journal of Family Violence, 11,* 411–423.

Fischer, R., & Ury, W. (1991). *Getting to yes: Negotiating agreement without giving in.* New York: Viking.

Friedman, R. A., Tidd, S. T., & Currall, S. C. (2000). What goes around comes around: The impact of personal conflict style on work conflict and stress. *The International Journal of Conflict Management, 11*(1), 32–55.

Garcia, W. (1996). Respecto: A Mexican base for interpersonal relationships. In S. Ting-Toomey (Ed.), *Communication in personal relationships across cultures* (pp. 137–155). Thousand Oaks, CA: Sage.

Gottman, J. M. (1994). *What predicts divorce? The relationship between marital processes and marital outcomes.* Hillsdale, NJ: Lawrence Erlbaum.

Gottman, J. M. (1995). What predicts divorce? *Family Relations, 44,* 116–32.

Gottman, J. M., & Levenson, R. W. (1988). The social psychophysiology of marriage. In P. Noller & M. A. Fitzpatrick (Eds.),

Perspectives on marital interaction (pp. 182–200). Philadelphia, PA: Multilingual Matters.

Guerrero, L. K. (1994). "I'm so mad I could scream": The effects of anger expression on relational satisfaction and communication competence. *Southern Communication Journal, 59*, 125–141.

Guerrero, L. K., & Andersen, P. A. (1998). Jealousy experience and expression in romantic relationships. In L. K. Guerrero & P. A. Andersen (Eds.), *Communication and emotion: Theory, research and application* (pp. 155–188). San Diego, CA: Academic Press.

Guerrero, L. K., Andersen, P. A., & Afifi, W. A. (2007). *Close encounters: Communicating in relationships* (2nd ed.). Mountain View, CA: Mayfield.

Guerrero, L. K., & La Valley, A. G. (2006). Conflict, emotion and communication. In J. G. Oetzel & S. Ting-Toomey (Eds.), *The Sage handbook of conflict communication* (pp. 69–96). Thousand Oaks, CA: Sage.

Impett, E. A., & Peplau, L. A. (2006). "His" and "her" relationships?: A review of the empirical evidence. In A. L. Vangelisti & D. Perlman (Eds.), *The Cambridge handbook of personal relationships* (pp. 273–292). Cambridge, NY: Cambridge University Press.

Infante, D. A., Chandler, T. A., & Rudd, J. E. (1989). Test of an argumentative skill deficiency model of interpersonal violence. *Communication Monograph, 56*, 163–177.

Jae-Yop, K., & Emery, C. (2003). Marital power, conflict, norm consensus, and marital violence in a nationally representative sample of Korean couples. *Journal of Interpersonal Violence, 18*(2), 197–219.

Johnson, D. W., Johnson, R. T., & Tjosvold, D. (2006). Constructive controversy: The value of intellectual opposition. In M. Deutsch & P. T. Coleman (Eds.), *The handbook of conflict resolution* (pp. 69–91). San Francisco: Jossey-Bass.

Johnson, M. P. (2006). Violence and abuse in personal relationships: Conflict, terror, and resistance in intimate partnerships. In A. L. Vangelisti & D. Perlman (Eds.), *The Cambridge handbook of personal relationships* (pp. 557–576). Cambridge, NY: Cambridge University Press.

Jones, T. S. (2000). Emotional communication in conflict: Essence and impact. In W. Eadie & P. Nelson (Eds.), *The language of conflict and resolution* (pp. 81–104). Thousand Oaks, CA: Sage.

Jones, W. H., & Burdette, M. P. (1994). Betrayal in relationships. In A. L. Weber & J. H. Harvey (Eds.), *Perspectives on close relationships* (pp. 243–262). Boston: Allyn & Bacon.

Kelley, H. H., Cunningham, J. D., Grisham, J. A., Lefebvre, L. M., Sink, C. R., & Yablon, G. (1978). Sex differences in comments made during conflict within close heterosexual pairs. *Sex Roles, 4*, 473–492.

Kilmann, R. H., & Thomas, K. W. (1975). Interpersonal conflict-handling behavior as a reflection of Jungian personality dimensions. *Psychology Reports, 37*, 309–325.

Kilmann, R. H., & Thomas, K. W. (1977). Developing a forced-choice measure of conflict-handling behavior: The "MODE" instrument. *Educational and Psychological Measurement, 37*, 971–980.

Kowalski, R. (2002). Whining, griping, and complaining: Positivity in the negativity. *Journal of Clinical Psychology, 58*(9), 1023–1035.

Kowalski, R., Walker, S., Wilkinson, R., Queen, A., & Sharpe, B. (2003). Lying, cheating, complaining, and other aversive interpersonal behaviors: A narrative examination of the dark side of relationships. *Journal of Social and Personal Relationships, 20*, 471–490.

Kurdek, L. A. (1994). Conflict resolution styles in gay, lesbian, heterosexual nonparent, and heterosexual parent couples. *Journal of Marriage and the Family, 56*, 705–722.

La France, M., & Harris, J. L. (2004). Gender and verbal and nonverbal communication. In M. A. Pauldi (Ed.), *Praeger Guide to the psychology of gender* (pp. 133–154). Santa Barbara, CA: Praeger Publishers.

Langer, E. J. (1989). *Mindfulness*. Reading, MA: Addison-Wesley.

Lazarus, R. S. (1991). *Emotion and adaptation*. New York: Oxford University Press.

Leung, K., Au, Y.-F., Fernandez-Dols, J. M., & Iwawaki, S. (1992). Preference for methods of conflict processing in two collectivistic cultures. *International Journal of Psychology, 27*, 195–209.

Lindner, E. G., (2006). Emotion and conflict: Why it is important to understand how emotions affect conflict and conflict affects emotions. In M. Deutsch & P. T. Coleman (Eds.), *The handbook of conflict resolution* (pp. 268–294). San Francisco: Jossey-Bass.

Marcus-Newhall, A., Pedersen, W. C., Carlson, M., & Miller, N. (2000). Displaced aggression is alive and well: A meta-analytic review. *Journal of Personality and Social Psychology, 78*, 670–689.

Margolin, G., & Wampold, B. E. (1981). Sequential analysis of conflict and accord in distressed and nondistressed marital partners. *Journal of Consulting and Clincial Psychology, 49*, 554–467.

Marshall, L. L. (1994). Physical and psychological abuse. In W. R. Cupach & B. H. Spitzberg (Eds.), *The dark side of interpersonal communication* (pp. 281–311). Hillsdale, NJ: Lawrence Erlbaum.

Marcus, A., & Gould, E. W. (2000). Cultural dimensions and global web user-interface design: What? So What? Now What? *Proceedings of the 6th Conference on Human Factors and the Web*. Austin, Texas. Retrieved October 5, 2005, from http://www.amanda.com/resources/hfweb2000/AMA_CultDim.pdf

Messman, S. J., & Mikesell, R. L. (2000). Competition and interpersonal conflict in dating relationships. *Communication Reports, 13*, 21–34.

Metts, S. (1994). Relational transgressions. In W. R. Cupach & B. H. Spitzberg (Eds.), *The dark side of interpersonal communication* (pp. 217–239). Hillsdale, NJ: Erlbaum.

Mikolic, J. M., Parker, J. C., & Pruitt, D. G. (1997). Escalation in response to persistent annoyance: Groups versus individuals and gender effects. *Journal of Personal and Social Psychology, 72*, 151–163.

Miller, R. S. (1997). We always hurt the ones we love: Aversive interactions in close relationships. In R. M. Kowalski (Ed.),

Aversive interpersonal behaviors (pp. 12–29). New York: Plenum.

Molm, L. (1997). *Coercive power in social exchange.* Cambridge, England: Cambridge University Press.

Mortenson, C. D. (1974). A transactional paradigm of social conflict. In G. R. Miller & H. W. Simones (Eds.), *Perspectives on communication in social contexts* (pp. 90–124). Englewood Cliffs, NJ: Prentice Hall.

Mullen, P. E., & Martin, J. L. (1994). Jealousy: A community study. *British Journal of Psychiatry, 164,* 35–43.

Nicotera, A. M. (1993). Beyond two dimensions: A grounded theory model of conflict-handling behavior. *Communication Monographs, 6,* 282–306.

Oetzel, J. G., & Ting-Toomey, S. (2006). *The Sage handbook of conflict communication.* Thousand Oaks, CA: Sage.

Osterman, K., et al. (1997). Sex difference in styles of conflict. In D. Fry & K. Bjorkqvist, *Cultural Variation in Conflict Resolution: Alternatives to Violence.* (pp. 185–197). Mahwah, NJ: Erlbaum.

Phinney, J. S., Kim-Jo, T., Osorto, S., & Vilhjalmsdottir, P. (2005). Autonomy and relatedness in adolescent-parent disagreements. *Journal of Adolescent Research, 20*(1), 8–39.

Putnam, L. L. (2006). Definitions and approaches to conflict and communication. In J. G. Oetzel & S. Ting-Toomey (Eds.), *The Sage handbook of conflict communication* (pp. 1–32). Thousand Oaks, CA: Sage.

Putnam, L. L., & Poole, M. S. (1987). Conflict and negotiation. In F. M. Jablin, L. L. Putnam, K. H. Roberts, & L. W. Porter (Eds.), *Handbook of organizational communication* (pp. 549–599). Newbury Park, CA: Sage.

Putnam, L. L., & Wilson, C. E. (1982). Communicative strategies in organizational conflicts: Reliability and validity of a measurement scale. In M. Burgoon (Ed.), *Communication yearbook.* Vol. 6. Beverly Hills, CA: Sage.

Rahim, M. A. (1986). *Managing conflict in organizations.* New York: Praeger.

Rahim, M. A., & Bonoma, T. V. (1979). Managing organizational conflict: A model for diagnosis and intervention, *Psychological Reports, 44,* 1023–1044.

Rahim, M. A., & Buntzman, G. F. (1990). Supervisory power bases, styles of handling conflict with subordinates, and subordinate compliance and satisfaction. *Journal of Psychology, 123,* 195–210.

Rennison, C. M., & Welchans, S. (2000). *Intimate partner violence special report* (NCJ 178247). Washington, DC: U.S. Department of Justice.

Roloff, M., & Soule, K. P. (2002). Interpersonal conflict. In M. L. Knapp & J. A. Daly (Eds.), *Handbook of interpersonal communication* (pp. 475–528). Thousand Oaks, CA: Sage.

Roloff, M., Soule, K. P., & Carey, C. M. (2001). Reasons for remaining in a relationship and responses to relational transgressions. *Journal of Social and Personal Relationships, 19,* 363–385.

Roseman, I. J., Wiest, C., & Swartz, T. S. (1994). Phenomenology, behaviors and goals differentiate discrete emotions. *Journal of Personality and Social Psychology, 67,* 206–221.

Rusbult, C. E., Verette, J., Whitney, G. A., Slovik, L. F., & Lipkus, I. (1991). Accommodation processes in close relationships: Theory and preliminary empirical evidence. *Journal of Personality and Social Psychology, 60,* 53–78.

Sabourin, T. C. (1996). The role of communication in verbal abuse between spouses. In D. D. Cahn & S. A. Lloyd (Eds.), *Family violence from a communication perspective* (pp. 199–217). Thousand Oaks, CA: Sage.

Sagrestano, L. M., Heavey, C. L., & Christensen, A. (2006). Individual differences versus social structural approaches to explaining demand-withdraw and social influence behaviors. In K. Dindia & D. J. Canary (Eds.), *Sex differences and similarities in communication* (pp. 379–395). Mawah, NJ: Lawrence Erlbaum.

Sillars, A. L. (1998). (Mis)Understandings. In B. H. Spitzberg & W. R. Cupach (Eds.), *The dark side of relationships* (pp. 73–102). Mahwah, NJ: Lawrence Erlbaum & Associates.

Sillars, A., Canary, D. J., & Tafoya, M. (2004). Communication, conflict, and the quality of family relationships. In A. L. Vangelisti (Ed.), *Handbook of family communication* (pp. 413–446). Mahwah, NJ: Erlbaum.

Simonelli, C. J., & Ingram, K. M. (1998). Psychological distress among men experiencing physical and emotional abuse in heterosexual dating relationships. *Journal of Interpersonal Violence, 13,* 667–681.

Simons, H. (1974). Prologue. In G. R. Miller & H. W. Simons (Eds.), *Perspectives on communication in social conflict* (pp. 1–13). Englewood Cliffs, NJ: Prentice Hall.

Spitzberg, B. H., Canary, D. J., & Cupach, W. R. (1994). A competence-based approach to the study of interpersonal conflict. In D. D. Cahn (Ed.), *Conflict in personal relationships* (pp. 183–202). Hillsdale, NJ: Lawrence Erlbaum.

Stone, D., Patton, B., & Heen, S. (1999). *Difficult conversations: How to discuss what matters most.* New York: Viking.

Ting-Toomey, S. (1985). Toward a theory of conflict and culture. In W. B. Gudykunst, L. P. Stewart, & S. Ting-Toomey (Eds.), *Communication, culture and organizational processes* (pp. 71–86). Beverly Hills, CA: Sage.

Ting-Toomey, S., & Oetzel, J. G. (2001). *Managing intercultural conflict effectively.* Thousand Oaks, CA: Sage.

Ting-Toomey, S., Yee-Jung, K. K., Shapiro, R. B., Garcia, W., Wright, T. J., & Oetzel, J. G. (2000). Ethnic/cultural identity salience and conflict styles in four US ethnic groups. *International Journal of Intercultural Relations, 24,* 47–81.

Trubinsky, P., Ting-Toomey, S., & Lin, S-L. (1991). The influence of individualism-collectivism and self-monitoring on conflict styles. *International Journal of Intercultural Relations, 15,* 65–84.

Vangelisti, A. L., & Sprague, R. J. (1998). Guilt and hurt: Similarities, distinctions, and conversational strategies. In P. A. Andersen & L. K. Guerrero (Eds.), *Handbook of communication and emotion: Research, theory, applications and contexts* (pp. 123–154). San Diego, CA: Academic Press.

Wayne, S. J., Liden, R. C., Graf, L. K., & Ferris, G. R. (1997). The role of upward influence tactics in human resource decisions. *Personnel Psychology, 50,* 979–1006.

Zillman, D. (1993). Mental control of angry aggression. In D. M. Wegner & J. W. Pennebaker (Eds.), *Handbook of mental control* (pp. 370–392). Englewood Cliffs, NJ: Prentice Hall.

Zuroff, D. C., & Duncan, N. (1999). Self-criticism and conflict resolution in romantic couples. *Journal of Behavioral Science, 31,* 137–149.

Chapter 11

Adams, K., & Galanes, G. J. (2003). *Communicating in groups: Applications and skills.* Boston, MA: McGraw-Hill.

Allen, T. H., & Plax, T. G. (2002). Exploring consequences of group communication in the classroom. In L. R. Frey (Ed.), *New directions in group communication* (pp. 219–234). Thousand Oaks, CA: Sage.

Alsop, R. (2003, September 9). Playing well with others. *Wall Street Journal* (Eastern Edition), p. R11.

Arrow, H., McGrath, J. E., & Berdahl, J. L. (2000). *Small groups as complex systems.* Thousand Oaks, CA: Sage.

Bantz, C. R. (1993). Cultural diversity and group cross-cultural team research. *Journal of Applied Communication Research, 21,* 1–20.

Benne, K. D., & Sheats, P. (1948). Functional roles of group members. *Journal of Social Issues, 4,* 41–49.

Bormann, E. G. (1975). *Discussion and group methods* (2nd ed.). New York: Harper & Row.

Bowers, C. A., Pharmer, J. A., & Salas, E. (2000). When member homogeneity is needed in work teams: A meta-analysis. *Small Group Research, 31,* 305–327.

Broome, B., J., & Chen, M. (1992). Guidelines for computer-assisted problem solving: Meeting the challenges of complex issues. *Small Group Research, 23,* 216–236.

Broome, B. J., & Fulbright, L. (1995). A multistage influence model of barriers to group problem solving: A participant-generated agenda for small group research. *Small Group Research, 26,* 24–55.

Cady, S. H., & Valentine. J. (1999). Team innovation and perceptions of consideration: What difference does diversity make? *Small Group Research, 30,* 730–750.

Cannaughton, S. L., & Shuffler, M. (2007). Multinational and multicultural distributed teams: A review and future agenda. *Small Group Research, 38(1),* 387–412.

Carwright, D. (1968). The nature of group cohesiveness. In D. Carwright & A. Zander (Eds.), *Group dynamics: Research and theory* (3rd ed., pp. 91–109). New York: Harper & Row.

Cox, T. (1994). *Cultural diversity in organizations: Theory, research and practice.* San Francisco: Berrett-Kochler.

Cragan, J. F. & Wright, D. W. (1999). *Communication in small groups: Theory, process, skills.* 5th ed. Belmont, CA: Wadsworth.

Crown, D. F. (2007). The use of group and groupcentric individual goals for culturally heterogeneous and homogeneous task groups: An assessment of European work teams. *Small Group Research, 38(4),* 489–508.

Dennis, A. R., & Wixom, B. H. (2001–2002). Investigating the moderators of the group support systems use with meta-analysis. *Journal of Management Information Systems, 18(3),* 235–257.

Fisher, B. A. (1970). Decision emergence: Phases in group decision-making. *Speech Monographs, 37,* 53–66.

Fisher, B. A. (1980). *Small group decision making: Communication and the group process* (2nd ed.). New York: McGraw-Hill.

Fisher, B. A., & Ellis, D. G. (1993). *Small group decision making: Communication and the group process.* Boston: McGraw-Hill.

French, J. R., Jr., & Raven, B. H. (1959). The bases of social power. In D. Cartwright (Ed.), *Studies in social power* (pp. 150–167). Ann Arbor, MI: Institute for Social Research.

Frey, L. R. (1994). The call of the field: Studying communication in natural groups. In L. R. Frey (Ed.), *Group communication in context: Studies of natural groups* (pp. ix–xiv). Hillsdale, NJ: Erlbaum.

Ilgen, D. R., Hollenbeck, J. R., Johnson, M., & Jundt, D. (2005). Teams in organizations: From input-process-output models to IMOI models. *Annual Review of Psychology, 56,* 517–543.

Gagné, M., & Zuckerman, M. (1999). Performance and learning goal orientations as moderators of social loafing and social facilitation. *Small Group Research, 30,* 524–541.

Gokhale, A. (1995). Collaborative learning enhances critical thinking. *Journal of Technology Education, 7,* 22–30.

Gouran, D. S., Hirokawa, R., & Martz, A. (1986). A critical analysis of factors related to the decisional processes involved in the *Challenger* disaster. *Central States Speech Journal, 37,* 119–135.

Hargrove, R. (1998). *Mastering the art of creative collaboration.* New York: Business Week Books.

Haslett, B. B., & Ruebush, J. (1999). What differences do individual differences in groups make? The effects of individuals, culture, and group composition. In L. R. Frey, D. S. Gouran, & M. S. Poole (Eds.), *The handbook of group communication theory and research* (pp. 115–138). Thousand Oaks, CA: Sage.

Henningsen, D. D. & Henningsen, M. L. M. (2006). Examining the symptoms of groupthink and retrospective sensemaking. *Small Group Research, 37(1),* 36–64.

Hirokawa, R. Y., & Salazar, A. J. (1999). Task-group communication and decision-making performance. In L. R. Frey, D. S. Gouran, & M. S. Poole (Eds.), *The handbook of group communication theory and research* (pp. 167–191). Thousand Oaks, CA: Sage.

Hobman, E. V., Bordia, P., Irmer, B., & Chang, A. (2002). The expression of conflict in computer-mediated and face-to-face groups, *Small Group Research, 33,* 439–465.

Hughes, L. (2003). How to be an effective team player. *Women in Business, 55,* 22.

Janis, I. L. (1982). *Groupthink: Psychological study of policy decisions and fiascoes.* Boston: Houghton-Mifflin.

Kent, M. V. (1994). The presence of others. In A. P. Hare, H. H. Blumberg, M. F. Davies, & M. V. Kent. *Small group research: A handbook* (pp. 81–106). Norwood, NJ: Ablex.

Keyton, J. (1999). Relational communication in groups. In L. R. Frey, D. S. Gouran, & M. S. Poole (Eds.), *Hand-book of group communication theory and research* (pp. 199–222). Thousand Oaks, CA: Sage.

Keyton, J. (2000). Introduction: The relational side of groups. *Small Group Research, 34,* 387–396.

King, N., & Anderson, N. (1990). Innovation in working groups. In M. A. West & J. F. Farr (Eds.), *Innovation and creativity at work: Psychological and organizational strategies* (pp. 110–135). Chichester, UK: Wiley.

Klocke, U. (2007). How to improved decision making in small groups: Effects of dissent and training interventions. *Small Group Research, 38*(3), 437–468.

Larson, J. R. (2007). Deep diversity and strong synergy: Modeling the impact of variability in members' problem solving strategies on group problem-solving performance. *Small Group Research, 38*(3), 413–436.

Li, S.-C. S. (2007). Computer-mediated communication and group decision making: A functional perspective. *Small Group Research, 38*(5), 593–614.

Lowry, P. B., Roberts, T. L., Romano, N. C., Cheney, P. D., & Hightower R. T. (2006). The impact of group size and social presence on small-group communication: Doescomputer–mediated communication make a difference? *Small Group Research, 37*(6), 631–661.

Littlejohn, S. W. (2002). *Theories of human communication* (7th ed.). Belmont, CA: Wadsworth.

Maznevski, M., & Chudoba, C. (2000). Bridging space over time: Global virtual team dynamics and effectiveness. *Organization Science, 11*(5), 473–492.

McLeod, P. L., Lobel, S. A., & Cox, T. H. (1996). Ethnic diversity and creativity in small groups. *Small Group Research, 27,* 248–264.

Mensch, G. O. (1993). A managerial tool for diagnosing structural readiness for breakthrough innovations in large bureaucracies (technocracies). In R. L. Kuhn (Ed.), *Generating creativity and innovation in large bureaucracies* (pp. 257–281). Westport, CT: Quorum.

Moore, R. M., III. (2000). Creativity of small groups and of persons working alone. *Journal of Social Psychology, 140,* 143–144.

Myers, S. A., & Goodboy, A. K. (2005). A study of grouphate in a course on small group communication. *Psychological Reports, 97*(2), 381–386.

Oetzel, J. G. (1998). Explaining individual communication processes in homogeneous and heterogeneous groups through individual-collectivism and self-construal. *Human Communication Research, 25,* 202–224.

Oetzel, J. G. (2001). Self-construals, communication processes, and group outcomes in homogeneous and heterogeneous groups. *Small Group Research, 32,* 19–54.

Oetzel, J. G. (2005). Effective intercultural workgroup communication theory. In W. B. Gudykunst (Ed.), *Theorizing about intercultural communication* (pp. 351–371). Thousand Oaks, CA: Sage.

Paletz, S. B. F., Peng, K., Erez, M., & Maslach, C. (2004). Ethnic composition and its differential impact on group processes in diverse teams. *Small Group Research, 35,* 128–158.

Pavitt, C. (1999). Theorizing about the group communication-leadership relationship. In L. R. Frey, D. S. Gouran, & M. S. Poole (Eds.), *Handbook of group communication theory and research* (pp. 313–334). Thousand Oaks, CA: Sage.

Peterson, R. S., & Behfar, K. J. (2003). The dynamic relationship between performance feedback, trust, and conflict in groups: A longitudinal study. *Organizational Behavior and Human Decision Processes, 92,* 102–112.

Polzer, J. T., Milton, L. P., & Swann, W. B., Jr. (2002). Capitalizing on diversity: Interpersonal congruence in small work groups. *Administrative Science Quarterly, 47,* 296–324.

Poole, M. S. (1983). Decision development in small groups: A study of multiple sequences in decision-making. *Communication Monographs, 50,* 206–232.

Poole, M. S., & Garner, J. T. (2006). Workgroup conflict and communication. In J. G. Oetzel & S. Ting-Toomey (Eds.), *The Sage handbook of conflict communication* (pp. 267–292). Thousand Oaks, CA: Sage.

Poole, M. S. (1999). Group communication theory. In L. R. Frey, D. S. Gouran, & M. S. Poole (Eds.), *Handbook of group communication theory and research* (pp. 37–70). Thousand Oaks, CA: Sage.

Propp, K. M. (1999). Collective information processing in groups. In L. R. Frey, D. S. Gouran, & M. S. Poole (Eds.), *Handbook of group communication theory and research* (pp. 225–250). Thousand Oaks, CA: Sage.

Putnam, L. L., & Stohl, C. (1996). Bona fide groups: An alternative perspective for communication and small group decision-making. In R. Y. Hirokawa & M.S. Poole (Eds.), *Communication and group decision-making* (2nd ed., pp. 147–178). Thousand Oaks, CA: Sage.

Riddle, B. L., Anderson, C. M., & Martin, M. M. (2000). Small group socialization scale: Development and validity. *Small Group Research, 31,* 554–572.

Rothwell, J. D. (1995). *In mixed company: Small group communication* (2nd ed.). Fort Worth, TX: Harcourt Brace.

Salazar, A. J. (1997). Communication effects in small group decision-making: Homogeneity and task as moderators of the communication performance relationship. *Western Journal of Communication, 61,* 35–65.

Sargent, L. D., & Sue-Chan, C. (2001). Does diversity affect group efficacy? *Small Group Research, 32,* 426–450.

Schiller, S. Z., & Mandviwalla, M. (2007). Virtual team research: An analysis of theory use and a framework for theory appropriation. *Small Group Research, 38*(1), 12–59.

Schultz, B. G. (1999). Improving group communication performance. In L. R. Frey, D. S. Gouran, & M. S. Poole (Eds.), *Handbook of group communication theory and research* (pp. 371–394). Thousand Oaks, CA: Sage.

Schwarz, A., & Schwarz, C. (2007). The role of latent beliefs and group cohesion in prediction group decision support systems success. *Small Group Research, 38*(1), 195–229.

Sell, J., Lovaglia, M. J., Mannix, E. A., Samuelson, C. D., & Wilson, R. K. (2004). Investigating conflict, power, and status within and among groups. *Small Group Research, 35,* 44–72.

Smith, P. G. (2001). Communication holds global teams together. *Machine Design, 73,* 70–73.

Sorensen, S. (1981, May). Grouphate. *A paper presented at the International Communication Association,* Minneapolis, MN.

Sunwolf & Seibold, D. R. (1999). The impact of formal procedure on group processes, members, and task outcomes. In L. R. Frey, D. S. Gouran, & M. S. Poole (Eds.), *Handbook of group communication theory and research* (pp. 394–431). Thousand Oaks, CA: Sage.

Valenti, M. A., & Rockett, R. (2008). The effects of demographic differences on forming intragroup relationships. *Small Group Research, 39*(2), 179–202.

van Knippenberg, D., De Dreu, C. K. W., & Homan, A. C. (2004). Work group diversity and group performance: An integrative model and research agenda. *Journal of Applied Psychology, 89*(6), 1008–1022.

Wellen, J. M., & Neale, M. (2006). Deviance, self-typicality and group cohesion: The corrosive effects of the bad apples on the barrel. *Small Group Research, 37*(2), 165–186.

Wheelan, S. A., Davidson, B., & Tilin, F. (2003). Group development across time: Reality or illusion? *Small Group Research, 34,* 223–245.

Chapter 12

Agle, B., Nagarajan, N., Srinivasan, D., & Sonnenfeld, J. (2006). Does CEO charisma matter? An empirical analysis of the relationships among organizational performance, environmental uncertainty, and top management teams' perceptions of CEO charisma. *Academy of Management Journal, 49*(1), 161–174.

Ardichvili, A., & Kuchinke, P. (2002). Leadership styles and cultural values among managers and subordinates: A comparative study of four countries of the former Soviet Union, Germany, and the US. *Human Resource Development International, 5*(1), 99–117.

Baldoni, J. (2004). Powerful leadership communication. *Leader to Leader, 32,* 20–21.

Barge. J. K. (1989). Leadership as medium: A leaderless group discussion model. *Communication Quarterly, 37,* 237–247.

Barnard, C. (1938). *The functions of an executive.* Cambridge, MA: Harvard University Press.

Behan, B. (2009, January 20). Time for diversity in the boardroom. *BusinessWeek.com.* Retrieved April 13, 2010, from http://www.businessweek.com/managing/content/jan2009/ca20090120_589700.htm

Benne, K. D., & Sheats, P. (1948). Functional roles of group members. *Journal of Social Issues, 4,* 41–49.

Bligh, M. C., & Kohles, J. C. (2009). The enduring allure of charisma: How Barack Obama won the historic 2008 presidential election. *The Leadership Quarterly, 20,* 483–492.

Bock, W. (2004). Great leaders do things differently: Why leadership is important. Retrieved July 23, 2009, from http://www.bockinfo.com/040720spia2.htm

Bono, J. E., & Judge, T. A. (2004). Personality and transformational and transactional leadership: A meta-analysis. *Journal of Applied Psychology, 89*(5), 901–910.

Broadbridge, A., & Hearn, J. (2008). Gender and management: New directions in research and continuing patterns in practice. *British Journal of Management, 19*(1), S38–S49.

Brooks, Carl (Interview with). (2009, April 6). Minorities in the C-Suite. *Workforce Management, 88*(4), 7.

Brown, M. E., & Treviño, L. K. (2006). Ethical leadership: A review and future directions. *The Leadership Quarterly, 17*(6), 595–616.

Catalyst. (2007, February). *2006 Catalyst census of women corporate officers and top earners of the Fortune 500.* New York: Catalyst. Retrieved May 24, 2009, from http:// www. catalyst.org/publication/18/2006-catalyst-census-of-women-corporate-officers-and-top-earners-of-the-fortune-500

Child, L. (2009, July 26). My good life after being fired. *Parade magazine,* p. 14.

Connaughton, S. L., & Daly, J. A. (2005). Leadership in the new millennium: Communication beyond temporal, spatial, and geographical boundaries. In P. Kalbfleisch (Ed.), *Communication yearbook 29* (pp. 187–213). Mahwah, NJ: Erlbaum.

Connaughton, S. L., & Shuffler, M. (2007). Multinational and multicultural distributed teams: A review and future agenda. *Small Group Research, 38,* 397–412.

Cooper, K. J. (2009, February 18). The presidential search "plateau". *Diverse: Issues in Higher Education, 15575411, 26*(1), 18–21.

Daft, R. L. (2008). *The leadership experience* (4th ed.). Mason, OH: Thomson Higher Education.

Denhardt, R. B., & Denhardt, J. V. (2004). *The dance of leadership.* Armonk, NJ: M. E. Sharpe.

Dunghy, T. (2009, February 20). Diversity everywhere but the sidelines. *New York Times,* 0362–4331, p. 31.

Eagly, A. H., & Carli, L. L. (2003). The female leadership advantage: An evaluation of the evidence. *Leadership Quarterly, 14,* 807–834.

Eagly, A. H., & Johnson, B. T. (1990). Gender and leadership style: A meta-analysis, *Psychological Bulletin, 108*(2), 233–256.

Early, P. C., & Ang, S. (2003). *Cultural Intelligence: Individual actions across cultures.* Stanford, CA: Stanford Books.

Early, P. C., & Mosakowski, E. (2004, October). Cultural Intelligence. *Harvard Business Review, 82*(10), 139–146.

Ely, R. (2003). Leadership: Overview. In R. Ely, E. Foldy, M. Scully, & the Centre for Gender in Organizations, Simmons School of Management (Eds.), *Reader in gender, work and organization* (pp. 153–158). Oxford: Blackwell.

Facts on Women in Congress 2010. (2010). Rutgers Center for American Women and Politics. Retrieved April 13, 2010, from, http://www.cawp.rutgers.edu/fast_facts/levels_of_office/Congress-CurrentFacts.php

Fatahi, K. (1996). *International management: A cross cultural and functional perspective.* Upper Saddle River, NJ: Prentice-Hall.

Fisher, A. (2005, August 8). Piercing the Bamboo Ceiling. *CNNMoney.com.* Retrieved August 2, 2009, from http://money.cnn.com/2005/08/08/news/economy/annie/fortune_annie080805/index.htm

Foels, R., Driskell, J. E., Mullen, B., & Salas, E. (2000). The effects of democratic leadership on group member satisfaction: An integration. *Small Group Research, 31,* 676–701.

Gastil, J. (1994). A meta-analytic review of the productivity and satisfaction of democratic and autocratic leadership. *Small Group Research, 25,* 384–399.

Gollent, M. (2007, June 6). Why are leadership skills important—for everyone? Retrieved July 23, 2009, from http://ezinearticles.com/?why-are-leadership-skills-important—for-everyone?&id=591333

Grant, H. M. & Crutchfield, L. (2008). The hub of leadership: Lessons from the social sector. *Leader to Leader, 48,* 45–52.

Greenleaf, R. K. (1991, 1977). *Servant leadership: A journey into the nature of legitimate power and greatness.* New York: Paulist Press.

Greenleaf, R. K. (2002). *Servant leadership: A journey into the nature of legitimate power and greatness* (25th anniversary ed.). New York: Paulist Press.

Groutage, H. (1999, October 10). Mother of slain student calls for tolerance. *Salt Lake Tribune,* p. A4.

Harned, P. J. (2009, April 27). Do the right things when times are tough. *Ethics Today.* Retrieved June 3, 2009, from http://www.ethics.org/ethics-today/0409/pat-column.asp

Harris, P. R., Moran, R. T., & Moran, S. V. (2004). *Managing cultural differences: Global leadership strategies for the 21st century* (6th ed.). Burlington, MA: Butterworth-Heinemann.

Heifetz, R. A. (1994). *Leadership without easy answers.* Cambridge: Harvard University Press.

Hofstede, G. (1997). *Cultures and organizations: Software of the mind* (Rev. ed.). New York: McGraw-Hill.

Hogan, R., Curphy, G. J., & Hogan, J. (1994). What we know about leadership: Effectiveness and personality. *American Psychologist, 29*(6), 493–504.

Hogan, R., Hogan, J., & Roberts, B. W. (1996). Personality measurement and employment decisions: Questions and answers. *American Psychologist, 51,* 469–477.

Hoyt, C. L., Simon, S., & Reid, L. (2009). Choosing the best (wo)man for the job: The effects of mortality salience, sex, and gender stereotypes on leader evaluations. *The Leadership Quarterly, 20,* 233–246.

Hymowitz, C., & Schellhardt, T. (1986, March 24). Corporate women: Special report. *Wall Street Journal,* p. 1.

Judge, T. A., Bono, J. E., Ilies, R., & Gerhardt, M. W. (2002). Personality and leadership: A qualitative and quantitative review. *Journal of Applied Psychology, 87,* 765–780.

Judge, T. A., & Cable, D. M. (2004). The effect of physical height on workplace success and income: Preliminary test of a theoretical model. *Journal of Applied Psychology, 89,* 428–441.

Judge, T. A., Colbert, A. E., & Ilies, R. (2004). Intelligence and leadership: A quantitative review and test of theoretical propositions. *Journal of Applied Psychology, 89,* 542–552.

Judge, T. A. & Livingston, B. A. (2008). Is the gap more than gender? A longitudinal analysis of gender, gender role orientation, and earnings. *Journal of Applied Psychology, 93,* 994–1012.

Jung, D. I., & Sosik, J. J. (2002). Transformational leadership in work groups: The role of empowerment, cohesiveness, and collective-efficacy on perceived group performance. *Small Group Research, 33,* 313–336.

Komives, S. R., Lucas, N., & McMahon, T. (1998). *Exploring leadership for college students who want to make a difference.* San Francisco: Jossey-Bass Publishers.

Ladkin, D. (2008). Leadership and Gender. In A. Marturano & J. Gosling, J. (Eds.). *Leadership: The key concepts 65–67.* New York: Routledge.

Lewin, K., Lippit, R., & White, R. K. (1939). Patterns of aggressive behavior in experimentally created "social climates." *Journal of Social Psychology, 10,* 271–279.

Lipman-Blumen, J. (2005). *The allure of toxic leaders: Why we follow destructive bosses and corrupt politicians—and how we can survive them.* Oxford, England: Oxford University Press.

Lyness, K. S., & Heilman, M. E. (2006). When fit is fundamental: Performance evaluations and promotions of upper-level female and male managers, *Journal of Applied Psychology, 91*(4), 777–785.

MacNeil, A., & McClanahan, A. (2005). Shared leadership, The Connexions Project. Retrieved May 21, 2008, from http://cnx.org/content/m12923/latest/

Martin, C. (2005). Management intercultural en Europe. *La Revue des Sciences de Gestion: Direction et Gestion, 40*(2), 25–34.

Marturano, A., & Gosling, J. (Eds.). (2008). *Leadership: The key concepts.* New York: Routledge.

Matha, B., & Boehm, M. (2008). *Beyond the babble: Leadership communication that drives results.* San Francisco: Jossey-Bass.

Meade, R. (1985). Experimental studies of authoritarian and democratic leadership in four cultures: American Indian, Chinese and Chinese-American. *High School Journal, 68,* 293–295.

Northouse, P. G. (2007). *Leadership: Theory and practice* (4th ed.). Thousand Oaks, CA: Sage.

Omatsu, G. (n.d.). *Student leadership training booklet.* California State University: Northridge.

Pavitt, C. (1999). Theorizing about the group communication-leadership relationship. In L. R. Frey, D. S. Gouran, & M. S. Poole (Eds.), *Handbook of group communication theory and research* (pp. 313–334). Thousand Oaks, CA: Sage.

Pavitt, C., High, A. C., Tressler, K. E., & Winslow, J. K. (2007). Leadership communication during group resource dilemmas. *Small Group Research, 38*(4), 509–531.

Pearce, C. L., & Conger, J. A. (2003). *Shared leadership: Reframing the hows and whys of leadership.* Thousand Oaks, CA: Sage.

Rauch, C. F., Jr., & Behling, O. (1984). Functionalism: Basis for alternative approach to the study of leadership. In J. G. Hunt, D.-M. H. Hosking, C. A. Schriesheim, & R. Stewart (Eds.), *Leaders and managers: International perspectives on managerial behavior and leadership* (pp. 45–62). New York: Pergamon.

Rosener, J. B. (1995). *America's competitive secret: utilizing women as a management strategy.* Oxford, UK: Oxford University Press.

Rost, J. C. (2008). Leadership definition. In A. Marturano & J. Gosling, J. (Eds.), *Leadership: The key concepts* (pp. 96–99). New York: Routledge.

Rowold, J., & Heinitz, K. (2007). Transformational and charismatic leadership: Assessing the convergent, divergent and criterion validity of the MLQ and the CKS. *The Leadership Quarterly, 18,* 121–133.

Savič, B. S., & Pagon, M. (2008). Individual involvement in health care organization: Differences between professional groups, leaders and employees. *Stress and Health, 24,* 71–84.

Schmid, R. E. (2000, August 6). Psychologist rate what helps make a president great. *Johnson City Press,* p. 10. (cited in Daft, p. 129).

Schneider, S. C., & Barsoux, J. L. (2003). Managing across cultures. New York: Prentice Hall.

Shipman, C., & Kay, K. (2009, May 25). Women will rule business, *TIME,* p. 47.

Singh, V., & Vinnicombe, S. (2006). *The female FTSE report.* Cranfield: Cranfield School of Management.

Steinheider, B., & Wuestewald, T. (2008). From the bottom-up: Sharing leadership in a police agency. *Police Practice & Research, 9*(2), 145–163.

Stogdill, R. M. (1974). *Handbook of leadership: A survey of theory and research.* New York: Free Press.

Strang, S. E., & Kuhnert, K. W. (2009). Personality and leadership: Developmental levels as predictors of leader performance. *The Leadership Quarterly, 20,* 421–433.

Thompson, J. A. (2000, September). Leading virtual teams. *Quality Digest.* Retrieved September 8, 2009, from http://www.qualitydigest.com/sept00/html/teams.html

Treviño, L. K., Brown, M., & Hartman, L. P. (2003). A qualitative investigation of perceived executive ethical leadership: Perceptions from inside and outside the executive suite. *Human Relations, 55,* 5–37.

Treviño, L. K., & Brown, M. E. (2004). Managing to be ethical: Debunking five business ethics myths. *Academy of Management Executive, 18,* 69–81.

Treviño, L. K., Hartman, L. P., & Brown, M. (2000). Moral person and moral manager: How executives develop a reputation for ethical leadership. *California Management Review, 42,* 128–142.

Uhl-Bien, M. (2006). Relational leadership theory: Exploring the social processes of leadership and organizing. *The Leadership Quarterly, 17,* 654–676.

Warkentin, M., Sayeed, L., & Hightower, R. (1997). Virtual teams versus face-to-face teams: An exploratory study of a web-based conference system. *Decision Sciences, 28*(4), 975–996.

Watson, C., & Hoffman, L. R. (2004). The role of task-related behavior in the emergence of leaders. *Group & Organization Management, 29*(6), 659–685.

Williams, L. (1995, February 5). A silk blouse on the assembly line? (Yes, the Boss's). *The New York Times,* Business Section, p. 7.

Chapter 13

Dyer, J. L. (2008, August). Fertility of American women: 2006, population characteristics. *U.S. Census Bureau.* Retrieved August 5, 2009 from: http://www.census.gov/prod/2008pubs/ p20-558.pdf

Gayle, B. M. (2004). Transformations in a civil discourse public speaking class: Speakers' and listeners' attitude change. *Communication Education, 53,* 174–185.

Lucas, S. E. (2004). *The art of public speaking* (8th ed.). Boston: McGraw Hill.

McKerrow, R. E., Gronbeck, B. E., Ehninger, D., & Monroe, A. H. (2003). *Principles of public speaking* (15th ed.). Boston: Allyn & Bacon.

Miller, A. N. (2002). An exploration of Kenyan public speaking patterns with implications for the American introductory public speaking course. *Communication Education, 51,* 168–182.

O'Hair, D., Stewart, R., & Rubenstein, H. (2010). *A speaker's guidebook* (4th ed.). Boston: Bedford/St.Martin's.

Osterman, R. (2005, May 23). "Soft skills" top list of what area employers desire. *Sacramento Bee,* p. D1.

Schutt, R. K. (2001). *Investigating the social world: The process and practice of research* (3rd ed.). Boston: Pine Forge Press.

Sprague, J., & Stuart, D. (2005). *The speaker's handbook.* Belmont, CA: Wadsworth/Thomson.

Webster, D. (1989). "Bunker Hill Monument Oration (1825)." In James Andrews and David Zarefsky (Eds.), *American Voices: Significant Speeches in American History, 1640–1945* (pp. 125–138). White Plains, NY: Longman.

Yook, E. L. (2004). Any questions? Knowing the audience through question types. *Communication Teacher, 18,* 91–93.

Chapter 14

Ayres, J. (1996). Speech preparation processes and speech apprehension. *Communication Education, 45,* 228–235.

Behnke, R., & Sawyer, C. (1999). Milestones of anticipatory public speaking anxiety. *Communication Education, 48,* 165–173.

Behnke, R., & Sawyer, C. (2004). Public speaking anxiety as a function of sensitization and habituation processes. *Communication Education, 53,* 164–173.

Bing, S. (2009, August 4). Geithner drops the F-Bomb, or now we know reform is on the way. *Fortune.* Retrieved August 4, 2009, from http://stanleybing.blogs.fortune.cnn.com/2009/08/04/geithner-drops-the-f-bomb-or-now-we-know-reform-is-on-the-way/#comments

Book, M. & Edelstein, M. (2009). *Stage Fright: 40 Stars Tell You How They Beat America's #1 Fear.* Tucson, AZ: See Sharp Press.

Bruce, T. J., & Saeed, S. A. (1999). Social anxiety disorder: A common underrecognized mental disorder. *American Family Physician, 60,* 2311–2320.

(2009, June 24). Gov. Sanford issues follow-up statement on today's media availability (Press Release). Retrieved September 26, 2009, from http://sc.statehouseblogs.com/2009/06/24/press-release-gov-sanford-issues-follow-up-statement-on-todays-media-availability/

Kennedy, J. F. (1961, January 9). Address delivered to a joint convention of the General Court of the Commonwealth of Massachusetts. The John F. Kennedy library. Retrieved September 28, 2009, from http://www.jfklibrary.org0/Historical+Resources/Archives/Reference+Desk/Speeches/JFK

Paletta, D. & Solomon, D. (2009, August 4). Geithner vents as overhaul stumbles. *The Wall Street Journal,* pp. A1, A4.

Processed foods—the cause of obesity (2006, August 20). Bio-Medicine.com. Retrieved September 27, 2009, from

http://www.bio-medicine.org/medicine-news/Processed-foods—u2013—22the-22-cause-of-obesity-21-13398-3/

Sanow, A. (1997). How I overcame the fear of public speaking. Retrieved June 23, 2010, from: http://www.arnoldsanow.com/uploads/article21.pdf

Sprague, J. & Stuart, D. (2005). *The speaker's handbook*. Belmont, CA: Wadsworth/Thomson.

Statistics you need to know. (2009, March 23). American Heart Association. Retrieved July 15, 2009, from http://www.americanheart.org/presenter.jhtml?identifier=107

U.S. obesity trends, 1985–2008. (2009, August 19). Centers for Disease Control and Prevention. Retrieved September 27, 2009, from http://www.cdc.gov/obesity/data/trends.html

Webster, D. (1989). Bunker Hill Monument Oration (1825). In J. Andrews and D. Zarefsky (Eds.), *American Voices: Significant Speeches in American History, 1640–1945* (pp. 125–138). White Plains, NY: Longman.

Chapter 15

"Arianna Huffington on Citizen Journalism." (28 June, 2009). Retrieved July 15, 2009, from http://www.youtube.com/watch?v=udJ0SVkuK44

Beyonceonline. The official Beyonce website. Retrieved July 15, 2009, from http://www.beyonceonline.com/us/home

Chan, M. (2009, June 11). World now at the start of 2009 influenza pandemic (Statement to the press by WHO Director). Retrieved July 15, 2009, from http://www.who.int/mediacentre/news/statements/2009/h1n1_pandemic_phase6_20090611/en/index.html

Gallo, C. (2007). Steve Jobs' greatest presentation. *Businessweek.com*. Retrieved July 15, 2009, from http://www.businessweek.com/smallbiz/content/jul2007/sb2007076_474371.htm

Gring, M. A. (2006). Epistemic and pedagogical assumptions for informative and persuasive speaking practices: Disinterring the dichotomy. *Argumentation and Advocacy, 43*, 41–50.

Herrick, J. (2004). *The history and theory of rhetoric: An introduction* (3rd ed.). Boston, Allyn & Bacon.

How to cook a perfect egg by Martha Stewart. Retrieved July 15, 2009, from http://www.youtube.com/watch?v=EHDFgFGXlWQ

Lucas, S. E. (2009). *The art of public speaking* (10th ed.). New York: McGraw Hill.

Macworld 2007—Steve Jobs introduces iPhone—Part I. (2007, January 9). Retrieved July 15, 2009, from http://www.youtube.com/watch?v=Svo45oepsI0

Major types of informative speeches. Retrieved July 15, 2009, from http://writing.colostate.edu/guides/speaking/infomod/pop2b.cfm

Minkin, T., & Renaud, B. (2009, July 15, 2009). America's top 10 healthiest fast food restaurants. Health.com. Retrieved September 27, 2009, from http://living.health.com/2009/02/19/americas-healthiest-fast-food-restaurants/

New England Aquarium. Retrieved July 15, 2009, from http://www.neaq.org/animals_and_exhibits/index.php

Nichols, G. (n.d.). Your gateway to the North End. Retrieved July 15, 2009, from http://www.northendboston.com/history.htm

Pausch, R., & Zaslow, J. (2008). *The last lecture*. New York: Hyperion.

Pausch, R. (2007). The last lecture. Retrieved July 15, 2009, from http://www.cmu.edu/uls/journeys/randy-pausch/index.html

Skype, http://www.skype.com/

Chapter 16

Beebe, S. A. B. & Beebe, S. J. (2010). *Public Speaking Handbook* (3rd ed.). Boston: Pearson.

Bounty Paper Towels. Retrieved April 26, 2010, from http://www.quickerpickerupper.com/en_US/index.shtml

Breslau, K. (2008, January 7). Hilary tears up: A Muskie moment, or a helpful glimpse of the real Hillary? Retrieved August 13, 2009, from http://www.newsweek.com/id/85609

Crouse, K. (2009, February 1). Phelps apologizes for marijuana pipe photograph. Retrieved August 13, 2009, from http://www.nytimes.com/2009/02/02/sports/othersports/02phelps.html

Dean, Howard. Retrieved August 13, 2009, from http://www.youtube.com/watch?v=KDwODbl3muE

Gallo, C. (2008, March 3). How to inspire people like Obama does. Businessweek.com. Retrieved September 27, 2009, from http://www.businessweek.com/smallbiz/content/mar2008/sb2008033_156351.htm

Goldsmith, B. (2008). Michael Phelps, the major advertising vehicle. *New York Times*. Retrieved August 13, 2009, from http://www.nytimes.com/2008/08/18/business/worldbusiness/18iht-sponsors.1.15385151.html

Gring, M. A. (2006). Epistemic and pedagogical assumptions for informative and persuasive speaking practices: Disinterring the dichotomy. *Argumentation and Advocacy, 43*, 41–50.

Hamilton, C. (2009). *Essentials of Public Speaking* (4th ed.). Boston: Wadsworth Cengage.

Herrick, J. (2004). *The History and Theory of Rhetoric: An Introduction* (3rd ed.). Boston: Allyn & Bacon.

Hornik, R. (2006). Personal Influence and the Effects of the National Youth Anti-Drug Media Campaign. *Annals of the American Academy of Political and Social Science*.

Honda. (2010). Environment. Retrieved April 26, 2010 from: http://automobiles.honda.com/insight-hybrid/environment.aspx

Jacobsohn, L. (2007, May 25). *The Role of Positive Outcome Expectancies in Boomerang Effects of the National Youth Antidrug Media Campaign*. Paper presented at the International Communication. Association, San Francisco.

Mac vs. Bloated PC. Retrieved August 13, 2009, from http://www.youtube.com/watch?v=1EbCyibkNB0&feature=related

Make It Right. Retrieved September 27, 2009, from http://makeitrightnola.org/

McConnell, M. (2010, March 3). The sales pitch may be new, but the bill isn't. Retrieved August 4, 2010 from: http://mcconnell.senate.gov/public/index.cfm?p=HealthCarePlan&ContentRecord_id=c6d689e3-5576-421a-b200-f43624960973&ContentType_id=f4c2c223-b5bb-41cf-9cab-3f5928c0c550&c19bc7a5-2bb9-4a73-b2ab-3c1b5191a72b&Group_id=c24be2ca-e186-424d-8cdf-1ba1284c0781&MonthDisplay=3&Year Display=2010

McLachlan, Sarah. BCSPCA Ad. Retrieved September 27, 2009, from http://www.youtube.com/watch?v=9gspElv1yvc

Obama, B. (2010, August 2). Remarks by the President at Disabled Veterans of America Conference in Atlanta, Georgia. Retrieved August 3, 2010 from: http://www.whitehouse.gov/the-press-office/remarks-president-disabled-veterans-america-conference-atlanta-georgia

ONDCP National Youth Anti-Drug Media Campaign. Retrieved August 13, 2009, from http://www.mediacampaign.org/

Pelosi, N. (2010, February 25). Pelosi remarks at bipartisan meeting at Blair House on health insurance reform.Retrieved on August 4, 2010 from: http://www.speaker.gov/ newsroom/speeches?id=0246

Rovell, D. (2009, February 5). Phelps' Kellogg Deal Won't Be Renewed. CNBC.com. Retrieved August 13, 2009, from http://www.cnbc.com/id/29041954/

Tecson, B. J. (2005, April 1). Black lack of 'truth': Teen smoking no longer on the decline. Retrieved August 13, 2009, from http://www.mtv.com/news/articles/1499460/20050401/index.jhtml? headlines=true

The Truth—Body Bags TV ad. Retrieved August 13, 2009, from http://www.youtube.com/watch?v=c4xmFcrJexk&feature=related

Yes We Can Barack Obama Music Video. Retrieved August 13, 2009, from http://www.youtube.com/watch?v=jjXyqcx-mYY

Wolburg, J. M. (2006). College students' responses to anti-smoking messages: Denial, defiance, and other boomerang effects. *Journal of Consumer Affairs, 40* (2), 294–323.

Zarefsky, D. (2008). *Public Speaking: Strategies for Success* (5th ed.). Boston: Pearson.

CREDITS

TEXT CREDITS

Chapter 1

p. 4, From "Prospective associations of co-rumination with friendship and emotional adjustment," July 16, 2007, New-Medical.Net, http://www.news-medical.net. Reprinted by permission; p. 6, From "Careers in Communication: An update," by A. D. Wolvin, *JACA: Journal of the Association for Communication Administration.* Copyright 1998 by Association for Communication Administration. Reproduced with permission of Association for Communication Administration in the format Textbook and Other Book via Copyright Clearance Center; p. 21, Reprinted with permission from www. legalworkplace. com. © Alexander Hamilton Institute, Inc., 70 Hilltop Rd., Ramsey, NJ 07446; p. 22, From "A Framework for Thinking Ethically," Markkula Center for Thinking Ethically (2010). Reprinted with permission of the Markkula Center for Applied Ethics at Santa Clara University, www.scu.edu/ethics.

Chapter 2

p. 35, From "The Smell Report: Sex Differences," by Kate Fox, Social Issues Research Centre, http://www.sirc.org. Reprinted by permission.

Chapter 3

p. 52, Courtesy of the American Dialect Society; p. 61, Reprinted by permission of Ryan Jones, www.noslang.com.

Chapter 4

p. 83, Courtesy Vayama; p. 88, From "Looking to Avoid Aggressive Drivers? Check Those Bumpers" by Shankar Vendantam. From *The Washington Post*, © June 16, 2008 *The Washington Post.* All rights reserved. Used by permission and protected by the Copyright Laws of the United States. The printing, copying, redistribution, or retransmission of the Material without express written permission is prohibited.

Chapter 5

p. 109, From *Listen Up: How to Improve Relationships, Reduce Stress, and Be More Productive by Using the Power of Listening* L. Baker and K. Watson, New York: St. Martin's Press, 2000; p. 111, From "Hearing Loss-Demographics-Deafness Statistics," by Jamie Berke, *About.com Guide,* December 2, 2007, http:// deafness.about.com; p. 113, From *Listen Up: How to Improve Relationships, Reduce Stress, and Be More Productive by Using the Power of Listening* by L. Baker and K. Watson, New York: St. Martin's Press, 2000.

Chapter 6

p. 123, Reprinted by permission of Allison Nafziger; p. 124, From "U. S. Populations Projections: 2005-2050," by J. S. Passel and D. V. Cohn, Washington, DC: Pew Hispanic Center, p. 9, www.pewhispanic.org/reports/report.php?ReportID=85. Reprinted by permission; p. 140, From "TV Reality Not Often Spoke of: Race," by Eric Deggans, ST. *Petersburg Times,* October 24, 2004. © *St. Petersburg Times* 2004. Reprinted by permission.

Chapter 7

p. 151, From "Love in the age of social networking too much text and not enough talk?" by N.R. Ritter, *Great Falls Tribune,* January 8, 2010. Reprinted by permission of *Great Falls Tribune,* www.greatfallstribune.com; p. 156, Excerpt posted by Steven Rothberg, CollegeRecruiter.com on September 26, 2008. Courtesy of CollegeRecruiter.com job board; p. 158, Adapted from "Guidelines for Using Social Networking Sites, 2006, Southampton Solent University, http://portal-live.solent.ac.uk. Reprinted by permission of Stephen Harding; p. 160, From "Romance on the Internet," *The Police Notebook,* University of Oklahoma Department of Public Safety, www.ou.edu. Reprinted by permission; p. 165, From RainiePew Internet and American Life Studies, http://www.pewinternet.org. Reprinted by permission of Pew Research Center's Internet and American Life Project; p. 168, "Ten Commandments of Computer Ethics" by Dr. Ramon C. Barquin, http://www.computerethics-institute.org. © 1991 Computer Ethics Institute. Used by permission of the author.

Chapter 8

p. 179, From "DNA dating site predicts chemical romance" by Ella Wenzel, *NewsBlog,* December 17, 2007, http://news.cnet.com. Reprinted by permission of CBS News; p. 189, From *Maintaining Relationships Through Communication: Relational, Contextual, and Cultural Variations* by D. Canary & M. Dainton. Copyright 2002 by Taylor & Francis Group LLC - Books. Reproduced with permission of Taylor & Francis Group LLC - Books in the format Textbook and Other Book via Copyright Clearance Center.

Chapter 9

p. 220, From "Abused men: The silent victims of domestic violence," by C. Lytle, *Examiner.com, Phoenix,* July 21, 2009. Reprinted by permission of Carmen Lytle.

Chapter 10

p. 239, From D.J. Canary (2003), "Managing interpersonal conflict," in J.O. Greene & B. Burleson, Eds., *Handbook of Communication and Social Interaction Skills,* pp. 530–531; p. 241: From "He Who Cast the First Stone Probably Didn't," *International Herald Tribune* from *The New York Times,* © July 24, 2006. *The New York Times.* All rights reserved. Used by permission and protected by the Copyright Laws of the United States. The printing, copying, redistribution, or retransmission of the Material without express written permission is prohibited.

Chapter 12

p. 284, From "Leadership as a philosophy . . . ," by Shawn M. Fouts, *The Student Affairs Blog,* http://www/thesablog.org, June 4, 2007, West Texas A & M University. Reprinted by permission of Shawn M. Fouts; p. 297, From Daft. *The Leadership Experience (with InfoTrac®),* 4e. © 2008 South-Western, a part of Cengage Learning, Inc. Reproduced by permission. www.cengage.com/permissions.

Chapter 14

p. 338, From "Deep Breathing", www.umm.edu. Reprinted by permission of the Sleep Disorders Center, University of Maryland Medical Center; p. 341, From "Enhance the image of those who will take your business to the next level." www.Professional- ImageDress .com. Reprinted by permission of Image Resource Group; p. 347, Adapted with permission from Cultural Savvy, 2009. www. culturalsavvy.com.

Chapter 15

pp. 359–360, From *The Last Lecture*, a speech delivered by Professor Randy Pausch of Carnegie Mellon University in 2007.

Chapter 16

p. 375, From "What Americans really want," by F. Luntz, *Los Angeles Times,* September 27, 2009. Reprinted by permission of Frank Luntz; p. 382, From "Common Fallacies in Reasoning," by Robert Gass, http://commfaculty.fullerton.edu. Used by permission of the author; pp. 386–387, From *Plastic Debris Rivers to Sea,* http:// plasticdebris.org

Inside Cover

From "150 Typical Job Interview Questions," copyright by Quintessential Careers. The original article can be found at http://www.quintcareers.com/interview_question_database/inter-view_questions.html. Reprinted with permission; From "Questions You Can Ask at the Job Interview," copyright by Quintessential Careers. The original article can be found at from http:// www.quintcareers.com/asking_interview_questions.html. Reprinted with permission.

PHOTO CREDITS

Chapter 1

p. 2, Shutterstock; p. 5, Photolibrary/Indexopen; p. 9, Alamy Images; p. 9, Alamy Images; p. 9, Newscom; p. 9, Alamy Images; p. 9, iStockphoto.com; p. 9, Alamy Images; p. 9, Alamy Images; p. 9, Alamy Images; p. 9, iStockphoto.com; p. 11, Photolibrary/Indexopen; p. 16, Fancy/Alamy.

Chapter 2

p. 26, Lewis J. Merrim/Photo Researchers, Inc.; p. 29, Rob Buskirk/Alamy.com; p. 36, Thinkstock; p. 37, Yoshikazu Tsuno/ Newscom; p. 41, Photos.com; p. 41, Photos.com; p. 41, Photos.com; p. 41, Photos.com; p. 45, Heidi Gutman/AP Wide World Photos.

Chapter 3

p. 50, David Young-Wolff/PhotoEdit Inc.; p. 54, Ariel Skelley/Alamy Images; p. 57, Kablonk/Alamy Images; p. 59, Jack Hollingsworth/ Photos.com; p. 72, Duane Osborn/Somos Images/Corbis RF.

Chapter 4

p. 76, SimplyMui/Masterfile Corporation; p. 80, Marmaduke St. John/Alamy Images; p. 87, Photos.com; p. 87, Photos.com; p. 87, Photos.com; p. 87, Dennis MacDonald/PhotoEdit Inc.; p. 93, iStockphoto.com; p. 94, Ted S. Warren/AP Wide World Photos.

Chapter 5

p. 100, Ryan Pierse/Getty Images Inc—Liaison p. 103, Photos.com; p. 103, Photos.com; p. 103, Photos.com; p. 103, Photos.com; p. 103, Photos.com; p. 104, Michael Keller/CORBIS—NY; p. 111, Ting Hoo/Getty Images, Inc—Liaison; p. 116, Matthias Tunger/ CORBIS— NY.

Chapter 6

p. 120, JAVIER SORIANO/Getty Images Inc. AFP; p. 127, Peter Turnley/CORBIS-NY; p. 127, Sebastian Bolesch/Das Fotoarchiv/ Photolibrary/Peter Arnold, Inc.; p. 127, Peter Turnley/CORBIS-NY; p. 127, KRISTIN MOSHER/Danita Delimont Photography; p. 128, Ariel Skelley/AGE Fotostock America, Inc.; p. 134, Preston Schlebusch/Getty Images Inc.—Image Bank; p. 137, Chuck Beckley/ Getty Images, Inc.—Liaison.

Chapter 7

p. 144, Newscom; p. 150, Photos.com; p. 150, Photos.com; p. 150, Shutterstock Images LLC; p. 150, Photos.com; p. 150, Superstock Royalty Free; p. 150, AP Wide World Photos; p. 155, Alamy Images; p. 155, Alamy Images; p. 163, Vanessa Vick/Redux Pictures; p. 169, AP Wide World Photos.

Chapter 8

p. 174, Hill Street Studios/Alamy Images; p. 181, Tara Moore/ Getty Images Inc—Stone Allstock; p. 186, Juice Images/Alamy Images Royalty Free; p. 186, Eric Raptosh/ Alamy Images; p. 186, Radius Images/Alamy Images; p. 186, Corbis/SuperStock, Inc.; p. 186, David Young-Wolff/PhotoEdit Inc.; p.187, Nicole Hill/Getty Images, Inc— Liaison; p. 196, Andy Tullis/AP Wide World Photos.

Chapter 9

p. 200, Thomas Northcut/Lifesize/Getty Images Royalty Free; p. 210, Laurence Mouton/Getty Images Inc. RF; p. 213, PhotoEdit Inc.; p. 213, LatinStock Collection/Alamy; p. 213, Alamy Images; p. 213, Superstock p. 213, Pixland/Jupiter Images–Pixland Royalty Free; p. 213, Masterfile; p. 215, Noel Hendrickson/Getty Images Inc.–Photo Disc; p. 222, ImageSource/AGE FOTOSTOCK.

Chapter 10

p. 226, Angela Hampton Picture Library/Alamy Images; p. 229, Westend 61 GmbH/Alamy Images; p. 234, Radius Images/Getty Images, Inc.—Liaison; p. 248, Jetta Productions/Getty Images— Iconica.

Chapter 11

p. 254, Robert Llewellyn/Photolibrary.com; p. 257, Ghislain & Marie David De Lossy/Photolibrary.com; p. 265, Everett Collection; p. 266, Dean Mitchell/iStockphoto; p. 272, Image Source/Alamy.

Chapter 12

p. 282, Michel Touraine/Jupiter Images Royalty Free; p. 285, Mary Kate Denny/PhotoEdit Inc.; p. 288, Alamy Images; p. 293, Mark Richards/PhotoEdit Inc.; p. 293, Alamy Images; p. 293, Library of Congress; p. 295, LaGrange College Servant Leadership Program.

Chapter 13

p. 304, Photolibrary/Indexopen; p. 311, Bob Daemmrich/The Image Works; p. 316, PhotoEdit Inc.; p. 327, PhotoEdit Inc.; p. 330, Photos.com; p. 330, Michael Newman/PhotoEdit Inc.; p. 330, K. Shamsi-Basha/The Image Works.

Chapter 14

p. 334, SuperStock, Inc.; p. 337, Getty Images, Inc.–Cornstock Images RF; p. 346, Mike Rozman/AP Wide World Photos; p. 348, SuperStock, Inc.; p. 350, David Young-Wolff/PhotoEdit Inc.; p. 350, SuperStock, Inc.; p. 350, Spencer Grant/PhotoEdit; p. 350, Mike Kahn/Green Stock Media/Alamy; p. 350, Juice Images/Alamy; p. 350, Scott J. Ferrell/Newscom; p. 350, Jamie Grill/Iconica/Getty; p. 350, iStockphoto.

Chapter 15

p. 354, AP Wide World Photos; p. 357, Richard Lord/PhotoEdit Inc.; p. 361, Newscom; p. 361, AP Wide World Photos; p. 361, Newscom; p. 366, Kayte Deioma/PhotoEdit Inc.; p. 367, Wikipedia images/Public Domain; p. 368, © Sarah Hadley/Alamy.

Chapter 16

p. 370, UPI/Roger L. Wollenberg/NewsCom; p. 373, AP Wide World Photos; p. 377, AP Wide World Photos; p. 377, AP Wide World Photos; p. 377, Honda Media Gallery/www. HondaNews.com; p. 377, Alamy Images; p. 380, Bob Daemmrich/The Image Works; p. 391, Alamy Images.

INDEX

A

Absolutism, 19–20
Accommodating style, 236
Accuracy
  honesty and, in language, 278, 289–299
  in informative speaking, 365–366
Acronyms, in public speaking, 342
Action
  interaction goals, 203–204
  in Monroe's motivated sequence, 386
  problem-solution-action pattern, 384
  transactionality, 13–14
  transactional model of human communication, 12
Action-oriented listening style, 106
Adaptors, 83, 297
Adolescent-parent conflicts, 230–231
Adrenaline, 337–338
Advocate, 375–376
Afghanistan, 371, 373, 381, 391
African American, 15, 65, 68, 80, 123–124, 129,
        141–142, 162, 193
  assimilation, 140
  Ebonics, 66
  ELC, 296
  executive/managerial roles for, 296
  legacy of slavery, 138–139
Age
  college culture, 114
  demographics of Internet users, 164–165
  elderly population, 123
  generational soundscapes, 115
  listening v., 109–110
  parental alienation, 235
  teenagers, 110, 128, 147–148, 163–164
  verbal communication influenced by, 58, 60–61
  vocabulary influenced by, 60
Aggressive touch, 90, 240–241
Aggressor role, 263
Agle, Bradley R., 292
Ahmadinejad, Mahmoud, 392
AIDS/HIV, 372
AIG. See American Insurance Group
Akhavi, Khody, 69
Alcohol consumption, 218
Alliteration, 342
Alternative solutions, 267
American Civil Liberties Union, 67–68
American Dialect Society, 52
American Insurance Group (AIG), 17
American Revolution, 339–340
America's Historical Newspapers, 319
Analysis paralysis, 267
Anecdotes, in public speaking, 327
Anger, 112
  apologies and, 223
  interpersonal violence, 215–217, 240
  persuasive power of, 378
  Proverbs on, 202
Animation, in PowerPoint, 343
Anonymity, 153–154

Anthony, Susan B., 321
Anticipation, of conflict situations, 249
Anti-smoking campaign, 378
Anxiety, 4–5
  arousal maintenance goal, 204–205
  communication apprehension, 336–337
Apologizing, 223
Appeal to authority, 383
Appeal to crowd, 383
Appeal to tradition, 383
Appearance, personal, 90–91
  importance for leadership, 299
  listening v. norms for, 114–115
  for public presentation, 341
The Apprentice, 140
Appropriateness
  in competence model of conflict, 249
  of style, 340–341
  of tone, 191, 339–340
Arab culture, 85
Argentina, 123
Aristotle, 4
Arousal maintenance goals, 204–205
Arthur Anderson Corporation, 17
Artifacts, 90–91
Artistic proofs, 351
Asian Americans, 68, 124, 129
  bamboo ceiling, 296
Assonance, 342
Asynchronous communication, 149–150, 152
Athletes, endorsement deals v. ethos, 376, 378
Attention-getting devices, 327
  in Monroe's motivated sequence, 386
Attribution (in perceptual process), 31, 40
Attributional bias, 31
Attributions theory, 31
Audience. See also Persuasive speaking
  adapting your ideas to, 366
  analysis, 312–314
  attention-getting devices tailored to, 327, 386
  attitude of, 380
  behavior of, 381–382
  boomerang effect, 378
  comprehension of your thesis statement, 328
  demographics, 311–312
  friendly face in, 337
  gender differences in addressing, 60
  involvement of your, 384
  respecting their ideas, 367
  using humor with your, 346–347
  values of, 381
Audience analysis, 312–314
Audiovisual aids, 327, 343–345
  ethics applied to, 351
  for informative speaking, 366–367
  Visual Aids Checklist, 344
Australia, 273
Authentic communication, 195–196, 278
Authoritarian leadership style, 291
  example of, 293

Authority, appeal to, 383
Automatic response, 206–207
Autonomy-connection dialectic, 184
Avatars, 155
Avoiding, 181–182, 191
Avoiding style (response to conflict), 237
Award ceremonies, 308

B

Baldwin, Alec, 235
Bamboo ceiling, 296
Basinger, Kim, 235
Battering, 216–217
Baxter, Leslie, 183
Bay of Pigs Invasion, 270
Beard, David, 115
"Bearing witness," 118
Behavior, speeches to impact audience, 381–382
Behavioral conflicts, 231–232
Behavioral de-escalation, 191
Beliefs, speeches to impact, 380–381
Belonging, 177
Betrayal, 208–210
Bible, 4, 202, 295
Bifurcation, 383
Bing, Stanley, 341
Bisexual Americans, 66
Black English, 66
Blagojevich, Rod, 17
Blocker role, 263, 265
Blog, 146–148, 168, 317
Bluesky, 155
Body, of your speech, 321
Body gestures, 83–84, 114. *See also*
        Nonverbal communication
    cultural diversity of nonverbal communication, 81–82
    verbal *v.* nonverbal messages, 96–97
Boehm, Macy, 286–287, 301
Bonding, 181–182
Book, Mick, 336
Books, as supporting materials source, 317
Boomerang effect, 378–379
Border dwellers, 126–127
    through relationships, 129, 131
    through socialization, 128–129
Boredom, 112
"Born leader," 285, 289
Boston, 367–368
Boy Scout troop, 285
Brainstorm, 267
Brazil, 83
Breadth, of topics, 180–181
Breathing exercises, 337–338
Brink, Uri ten, 320
Bulletin board systems, 146
Bumperstickers, 89
"Bunker Hill Monument Oration," 339–340
Bush, George W., 346, 373
Business relationships, 194
    employees, 272–273, 298, 357
    executive/managerial roles, 296
    financial transactions, 148
    managerial skills, 105, 110, 114

C

Canada, 163, 273
Canary, Dan, 249
Careers, in communication, 6–7
Carey, Mariah, 129
Carnegie Mellon University, 359–360
Cascade, 240
Cascade Model of Relational Conflict, 240–241
Catalyst study, 288–289
Categorization, 30
Catharsis, 231
Cause-effect pattern, 323
Celebrity advocates, 371–372
Census Bureau, U. S.
    on disability and employment, 111
    on ethnic/racial diversity, 123
    racial homogeneity in marriages, 193
Centers for Disease Control, 356
Certainty-focused communication, 71
Challenger space-shuttle explosion, 271
Challenges, relationship, 202, 208, 212–218, 236
Change-predictability dialectic, 184–185
Channels, 8–9, 11, 17
Charismatic leadership, 292–294
Chats, cyberspace, 146
Chávez, César, 293
Chewing gum, 348
Child, Lee, 300
Children, 110, 235
Chile, 163
China, 83, 163, 273, 314
Christianity, 134, 194. *See also* Bible
Chronemics, 85–86
Chronological pattern, 321
Church of Jesus Christ of Latter-Day Saints, 194
Cialdini, Robert, 206, 208
Cicero, 308
Cigarettes, 378
Circumscribing, 181–182
Citineni, Sindhura, 290
Clarity, 340
"Click, whirr response," 206–208
Clinton, Bill, 346, 373
Clinton, Hillary, 379
Clinton Bush Haiti Fund, 373
Closed questions, 312
Clothing, 90–91
CMC. *See* Computer-mediated communication
Cocultural theory, 64–65
Coercion, 274
    avoidance of, 247–248
Cognitive representation, 28–29
Cohesiveness, 275–276, 278–279
Cohort effect, 61
COINS. *See* Collaborative Innovation Networks
Collaboration, 288–289, 291
    virtual team, 272–273, 298
Collaborative Innovation Networks (COINS), 273
Collaborative leadership, 291
Collectivist attitude, 278
Collectivistic cultures, 245
Collectivistic orientation, 133
College culture, 114

College diploma, 164
Commitment, 183
Common good approach, 23
Communication, study of. *See also* Intercultural communication
　confirming communication, 72
　early linear model, 12
　Human Communication Societal Model, 16–17
　other social sciences *v.*, 4
personal goal attainment and, 4, 6
Communication apprehension, 336–337
Communication climate, 301
　Communication ethics, 18–19
　CMC and, 167–169
　crisis in United States, 17
　listening and, 116–117
　nonverbal, 96
　persuasive speaking and, 391
　in practice, 22–23
　receivers' responsibilities, 20–22
　suggestions for, 69–73
Ten Commandments of Computer Ethics, 168
Communication model, 181
Communication skills, six keys to improving
　　relationships, 243–244
Community organizations, 285
Competence, in responding to hurtful message, 213
Competence model of conflict, 249–251
Competitive fighting, 233, 240
Competitive style, 233
Compliance-gaining messages, 204–206
Compromiser role, 262
　Compromising style, 234–236
　Computer-mediated communication (CMC), 145
　anonymity and pseudoanonymity, 153–154
　ethics and, 167–169
　importance of, 147–148
　key channels of, 146
　media augmentation approach, 148, 152
　role in everyday life, 148–153
　romantic relationships, 159
　social context and, 161–167
　social network theory, 152–153
"speed of gossip," 151
work relationships, 159–161
Concessions, 235–236
　Conclusion, of your speech, 329–231
Confidentiality, 19
guidelines for private information, 116
　Confirming communication, 72
　Conflict, 228
　anticipation of situations, 249
　Cascade Model of Relational Conflict, 240–241
　causes of, 231–232
　choosing your response to, 237–239
　communication media *v.*, 151
　direct/nasty tactic response, 238
　direct/nice tactic response, 238
　in group meetings, 269
　from high diversity/low education group, 277
　humor/teasing or distraction response, 238
　importance of managing, 229–230
　indirect/nasty tactic response, 239
　indirect/nice tactic response, 238

intercultural communication *v.*, 124–125
interpersonal conflict principles, 250–251
listening *v.*, 110
negotiating borders, 131
problematic interactions, 240–244
purposes of, 230–231
refugees and other involuntary travelers, 127
responding to, 232–233
tactics, 233, 237–239
your strategic approach to managing, 248–250
Conflicting objectives, 113
Conflict phase, 268–269
Conflict strategy, 248–250
Conflict styles, 233
Conflict tactic, 233, 237–239
Congruency, between verbal and nonverbal messages, 97
Connotative meaning, 56
Consensus, groupthink, 270–271
Consensus decision-making style, 264–265
Consistency principle, 207, 209
Constructive marginal people, 131
Contemporary slang, 60–61
Contempt, 242–243
Content meaning, 10
Content-oriented listening style, 105–106
Context, 9, 16, 97
　CMC and, 161–167
　listening in, 115
　medical, 104
　of receiving hurtful message, 213
Contextual rules, 58
Continuum, of interpersonal communication, 177
Contradicting, of verbal and nonverbal messages, 97
Control, 293. *See also* Leadership styles
　regulation of, through conflict, 230
Conversation
　initiating, 188
　turn-taking in, 57–58, 93
Conversational rules, 57–58
Conversation starters, 202
Cooperative style, 233, 266
Coordinator role, 261
Co-ruminating, 4–5
Coulter, Ann, 389
Countdown with Keith Olbermann, 389
CQ. *See* Cultural intelligence
Craig, Larry, 380
Credibility
　ethos and, 351, 376, 378
　in persuasive speeches, 389–390
　in speech-making, 317, 368
Credit-taker role, 263
Critical listening, 105
Criticism, 202, 208, 229, 241–242
Cross-cultural marriage, advice for, 130
Crowd, appeal to, 383
Cruise, Tom, 84
Cuban American, 129
Cultural capital, 163–164
Cultural diversity, 9, 15–17, 64–65, 87, 121–122, 275, 297. *See also*
　　Intercultural communication; Nonverbal communication
　audience demographics, 311–312
　chronemics, 85–86

Cultural diversity (*Continued*)
  demographics, 277
  English as second language, 54, 62, 63
  eye contact, 84, 93, 95, 110, 114, 348
  haptics, 89
  how to encourage group cohesion, 276
  humor styles, 347
  intercultural communication *v.* conflict, 124–125
  related to attitudes and values, 277
  values influencing communication, 132–134
Cultural factors, in audience analysis, 314
Cultural identity, 42–43, 80, 123–124, 136
  perceptions influenced by, 44
Cultural-individual dialectic, 136
Cultural intelligence (CQ), 297
Cultural norms, 296–297
Cultural values, 132–134
Culture(s), 9, 15–17, 86–87, 122. *See also* Cultural diversity;
    Intercultural communication; *specific nation*
  adapting to new, 128
  Arab, 85
  cocultural theory, 64–65
  college, 114
  Japanese *v.* American, 121
  as learned patterns, 245
  perception/identity and, 42–43
  speech acts and, 57
  verbal communication influenced by, 58, 63
Culture shock, 126, 128
Custody battles, 235
Cyberbullying, 154
Cyberspace, 146
Cycle of blame and criticism, 208
Cypress, 125

D

Daft, Richard, 297
Dannen, Chris, 306
Dating
  DNA dating site, 179–180
  high school students, 202
  interethnic, 131
  meeting online, 160
  partner's aversive behaviors, 208
Dean, Howard, 379
Deception, 208–210
Decision-making, 267
  Group Decision Support Software, 272
  phases of, 268–270
  style of, 264–265
Decoding, 8
Deep breathing, 337–338
De-escalation, 191
Defensive communication, 70–71, 241–242
Defensive listening, 112
DeGeneres, Ellen, 346
Deggans, Eric, 140
Delivery, speech. *See* Speech delivery
Demagoguery, 379
Demand touching, 90
Democratic leadership style, 292, 293
Democratic process, 357
Demographics

audience, 311–312
  demographic analysis, 313
  demographic diversity, 277
  of Internet users, 164–165
  verbal communication influenced by, 62–63
Denhardt, Janet, 286
Denhardt, Robert, 286
Denmark, 83
Denotative meaning, 56
Depression, 4–5
Depth, of personal disclosure, 180–181
Devices, for speech-making
  attention-getting, 327, 386
  comparison, 342
  rhetorical, 342–343, 371, 373–374
  stylistic, 342
Devotion, 183
Dialect, regional/statewide, 61–62
Dialectical model of relationship development, 136–137, 184–185
  dialectic tension as relationship challenge, 202
Dialogue, promotion of, 301–302
Di Caprio, Leonardo, 373
Dichotomous thinking, 136
Diesel, Vin, 129
Differences-similarities dialectic, 137
Differentiating, 181–182
Diffusion of innovations, 166
Digital divide, 162–163
  closing of, 166–167
  globalization *v.*, 166
Digital media, 146
Dijk, Jan van, 166–167
Direct/nasty tactic response, 238
Direct/nice tactic response, 238
Disabilities, 112
  hearing, 111
  prejudice against those with, 115
Disappointment, 208, 229
Disconfirming communication, 71
Disengagement, 183
Disney Corporation, 124
Display rules, 221
Distance, regulation of, through conflict, 230
Distributed leadership, 291
Divorce rate, 202
Dominator role, 263
Donne, John, 343
Dress codes, 80
Duck, Steve, 5
Dungeons and Dragons, 155
Dyad, 176, 181

E

Eagle feathers, 134–135
Earley, Christopher, 297
Early linear model, of communication, 12
Ebonics, 66
Edelstein, Michael, 20, 336
Edwards, John, 380
Effectiveness, in competence model of conflict, 249
Efficacy, 275–276
Egypt, 83, 163
Elaborator role, 261

ELC. *See* Executive Leadership Council
Elderly population, 123
E-mail, 146–150
  etiquette for, 169
  rumors by, 154
  superior-subordinate communication via, 160–161
Emblems, 83
Emergence phase, 270
Emoticon, 149
Emotion, 191
  anger, 112, 202, 215–217, 223, 240, 378
  contempt, 242–243
  devotion, 183
  disappointment, 208, 229
  evoking, as purpose of speech, 315
  fear, 112, 222, 341, 378
  joy, 112
  love, 59, 89
  passion, 183
  pathos, 351, 378
  recognition of, 302
  relationship conflicts arousing, 239–240
  risk in appealing to, 379
  satisfaction, 213, 386
  social hierarchy *v.*, 221
  societal forces shaping, 220–221
Emotional flooding, 240
Emotional infidelity, 214
Emotional norms, 221
Emotional stability, 289
Emotional support, 197
Empathic communication, 71
  listening, 104
  between women and men, 109
Employees
  training sessions, 357
  in virtual teams, 272–273, 298
Empowerment, 376
  leadership conveying, to followers, 292
Encapsulated marginal people, 131
Enchallah (God willing), 134
Encoding, 8
Encourager role, 262
Endorsement deals, athletes in, 376, 378
Energizer role, 261
  leadership as, 286
English
  Ebonics, 66
  jargon, 63, 342
  LOL, 149
  metaphor, 342
  obscenities in public speaking, 341
  as second language, 54, 62–63
  slang, 60–61
  syntax, 55, 59
  television, 348
  vocabulary, 58, 60
Enron, 299
Entertainment
  celebrity advocates, 371–372
  CMC for, 147–148
  public speech for, 308
Entropia Universe, 154–155

Equality-oriented communication, 71
Equal participation, of group members, 264
Errors in reasoning, 382
Ethics, 18. *See also* Communication ethics
  applied to visual aids, 351
  CMC and, 167–169
  communication challenges and, 222–223
  demagoguery *v.*, 379
  informative speaking and, 368
  intercultural communication and, 140–141
  interpersonal communication and, 195–196
  of language use, 20
  leadership, 298–300
  in nonverbal communication, 96
  in offering feedback, 116–117
  in public speaking, 331
  in speech delivery, 352
Ethnic diversity, 123, 276–277
  intercultural communication *v.* conflict, 124–125
  multiracial Americans, 128–129
Ethnicity, 80, 95, 124
  verbal communication influenced by, 62–63
Ethnic slurs, 20
Ethos, 351
  sport endorsement deals *v.*, 376, 378
Etiquette, for world travelers, 83
Evaluating, 102–103
Evaluator-critic role, 261
EverQuest II, 154–155
Evocative speech, 308
  as general purpose, 315
Examples, using, in speeches, 320
Exclusivity, 183
Executive Leadership Council (ELC), 296
Expediter role, 262
Experimenting stage, 181
Expert testimony, 320
Expletives, in public speaking, 341
Expressiveness-privacy dialectic, 184
Extemporaneous speech, 346
External competition, 183
Extroversion, 289, 292–293
Eye contact, 84, 93, 348
  prejudice and, 95
  social status *v.*, 114
  with young people, 110

F

Facebook, 145, 147–148, 151, 196, 356
  identity management on, 153
Face-to-face communication, 150, 152
Facial expressions, 84
Fact finding checklist, 366
Fairness, justice and, 299–300
Fallacies of reasoning, 382
False dilemma, 383
Fatal attraction, 191
Faulty analogy, 383
Faulty cause, 382
Fear, 112
  persuasive power of, 378
  social hierarchy *v.*, 222
  use of, in public speaking, 341

Feedback, 8–9, 12
    about your identity communication, 40
    ethical choice in offering, 116–117
    healthy, 21
"*Feeling* of being heard," 115
Feeling rules, 221
"Feminine" leadership, 288–289, 302
Fey, Tina, 351
Fidgeting, 348
Field of experience, 14, 17
Filtered communication, 148–149
Financial transactions, 148
Follower role, 262, 292
Font size, in PowerPoint, 343
Foot-in-the-door technique, 207
"Forgive and forget," 223
Formal style, in speech tone, 340
Forrest Gump, 342–343
Fortune 500 company, 286, 289, 296
Fouts, Shawn M., 284
Frames (in perceptual process), 31
Framing, of hurtful message, 213
French fries, 137
Frequency, of communication exchanges, 180–181
Frey, Lawrence, 259
"Friendly thief," 208
Friendship
    betrayal in, 209–210
    communicating in, 185–192
    conflict within, 228
    ending of, 192
    "friendly thief," 208
    friendship touch, 89
    high school best friends, 202
    initiating, 188–189
    long-distance, 196–197
    relational maintenance, 189–190
    society/power and, 195
    via social networking sites, 157
Friendship touch, 89
Frustration, as indicative of conflict, 228
FtF. *See* Face-to-face communication
Fulbright scholarship, 125
Functional (situational) theory, 290–291
Functional touch, 89
Fundamental attribution error, 32
Funeral, public speech for, 308

G

Gaining assistance, as goal, 205
Gallo, Carmine, 355
Gass, Robert, 382–383
Gatekeeper role, 262
Gates, Bill, 289, 306, 314, 327
Gay and lesbian Americans, 16, 20, 66, 80, 194
GDSS. *See* Group Decision Support Software
Geithner, Timothy, 341
Gender(s), 86–87, 277. *See also* Romantic relationships; Women
    conflict strategies, 246–247
    dress/appearance for speech delivery, 341
    expressing jealousy, 210
    fighting, 244
    Genderwatch, 319

improved listening between, 109
Internet use, 164
interpersonal violence, 215
leadership and, 287–289
likelihood of straying from long-term partner, 214
listening styles, 108
-neutral language, 66
power of words, 65
SNS usage by, 162
societal images about, 220, 247
stereotypes, 60, 109, 287–288
verbal communication influenced by, 58, 60
Gender socialization, 220, 247
Genderwatch, 319
Generalized other, 37, 40
Geographical region, verbal communication
        influenced by, 61–62
Germany, 163, 246
Gestures, 81–84, 83, 114, 348. *See also* Nonverbal communication
    cultural diversity of nonverbal communication, 81–82
    verbal *v.* nonverbal messages, 96–97
Get-to-know time, 183
Gibson, Mel, 336
Gift-giving, 206–207
Giuliani, Rudy, 339, 374–375
Glass ceiling, 287, 296
Global Crossing, 17
Globalization, 166
Gloor, Peter, 273
Goals
    arousal maintenance, 205
    building community toward common, 300, 375
    identity, 203
    interaction, 203–204
    leadership with eye on, 299
    personal attainment, 4, 6
    personal resource, 204–205
    primary influence, 203, 205
    relational resource, 204
    secondary influence, 202–203, 205
Going Tribal, 79
Golden, Brenda, 134–135
Google, 318
Graduation ceremony, speech for, 308
Greece, 83, 125
Greenleaf, Robert K., 295
Gring, Mark, 357
Group Decision Support Software (GDSS), 272
Group enjoyment, 276, 278
    cultural diversity and, 277
Group meetings, conflicts in, 269
Group observer role, 262
Group processes, 276
Group Support Software (GSS), 272
Groupthink, 270–271
Grudge-holding, 236
GSS. *See* Group Support Software
Guilt, relationship conflicts causing, 240

H

Haiti, 373
"Halo effect," 208
Haptics, 89–90

Hasty generalization, 383
Hawaiians, 129
Health care, 373–374
Hearing disability, 111
Help seeker role, 263–264
Heterogeneous culture, 122
Heuristic function, 54
Hierarchy, 80, 114–115, 118, 221–222
    cultural diversity and group, 278
    haptics and, 90
    norms and views on leadership, 298
    power/perception/identity in, 42
    value, 15
High-context cultures, 245
High power distance, 245
Hispanic American, 123–124, 128–129, 162
History-past-present-future dialectic, 137
Hitler, Adolf, 294
Holy Bible, 4, 202, 295
Holzle, Eric, 180
Homogeneity, 193
Honda Insight advertisement, 378
Honesty, 278, 298–299
Hoover, J. Edgar, 296
Huffington, Arianna, 357
Huffington Post, 357
Hugging, 89
Human Communication Societal Model, 16–17
Humanitarian causes, 371–372
Human nature, 133
Human-nature value orientation, 134
Humor
    cautious use of, 347
    framing hurtful messages in, 211
    in public speaking, 346–347
    as response to conflict, 238
    styles of, per culture, 347
Hunger Lunch, 290
Hurricane Katrina, 126, 128, 371
Hurtful message, 210–211
    in competitive fighting, 240
    influences on perception of, 213
    sense of self *v.*, 212
    three responses to, 312
Hyperbole, in public speech, 342

Iceland, 163
Identity, self-, 5, 32–33, 205
    assault of, 240
    through communication, 41
    defensiveness as attempt to protect, 241
    Facebook and, 153
    looking-glass self, 36
    online, 155
    perception influenced by, 28, 34–36
    reflected appraisals, 36–37
    self-concept, 39–40
    social comparison, 37–38, 41
    verbal communication influenced by, 58
    view of hurtful message *v.*, 212
    your focus on, 40
Identity category, 45, 46, 48
Identity goals, 203

Identity group, 41, 46, 69
Identity labels, 68
Ignoring (avoidance style), 237
Illustrators, 83
Imagery, 342
Imaginative function, 53–54
Imagineer, 359–360
Immediacy, 83
Immigrants, 127–128
Impression management, online, 155
Impromptu speech, 345–346
Inauthentic communication, 195–196, 278
Incompatibilities, 229
India, 83, 163
Indirect conflict style, 233
Indirect fighting, 236
Indirect/nasty tactic response, 239
Indirect/nice tactic response, 238
Individual forces, 9, 17
Individualistic cultures, 245–246
Individualistic orientation, 132
Individual role, dysfunctionality of,
        in group, 263, 265
Infidelity, 210
    responding to, 216
Informal style, in speech tone, 340
Informational listening, 106
Information giver role, 261
Information seeker role, 261
Information sources, 171
Informative function, 53
Informative speeches, 308, 355
    about 'concepts,' 363
    about 'events,' 362–363
    about 'objects,' 362
    about 'processes,' 362
    adapting your ideas to
        your audience, 366
    chronological pattern, 364
    ethics and, 368
    fact finding checklist, 366
    four types of, 360
    geographical/spatial pattern, 364–365
    importance of, 357
    Obama's example, 356
    organizing, 363–365
    Pausch's example, 359–360
    persuasive speaking *v.*, 357–361
    rhetor, 356
    sample in outline form, 367–368
    tips for, 365–367
    topical pattern, 365
Informing, as purpose of your speech, 315
IngentaConnect, 319
Initiating stage, 181
Innovation, 275
    diversity and, 277
Instant messages, 146
Instrumental support, 197
Integrating stage, 181
Intensifying stage, 181
Intensity, of speaker's claim, 211
Intentionality, of hurtful message, 213
Intentional messages, 211

Interaction, 205
    goals, 203–204
    regulation of, 92–93
    virtual teams' leadership, 272–273, 298
Interactional function, 54
Intercultural communication, 58, 63, 124–125
    cultural intelligence, 297
    ethics and, 140–141
    etiquette for world travelers, 83
    improving your skills, 141–142
    intercultural couples, 193
    Japanese v. American, 121
    power and, 139
    reasons for studying, 122–123
    societal forces impacting, 138–139
Interdependent attitude, 278
Interdependent parties, 177, 228
Interests, 228
Interethnic dating, 131
Internet, 146–148, 165, 273
    COINS, 273
    digital divide, 162–163, 166–167
    DNA dating site, 179–180
    e-mail, 146–150, 154, 160–161, 169
    evaluating information sources, 171
    impression management, 155
    intercultural communication via, 123
    MMOGs, 146, 154–155
    socioeconomic status and, 164
    web sites, 146, 273, 317, 318, 357
Interpersonal communication, 176
    ethics and, 195–196
    friendships and romantic relationships, 185–192
    improving your skills, 223
    inauthentic communication, 195–196, 278
    influences on relationship development, 177–180
    long-distance friendships, 196–197
    models of relationship development, 180–185
    society/power/courtship/marriage, 193–194
    society/power/friendship, 195
Interpersonal conflict principles, 250–251
Interpersonal conflict styles, 233
Interpersonal script, 29–30
Interpersonal violence, 215–217
    jealousy causing, 240
Interpretation (in perceptual process), 28, 30–32
    refining your, 44
Interview
    separating yourself from source, 389
    as source for supporting materials, 317–318
Intimacy, 92–93, 222. See also
        Communication ethics
    CMS v., 151
    regulation of, through conflict, 230
Intimate distance, 86–87, 93
Intimidation, 296
Introduction, of your speech, 326–327
Introverts, 289
Involuntary long-term travelers, 126
Involuntary short-term travelers, 126
IPhone, 355, 357
Iran, 83
Iraq, 137, 388, 392

Irish American, 129
Islam, 80, 124–125, 129
Issue clarification, through conflict, 231
"I" statements, 72–73
Italy, 83

J
Japanese, 68, 121, 163
Jargon, 63, 342
Jealousy, 210, 240
Jefferson, Thomas, 293
Jesus, 194, 295
Jobs, Steve, 355, 357
"Joe Six-Pack," 351
"Joe the Plumber," 351
Johnson, Dwayne, 129
Joker, 263
Joking around (avoidance style), 237
Joy, 112
JSTOR (Journal Storage), 319
Judaism, 129
Justice, fairness and, 299–300
Justice approach, 23
Justifications, for ending relationships, 191

K
Kagemni, Precepts of, 4
Kant, Immanuel, 19–20
Karoke Revolution, 154–155
Kennedy, John F., 342
Kinesics, 82–84, 348
King, Martin Luther, Jr., 339, 343, 347
Kissing, 89, 183, 194
Knapp, Mark, 181–182
Knapp's Stage Model, 181–182
Kohonen, Susanna, 57
Kornacki, Martin, 105

L
Label, 30
LaGrange College Servant-Leadership Program, 295
Laissez-faire leadership style, 293
Language. *See also* English
    accuracy and honesty in, 278, 289–299
    avoiding gender bias in, 66
    components of, 55–58
    dialects, 61–62
    functions of, 53–55
    gender-neutral, 66
    humor v. knowledge of, 347
    misuse of persuasive, 391
    perception and, 64
    personal, 54
    sensitivity in speech delivery, 351
Language discrimination, 67
Laos, 163
Lao Tzu, 292, 294
Lateness, 85, 348
Latin American culture, 85, 123
Laughing, 114, 149, 347
Law and Order, 336
Lay, Ken, 299
Lay testimony, 320

Leadership, 284
  Boy Scout, 285
  components of studying, 285
  of diverse populations, 297
  effective, 300–302
  ethics in, 298–300
  Executive Leadership Council, 296
  with eye on goal, 299
  gender and, 287–289
  importance of, 285
  improving your skills, 300–302
  influences on, 287–290
  LaGrange College Servant-Leadership Program, 295
  leaders are made -not born, 285, 289
  listening skills, 301–302
  personal appearance, 299
  personality traits influencing, 289–290
  role of communication in, 286–287
  societal influences on, 296–298
  styles of, 291–293
  theories of, 290–296
  virtual team, 272–273, 298
  women underrepresented in, 287–288
Leadership styles, 291–293
Legitimate retribution, 241
Lesbian and gay Americans, 16, 66, 80, 194
Lexical choice, 58
LexisNexis Academic, 318
Libraries, 318–319, 368
Library of Congress, 319
License plates, 89
Lightner, Candy, 289
Liking (as weapon of influence), 208
  resisting, 209
Linear model of communication, 12
Listening, 101
  barriers to, 110–113
  as complex behavior, 110
  conflicts v., 110
  in context, 115
  ethics and, 116–117
  gender styles of, 108
  importance of, 102–103
  improving your skills, 117–118
  influences on, 106–110
  leadership requiring, 301–302
  mindful, 118
  poor habits in, 113
  social hierarchy and, 114–115
  stages of, 103
  strategies between genders, 109
  style, 106
Listening skills, improvement of, 117–118
Loewen, James, 138–139
Logical fallacy, 383
Logos, 351
  Honda Insight advertisement, 378
  logical fallacy, 383
LOL (laughing out loud), 149
Long term involuntary travelers, 127
Long-term orientation, short-term
    orientation v., 136
Long term voluntary travelers, 127

Looking-glass self, 36–37, 41
Love-intimate touch, 89
Low balling, 207
Low-context cultures, 245–246
Low power distance, 245–246
Luntz, Frank, 375
Lynch, James J., 105

M

Machiavellian tactics, 192
Mac-v.-PC ads, 375
MADD. See Mothers Against Drunk Driving
Magazines, as source for supporting materials, 317
Make It Right Foundation, 371
Making up, 183
Malaria, 306
Managerial skills, of listening, 105, 110, 114
Mandella, Nelson, 298–299
Manuscript speech, 346
Maps, 29
Marriage, request-making within, 206
Massachusetts, 296, 367–368
Massively Multi-Player Online Games (MMOGS), 146, 154–155
Matching hypothesis, 179
Mate guarding, 214
Matha, Bob, 286–287, 301
Mays, Billy, 85
McCain, John, 85, 339, 351
McConnell, Mitch, 374
McLachlan, Sarah, 378
Meaning creation, 8–10, 17
Media augmentation approach, 148, 152
Media deficit approach, 148
Media richness theory, 149, 150
Mediated communication, 116, 125
Mediation, 262
Media types, 150
Medical context, 104
Meditation, 384
Mehrabian, Albert, 78–79
Mentor, 291, 297
Message creation, 8
  in conflict management, 247
Meta-communication, 243
Metaphor, in public speech, 342
Mexican culture, 86
Mexico, 163
Middle East, 124–125
  digital divide, 162–163
  Enchallah, 134
Mindfulness, 46, 249
  in listening, 118
MMOGs. See Massively Multi-Player Online Games
MMR vaccine, 380–381
MMS. See Monroe's motivated sequence
Mobile phones, 146–148, 153
  etiquette for, 169–170
  iPhone, 355, 357
Monochronic time usage, 86
Monotheism, 136
Monroe's motivated sequence (MMS), 386
"Moochers," 206
Moral leadership, 300

"A More Perfect Union" speech, 308
Mosakowski, Elaine, 297
Mothers Against Drunk Driving (MADD), 289
Motivation, 297
    MMS, 386
    public speech for, 308
    talking to yourself for, 337–338
Mozilla Firefox, 273
Multicultural issues, leadership for, 297
Multiracial Americans, 128–129
Muscle tension, 337–338
Muslims, 80, 124–125, 129
Mussolini, Benito, 294
MySpace, 151, 155, 356

N

Name-calling, 247
The Nation, 318
National Counter-terrorism Center (NCTC), 69
Nationality, differences in listening, 110
National Review, 318
Native Americans, 84, 129, 134–135, 162
NCTC. *See* National Counter-terrorism Center
Need, in Monroe's motivated sequence, 386
Negative identity management, 191
Negative psychic change, 183
Negativity, 263
Nervousness, prior to public speaking, 337–338
Neutral communication, 65, 71
Neutral questions, 312
Newspapers, as source for supporting materials, 317
Nicaragua, 163
Nichols, Michael, 118
Nigeria, 83, 163
Noise, 8–9, 11–12, 17, 110–111
    Nonverbal codes, 82–83, 92
artifacts, 90–91
    Nonverbal communication, 78, 348
    body gestures, 81–84
    ethics of, 96
    facial expressions, 84
    functions of, 92–93
    importance of, 79
    influences on, 80–82
    paralinguistics, 84–85
    power and, 94–95
    prejudice/discrimination and, 95–96
    tips for, 91
your skills in, 96–97
Norway, 163
Note-taking, 390
Novelty, regulation of, through conflict, 230

O

Obama, Barack, 15, 85, 129, 284, 294, 341, 371
    "A More Perfect Union" speech, 308
    H1N1 Outbreak speech, 356
    use of alliteration, 342
Obama, Michelle, 81–82, 362
Objectivity, in informative speaking, 365–366
O'Brien, Soledad, 129
Obscenities, in public speaking, 341
Occupation, 63. *See also* Careers
Olbermann, Keith, 389

Olivier, Laurence, 336
Onomatopoeia, 343
Open-ended questions, 312
Openness, 184, 186–187, 189, 192, 196–197
    to diverse people, 297
Opinion giver role, 261
Opinion seeker role, 261
Organization (in perceptual process), 28
Organizational pattern, 321
Orientation phase, 268
Orienter role, 261
Ostracizing, 208, 229
Outline, of your speech, 323–326, 384
Outsourcing, 124
Overgeneralizing, 40
Overweight Americans, 351
Oxygen intake, 337–338

P

Pakistan, 126
Palin, Sarah, 284, 351
Paralinguistics, 84–85, 93
Parallelism, 343
Parental alienation, 235
Parry, Bruce, 79
Participants, 8–9, 11
Particular others, 37
Passion, 183
Passive-aggressiveness, 236
Pathos, 351, 378
Patterson, M. L., 78
Pausch, Randy, 340, 359–360
PDAs. *See* Personal Digital Assistants
Peace Corps, 125
Peer communication, 161
Pelosi, Nancy, 373–374
People-oriented listening style, 107
Perception, 34–36, 213
    culture/identity and, 42–43
    language and, 64
    refining your, 44
    research on gender differences in, 58, 60
    selective attention, 28
Performance (efficacy), 275–276
Persona, 345–348, 378
Personal-contextual dialectic, 137
Personal Digital Assistants (PDAs), 146
Personal distance, 86, 87
Personality conflicts, 232
Personality traits, leadership and, 289–290
Personal language, 54
Personal narrative, 320
Personal resource goals, 204–205
Personification, 343
Persuasion, 203, 357
    as general purpose of your speech, 315
Persuasive discourse, 230
Persuasive language, misuse of, 391
Persuasive speaking, 230
    arenas for, 374–375
    celebrity advocates for humanitarian causes, 371–372
    ethics of, 391
    influencing your audience, 372–373
    informative speaking *v.*, 357–361

organizing persuasive speeches, 382–387
power of, 376–379
tips for, 387–391
types of speeches, 379–382
Persuasive speech-making, 203, 308, 315
comprehensive research of both sides, 390
establishing your credibility in, 389–390
thesis statement organization, 388–389
Pew Global Attitudes Project, 319
Phelps, Michael, 376, 378
Phishing, 154
Phonology, 55, 59
Photographs, as source for supporting materials, 317
Physical attractiveness, 177, 179
Physical characteristics, 45
Physical condition, perceptions influenced by, 44
Physical environment, 16
Physical infidelity, 214
Physical separation, 183
Pitt, Brad, 371
PIXELearning, 155
Plato, 4, 19
Podcast, 147–148
Political discourse, 69
Polychronic time usage, 86
Polytheistic, 136
Positive psychic change, 183
Positive reinforcement, 337
Positive-tone strategies, 191
Positivity, 197
Post-traumatic stress disorder (PTSD), 385
Power, 195
as ability to influence others, 244–245
digital divide, 162–163, 166–167
empowerment, 292, 376
hierarchical, 42
identity labels and, 68
intercultural communication and, 139
language and, 64–65
low power distance, 245–246
nonverbal communication and, 94–95
persuasive speaking, 376–379
power distance, 136
ranting as indicative of loss of, 341
regulation of, through conflict, 230
small group communication and, 274–275
society/courtship/marriage, 193–194
society//friendship, 195
Power discourse, 245
Power distance, 136
PowerPoint, 343, 368
Pragmatics, 56, 59
Praising, 262
Precepts of Kagemni, 4
Precise language, 340
Preconceived ideas, 112
Predictability, regulation of, through conflict, 230
Preferred personality, 133
Prejudice/discrimination, 114
gender, 287–288
nonverbal communication and, 95–96
against persons with disabilities, 115
Preoccupation, 112
Primary identities, 42

Primary influence goals, 203, 205
Privacy, 184, 186–187, 189, 196
of public persons, 235
Privilege-disadvantage dialectic, 137–138
Problem analysis, 267
Problem definition/delineation, 267
Problem-solution-action pattern, 384
Problem-solution pattern, for your speech, 322
Problem-solving agenda, 266–267
prevention of groupthink, 271
Problem-solving pattern, 384
Problem-solving style, 234
Procedural technician role, 261
Product demonstrations, 357
Professional touch, 89
Project EUCLID, 319
Project MUSE, 319
Propositions, 388
ProQuest collection, 319
Prototype, 29
Proverbs, 202
Provisional communication, 71
Proxemics, 85, 87
Proximity, 177–179
Pseudoanonymity, 153–154
PsycARTICLES, 319
Psychological barriers, 112
PTSD. *See* Post-traumatic stress disorder
Public deliberation, 376
Public distance, 86–87
Public speaking
analyzing and relating to your audience, 311–314
attention-getting devices, 327, 386
developing your introduction, 326–327
establishing your reason for, 306–311
ethical, 331
event checklist, 307
general purpose of, 308
importance of, 306–307
main points of your speech, 315–316
organizing your speech, 321–326
phases of your speech, 330
sensitive topics, 318
speech development, 314–321
supporting materials, 317–321
thesis statement, 316–317
time limits for your speech, 345, 351
topical pattern for informative speeches, 365
topics for, 180–181, 308–310, 314–316, 387–388
transitions, 326

Q
Quality time, 183
Quotes, in pubic speaking, 327

R
Racial diversity, 276–277, 308
intercultural communication v. conflict, 124–125
Racial identity, 42–43, 45, 95, 124
barriers to listening, 112
verbal communication influenced by, 62–63
Racial slurs, 20, 116
Radio frequency identification (RFID), 160
Rallying crowds, 339

Rape, 217–218
Reality television shows, 140
Reasoned skepticism, 21
Reciprocity, 206, 209
Recognition seeker, 263–265
Recorder role, 261–262, 265
Reentry shock, 126
Reflected appraisals, 36–37
Refugees, 127
Regional culture, 16
    American Civil War, 115
Regionality, 61–62
Regulators, 83
Regulatory function, 53–54, 73
Reinforcement phase, 270–271
Rejection, 210
Relational infidelity, 214–215
Relationality, 177
Relational maintenance, 189–190
Relational resources, 205
Relational role, 261, 265
Relational temptations, 212, 214
Relational trajectory models, 183
Relational transgressions, 212
Relationship challenge, 202, 212–218. *See also* Conflict
    indirect fighting style as, 236
    partner's aversive behaviors, 208
Relationship meaning, 10, 65
Relationship rules, 232
Relationships, 10, 65. *See also* Interpersonal communication;
        Romantic relationships
    business, 105, 110, 114, 194, 272–273, 296, 298, 357
    challenges to, 202, 208, 212–218, 236
    communicating in friendships and romantic, 185–192
    conflicts arousing anger, 239–240
    dialectical model of relationship development, 184–185
    interpersonal communication influencing, 177–180
    justification for ending, 191
    models of relationship development, 180–185
    race *v.* romantic, 193
    relational maintenance, 189–190
    relational trajectory models, 183
    six keys to improving communication
        skills, 243–244
    sudden death of, 190
Relationship satisfaction, 213
Relationship threats, 212–218
Relativism, 19–20
Relaxation, 83
    meditation for, 384
    techniques for, 337–338
Religion, 45. *See also specific religion*
Repetition, as rhetorical device, 343
    in "A More Perfect Union" speech, 308
Request-making, 205–206
Research checklist, for persuasive speeches, 390
Research studies, as source for supportive
        materials, 318
Resources, 204–205
    limited, 229
Respect
    for audience's ideas, 367
    -ful communication style, 266
    service and, 299–300

Responding, 102–103
Retirement dinners, public speech for, 308
Reverse culture shock, 126
Reward-and-discipline system, 300
RFID. *See* Radio frequency identification
Rhetor, 356
Rhetorical devices, 342–343
    in "A More Perfect Union"
        speech, 308
    to compel change 371
Rights approach, 23
Ritter, Nicole Rosenleaf, 151
Robertson, Pat, 284
Roles, small group, 259–265
Romantic relationships, 159, 181–182, 184
    betrayal in, 209–210
    cheating, 215
    communicating in, 185–192
    ending of, 190–192
    "honeymoon" period, 237
    initiating, 185, 187–188
    making up, 183
    race and, in United States, 194
    relational infidelity, 214
    relational maintenance, 189–190
    relational transgressions, 212
    serious commitment, 183
    societal forces influencing, 219–220
Roosevelt, Franklin D., 293
Rose, Amanda, 4–5
Rowley, Coleen, 296
Rumors, 154

S
Sacrifice, 183
Sales pitch, 357
Sales presentations, 357
Samoan American, 129
Sanford, Mark, 351, 380
Sapir-Whorf hypothesis, 64
Sarcasm, 212, 296
Sartre, Jean-Paul, 20
Satisfaction
    in Monroe's motivated sequence, 386
    relationship, 213
Saturday Night Live, 351
Saving face, 269
Scientific Match dating site, 179–180
Search engines, 318–319
Secondary identities, 42
Secondary influence goals, 202–203, 205
Secondary questions, 312
Second Life, 154–155
Selection (in perceptual process), 28
Self-assessment, in leadership, 300–301
Self-awareness, 125
    of intercultural communication, 141–142
Self-concept, 39–41, 205
Self-confessor role, 263
Self-confidence, 297
Self-disclose, 184, 186–187, 189, 196
Self-esteem, 39–41, 45
    hurtful messages *v.*, 213
Self-fulfilling prophecy, 38–39, 41

Self-government movement, 375
Self-identity, 5, 32–33, 205. *See also* Identity, self-
     assault of, 240
     through communication, 41
     defensiveness as attempt to protect, 241
     Facebook and, 153
     looking-glass self, 36
     online, 155
     perception influenced by, 28, 34–36
     reflected appraisals, 36–37
     self-concept, 39–40
     self-fulfilling prophecy, 38–39, 41
     social comparison, 37–38, 41
     verbal communication influenced by, 58
     view of hurtful message *v.*, 212
     your focus on, 40
Self-serving bias, 32
Selling, public speech for, 308
Semantics, 56, 59
Sensing, 102–103
Sensitive topics, 318
Sensory model, 43
September 11, 2001, 138–139
Serious commitment, 183
Servant leadership theory, 294–295
Service
     to others, 299–300
     -task functions, 92–93
Setting, 8–11
Sex clubs, 155
Sexual coercion, 217–218
Sexual harassment, 20–21
Sexual infidelity, 214
Sexual orientation, 16, 20, 66, 80, 194
Shafir, Rebecca Z., 114, 118
Shared leadership, 291
Sharing activities, 205
Sharing information, 18. *See also*
     Communication ethics
Shepard, Judy, 290
Shepard, Matthew, 290
Short term involuntary travelers, 127
Short term orientation, 136
Short term voluntary travelers, 127
"Silent treatment," 236
Silver, Amy, 105
Similarity factor, 177, 179
Simile, as comparison device, 342
Simon, Carly, 336
Sincerity, 298
Situational couple violence, 217
Skype chat, 150
Slang, contemporary, 60–61
Slavery, 138–139
Small group communication, 256
     advantages and disadvantages of, 258–259
     effective sequencing of task and relational
          communication, 264–274
     ethics and, 278
     identifying roles in group situation, 262
     importance of, 257–258
     improving your skills, 278–279
     types of communications roles, 259–265
Small group roles, 259–264

Smiling, 84, 95, 97, 114
     mandated, 124
Smith, Matthew J., 154
Smoking, 378
SNS. *See* Social networking sites
Social comparison, 37–38, 41, 80, 112
Social control, 92–93
Social distance, 86–87
Social hierarchy, 80
     cultural diversity and group, 278
     emotional experience *v.*, 221
     fear *v.*, 222
     haptics and, 90
     listening influenced by, 114–115, 118
     norms and views on leadership, 298
     power/perception/identity in, 42
Social identity, 32–33, 42
     of North *v.* South in Civil War, 115
     perceptions influenced by, 44
Social influence, 202
Social influence skills, 202–203
Social networking sites (SNS), 146–148
     Facebook, 145, 147–148, 151, 153, 196, 356
     friendships via, 157
     guidelines for using, 158
     impression management on, 155–156, 168
     MySpace, 151, 155, 356
     sexual predators on, 155
     Twitter, 146–151, 163–164, 169, 356, 357
     usage frequency by gender, 162
Social network theory, 152–153
Social norms, 37, 43
Social penetration theory, 180
Social-polite touch, 89
Social presence, 148–149
Social presence theory, 149
Social proof, 207
     resisting, 209
Social status, 114
Social support, 197
Societal forces, 9, 12–17
     emotions shaped by, 220–221
     in gender socialization, 220, 247
     intercultural communication influenced
          by, 138–139
     leadership shaped by, 296–298
     listening in context of, 115
     romantic relationships influenced by, 219–220
     small group communication and, 274–278
     speech delivery influenced by, 351–352
Socioeconomic status, Internet use and, 164
Socrates, 4
Solutions, alternative, 267
Somalia, 163
Soundscapes, 115
South Africa, 125, 298–299
South Korea, 163
Spain, 163
Spam, 154
Spatial pattern, 321–322
Speaking rate, 347
Special-interest pleader, 263
Special occasion speech, 308
Specific purpose, of your speech, 310

Speech act theory, 56
    direct *v.* indirect, 57
Speech delivery, 335–336
    choosing your method, 345–346
    choosing your persona, 345–348, 378
    delivery method, 345
    dress/appearance for, 341
    ethics of, 352
    importance of, 336
    key issues in, 350
    language and style, 339–343
    overcoming anxiety, 336–337
    practicing, 348–350
    preparation before, 337
    relaxation techniques before, 337–338
    societal forces influencing, 351–352
    time limits, 345, 351
    tone, 191, 339–340
    visual aids, 343–345
"Speech to the Republican National
    Convention," 339, 374–375
"Speed of gossip," 151
Spell checker, 54
Spielberg, Steven, 289
Spitzberg, Brian, 249
Spontaneous communication, 70–71
Spoofing, 154
Sport endorsement deals, 376, 378
Sports, as healthy distraction, 5
Stage model, Knapp's, 181–182
Stagnating, 181–182
Standard setter role, 262
Statement of fact, 388
Statement of policy, 389
Statement of value, 389
Static-dynamic dialectic, 137
Statistical Abstract of the
    United States, 319–320
Statistical Universe, 318–319
Statistics, 319–320
    as attention-getters, 327
Stelle, Michael, 284
Stereotype threat, 38
Stereotyping, 30, 38–39, 45–46, 67,
    141–142, 287–288
    ameliorated by CMC, 152
    in audience analysis, 313
    ethnic slurs, 20
    by gender, 60, 109, 287–288
    online, 162
Stewart, Martha, 5
Stewart, Rod, 336
Stonewalling, 242–243
Strategic communication, 286–287
Strategy control, 250
Streisand, Barbra, 336
Stress indicators, 337–338
Students abroad, 128. *See also* Age
Style theory, 291–292
Stylistic devices, 342
Sudden death, of relationships, 190
Sullivan, William, 296

Superiority-focused communication, 71
Superior-subordinate communication, 160–161
Supporting materials, 317–321
Supportive communication, 70–71
Supportive listening, 107
Sweeping generalization, 382
Symbol, 8
Synchronous communication, 149
Syntax, 55, 59

T
Talking to yourself, 337–338
Talk-show hosts, 346
Tao Te Ching, 294
Task roles, 260–261, 265
Teaching, public speech for, 308
TEA party movement, 284
Teasing, 208, 229
Technocapital, 164, 166–167
Technology, 164–165. *See also* Audiovisual aids;
    Computer-mediated communication; Internet
    digital divide, 162–163, 166–167
    Group Support Software, 272
    Skype chat, 150
    small group communication and, 271–274
    for speeches, 344
    technocapital, 164, 166–167
Technology, Entertainment and Design
    (TED) conference, 306
TED. *See* Technology, Entertainment and Design conference
Teenagers, 128, 147–148, 163–164
    listening behaviors with, 110
Ten Commandments of Computer Ethics, 168
Terminating, stage of romantic relationship, 181–182
Territoriality, 88–89
Text messaging, 11, 60, 146, 149,
    150, 152, 170–171
Thailand, 83, 246
Thesis statement, 316–317
    helping audiences understand your, 328
    in Monroe's motivated sequence, 386
    in persuasive speech, 388–389
Time
    ease of public speaking over, 338
    get-to-know time, 183
    lateness, 85, 345, 348, 351
    monochronic time usage, 86
    -oriented listening style, 107–108
    polychronic time usage, 86
    quality, 183
    up to date research, 390
Time limits, 85, 345, 348, 351
Time-oriented listening style, 107–108
Tone, 191, 339–340
Topical pattern, 322
Topics, public speaking, 308–310
    breadth of, 180–181
    narrowing your, 314–316
    for persuasive speaking, 387–388
    sensitive topics, 318
    topical pattern for informative speeches, 365
"Toxic handlers," 296

Toxic leadership, 295–296
Tradition, appeal to, 383
Trait theory, 289
Transactionality, 13–14
Transformational leadership theory, 292–293
    charismatic *v.*, 294–295
Transitions, 326
"Truth" advertisements, 378
Truth bias, 209
Truthfulness, 18
    in conflict management, 247
    ethical leadership requiring, 298–299
    in informative speaking, 366
    in small group communication, 278
Tunisia, 163
Turkey, 125, 129
Turning point model, 183
Turn-taking, in conversation, 57–58, 93
Twitter, 146–151, 163–164, 169, 356, 357
Tyco, 17

U

Uncertainty reduction theory, 180
Understanding, listening and, 102–103
Uniforms, 91
Unintentional messages, 211
United Arab Emirates, 134
United States, 163, 246, 273. *See also specific group/organization/person*
    American Revolution, 339–340
    appearance and artifacts in, 90–91
    crisis in ethical communication, 17
    cultural diversity in, 123, 275–276
    eye contact importance in, 348
    haptics in, 89–90
    language discrimination, 67
    overweight, 351
    president's personality characteristics, 289
    public deliberation, 376
    race and romantic relationships, 193
    regional dialects, 61–62
    self-government movement, 376
Unwanted sex, 217–218
Urban legends, 154
Utilitarian approach, 23

V

Value hierarchy, 15
Value orientation, human-nature, 134
Values, audience's, 381
Van Dam, Andy, 357
Vangelisti, Anita L., 181–182
Vangelisti's Stages of Relational
    Development, 181–182
Venting, 249
Verbal attack
    from aggressor (in group setting), 263
    avoidance of, 247–248
    destructive nature of, 235
    ineffectiveness of, 234
    personality conflicts provoking, 232
    as response to hurtful message, 212

Verbal *v.* nonverbal messages, 96–97. *See also* Nonverbal communication
Video clips, 327
Video conference, 273
Vietnamese American, 16
Vietnam War, 270
View of human nature, 133
"Virtual reality" games, 146
Virtual teams, 272–273, 298
Virtue approach, 23
Visual aids, 327, 343, 345
    checklist of, 344
    ethics applied to, 351
    for informative speaking, 366–367
Visual Aids Checklist, 344
Visualization, in Monroe's motivated
    sequence, 386
Vitter, David, 380
Vocabulary, 58, 60
Vocalizations, 85
Vocal projection, 348
Vocal variety, 348
Voice qualities, 85
Voluntary short-term travelers, 126

W

Walther, Joseph, 158
Weakness, appeals to
    emotion seen as, 379
Weapons of influence, 206–209
Webblogs, 146–148, 168, 317
Web sites, 146, 273, 357
    as source for supporting materials, 317
    your library's, 318
Webster, Daniel, 339–340
Weddings, public speech for, 308
Whining, 236
Whites, 15, 42, 65, 80, 123–124, 129,
    141–142, 162, 193, 296
    eye contact, 84
    in South Africa, 125
Wikipedia, 273, 317
Window decals, 89
Withdrawal/avoidance strategy, 192, 237
Withholding information, 18
Wolburg, Joyce M., 379
Women, 33. *See also* Gender; Lesbian and
    gay Americans
    communicating in friendships and
        romantic relationships, 185–192
    empathic communication, 109
    executive and managerial roles for, 296
    haptics among, 90
    intercultural couples, 193
    interethnic dating, 131
    MADD, 289
    romantic relationships, 159, 160,
        181–182
    as targets, 168
    underrepresented in leadership
        positions, 287–288
    as video game players, 162

Wood, Andrew F., 154
WorldCom, 17
World of Warcraft, 154–155
World Wide Web (WWW), 146, 273, 357
WWW . *See* World Wide Web

X

Xerox, 273

Y

Yawning, 348
Yielding style, 236
"You have to give a little to get
a little," 235–236

Z

Zen Buddhism, 118